SURVEILLANCE AND INTELLIGENCE LAW HANDBOOK

GW00645598

SURVEILLANCE AND INTELLIGENCE LAW HANDBOOK

Dr Victoria Williams

OXFORD
UNIVERSITY PRESS

OXFORD

UNIVERSITY PRESS

Great Clarendon Street, Oxford OX2 6DP

Oxford University Press is a department of the University of Oxford.
It furthers the University's objective of excellence in research, scholarship,
and education by publishing worldwide in

Oxford New York

Auckland Cape Town Dar es Salaam Hong Kong Karachi
Kuala Lumpur Madrid Melbourne Mexico City Nairobi
New Delhi Shanghai Taipei Toronto

With offices in

Argentina Austria Brazil Chile Czech Republic France Greece
Guatemala Hungary Italy Japan Poland Portugal Singapore
South Korea Switzerland Thailand Turkey Ukraine Vietnam

Oxford is a registered trade mark of Oxford University Press
in the UK and in certain other countries

Published in the United States
by Oxford University Press Inc., New York

First published 2006

British Library Cataloguing in Publication Data

Data available

Library of Congress Cataloging in Publication Data

Data available

Typeset by Newgen Imaging Systems (P) Ltd., Chennai, India
Printed in Great Britain
on acid-free paper by
CPI Antony Rowe, Chippenham, Wiltshire

ISBN 978–0–19–928685–0

3 5 7 9 10 8 6 4 2

PREFACE

The history—though perhaps not the law—of surveillance, of coded messages and of people assuming identities to spy on others for the State is a long one, as is its counterpart in the domain of private activity hidden from State view. The capacity to speak freely using codes, or to meet in some private place out of sight, can serve ends as far apart, and yet as equally challenging to the State, as those of the anarchist on the one hand, and the escaping slave on the other. Whether secrecy is attained by 21st century encryption of a text message, or by directions hidden in 19th century African-American slave quilts, mapping the route north to freedom with visual metaphors lost to slave owners, secrecy in the hands of the individual is a controversial topic whenever, wherever, it arises.

This book focuses on the State's legal powers to impinge on individual privacy by covert action, and the individual's limited legal rights to scrutiny of that State action in the domestic jurisdiction. It endeavours to provide the key elements for an understanding and practical application of the procedural law in England and Wales relating to State covert activity, and to provide information about the Investigatory Powers Tribunal created to hear complaints in some areas. Where possible I have endeavoured to include notes on proposed developments in the law being discussed in 2005, and the selection of materials is intended to present what is useful in one volume without excessive length. The key Act covered is the Regulation of Investigatory Powers Act 2000, together with the significant statutory instruments and Tribunal Rules and Codes of Practice. Extracts from the Police Act 1997, Part III, Security Service Act 1989 and Intelligence Services Act 1994 also appear as do parts of other relevant statutes and materials such as the Anti-terrorism, Crime and Security Act 2001.

My thanks to Oxford University Press, and to Annie McCloud to whom this book is dedicated. (Extracts from) the Convention of 29 May 2000 on Mutual Assistance in Criminal Matters between the Member States of the European Union are reproduced with the kind permission of the European Union Publishers' Forum Secretariat.

This book aims to be up to date as at 1 October 2005.

Victoria Williams
2 Gray's Inn Square Chambers, October 2005

TABLE OF CONTENTS

PART IV RIPA FORMS AND NOTICES

PART V CODES OF PRACTICE

PART IX INTERNATIONAL MATERIALS

TABLE OF CASES

TABLE OF STATUTES

(Note: text of rules and regulations is tabled to page number.)

TABLE OF STATUTORY INSTRUMENTS

TABLE OF TREATIES AND CONVENTIONS

GLOSSARY OF COMMON TERMS

AO	Authorising Officer
CHIS	Covert Human Intelligence Source
CSP	Communications Service Provider
DP	Designated Person
ECHR	European Convention for the Protection of Human Rights and Fundamental Freedoms 1950
GCHQ	Government Communications Headquarters
HRA	Human Rights Act 1998
HMRC	HM Revenue and Customs
IPCC	Independent Police Complaints Commission
IPT	Investigatory Powers Tribunal
NCS	National Crime Squad
NCIS	National Criminal Intelligence Service
OFT	The Office of Fair Trading
PACE	The Police and Criminal Evidence Act 1984
RIPA	The Regulation of Investigatory Powers Act 2000
SIS	Secret Intelligence service (MI6)
SOCA	Serious Organised Crime Agency
SOCAP	The Serious Organised Crime and Police Act 2005
SPoC	Single Point of Contact
'The 1989 Act'	The Security Service Act 1989
'The 1994 Act'	The Intelligence Services Act 1994
'The 1997 Act'	The Police Act 1997
'The 1998 Act'	The Human Rights Act 1998

Part I

ENTERING AND INTERFERING WITH PROPERTY AND TELEGRAPHY

1

THE POLICE ACT 1997,[1] PART III

A. Bodies falling within Part III

Introduction

This section outlines the functions of the main bodies, *other than security and* **1.01**
intelligence services, which are entitled to seek authorisation to enter and interfere
with property and telegraphy (ie bodies operating within the Police Act 1997, Part
III authorisation arrangements)—which are functions linked to the use of surveillance.[2] They are described here as 'policing' bodies but note that they include
HM Revenue and Customs, and the Office of Fair Trading (OFT). In addition to
the bodies referred to here, the conventional police forces, including military
police forces, also fall within the scope of Part III of the 1997 Act.

The National Criminal Intelligence Service (NCIS) and the National Crime Squad
(NCS) will be replaced by the Serious Organised Crime Agency (SOCA) when the
Serious Organised Crime and Police Act 2005 (SOCAP) is brought into force but
the functions of NCIS and NCS are outlined here as background to SOCA.

The National Criminal Intelligence Service (NCIS)[3]

NCIS originated in drug intelligence work, but its role encompasses intelligence **1.02**
concerning serious and organised crime, for example money laundering, child
pornography, and football crime.[4] By s 2(2) of the 1997 Act, its functions are to
gather, store and analyse information to supply criminal intelligence to police
forces, NCS (see below) and 'other law enforcement agencies'. It also acts to support police forces, the Royal Ulster Constabulary, NCS and agencies carrying out
criminal intelligence activities.

---

[1] 'The 1997 Act'.   [2] Entry onto property is often essential to place surveillance devices.
[3] NCIS and NCS will be replaced by the Serious Organised Crime Agency (SOCA), planned to
start in 2006. The Regulation of Investigatory Powers Act 2000 (RIPA) and the 1997 Act are extensively amended by the SOCAP Act 2005.   [4] See s 2(3A) of the Police Act 1997 (as amended).

The expression 'other law enforcement agencies' is widely defined, and by s 2(3) includes any government department, police forces of Jersey, Guernsey and the Isle of Man, and any other person charged with the duty of investigating offences or charging offenders. It includes any other person engaged outside the UK in the carrying on of activities similar to any carried on by the NCIS Service Authority,[5] NCIS, police authorities and forces, the NCS Service Authority or NCS. Note that by s 1(4) of the Security Service Act 1989, one of the Security Service's functions is to act in support of the activities of NCS and other law enforcement agencies in the prevention and detection of serious crime.

1.03 The UK Europol National Unit[6] is based at NCIS as is the UK National Central Bureau of Interpol.[7] NCIS (or its successor) will operate the Home Office 'Sirene UK' gateway to the Schengen Information System and will enable UK officers via the Police National Computer to share information with organisations from EU member countries plus Norway and Iceland.[8]

By s 1(4) of the Security Service Act 1989, one of the Security Service's functions is to act in support of NCIS in the prevention and detection of serious crime.

The National Crime Squad[9]

1.04 The National Crime Squad was formed from the fusion of Regional Crime Squads which existed until April 1998. Its area of operation is serious and organised crime involving direct policing operations and surveillance. It carries out proactive targeted work against criminal organisations and is not solely 'reactive' to crime already committed. By s 48 of the 1997 Act its function is 'to prevent and detect serious crime of relevance to more than one police area in England and Wales'. It is also permitted to act in support of a police force[10] or other law enforcement agencies in the prevention and detection of serious crime, or act in support of NCIS (at the request of the Director General of NCIS).

---

[5] The NCIS Service Authority is established by s 1 of the 1997 Act and is the body responsible for setting up and operating NCIS. It has a duty to ensure that NCIS is efficient, effective and economical, including determination of the strategic direction of the service and objectives, and as the body which selects the senior staff of NCIS. It produces reports accessible via its website (see Appendix 1).

[6] Europol acts to assist EU agencies in relation to organised crime affecting two or more member states. See Appendix 1 for web links.

[7] The UK unit provides UK agencies with internationally sourced material and fulfils international requests exchange of information. See Appendix 1 for web links.

[8] The UK entered into 'partial but significant' membership of the Schengen Agreement in 2001, extending to the law enforcement aspects of the Agreement. The information involved, according to NCIS, relates to people wanted for extradition, missing persons, requests to locate people for court appearances, requests for information, stolen vehicles, trailers, firearms, identity documents and banknotes.

[9] SOCA will replace NCIS and the National Crime Squad when the SOCAP Act 2005 is brought into force.　　　　[10] At the request of a chief officer of police England and Wales.

As with NCIS, the scope of the expression 'other law enforcement agencies' is **1.05** wide, by s 48(4) of the 1997 Act this includes many of the same bodies as s 2(3) does in relation to NCIS. Much of its activity is focused on operations to disrupt and prevent drug and immigration crime, arms dealing, money laundering, contract killings and human trafficking. Like NCIS, it is operated by its own Service Authority (the NCS Service Authority), consisting of members appointed by the Secretary of State. NCS and NCIS cooperate, and the degree of co-operation presumably underpins the logic of the creation of the single Serious Organised Crime Agency (SOCA) from April 2006, to fuse NCIS and NCS.

The Serious Organised Crime Agency (SOCA)

The Serious Organised Crime and Police Act 2005 (SOCAP), Part I (expected to **1.06** be brought into force by 2006) creates the SOCA. By s 1:

(1) There shall be a body corporate to be known as the Serious Organised Crime Agency ("SOCA"). . . .
(3) Each of the following bodies shall cease to exist on such date as the Secretary of State appoints by order-
   (a) the National Criminal Intelligence Service and its Service Authority, and
   (b) the National Crime Squad and its Service Authority.

SOCA, headed by its Director General, is a fusion of the areas of operation of **1.07** NCIS and NCS, in particular being charged with 'preventing and detecting serious organised crime', and 'contributing to the reduction of such crime in other ways and to the mitigation of its consequences' (s 2). The main limitations imposed on its operation appear in s 2(3)–(4) in that if, in exercising its function of preventing and detecting serious organised crime, SOCA becomes aware of conduct appearing to involve serious or complex fraud, it may only function in that case with the agreement of the Serious Fraud Office, or if that agency declines to act. Likewise with revenue fraud, SOCA may exercise its functions only with the agreement of the Commissioners for Revenue and Customs.

SOCA is given (by s 3 of the SOCAP Act) a specific information remit, namely **1.08** gathering, storing, analysing and disseminating information relevant to the prevention, detection, investigation or prosecution of offences, the reduction of crime in other ways or mitigation of its consequences. (The categories echo the areas referred to in s 2.) SOCA is permitted to disseminate information gathered to certain police forces,[11] 'special police forces',[12] law enforcement

---

[11] Police forces in the United Kingdom, the States of Jersey Police Force, the salaried police force of the Island of Guernsey and the Isle of Man Constabulary.
[12] Ministry of Defence Police, British Transport Police Force, Civil Nuclear Constabulary, and Scottish Drug Enforcement Agency.

agencies,[13] or such other persons as it considers appropriate in connection with carrying out its functions as noted above.

1.09 SOCA's powers are defined in s 5 of the 2005 Act and encompass the powers to:

- institute criminal proceedings in England and Wales or Northern Ireland;
- act in support of activities of a police force at the request of the chief officer;
- act in support of activities of a law enforcement agency at the request of that law agency;
- enter into arrangements for cooperating with bodies or persons (in the UK or elsewhere) which it considers appropriate in connection with the exercise of any of its functions under ss 2 or 3;
- furnish 'such assistance as it considers appropriate in response to requests made by any government or other body exercising functions of a public nature in any country or territory outside the United Kingdom' (but not where the request being made could have been made under s 13 of the Crime (International Co-operation) Act 2003 (requests for evidence to be obtained)).[14]

1.10 Whist SOCA's remit is specific to serious organised crime, it may carry on activities in relation to other types of crime to further the purposes of its functions under ss 2 and 3.

Centre for Child Protection on the Internet

1.11 In April 2005 the Government announced 'Connecting the UK: the digital strategy' to set up a 'Centre for Child Protection on the Internet' to support police and child protection agencies targeting those using the internet to distribute illegal images and 'groom' children. It was said that the Centre would be 'attached to' SOCA and be operational by April 2006, staffed by police officers, child protection and internet experts. The extent and legal nature of its 'attachment' to SOCA remain to be ascertained but may be expected to include surveillance and intelligence work and processing of communications data.

---

[13] The law enforcement agencies referred to are the Commissioners for Revenue and Customs or any other government department, the Scottish Administration, any other person who is charged with the duty of investigating offences or charging offenders, and 'any other person who is engaged outside the United Kingdom in the carrying on of activities similar to any carried on by SOCA or a police force.' (s 3(4)).

[14] Unless the request is one where SOCA is given a function by virtue of an order (under s 27(2) of the Crime (International Co-operation) Act 2003).

HM Revenue and Customs (HMRC)

1.12 Formed in 2005 from a combination of HM Customs and Excise and the Inland Revenue, HMRC's remit incorporates the following areas:

- income tax, corporation tax, capital gains tax, inheritance tax, insurance premium tax, stamp tax, land and petroleum revenue taxes;
- VAT, customs duties and frontier protection, excise duties;
- national insurance;
- tax credits, child benefit and the child trust fund, enforcement of the national minimum wage, student loan repayments, developing lorry road user charging, environmental taxes.

1.13 HMRC's role in discovery and investigation of VAT and duty evasion (the former scope of operation of HM Customs and Excise) brings the need for surveillance work. Customs and Revenue functions fall within the authorisation scheme of the 1997 Act and of RIPA.

The Office of Fair Trading (OFT)

1.14 The OFT oversees statutorily regulated trade including:

- the Competition Act 1998, prohibiting anti-competitive behaviour (the Chapter I and II prohibitions);
- prohibitions on anti-competitive behaviour in Articles 81 and 82 of the EC Treaty;
- the Enterprise Act 2002, including cartel offences by which individuals who dishonestly engage in serious anti-competitive agreements can be prosecuted;
- the Consumer Credit Act 1974, imposing a licensing scheme for providing credit or lending money to consumers;
- enforcement of consumer protection legislation.

1.15 The OFT is a corporate body[15] and it carries out its functions on behalf of the Crown. Its functions are set out in ss 5–8 of the Enterprise Act 2002. The OFT is not a conventional policing body but in the context of this book a key area of operation is investigation and prosecution of cartel offences defined by s 188 and 189 of the Enterprise Act 2002, which amended RIPA and the 1997 Act so as to place the OFT in a position to authorise intrusive surveillance operations and enter and interfere with property or wireless telegraphy for the purposes of investigating cartel offences. It has powers to obtain search warrants and to require persons to provide information or documents (s 193 of the 2002 Act). However the OFT is also

---

[15] See s 1 of the Enterprise Act 2002. By s 2 of that Act the powers of the former 'Director General of Fair Trading' were transferred to the OFT.

an authorised public body for the purposes of directed surveillance[16] and may use that form of surveillance for its Competition Act operations.

1.16 The OFT published its own Codes of Practice (in 2004) available from its website (see Appendix 1) and which cover the use of surveillance and of covert human intelligence sources in cartel investigations.

Independent Police Complaints Commission (IPCC)

1.17 The IPCC assists with management of police complaint investigations where carried out by local forces, and carries out independent investigations into incidents involving death or serious injury, allegations of serious or organised corruption, allegations against senior officers, allegations of perverting the course of justice and racism. Its jurisdiction also covers NCIS and NCS, and in due course, SOCA.

1.18 Created by s 9 of the Police Reform Act 2002, the Commission replaced the Police Complaints Authority (which originated in the report following the Brixton riots in April 1981), and consists of a Chairman and a number of members appointed by the Secretary of State, none of whom may be or have been a constable in any part of the United Kingdom.[17] The IPCC is similar to a police force in terms of obtaining authorisation of intrusive surveillance, entry onto property and interference with property and wireless telegraphy (see the Independent Police Complaints Commission (Investigatory Powers) Order 2004 No 815).

B. The statutory framework

Introduction

1.19 The Police Act 1997, Part III provides an authorisation framework which prevents entry onto premises and interference with property or wireless telegraphy from being unlawful where it would otherwise be unlawful [18]– see s 92 of the 1997 Act. For the most intrusive forms of surveillance[19] it can be necessary to enter premises covertly, interfere with property (eg to place devices) and perhaps interfere with wireless telegraphy.[20] The scheme of Part III of the 1997 Act is the main route by which policing bodies may obtain authorisation for such actions.

---

[16] This expression is dealt with in Chapter 5.

[17] There are other related limitations upon who is eligible to serve on the IPCC, see s 9 of the Police Reform Act 2002 as amended.

[18] The Act of 1997 does not affect forms of surveillance which would otherwise be lawful.

[19] RIPA defines 'intrusive surveillance' in s 26 but at the core of its definition is that surveillance is intrusive if it is covert surveillance that (a) is carried out in relation to anything taking place on any residential premises or in any private vehicle; and (b) involves the presence of an individual on the premises or in the vehicle or is carried out by means of a surveillance device.

[20] An expression defined in the Wireless Telegraphy Act 1949 (as amended).

The person who may give authority under the 1997 Act for entry onto property, **1.20** interference with property or wireless telegraphy depends on the nature of the premises, risk of certain types information being obtained and the force or body seeking the authorisation. Thus whilst in all cases the authorisation of an 'authorising officer'[21] is required, in certain cases there is superimposed upon the basic authorisation requirement a *further* requirement for prior approval by a Commissioner who has held high judicial office.

The Covert Surveillance Code of Practice

Section 101(3) of the 1997 Act, now repealed, empowered the Secretary of State **1.21** to publish a Code of Practice as to applications under the 1997 Act and, prior to the advent of RIPA, a Code had been published in 1999. The present Covert Surveillance Code of Practice 2002 (see Chapter 15), published under powers in s 71 of RIPA to replace the former s 101 powers, provides guidance issued by the Secretary of State covering:

- covert surveillance under RIPA;
- entry on to and interference with property, etc under the 1997 Act;
- entry on to and interference with property, etc under s 5 of the Intelligence Services Act 1994 (MI5/Security Service, GCHQ and MI6/SIS).

The status of the Code

By s 72(1) of RIPA, 'a person exercising or performing any power or duty in rela- **1.22** tion to which provision may be made by a code of practice under section 71 shall, in doing so, have regard to the provisions (so far as they are applicable) of every code of practice for the time being in force under that section.'

The Code is admissible in criminal or civil proceedings, and by s 72(4) of RIPA if **1.23** it appears to:

- a court or tribunal conducting any civil or criminal proceedings,
- the Investigatory Powers Tribunal, a Commissioner under RIPA,
- a Surveillance Commissioner carrying out his functions under RIPA or the Police Act 1997,
- or any Assistant Surveillance Commissioner under RIPA,

that any provision of the Code is relevant then that provision 'shall be taken into account in determining that question'.

---

[21] Although Part III of RIPA is not in force, the authorising officer under the Police Act 1997 would, if that Part III of RIPA were in force, also be enabled to permit the service of a Part III Disclosure Notice on any person relating to any protected (encrypted or password protected) information obtained as a result of a Police Act 1997, Part III authorisation. See Chapter 6 for a discussion of Part III of RIPA.

Scope of authorisation

1.24 The types of actions which may be authorised appear in s 93(1) of the 1997 Act as follows:[22]

    (a)   the taking of such action, in respect of such property in the relevant area,[23] as he may specify,

    (ab) the taking of such action falling within subsection (1A), in respect of property outside the relevant area, as he may specify, or

    (b)   the taking of such action in the relevant area as he may specify, in respect of wireless telegraphy.

The reference to subs (1A) is to action for 'maintaining or retrieving any equipment, apparatus or device the placing or use of which in the relevant area has been authorised under this Part or Part II of the Regulation of Investigatory Powers Act 2000 . . .'[24]— in other words an authorising officer may authorise the taking of action outside the relevant area solely for the purpose of maintaining or retrieving any device, apparatus or equipment.[25] The references to 'relevant area', and the whole of (ab), are omitted if the authorising officer is a member of staff of SOCA,[26] a customs officer or officer of the OFT—emphasising the non-geographic nature of those bodies.

Authorisation must be for preventing or detecting serious crime, necessary and proportionate

1.25 Section 93 enables authorisation of interference or entry onto property provided that the authorising officer believes that it is:

- *necessary* for the action specified to be taken for the purpose of preventing or detecting serious crime,[27] and
- that the taking of the action is *proportionate* to what the action seeks to achieve.[28]

Crime is 'serious' if:

- it involves the use of violence,
- results in substantial financial gain, or

---

[22] 'Relevant area' is defined according to which State body seeks the authorization—see s 93(6) for the complex provisions. The references to 'he' are references to the authorising officer.

[23] Ibid.

[24] Or under any enactment contained in or made under an Act of the Scottish Parliament which makes provision equivalent to that made by Part II of that Act of 2000.

[25] Covert Surveillance Code of Practice, para 6.5.

[26] An amendment which has this effect is not yet in force—see the footnote to s 91(1B) to the 1997 Act.

[27] Different requirements apply to the Police Service of Northern Ireland and the OFT in terms of the nature of the crime. See s 93.

[28] Similar provisions, ss 28(2) and 32(2) appear in RIPA, Part II in relation to directed and intrusive surveillance, incorporating Convention law concepts of necessity and proportionality into the decision-making process.

- involves conduct by a large number of persons in pursuit of a common purpose,
- or the offence or one of the offences is an offence for which a person who has attained the age of 21 (18 in relation to England and Wales) and has no previous convictions could reasonably be expected to be sentenced to imprisonment for a term of three years or more (s 93(4)).[29]

In considering whether the interference is 'necessary', s 93(2B) requires the authorising officer to take into account whether what it is thought necessary to achieve by the authorised action could reasonably be achieved by other means. **1.26**

The Covert Surveillance Code of Practice stresses at paras 2.1–2.9 that in considering an authorisation the officer should be satisfied that the steps sought to be authorised are 'necessary in the circumstances of the particular case for one of the statutory grounds listed in section 93(2A) of the 1997 Act and section 5(2)(c) of the 1994 Act,[30] proportionate and when exercised steps should be taken to minimise collateral intrusion.' **1.27**

Collateral intrusion

Collateral intrusion, the risk of intrusion into the privacy of people who are not the subjects of the investigation, is dealt with in relation to RIPA in this book but is equally relevant to 1997 Act authorisations. Reference should be made to Chapter 5 of this work. **1.28**

Part 6 of the Covert Surveillance Code of Practice

Part 6 of the Code deals with 1997 Act authorisations. At para 6.2 (and also at para 2.11) the Code observes that in many cases an operation may involve both intrusive surveillance (under the authorisation scheme in RIPA) *and* entry on or interference with property or with wireless telegraphy (under the 1997 Act scheme or its Intelligence Services Act counterpart) and that this can be done within one combined authorisation. That does not remove the requirement for the authorising officers to be the appropriate people for both the RIPA and the Police Act application and does not relieve the applicant of the need to consider the requirements for both applications. **1.29**

---

[29] Where the Authorising Officer is a customs officer designated by the Commissioners of Customs and Excise, where the matter is an 'assigned matter' within the meaning of s 1(1) of the Customs and Excise Management Act 1979.

[30] Ie similar authorisations under the 1994 Act which applies to GCHQ, the Security Service/MI5 and the Secret Intelligence Service/MI6.

1.30 The Code indicates at para 6.4 that authorisations under the 1997 Act may not be necessary where the consent of a person able to give permission in respect of the property is available, although consideration should be given to the need to obtain an authorisation under RIPA for surveillance to be carried out (as opposed to obtaining authorisation merely to enter and place the equipment).

Authorising officer and applicant

1.31 Section 93(3) of the 1997 Act makes it clear that the Authorising Officer must refuse authorisation unless the applicant falls within the relevant category stated in s 93(5). The Code of Practice para, 6.3 states that authorisations require the personal authority of the Authorising Officer (or his designated deputy) except in urgent situations, where it is not reasonably practicable for the application to be considered by such person. The person entitled to act in those circumstances is set out in s 94 of the 1997 Act (see para 6.11 of the Code of Practice).

Section 93(5), authorising officers, and which applicants are permitted under s 93(3)

Police

The following may act as authorising officer[31] upon application by a member of his/her police force:

s 93 (5)

(a) the chief constable of a police force maintained under section 2 of the Police Act 1996 (maintenance of police forces for areas in England and Wales except London);

(b) the Commissioner, or an Assistant Commissioner, of Police of the Metropolis;

(c) the Commissioner of Police for the City of London;

(d) the chief constable of a police force maintained under or by virtue of section 1 of the Police (Scotland) Act 1967 (maintenance of police forces for areas in Scotland);

(e) the Chief Constable or a Deputy Chief Constable of the Royal Ulster Constabulary;

(ea)[32] the Chief Constable of the Ministry of Defence Police;

(ee) the Chief Constable of the British Transport Police;

---

[31] 'AO'.   [32] (ea) to (ee) added by RIPA, s 75.

Navy Regulating Branch/Royal Military Police/Royal Air Force Police

The following may act as AO upon application by a member of the Royal Navy Regulating Branch, the Royal Military Police or the Royal Air Force Police as appropriate:

(eb) the Provost Marshal of the Royal Navy Regulating Branch;
(ec) the Provost Marshal of the Royal Military Police;
(ed) the Provost Marshal of the Royal Air Force Police;

Independent Police Complaints Authority

The following may act as AO upon application by a member of staff of the Independent Police Complaints Commission who has been designated under paragraph 19(2) of Schedule 3 to the Police Reform Act 2002:

(ef)[33] the Chairman of the Independent Police Complaints Commission;

National Criminal Intelligence Service

The following may act as AO upon application by a member of the National Criminal Intelligence Service:

(f) the Director General of the National Criminal Intelligence Service.

National Crime Squad

The following may act as AO upon application by a member of the National Crime Squad:

(g)[34] the Director General of the National Crime Squad, or any person holding the rank of assistant chief constable in that Squad who is designated for the purposes of this paragraph by that Director General.

Customs

The following may act as AO upon application by a customs officer:

(h)[35] any customs officer designated by the Commissioners of Customs and Excise.

Office of Fair Trading

The following act as AO upon application by an officer of the Office of Fair Trading:

(i)[36] the chairman of the Office of Fair Trading.

SOCA

When the Serious Organised Crime Agency replaces NCIS and NCS, amendments to s 93(3)(b) and s 93(5)(f) of the Police Act 1997 have the effect that the

---

[33] Added by The Independent Police Complaints Commission (Investigatory Powers) Order 2004 (SI 2004 No 815) Art 2(2).   [34] Amended by RIPA, s 75.
[35] Amended by RIPA, s 75.   [36] Added by Enterprise Act 2000, s 200.

Director General of SOCA, or any member of the staff of that agency who is designated by the Director General for that purpose will be empowered to act as AO where the application is made by a member of the staff of SOCA.

Requirement for additional prior approval by a Surveillance Commissioner[37] in certain circumstances

1.32 By s 97(1) of the 1997 Act, warrants to enter property:

- used wholly or mainly as a dwelling or as a bedroom in a hotel, or
- which constitutes office premises

require prior approval by one of the surveillance commissioners.

The same prior approval is required for warrants for action which:

- is likely to result in any person acquiring knowledge of matters subject to *legal privilege* (defined in s *87), confidential personal information* (defined in s 99), *or confidential journalistic material* (defined in s 100).

Note that the requirement for commissioner approval is waived by s 97(3) where the person who gives the authorisation 'believes that the case is one of urgency'.

1.33 The Covert Surveillance Code of Practice, s 3 (sec Chapter 15) gives guidance on the subjects of confidential personal information, legal privilege and journalistic material.

Contents of an application for authorisation

1.34 Applications to the Authorising Officer for authorisation must generally[38] be made in writing and specify each of the following matters:[39]

- identities of those to be targeted (where known);
- property which the entry or interference with will affect;

---

[37] Section 91 creates the positions of Chief Surveillance Commissioner[37] and ordinary surveillance commissioners whose duties and powers are discussed here in the context of the 1997 Act. Section 62 of RIPA adds further duties to review the exercise of powers and duties under RIPA, Part III once that Part comes into force, and RIPA, Part II. By s 91(10) of the 1997 Act the decisions of the Chief Commissioner and other commissioners (including decisions as to their jurisdiction) 'shall not be subject to appeal or liable to be questioned in any court'. That provision was considered in *R v GS and Others* [2005] EWCA Crim 887 which is discussed further in Chapter 21.

[38] But application may be made orally in urgent cases: s 95(1). If it is not reasonably practicable for an AO to consider an application for authorisation under s 93 then there are detailed arrangements in s 94 for alternative persons to give authorisation.

[39] In urgent cases, the authorisation should record reasons why the authorising officer or deputy considered the case so urgent that an oral authorisation was given and why it was not reasonably practicable for the application to be considered by the authorising officer or the designated deputy (Code of Practice at paras 6.13–14).

- identity of individuals and/or categories of people, where known, who are likely to be affected by collateral intrusion;
- details of the offence planned or committed;
- details of the intrusive surveillance involved;
- how the authorisation criteria (as set out in paras 6.6 and 6.7) have been met;
- any action which may be necessary to retrieve any equipment used in the surveillance;
- in case of a renewal, the results obtained so far, or a full explanation of the failure to obtain any results; and
- whether an authorisation was given or refused, by whom and the time and date.

Duration and renewal of authorisation under the Police Act 1997

In the case of an authorisation made either: **1.35**

- orally in urgent circumstances under s 95(1) or
- by one of the alternative authorising officers listed in s 94 (ie where it was not reasonably practicable for an authorising officer to consider an application for an authorisation under s 93)

the authorisation will expire 72 hours after it took effect. In all other cases the authorisation expires after three months[40] (see s 95(2)).

In either case, under s 95(3) at any time before an authorisation would cease to have effect it may be renewed in writing for three months from the day on which it would cease to have effect, if the authorising officer considers it necessary to do so for the purpose for which it was originally issued. Authorisations may be renewed more than once.

Where a person gives, renews or cancels an authorisation, as soon as is reasonably **1.36** practicable he must give notice in writing to a commissioner (see s 96 for the notification requirements and the Police Act 1997 (Notification of Authorisations etc.) Order 1998 (SI 1998 No 3241) in Chapter 25 which stipulates the requirements as to the content of a notification).

Authorisation record

The Code of Practice, at para 6.27 requires that an authorisation record be kept **1.37** which records the following and is kept up to date (eg at review and cancellation stages—see later):

- the time and date when an authorisation is given;
- whether an authorisation is in written or oral form;

---

[40] Note that there is no requirement that an authorisation *must* remain in force for three months, indeed quite the opposite in that there are requirements (para 6.23 of the Code) for regular review—typically monthly, and immediate cancellation of the authorisation if no longer justified.

- the time and date when it was notified to a Surveillance commissioner;
- and the time and date when the Surveillance Commissioner notified his approval (where appropriate);
- every occasion when entry on or interference with property or with wireless telegraphy has occurred;
- the result of the periodic reviews of authorisation;
- the date of every renewal; and
- the time and date when any instruction was given by the Authorising Officer to cease the interference with property or with wireless telegraphy.

Reviewing authorisations periodically[41]

1.38 The Code of Practice, at para 6.23 stresses that authorising officers should regularly review authorisations to assess the need for the authorised activity to continue, and especially ensure regularity and frequency of renewals where entry or interference provides access to confidential information or involves collateral intrusion. Reviews, and the outcome of reviews, should be recorded on the authorisation record. Although it is for the Authorising Officer to determine how often a review should take place when giving an authorisation, the Code stresses that reviews should be done 'as frequently as is considered necessary and practicable and at no greater interval than one month'.

Obligation to cease activity when no longer authorised, and to cancel authorisations

1.39 The Authorising Officer who granted (or most recently renewed) the authorisation must cancel it if he is satisfied that the authorisation no longer meets the criteria upon which it was authorised. The cancellation must be notified to the Surveillance Commissioners (Code of Practice, para 6.24). It is not appropriate to allow an authorisation to run until expiry if it is found to be no longer necessary.

1.40 Once an authorisation or renewal expires or is cancelled or quashed,[42] the Authorising Officer is obliged to instruct those carrying out the operation to cease the actions authorised. The time and date of the instruction should be recorded in the authorisation record (Code of Practice, para 6.28).

Commissioners' powers to quash or cancel authorisations, and rights of appeal by authorising officers

1.41 Section 96(4) requires a commissioner to scrutinise each authorisation as soon as reasonably practicable after notification. Section 103 provides the commissioners

---

[41] See eg *R v Hans-Constantin Paulssen* [2003] EWCA Crim 3109 (discussed further in Chapter 21).
[42] See para **1.41** below.

with powers to quash or cancel authorisations which are unjustified or have ceased to be justified.

A commissioner may quash an authorisation if he is satisfied at any time that either: **1.42**

- there were no reasonable grounds for believing the matters specified in s 93(2) at the time the authorisation was made or renewed;[43] or
- there were reasonable grounds for believing any of the matters in s 97(2) (ie the circumstances in which a commissioner's prior approval is required) but no approval was obtained and there were no reasonable grounds for believing the case to be one of urgency for the purposes of s 97(3).

The commissioner may order the destruction of records relating to information **1.43** obtained, other than records required for pending criminal or civil proceedings. Similarly a commissioner may cancel an authorisation if satisfied that at any stage *after* the authorisation was made or renewed there were no reasonable grounds for believing the s 93(2) criteria were met (s 103(4)). Similar powers are available as to destruction of records (s 103(5)).

If a decision is made to quash, or to order the destruction of records then the order **1.44** does not take effect until a seven-day period for appealing has expired or any appeal is dismissed. (See para **1.46** below.) The fact that the Commissioner has exercised his powers to cancel or quash triggers the making of a report of his findings as soon as practicable to the Authorising Officer by whom the authorisation was made, and to the Chief Commissioner.

Removing devices after an authorisation is quashed or cancelled by a commissioner

If a commissioner cancels or quashes an authorisation, any covert devices will **1.45** need to be removed so as not to compromise investigations or officers. The commissioner may direct under s 103(6) that the authorisation will remain valid for a defined time to enable equipment to be retrieved, if he thinks there are reasonable grounds for so ordering.

Authorising Officer's right of appeal to the Chief Commissioner

Under s 104 an Authorising Officer may appeal to the Chief Commissioner against **1.46** a decision by a commissioner to refuse to approve an authorisation which requires prior approval (ie under s 97) or to quash an authorisation or renewal, or to cancel a renewal, to direct destruction of records, or to refuse to allow time to retrieve equipment. The time limit is seven days 'beginning with the day on which the

---

[43] Ie the action is necessary for the action specified to be taken for the purpose of preventing or detecting serious crime, and the taking of the action is proportionate to what the action seeks to achieve at the time the authorisation was made or renewed.

refusal, decision or, as the case may be, determination appealed against is reported to the authorising officer.' (s 104(2)).

1.47 If the Chief Commissioner determines an appeal he will give notice of his determination to the Authorising Officer concerned, and to the commissioner against whose decision the appeal was made. Unless he dismisses the appeal, he will give no reasons for his determination. If he does dismiss the appeal then he reports his findings to the Authorising Officer, the commissioner whose decision was appealed against, and the Prime Minister[44] (s 105).

C. Text of The Police Act 1997, Part III[45] as amended

PART III
AUTHORISATION OF ACTION IN RESPECT OF PROPERTY

The Commissioners

91. The Commissioners.

Authorisations

92. Effect of authorisation under Part III.
93. Authorisations to interfere with property etc.
94. Authorisations given in absence of authorising officer.
95. Authorisations: form and duration etc.
96. Notification of authorisations etc.

Authorisations requiring approval

97. Authorisations requiring approval.
98. Matters subject to legal privilege.
99. Confidential personal information.
100. Confidential journalistic material.

Code of Practice

101. *repealed*

Complaints etc.

102. *repealed*
103. Quashing of authorisations etc.

---

[44] The report may be via his annual report or at any other time—see s 107(2).
[45] The parts of the 1997 Act reproduced here are affected by the Police Act 1997 (Notification of Authorisations etc.) Order 1998, SI 1998 No 3241, discussed in Chapter 25.

Appeals

General

PART III

AUTHORISATION OF ACTION IN RESPECT OF PROPERTY

The Commissioners[46]

91.—(1) The Prime Minister shall appoint for the purposes of this Part—

    (a)   a Chief Commissioner, and

    (b)   such number of other Commissioners as the Prime Minister thinks fit.

(2) The persons appointed under subsection (1) shall be persons who hold or have held high judicial office within the meaning of the Appellate Jurisdiction Act 1876.

(3) Subject to subsections (4) to (7), each Commissioner shall hold and vacate office in accordance with the terms of his appointment.

(4) Each Commissioner shall be appointed for a term of three years.

(5) A person who ceases to be a Commissioner (otherwise than under subsection (7)) may be reappointed under this section.

(6) Subject to subsection (7), a Commissioner shall not be removed from office before the end of the term for which he is appointed unless a resolution approving his removal has been passed by each House of Parliament.

(7) A Commissioner may be removed from office by the Prime Minister if after his appointment—

    (a)   a bankruptcy order is made against him or his estate is sequestrated or he makes a composition or arrangement with, or grants a trust deed for, his creditors;

    (b)[47]   a disqualification order under the Company Directors Disqualification Act 1986 or Part II of the Companies (Northern Ireland) Order 1989, or an order under section 429(2)(b) of the Insolvency Act 1986 (failure

---

[46] Note that the role of the surveillance commissioners is expanded by RIPA, ss 62–64, in relation to covert surveillance and the Investigatory Powers Tribunal. The Intelligence Services Commissioner (under RIPA, s 59) is the reviewing authority for the analogous property interference provisions of the 1994 Act, which apply to the Intelligence Services.

[47] Amended by The Insolvency Act 2000 (Company Directors Disqualification Undertakings) Order 2004 (SI 2004/1491) and Insolvency Act 2000, Sch 4, Pt II, para 22(2).

to pay under county court administration order), is made against him or his disqualification undertaking is accepted under section 7 or 8 of the Company Directors Disqualification Act 1986 or under the Company Directors Disqualification (Northern Ireland) Order 2002; or

(c) he is convicted in the United Kingdom, the Channel Islands or the Isle of Man of an offence and has passed on him a sentence of imprisonment (whether suspended or not).

(8) The Secretary of State shall pay to each Commissioner such allowances as the Secretary of State considers appropriate.

(9)[48] The Secretary of State shall, after consultation with the Chief Commissioner and subject to the approval of the Treasury as to numbers, provide the Commissioners and any Assistant Surveillance Commissioners holding office under section 63 of the Regulation of Investigatory Powers Act 2000 with such staff as the Secretary of State considers necessary for the discharge of their functions.

(10) The decisions of the Chief Commissioner or, subject to sections 104 and 106, any other Commissioner (including decisions as to his jurisdiction) shall not be subject to appeal or liable to be questioned in any court.[49]

Effect of authorisations under Part III

92.[50] No entry on or interference with property or with wireless telegraphy shall be unlawful if it is authorised by an authorisation having effect under this Part.

Authorisations to interfere with property etc.

93.—(1)[51] Where subsection (2) applies, an authorising officer may authorise—
  (a) the taking of such action, in respect of such property in the relevant area, as he may specify,
  (ab) the taking of such action falling within subsection (1A), in respect of property outside the relevant area, as he may specify, or
  (b) the taking of such action in the relevant area as he may specify, in respect of wireless telegraphy.

(1A)[52] The action falling within this subsection is action for maintaining or retrieving any equipment, apparatus or device the placing or use of which in the relevant area has been authorised under this Part or Part II of the

---

[48] Amended by RIPA, Sch 4, Pt II, para 8(1).

[49] This subsection was discussed in *R v GS and Others* [2005] EWCA Crim 887 which is summarised in Chapter 21, in the context of intrusive surveillance.

[50] Activities not involving unlawful acts (eg entry with permission) are not rendered unlawful merely by reason of not being authorised. The Act provides a procedure whereby actions of physical entry onto property may be rendered lawful when they would *otherwise* be unlawful (such as by amounting to trespass).   [51] As amended by RIPA, s 75.

[52] Added by RIPA, s 75.

Regulation of Investigatory Powers Act 2000 or under any enactment contained in or made under an Act of the Scottish Parliament which makes provision equivalent to that made by Part II of that Act of 2000.

(1B)[53] Subsection (1) applies where the authorising officer is a *member of the staff of the Serious Organised Crime Agency,*[54] customs officer or an officer of the Office of Fair Trading with the omission of—

    (a) the words "in the relevant area", in each place where they occur; and

    (b) paragraph (ab).

(2)[55] This subsection applies where the authorising officer believes—

    (a) that it is necessary for the action specified to be taken for the purpose of preventing or detecting serious crime, and

    (b) that the taking of the action is proportionate to what the action seeks to achieve.

(2A)[56] Subsection (2) applies where the authorising officer is the Chief Constable or the Deputy Chief Constable of the Royal Ulster Constabulary as if the reference in subsection(2)(a) to preventing or detecting serious crime included a reference to the interests of national security.

(2AA)[57] Where the authorising officer is the chairman of the Office of Fair Trading, the only purpose falling within subsection (2)(a) is the purpose of preventing or detecting an offence under section 188 of the Enterprise Act 2002.

(2B)[58] The matters to be taken into account in considering whether the requirements of subsection (2) are satisfied in the case of any authorisation shall include whether what it is thought necessary to achieve by the authorised action could reasonably be achieved by other means.

(3)[59] An authorising officer shall not give an authorisation under this section except on an application made—

    (a) if the authorising officer is within subsection (5)(a) to (ea) or (ee), by a member of his police force,

    (aa) if the authorising officer is within subsection (5)(eb) to (ed), by a member, as the case may be, of the Royal Navy Regulating Branch, the Royal Military Police or the Royal Air Force Police;

    (ab)[60] if the authorising officer is within subsection (5)(ef), by a member of staff of the Independent Police Complaints Commission

---

[53] Added by RIPA, s 75 and by the Enterprise Act 2000, s 200.
[54] The text in italics will be added when Sch 4, para 97 of the SOCAP Act 2005 is in force.
[55] Amended by RIPA, s 75.   [56] Added by RIPA, s 75.
[57] Added by the Enterprise Act 2000, s 200.   [58] Added by RIPA, s 75.
[59] Amended by RIPA, Sch 4(1), Pt II, para 8(2).
[60] Added by the Independent Police Complaints Commission (Investigatory Powers) Order 2004 (SI 2004 No 815) Art 2(2).

who has been designated under paragraph 19(2) of Schedule 3 to the Police Reform Act 2002,

[(b) if the authorising officer is within subsection (5)(f), by a member of the National Criminal Intelligence Service,

(c) if the authorising officer is within subsection (5)(g), by a member of the National Crime Squad, or]

(b) if the authorising officer is within subsection (5)(f), by a member of the staff of the Serious Organised Crime Agency,[61]

(d) if the authorising officer is within subsection (5)(h), by a customs officer, or

(e)[62] if the authorising officer is within subsection (5)(i), by an officer of the Office of Fair Trading

(4) For the purposes of subsection (2), conduct which constitutes one or more offences shall be regarded as serious crime if, and only if,—

(a) it involves the use of violence, results in substantial financial gain or is conduct by a large number of persons in pursuit of a common purpose, or

(b)[63] the offence or one of the offences is an offence for which a person who has attained the age of twenty-one (eighteen in relation to England and Wales) and has no previous convictions could reasonably be expected to be sentenced to imprisonment for a term of three years or more,

and, where the authorising officer is within subsection (5)(h), it relates to an assigned matter within the meaning of section 1(1) of the Customs and Excise Management Act 1979.

(5) In this section "authorising officer" means—

(a) the chief constable of a police force maintained under section 2 of the Police Act 1996 (maintenance of police forces for areas in England and Wales except London);

(b) the Commissioner, or an Assistant Commissioner, of Police of the Metropolis;

(c) the Commissioner of Police for the City of London;

(d) the chief constable of a police force maintained under or by virtue of section 1 of the Police (Scotland) Act 1967 (maintenance of police forces for areas in Scotland);

(e) the Chief Constable or a Deputy Chief Constable of the Royal Ulster Constabulary;

---

[61] Text of (b) and (c) in square brackets will be replaced by new the text of (b) in italics when Sch 4, para 97 of the SOCAP Act 2005 is in force.   [62] Added by the Enterprise Act 2000, s 200.
[63] Amended by the Criminal Justice and Court Services Act 2000, Sch 7, para 149.

(ea)[64] the Chief Constable of the Ministry of Defence Police;

(eb) the Provost Marshal of the Royal Navy Regulating Branch;

(ec) the Provost Marshal of the Royal Military Police;

(ed) the Provost Marshal of the Royal Air Force Police;

(ee) the Chief Constable of the British Transport Police;

(ef)[65] the Chairman of the Independent Police Complaints Commission;

[(f) the Director General of the National Criminal Intelligence Service

(g)[66] the Director General of the National Crime Squad, [or any person holding the rank of assistant chief constable in that Squad who is designated for the purposes of this paragraph by that Director General];[67] or]

(f) *the Director General of the Serious Organised Crime Agency, or any member of the staff of that Agency who is designated for the purposes of this paragraph by that Director General;*[68]

(h)[69] any customs officer designated by the Commissioners of Customs and Excise for the purposes of this paragraph, or

(i)[70] the chairman of the Office of Fair Trading.

(6) In this section "relevant area"—

(a) in relation to a person within paragraph (a), (b) or (c) of subsection (5), means the area in England and Wales for which his police force is maintained;

(b) in relation to a person within paragraph (d) of that subsection means the area in Scotland for which his police force is maintained;

(c) in relation to a person within paragraph (e) of that subsection, means Northern Ireland;

(ca)[71] in relation to a person within paragraph (ea), means any place where, under section 2 of the Ministry of Defence Police Act 1987, the members of the Ministry of Defence Police have the powers and privileges of a constable;

(cb) in relation to a person within paragraph (ee), means the United Kingdom;

---

[64] (ea) to (ee) added by RIPA, s 75.

[65] Added by the Independent Police Complaints Commission (Investigatory Powers) Order 2004 (SI 2004 No 815) Art 2(2).   [66] Amended by RIPA, s 75.

[67] Text in square brackets (which had been inserted by s 75(6)(b) of RIPA will be removed by the repeal of that section by Sch 17, Part 2 of the SOCAP Act 2005 when that schedule is in force.

[68] (f) and (g) in square brackets will be replaced by the italicised text of (f) when Sch 4, para 97 of the SOCAP Act 2005 is in force.   [69] Amended by RIPA, s 75.

[70] Added by the Enterprise Act 2000, s 200.   [71] (ca) and (cb) added by RIPA, s 75.

[(d) in relation to the Director General of the National Criminal Intelligence Service, means the United Kingdom;

(e)[72] in relation to the Chairman of the Independent Police Complaints Commission or the Director General of the National Crime Squad, means England and Wales;][73]

(f)[74] and in each case includes the adjacent United Kingdom waters.

(6A)[75] For the purposes of any authorisation by a person within paragraph (eb), (ec) or (ed) of subsection (5) property is in the relevant area or action in respect of wireless telegraphy is taken in the relevant area if, as the case may be—

(a) the property is owned, occupied, in the possession of or being used by a person subject to service discipline; or

(b) the action is taken in relation to the use of wireless telegraphy by such a person.

(6B) For the purposes of this section a person is subject to service discipline—

(a) in relation to the Royal Navy Regulating Branch, if he is subject to the Naval Discipline Act 1957 or is a civilian to whom Parts I and II of that Act for the time being apply by virtue of section 118 of that Act;

(b) in relation to the Royal Military Police, if he is subject to military law or is a civilian to whom Part II of the Army Act 1955 for the time being applies by virtue of section 209 of that Act; and

(c) in relation to the Royal Air Force Police, if he is subject to air-force law or is a civilian to whom Part II of the Air Force Act 1955 for the time being applies by virtue of section 209 of that Act.

(7) The powers conferred by, or by virtue of, this section are additional to any other powers which a person has as a constable either at common law or under or by virtue of any other enactment and are not to be taken to affect any of those other powers.

Authorisations given in absence of authorising officer

94.—(1) Subsection (2) applies where it is not reasonably practicable for an authorising officer to consider an application for an authorisation under section 93 and—

(a)[76] if the authorising officer is within paragraph (b) [or (e)], *(e) or (f)*[77] of section 93(5), it is also not reasonably practicable for the application

---

[72] Amended by the Independent Police Complaints Commission (Investigatory Powers) Order 2004 (SI 2004 No 815) Art 2(2).

[73] The text of (d) and (e) in square brackets will be omitted when Sch 4, para 97 of the SOCAP Act 2005 is in force.   [74] Repealed by RIPA, Sch 5.

[75] (6A) and (6B) added by RIPA, s 75.   [76] Amended by RIPA, Sch 5.

[77] Text in square brackets will be replaced by the text in italics (and the word 'or' added at the end of (a)) when Sch 4, para 98 of the SOCAP Act 2005 is in force.

to be considered by any of the other persons within the paragraph concerned; *or*

(b)[78] if the authorising officer is within paragraph (a), (c), (d) (ef), [or (f)][79] of section 93(5), it is also not reasonably practicable for the application to be considered by his designated deputy, [or

(c)[80] if the authorising officer is within paragraph (g) of section 93(5), it is also not reasonably practicable for the application to be considered either—

    (i) by any other person designated for the purposes of that paragraph; or

    (ii) by the designated deputy of the Director General of the National Crime Squad.][81]

(2) Where this subsection applies, the powers conferred on the authorising officer by section 93 may, in an urgent case, be exercised—

    (a) where the authorising officer is within paragraph (a) or (d) of subsection (5) of that section, by a person holding the rank of assistant chief constable in his force;

    (b) where the authorising officer is within paragraph (b) of that subsection, by a person holding the rank of commander in the metropolitan police force;

    (c) where the authorising officer is within paragraph (c) of that subsection, by a person holding the rank of commander in the City of London police force;

    (d) where the authorising officer is within paragraph (e) of that subsection, by a person holding the rank of assistant chief constable in the Royal Ulster Constabulary;

  (da)[82] where the authorising officer is within paragraph (ea) of that subsection, by a person holding the rank of deputy or assistant chief constable in the Ministry of Defence Police;

  (db) where the authorising officer is within paragraph (eb) of that subsection, by a person holding the position of assistant Provost Marshal in the Royal Navy Regulating Branch;

  (dc) where the authorising officer is within paragraph(ec) or (ed) of that subsection, by a person holding the position of deputy Provost Marshal in the Royal Military Police or, as the case may be, in the Royal Air Force Police;

---

[78] Amended by the Crime and Disorder Act 1998, s 113(3), RIPA, Sch 4, para 8(3) and the Independent Police Complaints Commission (Investigatory Powers) Order 2004 (SI 2004 No 815) Art 2(3).

[79] The reference to (f) will be omitted when Sch 4, para 98 of the SOCAP Act 2005 is in force.   [80] Added by RIPA, Sch 4, para 8(3).

[81] The whole of (c) in square brackets will be omitted when Sch 4, para 98 of the SOCAP Act 2005 is in force.   [82] (da) to (dd) added by RIPA, Sch 4, para 8(4).

(dd) where the authorising officer is within paragraph (ee) of that subsection, by a person holding the rank of deputy or assistant chief constable in the British Transport Police;

(de)[83] where the authorising person is within paragraph (ef) of that subsection, by any other member of the Independent Police Complaints Commission;

[(e)[84] where the authorising officer is within paragraph (f) . . . of that subsection by a person designated for the purposes of this section by the Director General of the National Criminal Intelligence Service . . .;

(ea)[85] where the authorising officer is within paragraph (g) of that subsection, by a person designated for the purposes of this paragraph by the Director General of the National Crime Squad as a person entitled to act in an urgent case;]

(e) *where the authorising officer is within paragraph (f) of that subsection, by a person designated for the purposes of this section by the Director General of the Serious Organised Crime Agency;*[86]

(f) where the authorising officer is within paragraph (h) of that subsection, by a customs officer designated by the Commissioners of Customs and Excise for the purposes of this section.

(g)[87] where the authorising officer is within paragraph (i) of that subsection, by an officer of the Office of Fair Trading designated by it for the purposes of this section.

[(3)[88] A police member of the National Criminal Intelligence Service or the National Crime Squad appointed under section 9(1)(b) or 55(1)(b) may not be designated under subsection (2)(e) [or (2)(ea)][89] [unless he holds the rank of assistant chief constable in that Service or Squad.][90]

(4)[91] In subsection (1), "designated deputy"—

(a) in the case of an authorising officer within paragraph (a) or (d) of section 93(5), means the person holding the rank of assistant chief

---

[83] Added by the Independent Police Complaints Commission (Investigatory Powers) Order 2004 (SI 2004 No 815) Art 2(3). [84] Amended by RIPA, Sch 4, para 8(4).

[85] Added by RIPA, Sch 4, para 8(4)(c) (but see note below).

[86] The text of (e) and (ea) in square brackets will be repealed and replaced with the new (e) in italics when Sch 17, Part 2 and Sch 4, para 98 of the SOCAP Act 2005 is in force (which also repeals the amendment inserted by RIPA, Sch 4, para 8(4)(c)).

[87] Added by the Enterprise Act 2000, s 200.

[88] Amended by the Crime and Disorder Act 1998, s 113(3) and by RIPA, Sch 4, para 8(5).

[89] The reference to (2)(ea) in square brackets will be repealed when Sch 17, Part 2 of the SOCAP Act 2005 is in force (which repeals the amendment made by RIPA, Sch 4, para 8(5).

[90] Text in square brackets will be repealed when Sch 17, Part 2 and Sch 4, para 98 of the SOCAP Act 2005 is in force (which repeals the amendment made by the Crime and Disorder Act 1998, s 113). [91] Amended by RIPA, Sch 5.

constable designated to act . . . under section 12(4) of the Police Act 1996 or, as the case may be, section 5(4) of the Police (Scotland) Act 1967;

(b)[92] in the case of an authorising officer within paragraph (c) of section 93(5), means the person authorised to act . . . under section 25 of the City of London Police Act 1839;

[(c) in the case of an authorising officer within paragraph (f) or (g) of section 93(5), means the person designated to act . . . under section 8 or 54 and

(d)[93] in the case of an authorising officer within paragraph (ef) of section 93(5), means a person appointed as deputy chairman of the Independent Police Complaints Commission under paragraph 3(1) of Schedule 2 to the Police Reform Act 2002.][94]

Authorisations: form and duration etc.

95.[95]—(1) An authorisation shall be in writing, except that in an urgent case an authorisation (other than one given by virtue of section 94) may be given orally.

(2) An authorisation shall, unless renewed under subsection (3), cease to have effect—

(a) if given orally or by virtue of section 94, at the end of the period of 72 hours beginning with the time when it took effect;

(b) in any other case, at the end of the period of three months beginning with the day on which it took effect.

(3) If at any time before an authorisation would cease to have effect the authorising officer who gave the authorisation, or in whose absence it was given, considers it necessary for the authorisation to continue to have effect for the purpose for which it was issued, he may, in writing, renew it for a period of three months beginning with the day on which it would cease to have effect.

(4) A person shall cancel an authorisation given by him if satisfied that the authorisation is one in relation to which the requirements of paragraphs (a) and (b) of section 93(2) are no longer satisfied.

(5) An authorising officer shall cancel an authorisation given in his absence if satisfied that the authorisation is one in relation to which the requirements of paragraphs(a) and(b) of section 93(2) are no longer satisfied.

---

[92] Amended by the Crime and Disorder Act 1998, Sch 10.

[93] Added by the Independent Police Complaints Commission (Investigatory Powers) Order 2004 (SI 2004 No 815) Art 2(3).

[94] The text of (c) and (d) in square brackets will be repealed when Sch 17, Part 2 and Sch 4, para 98 of the SOCAP Act 2005 is in force (which also repeals the amendment made by the Crime and Disorder Act 1998, s 113).   [95] Subs (3), (4) and (6) amended by RIPA, Sch 4, para 8(6).

(6)   If the authorising officer who gave the authorisation is within paragraph (b), (e) [or (g)] *or (f)*[96] of section 93(5), the power conferred on that person by subsections (3) and (4) above shall also be exercisable by each of the other persons within the paragraph concerned.

(7)[97] Nothing in this section shall prevent a designated deputy from exercising the powers conferred on an authorising officer within paragraph (a), (c), [(d)], (ef), [(f) or (g)] *or (d)*[98] of section 93(5) by subsections (3), (4) and (5) above.

Notification of authorisations etc.

96.—(1) Where a person gives, renews or cancels an authorisation, he shall, as soon as is reasonably practicable and in accordance with arrangements made by the Chief Commissioner, give notice in writing that he has done so to a Commissioner appointed under section 91(1)(b).

(2) Subject to subsection (3), a notice under this section shall specify such matters as the Secretary of State may by order prescribe.[99]

(3) A notice under this section of the giving or renewal of an authorisation shall specify—

(a) whether section 97 applies to the authorisation or renewal, and

(b) where that section does not apply by virtue of subsection (3) of that section, the grounds on which the case is believed to be one of urgency.

(4) Where a notice is given to a Commissioner under this section, he shall, as soon as is reasonably practicable, scrutinise the notice.

(5) An order under subsection (2) shall be made by statutory instrument.

(6) A statutory instrument which contains an order under subsection (2) shall not be made unless a draft has been laid before, and approved by a resolution of, each House of Parliament.

Authorisations requiring approval

97.—(1) An authorisation to which this section applies shall not take effect until—

(a) it has been approved in accordance with this section by a Commissioner appointed under section 91(1)(b), and

---

[96] The reference to (g) in square brackets will be replaced by the reference to (f) when Sch 4, para 99 of the SOCAP Act 2005 is in force.

[97] Amended by the Independent Police Complaints Commission (Investigatory Powers) Order 2004 (SI 2004 No 815) Art 2(4).

[98] The reference to (d), (f) or (g) will be replaced with a reference to (d) only when Sch 4, para 99 of the SOCAP Act 2005 is in force. The precise amending text of Sch 4, para 99(3) of the SOCAP Act 2005 states 'In subsection (7) for, " (d), (f) or (g)" substitute "or (d)".'

[99] See the Police Act 1997 (Notification of Authorisations etc.) Order 1998 (SI 1998 No 3241) reproduced in Chapter 25.

(b) the person who gave the authorisation has been notified under subsection (4).

(2) Subject to subsection (3), this section applies to an authorisation if, at the time it is given, the person who gives it believes—

    (a) that any of the property specified in the authorisation—

        (i) is used wholly or mainly as a dwelling or as a bedroom in a hotel, or

        (ii) constitutes office premises, or

    (b) that the action authorised by it is likely to result in any person acquiring knowledge of—

        (i) matters subject to legal privilege,

        (ii) confidential personal information, or

        (iii) confidential journalistic material.

(3) This section does not apply to an authorisation where the person who gives it believes that the case is one of urgency.

(4) Where a Commissioner receives a notice under section 96 which specifies that this section applies to the authorisation, he shall as soon as is reasonably practicable—

    (a) decide whether to approve the authorisation or refuse approval, and

    (b) give written notice of his decision to the person who gave the authorisation.

(5) A Commissioner shall approve an authorisation if, and only if, he is satisfied that there are reasonable grounds for believing the matters specified in section 93(2).

(6)[100] Where a Commissioner refuses to approve an authorisation, he shall, as soon as is reasonably practicable, make a report of his findings to the authorising officer who gave it or in whose absence it was given. . . .

(6A)[101] The reference in subsection (6) to the authorising officer who gave the authorisation or in whose absence it was given shall be construed, in the case of an authorisation given by or in the absence of a person within paragraph (b), [(e) or (g)] *or (e)*[102] of section 93(5), as a reference to the Commissioner of Police, [Chief Constable or, as the case may be, Director General] *or, as the case may be, Chief Constable*[103] mentioned in the paragraph concerned.

(6B) *The reference in subsection (6) to the authorising officer who gave the authorisation or in whose absence it was given shall be construed—*

    (a) in the case of an authorisation given by a person within paragraph (f) of section 93(5), as a reference to that person, and

---

[100] Amended by RIPA, Sch 5.   [101] Added by RIPA, Sch 4, para 8(7).
[102] Text in square brackets will be replaced with the text in italics when Sch 4, para 100 of the SOCAP Act 2005 is in force.   [103] Ibid.

(b) in the case of an authorisation given in the absence of such a person, as a reference to a member of the staff of the Serious Organised Crime Agency who is designated for the purposes of this section by the Director General of that Agency. [104]

(7) This section shall apply in relation to a renewal of an authorisation as it applies in relation to an authorisation (the references in subsection (2)(a) and (b) to the authorisation being construed as references to the authorisation renewed).

(8) In this section—

"office premises" has the meaning given in section 1(2) of the Offices, Shops and Railway Premises Act 1963;

"hotel" means premises used for the reception of guests who desire to sleep in the premises.

Matters subject to legal privilege

98.—(1) Subject to subsection (5) below, in section 97 "matters subject to legal privilege" means matters to which subsection (2), (3) or (4) below applies.

(2) This subsection applies to communications between a professional legal adviser and—

(a) his client, or

(b) any person representing his client,

which are made in connection with the giving of legal advice to the client.

(3) This subsection applies to communications—

(a) between a professional legal adviser and his client or any person representing his client, or

(b) between a professional legal adviser or his client or any such representative and any other person,

which are made in connection with or in contemplation of legal proceedings and for the purposes of such proceedings.

(4) This subsection applies to items enclosed with or referred to in communications of the kind mentioned in subsection (2) or (3) and made—

(a) in connection with the giving of legal advice, or

(b) in connection with or in contemplation of legal proceedings and for the purposes of such proceedings.

(5) For the purposes of section 97—

(a) communications and items are not matters subject to legal privilege when they are in the possession of a person who is not entitled to possession of them, and

---

[104] The text in italics, (6B), will be inserted when Sch 4, para 100 of the SOCAP Act 2005 is in force.

(b) communications and items held, or oral communications made, with the intention of furthering a criminal purpose are not matters subject to legal privilege.

Confidential personal information

99.—(1) In section 97 "confidential personal information" means—
   (a) personal information which a person has acquired or created in the course of any trade, business, profession or other occupation or for the purposes of any paid or unpaid office, and which he holds in confidence, and
   (b) communications as a result of which personal information—
      (i) is acquired or created as mentioned in paragraph (a), and
      (ii) is held in confidence.
(2) For the purposes of this section "personal information" means information concerning an individual (whether living or dead) who can be identified from it and relating—
   (a) to his physical or mental health, or
   (b) to spiritual counselling or assistance given or to be given to him.
(3) A person holds information in confidence for the purposes of this section if he holds it subject—
   (a) to an express or implied undertaking to hold it in confidence, or
   (b) to a restriction on disclosure or an obligation of secrecy contained in any enactment (including an enactment contained in an Act passed after this Act).

Confidential journalistic material

100.—(1) In section 97 "confidential journalistic material" means—
   (a) material acquired or created for the purposes of journalism which—
      (i) is in the possession of persons who acquired or created it for those purposes,
      (ii) is held subject to an undertaking, restriction or obligation of the kind mentioned in section 99(3), and
      (iii) has been continuously held (by one or more persons) subject to such an undertaking, restriction or obligation since it was first acquired or created for the purposes of journalism, and
   (b) communications as a result of which information is acquired for the purposes of journalism and held as mentioned in paragraph (a)(ii).
(2) For the purposes of subsection (1), a person who receives material, or acquires information, from someone who intends that the recipient shall use it for the purposes of journalism is to be taken to have acquired it for those purposes.

Code of Practice

101.[105]

Complaints etc.

102.[106]

Quashing of authorisations etc.

103.—(1) Where, at any time, a Commissioner appointed under section 91(1)(b) is satisfied that, at the time an authorisation was given or renewed, there were no reasonable grounds for believing the matters specified in section 93(2), he may quash the authorisation or, as the case may be, renewal.

(2) Where, in the case of an authorisation or renewal to which section 97 does not apply, a Commissioner appointed under section 91(1)(b) is at any time satisfied that, at the time the authorisation was given or, as the case may be, renewed,—

    (a) there were reasonable grounds for believing any of the matters specified in subsection (2) of section 97, and

    (b) there were no reasonable grounds for believing the case to be one of urgency for the purposes of subsection (3) of that section,

he may quash the authorisation or, as the case may be, renewal.

(3) Where a Commissioner quashes an authorisation or renewal under subsection (1) or (2), he may order the destruction of any records relating to information obtained by virtue of the authorisation (or, in the case of a renewal, relating wholly or partly to information so obtained after the renewal) other than records required for pending criminal or civil proceedings.

(4) If a Commissioner appointed under section 91(1)(b) is satisfied that, at any time after an authorisation was given or, in the case of an authorisation renewed under section 95, after it was renewed, there were no reasonable grounds for believing the matters specified in section 93(2), he may cancel the authorisation.

(5) Where—

    (a) an authorisation has ceased to have effect (otherwise than by virtue of subsection (1) or (2)), and

    (b) a Commissioner appointed under section 91(1)(b) is satisfied that, at any time during the period of the authorisation, there were no reasonable grounds for believing the matters specified in section 93(2),

he may order the destruction of any records relating, wholly or partly, to information which was obtained by virtue of the authorisation after that time (other than records required for pending criminal or civil proceedings).

---

[105] Section 101 repealed by RIPA, Sch 5.   [106] Section 102 repealed by RIPA, Sch 5.

(6)   Where a Commissioner exercises his powers under subsection (1), (2) or (4), he shall, if he is satisfied that there are reasonable grounds for doing so, order that the authorisation shall be effective, for such period as he shall specify, so far as it authorises the taking of action to retrieve anything left on property in accordance with the authorisation.

(7)[107] Where a Commissioner exercises a power conferred by this section, he shall, as soon as is reasonably practicable, make a report of his findings—

(a) to the authorising officer who gave the authorisation or in whose absence it was given, and

(b) to the Chief Commissioner;

and subsection(6A) of section 97 shall apply for the purposes of this subsection as it applies for the purposes of subsection(6) of that section.

(8)   Where—

(a) a decision is made under subsection (1) or (2) and an order for the destruction of records is made under subsection (3), or

(b) a decision to order the destruction of records is made under subsection (5),

the order shall not become operative until the period for appealing against the decision has expired and, where an appeal is made, a decision dismissing it has been made by the Chief Commissioner.

(9)   A Commissioner may exercise any of the powers conferred by this section notwithstanding any approval given under section 97.

Appeals by authorising officers.

104.—(1) An authorising officer who gives an authorisation, or in whose absence it is given, may, within the prescribed period, appeal to the Chief Commissioner against—

(a)   any refusal to approve the authorisation or any renewal of it under section 97;

(b)   any decision to quash the authorisation, or any renewal of it, under subsection (1) of section 103;

(c)   any decision to quash the authorisation, or any renewal of it, under subsection (2) of that section;

(d)   any decision to cancel the authorisation under subsection (4) of that section;

(e)   any decision to order the destruction of records under subsection (5) of that section;

(f)   any refusal to make an order under subsection (6) of that section;

(g)[108] . . .

---

[107] Amended by RIPA, Sch 4, para 8(8).   [108] Repealed by RIPA, Sch 5.

(2) In subsection (1), "the prescribed period" means the period of seven days beginning with the day on which the refusal, decision or, as the case may be, determination appealed against is reported to the authorising officer.

(3) In determining an appeal within subsection (1)(a), the Chief Commissioner shall, if he is satisfied that there are reasonable grounds for believing the matters specified in section 93(2), allow the appeal and direct the Commissioner to approve the authorisation or renewal under that section.

(4) In determining—
   (a)   an appeal within subsection (1)(b),
   (b)[109] . . .

   the Chief Commissioner shall allow the appeal unless he is satisfied that, at the time the authorisation was given or, as the case may be, renewed there were no reasonable grounds for believing the matters specified in section 93(2).

(5) In determining—
   (a)   an appeal within subsection (1)(c),
   (b)[110] . . . ,

   the Chief Commissioner shall allow the appeal unless he is satisfied as mentioned in section 103(2).

(6) In determining—
   (a)   an appeal within subsection (1)(d) or (e),
   (b)[111] . . . ,

   the Chief Commissioner shall allow the appeal unless he is satisfied that at the time to which the decision relates there were no reasonable grounds for believing the matters specified in section 93(2).

(7) In determining an appeal within subsection (1)(f), the Chief Commissioner shall allow the appeal and order that the authorisation shall be effective to the extent mentioned in section 103(6), for such period as he shall specify, if he is satisfied that there are reasonable grounds for making such an order.

(8) Where an appeal is allowed under this section, the Chief Commissioner shall—
   (a)   in the case of an appeal within subsection (1)(b) or (c), also quash any order made by the Commissioner to destroy records relating to information obtained by virtue of the authorisation concerned,
   (b)[112] . . .

---

[109] Repealed by RIPA, Sch 5.   [110] Repealed by RIPA, Sch 5.
[111] Repealed by RIPA, Sch 5.   [112] Repealed by RIPA, Sch 5.

Appeals by authorising officers: supplementary

105.—(1) Where the Chief Commissioner determines an appeal under section 104—

   (a)[113] he shall give notice of his determination—

      (i) to the authorising officer concerned, and

      (ii) to the Commissioner against whose refusal, decision or determination the appeal was made,

      . . .

   (b) if he dismisses the appeal, he shall make a report of his findings—

      (i) to the authorising officer concerned,

      (ii) to the Commissioner against whose refusal, decision or determination the appeal was made, and

      (iii) under section 107(2), to the Prime Minister.

(2) Subject to subsection (1)(b), the Chief Commissioner shall not give any reasons for a determination under section 104.

(3)[114] Nothing in section 104 shall prevent a designated deputy from exercising the powers conferred by subsection (1) of that section on an authorising officer within paragraph (a), (c), [(d)], (ef), [(f) or (g)] *or (d)*[115] of section 93(5).

106.[116]

Supplementary provisions relating to Commissioners

107.—(1) The Chief Commissioner shall keep under review the performance of functions under this Part.

(2)[117] The Chief Commissioner shall make an annual report on the matters with which he is concerned to the Prime Minister and may at any time report to him on anything relating to any of those matters.

(3) The Prime Minister shall lay before each House of Parliament a copy of each annual report made by the Chief Commissioner under subsection (2) together with a statement as to whether any matter has been excluded from that copy in pursuance of subsection (4) below.

(4)[118] The Prime Minister may exclude a matter from the copy of a report as laid before each House of Parliament, if it appears to him, after consultation

---

[113] Part repealed by RIPA, Sch 5 and amended by RIPA, Sch 4, para 8(9).

[114] Amended by the Independent Police Complaints Commission (Investigatory Powers) Order 2004 (SI 2004 No 815) Art 2(5).

[115] The reference to (d), (f) or (g) will be replaced with a reference to (d) only when Sch 4, para 101 of the SOCAP Act 2005 is in force. The precise amending text of Sch 4, para 101 of the SOCAP Act 2005 is '. . . for ", (d), (f) or (g)" substitute "or (d)".'

[116] Section 106 repealed by RIPA, Sch 5.   [117] Amended by RIPA, Sch 4, para 8(10).

[118] Amended by RIPA, Sch 4, para 8(10).

with the Chief Commissioner, that the publication of that matter in the report would be prejudicial to any of the purposes for which authorisations may be given or granted under this Part of this Act or Part II of the Regulation of Investigatory Powers Act 2000 or under any enactment contained in or made under an Act of the Scottish Parliament which makes provision equivalent to that made by Part II of that Act of 2000 or to the discharge of—

(a) the functions of any police authority,

(b) the functions of the [Service Authority for the National Criminal Intelligence Service or the Service Authority for the National Crime Squad] *Serious Organised Crime Agency*,[119] or

(c) the duties of the Commissioners of Customs and Excise.

(5) Any person having functions under this Part, and any person taking action in relation to which an authorisation was given, shall comply with any request of a Commissioner for documents or information required by him for the purpose of enabling him to discharge his functions.

(5A)[120] It shall be the duty of—

(a) every person by whom, or on whose application, there has been given or granted any authorisation the function of giving or granting which is subject to review by the Chief Commissioner,

(aa)[121] the functions of the Independent Police Complaints Commission,

(b) every person who has engaged in conduct with the authority of such an authorisation,

(c) every person who holds or has held any office, rank or position with the same public authority as a person falling within paragraph(a),

(d) every person who holds or has held any office, rank or position with any public authority for whose benefit (within the meaning of Part II of the Regulation of Investigatory Powers Act 2000) activities which are or may be subject to any such review have been or may be carried out, and

(e) every person to whom a notice under section 49 of the Regulation of Investigatory Powers Act 2000 (notices imposing a disclosure requirement in respect of information protected by a key) has been given in relation to any information obtained by conduct to which such an authorisation relates,

---

[119] The references to the Service Agencies of NCIS and NCS in square brackets will be replaced with the reference to SOCA when Sch 4, para 102 of the SOCAP Act 2005 is in force.

[120] Subs (5A)–(5C) added by RIPA, Sch 4, para 8(11).

[121] Added by the Independent Police Complaints Commission (Investigatory Powers) Order 2004 (SI 2004 No 815) Art 2(6).

to disclose or provide to the Chief Commissioner all such documents and information as he may require for the purpose of enabling him to carry out his functions.

(5B) It shall be the duty of every Commissioner to give the tribunal established under section 65 of the Regulation of Investigatory Powers Act 2000 all such assistance (including his opinion as to any issue falling to be determined by that tribunal) as that tribunal may require—

(a) in connection with the investigation of any matter by that tribunal; or

(b) otherwise for the purposes of that tribunal's consideration or determination of any matter.

(5C) In this section "public authority" means any public authority within the meaning of section 6 of the Human Rights Act 1998 (acts of public authorities) other than a court or tribunal.

(6)[122] . . .

Interpretation of Part III

108.—(1) In this Part—

"Assistant Commissioner of Police of the Metropolis" includes the Deputy Commissioner of Police of the Metropolis;[123]

"authorisation" means an authorisation under section 93;

"authorising officer" has the meaning given by section 93(5);

"criminal proceedings" includes—

(a)[124] proceedings in the United Kingdom or elsewhere before a court-martial constituted under the Army Act 1955, the Air Force Act 1955 or the Naval Discipline Act 1957 . . . ,

(b) proceedings before the Courts-Martial Appeal Court, and

(c) proceedings before a Standing Civilian Court;

"customs officer" means an officer commissioned by the Commissioners of Customs and Excise under section 6(3) of the Customs and Excise Management Act 1979;

"designated deputy" has the meaning given in section 94(4);

"United Kingdom waters" has the meaning given in section 30(5) of the Police Act 1996; and

"wireless telegraphy" has the same meaning as in the Wireless Telegraphy Act 1949 and, in relation to wireless telegraphy, "interfere" has the same meaning as in that Act.

(2) Where, under this Part, notice of any matter is required to be given in writing, the notice may be transmitted by electronic means.

---

[122] Repealed by RIPA, Sch 5.   [123] Added by RIPA, Sch 4, para 8(12).
[124] Part repealed by the Armed Forces Act 2001, Sch 7, Pt 1.

(3) For the purposes of this Part, an authorisation (or renewal) given—

  (a) by the designated deputy of an authorising officer, or
  (b) by a person on whom an authorising officer's powers are conferred by section 94,

shall be treated as an authorisation (or renewal) given in the absence of the authorising officer concerned; and references to the authorising officer in whose absence an authorisation (or renewal) was given shall be construed accordingly.

2

THE INTELLIGENCE SERVICES ACT 1994[1] AND SECURITY SERVICE ACT 1989[2]

A. The intelligence and security organisations

Introduction

Only the UK national bodies are referred to here because they fall within the RIPA **2.01** scheme, and the 1989 and 1994 Acts. For links to the European Parliament's report on the international aspects of mass telecommunications interception by the 'ECHELON' programme operated under a signals intelligence agreement (the reputed 'UKUSA' agreement of 1948), the reader is referred to Appendix 1 which contains useful sources of information.[3]

GCHQ, SIS and the Security Service/MI5 fall under the scrutiny of the **2.02** Intelligence and Security Committee created by Sch 3 of the 1994 Act whose remit is 'to examine the expenditure, administration and policy of' those three bodies (s 10 of the 1994 Act). That committee does not necessarily receive all information where 'sensitive information' is involved (see Sch 3 to the 1994 Act, para 3).

Government Communications Headquarters (GCHQ)

GCHQ is an intelligence and security organisation and a department of the Civil **2.03** Service reporting to the Foreign Secretary. GCHQ's operations fall within the 1994 Act and RIPA. The 1994 Act, s 1 pointedly does not create GCHQ, but simply confirms that 'There shall continue to be a Government Communications Headquarters under the authority of the Secretary of State'.[4]

---

[1] 'The 1994 Act'.   [2] 'The 1989 Act'.
[3] Thus far, the signatory states have not officially acknowledged the existence of the UKUSA agreement.
[4] GCHQ evolved from the Government Code and Cipher School (GCCS) at Bletchley Park.

2.04 Information is typically supplied by GCHQ to bodies such as the MoD, Foreign and Commonwealth Office and other government departments, the Security Service and the Secret Intelligence Service. Its field of operation divides into signals intelligence and 'information assurance' relating to protection of governmental communication and information systems and non governmental systems essential to national functioning. Signals intelligence includes interception and monitoring of communications so to provide data for national security, law enforcement and military operations (and also to provide support for the UK's roles in NATO and European defence).

2.05 In accordance with the 1994 Act, s 3(2) the purposes for which GCHQ may intercept communications are limited to action in the interests of national security, safeguarding economic well-being of the United Kingdom in relation to the actions or intentions of persons outside the British Islands, and the prevention and detection of serious crime.[5]

2.06 Section 3 of the 1994 Act provides that GCHQ's functions are:

(a) to monitor or interfere with electromagnetic, acoustic and other emissions and any equipment producing such emissions and to obtain and provide information derived from or related to such emissions or equipment and from encrypted material; and

(b) to provide advice and assistance about—
   (i) languages, including terminology used for technical matters, and
   (ii) cryptography and other matters relating to the protection of information and other material, to the armed forces of the Crown, to Her Majesty's Government in the United Kingdom or to a Northern Ireland Department or to any other organisation which is determined for the purposes of this section in such manner as may be specified by the Prime Minister.

The Secret Intelligence Service (SIS), (MI6 or the Intelligence Service)

2.07 The SIS's existence is confirmed by s 1 of the 1994 Act. Section 1 states only that 'There shall continue to be a Secret Intelligence Service (in this Act referred to as "the Intelligence Service") under the authority of the Secretary of State'. Its operation is directed by the Chief of the Intelligence Service appointed by the Secretary of State. Its statutory functions are to 'obtain and provide information relating to the actions or intentions of persons outside the British Islands' and 'to perform other tasks relating to the actions or intentions of such persons'. SIS is statutorily obliged to exercise its functions only in the interests of national security, with particular reference to the defence and foreign policies of the Government in the UK or in the interests of the economic well-being of the UK, or in support of the prevention or detection of serious crime (defined by s 11(1)(a)

---

[5] Definitions of 'prevention' and 'detection' of serious crime appear in RIPA at s 81(5) and are applied to GCHQ and Secret Intelligence Service by s 11(1A) of the 1994 Act as amended by RIPA.

of the 1994 Act inserted by RIPA). In October 2005, SIS publicly referred to itself as MI6 and, for the first time, launched a website, for which see the Appendix.

The Security Service ('MI5')

The Security Service (which today also publicly refers to itself as MI5) is the **2.08** domestic secret intelligence service operating with a remit to act covertly to protect national security (including protecting the UK from the actions of persons outside the British Isles). Areas of interest include terrorism, counter-espionage, weapons of mass destruction and action in a support role with policing bodies such as NCIS, NCS, in due course SOCA, and conventional police forces in relation to preventing and detecting serious crime. It acts in a support role where necessary to assist SIS and GCHQ. It also includes within its publicly stated aims the protection of the Critical National Infrastructure.[6] Section 1 of the 1989 Act puts its functions on a statutory footing and the reader is referred to the text of the 1989 Act as amended, in Part C of this Chapter.

B. The statutory framework

Section 5 of 1994 Act enables GCHQ, SIS and MI5 to obtain warrants issued by **2.09** the Secretary of State (using the procedures set out in ss 5 and 6) authorising entry on to property or interference with property or interference with wireless telegraphy (actions akin to those authorised for police bodies under the 1997 Act). Note that this is one area—along with the provisions relating to the Intelligence and Security Committee—where the 1994 Act applies to the Security Service as well as to SIS and GCHQ.

The Secretary of State may issue a warrant[7] for property entry and interference if **2.10** he thinks it:

- *necessary* for the action to be taken for the purpose of assisting:
    - — the Security Service in carrying out any of its functions under the 1989 Act;
    - — the Intelligence Service in carrying out any of its functions under s 1 of the 1994 Act; or

---

[6] The Critical National Infrastructure comprises 'those assets, services and systems that support the economic, political and social life of the UK whose importance is such that any entire or partial loss or compromise could cause large scale loss of life, have a serious impact on the national economy, have other grave social consequences for the community, be of immediate concern to the national government' (quotation from the National Infrastructure Security Coordination Centre, see the Appendix for link). The CNI includes 10 sectors namely Communications, Emergency Services, Energy, Finance, Food, Government & Public Service, Health, Public Safety, Transport and Water.

[7] The warrant may be in respect of any specified property or in respect of wireless telegraphy specified in the warrant (cf the wider scope of overseas warrants under s 7). See s 5(2)(a)–(c) of the 1994 Act for the full requirements.

— GCHQ in carrying out any function which falls within s 3(1)(a) of the 1994 Act (ie monitoring in order to provide information);

and:

- is satisfied that the taking of the action is *proportionate* to what the action seeks to achieve; and
- is satisfied that satisfactory arrangements are in force in relation to the 'information safeguards' referred to below and will apply to the warrant in question.

The Secretary of State must take into account whether what it is thought necessary to achieve could reasonably be achieved by other means (s 5(2A)).

Information safeguards[8]

2.11   Under s 2(2)(a) of the 1989 Act (for the Security Service), s 2(2)(a) of the 1994 Act (for SIS), and s 4(2)(a) of the 1994 Act (for GCHQ), the heads of the respective services[9] are responsible for ensuring that there are arrangements for securing that:

- (in the case of SIS) no information is obtained other than is necessary for the proper discharge of its functions, and that no information is disclosed by it except so far as necessary for the proper discharge of its functions, in the interests of national security, for the purpose of the prevention or detection of serious crime or for the purpose of any criminal proceedings (s 2(2)(a) of the 1994 Act);
- (in the case of the Security Service) no information is obtained by the Service except so far as necessary for the proper discharge of its functions or disclosed by it except so far as necessary for the proper discharge of its functions or for the purpose of the prevention or detection of serious crime or for the purpose of any criminal proceedings (s 2(2)(a) of the 1989 Act);
- (in the case of GCHQ) no information is obtained by it except so far as necessary for the proper discharge of its functions and no information is disclosed by it except so far as necessary for the proper discharge of its functions or for the purpose of any criminal proceedings (s 4(2)(a)).

Limitations upon SIS and GCHQ warrants

2.12   SIS and GCHQ are not entitled to make use of the warrantry provisions of the 1994 Act to obtain a warrant for the purposes of the exercise of their functions in support of the prevention or detection of serious crime if the property relates to property in the British Islands (s 5(3) of the 1994 Act).

---

[8]   For each service there a restriction that the services must not act to further the interests of any UK political party (or any political party at all in the case of the Security Service): see s 2(2)(b) of the 1989 Act, and ss 2(2)(b) and 4(2)(b) of the 1994 Act.

[9]   For SIS, the Chief of the Intelligence Service, for GCHQ, the Director and for the Security Service, the Director-General.

Limitations upon Security Service warrants where assisting NCIS or National Crime Squad, etc

A warrant issued under the 1994 Act on an application by the Security Service in **2.13** order to act in support of the activities of police forces, NCIS, and the National Crime Squad and other law enforcement agencies (in the prevention and detection of serious crime)[10] may not relate to property in the British Islands *unless* the conduct being acted against is or would be offences:

- involving the use of violence,
- resulting in substantial financial gain,
- involving conduct by a large number of persons in pursuit of a common purpose;
- for which a person who has attained the age of 21 (18 in England and Wales) could reasonably be expected to be sentenced to imprisonment for a term of three years or more without previous convictions (s 5(3)(a)).

To summarise, the Security Service when assisting NCIS and NCS in the prevention or detection of serious crime is entitled to obtain a warrant for that purpose to the same extent as are NCIS and the National Crime Squad themselves (the provisions mirror s 93(4) of the Police Act 1997, discussed above). Note that when SOCA comes into being the references in the 1989 Act to NCIS and NCS are replaced with references to SOCA.

Security Service: limitations upon power to obtain warrants to act on behalf of SIS and GCHQ

The Security Service has additional provisions in relation to warrantry. It is pro- **2.14** vided by s 5(4) and (5) of the 1994 Act that the Security Service may make an application for a warrant to be issued authorising that Service to take action *on behalf of* the Intelligence Service or GCHQ but may not make an application unless the action proposed would be action in respect of which the SIS or GCHQ could make such an application, and is otherwise than in support of the prevention or detection of serious crime (s 5(5)).

Duration and renewal of Secretary of State warrants

By s 6 of the 1994 Act warrants must be issued by the Secretary of State personally **2.15** (or in an urgent case, by a senior official, provided that the Secretary of State has expressly authorised the issue of the warrant and that fact is endorsed on the warrant). A warrant normally expires after six months save that where a warrant is issued by a senior official it will expire at the end of the second working day

---

[10] Section 1(4) of the 1989 Act.

following the day of authorisation. The Secretary of State may renew a warrant before expiry if necessary for six months beginning with date of expiry, and is obliged by s 6(4) to cancel a warrant if he is satisfied that the action authorised by it is no longer necessary.

2.16 In September 2005 the Home Secretary published a draft Bill (the Terrorism Bill 2005), cl 25 of which would amend ss 6 and 7 of the 1994 Act. The draft amendments are noted in the footnotes to the text of ss 6 and 7.

Overseas Secretary of State warrants

2.17 Section 7 of the 1994 Act enables SIS and GCHQ to obtain a warrant from the Secretary of State to carry out actions to enter or interfere with property and wireless telegraphy in overseas locations (outside the British Isles) and escape liability in the UK for those overseas activities. Proposed amendments to s 7 published in September 2005 deal with situations where property was believed to be outside the British Isles but in fact was not. (See footnotes to ss 6 and 7 of the 1994 Act).

Scope and requirements of overseas warrants

2.18 Authorisations may relate to a particular activity, or activities fitting a particular description or undertaken in the course of some specified operation or they or may be limited to a person or persons fitting a given description. (Therefore in particular the authorised activities need not relate to specific premises but may be person-specific).

2.19 Before issuing an overseas warrant the Secretary of State must be satisfied that:

- acts done in reliance on the authorisation, or the operation in the course of which the acts may be done, will be necessary for the proper discharge of a function of the Intelligence Service or GCHQ; and
- there are satisfactory arrangements in force to secure that nothing will be done in reliance on the authorisation beyond what is necessary for the proper discharge of a function of the Intelligence Service or GCHQ; and
- in so far as any acts may be done in reliance on the authorisation, their nature and likely consequences will be reasonable, having regard to the purposes for which they are carried out; and
- the same 'information safeguards' as were referred to above in relation to domestic warrants are in place (see s 7(3)(c) for details).

The rules as to renewal and cancellation of overseas Secretary of State warrants are the same as those referred to above for domestic warrants.

The Intelligence Services Commissioner

2.20 Section 59 of RIPA replaces the previous provisions of the 1989 Act and the 1994 Act (which established commissioners for both the Intelligence Services and the

Security Service), with provision for a single Intelligence Services Commissioner, whose remit (among other matters)[11] is to keep under review the exercise of the Secretary of State's powers under ss 5–7 of the 1994 Act, ie the warrantry arrangements for authorising interference with property by SIS, the Security Service or GCHQ in certain circumstances. His obligations include the provision of assistance to the Investigatory Powers Tribunal and the provision of at least an annual report to the Prime Minister (which, subject to editing, is then laid before Parliament: s 59(3)–(5)).

Every member of the Intelligence Services, every official of the department of the Secretary of State and every member of HM forces is under a statutory duty (s 60) to disclose to and provide the Intelligence Services Commissioner with all documents and information which he may require to enable him to carry out his functions. **2.21**

C. Text of The Intelligence Services Act 1994[12] as amended

ARRANGEMENT OF SECTIONS

The Secret Intelligence Service

1. The Secret Intelligence Service.
2. The Chief of the Intelligence Service.

GCHQ

3. The Government Communications Headquarters.
4. The Director of GCHQ.

Authorisation of certain actions

5. Warrants: general.
6. Warrants: procedure and duration, etc.
7. Authorisation of acts outside the British Islands.
8. *repealed*
9. *repealed*

The Intelligence and Security Committee

10. The Intelligence and Security Committee.

---

[11] Eg reviewing the Secretary of State's exercise of his powers under RIPA, Parts II and III, and the exercise and performance of powers and duties by the Intelligence Services, MoD, and HM Forces, under Parts II and III of RIPA other than in Northern Ireland (s 59).

[12] Act passed on 26 May 1994, in force on 5 December 1994 as regards the sections here (the Intelligence Services Act 1994 (Commencement) Order 1994 (SI 1994 No 2734)).

Supplementary

11. Interpretation and consequential amendments.
12. Short title, commencement and extent.
[. . .]

The Secret Intelligence Service

The Secret Intelligence Service

1. (1) There shall continue to be a Secret Intelligence Service (in this Act referred to as "the Intelligence Service") under the authority of the Secretary of State; and, subject to subsection (2) below, its functions shall be—

    (a) to obtain and provide information relating to the actions or intentions of persons outside the British Islands; and

    (b) to perform other tasks relating to the actions or intentions of such persons.

(2) The functions of the Intelligence Service shall be exercisable only—

    (a) in the interests of national security, with particular reference to the defence and foreign policies of Her Majesty's Government in the United Kingdom; or

    (b) in the interests of the economic well-being of the United Kingdom; or

    (c) in support of the prevention or detection of serious crime.

The Chief of the Intelligence Service

2. (1) The operations of the Intelligence Service shall continue to be under the control of a Chief of that Service appointed by the Secretary of State.

(2) The Chief of the Intelligence Service shall be responsible for the efficiency of that Service and it shall be his duty to ensure—

    (a) that there are arrangements for securing that no information is obtained by the Intelligence Service except so far as necessary for the proper discharge of its functions and that no information is disclosed by it except so far as necessary—

        (i) for that purpose;

        (ii) in the interests of national security;

        (iii) for the purpose of the prevention or detection of serious crime; or

        (iv) for the purpose of any criminal proceedings; and

    (b) that the Intelligence Service does not take any action to further the interests of any United Kingdom political party.

(3) Without prejudice to the generality of subsection (2)(a) above, the disclosure of information shall be regarded as necessary for the proper discharge of the functions of the Intelligence Service if it consists of—

    (a) the disclosure of records subject to and in accordance with the Public Records Act 1958; or

(b) the disclosure, subject to and in accordance with arrangements approved by the Secretary of State, of information to the Comptroller and Auditor General for the purposes of his functions.

(4) The Chief of the Intelligence Service shall make an annual report on the work of the Intelligence Service to the Prime Minister and the Secretary of State and may at any time report to either of them on any matter relating to its work.

GCHQ

The Government Communications Headquarters

3. (1) There shall continue to be a Government Communications Headquarters under the authority of the Secretary of State; and, subject to subsection (2) below, its functions shall be—

(a) to monitor or interfere with electromagnetic, acoustic and other emissions and any equipment producing such emissions and to obtain and provide information derived from or related to such emissions or equipment and from encrypted material; and

(b) to provide advice and assistance about—

(i) languages, including terminology used for technical matters, and

(ii) cryptography and other matters relating to the protection of information and other material, to the armed forces of the Crown, to Her Majesty's Government in the United Kingdom or to a Northern Ireland Department or to any other organisation which is determined for the purposes of this section in such manner as may be specified by the Prime Minister.

(2) The functions referred to in subsection (1)(a) above shall be exercisable only—

(a) in the interests of national security, with particular reference to the defence and foreign policies of Her Majesty's Government in the United Kingdom; or

(b) in the interests of the economic well-being of the United Kingdom in relation to the actions or intentions of persons outside the British Islands; or

(c) in support of the prevention or detection of serious crime.

(3) In this Act the expression "GCHQ" refers to the Government Communications Headquarters and to any unit or part of a unit of the armed forces of the Crown which is for the time being required by the Secretary of State to assist the Government Communications Headquarters in carrying out its functions.

The Director of GCHQ

4. (1) The operations of GCHQ shall continue to be under the control of a Director appointed by the Secretary of State.

(2) The Director shall be responsible for the efficiency of GCHQ and it shall be his duty to ensure—

(a) that there are arrangements for securing that no information is obtained by GCHQ except so far as necessary for the proper discharge of its functions and that no information is disclosed by it except so far as necessary for that purpose or for the purpose of any criminal proceedings; and

(b) that GCHQ does not take any action to further the interests of any United Kingdom political party.

(3) Without prejudice to the generality of subsection (2)(a) above, the disclosure of information shall be regarded as necessary for the proper discharge of the functions of GCHQ if it consists of—

(a) the disclosure of records subject to and in accordance with the Public Records Act 1958; or

(b) the disclosure, subject to and in accordance with arrangements approved by the Secretary of State, of information to the Comptroller and Auditor General for the purposes of his functions.

(4) The Director shall make an annual report on the work of GCHQ to the Prime Minister and the Secretary of State and may at any time report to either of them on any matter relating to its work.

Authorisation of certain actions

Warrants: general

5. (1) No entry on or interference with property or with wireless telegraphy shall be unlawful if it is authorised by a warrant issued by the Secretary of State under this section.

(2) The Secretary of State may, on an application made by the Security Service, the Intelligence Service or GCHQ, issue a warrant under this section authorising the taking, subject to subsection (3) below, of such action as is specified in the warrant in respect of any property so specified or in respect of wireless telegraphy so specified if the Secretary of State—

(a)[13] thinks it necessary for the action to be taken for the purpose of assisting, as the case may be,—

(i) the Security Service in carrying out any of its functions under the 1989 Act; or

(ii) the Intelligence Service in carrying out any of its functions under section 1 above; or

(iii) GCHQ in carrying out any function which falls within section 3(1)(a) above; and

---

[13] Amended by RIPA, s 74(1).

(b)[14] is satisfied that the taking of the action is proportionate to what the action seeks to achieve; and

(c) is satisfied that satisfactory arrangements are in force under section 2(2)(a) of the 1989 Act (duties of the Director-General of the Security Service), section 2(2)(a) above or section 4(2)(a) above with respect to the disclosure of information obtained by virtue of this section and that any information obtained under the warrant will be subject to those arrangements.

(2A)[15] The matters to be taken into account in considering whether the requirements of subsection (2)(a) and (b) are satisfied in the case of any warrant shall include whether what it is thought necessary to achieve by the conduct authorised by the warrant could reasonably be achieved by other means.

(3)[16] A warrant issued on the application of the Intelligence Service or GCHQ for the purposes of the exercise of their functions by virtue of section 1(2)(c) or 3(2)(c) above may not relate to property in the British Islands.

(3A) A warrant issued on the application of the Security Service for the purposes of the exercise of their function under section 1(4) of the Security Service Act 1989 may not relate to property in the British Islands unless it authorises the taking of action in relation to conduct within subsection (3B) below.

(3B) Conduct is within this subsection if it constitutes (or, if it took place in the United Kingdom, would constitute) one or more offences, and either-

(a) it involves the use of violence, results in substantial financial gain or is conduct by a large number of persons in pursuit of a common purpose; or

(b)[17] the offence or one of the offences is an offence for which a person who has attained the age of twenty-one (eighteen in relation to England and Wales) and has no previous convictions could reasonably be expected to be sentenced to imprisonment for a term of three years or more.

(4) Subject to subsection (5) below, the Security Service may make an application under subsection (2) above for a warrant to be issued authorising that Service (or a person acting on its behalf) to take such action as is specified in the warrant on behalf of the Intelligence Service or GCHQ and, where such a warrant is issued, the functions of the Security Service shall include the carrying out of the action so specified, whether or not it would otherwise be within its functions.

---

[14] Amended by RIPA, s 74(2).   [15] Added by RIPA, s 74.
[16] Subs (3) replaced and (3A) and (3B) added by Security Service Act 1996, s 2.
[17] Amended by the Criminal Justice and Court Services Act 2000, Sch 7, Pt II, para 119.

(5) The Security Service may not make an application for a warrant by virtue of subsection (4) above except where the action proposed to be authorised by the warrant—

  (a) is action in respect of which the Intelligence Service or, as the case may be, GCHQ could make such an application; and

  (b) is to be taken otherwise than in support of the prevention or detection of serious crime.

Warrants: procedure and duration, etc.

6[18] (1) A warrant shall not be issued except—

  (a) under the hand of the Secretary of State; or

  (b)[19] in an urgent case where the Secretary of State has expressly authorised its issue and a statement of that fact is endorsed on it, under the hand of a senior official .

(2) A warrant shall, unless renewed under subsection (3) below, cease to have effect—

  (a) if the warrant was under the hand of the Secretary of State, at the end of the period of six months beginning with the day on which it was issued; and

  (b) in any other case, at the end of the period ending with the second[20] working day following that day.

(3) If at any time before the day on which a warrant would cease to have effect the Secretary of State considers it necessary for the warrant to continue to have effect for the purpose for which it was issued, he may by an instrument under his hand renew it for a period of six months beginning with that day.

(4) The Secretary of State shall cancel a warrant if he is satisfied that the action authorised by it is no longer necessary.

(5) In the preceding provisions of this section "warrant" means a warrant under section 5 above.

(6) As regards the Security Service, this section and section 5 above have effect in place of section 3 (property warrants) of the 1989 Act, and accordingly—

  (a) a warrant issued under that section of the 1989 Act and current when this section and section 5 above come into force shall be treated as a warrant

---

[18] Section 25 of the draft Terrorism Bill 2005, in September 2005 proposed addition of s 6(1)(d) and new subsections (1A) and (1B) as follows: 'or (d) in an urgent case where the Secretary of State has expressly authorised the issue of warrants in accordance with this paragraph by specified senior officials and a statement of that fact is endorsed on the warrant, under the hand of any of the specified officials.' '(1A) But a warrant issued in accordance with subsection (1)(d) may authorise the taking of an action only if the action is an action in relation to property which, immediately before the issue of the warrant, would, if done outside the British Islands, have been authorised by virtue of an authorisation under section 7 that was in force at that time. (1B) A senior official who issues a warrant in accordance with subsection (1)(d) must inform the Secretary of State about the issue of the warrant as soon as practicable after issuing it'.   [19] Part repealed by RIPA, Sch 5.

[20] Section 25 of the draft Terrorism Bill 2005 in September 2005 proposed that the reference to 'second' be amended to 'fifth'.

under section 5 above, but without any change in the date on which the warrant was in fact issued or last renewed; and

(b) section 3 of the 1989 Act shall cease to have effect.

Authorisation of acts outside the British Islands

7. (1) If, apart from this section, a person would be liable in the United Kingdom for any act done outside the British Islands, he shall not be so liable if the act is one which is authorised to be done by virtue of an authorisation given by the Secretary of State under this section.

(2) In subsection (1) above "liable in the United Kingdom" means liable under the criminal or civil law of any part of the United Kingdom.

(3) The Secretary of State shall not give an authorisation under this section unless he is satisfied—

(a)[21] that any acts which may be done in reliance on the authorisation or, as the case may be, the operation in the course of which the acts may be done will be necessary for the proper discharge of a function of the Intelligence Service or GCHQ; and

(b) that there are satisfactory arrangements in force to secure—

(i) that nothing will be done in reliance on the authorisation beyond what is necessary for the proper discharge of a function of the Intelligence Service or GCHQ; and

(ii) that, in so far as any acts may be done in reliance on the authorisation, their nature and likely consequences will be reasonable, having regard to the purposes for which they are carried out; and

(c) that there are satisfactory arrangements in force under section 2(2)(a) or 4(2)(a) above with respect to the disclosure of information obtained by virtue of this section and that any information obtained by virtue of anything done in reliance on the authorisation will be subject to those arrangements.

(4) Without prejudice to the generality of the power of the Secretary of State to give an authorisation under this section, such an authorisation—

(a) may relate to a particular act or acts, to acts of a description specified in the authorisation or to acts undertaken in the course of an operation so specified;

(b) may be limited to a particular person or persons of a description so specified; and

(c) may be subject to conditions so specified.

---

[21] (a), (b) and (c) amended by the Anti-Terrorism, Crime and Security Act 2001, s 116(1).

(5)   An authorisation shall not be given under this section except—

    (a)   under the hand of the Secretary of State; or

    (b)[22] in an urgent case where the Secretary of State has expressly authorised it to be given and a statement of that fact is endorsed on it, under the hand of a senior official. . . .

(6)   An authorisation shall, unless renewed under subsection (7) below, cease to have effect—

    (a)   if the authorisation was given under the hand of the Secretary of State, at the end of the period of six months beginning with the day on which it was given;

    (b)   in any other case, at the end of the period ending with the second[23] working day following the day on which it was given.

(7)   If at any time before the day on which an authorisation would cease to have effect the Secretary of State considers it necessary for the authorisation to continue to have effect for the purpose for which it was given, he may by an instrument under his hand renew it for a period of six months beginning with that day.

(8)   The Secretary of State shall cancel an authorisation if he is satisfied that any act authorised by it is no longer necessary.

(9)[24] For the purposes of this section the reference in subsection (1) to an act done outside the British Islands includes a reference to any act which-

    (a)   is done in the British Islands; but

    (b)   is or is intended to be done in relation to apparatus that is believed to be outside the British Islands, or in relation to anything appearing to originate from such apparatus;

and in this subsection "apparatus" has the same meaning as in the Regulation of Investigatory Powers Act 2000 (c. 23).

(10)–(14) [*proposed, see note*][25]

---

[22] Part repealed by RIPA, Sch 5.

[23] Section 25 of the draft Terrorism Bill 2005 published at time of writing proposed that the reference to 'second' working day be amended to state 'fifth'.

[24] Added by the Anti-Terrorism, Crime and Security Act 2001, s 116(2).

[25] Section 25 of the draft Terrorism Bill 2005, in September 2005 proposed the following additions to s 7, namely new subsections (10)–(14):

    (10) Where—

        (a)   a person is authorised by virtue of this section to do an act outside the British Islands in relation to property,

        (b)   the act is one which, in relation to property within the British Islands, is capable of being authorised by a warrant under section 5,

        (c)   a person authorised by virtue of this section to do that act outside the British Islands, does the act in relation to that property while it is within the British Islands, and

        (d)   the act is done in circumstances falling within subsection (11) or (12) this section shall have effect as if the act were done outside the British Islands in relation to that property.

8.[26]

9.[27]

The Intelligence and Security Committee

10. (1) There shall be a Committee, to be known as the Intelligence and Security Committee and in this section referred to as "the Committee", to examine the expenditure, administration and policy of—

 (a) the Security Service;

 (b) the Intelligence Service; and

 (c) GCHQ.

(2) The Committee shall consist of nine members—

 (a) who shall be drawn both from the members of the House of Commons and from the members of the House of Lords; and

 (b) none of whom shall be a Minister of the Crown.

(3) The members of the Committee shall be appointed by the Prime Minister after consultation with the Leader of the Opposition, within the meaning of the Ministerial and other Salaries Act 1975; and one of those members shall be so appointed as Chairman of the Committee.

(4) Schedule 3 to this Act shall have effect with respect to the tenure of office of members of, the procedure of and other matters relating to, the Committee; and in that Schedule "the Committee" has the same meaning as in this section.

(5) The Committee shall make an annual report on the discharge of their functions to the Prime Minister and may at any time report to him on any matter relating to the discharge of those functions.

---

(11) An act is done in circumstances falling within this subsection if it is done in relation to the property at a time when it is believed to be outside the British Islands.

(12) An act is done in circumstances falling within this subsection if it -

 (a) is done in relation to property which was mistakenly believed to be outside the British Islands either when the authorisation under this section was given or at a subsequent time or which has been brought within the British Islands since the giving of the authorisation; but

 (b) is done before the end of the fifth working day after the day on which the presence of the property in the British Islands first becomes known.

(13) In subsection (12) the reference to the day on which the presence of the property in the British Islands first becomes known is a reference to the day on which it first appears to a member of the Intelligence Service or of GCHQ, after the relevant time -

 (a) that the belief that the property was outside the British Islands was mistaken; or

 (b) that the property is within those Islands.

(14) In subsection (13) .the relevant time. means, as the case may be -

 (a) the time of the mistaken belief mentioned in subsection (12)(a); or

 (b) the time at which the property was, or was most recently, brought within the British Islands.

[26] Section 8 repealed by RIPA, Sch 5.   [27] Section 9 repealed by RIPA, Sch 5.

(6) The Prime Minister shall lay before each House of Parliament a copy of each annual report made by the Committee under subsection (5) above together with a statement as to whether any matter has been excluded from that copy in pursuance of subsection (7) below.

(7) If it appears to the Prime Minister, after consultation with the Committee, that the publication of any matter in a report would be prejudicial to the continued discharge of the functions of either of the Services or, as the case may be, GCHQ, the Prime Minister may exclude that matter from the copy of the report as laid before each House of Parliament.

Supplementary

Interpretation and consequential amendments

11. (1) In this Act—

   (a) "the 1989 Act" means the Security Service Act 1989;

   (b)[28] . . .;

   (c) "Minister of the Crown" has the same meaning as in the Ministers of the Crown Act 1975;

   (d)[29] "senior official" has the same meaning as in the Regulation of Investigatory Powers Act 2000;

   (e) "wireless telegraphy" has the same meaning as in the Wireless Telegraphy Act 1949[30] and, in relation to wireless telegraphy, "interfere" has the same meaning as in that Act;

   (f) "working day" means any day other than a Saturday, a Sunday, Christmas Day, Good Friday or a day which is a bank holiday under the Banking and Financial Dealings Act 1971 in any part of the United Kingdom.

(1A)[31] Section 81(5) of the Regulation of Investigatory Powers Act 2000 (meaning of "prevention" and "detection"), so far as it relates to serious crime, shall apply

   (a)[32] for the purposes of section 3 above, as it applies for the purposes of Chapter 1 of Part 1 of that Act; and

   (b) for the other purposes of this Act, as it applies for the purposes of the provisions of that Act not contained in that Chapter.

(2) In consequence of the preceding provisions of this Act, the 1989 Act, the Official Secrets Act 1989 and the Official Secrets Act 1989 (Prescription) Order 1990 shall have effect subject to the amendments in Schedule 4 to this Act.

---

[28] Repealed by RIPA, Sch 5.   [29] Replaced by RIPA, s 74(4).

[30] See s 19 of the Wireless Telegraphy Act 1949.   [31] Added by RIPA, Sch 4, para 6.

[32] (a) and (b) substituted by by the Anti-Terrorism, Crime and Security Act 2001, s 116(3).

Short title, commencement and extent

12. (1) This Act may be cited as the Intelligence Services Act 1994.

(2) This Act shall come into force on such day as the Secretary of State may by an order made by statutory instrument appoint, and different days may be so appointed for different provisions or different purposes.

(3) This Act extends to Northern Ireland.

(4) Her Majesty may by Order in Council direct that any of the provisions of this Act specified in the Order shall extend, with such exceptions, adaptations and modifications as appear to Her to be necessary or expedient, to the Isle of Man, any of the Channel Islands or any colony.

SCHEDULES

SCHEDULE 1—*repealed by Sch. 5 of RIPA 2000*
SCHEDULE 2—*repealed by Sch. 5 of RIPA 2000*

SCHEDULE 3 SECTION 10(4)

The Intelligence and Security Committee

Tenure of office

1. (1) Subject to the provisions of this paragraph, a member of the Committee shall hold office for the duration of the Parliament in which he is appointed.

(2) A member of the Committee shall vacate office—

   (a) if he ceases to be a member of the House of Commons;

   (b) if he ceases to be a member of the House of Lords;

   (c) if he becomes a Minister of the Crown; or

   (d) if he is required to do so by the Prime Minister on the appointment, in accordance with section 10(3) of this Act, of another person as a member in his place.

(3) A member of the Committee may resign at any time by notice to the Prime Minister.

(4) Past service is no bar to appointment as a member of the Committee.

Procedure

2. (1) Subject to the following provisions of this Schedule, the Committee may determine their own procedure.

(2) If on any matter there is an equality of voting among the members of the Committee, the Chairman shall have a second or casting vote.

(3) The Chairman may appoint one of the members of the Committee to act, in his absence, as chairman at any meeting of the Committee, but sub-paragraph (2) above shall not apply to a chairman appointed under this sub-paragraph.

(4) The quorum of the Committee shall be three.

Access to information

3. (1) If the Director-General of the Security Service, the Chief of the Intelligence Service or the Director of GCHQ is asked by the Committee to disclose any information, then, as to the whole or any part of the information which is sought, he shall either—
   (a) arrange for it to be made available to the Committee subject to and in accordance with arrangements approved by the Secretary of State; or
   (b) inform the Committee that it cannot be disclosed either—
       (i) because it is sensitive information (as defined in paragraph 4 below) which, in his opinion, should not be made available under paragraph (a) above; or
       (ii) because the Secretary of State has determined that it should not be disclosed.

(2) The fact that any particular information is sensitive information shall not prevent its disclosure under sub-paragraph (1)(a) above if the Director-General, the Chief or the Director (as the case may require) considers it safe to disclose it.

(3) Information which has not been disclosed to the Committee on the ground specified in sub-paragraph (1)(b)(i) above shall be disclosed to them if the Secretary of State considers it desirable in the public interest.

(4) The Secretary of State shall not make a determination under sub-paragraph (1)(b)(ii) above with respect to any information on the grounds of national security alone and, subject to that, he shall not make such a determination unless the information appears to him to be of such a nature that, if he were requested to produce it before a Departmental Select Committee of the House of Commons, he would think it proper not to do so.

(5) The disclosure of information to the Committee in accordance with the preceding provisions of this paragraph shall be regarded for the purposes of the 1989 Act or, as the case may be, this Act as necessary for the proper discharge of the functions of the Security Service, the Intelligence Service or, as the case may require, GCHQ.

Sensitive information

4. The following information is sensitive information for the purposes of paragraph 3 above—
   (a) information which might lead to the identification of, or provide details of, sources of information, other assistance or operational methods available to the Security Service, the Intelligence Service or GCHQ;
   (b) information about particular operations which have been, are being or are proposed to be undertaken in pursuance of any of the functions of those bodies; and

(c) information provided by, or by an agency of, the Government of a territory outside the United Kingdom where that Government does not consent to the disclosure of the information.

D. Text of The Security Service Act 1989 as amended

Arrangement of Sections

1 The Security Service.
2 The Director-General.
3 *ceased to have effect.*
4 *repealed*
5 *repealed*
6 Expenses.
7 Short title, commencement and extent.
Schedules *repealed*

The Security Service.

1. (1) There shall continue to be a Security Service (in this Act referred to as "the
Service") under the authority of the Secretary of State.

(2) The function of the Service shall be the protection of national security and,
in particular, its protection against threats from espionage, terrorism and
sabotage, from the activities of agents of foreign powers and from actions
intended to overthrow or undermine parliamentary democracy by political,
industrial or violent means.

(3) It shall also be the function of the Service to safeguard the economic well-
being of the United Kingdom against threats posed by the actions or intentions of persons outside the British Islands.

(4)[33] It shall also be the function of the Service to act in support of the activities
of police forces, [the National Criminal Intelligence Service, the National
Crime Squad], *the Serious Organised Crime Agency* [34] and other law enforcement agencies in the prevention and detection of serious crime.

(5)[35] Section 81(5) of the Regulation of Investigatory Powers Act 2000 (meaning
of "prevention" and "detection"), so far as it relates to serious crime, shall
apply for the purposes of this Act as it applies for the purposes of the provisions of that Act not contained in Chapter I of Part I.

---

[33] Added by the Security Service Act 1996, s 1 and amended by the Police Act 1997, Sch 9, para 60.
[34] The reference to SOCA will be inserted when Sch 4, para 56 of the SOCAP Act 2005 is in
force, replacing the text in square brackets.   [35] Added by RIPA, Sch 4, para 4.

The Director-General

2. (1) The operations of the Service shall continue to be under the control of a Director-General appointed by the Secretary of State.

(2) The Director-General shall be responsible for the efficiency of the Service and it shall be his duty to ensure—

(a)[36] that there are arrangements for securing that no information is obtained by the Service except so far as necessary for the proper discharge of its functions or disclosed by it except so far as necessary for that purpose or for the purpose of the prevention or detection of serious crime or for the purpose of any criminal proceedings; and

(b) that the Service does not take any action to further the interests of any political party; and

(c)[37] that there are arrangements, agreed with [the Director General of the National Criminal Intelligence Service] *the Director General of the Serious Organised Crime Agency,* for coordinating the activities of the Service in pursuance of section 1(4) of this Act with the activities of police, [the National Criminal Intelligence Service, the National Crime Squad], *the Serious Organised Crime Agency* and other law[38] enforcement agencies

(3) The arrangements mentioned in subsection (2)(a) above shall be such as to ensure that information in the possession of the Service is not disclosed for use in determining whether a person should be employed, or continue to be employed, by any person, or in any office or capacity, except in accordance with provisions in that behalf approved by the Secretary of State.

(3A)[39] Without prejudice to the generality of subsection(2)(a) above, the disclosure of information shall be regarded as necessary for the proper discharge of the functions of the Security Service if it consists of-

(a) the disclosure of records subject to and in accordance with the Public Records Act 1958; or

(b) the disclosure, subject to and in accordance with arrangements approved by the Secretary of State, of information to the Comptroller and Auditor General for the purposes of his functions.

(3B) . . .[40]

---

[36] Amended by the Intelligence Services Act 1994, Sch 4, para 1 and by RIPA, Sch 4, para 4(2).

[37] Added by the Security Service Act 1996, s 1 and amended by the Police Act 1997, s 12 and Sch 9, para 61.

[38] The references to the Director General of SOCA and to SOCA in (2)(c) will be inserted when Sch 4, para 57 of the SOCAP Act 2005 is in force, replacing the text in square brackets.

[39] Added by the Intelligence Services Act 1994, Sch 4, para 1.

[40] Added by the Security Services Act 1996, s 1 and repealed by the Police Act 1997, Sch 10.

(4) The Director-General shall make an annual report on the work of the Service to the Prime Minister and the Secretary of State and may at any time report to either of them on any matter relating to its work.

Warrants.

3.[41]

4.[42]

5.[43]

Expenses.

6. Any expenses incurred by the Secretary of State under this Act shall be defrayed out of money provided by Parliament.

Short title, commencement and extent.

7. (1) This Act may be cited as the Security Service Act 1989.

(2) This Act shall come into force on such day as the Secretary of State may by an order made by statutory instrument appoint, and different days may be appointed for different provisions or different purposes.

(3) This Act extends to Northern Ireland.

(4) Her Majesty may by Order in Council direct that any of the provisions of this Act specified in the Order shall extend, with such exceptions, adaptations and modifications as may be so specified, to the Isle of Man, any of the Channel Islands or any colony.

---

[41] By s 6 of the Intelligence Services Act 1994 this section has ceased to have effect and is replaced by ss 5 and 6 of that Act.   [42] Section 4 repealed by RIPA, Sch 5.

[43] Section 5 repealed by RIPA, Sch 5.

PART II

THE REGULATION OF INVESTIGATORY POWERS ACT 2000 (AS AMENDED)

LIST OF STATUTORY SECTIONS

Regulation of Investigatory Powers Act 2000[1] (2000 c. 23)

Royal Assent 28 July 2000

PART I

COMMUNICATIONS

CHAPTER I

INTERCEPTION

Unlawful and authorised interception

Section

1. Unlawful interception.
2. Meaning and location of "interception" etc.
3. Lawful interception without an interception warrant.
4. Power to provide for lawful interception.
5. Interception with a warrant.

Interception warrants

6. Application for issue of an interception warrant.
7. Issue of warrants.
8. Contents of warrants.
9. Duration, cancellation and renewal of warrants.
10. Modification of warrants and certificates.
11. Implementation of warrants.

---

[1] As to surveillance in Scotland see the Scotland Act 1998 (Transfer of Functions to the Scottish Ministers etc.) (No 2) Order 2000 (SI 2000 No 2000/3253) Art 2 and Sch 1 and the Scotland Act 1998 (Transfer of Functions to the Scottish Ministers etc.) (No 2) Order 2003 (SI 2003/2617 (s 12), Arts 2 and 3, Sch 1, para 2, Sch 2). See also the Scotland Act 1998, s 63. For Surveillance under Scots law see the RIPA (Scotland) Act 2000 which mirrors Parts II and IV of RIPA. Complaints under the Scottish version of RIPA may be made to the Investigatory Powers Tribunal (there is no separate Tribunal for Scotland).

---

[2] This section is 'treated as if inserted' into the Act in its application to the detection of television receivers only. See The RIPA (British Broadcasting Corporation) Order 2001 (SI 2001/1057), Art 3.

PART III
INVESTIGATION OF ELECTRONIC DATA PROTECTED BY ENCRYPTION ETC.

3

INTERCEPTION OF COMMUNICATIONS: RIPA, PART I, CHAPTER I, SS 1–20

A. Discussion

Introduction

Chapter I of Part I of RIPA (ss 1–20) governs the interception of communications **3.01**
It is the successor to the Interception of Communications Act 1985, replacement
of which was prompted by *Halford v UK*[1] when the 1985 Act was found to be
wanting. In human rights terms the Human Rights Act 1998 meant that the
issues highlighted in *Halford* were drawn into focus because there was the real
prospect that intercepted communications obtained otherwise than under a
properly formulated legal code (and so not 'in accordance with the law' for
Convention purposes) would be found to be unlawfully obtained as a result of s
6(2) of the 1998 Act, which provides that it is unlawful for public authorities to
act in a way which is incompatible with Convention rights.[2]

EU Directive on Privacy and Electronic Communications

Change, in the form of a fully codified piece of legislation, was also prompted by **3.02**
the Telecoms Data Protection Directive (97/66 EC) which required Member
States to legislate to protect the confidentiality of communications over public
networks, subject to various exceptions. That Directive was later updated and
replaced by the EU Directive on Privacy and Electronic Communications

---

[1] (1997) 24 EHRR 523. The 1985 Act was aimed at interception of communications in public
systems and did not cover private telephone networks. A telephone intercept attached to a private
network fell outside the Act and it was found that interception had been 'otherwise than in accordance with the law' for the purposes of the Convention. It was in part to plug the legislative gap that
RIPA, Part I was enacted. See also *R v Effick* [1995] 1 AC 309 HL.

[2] The prime candidates of relevance in interception cases are Arts 8 and 6.

(2002/58/EC), see the Privacy and Electronic Communications (EC Directive) Regulations 2003 (SI 2003 No 2426).[3]

Overview

3.03 Chapter I of RIPA, Part I creates offences (akin to those previously created by the 1985 Act) of unlawful interception, and also a tort of unlawful interception which in some circumstances arises in relation to the interception of communications over private telecommunications systems.[4] Sections 3 and 4 allow interception in some instances without a warrant, and in other circumstances s 5 provides a mechanism for obtaining a warrant from the Secretary of State (ss 5–11). The remaining sections of Chapter I provide a system for compensating service providers who incur cost in intercepting communications at the request of the State, and retains a restriction which the 1985 Act created whereby material obtained by interception under warrant may not be adduced in evidence.

The Interception of Communications Code of Practice and the Interception of Communications Commissioner[5]

3.04 The Interception of Communications Code of Practice has been issued by the Secretary of State and is discussed in Chapter 18. It should be consulted alongside the statutory provisions. RIPA provides (at s 72) that Codes of Practice are admissible as evidence in criminal and civil proceedings. If any provision of the Code appears relevant before any court or tribunal considering any such proceedings or to one of the commissioners responsible for overseeing the powers conferred by RIPA (see Part IV of the Act), it *must* be taken into account.

The offences of unlawful interception

3.05 By s 1(1) and (2) of RIPA it is an offence intentionally and without lawful authority[6] to intercept, at any place in the United Kingdom,[7] any communication *in the course*

---

[3] This Directive addresses consumer and technological changes since the 1997 Directive, introducing controls on the use of 'cookies' on websites which were rendered subject to a 'transparency' requirement whereby those who use such code devices must provide information on them and allow users to refuse them.

[4] 'Traffic data' as opposed to the content of communications is excluded from the regime of Chapter I and is regulated by the scheme of Chapter II.

[5] The Interception of Communications Commissioner is appointed by the Prime Minister under s 57 of RIPA and his duties, set out in s 57, include keeping under review the performance by the Secretary of State of his various duties under ss 1–11, assisting the Investigatory Powers Tribunal and reporting breaches of the Act to the Prime Minister. A similar arrangement was in place under s 8 of the Interception of Communications Act 1985 and on the coming into force of RIPA, the IOCA 1985 Commissioner became the RIPA Interception of Communications Commissioner (s 57(8)).

[6] See the summary of *R v Ipswich Crown Court ex parte NTL Group Ltd* [2002] EWHC 1585 (Divisional Court) (discussed in Chapter 20).

[7] Section 2(4) defines the circumstances when interception occurs in the UK, to the effect that the interception must be effected by conduct which takes place in the UK. In the case of interception

of its transmission by means of a *public postal service*,[8] or a *public telecommunication system* or a *private telecommunication system*. This is subject to the exception that in the case of a *private* telecommunication system, no *criminal* liability arises where the interception was done by, or with the implied or express consent of, a person who has a right to control the private system being intercepted (even if there was no lawful authority for the interception): s 1(6). Tortious liability may arise in such circumstances: see s 1(3).

The above offences are punishable by imprisonment for up to two years, or a fine **3.06** or both, see s 1(7), subject to the safeguard that any proceedings must be commenced by the Director of Public Prosecutions.

'Private telecommunication system'

The Act defines private telecommunication systems in s 2(1) as including any **3.07** telecommunication system which 'without itself being a public telecommunication system' satisfies the twin criteria:

> being 'attached, directly or indirectly and whether or not for the purposes of the communication in question, to a public telecommunication system' and that 'there is apparatus comprised in the system which is both located in the United Kingdom and used (with or without other apparatus) for making the attachment to the public telecommunication system'.

In other words the system has to be connected, ultimately, to a public telecommunication system via equipment in the UK, excluding cases where a wholly internal system is used without the capacity to make external connections.

As to the justiciability of the 'public v private' issue, see the summary of *AG's Ref No 5 of 2002 sub nom W* [2004] UKHL 40 in Chapter 20.

Interception of a communication in the course of transmission

The authorisation scheme of Chapter I applies to interception of communica- **3.08** tions 'in the course of their transmission', which calls for definitions of the component terms 'interception', 'communication' and 'in the course of transmission'.

---

involving private telecommunications systems the sender or the intended recipient must also be in the UK.

[8] Ie any service which 'consists in . . . the collection, sorting, conveyance, distribution and delivery (whether in the United Kingdom or elsewhere) of postal items; and . . . is offered or provided as a service the main purpose of which, or one of the main purposes of which, is to make available, or to facilitate, a means of transmission from place to place of postal items containing communications' and which is 'offered or provided to, or to a substantial section of, the public in any one or more parts of the United Kingdom' (s 2(1)).

Sections 2(2), (3), (5) and 81(1) provide operational definitions at some length; a shortened summary of the definition in the context of telecommunications, simplifying the language is that:

'communication' includes anything comprising speech, music, sounds, visual images or data of any description, signals which impart anything *between persons, between a person and a thing*, or *between things*, or signals for the actuation or control of any apparatus (see s 81(1) for the full definition).

a person intercepts a communication in the course of its transmission if he modifies or interferes with a telecommunication system,[9] or its operation, or monitors transmissions made via the system, or monitors transmissions made by wireless telegraphy to or from the system, so as to make some or all of the content of the communication available 'while being transmitted', to a person other than the sender or intended recipient of the communication[10] (s 2(2), (3)).

3.09 The position of a police officer who is a party to a telephone conversation tape-recorded with his knowledge, is not that of telephone interception but is surveillance within RIPA, Part II. See *R v Hardy and Hardy* [2002] EWCA Crim 3012 (in Chapter 20). A conversation recorded by a covert device in a vehicle, which picks up one side of a telephone call is not 'interception of a communication' in the course of its transmission: see *R v E* [2004] EWCA Crim, 1243 and *R v Allsopp and Others* [2005] EWCA Crim 703, summarised in Chapters 20 and 21.

Speaking in the House of Lords during passage of the Bill, Lord Bassam of Brighton indicated:

The course of transmission begins where a postal service or telecommunication system first begins to transmit a communication. In a telephone, the sound waves from the human voice first begin to be in the course of their transmission by means of a telephone communication when they are received by the microphone in the hand set. They continue to be in the course of their transmission until they are emitted by the speaker. . . . listening to a voice from a speakerphone is not interception: the sound waves have left the communication system on which they were transmitted and hence no longer technically in the course of their transmission.[11]

3.10 Section 2(7) expands the meaning of 'while being transmitted' to include times when the system stores a message for later collection, for example e-mails stored

---

[9] 'Telecommunication system' is widely defined in terms of communication by means of electrical or electromagnetic energy, see s 2(1).

[10] Section 2(3) specifically excludes from the definition any communications broadcast for public reception, such as public radio or television.

[11] Lord Bassam of Brighton, Hansard (House of Lords) 12 June 2000 Col 1435.

on a server for downloading. Similarly s 2(8) expands the meaning of 'make some or all of the content available' to include storage of intercepted material, so that the person doing the interception may receive it later.

'Traffic data'

'Interception of a communication' does *not* include conduct which accesses only **3.11** so-called 'traffic data' or conduct which enables access to the content of the communication only to the extent necessary to identify the traffic data so that it can be accessed (s 2(5)). This calls for its own definition which is provided at length by s 2(9). Expressed in simpler language this is the data which is carried with or attached to ('logically associated with': s 2(10)) the communication and which serves to identify its source, destination, sender or sending and receiving equipment, and other message attributes. It can be seen as the operating information supplied by the system as opposed to the content of the message being sent. In the context of postal items, s 2 indicates that 'data' means anything written on the outside of the item. Chapter II of Part I provides a separate and regulatory regime for accessing traffic data.

Lawful authority to intercept and the limits on criminal liability

The offences created by s 1 do not arise where either: **3.12**

- the interception is carried out with lawful authority (s 1(1) and (2)); or
- the interception—in respect of a private telecommunications system only[12]— is carried out by, or with the implied or express consent of, a person having the right to control the operation of the system or its use (s 1(6)). (If carried out with permission but without lawful authority, a tort arises: s 1(3).)

'Lawful authority' appertains if one or more of three criteria are satisfied (see **3.13** s 1(5)(a)–(c)):

that the inteception is:

(a) authorised by s 3 or s 4 of RIPA—without the need for a warrant; or
(b) authorised by means of a warrant issued by the Secretary of State under s 5 of RIPA; or
(c) carried out in relation to a stored communication, in the exercise of any statutory power for the purpose of obtaining information or obtaining possession of any document or other property. See *R v Ipswich Crown Court ex parte NTL Group Ltd* [2002] EWHC 1585 (in Chapter 20).

---

[12] See above for definition, and s 2(1).

The first class of lawful interception: without warrant in some cases: s 1(5)(a) and ss 3 and 4

Section 3

3.14 Section 3 permits interception without a warrant if any of the following circumstances apply:

- there are reasonable grounds to believe that the sender and the recipient *both* consent to the interception (s 3(1)); or
- where *either* the sender *or* the intended recipient consents *and* the interception has been authorised under Part II of RIPA[13] (directed surveillance) (see s 3(2) and Part II of RIPA, especially s 27); or
- where the interception is connected with the provision or operation of a postal or telecommunication service, or for the purpose of enforcement Acts governing the use of such services and the interception is done by or on behalf of a person who provides that service (s 3(3)); or
- where the interception is done under s 5 of the Wireless Telegraphy Act 1949[14] (interception of misleading messages, etc), or is connected with the issue of licences under that Act, and certain other purposes (see s 3(4), (5)).

Section 4

3.15 Section 4 allows interception of communications without warrant where any of the following applies.

- the interception is for the purpose of obtaining information about the communications of someone overseas, and relates to the use of a public telecommunication service provided to persons in that country, and the person who provides the service is required by the law of that country or territory to carry out (or secure or facilitate) the interception (s 4(1));[15]
- where the interception is authorised by the regulations made by the Secretary of State as 'a legitimate business practice' which is 'reasonably required for the purpose, in connection with the carrying on of any business,[16] of monitoring

---

[13] Eg where the police are monitoring a call between an officer and an unwitting suspect.
[14] Section 5 of the Act is amended by s 73 of RIPA—see notes to s 73 in this work.
[15] The Secretary of State can impose further requirements: s 4(1)(d), (e). See the RIPA (Conditions for the Lawful Interception of Persons outside the United Kingdom) Order 2004 (SI 2004 No 157) which imposes the restriction that the interception must be carried out 'for the purposes of a criminal investigation . . . in a country or territory that is party to a designated international agreement'. See the RIPA (Designation of an International Agreement) Order 2004 (SI 2004 No 158) designating the EU Convention on Mutual Assistance in Criminal Matters (see Chapter 32 of this book) as such an agreement.
[16] 'Business' includes the activities of government departments, public authorities, etc (s 4(7)).

or keeping a record' of communications in the course of which business is transacted or which relate to that business (s 4(2)); any regulations may only authorise interception over systems provided by or to the person carrying out the interception: see s 4(3). See the Telecommunications (Lawful Business Practice) (Interception of Communications) Regulations 2000 (SI 2000 No 2699).[17]

- where the interception is done in the exercise of powers under s 47 of the Prison Act 1952, or in relation to high security psychiatric hospitals (see s 4(4)–4(8)).

The second class of lawful interception: interception with warrant: see s 1(5)(b) and s 5

Interception warrants are issued normally by the Secretary of State, upon applica- **3.16**
tion by any of the specific authorised bodies or individuals defined by s 6[18] including the Security and Intelligence Services, GCHQ, Customs, NCIS (soon to be
replaced by SOCA), and persons who are the competent authority of an overseas
country under an international mutual assistance agreement. By s 5(1) a warrant
may authorise any of the following:

- the interception in the course of their transmission by means of a postal service or telecommunication system of the communications described in the warrant;
- the making, in accordance with an international mutual assistance agreement, of a request for the provision assistance in connection with, or in the form of, an interception of communications;
- the disclosure of intercepted material obtained by any interception authorised or required by the warrant, and of related communications data.

Contents of an application for a warrant

The Interception Code provides guidance on the contents of an application, for **3.17**
both domestic warrants (s 8(1)) and what might be called 'external' warrants
under s 8(4). See paras 4.2 and 5.2 of the Code, discussed in Chapter 18.

---

[17] This Order allows monitoring to ascertain compliance with regulatory practices and matters such as quality control and training, monitoring which is in the interests of national security (in which case only certain specified public officials under s 6(2)(a)–(i) of RIPA may make the interception—see reg 3(2)(d)(i)), to prevent or detect crime, investigate or detect unauthorised use of telecommunication systems and certain other purposes. The controller of the system has to have made all reasonable efforts to inform potential users that interceptions may be made (reg 3(2)(c)).   [18] See s 6 for the detailed list.

Grounds for granting an application for a warrant

3.18 Before granting an application, the Secretary of State must be satisfied that what the action seeks to achieve is:

(1)   *Necessary*[19] for one or more of the following reasons:
- in the interests of national security;
- for the purpose of preventing or detecting serious crime;[20] or
- for the purpose of safeguarding the economic well-being of the UK (but only where the information sought relates to acts or intentions of persons outside the British Isles: s 5(5)); or
- for the purpose, in circumstances appearing to the Secretary of State to be equivalent to those in which he would issue a warrant for the purpose of preventing or detecting serious crime, of giving effect to the provisions of any international mutual assistance agreement[21] (see s 5(3)).

and

(2)   that the conduct authorised by the warrant is *proportionate* to what is sought to be achieved.

Cases where a senior official may issue the warrant

3.19 The one exception is that a senior official may issue a warrant in the absence of the Secretary of State in:

- a case of urgency, (but the Secretary of State must still expressly authorise the warrant (s 7(2)(a))); and
- where the warrant is sought for the purposes of helping a foreign state under the terms of an international mutual legal assistance agreement, provided that it appears the subject is outside the UK or the interception will take place only in relation to premises outside the UK (s 7(2)(b)).

The two types of warrant (s 8(1) and s 8(4))

The s 8(1) warrant

3.20 A s 8(1) warrant must name or describe either one person[22] as the interception subject or a single set of premises in relation to which the interception is to take

---

[19] By s 5(4) one matter to be considered is whether the information could reasonably be obtained by other means.

[20] Section 81(5) of RIPA excludes from the scope of 'detecting' serious crime (in Part I of the Act only) the gathering of evidence for legal proceedings. See RIPA, s. 81(2) and (3) as amended for definition of 'serious crime'.

[21] This ground is omitted for 'certificated' warrants, which relate to communications outside the British Isles: see the discussion of the two available types of warrant, below, and s. 8(4)(b).

[22] Counterintuitively, s 81(1) defines 'person' as including a combination of persons.

place. The effect is that one authorisation can authorise interception at any number of physical premises if it names the individual who is the target. By s 8(2) it must also set out in one or more schedules a description of the communications which are authorised to be intercepted, stating the address, numbers, apparatus, or other factors or combination of factors[23] to be used to identify the communications which are authorised to be intercepted.

The s 8(4) (or 'certificated') warrant

This is a broader warrant, and may be issued without the requirements of naming   **3.21**
a subject or premises and without the required schedules of s 8(2) but only if:

* the warrant is confined to interception of 'external communications' (and all necessary related conduct—see s 5(6)). ('External Communication' is defined in s 20 as 'a communication sent or received outside the British Islands') and
* the Secretary of State certifies the descriptions of material the interception of which he considers necessary, and certifies that he considers the examination of material of those descriptions necessary in the interests of national security, for the purpose of preventing or detecting serious crime, or for the purpose of safeguarding the economic well-being of the United Kingdom.

Duration, renewal, modification and cancellation of warrants[24]

Duration

Warrants (or renewed warrants) normally cease to have effect after three months   **3.22**
from date of issue or renewal, unless renewed (or re-renewed) before expiry: s 9(6)(c).

In the case of warrants issued by senior officials on grounds of urgency, the warrant expires at the end of the fifth working day following day of issue (s 9(6)(a)). At the time of writing a draft Terrorism Bill 2005 had been published, s 26 of which proposed an extended initial period of validity in certain circumstances. See footnotes to the text of RIPA, s 9.

Renewal

The Secretary of State may renew any warrant if he believes that it continues to be   **3.23**
necessary on any of the grounds referred to at para **3.17** above (and see s 5(3)).[25]
In the case of warrants issued by the Secretary of State where the grounds are those

---

[23] These are descriptive factors which can be used to identify communications 'likely' to be from or intended for the identified subject of the warrant, or communications from or intended to be transmitted to the identified premises (s 8(3)).

[24] See Interception Code of Practice at paras 4.13–4.17 (for s 8(1) warrants) and paras 5.12–5.16 (for s 8(4) certificated warrants).

[25] See s 9(1)(b) and s 7(2)(b) for the situation where a senior official may renew a warrant.

of interests of national security or preserving the economic well-being of the UK, a renewal is for six months at a time: s 9(6)(b).

Modification of warrants

3.24 The Secretary of State (or under narrow circumstances a senior official) may modify a warrant or a certificate in a certificated warrant (s 8(4)) in the circumstances set out in s 10. See the Interception Code of Practice, paras 4.10–4.12 (for s 8(1) warrants), and paras 5.10–5.11 in the case of s 8(4) 'certificated' warrants. A draft Terrorism Bill 2005 was published in September 2005, which proposed amendments to s 10 (see footnotes to s 10).

Cancellation

3.25 The Secretary of State must cancel a warrant if he is satisfied that it is no longer necessary (s 9(3)). He must[26] also cancel a warrant if he is satisfied that the interception subject is in the UK, if the warrant was one issued or renewed by a senior official for the purposes of helping a foreign state under an international mutual assistance agreement when it appeared that the subject was outside the UK (s 9(4)(a)). The Code, at para 5.15, indicates that in practice a senior official will sign the cancellation instrument.

The 'general safeguards' on use of intercepted material

3.26 The Secretary of State is under a duty[27] (s 15(1)(a)) to ensure that arrangements[28] are in place for securing that the number of people to whom intercepted material or its related communications data is disclosed, the extent of disclosure and number of copies are restricted to the 'minimum that is necessary for the authorised purposes' (s 15(2)). 'Necessary' has an expanded definition in s 15(4). He must ensure that arrangements are in place to secure the destruction of intercepted material and related communications data, and copies,[29] as soon as there are no longer grounds for retaining it as 'necessary for the authorised purpose' (s 15(3)). This can pose problems for the retention of intercepted material in the context of prosecution of offences,[30] since the purposes authorised under the Act are the 'prevention or detection' of serious crime, not its prosecution (the data may have been destroyed before a prosecution comes about). See comments at para **3.32** below.

---

[26] Unless he has already authorised renewal under his own hand: s 9(4)(b).

[27] In relation to material sought in order to be sent to overseas authorities under a mutual assistance agreement, the duties are modified: see s 15(6) and (7).

[28] 'Arrangements' includes ensuring security of storage (s 15(5)).

[29] Including copies of records of the identities of the persons intercepted or doing the intercepting, or to whom the data relates (s 15(8)).

[30] Such material is not generally admissible in most proceedings but disclosure may be necessary to a prosecutor in the interest of ensuring that the duty to act fairly in prosecuting is complied with: see RIPA, ss 17(1) and 18(7). Once a prosecution is actually underway the obligation to ensure destruction is suspended, if the data needs to be retained for the purpose of enabling a prosecutor to discharge his duty to act fairly (s 15(4(d)).

The 'extra safeguards' on the use of material in the case of certificated warrants (s 8(4))

Section 15(1)(b) imposes a duty upon the Secretary of State to ensure that as **3.27** regards certificated warrants additional 'safeguards' set out in s 16 are in place. In particular s 16(1) requires him to ensure that arrangements are in force so that that the intercepted material is *looked at or listened to* only to the extent that it has been certified as material for which examination is necessary, and to ensure that the material is selected otherwise than according to a factor which is referable to an individual who is known to be in the British Islands and is a factor with the purpose of identification of material contained in communications sent by or intended for him.

The above restriction is subject to an exception that the Secretary of State may **3.28** authorise the inspection of the material provided it relates to a period of no more than three months of interception, and it is necessary to inspect it on grounds of national security, preventing or detecting serious crime or for the purpose of safeguarding the economic well-being of the UK (ie the s 5(3)(a)–(c) criteria). (See s 16(3).) Such an exception might be made where an overseas target individual is engaging in communications which are 'external' for the purpose of s 8(4) but who is in communication with a person located in the UK who is himself making related internal communications not normally capable of being intercepted under a certificated warrant. At the time of writing, the draft Terrorism Bill 2005 proposed amendments to s 16 (see footnotes to s 16).

Unauthorised disclosure

Section 19 creates an offence, committed if (broadly) any details contained in a **3.29** warrant are disclosed by any person listed in s 19(2)—essentially those involved in the organisations undertaking interception, or providing public postal services or public telecommunications. There are exceptions for disclosure for the purpose of obtaining legal advice concerning Chapter 1 of RIPA, or by a legal adviser for the purpose of actual or contemplated legal proceedings, or disclosure to the Interception of Communications Commissioner (or at his direction). See s 19 for specific details of the available defences, which are wider than the short summary here.

The third class of lawful interception: where interception is in relation to a stored communication under any statutory power for the purpose of obtaining information or obtaining possession of any document, etc, s 1(5)(c)

This exception, referred to in s 1(5)(c) applies where an *existing* power allows **3.30** access to material, such as stored messages, for the purpose of taking possession of it or obtaining information. An example would be an order of a Circuit Judge under PACE 1984, Sch 1 for accessing 'special procedure' material stored on

See *R v Ipswich Crown Court ex parte NTL Group Ltd* [2002] EWHC
isional Court) (discussed) in Chapter 20).

of intercepted evidence in court

ial lawfully intercepted *without* a warrant (ie under s 1(5)(c), s 3 or s 4 of
.) may be used[31] in court proceedings including as to the disclosure of the
contents of what has been intercepted: s 18(4).

On the other hand material which has been intercepted *with* a warrant is subject
to a non-disclosure regime. The effect of s 18(1) of RIPA read with s 17 (which is
the descendant of s 9 of the Interception of Communications Act 1985), is that,
except in certain types of case set out later,

> . . . no evidence shall be adduced, question asked, assertion or disclosure made or other
> thing done in, for the purposes of or in connection with any legal proceedings[32] . . .

which (departing from the statutory language for the sake of explanation):

- discloses any of the contents of an intercepted communication or related communications data, in circumstances where it may be inferred that the origin of
  the information is one of several specific activities by the State (see below); or
- tends to suggest that any of the specific activities discussed below have, or may
  have, occurred or may be going to occur.

3.32 The activities referred to are listed in s 17(2) and fall into five categories, which
may be summarised (again, in simplified language) as being:

- illegal interception[33] by any of a range of (broadly) state bodies[34] or officials
  listed in s 17(3);
- breach of duty by the Secretary of State under s 1(4) of the Act;[35]
- issue of an interception warrant under RIPA (or under its predecessor, the
  1985 Act);
- making of an application for a warrant;
- imposition of any requirements on any person to provide assistance in giving
  effect to an interception warrant.

---

[31] This may be affected by exclusionary rules of evidence, s 78 of PACE 1984, and in appropriate circumstances also the HRA 1998.

[32] Ie civil or criminal proceedings. See *AG's Ref No. 5 of 2002 sub nom W* [2004] UKHL 40 (discussed in Chapter 20) in relation to investigation of lawfulness of interception and whether an intercept was in respect of private or public systems.

[33] Ie offences under s 1(1) or (2) of RIPA, but s 17(2) also includes expressly the former offence
under s 1 of the Interception of Communications Act 1985, the predecessor to RIPA.

[34] Including, for example, SOCA.

[35] The section referred to places the Secretary of State under a duty to ensure that no request for
assistance from a foreign state under the terms of an international agreement is made on behalf of a
person in the UK except with lawful authority (s 17(2)(a)–(e)).

Disclosure allowed for some purposes

The restriction in s 17(1) upon the disclosure of intercepted material obtained **3.33** under warrant does not apply to proceedings for criminal offences listed in s 18(12) (largely communications offences, offences under RIPA, or offences under the Official Secrets Acts). Nor does the restriction apply to proceedings before the Investigatory Powers Tribunal or appeals from it,[36] or proceedings for control orders under the Prevention of Terrorism Act 2005 (where disclosure would be to the Secretary of State or his representative)[37] nor, as regards parties other than the appellant/applicant, proceedings before the Special Immigration Appeals Commission, or Proscribed Organisations Appeals Commission (see s 18(1) for the full list). An exception is also made by s 18(3) allowing disclosure where the proceedings relate to unfair dismissal of a person for allegedly committing one of the offences created by the interception provisions of RIPA.

The existence and contents of an interception of any sort may be disclosed to a **3.34** prosecutor for the purpose of enabling him to determine what must be done to ensure fairness of the prosecution. On this point the Interception Code, at para 7.7, dryly observes that:

> The exception does not mean that intercepted material should be retained against a remote possibility that it might be relevant to future proceedings. . . . The exceptions only come into play if such material has, in fact, been retained for an authorised purpose. Because the authorised purpose given in section 5(3)(b) ("for the purpose of preventing or detecting serious crime") does not extend to gathering evidence for the purpose of a prosecution, material intercepted for this purpose may not have survived to the prosecution stage, as it will have been destroyed in accordance with the section 15(3) safeguards. There is, in these circumstances, no need to consider disclosure to a prosecutor if, in fact, no intercepted material remains in existence.[38]

The Code gives guidance as to what should happen *if* material has been retained **3.35** which ought to be disclosed to a prosecutor: see paras 7.8 onwards of the Code of Practice, in Chapter 18. The material may also be disclosed, by the prosecutor, by means of his inviting the judge to make an order for disclosure to him alone, which the judge may grant under s 18(7) if the exceptional circumstances of the case make disclosure to him essential in the interests of justice. The judge may then direct the prosecution to make 'any such admission of fact as that judge thinks essential in the interests of justice' if there are exceptional circumstances requiring him to do so.

---

[36] Presently there is no such route of appeal but see s 67(8).

[37] Prevention of Terrorism Act 2005, Schedule, Art 11.

[38] See s 15(4)(d) which suspends the Secretary of State's duty to ensure that arrangements are in place to destroy data, if the retention of the data is needed for the purpose of ensuring that a prosecutor can discharge his duty to act fairly. But the data may have been destroyed prior to any prosecution.

The duty to maintain interception capability

3.36 Telecommunications service providers are intimately involved in any interception, and s 12 puts in place a means by which businesses may be required to take certain steps in the operation of their systems so as to ensure that when an interception is required, it may be carried out. Section 12(1) confers on the Secretary of State the power to provide that persons providing public telecommunications or postal services must fulfil obligations aimed at ensuring that it remains practicable for them to assist in interception. This is generally referred to as the 'maintenance of interception capability' since the requirements which may be imposed are those aimed at ensuring that there is the practical capability to assist in carrying out interception warrants: s 12(3)).

3.37 The present requirements appear in the Regulation of Investigatory Powers (Maintenance of Interception Capability) Order 2002 (SI 2002 No 1931) which provides that the Secretary of State may serve a notice on a service provider requiring it to take the steps specified in the notice, which may be any or all of the steps set out in the Schedule to the Order. The telecommunications provisions do not apply if the service is provided to fewer than 10,000 persons in the United Kingdom or to service providers who only provide, or propose to provide, a public telecommunications service in relation to the provision of banking, insurance, investment or other financial services: see reg 2).

3.38 The table in the Schedule to the Order (at Chapter 28, Part C of this work) lists the possible requirements which may be imposed by the Secretary of State. Part I applies only to public postal service providers who intend to or who in fact do provide a public postal service and Part II applies only to service providers providing a public telecommunications service.

3.39 Unless the matter is referred to the Technical Advisory Board (see later), s 12(7) makes it the duty of anyone served with such a notice to comply with it, and an injunction may be obtained requiring them to comply.

Referral of notices to the Technical Advisory Board

3.40 Regulation 4 of the Regulation of Investigatory Powers (Maintenance of Interception Capability) Order 2002 permits a service provider who has been served with a Notice requiring it to comply with any of the possible obligations to refer the notice to the Technical Advisory Board[39] within 28 days. The Board is created by s 13, and consists of people appointed by the Secretary of State, including those able to represent the interests of both service providers and those seeking interception warrants.

---

[39] The RIPA (Technical Advisory Board) Order 2001 (SI 2001 No 3734).

If a Notice is referred to the Board then the obligations are suspended until the Board **3.41** has considered and reported to the Secretary of State about the technical requirements and the financial consequences for the service provider. The Secretary of State may withdraw the Notice or issue a further Notice (in the same form or modified: s 12(6(c), in which event the Service Provider must comply whether or not he then refers that Notice to the Board (s 12(6)(a)). There are provisions requiring fair contributions towards the costs of compliance to be paid to service providers (s 14).

The text of RIPA, Part I, Chapter I as amended follows.

B. Text of Part I, Chapter I

REGULATION OF INVESTIGATORY POWERS ACT 2000 (AS AMENDED)

PART I
COMMUNICATIONS
CHAPTER I
INTERCEPTION

Unlawful and authorised interception

Unlawful interception

1.[40]—(1) It shall be an offence for a person intentionally and without lawful authority to intercept, at any place in the United Kingdom, any communication in the course of its transmission[41] by means of—

(a) a public postal service; or

(b) a public telecommunication system.

(2) It shall be an offence for a person—

(a) intentionally and without lawful authority, and

(b) otherwise than in circumstances in which his conduct is excluded by subsection (6) from criminal liability under this subsection,

to intercept, at any place in the United Kingdom, any communication in the course of its transmission by means of a private telecommunication system.

(3) Any interception of a communication which is carried out at any place in the United Kingdom by, or with the express or implied consent of, a person

---

[40] Commencement: most of section: 2/10/2000 (SI 2000 No 2543) but note that s 1(3) commenced 24/10/00 by the same SI.

[41] *R v E* [2004] EWCA Crim 1243 and *R v Allsopp and Others* [2005] EWCA Crim 703, discussed in Chapter 20.

having the right to control the operation or the use of a private telecommunication[42] system shall be actionable at the suit or instance of the sender or recipient, or intended recipient, of the communication if it is without lawful authority and is either—

(a) an interception of that communication in the course of its transmission[43] by means of that private system; or

(b) an interception of that communication in the course of its transmission, by means of a public telecommunication system, to or from apparatus comprised in that private telecommunication system.

(4) Where the United Kingdom is a party to an international agreement which—

(a) relates to the provision of mutual assistance in connection with, or in the form of, the interception of communications,

(b) requires the issue of a warrant, order or equivalent instrument in cases in which assistance is given, and

(c) is designated for the purposes of this subsection by an order made by the Secretary of State,

it shall be the duty of the Secretary of State to secure that no request for assistance in accordance with the agreement is made on behalf of a person in the United Kingdom to the competent authorities of a country or territory outside the United Kingdom except with lawful authority.

(5)[44] Conduct has lawful authority for the purposes of this section if, and only if—

(a) it is authorised by or under section 3 or 4;

(b) it takes place in accordance with a warrant under section 5 ("an interception warrant"); or

(c) it is in exercise, in relation to any stored communication, of any statutory power that is exercised (apart from this section) for the purpose of obtaining information or of taking possession of any document or other property;

and conduct (whether or not prohibited by this section) which has lawful authority for the purposes of this section by virtue of paragraph (a) or (b) shall also be taken to be lawful for all other purposes.

(6) The circumstances in which a person makes an interception of a communication in the course of its transmission by means of a private telecommunication system are such that his conduct is excluded from criminal liability under subsection (2) if—

(a) he is a person with a right to control the operation or the use of the system; or

---

[42] *AG's Ref No 5 of 2002 sub nom W [2004] UKHL 40*, discussed in Chapter 20.

[43] *R v Hardy and Hardy* [2002] EWCA Crim 3012 and *R v E* [2004] EWCA Crim 1243, discussed in Chapter 20 and *R v Allsopp and Others* [2005] EWCA Crim 703, discussed in Chapter 21.

[44] *R v Ipswich Crown Court ex parte NTL Group Ltd* [2002] EWHC 1585 (Divisional Court), discussed in Chapter 20.

(b) he has the express or implied consent of such a person to make the interception.

(7) A person who is guilty of an offence under subsection (1) or (2) shall be liable—

    (a) on conviction on indictment, to imprisonment for a term not exceeding two years or to a fine, or to both;

    (b) on summary conviction, to a fine not exceeding the statutory maximum.

(8) No proceedings for any offence which is an offence by virtue of this section shall be instituted—

    (a) in England and Wales, except by or with the consent of the Director of Public Prosecutions;

    (b) in Northern Ireland, except by or with the consent of the Director of Public Prosecutions for Northern Ireland.

Meaning and location of "interception" etc.

2.[45]—(1) In this Act—

"*postal service*" means any service which—

    (a) consists in the following, or in any one or more of them, namely, the collection, sorting, conveyance, distribution and delivery (whether in the United Kingdom or elsewhere) of postal items; and

    (b) is offered or provided as a service the main purpose of which, or one of the main purposes of which, is to make available, or to facilitate, a means of transmission from place to place of postal items containing communications;

"*private telecommunication system*" means any telecommunication system which, without itself being a public telecommunication system, is a system in relation to which the following conditions are satisfied—

    (a) it is attached, directly or indirectly and whether or not for the purposes of the communication in question, to a public telecommunication system; and

    (b) there is apparatus comprised in the system which is both located in the United Kingdom and used (with or without other apparatus) for making the attachment to the public telecommunication system;

"*public postal service*" means any postal service which is offered or provided to, or to a substantial section of, the public in any one or more parts of the United Kingdom;

"*public telecommunications service*" means any telecommunications service which is offered or provided to, or to a substantial section of, the public in any one or more parts of the United Kingdom;

"*public telecommunication system*" means any such parts of a telecommunication system by means of which any public telecommunications service is provided as are located in the United Kingdom;[46]

---

[45] Commencement: 2/10/00 by SI 2000 No 2543.
[46] *AG's Ref No. 5 of 2002 sub nom W* [2004] UKHL 40, discussed in Chapter 20.

"*telecommunications service*" means any service that consists in the provision of access to, and of facilities for making use of, any telecommunication system (whether or not one provided by the person providing the service); and

"*telecommunication system*" means any system (including the apparatus comprised in it) which exists (whether wholly or partly in the United Kingdom or elsewhere) for the purpose of facilitating the transmission of communications by any means involving the use of electrical or electro-magnetic energy.

(2) For the purposes of this Act, but subject to the following provisions of this section, a person intercepts a communication in the course of its transmission by means of a telecommunication system if, and only if, he—

(a) so modifies or interferes with the system, or its operation,

(b) so monitors transmissions made by means of the system, or

(c) so monitors transmissions made by wireless telegraphy to or from apparatus comprised in the system,

as to make some or all of the contents of the communication available, while being transmitted,[47] to a person other than the sender or intended recipient of the communication.

(3) References in this Act to the interception of a communication do not include references to the interception of any communication broadcast for general reception.

(4) For the purposes of this Act the interception of a communication takes place in the United Kingdom if, and only if, the modification, interference or monitoring or, in the case of a postal item, the interception is effected by conduct within the United Kingdom and the communication is either—

(a) intercepted in the course of its transmission by means of a public postal service or public telecommunication system; or

(b) intercepted in the course of its transmission by means of a private telecommunication system in a case in which the sender or intended recipient of the communication is in the United Kingdom.

(5) References in this Act to the interception of a communication in the course of its transmission by means of a postal service or telecommunication system do not include references to—

(a) any conduct that takes place in relation only to so much of the communication as consists in any traffic data comprised in or attached to a communication (whether by the sender or otherwise) for the purposes of any postal service or telecommunication system by means of which it is being or may be transmitted; or

(b) any such conduct, in connection with conduct falling within paragraph (a), as gives a person who is neither the sender nor the intended recipient only so much access to a communication as is necessary for the purpose of identifying traffic data so comprised or attached.

---

[47] *R v Hardly and Hardy* [2002] EWCA Crim 3012, discussed in Chapter 20.

(6) For the purposes of this section references to the modification of a telecommunication system include references to the attachment of any apparatus to, or other modification of or interference with—

    (a) any part of the system; or

    (b) any wireless telegraphy apparatus used for making transmissions to or from apparatus comprised in the system.

(7) For the purposes of this section the times while a communication is being transmitted by means of a telecommunication system shall be taken to include any time when the system by means of which the communication is being, or has been, transmitted is used for storing it in a manner that enables the intended recipient to collect it or otherwise to have access to it.

(8) For the purposes of this section the cases in which any contents of a communication are to be taken to be made available to a person while being transmitted shall include any case in which any of the contents of the communication, while being transmitted, are diverted or recorded so as to be available to a person subsequently.

(9) In this section "traffic data", in relation to any communication, means—

    (a) any data identifying, or purporting to identify, any person, apparatus or location to or from which the communication is or may be transmitted,

    (b) any data identifying or selecting, or purporting to identify or select, apparatus through which, or by means of which, the communication is or may be transmitted,

    (c) any data comprising signals for the actuation of apparatus used for the purposes of a telecommunication system for effecting (in whole or in part) the transmission of any communication, and

    (d) any data identifying the data or other data as data comprised in or attached to a particular communication,

but that expression includes data identifying a computer file or computer program access to which is obtained, or which is run, by means of the communication to the extent only that the file or program is identified by reference to the apparatus in which it is stored.

(10) In this section—

    (a) references, in relation to traffic data comprising signals for the actuation of apparatus, to a telecommunication system by means of which a communication is being or may be transmitted include references to any telecommunication system in which that apparatus is comprised; and

    (b) references to traffic data being attached to a communication include references to the data and the communication being logically associated with each other;

and in this section "data", in relation to a postal item, means anything written on the outside of the item.

(11) In this section "postal item" means any letter, postcard or other such thing in writing as may be used by the sender for imparting information to the recipient, or any packet or parcel.

Lawful interception without an interception warrant

3.[48]—(1) Conduct by any person consisting in the interception of a communication is authorised by this section if the communication is one which, or which that person has reasonable grounds for believing, is both—

    (a) a communication sent by a person who has consented to the interception; and

    (b) a communication the intended recipient of which has so consented.

(2) Conduct by any person consisting in the interception of a communication is authorised by this section if—

    (a) the communication is one sent by, or intended for, a person who has consented to the interception; and

    (b) surveillance by means of that interception has been authorised under Part II.

(3) Conduct consisting in the interception of a communication is authorised by this section if—

    (a) it is conduct by or on behalf of a person who provides a postal service or a telecommunications service; and

    (b) it takes place for purposes connected with the provision or operation of that service or with the enforcement, in relation to that service, of any enactment relating to the use of postal services or telecommunications services.

(4) Conduct by any person consisting in the interception of a communication in the course of its transmission by means of wireless telegraphy is authorised by this section if it takes place—

    (a) with the authority of a designated person under section 5 of the Wireless Telegraphy Act 1949 (misleading messages and interception and disclosure of wireless telegraphy messages); and

    (b) for purposes connected with anything falling within subsection (5).

(5) Each of the following falls within this subsection—

    (a) the issue of licences under the Wireless Telegraphy Act 1949;

    (b) the prevention or detection of anything which constitutes interference with wireless telegraphy; and

    (c) the enforcement of any enactment contained in that Act or of any enactment not so contained that relates to such interference.

---

[48] Commencement: 2/10/00 by SI 2000 No 2543.

Power to provide for lawful interception

4.[49]—(1) Conduct by any person ("the interceptor") consisting in the interception of a communication in the course of its transmission by means of a telecommunication system is authorised by this section if—

(a) the interception is carried out for the purpose of obtaining information about the communications of a person who, or who the interceptor has reasonable grounds for believing, is in a country or territory outside the United Kingdom;

(b) the interception relates to the use of a telecommunications service provided to persons in that country or territory which is either—

(i) a public telecommunications service; or

(ii) a telecommunications service that would be a public telecommunications service if the persons to whom it is offered or provided were members of the public in a part of the United Kingdom;

(c) the person who provides that service (whether the interceptor or another person) is required by the law of that country or territory to carry out, secure or facilitate the interception in question;

(d) the situation is one in relation to which such further conditions as may be prescribed by regulations made by the Secretary of State are required to be satisfied before conduct may be treated as authorised by virtue of this subsection; and

(e) the conditions so prescribed are satisfied in relation to that situation.

(2) Subject to subsection (3), the Secretary of State may by regulations authorise any such conduct described in the regulations as appears to him to constitute a legitimate practice reasonably required for the purpose, in connection with the carrying on of any business, of monitoring or keeping a record of—

(a) communications by means of which transactions are entered into in the course of that business; or

(b) other communications relating to that business or taking place in the course of its being carried on.

(3) Nothing in any regulations under subsection (2) shall authorise the interception of any communication except in the course of its transmission using apparatus or services provided by or to the person carrying on the business for use wholly or partly in connection with that business.

(4) Conduct taking place in a prison is authorised by this section if it is conduct in exercise of any power conferred by or under any rules made under section 47 of the Prison Act 1952, section 39 of the Prisons (Scotland) Act 1989 or section 13 of the Prison Act (Northern Ireland) 1953 (prison rules).

(5) Conduct taking place in any hospital premises where high security psychiatric services are provided is authorised by this section if it is conduct in

---

[49] Commencement: 2/10/00 by SI 2000 No 2543.

pursuance of, and in accordance with, any direction given under section 17 of the National Health Service Act 1977 (directions as to the carrying out of their functions by health bodies) to the body providing those services at those premises.

(6) Conduct taking place in a state hospital is authorised by this section if it is conduct in pursuance of, and in accordance with, any direction given to the State Hospitals Board for Scotland under section 2(5) of the National Health Service (Scotland) Act 1978 (regulations and directions as to the exercise of their functions by health boards) as applied by Article 5(1) of and the Schedule to The State Hospitals Board for Scotland Order 1995 (which applies certain provisions of that Act of 1978 to the State Hospitals Board).

(7) In this section references to a business include references to any activities of a government department, of any public authority or of any person or office holder on whom functions are conferred by or under any enactment.

(8) In this section—

"government department" includes any part of the Scottish Administration, a Northern Ireland department and the National Assembly for Wales;

"high security psychiatric services" has the same meaning as in the National Health Service Act 1977;

"hospital premises" has the same meaning as in section 4(3) of that Act; and

"state hospital" has the same meaning as in the National Health Service (Scotland) Act 1978.

(9) In this section "prison" means—

(a) any prison, young offender institution, young offenders centre or remand centre which is under the general superintendence of, or is provided by, the Secretary of State under the Prison Act 1952 or the Prison Act (Northern Ireland) 1953, or

(b) any prison, young offenders institution or remand centre which is under the general superintendence of the Scottish Ministers under the Prisons (Scotland) Act 1989,

and includes any contracted out prison, within the meaning of Part IV of the Criminal Justice Act 1991 or section 106(4) of the Criminal Justice and Public Order Act 1994, and any legalised police cells within the meaning of section 14 of the Prisons (Scotland) Act 1989.

Interception with a warrant

5.[50]—(1) Subject to the following provisions of this Chapter, the Secretary of State may issue a warrant authorising or requiring the person to whom it is

---

[50] Commencement: 2/10/00 by SI 2000 No 2543.

addressed, by any such conduct as may be described in the warrant, to secure any one or more of the following—

(a) the interception in the course of their transmission by means of a postal service or telecommunication system of the communications described in the warrant;

(b) the making, in accordance with an international mutual assistance agreement, of a request for the provision of such assistance in connection with, or in the form of, an interception of communications as may be so described;

(c) the provision, in accordance with an international mutual assistance agreement, to the competent authorities of a country or territory outside the United Kingdom of any such assistance in connection with, or in the form of, an interception of communications as may be so described;

(d) the disclosure, in such manner as may be so described, of intercepted material obtained by any interception authorised or required by the warrant, and of related communications data.

(2) The Secretary of State shall not issue an interception warrant unless he believes—

(a) that the warrant is necessary on grounds falling within subsection (3); and

(b) that the conduct authorised by the warrant is proportionate to what is sought to be achieved by that conduct.

(3) Subject to the following provisions of this section, a warrant is necessary on grounds falling within this subsection if it is necessary—

(a) in the interests of national security;

(b) for the purpose of preventing or detecting serious crime;

(c) for the purpose of safeguarding the economic well-being of the United Kingdom; or

(d) for the purpose, in circumstances appearing to the Secretary of State to be equivalent to those in which he would issue a warrant by virtue of paragraph (b), of giving effect to the provisions of any international mutual assistance agreement.

(4) The matters to be taken into account in considering whether the requirements of subsection (2) are satisfied in the case of any warrant shall include whether the information which it is thought necessary to obtain under the warrant could reasonably be obtained by other means.

(5) A warrant shall not be considered necessary on the ground falling within subsection (3)(c) unless the information which it is thought necessary to obtain is information relating to the acts or intentions of persons outside the British Islands.

(6) The conduct authorised by an interception warrant shall be taken to include—

(a) all such conduct (including the interception of communications not identified by the warrant) as it is necessary to undertake in order to do what is expressly authorised or required by the warrant;

(b) conduct for obtaining related communications data; and

(c) conduct by any person which is conduct in pursuance of a requirement imposed by or on behalf of the person to whom the warrant is addressed to be provided with assistance with giving effect to the warrant.

Interception warrants

Application for issue of an interception warrant

6.[51]—(1) An interception warrant shall not be issued except on an application made by or on behalf of a person specified in subsection (2).

(2) Those persons are—

(a) the Director-General of the Security Service;

(b) the Chief of the Secret Intelligence Service;

(c) the Director of GCHQ;

(d) the Director General of the National Criminal Intelligence Service;[52]

(e) the Commissioner of Police of the Metropolis;

(f) the Chief Constable of the Royal Ulster Constabulary;

(g) the chief constable of any police force maintained under or by virtue of section 1 of the Police (Scotland) Act 1967;

(h) the Commissioners of Customs and Excise;

(i) the Chief of Defence Intelligence;

(j) a person who, for the purposes of any international mutual assistance agreement, is the competent authority of a country or territory outside the United Kingdom.

(3) An application for the issue of an interception warrant shall not be made on behalf of a person specified in [*paragraph (a), (b), (c), (e), (f), (g), (h), (i) or (j)*][53] subsection (2) except by a person holding office under the Crown.

Issue of warrants

7.[54]—(1)[55] An interception warrant shall not be issued except—

(a) under the hand of the Secretary of State or, in the case of a warrant issued by the Scottish Ministers (by virtue of provision made under section 63 of the Scotland Act 1998), a member of the Scottish Executive; or

(b) in a case falling within subsection (2) (a) or (b), under the hand of a senior official; or

---

[51] Commencement: 2/10/00 by SI 2000 No 2543.

[52] The reference to NCIS will be replaced by a reference to SOCA when Sch 4, para 132 of the SOCAP Act 2005 is in force.

[53] Words in italics will be added when Sch 4, para 132 of the SOCAP Act 2005 is in force.

[54] Commencement: 2/10/00 by SI 2000 No 2543.

[55] Amended by Scotland Act 1998 (Transfer of Functions to the Scottish Ministers etc.) (No 2) Order 2000 (SI 2000 No 3253) Sch 3, para 4(a)–4(c).

    (c) in a case falling within subsection (2)(aa), under the hand of a member of the staff of the Scottish Administration who is a member of the Senior Civil Service and who is designated by the Scottish Ministers as a person under whose hand a warrant may be issued in such a case.

(2)[56] Those cases are—

    (a) an urgent case in which the Secretary of State has himself expressly authorised the issue of the warrant in that case; and

    (aa) an urgent case in which the Scottish Ministers have themselves (by virtue of provision made under section 63 of the Scotland Act 1998) expressly authorised the use of the warrant in that case and a statement of that fact is endorsed on the warrant; and

    (b) a case in which the warrant is for the purposes of a request for assistance made under an international mutual assistance agreement by the competent authorities of a country or territory outside the United Kingdom and either—

        (i) it appears that the interception subject is outside the United Kingdom; or

        (ii) the interception to which the warrant relates is to take place in relation only to premises outside the United Kingdom.

(3) An interception warrant—

    (a) must be addressed to the person falling within section 6(2) by whom, or on whose behalf, the application for the warrant was made; and

    (b) in the case of a warrant issued under the hand of a senior official, must contain, according to whatever is applicable-

        (i) one of the statements set out in subsection (4); and

        (ii) if it contains the statement set out in subsection (4)(b), one of the statements set out in subsection (5).

(4) The statements referred to in subsection (3)(b)(i) are—

    (a) a statement that the case is an urgent case in which the Secretary of State has himself expressly authorised the issue of the warrant;

    (b) a statement that the warrant is issued for the purposes of a request for assistance made under an international mutual assistance agreement by the competent authorities of a country or territory outside the United Kingdom.

(5) The statements referred to in subsection (3)(b)(ii) are—

    (a) a statement that the interception subject appears to be outside the United Kingdom;

    (b) a statement that the interception to which the warrant relates is to take place in relation only to premises outside the United Kingdom.

---

[56] Amended by Scotland Act 1998 (Transfer of Functions to the Scottish Ministers etc.) (No 2) Order 2000 (SI 2000 No 3253) Sch 3, para 4(d).

Contents of warrants

8.[57]—(1) An interception warrant must name or describe either—

(a) one person as the interception subject; or

(b) a single set of premises as the premises in relation to which the interception to which the warrant relates is to take place.

(2) The provisions of an interception warrant describing communications the interception of which is authorised or required by the warrant must comprise one or more schedules setting out the addresses, numbers, apparatus or other factors, or combination of factors, that are to be used for identifying the communications that may be or are to be intercepted.

(3) Any factor or combination of factors set out in accordance with subsection (2) must be one that identifies communications which are likely to be or to include-

(a) communications from, or intended for, the person named or described in the warrant in accordance with subsection (1); or

(b) communications originating on, or intended for

transmission to, the premises so named or described.

(4) Subsections (1) and (2) shall not apply to an interception warrant if—

(a) the description of communications to which the warrant relates confines the conduct authorised or required by the warrant to conduct falling within subsection (5); and

(b) at the time of the issue of the warrant, a certificate applicable to the warrant has been issued by the Secretary of State certifying—

(i) the descriptions of intercepted material the examination of which he considers necessary; and

(ii) that he considers the examination of material of those descriptions necessary as mentioned in section 5(3)(a), (b) or (c).

(5) Conduct falls within this subsection if it consists in—

(a) the interception of external communications in the course of their transmission by means of a telecommunication system; and

(b) any conduct authorised in relation to any such interception by section 5(6).

(6) A certificate for the purposes of subsection (4) shall not be issued except under the hand of the Secretary of State.

Duration, cancellation and renewal of warrants

9. [58,59]—(1) An interception warrant—

(a) shall cease to have effect at the end of the relevant period; but

(b) may be renewed, at any time before the end of that period, by an instrument under the hand of the Secretary of State or, in the case of a warrant

---

[57] Commencement: 2/10/00 by SI 2000 No 2543.

[58] Commencement: 2/10/00 by SI 2000 No 2543.

[59] Amended by Scotland Act 1998 (Transfer of Functions to the Scottish Ministers etc.) (No 2) Order 2000 (SI 2000 No 3253) Sch 3, para 5.

issued by the Scottish Ministers (by virtue of provision made under section 63 of the Scotland Act 1998), a member of the Scottish Executive or, in a case falling within section 7(2)(b), under the hand of a senior official.

(2) An interception warrant shall not be renewed under subsection (1) unless the Secretary of State believes that the warrant continues to be necessary on grounds falling within section 5(3).

(3) The Secretary of State shall cancel an interception warrant if he is satisfied that the warrant is no longer necessary on grounds falling within section 5(3).

(4) The Secretary of State shall cancel an interception warrant if, at any time before the end of the relevant period, he is satisfied in a case in which-

    (a) the warrant is one which was issued containing the statement set out in section 7(5)(a) or has been renewed by an instrument containing the statement set out in subsection (5)(b)(i) of this section, and

    (b) the latest renewal (if any) of the warrant is not a renewal by an instrument under the hand of the Secretary of State, that the person named or described in the warrant as the interception subject is in the United Kingdom.

(5) An instrument under the hand of a senior official that renews an interception warrant must contain—

    (a) a statement that the renewal is for the purposes of a request for assistance made under an international mutual assistance agreement by the competent authorities of a country or territory outside the United Kingdom; and

    (b) whichever of the following statements is applicable-

        (i) a statement that the interception subject appears to be outside the United Kingdom;

        (ii) a statement that the interception to which the warrant relates is to take place in relation only to premises outside the United Kingdom.

(6) In this section "the relevant period"—

    (a) in relation to an unrenewed warrant issued in a case falling within section 7(2)(a) under the hand of a senior official, means the period ending with the fifth working day following the day of the warrant's issue;

    [(ab) *proposed, see footnotes*][60]

    (b) in relation to a renewed warrant the latest renewal of which was by an instrument endorsed under the hand of the Secretary of State with a statement that the renewal is believed to be necessary on grounds falling within section 5(3)(a) or (c), means the period of six months beginning with the day of the warrant's renewal; and

---

[60] The draft Terrorism Bill 2005 in September 2005 proposed the addition of a new subpara (ab) as follows:

'(ab) in relation to an unrenewed warrant which is endorsed under the hand of the Secretary of State with a statement that the issue of the warrant is believed to be necessary on grounds falling within section 5(3)(a) or (c), means the period of six months beginning with the day of the warrant's issue;'

(c) in all other cases, means the period of three months beginning with the day of the warrant's issue or, in the case of a warrant that has been renewed, of its latest renewal.

Modification of warrants and certificates

10.[61,62]—(1) The Secretary of State may at any time—

    (a) modify the provisions of an interception warrant; or

    (b) modify a section 8(4) certificate so as to include in the certified material any material the examination of which he considers to be necessary as mentioned in section 5(3)(a), (b) or (c).

(2) If at any time the Secretary of State considers that any factor set out in a schedule to an interception warrant is no longer relevant for identifying communications which, in the case of that warrant, are likely to be or to include communications falling within section 8(3)(a) or (b), it shall be his duty to modify the warrant by the deletion of that factor.

(3) If at any time the Secretary of State considers that the material certified by a section 8(4) certificate includes any material the examination of which is no longer necessary as mentioned in any of paragraphs (a) to (c) of section 5(3), he shall modify the certificate so as to exclude that material from the certified material.

(4) Subject to subsections (5) to (8), a warrant or certificate shall not be modified under this section except by an instrument under the hand of the Secretary of State or of a senior official.

(4A) Subject to subsections (5A), (6) and (8), a warrant issued by the Scottish Ministers (by virtue of provision made under section 63 of the Scotland Act 1998) shall not be modified under this section except by an instrument under the hand of a member of the Scottish Executive or a member of the staff of the Scottish Administration who is a member of the Senior Civil Service and is designated by the Scottish Ministers as a person under whose hand an instrument may be issued in such a case (in this section referred to as "a designated official")

(5) Unscheduled parts of an interception warrant shall not be modified under the hand of a senior official except in an urgent case in which—

    (a) the Secretary of State has himself expressly authorised the modification; and

    (b) a statement of that fact is endorsed on the modifying instrument.

---

[61] Commencement: 2/10/00 by SI 2000 No 2543.
[62] Amended by Scotland Act 1998 (Transfer of Functions to the Scottish Ministers etc.) (No 2) Order 2000 (SI 2000 No 3253), Sch 3, para 6.

(5A) Unscheduled parts of an interception warrant issued by the Scottish Ministers shall not be modified under the hand of a designated official except in an urgent case in which—

    (a) they have themselves (by virtue of provision made under section 63 of the Scotland Act 1998) expressly authorised the modification; and

    (b) a statement of that fact is endorsed on the modifying instrument

(6)[63] Subsection (4) or (4A) shall not authorise the making under the hand of either—

    (a) the person to whom the warrant is addressed, or

    (b) any person holding a position subordinate to that person,

of any modification of any scheduled parts of an interception warrant.

(7) A section 8(4) certificate shall not be modified under the hand of a senior official except in an urgent case in which—

    (a) the official in question holds a position in respect of which he is expressly authorised by provisions contained in the certificate to modify the certificate on the Secretary of State's behalf; or

    (b) the Secretary of State has himself expressly authorised the modification and a statement of that fact is endorsed on the modifying instrument.

(8) Where modifications in accordance with this subsection are expressly authorised by provision contained in the warrant, the scheduled parts of an interception warrant may, in an urgent case, be modified by an instrument under the hand of—

    (a) the person to whom the warrant is addressed; or

    (b) a person holding any such position subordinate to that person as may be identified in the provisions of the warrant.

(9) Where—

    (a) a warrant or certificate is modified by an instrument under the hand of a person other than the Secretary of State or, as the case may be, the Scottish Ministers (by virtue of provision made under section 63 of the Scotland Act 1998), and

---

[63] The draft Terrorism Bill 2005 in September 2005 proposed that subs (6) be substituted with the following text:

'(6) Subsection (4) authorises the modification of the scheduled parts of an interception warrant under the hand of a senior official who is either—
    (a) the person to whom the warrant is addressed, or
    (b) a person holding a position subordinate to that person,
only if the applicable condition specified in subsection (6A) is satisfied and a statement that the condition is satisfied is endorsed on the modifying instrument.

(6A) The applicable condition is—
    (a) in the case of an unrenewed warrant, that the warrant is endorsed with a statement that the issue of the warrant is believed to be necessary in the interests of national security; and
    (b) in the case of a renewed warrant, that the instrument by which it was last renewed is endorsed with a statement that the renewal is believed to be necessary in the interests of national security.'

(b) a statement for the purposes of subsection (5)(b), (5A)(b)[64] or (7)(b) is endorsed on the instrument, or the modification is made under subsection (8),

that modification shall cease to have effect at the end of the fifth working day following the day of the instrument's issue.

(10) For the purposes of this section—

(a) the scheduled parts of an interception warrant are any provisions of the warrant that are contained in a schedule of identifying factors comprised in the warrant for the purposes of section 8(2); and

(b) the modifications that are modifications of the scheduled parts of an interception warrant include the insertion of an additional such schedule in the warrant;

and references in this section to unscheduled parts of an interception warrant, and to their modification, shall be construed accordingly.

Implementation of warrants

11.[65]—(1) Effect may be given to an interception warrant either—

(a) by the person to whom it is addressed; or

(b) by that person acting through, or together with, such other persons as he may require (whether under subsection (2) or otherwise)

to provide him with assistance with giving effect to the warrant.

(2) For the purpose of requiring any person to provide assistance in relation to an interception warrant the person to whom it is addressed may—

(a) serve a copy of the warrant on such persons as he considers may be able to provide such assistance; or

(b) make arrangements under which a copy of it is to be or may be so served.

(3) The copy of an interception warrant that is served on any person under subsection (2) may, to the extent authorised—

(a) by the person to whom the warrant is addressed, or

(b) by the arrangements made by him for the purposes of that subsection,

omit any one or more of the schedules to the warrant.

(4) Where a copy of an interception warrant has been served by or on behalf of the person to whom it is addressed on—

(a) a person who provides a postal service,

(b) a person who provides a public telecommunications service, or

(c) a person not falling within paragraph (b) who has control of the whole or any part of a telecommunication system located wholly or partly in the United Kingdom, it shall (subject to subsection (5)) be the duty of

---

[64] The draft Terrorism Bill 2005 in September 2005 proposed the insertion of ', (6)' after the reference to '(5)(b)'.   [65] Commencement: 2/10/00 by SI 2000 No 2543.

that person to take all such steps for giving effect to the warrant as are notified to him by or on behalf of the person to whom the warrant is addressed.

(5) A person who is under a duty by virtue of subsection (4) to take steps for giving effect to a warrant shall not be required to take any steps which it is not reasonably practicable for him to take.

(6) For the purposes of subsection (5) the steps which it is reasonably practicable for a person to take in a case in which obligations have been imposed on him by or under section 12 shall include every step which it would have been reasonably practicable for him to take had he complied with all the obligations so imposed on him.

(7) A person who knowingly fails to comply with his duty under subsection (4) shall be guilty of an offence and liable—

(a) on conviction on indictment, to imprisonment for a term not exceeding two years or to a fine, or to both;

(b) on summary conviction, to imprisonment for a term not exceeding six months or to a fine not exceeding the statutory maximum, or to both.

(8) A person's duty under subsection (4) to take steps for giving effect to a warrant shall be enforceable by civil proceedings by the Secretary of State for an injunction, or for specific performance of a statutory duty under section 45 of the Court of Session Act 1988, or for any other appropriate relief.

(9) For the purposes of this Act the provision of assistance with giving effect to an interception warrant includes any disclosure to the person to whom the warrant is addressed, or to persons acting on his behalf, of intercepted material obtained by any interception authorised or required by the warrant, and of any related communications data.

Interception capability and costs

Maintenance of interception capability

12.[66]—(1) The Secretary of State may by order provide for the imposition by him on persons who—

(a) are providing public postal services or public telecommunications services, or

(b) are proposing to do so,

of such obligations as it appears to him reasonable to impose for the purpose of securing that it is and remains practicable for requirements to provide assistance in relation to interception warrants to be imposed and complied with.

(2) The Secretary of State's power to impose the obligations provided for by an order under this section shall be exercisable by the giving, in accordance

---

[66] Commencement: 2/10/00 by SI 2000 No 2543.

with the order, of a notice requiring the person who is to be subject to the obligations to take all such steps as may be specified or described in the notice.

(3) Subject to subsection (11), the only steps that may be specified or described in a notice given to a person under subsection (2) are steps appearing to the Secretary of State to be necessary for securing that that person has the practical capability of providing any assistance which he may be required to provide in relation to relevant interception warrants.

(4) A person shall not be liable to have an obligation imposed on him in accordance with an order under this section by reason only that he provides, or is proposing to provide, to members of the public a telecommunications service the provision of which is or, as the case may be, will be no more than—

   (a) the means by which he provides a service which is not a telecommunications service; or

   (b) necessarily incidental to the provision by him of a service which is not a telecommunications service.

(5) Where a notice is given to any person under subsection (2) and otherwise than by virtue of subsection (6)(c), that person may, before the end of such period as may be specified in an order under this section, refer the notice to the Technical Advisory Board.

(6) Where a notice given to any person under subsection (2) is referred to the Technical Advisory Board under subsection (5)—

   (a) there shall be no requirement for that person to comply, except in pursuance of a notice under paragraph (c)(ii), with any obligations imposed by the notice;

   (b) the Board shall consider the technical requirements and the financial consequences, for the person making the reference, of the notice referred to them and shall report their conclusions on those matters to that person and to the Secretary of State; and

   (c) the Secretary of State, after considering any report of the Board relating to the notice, may either—

     (i) withdraw the notice; or

     (ii) give a further notice under subsection (2) confirming its effect, with or without modifications.

(7) It shall be the duty of a person to whom a notice is given under subsection (2) to comply with the notice; and that duty shall be enforceable by civil proceedings by the Secretary of State for an injunction, or for specific performance of a statutory duty under section 45 of the Court of Session Act 1988, or for any other appropriate relief.

(8) A notice for the purposes of subsection (2) must specify such period as appears to the Secretary of State to be reasonable as the period within which the steps specified or described in the notice are to be taken.

(9) Before making an order under this section the Secretary of State shall consult with—

(a) such persons appearing to him to be likely to be subject to the obligations for which it provides,

(b) the Technical Advisory Board,

(c) such persons representing persons falling within paragraph (a), and

(d) such persons with statutory functions in relation to persons falling within that paragraph,

as he considers appropriate.

(10) The Secretary of State shall not make an order under this section unless a draft of the order has been laid before Parliament and approved by a resolution of each House.

(11) For the purposes of this section the question whether a person has the practical capability of providing assistance in relation to relevant interception warrants shall include the question whether all such arrangements have been made as the Secretary of State considers necessary—

(a) with respect to the disclosure of intercepted material;

(b) for the purpose of ensuring that security and confidentiality are maintained in relation to, and to matters connected with, the provision of any such assistance; and

(c) for the purpose of facilitating the carrying out of any functions in relation to this Chapter of the Interception of Communications Commissioner;

but before determining for the purposes of the making of any order, or the imposition of any obligation, under this section what arrangements he considers necessary for the purpose mentioned in paragraph (c) the Secretary of State shall consult that Commissioner.

(12) In this section "relevant interception warrant"—

(a) in relation to a person providing a public postal service, means an interception warrant relating to the interception of communications in the course of their transmission by means of that service; and

(b) in relation to a person providing a public telecommunications service, means an interception warrant relating to the interception of communications in the course of their transmission by means of a telecommunication system used for the purposes of that service.

Technical Advisory Board

13.[67]—(1) There shall be a Technical Advisory Board consisting of such number of persons appointed by the Secretary of State as he may by order provide.

---

[67] Commencement: 2/10/00 by SI 2000 No 2543.

(2) The order providing for the membership of the Technical Advisory Board must also make provision which is calculated to ensure—

(a) that the membership of the Technical Advisory Board includes persons likely effectively to represent the interests of the persons on whom obligations may be imposed under section 12;

(b) that the membership of the Board includes persons likely effectively to represent the interests of the persons by or on whose behalf applications for interception warrants may be made;

(c) that such other persons (if any) as the Secretary of State thinks fit may be appointed to be members of the Board; and

(d) that the Board is so constituted as to produce a balance between the representation of the interests mentioned in paragraph (a) and the representation of those mentioned in paragraph (b).

(3) The Secretary of State shall not make an order under this section unless a draft of the order has been laid before Parliament and approved by a resolution of each House.

Grants for interception costs

14.[68]—(1) It shall be the duty of the Secretary of State to ensure that such arrangements are in force as are necessary for securing that a person who provides—

(a) a postal service, or

(b) a telecommunications service,

receives such contribution as is, in the circumstances of that person's case, a fair contribution towards the costs incurred, or likely to be incurred, by that person in consequence of the matters mentioned in subsection (2).

(2) Those matters are—

(a) in relation to a person providing a postal service, the issue of interception warrants relating to communications transmitted by means of that postal service;

(b) in relation to a person providing a telecommunications service, the issue of interception warrants relating to communications transmitted by means of a telecommunication system used for the purposes of that service;

(c) in relation to each description of person, the imposition on that person of obligations provided for by an order under section 12.

(3) For the purpose of complying with his duty under this section, the Secretary of State may make arrangements for payments to be made out of money provided by Parliament.

---

[68] Commencement: 2/10/00 by SI 2000 No 2543.

Restrictions on use of intercepted material etc.

General safeguards

15.[69]—(1) Subject to subsection (6), it shall be the duty of the Secretary of State to ensure, in relation to all interception warrants, that such arrangements are in force as he considers necessary for securing—

(a) that the requirements of subsections (2) and (3) are satisfied in relation to the intercepted material and any related communications data; and

(b) in the case of warrants in relation to which there are section 8(4) certificates, that the requirements of section 16 are also satisfied.

(2) The requirements of this subsection are satisfied in relation to the intercepted material and any related communications data if each of the following—

(a) the number of persons to whom any of the material or data is disclosed or otherwise made available,

(b) the extent to which any of the material or data is disclosed or otherwise made available,

(c) the extent to which any of the material or data is copied, and

(d) the number of copies that are made,

is limited to the minimum that is necessary for the authorised purposes.

(3) The requirements of this subsection are satisfied in relation to the intercepted material and any related communications data if each copy made of any of the material or data (if not destroyed earlier) is destroyed as soon as there are no longer any grounds for retaining it as necessary for any of the authorised purposes.

(4) For the purposes of this section something is necessary for the authorised purposes if, and only if—

(a) it continues to be, or is likely to become, necessary as mentioned in section 5(3);

(b) it is necessary for facilitating the carrying out of any of the functions under this Chapter of the Secretary of State;

(c) it is necessary for facilitating the carrying out of any functions in relation to this Part of the Interception of Communications Commissioner or of the Tribunal;

(d) it is necessary to ensure that a person conducting a criminal prosecution has the information he needs to determine what is required of him by his duty to secure the fairness of the prosecution; or

(e) it is necessary for the performance of any duty imposed on any person by the Public Records Act 1958 or the Public Records Act (Northern Ireland) 1923.

(5) The arrangements for the time being in force under this section for securing that the requirements of subsection (2) are satisfied in relation to the intercepted

---

[69] Commencement: 2/10/00 by SI 2000 No 2543.

material or any related communications data must include such arrangements as the Secretary of State considers necessary for securing that every copy of the material or data that is made is stored, for so long as it is retained, in a secure manner.

(6) Arrangements in relation to interception warrants which are made for the purposes of subsection (1)—

(a) shall not be required to secure that the requirements of subsections (2) and (3) are satisfied in so far as they relate to any of the intercepted material or related communications data, or any copy of any such material or data, possession of which has been surrendered to any authorities of a country or territory outside the United Kingdom; but

(b) shall be required to secure, in the case of every such warrant, that possession of the intercepted material and data and of copies of the material or data is surrendered to authorities of a country or territory outside the United Kingdom only if the requirements of subsection (7) are satisfied.

(7) The requirements of this subsection are satisfied in the case of a warrant if it appears to the Secretary of State—

(a) that requirements corresponding to those of subsections (2) and (3) will apply, to such extent (if any) as the Secretary of State thinks fit, in relation to any of the intercepted material or related communications data possession of which, or of any copy of which, is surrendered to the authorities in question; and

(b) that restrictions are in force which would prevent, to such extent (if any) as the Secretary of State thinks fit, the doing of anything in, for the purposes of or in connection with any proceedings outside the United Kingdom which would result in such a disclosure as, by virtue of section 17, could not be made in the United Kingdom.

(8) In this section "copy", in relation to intercepted material or related communications data, means any of the following (whether or not in documentary form)-

(a) any copy, extract or summary of the material or data which identifies itself as the product of an interception, and

(b) any record referring to an interception which is a record of the identities of the persons to or by whom the intercepted material was sent, or to whom the communications data relates,

and "copied" shall be construed accordingly.

Extra safeguards in the case of certificated warrants

16.[70]—(1) For the purposes of section 15 the requirements of this section, in the case of a warrant in relation to which there is a section 8(4) certificate, are that the

---

[70] Commencement: 2/10/00 by SI 2000 No 2543.

intercepted material is read, looked at or listened to by the persons to whom it becomes available by virtue of the warrant to the extent only that it—

    (a) has been certified as material the examination of which is necessary as mentioned in section 5(3)(a), (b) or (c); and

    (b) falls within subsection (2).

  (2) Subject to subsections (3) and (4), intercepted material falls within this subsection so far only as it is selected to be read, looked at or listened to otherwise than according to a factor which—

    (a) is referable to an individual who is known to be for the time being in the British Islands; and

    (b) has as its purpose, or one of its purposes, the identification of material contained in communications sent by him, or intended for him.

  (3) Intercepted material falls within subsection (2), notwithstanding that it is selected by reference to any such factor as is mentioned in paragraph (a) and (b) of that subsection, if—

    (a) it is certified by the Secretary of State for the purposes of section 8(4) that the examination of material selected according to factors referable to the individual in question is necessary as mentioned in subsection 5(3)(a), (b) or (c); and

    (b) the material relates only to communications sent during a period of not more than three months specified in the certificate.[71]

(3A) [*proposed, see footnote*][72]

  (4) Intercepted material also falls within subsection (2), notwithstanding that it is selected by reference to any such factor as is mentioned in paragraph (a) and (b) of that subsection, if—

    (a) the person to whom the warrant is addressed believes, on reasonable grounds, that the circumstances are such that the material would fall within that subsection; or

    (b) the conditions set out in subsection (5) below are satisfied in relation to the selection of the material.

  (5) Those conditions are satisfied in relation to the selection of intercepted material if—

    (a) it has appeared to the person to whom the warrant is addressed that there has been such a relevant change of circumstances as, but for

---

[71] The draft Terrorism Bill 2005 in September 2005 proposed replacement of the expression 'a period of not more than three months specified in the certificate' with the expression 'a period specified in the certificate that is no longer than the permitted maximum'.

[72] The draft Terrorism Bill 2005 proposed insertion of the following:

'(3A) In subsection (3)(b) "the permitted maximum" means—

    (a) in the case of material the examination of which is certified for the purposes of section 8(4) as necessary in the interests of national security, six months; and

    (b) in any other case, three months.'

subsection (4)(b), would prevent the intercepted material from falling within subsection (2);

    (b) since it first so appeared, a written authorisation to read, look at or listen to the material has been given by a senior official; and

    (c) the selection is made before the end of the[73] first working day after the day on which it first so appeared to that person.

(5A) [*proposed, see footnotes*][74]

(6) References in this section to its appearing that there has been a relevant change of circumstances are references to its appearing either—

    (a) that the individual in question has entered the British Islands; or

    (b) that a belief by the person to whom the warrant is addressed in the individual's presence outside the British Islands was in fact mistaken.

 Exclusion of matters from legal proceedings

17.[75]—(1) Subject to section 18, no evidence shall be adduced, question asked, assertion or disclosure made or other thing done in, for the purposes of or in connection with any legal proceedings which (in any manner)—

    (a) discloses, in circumstances from which its origin in anything falling within subsection (2) may be inferred, any of the contents of an intercepted communication or any related communications data; or

    (b) tends (apart from any such disclosure) to suggest that anything falling within subsection (2) has or may have occurred or be going to occur.

(2) The following fall within this subsection-

    (a) conduct by a person falling within subsection (3) that was or would be an offence under section 1(1) or (2) of this Act or under section 1 of the Interception of Communications Act 1985;

    (b) a breach by the Secretary of State of his duty under section 1(4) of this Act;

    (c) the issue of an interception warrant or of a warrant under the Interception of Communications Act 1985;

---

[73] The draft Terrorism Bill 2005 proposed replacement of the expression 'first working day after the day on which it first so appeared to that person' with the expression 'the permitted maximum'.

[74] The draft Terrorism Bill 2005 proposed insertion of the following subsection:

'(5A) In subsection (5)(c) "the permitted period" means —

    (a) in the case of material the examination of which is certified for the purposes of section 8(4) as necessary in the interests of national security, the period ending with the end of the fifth working day after it first appeared as mentioned in subsection (5)(a) to the person to whom the warrant is addressed; and

    (b) in any other case, the period ending with the end of the first working day after it first so appeared to that person.'

[75] Commencement: 2/10/00 by SI 2000 No 2543. See *AG's Ref No. 5 of 2002 sub nom W* [2004] UKHL 40, discussed in Chapter 20.

    (d) the making of an application by any person for an interception warrant, or for a warrant under that Act;

    (e) the imposition of any requirement on any person to provide assistance with giving effect to an interception warrant.

(3) The persons referred to in subsection (2)(a) are—

    (a) any person to whom a warrant under this Chapter may be addressed;

    (b) any person holding office under the Crown;

    [(c) any member of the National Criminal Intelligence Service;

    (d) any member of the National Crime Squad];

    (c) any member of the staff of the Serious Organised Crime Agency;[76]

    (e) any person employed by or for the purposes of a police force;

    (f) any person providing a postal service or employed for the purposes of any business of providing such a service; and

    (g) any person providing a public telecommunications service or employed for the purposes of any business of providing such a service.

(4) In this section "intercepted communication" means any communication intercepted in the course of its transmission by means of a postal service or telecommunication system.

Exceptions to section 17

18.[77]—(1) Section 17(1) shall not apply in relation to—

    (a)   any proceedings for a relevant offence;

    (b)   any civil proceedings under section 11(8);

    (c)   any proceedings before the Tribunal;

    (d)   any proceedings on an appeal or review for which provision is made by an order under section 67(8);

    (da)[78] any control order proceedings (within the meaning of the Prevention of Terrorism Act 2005) or any proceedings arising out of such proceedings;

    (e)   any proceedings before the Special Immigration Appeals Commission or any proceedings arising out of proceedings before that Commission; or

    (f)   any proceedings before the Proscribed Organisations Appeal Commission or any proceedings arising out of proceedings before that Commission.

---

[76] Words in italics will be added (replacing the words in square brackets) when Sch 4, para 133 of the SOCAP Act 2005 is in force. The amendment will not affect the operation of s 17 in relation to conduct by NICS or NCS which took place before the amendment comes into force.

[77] Commencement: 2/10/00 by SI 2000 No 2543.

[78] (da) inserted by Schedule to the Prevention of Terrorism Act 2005, Art 6, with effect from 11/3/2005.

(2)[79] Subsection (1) shall not, by virtue of paragraph (da) to (f), authorise the disclosure of anything—

   (a) in the case of any proceedings falling within paragraph (e), to—

      (i) the appellant to the Special Immigration Appeals Commission; or

      (ii) any person who for the purposes of any proceedings so falling (but otherwise than by virtue of an appointment under section 6 of the Special Immigration Appeals Commission Act 1997) represents that appellant;

   (za) in the case of any proceedings falling within paragraph (da) to—

      (i) a person who, within the meaning of the Schedule to the Prevention of Terrorism Act 2005, is or was a relevant party to the control order proceedings; or

      (ii) any person who for the purposes of any proceedings so falling (but otherwise than by virtue of an appointment under paragraph 7 of that Schedule) represents a person falling within sub-paragraph (i);

or

   (b) in the case of proceedings falling within paragraph (f), to—

      (i) the applicant to the Proscribed Organisations Appeal Commission;

      (ii) the organisation concerned (if different);

      (iii) any person designated under paragraph 6 of Schedule 3 to the Terrorism Act 2000 to conduct proceedings so falling on behalf of that organisation; or

      (iv) any person who for the purposes of any proceedings so falling (but otherwise than by virtue of an appointment under paragraph 7 of that Schedule) represents that applicant or that organisation.

(3) Section 17(1) shall not prohibit anything done in, for the purposes of, or in connection with, so much of any legal proceedings as relates to the fairness or unfairness of a dismissal on the grounds of any conduct constituting an offence under section 1(1) or (2), 11(7) or 19 of this Act, or section 1 of the Interception of Communications Act 1985.

(4) Section 17(1)(a) shall not prohibit the disclosure of any of the contents of a communication if the interception of that communication was lawful by virtue of section 1(5)(c), 3 or 4.

(5) Where any disclosure is proposed to be or has been made on the grounds that it is authorised by subsection (4), section 17(1) shall not prohibit the doing of anything in, or for the purposes of, so much of any legal proceedings as relates to the question whether that disclosure is or was so authorised.

---

[79] Reference to (da), and new subpara (za) inserted by the Prevention of Terrorism Act 2005 Schedule, Art 6. with effect from 11/3/2005.

(6) Section 17(1)(b) shall not prohibit the doing of anything that discloses any conduct of a person for which he has been convicted of an offence under section 1(1) or (2), 11(7) or 19 of this Act, or section 1 of the Interception of Communications Act 1985.

(7) Nothing in section 17(1) shall prohibit any such disclosure of any information that continues to be available for disclosure as is confined to—

    (a) a disclosure to a person conducting a criminal prosecution for the purpose only of enabling that person to determine what is required of him by his duty to secure the fairness of the prosecution;[80] or

    (b) a disclosure to a relevant judge in a case in which that judge has ordered the disclosure to be made to him alone.

(8) A relevant judge shall not order a disclosure under subsection (7)(b) except where he is satisfied that the exceptional circumstances of the case make the disclosure essential in the interests of justice.

(9) Subject to subsection (10), where in any criminal proceedings-

    (a) a relevant judge does order a disclosure under subsection (7)(b), and

    (b) in consequence of that disclosure he is of the opinion that there are exceptional circumstances requiring him to do so,

he may direct the person conducting the prosecution to make for the purposes of the proceedings any such admission of fact as that judge thinks essential in the interests of justice.

(10) Nothing in any direction under subsection (9) shall authorise or require anything to be done in contravention of section 17(1).

(11) In this section "a relevant judge" means—

    (a) any judge of the High Court or of the Crown Court or any Circuit judge;

    (b) any judge of the High Court of Justiciary or any sheriff;

    (c) in relation to a court-martial, the judge advocate appointed in relation to that court-martial under section 84B of the Army Act 1955, section 84B of the Air Force Act 1955 or section 53B of the Naval Discipline Act 1957; or

    (d) any person holding any such judicial office as entitles him to exercise the jurisdiction of a judge falling within paragraph (a) or (b).

(12) In this section "relevant offence" means—

    (a) an offence under any provision of this Act;

    (b) an offence under section 1 of the Interception of Communications Act 1985;

    (c) an offence under section 5 of the Wireless Telegraphy Act 1949;

    (d)[81] an offence under section section 83 or 84 of the Postal Services Act 2000;

---

[80] See para 7.7 of the Interception Code of Practice in Chapter 18.

[81] Amended by the Postal Services Act 2000 (Consequential Modifications No 1) Order 2001 (SI 2001 No 1149) Sch 2 and Sch 1, para 135.

(e) an offence under section 45 of the Telecommunications Act 1984;

(f)[82] *repealed*;

(g) an offence under section 1 or 2 of the Official Secrets Act 1911 relating to any sketch, plan, model, article, note, document or information which incorporates or relates to the contents of any intercepted communication or any related communications data or tends to suggest as mentioned in section 17(1)(b) of this Act;

(h) perjury committed in the course of any proceedings mentioned in subsection (1) or (3) of this section;

(i) attempting or conspiring to commit, or aiding, abetting, counselling or procuring the commission of, an offence falling within any of the preceding paragraphs; and

(j) contempt of court committed in the course of, or in relation to, any proceedings mentioned in subsection (1) or (3) of this section.

(13) In subsection (12) "intercepted communication" has the same meaning as in section 17.

Offence for unauthorised disclosures

19.[83]—(1) Where an interception warrant has been issued or renewed, it shall be the duty of every person falling within subsection (2) to keep secret all the matters mentioned in subsection (3).

(2) The persons falling within this subsection are—

(a) the persons specified in section 6(2);

(b) every person holding office under the Crown;

[(c) every member of the National Criminal Intelligence Service;

(d) every member of the National Crime Squad];

(c) *every member of the staff of the Serious Organised Crime Agency;*[84]

(e) every person employed by or for the purposes of a police force;

(f) persons providing postal services or employed for the purposes of any business of providing such a service;

(g) persons providing public telecommunications services or employed for the purposes of any business of providing such a service;

(h) persons having control of the whole or any part of a telecommunication system located wholly or partly in the United Kingdom.

(3) Those matters are—

(a) the existence and contents of the warrant and of any section 8(4) certificate in relation to the warrant;

---

[82] Repealed by the Communications Act 2003, Sch 19.

[83] Commencement: 2/10/00 by SI 2000 No 2543.

[84] Words in italics will be added (replacing the words in square brackets) when Sch 4, para 134 of the SOCAP Act 2005 is in force. The amendment will not affect the operation of s 19 in relation to conduct by NCIS or NCS which took place before the amendment comes into force.

    (b) the details of the issue of the warrant and of any renewal or modification of the warrant or of any such certificate;

    (c) the existence and contents of any requirement to provide assistance with giving effect to the warrant;

    (d) the steps taken in pursuance of the warrant or of any such requirement; and

    (e) everything in the intercepted material, together with any related communications data.

(4) A person who makes a disclosure to another of anything that he is required to keep secret under this section shall be guilty of an offence and liable—

    (a) on conviction on indictment, to imprisonment for a term not exceeding five years or to a fine, or to both;

    (b) on summary conviction, to imprisonment for a term not exceeding six months or to a fine not exceeding the statutory maximum, or to both.

(5) In proceedings against any person for an offence under this section in respect of any disclosure, it shall be a defence for that person to show that he could not reasonably have been expected, after first becoming aware of the matter disclosed, to take steps to prevent the disclosure.

(6) In proceedings against any person for an offence under this section in respect of any disclosure, it shall be a defence for that person to show that—

    (a) the disclosure was made by or to a professional legal adviser in connection with the giving, by the adviser to any client of his, of advice about the effect of provisions of this Chapter; and

    (b) the person to whom or, as the case may be, by whom it was made was the client or a representative of the client.

(7) In proceedings against any person for an offence under this section in respect of any disclosure, it shall be a defence for that person to show that the disclosure was made by a legal adviser—

    (a) in contemplation of, or in connection with, any legal proceedings; and

    (b) for the purposes of those proceedings.

(8) Neither subsection (6) nor subsection (7) applies in the case of a disclosure made with a view to furthering any criminal purpose.

(9) In proceedings against any person for an offence under this section in respect of any disclosure, it shall be a defence for that person to show that the disclosure was confined to a disclosure made to the Interception of Communications Commissioner or authorised—

    (a) by that Commissioner;

    (b) by the warrant or the person to whom the warrant is or was addressed;

    (c) by the terms of the requirement to provide assistance; or

    (d) by section 11(9).

Interpretation of Chapter I

Interpretation of Chapter I

20.[85] In this Chapter—

"certified", in relation to a section 8(4) certificate, means of a description certified by the certificate as a description of material the examination of which the Secretary of State considers necessary;

"external communication" means a communication sent or received outside the British Islands;

"intercepted material", in relation to an interception warrant, means the contents of any communications intercepted by an interception to which the warrant relates;

"the interception subject", in relation to an interception warrant, means the person about whose communications information is sought by the interception to which the warrant relates;

"international mutual assistance agreement" means an international agreement designated for the purposes of section 1(4);

"related communications data", in relation to a communication intercepted in the course of its transmission by means of a postal service or telecommunication system, means so much of any communications data (within the meaning of Chapter II of this Part) as—

(a) is obtained by, or in connection with, the interception; and

(b) relates to the communication or to the sender or recipient, or intended recipient, of the communication;

"section 8(4) certificate" means any certificate issued for the purposes of section 8(4).

---

[85] Commencement: 2/10/00 by SI 2000 No 2543.

4

ACQUISITION AND DISCLOSURE OF COMMUNICATIONS DATA: RIPA, PART I, CHAPTER II, SS 21–25

A. Discussion

Introduction: 'communications data'

It will be recalled that in Chapter I of Part I of RIPA a distinction is drawn between **4.01** the message content of communications, interception of which is regulated by Chapter I, and 'traffic data' defined by s 2(9) and (10) for the purposes of Chapter I. That distinction is widened in Chapter II where the notion of 'Communications Data' is coined in s 21(4)(a)–(c) as including:

- 'traffic data'[1] comprised in or attached to a communication for the purposes of the service by which it is being transmitted; and
- information which includes none of the contents of a communication (save for the type of traffic data above) which is 'about' the use made by any person of a postal/telecommunication service or is in connection with the provision to or use by anyone of any telecommunication system or service; and
- any other information which is held by a service provider in relation to persons to whom the service is provided.

'Communications Data' is therefore information such as numbers dialled, times **4.02** of calls, details of callers and receivers, website addresses, email addresses, etc. On postal items the Communications Data includes anything written on the outside of the item (s. 21(7)). See the discussion at para **4.04** below.

Chapter II of Part I applies to Communications Data as defined above and pro- **4.03** vides a means by which certain classes of authorised person or public body can obtain access to it whilst ensuring that such access is lawful for all purposes

---

[1] Section 21(6) and (7) reproduces the definition in s 2(9) and (10).

(s 21(2)). Communications Data is subject to a substantially different regime to the message content, which is subject to the strictures of RIPA, Chapter I. Such data is more readily obtained, and lawfully obtained communications data is not subject to the restrictions on use which are imposed upon the use of communications intercepted under Chapter I. This difference was subject to criticism by the Data Protection Commissioner prior to the passage of the Act in the following terms in her 'Response of the Data Protection Commissioner to the Government's Regulation of Investigatory Powers Bill' 'March' 2000, at para 8:

> 8. The Commissioner questions the distinction . . . between the requirements for gaining access to data contained within an intercepted communication and those for gaining access to other communications data . . . Both sets of data provide insight into the private lives of individuals and should therefore be subject to equivalent controls and safeguards.

Accessing communications data (pre-consultation text of Code of Practice)

4.04 A Code of Practice on the accessing of communications data exists in two informal forms, neither of which had been formally brought into force at time of writing. The first was released in 2001 as the 'Accessing Communications Data Draft Code Of Practice' (Home Office Circular 32/2001) which had the status of being a consultative document draft Code. A new text was released in 2005, namely the 'Acquisition and Disclosure of Communications Revised Code of Practice' (Home Office pre-consultative document, 2005). That may or may not in due course become the Code of Practice, but at the time of writing it was a pre-consultative text.

Of interest at this stage is para 2.13 of the 2005 pre-consultative Code which provides the following definition of Communications Data:

> 2.13 The term 'communications data' embraces the 'who', 'when' and 'where' of a communication but not the content, not what was said or written. It includes the manner in which, and by what method, a person or machine communicates with another person or machine. It excludes what they say or what data they pass on within that communication (with the exception of data required to investigate crimes such as 'dial through' fraud, where data is passed on to activate communications equipment in order to fraudulently obtain communications services).'[2]

The Voluntary Code of Practice on the retention of communications data under the Anti-terrorism Crime and Security Act 2001

4.05 By Part 11 of the Anti-Terrorism, Crime and Security Act 2001, the Secretary of State may publish a Code of Practice governing the provision which communication service providers are requested to make for the retention of communications data,

---

[2] The 2005 document also provides examples of 'traffic data' (which is one category of Communications Data) at para 2.19.

and a Code of Practice (reproduced in Chapter 17) was published which was brought into force by the Retention of Communications Data (Code of Practice) Order 2003 (SI 2003 No 3175) with effect from 5 December 2001.

The provisions of the Code under the 2001 Act are too detailed to be discussed **4.06** further but the reader is referred to the copy of the Code in Chapter 17. The Code makes detailed provision for periods of time for which communications providers may retain certain types of Communications Data such as log-on details, and sent and received email details.

The public authorities which may access communications data

The public authorities which may access communications data are set out in **4.07** s 25(1) under 'relevant public authority':

(a)   a police force;
[(b)   the National Criminal Intelligence Service;
(c)   the National Crime Squad;
(d)   the Commissioners of Customs and Excise]
(b)   the Serious Organised Crime Agency;[3]
(e)   the Commissioners of Inland Revenue;
(f)   any of the intelligence services;
(g)   any public authority not listed above as may be specified by the Secretary of State ('the additional public authorities').

The current SI specifying the various 'additional public authorities', which also **4.08** lists limitations in terms of the grounds on which any of the public authorities may obtain access to data, and what types of data may be sought is the Regulation of Investigatory Powers (Communications Data) Order 2003 (SI 2003 No 3172) amended by the Regulation of Investigatory Powers (Communications Data) (Amendment) Order 2005 (SI 2005 No. 1083).[4]

The Designated Person

Under s 22 of RIPA it is the 'Designated Person' within each public authority who **4.09** is responsible for considering and approving or rejecting applications by members of the same authority to obtain access to communications data from service providers. The Designated Persons (typically senior ranks or officers in public bodies) who are entitled to grant authorisation to obtain communications data or issue Notices for service on CSPs are set out in the Regulation of Investigatory

---

   [3] Words in italics will be added (replacing the words in square brackets) when Sch 4, para 135 of the SOCAP Act 2005 is in force.
   [4] The Schedules to the Order are complex and require careful reading.

Powers (Communications Data) Order 2003 (SI 2003 No 3172) amended by the Regulation of Investigatory Powers (Communications Data) (Amendment) Order 2005 (SI 2005 No 1083).

4.10 Perhaps the most significant matter is that the Designated Persons capable of granting authorisation are members of the bodies proposing to obtain the data (cf interception warrants under Chapter I where the Secretary of State's authorisation is necessary).

The single point of contact[5]

4.11 In order to ensure that there is a coherent administration of the communications data regime, and that there is one verifiable individual in any authority whose credentials can be checked by service providers, following Government consultation, a 'Single Point of Contact' or SPoC system was put into place. The SPoC is a trained person (there are several approved training providers) to whom staff within authorities may pass their applications for access to communications data, and who will liase with CSPs as well as serving the notices described below if they are authorised by the Designated Person.[6] The 2005 pre-consultative Acquisition and Disclosure of Communications Data Revised Code Of Practice ('the draft Code') at para 3.15 states:

> 3.15 Public authorities unable to call upon the services of an accredited SPoC should not undertake the acquisition of communications data.

4.12 The SPoC checks applications for compliance with the Act before, if appropriate, passing them on to the Designated Person ('DP') to seek authorisation. If the DP approves the application then the SPoC becomes responsible for service of Notices on CSPs or for administration of Authorisations (as the case may be—see para **4.13** below). The SPoC will retain and keep secure the information associated with the application (which may of course later be needed as evidence if for example a prosecution results).

4.13 The draft Code gives the following guidance on the role of the SPoC:

> 3.14 The SPoC should be in a position to:
> - assess whether the acquisition of specific communications data from a CSP is reasonably practical or whether the specific data required is inextricably linked to other data;
> - advise applicants and Designated Persons on the interpretation of the Act, particularly whether an authorisation or notice is appropriate;
> - provide assurance to Designated Persons that authorisations and notices are lawful under the Act and free from errors;

---

[5] The SPoC arrangement is essentially a practical arrangement to enable the statutory provisions to work manageably.

[6] The SPoC and the Designated Person may be one and the same individual: Code, para 3.15.

- provide assurance to CSPs that authorisations and notices are authentic and lawful;
- assess any cost and resource implications to both the public authority and the CSP of data requirements.

> **Standard forms available in Chapter 13 of this work which are relevant to access to Communications Data (forms are for *additional public authorities* only: see paras 4.06–4.07):[7]**
> A Application for communications data (under Part I, Chapter II of RIPA)
> B Application for Communications Data—SPoC Rejection Form
> C Designated Person's Consideration Form in respect of an Application for Communications Data
> D Notice under s 22(4) of the Regulation of Investigatory Powers Act 2000 requiring Communications Data to be obtained and disclosed
> E Applicant's Cancellation request form under s 22(4) & (8) of RIPA
> F SPoC's Cancellation Notice under s 22 (4) & (8) of RIPA

Authorisations v Notices

RIPA permits two ways of accessing communications data if an application for access is approved by the DP, as follows. **4.14**

(1) Section 22(4) provides that where a CSP may be in possession of, or is capable of obtaining communications data, then the DP within that authority may (if he approves the application) serve a *Notice* in standard form requiring that CSP to obtain and disclose the data. Any operator served with such a notice is under a duty to comply: s 22(6), unless it is not reasonably practicable (s 22(7)). The duty is enforceable: s 2(8). The notice is given by the DP but in practical terms it is the SPoC who serves it (thereby maintaining the integrity of the SPoC system).

(2) Section 22(3) provides that a DP may grant an Authorization allowing a member of the same authority to collect or retrieve the data from the CSP's records themselves.[8] Authorisation can only be given to someone holding an office, rank or position within the same authority (s 22(3)). The DP will only grant an authorisation,[9] when he believes that one or more of the following apply (see the notes for guidance on the DP's consideration form):
- the CSP would be incapable of complying with a notice;
- if a Notice is given the enquiry would be likely to be prejudiced;
- there is an existing arrangement in place between the public authority and the CSP for the exchange of data, and the SPoC can retrieve the data using an automated system within the public authority.

---

[7] Where forms are referred to here, the titles given to them are intended to be descriptive and are not official titles.

[8] See Code of Practice for the retention of Communications Data under the Anti-Terrorism, Crime and Security Act 2001 dealing with the periods of time for which CSPs should retain various types of Communications Data if adopting that Code.

[9] Authorisations are a greater intrusion by the State because they allow the public authority to access the data rather than the access being performed by the CSP.

4.15 The draft Code gives the following guidance:

> 3.20 An authorisation may be appropriate where:
> - a CSP is not capable of obtaining or disclosing the communications data;
> - a designated person believes the investigation or operation may be prejudiced if the CSP is required to obtain or disclose the data;
> - there is an agreement in place between a public authority and a CSP relating to appropriate mechanisms for disclosure of communications data, or
> - a designated person considers there is a requirement to conduct a telephone subscriber check but a CSP has yet to be conclusively determined as the holder of the communications data.
>
> 3.21 An authorisation is not served upon a CSP, although there may be circumstances where a CSP may require or may be given an assurance that conduct being undertaken is lawful. That assurance may be given by disclosing details of the authorisation or the authorisation itself.

4.16 The procedure is that an authorisation is granted by the DP, but is administered by the SPoC, again thereby protecting the integrity of the SPoC system.

Grounds for granting Authorisations or giving Notices

4.17 An Authorisation may be granted—or Notice given—if the DP believes that it is *necessary* on one of the following grounds[10] for the data to be obtained *and* he believes that obtaining the data required is *proportionate*[11] to what is sought to be achieved by obtaining it:

(a) in the interests of national security;

(b) for the purpose of preventing or detecting crime or of preventing disorder;

(c) in the interests of the economic well-being of the United Kingdom;

(d) in the interests of public safety;

(e) for the purpose of protecting public health;

(f) for the purpose of assessing or collecting any tax, duty, levy or other imposition, contribution or charge payable to a government department;

(g) for the purpose, in an emergency, of preventing death or injury or any damage to a person's physical or mental health, or of mitigating any injury or damage to a person's physical or mental health;[12] or

(h) for any purpose (not falling within paras (a)–(g)) which is specified by an order made by the Secretary of State.

But the reader will recall that not all authorities may rely on all possible grounds, especially as regards the additional public authorities: see the Regulation of Investigatory Powers (Communications Data) Order 2003 (SI 2003 No 3172).

---

[10] Section 22(2), but note that not all grounds available to all public authorities.

[11] Section 22(5).

[12] The most obvious example being the accessing of location data following a 999 emergency call so as to locate the caller.

Form and duration of Authorisation or Notice (s 23)

Sections 23(1) and 23(2) set out the matters which must be stated in an authori- **4.18**
sation or the record of an authorisation. By virtue of s 23(4), Authorisations (or
Notices) may not in the first instance be granted for more than one month, but
s 23(5) permits renewal for up to a month at a time—from the end of the current
period of validity rather than from date of renewal—provided renewal takes place
before the Authorisation or Notice expires.

A Notice must be cancelled if the person who gave it is satisfied that it is no longer **4.19**
necessary under any of the grounds in s 22(2) or the conduct required is no longer
proportionate to what is sought to be achieved (s 22(8)). The process for cancellation of a notice would typically be that the applicant would (in addition to tele-
phoning the SPoC if appropriate to reduce the invasion of privacy of the person
whose data is being accessed), send a cancellation form to the SPoC. The SPoC,
having obtained approval of the cancellation form from the DP would serve
a Cancellation Notice on the CSP, and may telephone the CSP to cease access
without delay.

Urgent cases (Notices and Authorisations)

In exceptional urgent circumstances, application may be made by an applicant, **4.20**
approved by a DP and notice given or authorisation granted orally. This may be
appropriate where there is an immediate threat to life such that a person's life
might be endangered if the application procedure were undertaken in writing
from the outset.

The 2005 draft Code states:[13]

> 3.43 Particular care must be given to the use of the urgent oral process. When notice
> is given orally, the SPoC or (in the case of an emergency call) the emergency service
> controller must provide a unique reference number for the notice (or emergency call)
> and provide the name of the designated person (or authorising officer in the case of
> an emergency call). Where telephone numbers (or other identifiers) are being
> relayed, the relevant number must be read twice and repeated back by the CSP to
> confirm the correct details have been taken.

Emergency calls and other special cases

Certain CSPs have obligations under the Communications Act 2003 in respect of **4.21**
calls to emergency numbers. They must ensure that any service user can access the
emergency authorities by using emergency numbers and, if feasible, make caller
location information available for all 999/112 calls. The 2005 draft Code provides

---

[13] See also the subsequent paragraphs of the draft Code, in Chapter 19.

information as to the handling of Communications Data in such circumstances, and in other cases, at para 4.1.

Compensation to CSPs

4.22 Chapter II of RIPA provides that the Secretary of State is under a duty to put in place arrangements to allow payments to service providers of 'appropriate contributions'[14] towards the costs of complying with Notices under s 22(4).

The role of the Interception of Communications Commissioner

4.23 The Interception of Communications Commissioner appointed under s 57 plays a reporting role in relation to the access of communications data: by s 57(2)(b) he must keep under review the exercise and performance of powers and duties given to persons under Chapter II.

The text of RIPA, Part I, Chapter II as amended follows.

B. Text of Part I, Chapter II

REGULATION OF INVESTIGATORY POWERS ACT 2000 (AS AMENDED)

CHAPTER II

ACQUISITION AND DISCLOSURE OF COMMUNICATIONS DATA

Lawful acquisition and disclosure of communications data

21.[15]—(1) This Chapter applies to—
  (a) any conduct in relation to a postal service or telecommunication system for obtaining communications data, other than conduct consisting in the interception of communications in the course of their transmission by means of such a service or system; and
  (b) the disclosure to any person of communications data.

---

[14] Contrast RIPA, Part I, Chapter I which provided for payment of a 'fair contribution' and had an elaborate scheme for protecting service providers from excessive cost of interception via the Technical Advisory Board.

[15] Commencement: s 21(4), for the purpose of giving effect to the definition of 'related communications data' in s 20, came into force on 2/10/00 by SI 2000 No 2543. Remainder commenced on 5/1/2004 by SI 2003 No 3140.

(2) Conduct to which this Chapter applies shall be lawful for all purposes if—

    (a) it is conduct in which any person is authorised or required to engage by an authorisation or notice granted or given under this Chapter; and

    (b) the conduct is in accordance with, or in pursuance of, the authorisation or requirement.

(3) A person shall not be subject to any civil liability in respect of any conduct of his which-

    (a) is incidental to any conduct that is lawful by virtue of subsection (2); and

    (b) is not itself conduct an authorisation or warrant for which is capable of being granted under a relevant enactment and might reasonably have been expected to have been sought in the case in question.

(4) In this Chapter "communications data" means any of the following—

    (a) any traffic data comprised in or attached to a communication (whether by the sender or otherwise) for the purposes of any postal service or telecommunication system by means of which it is being or may be transmitted;

    (b) any information which includes none of the contents of a communication (apart from any information falling within paragraph (a)) and is about the use made by any person-

      (i) of any postal service or telecommunications service; or

      (ii) in connection with the provision to or use by any person of any telecommunications service, of any part of a telecommunication system;

    (c) any information not falling within paragraph (a) or (b) that is held or obtained, in relation to persons to whom he provides the service, by a person providing a postal service or telecommunications service.

(5) In this section "relevant enactment" means-

    (a) an enactment contained in this Act;

    (b) section 5 of the Intelligence Services Act 1994 (warrants for the intelligence services); or

    (c) an enactment contained in Part III of the Police Act 1997 (powers of the police and of customs officers).

(6) In this section "traffic data", in relation to any communication, means—

    (a) any data identifying, or purporting to identify, any person, apparatus or location to or from which the communication is or may be transmitted,

    (b) any data identifying or selecting, or purporting to identify or select, apparatus through which, or by means of which, the communication is or may be transmitted,

    (c) any data comprising signals for the actuation of apparatus used for the purposes of a telecommunication system for effecting (in whole or in part) the transmission of any communication, and

(d) any data identifying the data or other data as data comprised in or attached to a particular communication,

but that expression includes data identifying a computer file or computer program access to which is obtained, or which is run, by means of the communication to the extent only that the file or program is identified by reference to the apparatus in which it is stored.

(7) In this section—

    (a) references, in relation to traffic data comprising signals for the actuation of apparatus, to a telecommunication system by means of which a communication is being or may be transmitted include references to any telecommunication system in which that apparatus is comprised; and

    (b) references to traffic data being attached to a communication include references to the data and the communication being logically associated with each other;

and in this section "data", in relation to a postal item, means anything written on the outside of the item.

Obtaining and disclosing communications data

22.[16]—(1) This section applies where a person designated for the purposes of this Chapter believes that it is necessary on grounds falling within subsection (2) to obtain any communications data.

(2) It is necessary on grounds falling within this subsection to obtain communications data if it is necessary—

    (a) in the interests of national security;

    (b) for the purpose of preventing or detecting crime or of preventing disorder;

    (c) in the interests of the economic well-being of the United Kingdom;

    (d) in the interests of public safety;

    (e) for the purpose of protecting public health;

    (f) for the purpose of assessing or collecting any tax, duty, levy or other imposition, contribution or charge payable to a government department;

    (g) for the purpose, in an emergency, of preventing death or injury or any damage to a person's physical or mental health, or of mitigating any injury or damage to a person's physical or mental health; or

    (h) for any purpose (not falling within paragraphs (a) to (g)) which is specified for the purposes of this subsection by an order made by the Secretary of State.

---

[16] Commencement: 5/1/2004 by SI 2003 No 3140.

(3) Subject to subsection (5), the Designated Person may grant an authorisation for persons holding offices, ranks or positions with the same relevant public authority as the Designated Person to engage in any conduct to which this Chapter applies.

(4) Subject to subsection (5), where it appears to the Designated Person that a postal or telecommunications operator is or may be in possession of, or be capable of obtaining, any communications data, the Designated Person may, by notice to the postal or telecommunications operator, require the operator-

(a) if the operator is not already in possession of the data, to obtain the data; and

(b) in any case, to disclose all of the data in his possession or subsequently obtained by him.

(5) The Designated Person shall not grant an authorisation under subsection (3), or give a notice under subsection (4), unless he believes that obtaining the data in question by the conduct authorised or required by the authorisation or notice is proportionate to what is sought to be achieved by so obtaining the data.

(6) It shall be the duty of the postal or telecommunications operator to comply with the requirements of any notice given to him under subsection (4).

(7) A person who is under a duty by virtue of subsection (6) shall not be required to do anything in pursuance of that duty which it is not reasonably practicable for him to do.

(8) The duty imposed by subsection (6) shall be enforceable by civil proceedings by the Secretary of State for an injunction, or for specific performance of a statutory duty under section 45 of the Court of Session Act 1988, or for any other appropriate relief.

(9) The Secretary of State shall not make an order under subsection (2)(h) unless a draft of the order has been laid before Parliament and approved by a resolution of each House.

Form and duration of Authorisations and Notices

23.[17]—(1) An authorisation under section 22(3)—

(a) must be granted in writing or (if not in writing) in a manner that produces a record of its having been granted;

(b) must describe the conduct to which this Chapter applies that is authorised and the communications data in relation to which it is authorised;

(c) must specify the matters falling within section 22(2) by reference to which it is granted; and

---

[17] Commencement: 5/1/2004 by SI 2003 No 3140.

(d) must specify the office, rank or position held by the person granting the authorisation.

(2) A notice under section 22(4) requiring communications data to be disclosed or to be obtained and disclosed—

(a) must be given in writing or (if not in writing) must be given in a manner that produces a record of its having been given;

(b) must describe the communications data to be obtained or disclosed under the notice;

(c) must specify the matters falling within section 22(2) by reference to which the notice is given;

(d) must specify the office, rank or position held by the person giving it; and

(e) must specify the manner in which any disclosure required by the notice is to be made.

(3) A notice under section 22(4) shall not require the disclosure of data to any person other than—

(a) the person giving the notice; or

(b) such other person as may be specified in or otherwise identified by, or in accordance with, the provisions of the notice;

but the provisions of the notice shall not specify or otherwise identify a person for the purposes of paragraph (b) unless he holds an office, rank or position with the same relevant public authority as the person giving the notice.

(4) An authorisation under section 22(3) or notice under section 22(4)—

(a) shall not authorise or require any data to be obtained after the end of the period of one month beginning with the date on which the authorisation is granted or the notice given; and

(b) in the case of a notice, shall not authorise or require any disclosure after the end of that period of any data not in the possession of, or obtained by, the postal or telecommunications operator at a time during that period.

(5) An authorisation under section 22(3) or notice under section 22(4) may be renewed at any time before the end of the period of one month applying (in accordance with subsection (4) or subsection (7)) to that authorisation or notice.

(6) A renewal of an authorisation under section 22(3) or of a notice under section 22(4) shall be by the grant or giving, in accordance with this section, of a further authorisation or notice.

(7) Subsection (4) shall have effect in relation to a renewed authorisation or renewal notice as if the period of one month mentioned in that subsection did not begin until the end of the period of one month applicable to the authorisation or notice that is current at the time of the renewal.

(8) Where a person who has given a notice under subsection (4) of section 22 is satisfied—

(a) that it is no longer necessary on grounds falling within subsection (2) of that section for the requirements of the notice to be complied with, or

    (b) that the conduct required by the notice is no longer proportionate to what is sought to be achieved by obtaining communications data to which the notice relates,

he shall cancel the notice.

(9) The Secretary of State may by regulations provide for the person by whom any duty imposed by subsection (8) is to be performed in a case in which it would otherwise fall on a person who is no longer available to perform it; and regulations under this subsection may provide for the person on whom the duty is to fall to be a person appointed in accordance with the regulations.

Arrangements for payments

24.[18]—(1) It shall be the duty of the Secretary of State to ensure that such arrangements are in force as he thinks appropriate for requiring or authorising, in such cases as he thinks fit, the making to postal and telecommunications operators of appropriate contributions towards the costs incurred by them in complying with notices under section 22(4).

(2) For the purpose of complying with his duty under this section, the Secretary of State may make arrangements for payments to be made out of money provided by Parliament.

Interpretation of Chapter II

25.[19]—(1)   In this Chapter—

"communications data" has the meaning given by section 21(4);

"designated" shall be construed in accordance with subsection (2);

"postal or telecommunications operator" means a person who provides a postal service or telecommunications service;

"relevant public authority" means (subject to subsection (4)) any of the following—

(a) a police force;

[(b) the National Criminal Intelligence Service;

(c) the National Crime Squad;

(d) the Commissioners of Customs and Excise]

(b) the Serious Organised Crime Agency [20]

(e) the Commissioners of Inland Revenue;

(f) any of the intelligence services;

---

[18] Commencement: 5/1/2004 by SI 2003 No 3140.

[19] Commencement: 5/1/2004 by SI 2003 No 3140.

[20] Words in italics will be added (replacing the words in square brackets) when Sch 4, para 135 of the SOCAP Act 2005 is in force.

(g) any such public authority not falling within paragraphs (a) to (f) as may be specified for the purposes of this subsection by an order made by the Secretary of State.

(2) Subject to subsection (3), the persons designated for the purposes of this Chapter are the individuals holding such offices, ranks or positions with relevant public authorities as are prescribed for the purposes of this subsection by an order made by the Secretary of State.

(3) The Secretary of State may by order impose restrictions—

   (a) on the authorisations and notices under this Chapter that may be granted or given by any individual holding an office, rank or position with a specified public authority; and

   (b) on the circumstances in which, or the purposes for which, such authorisations may be granted or notices given by any such individual.

(3A) *References in this Chapter to an individual holding an office or position with the Serious Organised Crime Agency include references to any member of the staff of that Agency.*[21]

[(4) The Secretary of State may by order remove any person from the list of persons who are for the time being relevant public authorities for the purposes of this Chapter.

(5) The Secretary of State shall not make an order under this section that adds any person to the list of persons who are for the time being relevant public authorities for the purposes of this Chapter unless a draft of the order has been laid before Parliament and approved by a resolution of each House.]

(4) *The Secretary of State may by order—*

   (a) *remove any person from the list of persons who are for the time being relevant public authorities for the purposes of this Chapter; and*

   (b) *make such consequential amendments, repeals or revocations in this or any other enactment as appear to him to be necessary or expedient.*

(5) *The Secretary of State shall not make an order under this section—*

   (a) *that adds any person to the list of persons who are for the time being relevant public authorities for the purposes of this Chapter, or*

   (b) *that by virtue of subsection (4)(b) amends or repeals any provision of an Act, unless a draft of the order has been laid before Parliament and approved by a resolution of each House.*[22]

---

[21] Words in italics will be added when Sch 4, para 135 of the SOCAP Act 2005 is in force.
[22] Words in italics will be added (replacing words in square brackets at subs (4) and (5)) when Sch 4, para 135 of the SOCAP Act 2005 is in force.

5

SURVEILLANCE AND COVERT HUMAN INTELLIGENCE SOURCES: RIPA, PART II, SS 26–48

A. Introduction

Introduction

RIPA, Part II covers three areas, namely directed surveillance, Intrusive Surveillance **5.01** and Covert Human Intelligence Sources ('CHIS') and provides authorisation procedures in each of those areas. It is important to note that Part II creates what is essentially a voluntary scheme for authorisation (often wholly internally to the public bodies concerned) of surveillance or use of CHIS. Thus in contrast to the position which was discussed in the earlier parts of this work relating to interception of communications, RIPA does not impose any form of legal duty or obligation upon public authorities to obtain prior authorisation of surveillance or CHIS activities. The 'penalty' which a public authority might face if it failed to follow the procedures in Part II of RIPA would be the risk of the activities in question being found to breach s 6 of the Human Rights Act 1998 (HRA) or of having evidence excluded by a court. The forum for a s 7 HRA claim in the context of RIPA would be the Investigatory Powers Tribunal whose rules and procedures were considered in Chapter 11.

Overview

The use of CHIS and of directed surveillance[1] are subject to an internal form **5.02** of authorisation and record keeping process within the public body carrying out the surveillance, which is subject to post hoc oversight by the Surveillance

---

[1] Directed Surveillance is covert surveillance for the purposes of a specific investigation which is likely to reveal private information, other than surveillance amounting to intrusive surveillance—see n2 below and s 26(2) of RIPA. The full definition includes exceptions.

Commissioner in the case of non-Intelligence Services authorisations. The Intelligence Services Commissioner has a remit to provide oversight of the Security Service, Secret Intelligence Service, GCHQ and the Ministry of Defence and HM Forces (excluding the military police forces, and in Northern Ireland officials of the Ministry of Defence and HM Forces). The range of authorities entitled to carry out directed surveillance or make use of CHIS is wide.

5.03 By contrast intrusive surveillance[2] is subject to an authorisation process with a higher degree of supervision, and the authorisation mechanism is available to a shorter list of public authorities, principally the police and the other law enforcement and intelligence bodies. In the case of police and Customs authorisations the process involves senior authorising officers within the public bodies coupled with reporting and (usually) the need for prior approval by a Surveillance Commissioner.[3] For the Intelligence Services, authorisation is sought from the Secretary of State by way of warrant combined with oversight by the Intelligence Services Commissioner.

5.04 Ultimately conduct under RIPA, Part II (directed or intrusive surveillance or use of CHIS) may be subject to a complaint to the Investigatory Powers Tribunal by an aggrieved person.

The Codes of Practice

The Covert Surveillance: Code of Practice 2002[4]

5.05 The Covert Surveillance: Code of Practice (in Chapter 15) establishes guidance relevant to both types of surveillance, but note that in relation to the use of covert surveillance and CHIS the OFT has published versions of the Code in relation to its investigations into 'cartel offences' under the Enterprise Act 2002 and Competition Act 1998. See the OFT website, www.oft.gov.uk. However the Home Office version is the one which is binding.[5]

The Covert Human Intelligence Sources: Code Of Practice 2002[6]

5.06 The CHIS: Code of Practice 2002, appearing in Chapter 16, establishes a comprehensive Code in relation to the use of CHIS.

---

[2] Intrusive surveillance is covert surveillance in relation to anything taking place on private premises or vehicles which involves the presence of a person on the premises/vehicle or which makes use of a surveillance device, but see the detailed definitions later in this chapter and s 26(3) of RIPA.

[3] However there is no provision in RIPA, Part II which renders unauthorised Intrusive Surveillance actionably illegal.

[4] The RIPA (Covert Surveillance: Code of Practice) Order 2002 (SI 2002 No 1933) which came into force on 1 August 2002.

[5] The press release accompanying the publication of the OFT Codes confirmed this point.

[6] The RIPA (Covert Human Intelligence Sources: Code of Practice) Order 2002 (SI 2002 No 1932) which came into force on 1 August 2002.

The status of the Codes: a reminder

By s 72(1): **5.07**

> . . . a person exercising or performing any power or duty in relation to which provision may be made by a code of practice under section 71 shall, in doing so, have regard to the provisions (so far as they are applicable) of every code of practice for the time being in force under that section.

The Code is admissible in criminal or civil proceedings, and by s 72(4) if it appears **5.08** to a court or tribunal, the Investigatory Powers Tribunal, a commissioner under RIPA, a Surveillance Commissioner carrying out his functions under RIPA or the Police Act 1997 or any Assistant Surveillance Commissioner under RIPA, that any provision of the Code is relevant then that provision of the code '. . . shall be taken into account in determining that question'.

B. Directed and Intrusive Covert Surveillance (overview)

Definitions and exceptions

It is logical to begin with some core definitions (RIPA, s 26(2) and (3)): **5.09**

'Surveillance' generally includes, (subject to some exceptions which will become clear below), any or all of the following:

(a) monitoring, observing or listening to persons,[7] their movements, their conversations or their other activities or communications;
(b) recording anything monitored, observed or listened to in the course of surveillance; and
(c) surveillance by or with the assistance of a surveillance device.[8]

'Covert'

It is of the essence that the surveillance dealt with under RIPA falls within the Act **5.10** only if it is done covertly. Section 26(9)(a) defines 'covert' in the context of surveillance such that surveillance is covert only if:

> . . . it is carried out in a manner that is calculated to ensure that the persons who are subject to the surveillance are unaware that it is or may be taking place.

It follows that where surveillance is obvious—such as with CCTV cameras in the street which are known to be taking images—it will not amount to 'covert'

---

[7] 'Person' includes any organisation and any association or combination of persons, such as companies and partnerships. See s 81(1).

[8] Section 48(2)(a)–(c). 'Surveillance device' is defined in s 48(1), ie 'any apparatus designed or adapted for use in surveillance'.

surveillance unless the use to which it is put changes covertly to being more directed in nature. See the discussion below at para 5.17.

5.11 There is some ground for concern that the definition above relies upon the perception of the person carrying out the surveillance as opposed to the state of knowledge of the person observed. One can envisage a situation where a person was unaware of being observed *in fact*—making the surveillance 'covert' for all practical purposes—whilst the activity in question was not 'calculated to ensure' that he was unaware, and was therefore not legally speaking 'covert' within the meaning of Part II. See the 'Response of the Data Protection Commissioner to the Government's Regulation of Investigatory Powers Bill' March 2000, para 12 which made the point thus:

> It is the view of the Commissioner that the surveillance should be regarded as covert if the effect is that persons are unaware that it is being carried out. It should not be defined on the basis of whether it is the intention of those carrying out the surveillance to ensure that the persons are unaware.

Intrusive surveillance (s 26(3))

5.12 Section 26(3) defines intrusive surveillance thus:

> . . . surveillance is intrusive . . . if, and only if, it is covert surveillance that—
> (a) is carried out in relation to anything taking place on any residential premises[9] or in any private vehicle; and
> (b) involves the presence of an individual on the premises or in the vehicle or is carried out by means of a surveillance device.

Exceptions:

(a) Surveillance is not intrusive (ie it is treated as merely directed surveillance, see below) if:
   • it is carried out by means only of a surveillance device 'designed or adapted principally for the purpose of providing information about the location of a vehicle', see s 26(4)(a); or
   • if it is surveillance in the form of interception of a communication *and* the person sending the communication or the person for whom it was intended, has consented to its interception (and no interception warrant has been obtained). See s 48(4) and 26(4)(b).

(b) Surveillance is also deemed *not* to be intrusive if it is carried out using a surveillance device which is not physically present on the premises or vehicle being observed, unless the device 'is such that it consistently provides

---

[9] The 'Response of the Data Protection Commissioner to the Government's RIPA Bill' March 2000, para 10 recommended that this definition ought to have been extended to any place where the person concerned has a legitimate expectation of privacy.

information of the same quality and detail as might be expected to be obtained from a device actually present on the premises or in the vehicle'[10] (s 26(5)).

(c) Surveillance which is carried out by means of apparatus for the purpose of detecting television receivers installed or used on residential premises and which is carried out from outside those premises, and exclusively for that purpose, is treated as neither intrusive nor directed surveillance (s 26(6)).

Directed surveillance (s 26(2))

Section 26(2) defines directed surveillance thus: **5.13**

> . . . surveillance is directed . . . if it is covert but not intrusive and is undertaken-
> (a) for the purposes of a specific investigation or a specific operation;
> (b) in such a manner as is likely to result in the obtaining of private information[11] about a person (whether or not one specifically identified for the purposes of the investigation or operation); and
> (c) otherwise than by way of an immediate response to events or circumstances the nature of which is such that it would not be reasonably practicable for an authorisation . . . to be sought for the carrying out of the surveillance.

Exception (in addition to (c) above):

(a) Surveillance which is carried out by means of apparatus for the purpose of detecting television receivers installed or used on residential premises and which is carried out from outside those premises, and exclusively for that purpose, is treated as *neither* intrusive nor directed surveillance (s 26(6)).

'Private information' and 'family life'

The concept of 'private information' is broad. See s 26(10) which confirms that **5.14** 'private information' includes information relating to the private or family life of the person in question. The Code, at para 4.1, confirms that the concept should:

> . . . include an individual's private or personal relationship with others. Family life should be treated as extending beyond the formal relationships created by marriage.

The issue of whether same sex relationships attract the protection of the 'family life' limb of Article 8 of the Convention appears to have been settled in the affirmative in the UK (*Secretary of State for Work & Pensions v M; and Cynthia Langley v (1) Bradford Metropolitan District Council and Others.*).[12] As to whether the

---

[10] This is open to criticism that the notions of 'quality', 'detail' and 'consistency' are very subjective. In an ECHR, Art 8 context one might expect *degree of intrusion* into privacy to be the criterion. Furthermore no express consideration is given to the status of poor quality device data which is digitally enhanced.

[11] 'Private information' includes information relating to private or family life of the echoing part of the wording of Art 8 of the Convention. See s 26(10).

[12] [2004] EWCA Civ 1343. The background is that in *Estevez v Spain* (app no 56501/00; 10 May 2001) concerning the withholding of a survivor's pension from the deceased's long term homosexual

expression 'family life' would be interpreted more or less liberally where it appears in RIPA, the expectation would be that the courts would adopt an interpretation consistent with the Article 8 interpretation in *Langley*.

The use of a person either to carry a surveillance device or to record information while present: is this covert surveillance?

5.15 By s 48(3)(a) and (b), conduct which involves the use of Covert Human Intelligence Sources to obtain information while the source is physically present—for example to carry a 'wire' to record information given in a conversation—is treated as being the use of CHIS (and therefore subject to the authorisation scheme for CHIS), as opposed to surveillance. Section 48(3) thus resolves a conceptual difficulty which might otherwise arise where a human source is used as a type of human 'surveillance device'. The Act places such activity outside the scope of surveillance and leaves it firmly within the scope of CHIS:[13]

> 48 . . . (3) References in this Part to surveillance do not include references to-
>> (a) any conduct of a covert human intelligence source for obtaining or recording (whether or not using a surveillance device) any information which is disclosed in the presence of the source;
>> (b) the use of a covert human intelligence source for so obtaining or recording information; . . .

Where surveillance involves entry onto private property (or vehicles) or interference with wireless telegraphy

5.16 If surveillance involves covert entry onto private premises or interference with wireless telegraphy which must be authorised under s 5 of the 1994 Act or Part III of the 1997 Act then the activity is deemed not to amount to surveillance under Part II of RIPA, and falls instead within the authorisation regimes of the 1994 or 1997 Acts as appropriate.[14]

> 48 . . . (3) References in this Part to surveillance do not include references to- . . .
>> (c) any such entry on or interference with property or with wireless telegraphy as would be unlawful unless authorised under—
>>> (i) section 5 of the Intelligence Services Act 1994 (warrants for the intelligence services); or
>>> (ii) Part III of the Police Act 1997 (powers of the police and of customs officers).

---

partner, the court, declared an application under Arts 8 and 14 inadmissible. However considering the specific position of the UK, the Court of Appeal in the *Langley* case stated, per Lord Justice Neuberger: 'I have reached the conclusion that, in light of the margin of appreciation accorded by the ECtHR, a stable, same-sex relationship between two persons living together should, at least in most contexts, in this country in 2004, be treated as a family relationship, and therefore in principle within the ambit of Article 8'.

[13] But see *R v Hardy and Hardy* [2002] EWCA Crim 3012 (discussed in Chapter 20).
[14] This is the effect of s 48(3)(c) of RIPA.

The status of general observation and responsive surveillance

It is worth noting that the Covert Surveillance Code of Practice confirms at **5.17** para 1.3 that:

> General observation forms part of the duties of many law enforcement officers and other public authorities and is not usually regulated by the 2000 Act. . . . Such observation may involve the use of equipment to merely reinforce normal sensory perception, such as binoculars, or the use of cameras, where this does not involve systematic surveillance of an individual.

The above underlines the purpose of the regulatory scheme of Part II of RIPA to **5.18** ensure that Convention rights of individuals are not disproportionately interfered with. The intended subject matter of RIPA Part II is *planned* or *systematic* (or at least foreseeable) surveillance of individuals as opposed to unforeseeable surveillance which is essentially responsive such as might arise where a CCTV image of a street scene—taken via an obvious CCTV camera—leads to a spontaneous observation of a suspicious person or an incident for a short time.

Where an essentially immediate response to circumstances develops into a more **5.19** prolonged surveillance (eg systematically tracking a person from camera to camera down a street over an extended period) a decision has to be made whether the activity has moved within the ambit of RIPA. The Code notes at para 1.4 in relation to CCTV that:

> Although the provisions of the 2000 Act or of this code of practice do not normally cover the use of overt CCTV surveillance systems, since members of the public are aware that such systems are in use, there may be occasions when public authorities use overt CCTV systems for the purposes of a specific investigation or operation. In such cases, authorisation for intrusive or directed surveillance may be necessary.

The Code emphasises at para 2.3 that authorisation is advisable in any case where **5.20** the surveillance is likely to interfere with a person's Article 8 rights by obtaining private information, whether or not that person is the subject of the investigation or operation.

The effect of proper authorisation on lawfulness

Section 27(1) provides that conduct falling within the scope of Part II (directed **5.21** surveillance, intrusive surveillance and CHIS) are lawful 'for all purposes' provided the authorisation process is followed and the activities are carried out in accordance with the authorisation. The general nature of the defence provided by s 27 is extended partially to conduct which is incidental to any authorised conduct, in that s 27(2) provides that a person may not be subject to any civil penalty for conduct incidental to that which was authorised. The scope of s 27 in the context of a defence application for disclosure was considered in *R v GS and Others*.[15] which appears in Chapter 21.

5.22 The defence to civil liability for incidental conduct does not apply if the incidental conduct in question might reasonably have been expected to be the subject of an application for a warrant or authorisation under Part III of the 1997 Act, the 1994 Act or any part of RIPA. Thus one would not expect a defence to civil liability relying on s 27(2) to be successful where the police covertly entered premises to place a recording device but omitted to obtain a warrant to do so. The entry onto the premises (a trespass) would not fairly be said to be 'incidental' to the surveillance activity even if that surveillance itself was authorised under Part II of RIPA.

5.23 The lawfulness conferred by authorisation under Part II is without territorial limit, ie if a RIPA, Part II authorisation permits surveillance overseas then at least for the purposes of domestic law the activity is lawful (it may however be unlawful in the local law of the foreign territory). See s 27(3).

Record keeping

5.24 The Code of Practice requires that a centrally retrievable—and up to date—record of all authorisations should be held by each public authority. The record should be made available to the relevant commissioner or an inspector from the Office of Surveillance Commissioners, upon request and must be kept sufficiently up to date to reflect all applications, renewals and cancellations of applications within that authority. The Code requires that the records be retained for at least three years from the ending of the authorisation.

Minimum information to be kept in centrally retrievable records by each authority

- type of authorisation;
- date the authorisation was given;
- name and rank/grade of the authorising officer;
- unique reference number (URN) of the investigation or operation;
- title of the investigation or operation, including a brief description and names of subjects, if known;
- whether the urgency provisions were used, and if so why;
- if the authorisation is renewed, when it was renewed and who authorised the renewal, including the name and rank/grade of the authorising officer;
- whether the investigation or operation is likely to result in obtaining confidential information as defined in this code of practice;
- date the authorisation was cancelled.

(See Covert Surveillance Code of Practice, para. 2.14).

---

[15] [2005] EWCA Crim 887.

Outside the records referred to above, the authority should also retain additional **5.25** information—which may be filed rather than kept in a centrally retrievable form namely:

- a copy of the application and authorisation with any supplementary documentation, and notification of the approval given by the authorising officer;
- a record of the period over which surveillance has taken place;
- a record of the frequency of reviews prescribed by the authorising officer;
- a record of the result of each review of the authorisation;
- a copy of any renewal of an authorisation, together with the supporting documentation submitted when the renewal was requested;
- the date and time when any instruction was given by the authorising officer.

Retention and destruction of the material obtained, and the Criminal Procedure and Investigations Act 1996

The Covert Surveillance Code of Practice is clear that where the so-called **5.26** 'product' of surveillance could be relevant to pending or future criminal or civil proceedings, 'it should be retained in accordance with established disclosure requirements for a suitable further period, commensurate to any subsequent review' (para 2.16).

In the context of law enforcement the Code of Practice issued under the Criminal **5.27** Procedure and Investigations Act 1996 requires that material which is obtained in the course of a criminal investigation and which may be relevant to the investigation must be recorded and retained.

C. Directed Surveillance

Forms available in Chapter 14 of this work which are relevant to directed surveillance. (Original forms are available from Home Office or its website.)

A Application for authorisation to carry out Directed Surveillance
B Review of a Directed Surveillance Authorisation
C Application for renewal of a Directed Surveillance Authorisation
D Cancellation of a Directed Surveillance Authorisation

NB the above forms are for use by public authorities listed in Sch 1 of RIPA in relation to Directed Surveillance but do not apply to police forces, the intelligence services, the armed forces, HM Customs and Excise and the Ministry of Defence who have separate arrangements for the grant of authorisations under Part II of RIPA.

The authorisation scheme for directed surveillance is essentially one of internal **5.28** authorisation and record keeping by the public authority carrying out the surveillance. The classes of public authorities which are entitled to the benefit of the s 27 defence in respect of *directed surveillance*—ie that surveillance by them will be lawful if authorised and done in accordance with the authorisation—are set out in Sch 1 to RIPA, which has been amended from time to time under the Secretary of State's powers.[16] The relevant authorities, taking into account amendments to Sch 1 of RIPA made by the Regulation of Investigatory Powers (Directed Surveillance and Covert Human Intelligence Sources) Order 2003 (SI 2003 No 3171), and the Regulation of Investigatory Powers (Directed Surveillance and Covert Human Intelligence Sources) (Amendment) Order 2005 (SI 2005 No 1084) appear in the copy of Sch 1 as amended,[17] set out in Chapter 10. Section 28 governs the authorisation process for directed surveillance.

Who may authorise directed surveillance (the Designated Person (DP))?

5.29 The Orders referred to above specify, for each authority, which types of officer or member of staff are those designated with power to consider and then grant (or refuse) an application within that authority for the use of directed surveillance. The Orders[18] provide for alternative officers who are empowered to grant authorisations in urgent[19] cases. Article 5 of the Regulation of Investigatory Powers (Directed Surveillance and Covert Human Intelligence Sources) Order 2003 (SI 2003 No 3171) (the 2003 Order) provides that officers *more senior* than those set out in the order as being Designated Persons are also designated.

Combined authorisations for use of directed surveillance and intrusive surveillance

5.30 By s 30(2) the Secretary of State is added to the list of persons permitted to grant authorisations for directed surveillance (or use of CHIS) where the application is combined with an application for the use of intrusive surveillance.

Confidential information: higher level of authorisation required

5.31 In cases where it is thought that confidential information is likely to be obtained, the Covert Surveillance Code of Practice, at para. 3.2, and Annex A requires

---

[16] Ie under s 30(5). By s 31 of RIPA special arrangements apply to the making of orders designating authorities and persons for the purposes of s 28 (and s 29 in relation to CHIS) in Northern Ireland. See the RIPA (Prescription of Offices, Ranks and Positions) Order (Northern Ireland) 2002 (SR 2002 No 292).

[17] The authorities in both Parts I and II of the Schedule are relevant for Directed Surveillance authorisations whereas only the authorities in Part I of the Schedule are also relevant for CHIS.

[18] See Chapters 29 and 31.

[19] Article 6 of the 2003 Order provides that the various additional persons listed in the schedule to the Order (generally being slightly more junior members of staff or officers in the various authorities) may grant authorisations '. . . where it is not reasonably practicable, having regard to the urgency of the case, for the application to be considered by' the Designated Person within that part of the public authority.

a higher level of authorisation (more senior officers within each public authority) than would normally be the case. Box 15 of the form in Part A of Chapter 14 contains a box for authorisation where confidential information is involved.

'Confidential information' includes matters subject to legal privilege, confidential personal information and confidential journalistic material. The Code indicates that extra care should be taken where surveillance may acquire knowledge of discussions between a minister of religion and a person relating to spiritual welfare, or where matters of medical or journalistic confidentiality or legal privilege may be involved.

The BBC

Section 27A was inserted by the Regulation of Investigatory Powers (British **5.32** Broadcasting Corporation) Order 2001 (SI 2001 No 1057) which provides for authorisation of television detection by licensing officers in the BBC, using externally located equipment.

The contents of an application and the requirements for granting an authorisation for directed surveillance

The applicant should complete the application form for directed surveillance (see **5.33** the form in Part A of Chapter 14),[20] and the various spaces on it for stating the key information required by the Covert Surveillance Code of Practice, para 4.16. In urgent cases there is additional information which must be stated (see para 4.17 of the Code).

The power to grant an authorisation for directed surveillance does not arise unless **5.34** the Designated Person believes that:

- the authorisation is *necessary* on one or more statutory grounds listed in s 28(3) (but by s 30(3), not all grounds need be available to all public authorities). One would expect necessity to encompass consideration of whether alternative means are available and whether the expected outcome will have a meaningful bearing on the operation. The grounds are set out later in this section. Boxes 3 and 4 of the form in Part A of Chapter 14 provide space for the applicant to state the grounds why surveillance is thought necessary.

- the surveillance is *proportionate* to what is sought to be achieved by carrying it out (s 28(2)). Considerations would include whether the extent of the proposed invasion of privacy and the proposed methods to be used are appropriate in comparison with the matter under investigation. Box 5 of the form provides

---

[20] The standard forms do not apply to police forces, intelligence services, armed forces, HM Customs and the MoD who have separate arrangements of their own.

space for the applicant to state why the specific Directed Surveillance sought is said to be proportionate to what it seeks to achieve.

The statutory grounds

5.35 The DP's decision is not a 'box ticking' exercise, in that he must record in Box 13 of the application form exactly *why* the directed surveillance which is sought by the applicant is, both necessary and proportionate, prior to signing the authorisation box (Box 14).

Section 28(3) elaborates on the necessity test by setting out a list of grounds on which the surveillance must be believed to be necessary. (Matters are not as simple as may appear because s 30(1) and (3) empowers the Secretary of State to restrict the grounds which may be relied upon by different public authorities. Hence whilst the Act lists grounds from (a)–(g), in practice most public authorities are limited by Order to making use of only one or two of the potentially available grounds.

5.36 The current Orders which define the available grounds for each public authority are the Regulation of Investigatory Powers (Directed Surveillance and Covert Human Intelligence Sources) Order 2003 (SI 2003 No 3171),[21] and the Regulation of Investigatory Powers (Directed Surveillance and Covert Human Intelligence Sources) (Amendment) Order 2005 (SI 2005 No 1084).[22]

Limitations upon the grounds available[23]

5.37 Probably the most commonly encountered limitations imposed by the above Orders are that county and district councils may only rely on ground (b) in the list above (preventing or detecting crime or of preventing disorder). Other examples include the Food Standards Agency which, as one might expect, is entitled to rely on grounds (b), (d) and (e) namely preventing or detecting crime or of preventing disorder, interests of public safety and for the purpose of protecting public health. Law enforcement and tax collecting agencies are permitted to make use of a less restricted range of grounds within the list above. Police forces may rely on grounds (a) to (e) for example. It is *essential* that in seeking an authorisation (or in granting it), the grounds must be ones which are statutorily available to the public authority in question. The full range of possible grounds is as follows: the Designated Person

---

[21] 'The 2003 Order'.
[22] The Independent Police Complaints Commission (Investigatory Powers) Order 2004 (SI 2004 No 815) prescribes other individuals in police complaints cases.
[23] It makes no difference to the available grounds if a more senior officer than strictly necessary grants the authorisation: Art 10 of the 2003 Order.

must be satisfied that the proposed surveillance is *necessary* on one or more of the grounds (s 28(3))[24]

. . . (a) in the interests of national security;
(b) for the purpose of preventing or detecting crime or of preventing disorder;
(c) in the interests of the economic well-being of the United Kingdom;
(d) in the interests of public safety;
(e) for the purpose of protecting public health;
(f) for the purpose of assessing or collecting any tax, duty, levy or other imposition, contribution or charge payable to a government department; or
(g) for any purpose (not falling within paragraphs (a) to (f)) which is specified for the purposes of this subsection by an order made by the Secretary of State.

Note that ground (b) is wider than its sister in s 5(3)(b) (in relation to interception warrants) in that it includes a reference to 'preventing disorder' and omits reference to 'serious' crime, and ground (c) refers to the 'interests of the economic well-being of the United Kingdom' as opposed to the test which appears in s 5(3)(c) for interception warrants, namely 'safeguarding' the economic well-being of the UK.   **5.38**

What if the information could reasonably be obtained by other means?

In the context of interception of communications there was an additional require-   **5.39**
ment under s 5(4) for the Secretary of State to consider whether the information could reasonably be obtained by other means. It is notable that *no* such express requirement is imposed in the context of directed surveillance. One would expect that issues of proportionality and necessity would still arise if in fact the information could reasonably have been obtained by other means irrespective of the absence of an express reference in s 28.

The Surveillance Code, para 2.5 states when discussing proportionality: **5.40**

. . . This involves balancing the intrusiveness of the activity on the target and others who might be affected by it against the need for the activity in operational terms. . . . All such activity should be carefully managed to meet the objective in question and must not be arbitrary or unfair . . .

Collateral intrusion as a factor when considering proportionality

The person responsible for authorising surveillance must take into account the   **5.41**
risk of intrusion into the privacy of people who are not the subjects of the investigation or operation. That incidental invasion of privacy is referred to in the Surveillance Code as collateral intrusion. Although the Act itself does not refer to collateral intrusion, the Surveillance Code imposes several specific requirements.

---

[24] The same list appears in s 29(3) in relation to authorisation for the conduct or use of covert human intelligence sources.

Collateral intrusion: key duties under the Covert Surveillance Code

- By para 2.7, the application itself should include an assessment of the risk of any collateral intrusion.[25] The authorising officer should take this into account, when considering the proportionality of the surveillance.[26]
- By para 2.8, 'those carrying out the surveillance should inform the authorising officer if the investigation or operation unexpectedly interferes with the privacy of individuals who are not covered by the authorisation. . . . consideration should be given to whether the authorisation needs to be amended and reauthorised or a new authorisation is required.'
- By para 2.9, any person granting or applying for an authorisation is required to be aware of 'particular sensitivities in the local community where the surveillance is taking place and of similar activities being undertaken by other public authorities which could impact on the deployment of surveillance.'
- The above also applies to applications for warrants for entry on or interference with property or with wireless telegraphy (see Part I of this work).

Written v oral authorisations

5.42 The usual rule, under s 43(1)(b) is that authorisations for any Part II activity should be in writing, and may include authorisations for more than one activity provided that the criteria for authorisation are met for each activity being autho-rised (s 43(2)). Oral authorisations may be granted in urgent cases unless the authority of the person granting the authorisation is confined only to urgent cases. (Sch 1, Col 3 to the 2003 Order lists officers who may authorise only in urgent cases.) The Code para. 4.13, defines an urgent case as being one where 'the time that would elapse before the authorising officer was available . . . would, in the judgment of the person giving the authorisation, be likely to endanger life or jeopardise the investigation or operation . . .'

If oral authorisation is given, the details listed at paras 4.16 and 4.17 of the Code must be recorded in writing by the applicant as soon as practicable (para 4.18).

The duration, review, renewal and cancellation of authorisations for directed surveillance

5.43 Part II authorisations once granted, unless cancelled or renewed for a further period, cease to have effect after a time which is set out below.

---

[25] For directed surveillance by bodies other than the police, etc Box 9 of the standard authorisation form (Part A of Chapter 14) provides space for the applicant to state the extent of potential collateral intrusion, why it is unavoidable, and to give a written plan for minimisation.

[26] The Code stresses that 'Measures should be taken, wherever practicable, to avoid or minimise unnecessary intrusion into the lives of those not directly connected with the investigation or operation.'

Duration of authorisation for Directed Surveillance

Type of authorisation	Ceases to have effect after:
(A) Oral & urgent cases	
Oral authorisations & oral renewals	**72 hours** from grant or renewal (s 43(3)(a)(i))
Authorisations & renewals by a person who is only empowered to authorise/renew in urgent cases	**72 hours** from grant (s 43(3)(a)(i))
(B) Other cases (not falling within (A) above) (s. 43(3)(c))	**3 months** from grant or latest renewal

Review and renewal

Renewal of an authorisation for directed surveillance may only be granted by a **5.44** person who could have granted the authorisation, but there is no requirement for the renewing officer to be the same individual as the original authorising officer (s 43(4)). The application form[27] for applying to renew an existing authorisation for directed surveillance appears in Part C of Chapter 14. It embodies the information which is required by the Code. The requirements for renewal of an authorisation are the same as those for the original grant of the authorisation. Paragraphs 4.21–4.22 of the Code require that there must be a regular review carried out as often as the authorising officer decides is necessary and practicable. The Code stresses the need for especially frequent reviews where the activity accesses confidential information or causes collateral intrusion (para 4.21). The results of reviews must also be recorded on the central record of surveillance authorisations held by the authority.

The form in Part B of Chapter 14 is a review form which provides space for the **5.45** applicant to record the current state of the activity, including changes in material matters, reasons why the operation remains necessary and proportionate, and details of collateral intrusion. The authorisation form in Part A of Chapter 14 also provides space for recording dates of reviews.

How long may an authorisation for directed surveillance be renewed for?

The duration of any renewal follows the same rules as were set out above in respect **5.46** of the duration of the original authorisation, and the renewed period runs from the date when the authorisation would expire. This is subject to the exception in

---

[27] Used by bodies other than police forces, the intelligence services, the armed forces, HM Customs and Excise and the Ministry of Defence.

s 44(5) that in the case of an authorisation for directed surveillance granted by a member of the Intelligence Services on grounds of interests of national security or economic welfare of UK, the renewed period may be six months. See the Code at paras 4.23–4.26.

Cancellation if grounds cease to exist

5.47 The officer who granted the most recent renewal or the original grant of the authorisation is obliged to cancel the authorisation if at any stage he is satisfied that the grounds of necessity and proportionality no longer apply—see s 45(1)(a) and para 4.28 of the Code. As soon as the decision is taken to cease the surveillance, instructions must be given to those involved to stop, and the time and date of instruction must be recorded in the central record held by the public authority. (Code, para 4.29). If the outcome of a review is that grounds no longer exist then cancellation would follow at that stage rather than being delayed until an application for renewal. The form in Part D of Chapter 14 is a cancellation form.

D. Intrusive Surveillance

Who may authorise intrusive surveillance?

5.48 Section 31(1) provides that the Secretary of State[28] and the 'Senior Authorising Officers' have the power to grant authorisation for intrusive surveillance. The Secretary of State's role is discussed later (see para **5.62** below) but note that applications for the use of intrusive surveillance by the Intelligence Services (ie Security Service, SIS and GCHQ) are granted by means of the Secretary of State's warrant.

5.49 The identities of the senior authorising officers—ie for authorisation in the case of non-Intelligence Services and non-Military Intrusive Surveillance work—appear in s 32(6), and they may only grant authorisations made from within their own force. Where the authorising officer is a member of a police force, NCIS, or NCS, then authorisations for intrusive surveillance in relation to residential premises may only relate to premises within that force's area. See s 33(1)–(4). Subsection (6) defines the areas of operation of the various types of forces involved.

Identifying the Senior Authorising Officers (police and Customs)

5.50 The list below indicates the Senior Authorising Officers from s 31(1)(6) as amended. Note the absence of the Intelligence Services, whose applications

---

[28] The Code, para 5.25 notes that this may mean any Secretary of State, though it also states that the Secretary of State should be the one for the relevant Department of State in question.

for intrusive surveillance are subject to authorisation by Secretary of State's warrant—see later).

Senior Authorising Officers for intrusive surveillance

   (a)   the chief constable of every police force maintained under s 2 of the Police Act 1996 (police forces in England and Wales outside London);
   (b)   the Commissioner of Police of the Metropolis and every Assistant Commissioner of Police of the Metropolis;
   (c)   the Commissioner of Police for the City of London;
   (d)   the chief constable of every police force maintained under or by virtue of s 1 of the Police (Scotland) Act 1967 (police forces for areas in Scotland);
   (e)   the Chief Constable of the Royal Ulster Constabulary and the Deputy Chief Constable of the Royal Ulster Constabulary;
   (f)   the Chief Constable of the Ministry of Defence Police;
   (g)   the Provost Marshal of the Royal Navy Regulating Branch;
   (h)   the Provost Marshal of the Royal Military Police;
   (i)   the Provost Marshal of the Royal Air Force Police;
   (j)   the Chief Constable of the British Transport Police;
   (ja)[29] the Chairman of the Independent Police Complaints Commission;
   [(k)   the Director General of the National Criminal Intelligence Service;
   (l)[30] the Director General of the National Crime Squad and any person holding the rank of assistant chief constable in that Squad who is designated for the purposes of this paragraph by that Director General;]
   (k)   the Director General of the Serious Organised Crime Agency and any member of the staff of that Agency who is designated for the purposes of this paragraph by that Director General;[31]
   (m)   any customs officer designated for the purposes of this paragraph by the Commissioners of Customs and Excise.
   (n)[32] the Chairman of the OFT.[33]

Confidential Information
In cases where it is thought that confidential information is likely to be obtained the Covert Surveillance Code of Practice at para. 3.2 and Annex A requires a higher level of authorisation.

Additional requirement for approval by a Surveillance Commissioner in Police/Customs cases

5.51   For Police, NCIS, NCS, SOCA, OFT, Customs and IPCC authorisations (hereafter 'Police and Customs Authorisations'), there is an additional requirement for the approval of a Surveillance Commissioner before the authorisation can take effect. Therefore, the requirement involves authorisation by the Senior

---

[29] Inserted by the Independent Police Complaints Commission (Investigatory Powers) Order 2004 (SI 2004 No 815), Art 3(2).
[30] Amended by the Enterprise Act 2002, Sch 26.
[31] Words in italics at (k) will be added (replacing the words in square brackets at (k) and (l)) when Sch 4, para 136 of the SOCAP Act 2005 is in force.
[32] Inserted by the Enterprise Act 2002, s 199(2)(b).
[33] In the case of an authorisation granted by the Chairman of the OFT, the only ground permitted is that the Intrusive Surveillance is necessary for the purpose of preventing or detecting an offence under s 188 of the Enterprise Act 2002 (cartel offences). See s 32(3A).

Authorising Officer *as well as* subsequent approval by a Surveillance Commissioner in such cases[34] before the authorisation takes effect. See s 36(2) and the Notice requirements discussed later.

5.52 If the application is refused, the commissioner must report his findings to the 'most relevant senior person' in the authority which made the application (a list appears in s 35(6)). His decision must also be reported in writing to the person who gave the authorisation, as soon as reasonably practicable (s 35(4)(b)).

The form of an application for intrusive surveillance

5.53 The Covert Surveillance Code, para 5.16 sets out the requirements for the content of an application for authorisation of intrusive surveillance. Applications should normally be in writing and describe:

- the conduct to be authorised and the purpose of the investigation or operation;
- the reasons why the authorisation is necessary in the particular case and on the grounds listed in s 32(3) of the 2000 Act;
- the reasons why the surveillance is considered proportionate to what it seeks to achieve;
- the nature of the surveillance;
- the residential premises or private vehicle in relation to which the surveillance will take place;
- the identities, where known, of those to be the subject of the surveillance;
- an explanation of the information which it is desired to obtain as a result of the surveillance;
- details of any potential collateral intrusion and why the intrusion is justified;
- details of any confidential information that is likely to be obtained as a consequence of the surveillance.

A subsequent record should be made of whether authority was given or refused, by whom and the time and date.

Where the application is oral, the detail above is required to be recorded in writing as soon as reasonably practicable (Code, para 5.18).

The requirements for granting an authorisation for intrusive surveillance

5.54 The power to grant an authorisation for intrusive surveillance does not arise unless the person authorising it believes that:

- the authorisation is *necessary* on one or more statutory grounds listed in s.32(2)(a), s 32(3); and

---

[34] Different arrangements apply in urgent cases, see s 36(3).

- the surveillance is proportionate to what is sought to be achieved by carrying it out (s 32(2)(b)).

It will be apparent from the above that the twin tests of necessity and proportionality are applied to Intrusive Surveillance as they were to Directed Surveillance.

The statutory grounds

Section 32(3) elaborates on the necessity test by setting out a list of grounds on **5.55** which the surveillance must be believed to be necessary. The list is far narrower than the equivalent one in s 28(3) in relation to grounds for authorising Directed Surveillance:

(a) in the interests of national security;
(b) for the purpose of preventing or detecting serious crime;
(c) in the interests of the economic well-being of the United Kingdom

Note that the above list is not identical to grounds (a) to (c) under s 28(3) in that ground (b) omits reference to preventing disorder, and imposes the higher criterion of 'serious' in relation to crime.

The grounds are similar to those for the grant of interception warrants under s 5(3), for which see Chapter 3, but first the scope of 'detecting serious crime' in s 32(3)(b) includes gathering evidence for use in legal proceedings (see s 81(5)) whereas such use is expressly outside the scope of s 5(3)(b) of the Act. Secondly the test in s 5(c) for granting an interception warrant ('safeguarding' the economic well-being of the UK) is higher than the test appearing in s 32(3)(c) which merely states 'in the interests of the economic well-being' of the UK.

Requirement for notification to a Surveillance Commissioner in respect of a police or Customs application grant or cancellation

By s 35 all grants and cancellations of police and Customs authorisations must be **5.56** notified to an ordinary Surveillance Commissioner in writing as soon as reasonably practicable after the grant or cancellation. The notification must state either that the approval of a Surveillance Commissioner is required, or that the case is urgent and the reasons why. A Surveillance Commissioner will scrutinise the authorisation as soon as practicable (and in non-urgent cases either grant or refuse approval).

The Secretary of State is empowered by s 35(2)(c) to prescribe the contents of **5.57** such Notification and the current Order of relevance is SI 2000 No 2563 (the Regulation of Investigatory Powers (Notification of Authorisations etc.)

Order 2000) requiring the following to be stated in the notification to the Commissioner in the case of a grant[35] of an application:

(a) grounds on which the person granting the application believes the matters specified in s 32(2)(a) and (b)[36] of the 2000 Act;
(b) nature of the authorised conduct including the residential premises or private vehicle in relation to which the conduct is authorised and the identity, where known, of persons to be the subject of the authorised conduct; and
(c) whether the conduct to be authorised is likely to lead to intrusion on the privacy of persons other than any person who is to be the subject of that conduct.

5.58 Where a person cancels an authorisation, the Order requires the notice to a commissioner to state:

(a) the date and time when he gave the instructions to cease the conduct authorised;
(b) reasons for cancelling the authorisation;
(c) outcome of the investigation to which the authorisation related, and details of any criminal proceedings instituted or intended to be instituted; and
(d) what arrangements have been made for the storage of material obtained as a result of the conduct authorised, for its review and its destruction when its retention is no longer required, and for the immediate destruction of any material unrelated to the purposes for which the conduct was authorised.

5.59 By s 40, certain people[37] are under a duty to comply with any request of a Surveillance Commissioner for documents or information required for the purpose of his functions.

Oral authorisations in urgent cases, and cases where the Senior Authorising Officer is unavailable

5.60 The usual rule, under s 43(1)(b) is that authorisations should be in writing, and may include authorisations for more than one activity if the criteria for authorisation are met for each activity (s 43(2)). Again, oral authorisations may be granted in urgent cases, unless the authority of the person granting the authorisation is confined to urgent cases.

---

[35] The Order also imposes requirements in the case of a renewal of an authorisation.
[36] Necessity and proportionality.
[37] For example, every member of a police force, IPCC, NICS, NCS, or SOCA, every Customs and OFT officer. See s 40.

If an oral authorisation is given, the details at para 5.16 of the Code should be **5.61** recorded in writing as soon as practicable but in addition, the authorisation should record reasons why:

- the authorising officer or designated deputy considered the case so urgent that an oral instead of a written authorisation was given; and/or
- it was not reasonably practicable for the application to be considered by the senior authorising officer or the designated deputy.

Section 34 puts in place rules for who may authorise an intrusive surveillance **5.62** application made by the police, NCIS, NCS, SOCA, Customs or the IPCC, if the senior authorising officer or deputy is unavailable *and* the case is urgent.[38] See s 34(4) for the list of authorised alternatives—for example, a person is entitled to act for the chief constable of a police force if he holds the rank of assistant chief constable in that force.

Secretary of State authorisations: limited in terms of applicant and available grounds (Intelligence Services and military)

The Secretary of State is limited in terms of both the grounds upon which he may **5.63** grant an authorisation and to whom. Section 41(1) provides that the Secretary of State may grant authorisations only upon application by:

(a) a member of any of the intelligence services;
(b) an official of the Ministry of Defence;
(c) a member of Her Majesty's forces;[39]
(d) an individual holding an office, rank or position with any such public authority as may be designated for the purposes of this section as an authority whose activities may require the carrying out of intrusive surveillance.[40]

Furthermore when the Secretary of State considers an application from the MoD or HM Forces,[41] the grounds available are restricted solely to:

- the interests of national security;
- the purpose of preventing or detecting serious crime (s 41(2)).

In the case of applications for intrusive surveillance made by the Intelligence **5.64** Services, the form of the authorisation must be that of a warrant (which may be

---

[38] 'Urgent' is not defined but the Code, para. 5.13 defines an urgent case in the context of Intrusive Surveillance as being one where '. . . the time that would elapse before the authorising officer was available . . . would, in the judgment of the person giving the authorisation, be likely to endanger life or jeopardise the investigation or operation . . .'.

[39] By s 81(1) the military police forces are treated as being police forces, which implies that the procedures of ss 33–40 are appropriate for them.

[40] At the time of writing no orders had been made.

[41] Not including members of the military police forces: s 41(7).

combined a warrant under the Intelligence Services Act 1994 if the appropriate grounds apply). Authorisation is available to the SIS and GCHQ only on grounds of interests of national security and interests of the economic well-being of the UK, s 32(3)(a) and (c): see s 42(3)–(5). By s 44(1) and (2) the warrant must be issued under the hand of the Secretary of State but in an urgent case, if the Secretary of State has expressly authorised, a senior official may sign the warrant (which will then expire after the second working day).

What if the information could reasonably be obtained by other means?

5.65 Section 32(4) imposes a requirement upon Senior Authorising Officers and the Secretary of State, in relation to intrusive surveillance, similar to that which was imposed on the Secretary of State by s 5(4) for interception of communications, namely to consider whether the information could reasonably be obtained by other means. See also para 2.5 of the Code.

Collateral intrusion

5.66 The Surveillance Code imposes requirements to limit the extent of collateral intrusion. See para **5.40** above.

The duration, review, renewal and cancellation of authorisations for intrusive surveillance (including Secretary of State Authorisations for bodies *other than* the Intelligence Services)

5.67 Part II authorisations, unless cancelled or renewed for a further period, cease to have effect after a time which is set out in the table below. (NB in relation to the BBC see footnotes to s 43.)

Duration

(A) **Oral & urgent cases**

Oral authorizations & oral renewals	**72 hours** from grant or renewal (s 43(3)(a)(i))
Authorisations & renewals by a person who is only empowered to authorise/renew in urgent cases	**72 hours** from grant (s 43(3)(a)(i))

(B) **Other cases** (not falling within (A) above) (s 43(3)(c)) — **3 months** from grant or latest renewal

5.68 If at any time before an authorisation expires the senior authorising officer or, in his absence, the designated deputy considers the authorisation should continue to have effect, he may renew it in writing for a further period of three months. See s 43(4) and the Code at para 5.33. The same requirements for approval by a Surveillance Commissioner apply to a renewal as applied to the initial grant.

In the case of Secretary of State authorisations other than Intelligence Services authorisations, if the Secretary of State considers it necessary for the warrant to be renewed for the purpose for which it was issued, he may renew for a further period of three months (s 43(4) and the Code, para 5.35).

Renewal of an authorisation for intrusive surveillance may only be granted by a person who could have granted the authorisation in the first place, but there is no requirement for the renewing officer to be the same individual as the original authorising officer (s 43(4)).

The duration, review, renewal and cancellation of Secretary of State Intelligence Services authorisations

5.69

(A) **Warrants issued by a Secretary of State**
A warrant issued by the Secretary of State ceases to have effect six months beginning with the day of issue. See s 44(4).

(B) **Warrants expressly authorised by a Secretary of State, and signed on his behalf by a senior civil servant**
These cease to have effect at the end of the second working day following the day of issue unless renewed by the Secretary of State. See s 44(3).

The Code, at para 5.36 provides that if at any time before an Intelligence Service **5.70** warrant expires, the Secretary of State considers it necessary for the warrant to be renewed for the purpose for which it was issued, he may renew it in writing for a further period of six months. All applications for a renewal of an Intelligence Services warrant should record whether this is the first renewal, and every occasion on which it has been renewed previously, any significant changes to the information, the reasons why it is necessary to continue, the content and value to the investigation or operation of the product so far obtained, and the results of regular reviews. (See the Code at para 5.37).

The requirement for regular review of intrusive surveillance authorisations

Paragraphs 5.39–5.40 of the Code require that the senior authorising officer or, **5.71** for those subject to Secretary of State authorisation, the person who made the application should determine how often a review should take place. The Code states that this should be as frequently as is considered necessary and practicable. As with directed surveillance, the Code stresses the need for frequent reviews where the activity accesses confidential information or causes collateral intrusion (para 5.39) and the results of reviews must also be recorded on the central record (see Code, paras 2.14–2.15 and 5.39).

Cancellation if grounds cease to exist

5.72 The Senior Authorising Officer[42] who granted the most recent renewal or the grant of the authorisation, or the person who made the application to the Secretary of State must apply for its cancellation, if he is satisfied that the surveillance no longer meets the criteria on which it was authorised. (A Surveillance Commissioner must be also notified where police, NCIS, NCS, SOCA, OFT, Customs or IPCC authorisations are cancelled (the Regulation of Investigatory Powers (Notification of Authorisations etc.) Order 2000 (SI No 2563)), see para 5.51 above. As soon as the decision is taken that the Intrusive Surveillance should be discontinued, instructions must be given to those involved to stop all surveillance and the date and time of the instruction should be recorded in the central record (see Code, paras 2.14–2.15).

The quashing and cancellation of Police and Customs authorisations and the appeal process

Quashing and cancellation by a Surveillance Commissioner

5.73 In the case of applications made and granted by the Police, NCIS, NCS, SOCA, OFT, Customs and IPCC, s 37 provides that:

- if an ordinary Surveillance Commissioner is (at any time) satisfied that at the time when an authorisation was granted or at the time of any renewal there were no reasonable grounds for believing that the requirements of s 32(2)(a) and (b) were satisfied (ie the requirements of necessity on the stautory grounds, and proportionality) (s 37(2)); or

- in the case of an authorisation granted without approval of a Surveillance Commissioner in urgent cases, if an ordinary Surveillance Commissioner is satisfied that at the date of the authorisation there were no reasonable grounds for believing that the case was one of urgency (s 37(4))

then he may *quash* the authorisation with effect from the date of grant or renewal.[43]

5.74 If the authorisation in force and a Surveillance Commissioner forms the view that there are no longer any reasonable grounds for believing that the statutory requirements of necessity and proportionality are met, then he may *cancel* (as opposed to quash) the authorisation with effect from the time when it appears to him that the requirements ceased to be met (s 37(2)).

---

[42] Or whoever has taken his place if he is unavailable—Code, para 5.41.
[43] Including retrospectively with effect from the date of the original grant or renewal: s 37(2).

It will be recalled that for all Police and Customs authorisations (an umbrella term **5.75** including Police, NCIS, NCS, SOCA, OFT, Customs and IPCC), any authorisation must be notified to a Surveillance Commissioner and that, save in urgent cases, his approval is required before the authorisation takes effect. Those requirements mean that all Police and Customs authorisations come to the attention of a Surveillance Commissioner. The power to quash illegitimate authorisations accordingly meshes with the notice requirements.

Consequential orders for destruction of records

The ordinary Surveillance Commissioners are given the power (s 37(5)) to order **5.76** destruction of records relating to information obtained after the date when a quashing or cancellation decision took effect. If the authorisation has already ceased to have effect then the order may require destruction of records of information obtained once reasonable grounds for the authorisation had ceased to exist (s 37(6)). Any destruction order does not take effect until either the time limit for appealing has expired (see below) or any appeal has been dismissed (s 37(9)). But no such order may be made when the records relate to pending civil or criminal proceedings (s 37(7)).

If a quashing or record destruction order is made then the commissioner making **5.77** it is obliged to make a report to the Chief Surveillance Commissioner as well as to the most senior person in the applicant authority (a list is set out in s 36(6)).

The right of appeal and grounds

The quashing of an authorisation, possibly coupled with an order for destruction **5.78** of records, has possibly irreversible consequences. Even a refusal to approve authorisation could have serious consequences for an investigation. Section 38 provides for a right of appeal by the senior authorising officer against a decision of an Ordinary Surveillance Commissioner, to the Chief Surveillance Commissioner where the decision in question was one of the following:

(a) refusal to approve a police or customs authorisation;
(b) any decision to quash or cancel an authorisation;
(c) any decision to order the destruction of records under s 37.

By s 38 the appeal must be brought within seven days from the day when the deci- **5.79** sion in question was reported by the commissioner to the appellant. The appeal must be granted by the Chief Surveillance Commissioner if he is satisfied that (contrary to the decision of the ordinary commissioner):

(a) there *were* reasonable grounds for believing that the requirements of necessity and proportionality under s 32(2)(a) and (b) were met in relation to the authorisation at the time in question; and

(b) the Chief Surveillance Commissioner is not satisfied that the authorisation is one in respect a notice of urgency was given in the absence of reasonable grounds for believing that the case was one of urgency. (s 38(4)).

5.80 The Chief Surveillance Commissioner has a power under s 38(5) to *vary* the date from which a quashing or cancellation takes effect, if he is satisfied that a quashing order or cancellation was appropriate but that the order should have taken effect from a different date.

5.81 If the appeal succeeds, and the result is the setting aside of a quashing or cancellation decision then the Chief Surveillance Commissioner is obliged by s 38(6) also to set aside any order which was made for the destruction of records.

Notice of appeal decision

5.82 The outcome of an appeal to the Chief Surveillance Commissioner is required to be notified to both the appellant and to the ordinary Surveillance Commissioner whose decision was appealed. If the decision was to dismiss the appeal a report of the Chief Surveillance Commissioner's findings is sent to the appellant, the ordinary Surveillance Commissioner whose decision was upheld *and* to the Prime Minister (s 39(1)–(2)). Other than where such a report is made the Chief Surveillance Commissioner *must not* give reasons for his appeal decision (s 38(4)).

E. Covert Human Intelligence Sources

(It is suggested that it would assist the reader to have read Part B of this Chapter before consulting this part of this work).

Forms available in Chapter 14 which are relevant to the use of Covert Human Intelligence Sources. (Original forms are available from Home Office or its website.)

E   Application for Authorisation of the use or conduct of a Covert Human Intelligence Source
F   Review of an Authorisation for the use or conduct of a Covert Human Intelligence Source
G   Application for renewal of an Authorisation for the use or conduct of a Covert Human Intelligence Source
H   Cancellation of an Authorisation for the use or conduct of a Covert Human Intelligence Source

NB the above forms are for use by all public authorities listed in Sch 1, Part I of RIPA in relation to the use of Covert Human Intelligence Source under s 29. The forms do not apply to police forces, the Intelligence Services, the armed forces, HM Customs and Excise and the Ministry of Defence who have separate arrangements for the grant of authorisations under Part II of RIPA.

Introduction

5.83 Before turning to the Act's definition of what comprises the use of a Covert Human Intelligence Source, or CHIS, it is as well to note that the CHIS Code of

Practice 2002, para 1.3 makes it clear what *does not* fall within the scope of CHIS under Part II of RIPA, as follows:

> The provisions of the 2000 Act are not intended to apply in circumstances where members of the public volunteer information to the police or other authorities, as part of their normal civic duties, or to contact numbers set up to receive information (such as Crimestoppers, Customs Confidential, the Anti Terrorist Hotline, or the Security Service Public Telephone Number). Members of the public acting in this way would not generally be regarded as sources.

Covert Human Intelligence Sources (s 26(8))

Section 26(8) defines 'Covert Human Intelligence Source' thus: **5.84**

> . . . a person is a Covert Human Intelligence Source if-
> (a) he establishes or maintains a personal or other relationship with a person for the covert purpose of facilitating the doing of anything falling within paragraph (b) or (c);
> (b) he covertly uses such a relationship to obtain information or to provide access to any information to another person; or
> (c) he covertly discloses information obtained by the use of such a relationship, or as a consequence of the existence of such a relationship.

The key feature of the expression 'covert' in the context of human intelligence   **5.85**
sources, under s 26(9)(a) and (b), is that the relationship is conducted in a manner calculated to keep one party to the relationship unaware of the purpose for which it is being maintained, or unaware of the disclosure or use of information obtained.

As with the other Part II activities RIPA does not impose a *requirement* on public   **5.86**
authorities obtain an authorisation for CHIS but where there is an interference by a public authority with the Article 8 rights of the subject, and there is no authorisation and no other lawful justification then the exclusionary rules of evidence (at least in criminal cases) could lead to material obtained being excluded. The Intelligence Services Commissioner oversees the authorisation arrangements for the use of CHIS by the Intelligence Services, and the Surveillance Commissioners oversee the use of CHIS by other bodies. See Chapter 7 which sets out the roles of the various commissioners in detail.

Codes of Practice

The relevant Code of Practice in relation to CHIS for most purposes is the CHIS   **5.87**
Code of Practice (see Chapter 16) but note that the OFT has published a version of the Code in relation to its own investigations into 'cartel offences'. (The text of the OFT Code (dated August 2004) is heavily based on the text of the CHIS Code, and the OFT version may be found via the OFT website.)

The use of a person carrying a surveillance device: is this covert surveillance or the use of CHIS?

5.88 By s 48(3)(a) and (b), conduct which involves the use of a CHIS to carry a surveillance device or to record information while physically present, is treated as use of the CHIS rather than as surveillance. See Part B of this Chapter and the CHIS Code of Practice at paras 4.39–4.42 which among other things reminds the reader at paras 4.41–4.42 that:

> . . . if a surveillance device is to be used, other than in the presence of the source, an intrusive surveillance authorisation and if applicable an authorisation for interference with property should be obtained.

Telephone calls involving CHIS sources

5.89 In relation to recording of telephone conversations where the CHIS is a party to the call and consents to it being recorded, unless there is already an interception warrant in place under RIPA, Part I, the activity will amount to directed surveillance (ie under Part II) and not to interception of communications under Part I. See s 48(4) of RIPA.

What about surveillance before recruitment of a source?

5.90 The use of CHIS requires the pre-selection of a suitable source. It may well be necessary to carry out surveillance in respect of a potential source prior to approaching that individual with a view to seeking to involve him as a CHIS. The CHIS Code at para 2.12 indicates that:

> . . . an authorisation authorising an officer to establish a covert relationship with a potential source could be combined with a directed surveillance authorisation so that both the officer and potential source could be followed.

Lawfulness of authorised use of CHIS

5.91 Section 27(1) provides that conduct falling within the scope of Part II (including CHIS) is lawful 'for all purposes' provided the authorisation process is followed and provided the activities carried out are in accordance with the authorisation obtained. The reader is referred to the discussion at para **5.19** above where this subject is dealt with in relation to all three types of Part II conduct.

Which public authorities, and who may authorise the use of CHIS?

5.92 As with directed surveillance, the use of CHIS falls within a self-authorisation regime whereby a Designated Person (under s 29) within a part of an authority is entitled to apply the RIPA criteria for the use of CHIS and effectively certify that the use is legitimate (the authority authorising itself). The arrangements for CHIS and for Directed Surveillance are very similar and much reference is made in this part of this work to the earlier discussion of directed surveillance. It is arguable that since in some circumstances the use of CHIS can be extremely intrusive that the voluntary and effectively internal self-authorisation of CHIS may be an inadequate protection in human rights terms and that similar strictures to those imposed for intrusive surveillance might have offered better protection.

The classes of authorities to which the CHIS authorisation process is available are **5.93** set out in Part I of Sch 1 to RIPA. The relevant authorities, taking into account amendments to Sch 1 of RIPA made by the Regulation of Investigatory Powers (Directed Surveillance and Covert Human Intelligence Sources) Order 2003 (SI 2003 No 3171) and the Regulation of Investigatory Powers (Directed Surveillance and Covert Human Intelligence Sources) (Amendment) Order 2005 (SI 2005 No 1084) appear in the copy of Sch 1 (as amended).[44]

The Orders specify the types of officer or employee who may act as Designated **5.94** Persons considering applications within that authority, and they also provide alternative persons who are empowered to grant authorisations in urgent cases.[45] Article 5 of the Regulation of Investigatory Powers (Directed Surveillance and Covert Human Intelligence Sources) Order 2003 (SI 2003 No 3171) ('The 2003 Order') provides that officers *more senior* than those set out in the order as being Designated Persons are also designated.

Combined authorisations for use of CHIS and intrusive surveillance

By s 30(2) the Secretary of State is added to the list of persons permitted to grant **5.95** authorisations for CHIS (or for directed surveillance) in cases where the application is combined with an application for the use of intrusive surveillance.

Use of material in evidence

The CHIS Code confirms that as for material gathered via the other Part II **5.96** activities, material obtained may be used as evidence in criminal proceedings (subject to s 78 of PACE 1984 and the Human Rights Act 1998). Information obtained by use of CHIS is subject to the rules for retention and disclosure of material under the Criminal Procedure and Investigations Act 1996, where those rules apply to the law enforcement body in question. There is nothing in

---

[44] Only the authorities in Part I of the Schedule are relevant for CHIS.

[45] Article 6 of the 2003 Order provides that the various additional persons listed in the Schedule (generally being more junior members of staff in the various authorities) may grant authorisations 'where it is not reasonably practicable, having regard to the urgency of the case, for the application to be considered by' the Designated Person.

RIPA which prevents material obtained from use of a source being used in other investigations if the information is properly handled (eg as to data protection considerations).

The contents of an application and the three requirements for granting an authorisation for the use of CHIS

5.97 The power to grant an authorisation does not arise unless the Designated Person considering it believes that each of the following *three* matters are true (note that (c) is an additional set of requirements included for CHIS).

(a) The authorisation is *necessary* on one or more grounds listed in s 29(3) and discussed below (but by s 30(3), not all grounds may be available to all public authorities).
    Boxes 2 and 3 of the standard application form in Part E of Chapter 15 provide space for the applicant to state the grounds why surveillance is thought necessary.

(b) The conduct or use of the source is *proportionate* to what is sought to be achieved through use of that source (s 29(2)(b)). Box 4 of the standard application form provides space for the applicant to state why the specific directed surveillance sought is said to be proportionate to what it seeks to achieve.

(c) Arrangements exist for the source's case that satisfy the requirements below (set out in s 29(5)) and such other requirements as may be imposed by order made by the Secretary of State:
    (a) that there will at all times be a person holding an office, rank or position with the relevant investigating authority who will have day-to-day responsibility for dealing with the source on behalf of that authority, and for the source's security and welfare;
    (b) that there will at all times be another person holding an office, rank or position with the relevant investigating authority who will have general oversight of the use made of the source;
    (c) that there will at all times be a person holding an office, rank or position with the relevant investigating authority who will have responsibility for maintaining a record of the use made of the source;
    (d) that the records relating to the source that are maintained by the relevant investigating authority will always contain particulars of all such matters (if any) as may be specified for the purposes of this paragraph in regulations made by the Secretary of State; and
    (e) that records maintained by the relevant investigating authority that disclose the identity of the source will not be available to persons except to the extent that there is a need for access to them to be made available to those persons.

In urgent cases there is certain additional information which must be stated (see para 4.17 of the Code of Practice).

The statutory grounds

Section 29(3) elaborates on the necessity test by setting out a list of grounds on **5.98** which the use of a CHIS must be believed to be necessary. (But s 30(1) and (3) empower the Secretary of State to restrict the grounds which may be relied upon by different public authorities.) The current Orders of relevance which define the available grounds for each public authority are the Regulation of Investigatory Powers (Directed Surveillance and Covert Human Intelligence Sources) Order 2003 (SI 2003 No 3171)[46] and the Regulation of Investigatory Powers (Directed Surveillance and Covert Human Intelligence Sources) (Amendment) Order 2005 (SI 2005 No 1084).[47]

Limitations upon the grounds available

The full range of possible grounds appear in s 29(3), subject to the reality that **5.99** most public authorities are limited by the 2003 Order to using only a small subset of the grounds listed in the Act.[48] The grounds available for Directed Surveillance and CHIS are identical (s 29(3) for CHIS, s 28(3) for Directed Surveillance) and the reader should see para **5.36** above for a list.

Collateral intrusion as a factor when considering proportionality in relation to the use of CHIS

The reader is referred to the discussion of collateral intrusion at para **5.40** above. **5.100** The CHIS Code at paras 2.7–2.9 stresses that an application for an authorisation should include an assessment of the risk of any collateral intrusion and that the authorising officer should take this into account, when considering the proportionality of the use and conduct of a source. Those tasking a source should inform the authorising officer if the investigation or operation unexpectedly interferes with the privacy of individuals who are not covered by the authorisation.

Risk assessment before authorisation

The officer who authorises use of CHIS must first ensure that a risk assessment is **5.101** carried out (generally by the applicant) in terms of the risk to the source, and the consequences if the role of the source were to become known. The ongoing security and welfare of the Source after cancellation of the authorisation must also be

---

[46] 'The 2003 Order'.
[47] The Independent Police Complaints Commission (Investigatory Powers) Order 2004 (SI 2004 No 815) also prescribes certain other individuals in Arts 4 and 5 in police complaints cases.
[48] It makes no difference to the available grounds if a more senior officer than strictly necessary grants the authorisation: Art 10 of the 2003 Order.

considered: see the CHIS Code at para 4.36 and note that there is space in Box 8 of the form in Part E of Chapter 15 for the risk assessment. (Box 7 should set out the proposed details of the tasking for that source).[49]

Confidential information obtained by use of CHIS

5.102   As with other Part II activities, the CHIS Code stresses that care should be taken when confidential information might be obtained via the use of a CHIS (see para **5.30**) above. The Code requires a higher degree of seniority of authorising officer in cases where through the use or conduct of a source it is likely that knowledge of confidential information will be acquired. Annex A of the Code lists the authorising officer for each public authority permitted to authorise such use or conduct of a source. Note that Box 17 of the standard CHIS application form contains space for authorisation where confidential information is involved.

The use of vulnerable individuals[50] and juveniles as sources

5.103   The CHIS Code provides guidance for the protection of vulnerable people, and juveniles. It stresses at paras 3.13 and 3.14 that vulnerable people should not be authorised to act as sources save in 'the most exceptional circumstances'. In such cases Annex A to the Code provides a separate column of types of authorising officer for each public authority permitted to authorise the use of a vulnerable individual as a source.

5.104   In the context of juveniles (those under 18 years) the Code provides a list of authorising officers in Annex A. The Code requires that 'On no occasion should the use or conduct of a source under 16 years of age be authorised to give information against his parents or any person who has parental responsibility for him.'

5.105   Further special safeguards are set out in the Regulation of Investigatory Powers (Juveniles) Order 2000 (SI No 2793) (see Chapter 26). In particular the duration of an authorisation where a juvenile source is authorised is *one* month and not 12 months as it is for adults (CHIS Code, para 3.14; Article 6 of the 2000 Order). The other requirements of the 2000 Order are set out in summary in the table below.

---

[49] The Code advises that the description need not be so narrow that a separate authorisation is required each time the source is tasked.

[50] A vulnerable individual is a person who is or may be in need of community care services by reason of mental or other disability, age or illness and who is or may be unable to take care of himself, or unable to protect himself against significant harm or exploitation.

Additional Code requirements for juvenile sources

Sources under 16

No authorisation may be granted for the conduct or use of a source if the source is under the age of 16 and the relationship to which the conduct or use would relate is between the source and his parent or any person who has parental responsibility for him.

Where a source is under the age of 16, the arrangements which the authorising officer must believe to be satisfied include that there must be at all times a person holding an office, rank or position with a relevant investigating authority who has responsibility for ensuring that an appropriate adult[51] is present at meetings.

Sources under 18[52]

An authorisation may not be granted or renewed in any case where the source is under the age of 18 unless a person holding an office, rank or position with a relevant investigating authority has made or updated a risk assessment sufficient to demonstrate that:

the nature and magnitude of any risk of physical injury to the source arising in the course of, or as a result of, carrying out the conduct described in the authorisation have been identified and evaluated; and

the nature and magnitude of any risk of psychological distress to the source arising in the course of, or as a result of, carrying out the conduct described in the authorisation have been identified and evaluated

And:

The person granting or renewing the authorisation has considered the risk assessment and has satisfied himself that any risks identified in it are justified and, if they are, that they have been properly explained to and understood by the source; and

The person granting or renewing the authorisation knows whether the relationship to which the conduct or use would relate is between the source and a relative, guardian or person who has for the time being assumed responsibility for the source's welfare, and, if it is, has given particular consideration to whether the authorisation is justified in the light of that fact.

Central record of all authorisations, and other mandatory requirements in relation to the handling of a source

As with covert surveillance, the Code of Practice, para 2.13 requires that:　　　　**5.106**

. . . a centrally retrievable record of all authorisations should be held by each public authority and regularly updated whenever an authorisation is granted, renewed or cancelled.

The minimum suggested records retention time is three years after the end of the period of authorisation. In terms of record content, in addition to a record being

---

[51] 'Appropriate adult' means the parent or guardian of the source; or any other person who has for the time being assumed responsibility for his welfare; failing which any responsible person aged 18 years or over who is neither a member of nor employed by any relevant investigating authority (Art 3(3) of the 2000 Order).

[52] See Art 5 of the 2000 Order.

kept of the matters listed, s 29(5) (detailed at para **5.96**) above the Regulation of Investigatory Powers (Source Records) Regulations 2000 (SI No 2725) and the CHIS Code, at para 2.15 detail what must be included in the central records relating to each source.

The duration, review, renewal and cancellation of authorisations for use or conduct of CHIS

Duration of authorisations

5.107 A written authorisation in respect of an adult source will, unless renewed, cease to have effect at the end of a period of 12 months beginning with the day on which it took effect (s 43(3)(b)) but urgent oral authorisations or authorisations by a person who is entitled to act only in urgent cases will, unless renewed, cease to have effect after 72 hours (s 43(3)(a)), beginning with the time when the authorisation was granted or renewed.

5.108 For juveniles the duration in non-urgent cases is reduced to one month (CHIS Code, para 3.14 and Article 6 of the Regulation of Investigatory Powers (Juveniles) Order 2000 (SI No 2793)).

Review and renewal

5.109 In the case of CHIS authorisation renewals, there is a statutory requirement[53] (in s 46(6) and (7)) that renewal may only take place if there has been a review of the use made of the source, the tasks given to him and information obtained, and the outcome of the review has been considered by the person granting the renewal. Renewal may be for the same length of time as the original authorisation (depending on whether it was an urgent authorisation or not).

5.110 The CHIS Code stresses the need for especially frequent reviews where the activity accesses confidential information or causes collateral intrusion (para 4.19). A standard review form appears in Part F of Chapter 15 with spaces for the necessary details and for comments by the reviewing officer and for a statement as to whether he authorises the use to continue after the review.

5.111 The results of reviews must also be recorded on the central record of CHIS authorisations held by each authority. Paragraph 4.24 of the CHIS Code gives a list of matters which must be stated on an application for renewal. A standard renewal form for use when an existing authorisation is sought to be renewed with effect from its expiry date is in Part G of Chapter 15.

---

[53] Contrast this with the review requirements for directed and intrusive surveillance, which are found within the Covert Surveillance Code of Practice but not statutorily.

See *R v Hans-Constantin Paulssen*[54] (discussed in Chapter 21) in relation to the use of CHIS evidence where an operation continued without the authorisation being reviewed or renewed after expiry.

Cancellation

The officer who granted or renewed the authorisation[55] must cancel it if he is satisfied that the use or conduct of the source: **5.112**

• no longer satisfies the criteria for authorisation; or
• that satisfactory arrangements for the source's case no longer exist.

The form in Part H of Chapter 15 is a standard cancellation form. Where necessary, the safety and welfare of the source should continue to be taken into account after the authorisation has been cancelled.

Tasking, management and welfare issues

It will be recalled that in addition to the twin requirements of necessity and proportionality, s 29(3)(c) imposed a set of requirements (listed in s 29(5)) broadly in terms of the presence of proper arrangements for the tasking[56] and management of the source. The first three of those requirements in s 29(5) requires the appointment of specific people with responsibilities as follows: **5.113**

(a) . . . a person holding an office, rank or position with the relevant investigating authority who will have day-to-day responsibility for dealing with the source on behalf of that authority, and for the source's security and welfare;[57]
(b) . . . another person holding an office, rank or position with the relevant investigating authority who will have general oversight of the use made of the source;
(c) . . . a person holding an office, rank or position with the relevant investigating authority who will have responsibility for maintaining a record of the use made of the source.

The Code, para 4.32 stresses that where it is intended to task a source 'in a new way or significantly greater way than previously identified', the persons at (a) and (b) 'must refer the proposed tasking to the authorising officer, who should consider whether a separate authorisation is required. This should be done in advance of any tasking and the details of such referrals must be recorded.'

---

[54] [2003] EWCA Crim 3109.

[55] If he is no longer available, the cancellation must be carried out by the person who has taken over the role of authorising officer, or a person listed in the RIPA (Cancellation of Authorisations) Order 2000 (SI No 2794) as entitled to act as authorising officer.

[56] The Code, para 4.26 defines 'tasking' as '. . . the assignment given to the source by the persons defined at sections 29(5)(a) and (b) of the 2000 Act, asking him to obtain information, to provide access to information or to otherwise act, incidentally, for the benefit of the relevant public authority.'

[57] The Code suggests that this person will usually be of a rank or position below that of the authorising officer.

5.114 Given that the person at (a) is in day to day contact with the source it is likely to be that person who becomes aware of issues which might affect the source's welfare. Unsurprisingly he is, under the Code, para 4.37 made responsible for bringing to the attention of the person defined at s 29(5)(b)[58] any concerns about the personal circumstances of the source insofar as they might affect the validity of the risk assessment, the conduct, safety and welfare of the source.

The text of RIPA Part II as amended follows.

F. Text of Part II

REGULATION OF INVESTIGATORY POWERS ACT 2000 (AS AMENDED)

PART II

SURVEILLANCE AND COVERT HUMAN INTELLIGENCE SOURCES

Introductory

Conduct to which Part II applies.[59]

26.[60]—(1) This Part applies to the following conduct—
  (a) directed surveillance;
  (b) intrusive surveillance; and
  (c) the conduct and use of covert human intelligence sources.

(2) Subject to subsection (6), surveillance is directed for the purposes of this Part if it is covert but not intrusive and is undertaken—
  (a) for the purposes of a specific investigation or a specific operation;
  (b) in such a manner as is likely to result in the obtaining of private information about a person (whether or not one specifically identified for the purposes of the investigation or operation); and
  (c) otherwise than by way of an immediate response to events or circumstances the nature of which is such that it would not be reasonably practicable for an authorisation under this Part to be sought for the carrying out of the surveillance.

---

[58] Ie the person who might decide that the authorisation ought to come to an end.

[59] The Secretary of State has limited power under s 47 to alter the definitions in s 26. As to the fact that general observation techniques do not usually fall within RIPA, see the Covert Surveillance Code of Practice at para 1.3. Note that by virtue of s 48(3)(c), where surveillance involves the entry onto property or interference with wireless telegraphy then the authorisation provisions of Part III of the Police Act 1997 will apply.

[60] Commencement: 25/9/2000 by SI 2000 No 2543.

(3)   Subject to subsections (4) to (6), surveillance is intrusive for the purposes of this Part if, and only if, it is covert surveillance that—

(a) is carried out in relation to anything taking place on any residential premises or in any private vehicle; and

(b) involves the presence of an individual on the premises or in the vehicle or is carried out by means of a surveillance device.

(4)   For the purposes of this Part surveillance is not intrusive to the extent that—

(a) it is carried out by means only of a surveillance device designed or adapted principally for the purpose of providing information about the location of a vehicle; or

(b) it is surveillance consisting in any such interception of a communication as falls within section 48(4).

(5)   For the purposes of this Part surveillance which—

(a) is carried out by means of a surveillance device in relation to anything taking place on any residential premises or in any private vehicle, but

(b) is carried out without that device being present on the premises or in the vehicle,

is not intrusive unless the device is such that it consistently provides information of the same quality and detail as might be expected to be obtained from a device actually present on the premises or in the vehicle.

(6)[61]   For the purposes of this Part surveillance which—

(a) is carried out by means of apparatus designed or adapted for the purpose of detecting the installation or use in any residential or other premises of a television receiver (within the meaning of Part 4 of the Communications Act 2003), and

(b) is carried out from outside those premises exclusively for that purpose, is neither directed nor intrusive.

(7) In this Part—

(a) references to the conduct of a covert human intelligence source are references to any conduct of such a source which falls within any of paragraphs (a) to (c) of subsection (8), or is incidental to anything falling within any of those paragraphs; and

(b) references to the use of a covert human intelligence source are references to inducing, asking or assisting a person to engage in the conduct of such a source, or to obtain information by means of the conduct of such a source.

---

[61] Amended by Communications Act 2003, Sch 17, para. 161(2).

(8) For the purposes of this Part a person is a covert human intelligence source if—

    (a) he establishes or maintains a personal or other relationship with a person for the covert purpose of facilitating the doing of anything falling within paragraph (b) or (c);

    (b) he covertly uses such a relationship to obtain information or to provide access to any information to another person; or

    (c) he covertly discloses information obtained by the use of such a relationship, or as a consequence of the existence of such a relationship.

(9) For the purposes of this section—

    (a) surveillance is covert if, and only if, it is carried out in a manner that is calculated to ensure that persons who are subject to the surveillance are unaware that it is or may be taking place;[62]

    (b) a purpose is covert, in relation to the establishment or maintenance of a personal or other relationship, if and only if the relationship is conducted in a manner that is calculated to ensure that one of the parties to the relationship is unaware of the purpose; and

    (c) a relationship is used covertly, and information obtained as mentioned in subsection (8)(c) is disclosed covertly, if and only if it is used or, as the case may be, disclosed in a manner that is calculated to ensure that one of the parties to the relationship is unaware of the use or disclosure in question.

(10) In this section "private information", in relation to a person, includes any information relating to his private or family life.[63]

(11) References in this section, in relation to a vehicle, to the presence of a surveillance device in the vehicle include references to its being located on or under the vehicle and also include references to its being attached to it.

Authorisation of surveillance and human intelligence sources

Lawful surveillance etc.

27.[64]—(1) Conduct to which this Part applies shall be lawful for all purposes if—

    (a) an authorisation under this Part confers an entitlement to engage in that conduct on the person whose conduct it is; and

    (b) his conduct is in accordance with the authorisation.

---

[62] But note that s 48(3)(a) and (b) *exclude* from the definition of surveillance the use of CHIS to obtain information in person, such as by carrying a covert recording device about the person. Such conduct is treated as the use of CHIS, and subject to the CHIS authorisation procedures.

[63] Echoing the words of (part of) ECHR, Art 8.

[64] Commencement: 25/9/2000 by SI 2000 No 2543.

(2) A person shall not be subject to any civil liability in respect of any conduct of his which—

    (a) is incidental to any conduct that is lawful by virtue of subsection (1); and

    (b) is not itself conduct an authorisation or warrant for which is capable of being granted under a relevant enactment and might reasonably have been expected to have been sought in the case in question.

(3) The conduct that may be authorised under this Part includes conduct outside the United Kingdom.

(4) In this section "relevant enactment" means—

    (a) an enactment contained in this Act;

    (b) section 5 of the Intelligence Services Act 1994 (warrants for the intelligence services); or

    (c) an enactment contained in Part III of the Police Act 1997 (powers of the police and of Customs officers).

27A[65] Authorisation of detection of television receivers

27A—(1) Subject to the following provisions of this Part, the persons designated for the purposes of this section shall each have power to grant authorisations for the detection of television receivers, that is to say, surveillance which—

    (a) is carried out by means of apparatus designed or adapted for the purpose of detecting the installation or use in any residential or other premises of a television receiver (within the meaning of section 1 of the Wireless Telegraphy Act 1949), and

    (b) is carried out from outside those premises exclusively for that purpose.

(2) The persons designated for the purposes of this section are—

    (a) any person holding the position of head of sales or head of marketing within the Television Licence Management Unit of the British Broadcasting Corporation, and

    (b) any person holding a position within that Unit which is more senior than the positions mentioned in paragraph (a).

(3) A person shall not grant an authorisation for the detection of television receivers unless he believes—

    (a) that the authorisation is necessary—

        (i) for the purpose of preventing or detecting crime constituting an offence under section 1 or 1A of the Wireless Telegraphy Act 1949; or

---

[65] Commencement 16/3/01 by SI 2001 No 1057. This section is treated 'as if inserted' into the Act by the RIPA (British Broadcasting Corporation) Order 2001 (SI 2001 No 1057), Art 3.

(ii) for the purpose of assessing or collecting sums payable to the British Broadcasting Corporation under regulations made under section 2 of the Wireless Telegraphy Act 1949; and

(b) that the authorised surveillance is proportionate to what is sought to be achieved by carrying it out.

(4) The conduct that is authorised by an authorisation for the detection of television receivers is any conduct that—

(a) consists in the carrying out of the detection of television receivers, and

(b) is carried out by the persons described in the authorisation in the circumstances described in the authorisation.

Authorisation of directed surveillance

28.[66]—(1) Subject to the following provisions of this Part, the persons designated for the purposes of this section shall each have power to grant authorisations for the carrying out of directed surveillance.

(2) A person shall not grant an authorisation for the carrying out of directed surveillance unless he believes—

(a) that the authorisation is necessary on grounds falling within subsection (3); and

(b) that the authorised surveillance is proportionate to what is sought to be achieved by carrying it out.

(3) An authorisation is necessary on grounds falling within this subsection if it is necessary—

(a) in the interests of national security;

(b) for the purpose of preventing or detecting crime or of preventing disorder;

(c) in the interests of the economic well-being of the United Kingdom;

(d) in the interests of public safety;

(e) for the purpose of protecting public health;

(f) for the purpose of assessing or collecting any tax, duty, levy or other imposition, contribution or charge payable to a government department; or

(g) for any purpose (not falling within paragraphs (a) to (f)) which is specified for the purposes of this subsection by an order made by the Secretary of State.

(4) The conduct that is authorised by an authorisation for the carrying out of Directed Surveillance is any conduct that—

(a) consists in the carrying out of Directed Surveillance of any such description as is specified in the authorisation; and

---

[66] Commencement: 25/9/2000 by SI 2000 No 2543.

(b) is carried out in the circumstances described in the authorisation and for the purposes of the investigation or operation specified or described in the authorisation.[67]

(5) The Secretary of State shall not make an order under subsection (3)(g) unless a draft of the order has been laid before Parliament and approved by a resolution of each House.

Authorisation of covert human intelligence sources

29.[68]—(1) Subject to the following provisions of this Part, the persons designated for the purposes of this section shall each have power to grant authorisations for the conduct or the use of a covert human intelligence source.

(2) A person shall not grant an authorisation for the conduct or the use of a covert human intelligence source unless he believes—

(a) that the authorisation is necessary on grounds falling within subsection (3);

(b) that the authorised conduct or use is proportionate to what is sought to be achieved by that conduct or use; and

(c) that arrangements exist for the source's case that satisfy the requirements of subsection (5) and such other requirements as may be imposed by order made by the Secretary of State.

(3) An authorisation is necessary on grounds falling within this subsection if it is necessary—

(a) in the interests of national security;

(b) for the purpose of preventing or detecting crime or of preventing disorder;

(c) in the interests of the economic well-being of the United Kingdom;

(d) in the interests of public safety;

(e) for the purpose of protecting public health;

(f) for the purpose of assessing or collecting any tax, duty, levy or other imposition, contribution or charge payable to a government department; or

(g) for any purpose (not falling within paragraphs (a) to (f)) which is specified for the purposes of this subsection by an order made by the Secretary of State.

(4) The conduct that is authorised by an authorisation for the conduct or the use of a covert human intelligence source is any conduct that—

(a) is comprised in any such activities involving conduct of a covert human intelligence source, or the use of a covert human intelligence source, as are specified or described in the authorisation;

---

[67] Note that s 27(2) exempts from civil liability actions which, whilst not authorised by this section, are 'incidental' to it.

[68] Commencement: 25/9/2000 by SI 2000 No 2543.

(b) consists in conduct by or in relation to the person who is so specified or described as the person to whose actions as a covert human intelligence source the authorisation relates; and

(c) is carried out for the purposes of, or in connection with, the investigation or operation so specified or described.

(5) For the purposes of this Part there are arrangements for the source's case that satisfy the requirements of this subsection if such arrangements are in force as are necessary for ensuring—

(a) that there will at all times be a person holding an office, rank or position with the relevant investigating authority who will have day-to-day responsibility for dealing with the source on behalf of that authority, and for the source's security and welfare;

(b) that there will at all times be another person holding an office, rank or position with the relevant investigating authority who will have general oversight of the use made of the source;

(c) that there will at all times be a person holding an office, rank or position with the relevant investigating authority who will have responsibility for maintaining a record of the use made of the source;

(d) that the records relating to the source that are maintained by the relevant investigating authority will always contain particulars of all such matters (if any) as may be specified for the purposes of this paragraph in regulations made by the Secretary of State; and

(e) that records maintained by the relevant investigating authority that disclose the identity of the source will not be available to persons except to the extent that there is a need for access to them to be made available to those persons.

(6) The Secretary of State shall not make an order under subsection (3)(g) unless a draft of the order has been laid before Parliament and approved by a resolution of each House.

(7) The Secretary of State may by order—

(a) prohibit the authorisation under this section of any such conduct or uses of covert human intelligence sources as may be described in the order; and

(b) impose requirements, in addition to those provided for by subsection (2), that must be satisfied before an authorisation is granted under this section for any such conduct or uses of covert human intelligence sources as may be so described.

(8) In this section "relevant investigating authority", in relation to an authorisation for the conduct or the use of an individual as a covert human intelligence source, means (subject to subsection (9)) the public authority for whose benefit the activities of that individual as such a source are to take place.

(9) In the case of any authorisation for the conduct or the use of a covert human intelligence source whose activities are to be for the benefit of more than one public authority, the references in subsection (5) to the relevant investigating authority are references to one of them (whether or not the same one in the case of each reference).

Persons entitled to grant authorisations under ss. 28 and 29

30.[69]—(1) Subject to subsection (3), the persons designated for the purposes of sections 28 and 29 are the individuals holding such offices, ranks or positions with relevant public authorities as are prescribed for the purposes of this subsection by an order under this section.

(2) For the purposes of the grant of an authorisation that combines—
  (a) an authorisation under section 28 or 29, and
  (b) an authorisation by the Secretary of State for the carrying out of intrusive surveillance,
the Secretary of State himself shall be a person designated for the purposes of that section.

(3) An order under this section may impose restrictions—
  (a) on the authorisations under sections 28 and 29 that may be granted by any individual holding an office, rank or position with a specified public authority; and
  (b) on the circumstances in which, or the purposes for which, such authorisations may be granted by any such individual.

(4) A public authority is a relevant public authority for the purposes of this section—
  (a) in relation to section 28 if it is specified in Part I or II of Schedule 1; and
  (b) in relation to section 29 if it is specified in Part I of that Schedule.

(5) An order under this section may amend Schedule 1 by—
  (a) adding a public authority to Part I or II of that Schedule;
  (b) removing a public authority from that Schedule;
  (c) moving a public authority from one Part of that Schedule to the other;
  (d) making any change consequential on any change in the name of a public authority specified in that Schedule.

(6) Without prejudice to section 31, the power to make an order under this section shall be exercisable by the Secretary of State.

(7) The Secretary of State shall not make an order under subsection (5) containing any provision for—
  (a) adding any public authority to Part I or II of that Schedule, or

---

[69] Commencement: 25/9/2000 by SI 2000 No 2543.

(b) moving any public authority from Part II to Part I of that Schedule, unless a draft of the order has been laid before Parliament and approved by a resolution of each House.

Orders under s. 30 for Northern Ireland

31.[70]—(1) Subject to subsections (2) and (3), the power to make an order under section 30 for the purposes of the grant of authorisations for conduct in Northern Ireland shall be exercisable by the Office of the First Minister and deputy First Minister in Northern Ireland (concurrently with being exercisable by the Secretary of State).

(2) The power of the Office of the First Minister and deputy First Minister to make an order under section 30 by virtue of subsection (1) or (3) of that section shall not be exercisable in relation to any public authority other than—

(a) the Food Standards Agency;

(b)[71] *repealed*

(c) an authority added to Schedule 1 by an order made by that Office;

(d) an authority added to that Schedule by an order made by the Secretary of State which it would (apart from that order) have been within the powers of that Office to add to that Schedule for the purposes mentioned in subsection (1) of this section.

(3) The power of the Office of the First Minister and deputy First Minister to make an order under section 30—

(a) shall not include power to make any provision dealing with an excepted matter;

(b) shall not include power, except with the consent of the Secretary of State, to make any provision dealing with a reserved matter.

(4) The power of the Office of the First Minister and deputy First Minister to make an order under section 30 shall be exercisable by statutory rule for the purposes of the Statutory Rules (Northern Ireland) Order 1979.

(5) A statutory rule containing an order under section 30 which makes provision by virtue of subsection (5) of that section for—

(a) adding any public authority to Part I or II of Schedule 1, or

(b) moving any public authority from Part II to Part I of that Schedule, shall be subject to affirmative resolution (within the meaning of section 41(4) of the Interpretation Act (Northern Ireland) 1954).

(6) A statutory rule containing an order under section 30 (other than one to which subsection (5) of this section applies) shall be subject to negative resolution (within the meaning of section 41(6) of the Interpretation Act (Northern Ireland) 1954).

---

[70] Commencement: 25/9/2000 by SI 2000 No 2543.
[71] Repealed by the Intervention Board for Agricultural Produce (Abolition) Regulations 2001 (SI 2001 No 3686), Art 6(17).

(7) An order under section 30 made by the Office of the First Minister and Deputy First Minister may—

    (a) make different provision for different cases;

    (b) contain such incidental, supplemental, consequential and transitional provision as that Office thinks fit.

(8) The reference in subsection (2) to an addition to Schedule 1 being within the powers of the Office of the First Minister and deputy First Minister includes a reference to its being within the powers exercisable by that Office with the consent for the purposes of subsection (3)(b) of the Secretary of State.

(9) In this section "excepted matter" and "reserved matter" have the same meanings as in the Northern Ireland Act 1998; and, in relation to those matters, section 98(2) of that Act (meaning of "deals with") applies for the purposes of this section as it applies for the purposes of that Act.

Authorisation of intrusive surveillance

32.[72]—(1) Subject to the following provisions of this Part, the Secretary of State and each of the senior authorising officers shall have power to grant authorisations for the carrying out of intrusive surveillance.

    (2) Neither the Secretary of State nor any senior authorising officer shall grant an authorisation for the carrying out of intrusive surveillance unless he believes—

        (a) that the authorisation is necessary on grounds falling within subsection (3); and

        (b) that the authorised surveillance is proportionate to what is sought to be achieved by carrying it out.

    (3) Subject to the following provisions of this section, an authorisation is necessary on grounds falling within this subsection if it is necessary—

        (a) in the interests of national security;

        (b) for the purpose of preventing or detecting serious crime; or

        (c) in the interests of the economic well-being of the United Kingdom.

(3A)[73] In the case of an authorisation granted by the chairman of the OFT, the authorisation is necessary on grounds falling within subsection (3) only if it is necessary for the purpose of preventing or detecting an offence under section 188 of the Enterprise Act 2002 (cartel offence).

    (4) The matters to be taken into account in considering whether the requirements of subsection (2) are satisfied in the case of any authorisation shall include whether the information which it is thought necessary to obtain by the authorised conduct could reasonably be obtained by other means.

---

[72] Commencement: 25/9/2000 by SI 2000 No 2543.
[73] Inserted by the Enterprise Act 2003, s 199(2)(a).

(5) The conduct that is authorised by an authorisation for the carrying out of intrusive surveillance is any conduct that—

(a) consists in the carrying out of intrusive surveillance of any such description as is specified in the authorisation;

(b) is carried out in relation to the residential premises specified or described in the authorisation or in relation to the private vehicle so specified or described; and

(c) is carried out for the purposes of, or in connection with, the investigation or operation so specified or described.

(6) For the purposes of this section the senior authorising officers are—

(a) the chief constable of every police force maintained under section 2 of the Police Act 1996 (police forces in England and Wales outside London);

(b) the Commissioner of Police of the Metropolis and every Assistant Commissioner of Police of the Metropolis;

(c) the Commissioner of Police for the City of London;

(d) the chief constable of every police force maintained under or by virtue of section 1 of the Police (Scotland) Act 1967 (police forces for areas in Scotland);

(e) the Chief Constable of the Royal Ulster Constabulary and the Deputy Chief Constable of the Royal Ulster Constabulary;

(f) the Chief Constable of the Ministry of Defence Police;

(g) the Provost Marshal of the Royal Navy Regulating Branch;

(h) the Provost Marshal of the Royal Military Police;

(i) the Provost Marshal of the Royal Air Force Police;

(j) the Chief Constable of the British Transport Police;

(ja)[74] the Chairman of the Independent Police Complaints Commission;

[(k) the Director General of the National Criminal Intelligence Service;

(l)[75] the Director General of the National Crime Squad and any person holding the rank of assistant chief constable in that Squad who is designated for the purposes of this paragraph by that Director General;]

(k) *the Director General of the Serious Organised Crime Agency and any member of the staff of that Agency who is designated for the purposes of this paragraph by that Director General;*[76]

---

[74] Inserted by the Independent Police Complaints Commission (Investigatory Powers) Order 2004 (SI 2004 No 815), Art 3(2).   [75] Amended by the Enterprise Act 2002, Sch 26.
[76] Words in italics at (k) will be added (replacing the words in square brackets at (k) and (l)) when Sch 4, para 136 of the SOCAP Act 2005 is in force.

(m) any Customs officer designated for the purposes of this paragraph by the Commissioners of Customs and Excise.

(n)[77] the chairman of the OFT.

Police and Customs authorisations

Rules for grant of authorisations

33.[78]—(1) A person who is a Designated Person for the purposes of section 28 or 29 by reference to his office, rank or position with a police force, [the National Criminal Intelligence Service or the National Crime Squad] shall not grant an authorisation under that section except on an application made by a member of the same force [, Service or Squad].[79]

(1A)[80] A person who is a designated person for the purposes of section 28 or 29 by reference to his office or position with the Independent Police Complaints Commission shall not grant an authorisation under that section except on an application made by a member of staff of the Commission who has been designated under paragraph 19(2) of Schedule 3 to the Police Reform Act 2002.

(1A) *A person who is a designated person for the purposes of section 28 or 29 by reference to his office or position with the Serious Organised Crime Agency shall not grant an authorisation under that section except on an application made by a member of the staff of the Agency.*[81]

(2) A person who is designated for the purposes of section 28 or 29 by reference to his office, rank or position with the Commissioners of Customs and Excise shall not grant an authorisation under that section except on an application made by a customs officer.

(3) A person who is a senior authorising officer by reference to a police force, [the National Criminal Intelligence Service or the National Crime Squad] shall not grant an authorisation for the carrying out of intrusive surveillance except—

(a) on an application made by a member of the same force, Service or Squad; and

(b) in the case of an authorisation for the carrying out of intrusive surveillance in relation to any residential premises, where those premises are in the area of operation of that force[, Service or Squad].[82]

---

[77] Inserted by the Enterprise Act 2002, s 199(2)(b).

[78] Commencement: 25/9/2000 by SI 2000 No 2543.

[79] The words in square brackets in this subsection will be omitted when Sch 4 of the SOCAP Act 2005, para 137 comes into force.

[80] Inserted by the Independent Police Complaints Commission (Investigatory Powers) Order 2004 (SI 2004 No 815), Art 3(3).

[81] The words in italics will be inserted when Sch 4 of the SOCAP Act 2005, para 137 comes into force.

[82] The words in square brackets in this subsection will be omitted when Sch 4 of the SOCAP Act 2005, para 137 comes into force.

(3A)[83] A person who is a senior authorising officer by reference to the Independent Police Complaints Commission shall not grant an authorisation for the carrying out of intrusive surveillance except—

    (a) on an application made by a member of staff of the Commission who has been designated under paragraph 19(2) of Schedule 3 to the Police Reform Act 2002; and

    (b) in the case of an authorisation for the carrying out of intrusive surveillance in relation to any residential premises, where those premises are in England and Wales.

(3A) *The Director General of the Serious Organised Crime Agency or a person designated for the purposes of section 32(6)(k) by that Director General shall not grant an authorisation for the carrying out of intrusive surveillance except on an application made by a member of the staff of the Agency.*[84]

  (4) A person who is a senior authorising officer by virtue of a designation by the Commissioners of Customs and Excise shall not grant an authorisation for the carrying out of intrusive surveillance except on an application made by a customs officer.

(4A)[85] The chairman of the OFT shall not grant an authorisation for the carrying out of intrusive surveillance except on an application made by an officer of the OFT.

  (5)[86] A single authorisation may combine both—

    (a) an authorisation granted under this Part by, or on the application of, an individual who is a member of a police force, [the National Criminal Intelligence Service or the National Crime Squad] *a member of the staff of the Serious Organised Crime Agency*,[87] or who is a member of staff of the Independent Police Complaints Commission, or who is a customs officer or the chairman or an officer of the OFT; and

    (b) an authorisation given by, or on the application of, that individual under Part III of the Police Act 1997; but the provisions of this Act or that Act that are applicable in the case of each of the authorisations shall apply separately in relation to the part of the combined authorisation to which they are applicable.

---

[83] The Independent Police Complaints Commission (Investigatory Powers) Order 2004 (SI 2004 No 815), Art 3(3).

[84] The words in italics will be inserted when Sch 4 of the SOCAP Act 2005, para 137 comes into force.

[85] Inserted by the Enterprise Act 2002, s 199(3).

[86] Inserted by the Enterprise Act 2002, s 199(3), amended by the Independent Police Complaints Commission (Investigatory Powers) Order 2004 (SI 2004 No 815), Art 3(3).

[87] The words in square brackets will be replaced by the words in italics when Sch 4 of the SOCAP Act 2005, para 137 comes into force.

(6) For the purposes of this section—

    (a) the area of operation of a police force maintained under section 2 of the Police Act 1996, of the Metropolitan police force, of the City of London police force or of a police force maintained under or by virtue of section 1 of the Police (Scotland) Act 1967 is the area for which that force is maintained;

    (b) the area of operation of the Royal Ulster Constabulary is Northern Ireland;

    (c) residential premises are in the area of operation of the Ministry of Defence Police if they are premises where the members of that police force, under section 2 of the Ministry of Defence Police Act 1987, have the powers and privileges of a constable;

    (d) residential premises are in the area of operation of the Royal Navy Regulating Branch, the Royal Military Police or the Royal Air Force Police if they are premises owned or occupied by, or used for residential purposes by, a person subject to service discipline;

    (e) the area of operation of the British Transport Police [and also of the National Criminal Intelligence Service][88] is the United Kingdom;

    [(f) the area of operation of the National Crime Squad is England and Wales];
and references in this section to the United Kingdom or to any part or area of the United Kingdom include any adjacent waters within the seaward limits of the territorial waters of the United Kingdom.

(7) For the purposes of this section a person is subject to service discipline—

    (a) in relation to the Royal Navy Regulating Branch, if he is subject to the Naval Discipline Act 1957 or is a civilian to whom Parts I and II of that Act for the time being apply by virtue of section 118 of that Act;

    (b) in relation to the Royal Military Police, if he is subject to military law or is a civilian to whom Part II of the Army Act 1955 for the time being applies by virtue of section 209 of that Act; and

    (c) in relation to the Royal Air Force Police, if he is subject to air-force law or is a civilian to whom Part II of the Air Force Act 1955 for the time being applies by virtue of section 209 of that Act.

Grant of authorisations in the senior officer's absence

34.[89]—(1)[90] This section applies in the case of an application for an authorisation for the carrying out of intrusive surveillance where—

    (a) the application is one made by a member of a police force, [of the National Criminal Intelligence Service or of the National Crime Squad]

---

[88] The words in square brackets at (e) and (f) will be omitted when Sch 4 of the SOCAP Act 2005, para 137 comes into force.   [89] Commencement: 25/9/2000 by SI 2000 No 2543.
[90] Amended by the Enterprise Act 2002, s 199(5) and by the Independent Police Complaints Commission (Investigatory Powers) Order 2004 (SI 2004 No 815), Art 3(4).

> *a member of the staff of the Serious Organised Crime Agency*[91] or by a member of staff of the Independent Police Complaints Commission who has been designated under paragraph 19(2) of Schedule 3 to the Police Reform Act 2002 or by an officer of the OFT or a customs officer; and

    (b) the case is urgent.

(2)[92] If—

    (a) it is not reasonably practicable, having regard to the urgency of the case, for the application to be considered by any person who is a senior authorising officer by reference to the force, [Service or Squad] *or Agency*[93] in question or the Independent Police Complaints Commission or, as the case may be as chairman of the OFT or, by virtue of a designation by the Commissioners of Customs and Excise, and

    (b) it also not reasonably practicable, having regard to the urgency of the case, for the application to be considered by a person (if there is one) who is entitled, as a designated deputy of a senior authorising officer, to exercise the functions in relation to that application of such an officer,

the application may be made to and considered by any person who is entitled under subsection (4) to act for any senior authorising officer who would have been entitled to consider the application.

(3) A person who considers an application under subsection (1) shall have the same power to grant an authorisation as the person for whom he is entitled to act.

(4) For the purposes of this section—

    (a) a person is entitled to act for the chief constable of a police force maintained under section 2 of the Police Act 1996 if he holds the rank of assistant chief constable in that force;

    (b) a person is entitled to act for the Commissioner of Police of the Metropolis, or for an Assistant Commissioner of Police of the Metropolis, if he holds the rank of commander in the Metropolitan police force;

    (c) a person is entitled to act for the Commissioner of Police for the City of London if he holds the rank of commander in the City of London police force;

    (d) a person is entitled to act for the Chief Constable of a police force maintained under or by virtue of section 1 of the Police (Scotland) Act 1967 if he holds the rank of Assistant Chief Constable in that force;

---

[91] The words in italics will be added (replacing the words in square brackets) when Sch 4, para 138 of the SOCAP Act 2005 is in force.

[92] Amended by the Enterprise Act 2002, s 199(5) and by the Independent Police Complaints Commission (Investigatory Powers) Order 2004 (SI 2004 No 815), Art 3(4).

[93] The words in italics will be added (replacing the words in square brackets) when Sch 4, para 138 of the SOCAP Act 2005 is in force.

    (e)   a person is entitled to act for the Chief Constable of the Royal Ulster Constabulary, or for the Deputy Chief Constable of the Royal Ulster Constabulary, if he holds the rank of Assistant Chief Constable in the Royal Ulster Constabulary;

    (f)   a person is entitled to act for the Chief Constable of the Ministry of Defence Police if he holds the rank of Deputy or Assistant Chief Constable in that force;

    (g)   a person is entitled to act for the Provost Marshal of the Royal Navy Regulating Branch if he holds the position of assistant Provost Marshal in that Branch;

    (h)   a person is entitled to act for the Provost Marshal of the Royal Military Police or the Provost Marshal of the Royal Air Force Police if he holds the position of deputy Provost Marshal in the police force in question;

    (i)   a person is entitled to act for the Chief Constable of the British Transport Police if he holds the rank of deputy or assistant chief constable in that force;

    (j)   a person is entitled to act for the Director General of the National Criminal Intelligence Service if he is a person designated for the purposes of this paragraph by that Director General;

    (k)   a person is entitled to act for the Director General of the National Crime Squad if he is designated for the purposes of this paragraph by that Director General as a person entitled so to act in an urgent case;

    (l)   a person is entitled to act for a person who is a senior authorising officer by virtue of a designation by the Commissioners of Customs and Excise, if he is designated for the purposes of this paragraph by those Commissioners as a person entitled so to act in an urgent case.

    (m)[94]   a person is entitled to act for the chairman of the OFT if he is an officer of the OFT designated by it for the purposes of this paragraph as a person entitled so to act in an urgent case.

    (n)[95]   person is entitled to act for the Chairman of the Independent Police Complaints Commission if he is any other member of the Independent Police Complaints Commission.

[(5)   A police member of the National Criminal Intelligence Service or the National Crime Squad appointed under section 9(1)(b) or 55(1)(b) of the Police Act 1997 (police members) may not be designated under subsection (4)(j) or (k) unless he holds the rank of assistant chief constable in that Service or Squad.][96]

---

[94] Inserted by the Enterprise Act 2002, s 199(5).

[95] Inserted by the Independent Police Complaints Commission (Investigatory Powers) Order 2004 (SI 2004 No 815), Art 3(4).

[96] Subsection (5) will be omitted when Sch 4, para 138 of the SOCAP Act 2005 is in force.

(6) In this section "designated deputy"—

    (a)   in relation to a chief constable, means a person holding the rank of assistant chief constable who is designated to act under section 12(4) of the Police Act 1996 or section 5(4) of the Police (Scotland) Act 1967;

    (b)   in relation to the Commissioner of Police for the City of London, means a person authorised to act under section 25 of the City of London Police Act 1839;

    [(c)   in relation to the Director General of the National Criminal Intelligence Service or the Director General of the National Crime Squad, means a person designated to act under section 8 or, as the case may be, section 54 of the Police Act 1997.][97]

    (d)[98]   in relation to the Chairman of the Independent Police Complaints Commission, means a person appointed as deputy chairman of the Independent Police Complaints Commission under paragraph 3(1) of Schedule 2 to the Police Reform Act 2002.

Notification of authorisations for intrusive surveillance

35.[99]—(1)[100]   Where a person grants or cancels a police, *SOCA*,[101] customs or OFT authorisation for the carrying out of intrusive surveillance, he shall give notice that he has done so to an ordinary Surveillance Commissioner.

(2) A notice given for the purposes of subsection (1)—

    (a)   must be given in writing as soon as reasonably practicable after the grant or, as the case may be, cancellation of the authorisation to which it relates;

    (b)   must be given in accordance with any such arrangements made for the purposes of this paragraph by the Chief Surveillance Commissioner as are for the time being in force; and

    (c)   must specify such matters as the Secretary of State may by order prescribe.

(3) A notice under this section of the grant of an authorisation shall, as the case may be, either—

    (a)   state that the approval of a Surveillance Commissioner is required by section 36 before the grant of the authorisation will take effect; or

    (b)   state that the case is one of urgency and set out the grounds on which the case is believed to be one of urgency.

---

[97] Subsection (6)(c) will be omitted when Sch 4, para 138 of the SOCAP Act 2005 is in force.

[98] Inserted by the Independent Police Complaints Commission (Investigatory Powers) Order 2004 (SI 2004 No 815), Art 3(4).   [99] Commencement: 25/9/2000 by SI 2000 No 2543.

[100] Amended by the Enterprise Act 2002, s 199(6).

[101] The reference to SOCA will be inserted from date of commencement of Sch 4, para 139 of the SOCAP Act 2005.

(4) Where a notice for the purposes of subsection (1) of the grant of an authorisation has been received by an ordinary Surveillance Commissioner, he
shall, as soon as practicable—
(a) scrutinise the authorisation; and
(b) in a case where notice has been given in accordance with subsection
(3)(a), decide whether or not to approve the authorisation.

(5) Subject to subsection (6), the Secretary of State shall not make an order
under subsection (2)(c) unless a draft of the order has been laid before
Parliament and approved by a resolution of each House.

(6) Subsection (5) does not apply in the case of the order made on the first
occasion on which the Secretary of State exercises his power to make an
order under subsection (2)(c).

(7) The order made on that occasion shall cease to have effect at the end of the
period of forty days beginning with the day on which it was made unless,
before the end of that period, it has been approved by a resolution of each
House of Parliament.

(8) For the purposes of subsection (7)—
(a) the order's ceasing to have effect shall be without prejudice to anything previously done or to the making of a new order; and
(b) in reckoning the period of forty days no account shall be taken
of any period during which Parliament is dissolved or prorogued
or during which both Houses are adjourned for more than four
days.

(9) Any notice that is required by any provision of this section to be given in
writing may be given, instead, by being transmitted by electronic means.

(10)[102] In this section references to a police, *SOCA*[103] customs or OFT authorisation are references to an authorisation granted by—
(a) a person who is a senior authorising officer by reference to a police
force the Independent Police Complaints Commission, [the
National Criminal Intelligence Service or the National Crime
Squad] *or the Serious Organised Crime Agency*;
(b) a person who is a senior authorising officer by virtue of a designation
by the Commissioners of Customs and Excise;
(ba) the chairman of the OFT; or
(c) a person who for the purposes of section 34 is entitled to act for a
person falling within paragraph (a) or for a person falling within
paragraph (b) or for a person falling within paragraph (ba).

---

[102] Amended by the Enterprise Act 2002, s 199(6) and Sch 26, and by the Independent Police
Complaints Commission (Investigatory Powers) Order 2004 (SI 2004 No 815), Art 3(5).
[103] The references to SOCA will be inserted and words in square brackets in (a) replaced from
date of commencement of Sch 4, para 139 of the SOCAP Act 2005.

Approval required for authorisations to take effect

36.[104]—(1)[105] This section applies where an authorisation for the carrying out of intrusive surveillance has been granted on the application of—

   (a) a member of a police force;

   (aa) a member of staff of the Independent Police Complaints Commission who has been designated under paragraph 19(2) of Schedule 3 to the Police Reform Act 2002;

   [(b) a member of the National Criminal Intelligence Service;

   (c) a member of the National Crime Squad;]

   (b) a member of the staff of the Serious Organised Crime Agency;[106]

   (d) a customs officer; or

   (e) an officer of the OFT.

(2) Subject to subsection (3), the authorisation shall not take effect until such time (if any) as—

   (a) the grant of the authorisation has been approved by an ordinary Surveillance Commissioner; and

   (b) written notice of the Commissioner's decision to approve the grant of the authorisation has been given, in accordance with subsection (4), to the person who granted the authorisation.

(3) Where the person who grants the authorisation—

   (a) believes that the case is one of urgency, and

   (b) gives notice in accordance with section 35(3)(b), subsection (2) shall not apply to the authorisation, and the authorisation shall have effect from the time of its grant.

(4) Where subsection (2) applies to the authorisation—

   (a) a Surveillance Commissioner shall give his approval under this section to the authorisation if, and only if, he is satisfied that there are reasonable grounds for believing that the requirements of section 32(2)(a) and (b) are satisfied in the case of the authorisation; and

   (b) a Surveillance Commissioner who makes a decision as to whether or not the authorisation should be approved shall, as soon as reasonably practicable after making that decision, give written notice of his decision to the person who granted the authorisation.

(5) If an ordinary Surveillance Commissioner decides not to approve an authorisation to which subsection (2) applies, he shall make a report of his findings to the most senior relevant person.

---

[104] Commencement: 25/9/2000 by SI 2000 No 2543.

[105] Amended by the Enterprise Act 2002, s 199(7) and Sch 26, and by the Independent Police Complaints Commission (Investigatory Powers) Order 2004 (SI 2004 No 815), Art 3(6).

[106] The words in italics will be added (replacing the words in square brackets) when Sch 4, para 140 of the SOCAP Act 2005 is in force.

(6)[107] In this section "the most senior relevant person" means—

(a) where the authorisation was granted by the senior authorising officer with any police force who is not someone's deputy, that senior authorising officer;

(b) where the authorisation was granted by the Director General of the [National Criminal Intelligence Service or the Director General of the National Crime Squad,] *Serious Organised Crime Agency,*[108] that Director General;

(ba) where the authorisation was granted by the Chairman of the Independent Police Complaints Commission, by the designated deputy of the Chairman of the Independent Police Complaints Commission or by another member of that Commission entitled to act for that Chairman by virtue of section 34(4)(m), that Chairman;

(c) where the authorisation was granted by a senior authorising officer with a police force who is someone's deputy, the senior authorising officer whose deputy granted the authorisation;

[(d) where the authorisation was granted by the designated deputy of the Director General of the National Criminal Intelligence Service or a person entitled to act for him by virtue of section 34(4)(j), that Director General;

(e) where the authorisation was granted by the designated deputy of the Director General of the National Crime Squad or by a person designated by that Director General for the purposes of section 32(6)(l) or 34(4)(k), that Director General;]

(d) *where the authorisation was granted by a person designated for the purposes of section 32(6)(k), or by a person entitled to act for the Director General of the Serious Organised Crime Agency by virtue of section 34(4)(j), that Director General;*[109]

(f) where the authorisation was granted by a person entitled to act for a senior authorising officer under section 34(4)(a) to (i), the senior authorising officer in the force in question who is not someone's deputy;

(g) where the authorisation was granted by a customs officer, the Customs officer for the time being designated for the purposes of this paragraph by a written notice given to the Chief Surveillance Commissioner by the Commissioners of Customs and Excise; and

---

[107] Amended by the Enterprise Act 2002, s 199(7) and Sch 26 and by the Independent Police Complaints Commission (Investigatory Powers) Order 2004 (SI 2004 No 815), Art 3(6).

[108] The words in italics will be added (replacing the words in square brackets) when Sch 4, para 140 of the SOCAP Act 2005 is in force.

[109] The words in italics in (d) will be added (replacing the words in square brackets in (d) and (e)) when Sch 4, para 140 of the SOCAP Act 2005 is in force.

(h) where the authorisation was granted by the chairman of the OFT or a person entitled to act for him by virtue of section 34(4)(m), that chairman.

(7) The references in subsection (6) to a person's deputy are references to the following—

(a) in relation to—

(i) a chief constable of a police force maintained under section 2 of the Police Act 1996,

(ii) the Commissioner of Police for the City of London, or

(iii) a chief constable of a police force maintained under or by virtue of section 1 of the Police (Scotland) Act 1967,

to his designated deputy;

(b) in relation to the Commissioner of Police of the Metropolis, to an Assistant Commissioner of Police of the Metropolis; and

(c) in relation to the Chief Constable of the Royal Ulster Constabulary, to the Deputy Chief Constable of the Royal Ulster Constabulary;

and in this subsection and that subsection "designated deputy" has the same meaning as in section 34.

(8) Any notice that is required by any provision of this section to be given in writing may be given, instead, by being transmitted by electronic means.

Quashing of police and customs authorisations etc.

37.[110]—(1)[111] This section applies where an authorisation for the carrying out of Intrusive Surveillance has been granted on the application of—

(a) a member of a police force;

(aa) a member of staff of the Independent Police Complaints Commission who has been designated under paragraph 19(2) of Schedule 3 to the Police Reform Act 2002;

[(b) a member of the National Criminal Intelligence Service;

(c) a member of the National Crime Squad;]

(b) a member of the staff of the Serious Organised Crime Agency;[112]

(d) a Customs officer; or

(e) an officer of the OFT.

(2) Where an ordinary Surveillance Commissioner is at any time satisfied that, at the time when the authorisation was granted or at any time when it was renewed, there were no reasonable grounds for believing that the requirements

---

[110] Commencement: 25/9/2000 by SI 2000 No 2543.

[111] Amended by the Enterprise Act 2002, s 199(8) and Sch 26 and by the Independent Police Complaints Commission (Investigatory Powers) Order 2004 (SI 2004 No 815), Art 3(7).

[112] The words in italics in (b) will be added (replacing the words in square brackets in (b) and (c)) when Sch 4, para 141 of the SOCAP Act 2005 is in force.

of section 32(2)(a) and (b) were satisfied, he may quash the authorisation with effect, as he thinks fit, from the time of the grant of the authorisation or from the time of any renewal of the authorisation.

(3) If an ordinary Surveillance Commissioner is satisfied at any time while the authorisation is in force that there are no longer any reasonable grounds for believing that the requirements of section 32(2)(a) and (b) are satisfied in relation to the authorisation, he may cancel the authorisation with effect from such time as appears to him to be the time from which those requirements ceased to be so satisfied.

(4) Where, in the case of any authorisation of which notice has been given in accordance with section 35(3)(b), an ordinary Surveillance Commissioner is at any time satisfied that, at the time of the grant or renewal of the authorisation to which that notice related, there were no reasonable grounds for believing that the case was one of urgency, he may quash the authorisation with effect, as he thinks fit, from the time of the grant of the authorisation or from the time of any renewal of the authorisation.

(5) Subject to subsection (7), where an ordinary Surveillance Commissioner quashes an authorisation under this section, he may order the destruction of any records relating wholly or partly to information obtained by the authorised conduct after the time from which his decision takes effect.

(6) Subject to subsection (7), where—
   (a) an authorisation has ceased to have effect (otherwise than by virtue of subsection (2) or (4)), and
   (b) an ordinary Surveillance Commissioner is satisfied that there was a time while the authorisation was in force when there were no reasonable grounds for believing that the requirements of section 32(2)(a) and (b) continued to be satisfied in relation to the authorisation,
he may order the destruction of any records relating, wholly or partly, to information obtained at such a time by the authorised conduct.

(7) No order shall be made under this section for the destruction of any records required for pending criminal or civil proceedings.

(8) Where an ordinary Surveillance Commissioner exercises a power conferred by this section, he shall, as soon as reasonably practicable, make a report of his exercise of that power, and of his reasons for doing so—
   (a) to the most senior relevant person (within the meaning of section 36); and
   (b) to the Chief Surveillance Commissioner.

(9) Where an order for the destruction of records is made under this section, the order shall not become operative until such time (if any) as—
   (a) the period for appealing against the decision to make the order has expired; and
   (b) any appeal brought within that period has been dismissed by the Chief Surveillance Commissioner.

(10) No notice shall be required to be given under section 35(1) in the case of a cancellation under subsection (3) of this section.

Appeals against decisions by Surveillance Commissioners

38.[113]—(1) Any senior authorising officer may appeal to the Chief Surveillance Commissioner against any of the following—

(a) any refusal of an ordinary Surveillance Commissioner to approve an authorisation for the carrying out of intrusive surveillance;

(b) any decision of such a Commissioner to quash or cancel such an authorisation;

(c) any decision of such a Commissioner to make an order under section 37 for the destruction of records.

(2) In the case of an authorisation granted by the designated deputy of a senior authorising office or by a person who for the purposes of section 34 is entitled to act for a senior authorising officer, that designated deputy or person shall also be entitled to appeal under this section.

(3) An appeal under this section must be brought within the period of seven days beginning with the day on which the refusal or decision appealed against is reported to the appellant.

(4) Subject to subsection (5), the Chief Surveillance Commissioner, on an appeal under this section, shall allow the appeal if—

(a) he is satisfied that there were reasonable grounds for believing that the requirements of section 32(2)(a) and (b) were satisfied in relation to the authorisation at the time in question; and

(b) he is not satisfied that the authorisation is one of which notice was given in accordance with section 35(3)(b) without there being any reasonable grounds for believing that the case was one of urgency.

(5) If, on an appeal falling within subsection (1)(b), the Chief Surveillance Commissioner—

(a) is satisfied that grounds exist which justify the quashing or cancellation under section 37 of the authorisation in question, but

(b) considers that the authorisation should have been quashed or cancelled from a different time from that from which it was quashed or cancelled by the ordinary Surveillance Commissioner against whose decision the appeal is brought,

he may modify that Commissioner's decision to quash or cancel the authorisation, and any related decision for the destruction of records, so as to give effect to the decision under section 37 that he considers should have been made.

---

[113] Commencement: 25/9/2000 by SI 2000 No 2543.

(6) Where, on an appeal under this section against a decision to quash or cancel an authorisation, the Chief Surveillance Commissioner allows the appeal he shall also quash any related order for the destruction of records relating to information obtained by the authorised conduct.

(7) In this section "designated deputy" has the same meaning as in section 34.

Appeals to the Chief Surveillance Commissioner: supplementary

39.[114]—(1) Where the Chief Surveillance Commissioner has determined an appeal under section 38, he shall give notice of his determination to both—

(a) the person by whom the appeal was brought; and

(b) the ordinary Surveillance Commissioner whose decision was appealed against.

(2) Where the determination of the Chief Surveillance Commissioner on an appeal under section 38 is a determination to dismiss the appeal, the Chief Surveillance Commissioner shall make a report of his findings—

(a) to the persons mentioned in subsection (1); and

(b) to the Prime Minister.

(3) Subsections (3) and (4) of section 107 of the Police Act 1997 (reports to be laid before Parliament and exclusion of matters from the report) apply in relation to any report to the Prime Minister under subsection (2) of this section as they apply in relation to any report under subsection (2) of that section.

(4) Subject to subsection (2) of this section, the Chief Surveillance Commissioner shall not give any reasons for any determination of his on an appeal under section 38.

Information to be provided to Surveillance Commissioners

40.[115]—It shall be the duty of—

(a) every member of a police force,

(aa) every member and every employee of the Independent Police Complaints Commission,

[(b) every member of the National Criminal Intelligence Service,

(c) every member of the National Crime Squad, and]

(b) *every member of the staff of the Serious Organised Crime Agency*,[116]

(d) every Customs officer, and

(e) every officer of the OFT,

---

[114] Commencement: 25/9/2000 by SI 2000 No 2543.

[115] Commencement: 25/9/2000 by SI 2000 No 2543. Amended by the Enterprise Act 2002; s 199(9) and by the Independent Police Complaints Commission (Investigatory Powers) Order 2004 (SI 2004 No 815), Art 3(8).

[116] The words in italics in (b) will be added (replacing the words in square brackets in (b) and (c)) when Sch 4, para 142 of the SOCAP Act 2005 is in force.

to comply with any request of a Surveillance Commissioner for documents or information required by that Commissioner for the purpose of enabling him to carry out the functions of such a Commissioner under sections 35 to 39.

Other authorisations

Secretary of State authorisations

41.[117]—(1) The Secretary of State shall not grant an authorisation for the carrying out of intrusive surveillance except on an application made by—

   (a) a member of any of the intelligence services;

   (b) an official of the Ministry of Defence;

   (c) a member of Her Majesty's forces;[118]

   (d) an individual holding an office, rank or position with any such public authority as may be designated for the purposes of this section as an authority whose activities may require the carrying out of Intrusive Surveillance.

(2) Section 32 shall have effect in relation to the grant of an authorisation by the Secretary of State on the application of an official of the Ministry of Defence, or of a member of Her Majesty's forces, as if the only matters mentioned in subsection (3) of that section were—

   (a) the interests of national security; and

   (b) the purpose of preventing or detecting serious crime.

(3) The designation of any public authority for the purposes of this section shall be by order made by the Secretary of State.

(4) The Secretary of State may by order provide, in relation to any public authority, that an application for an authorisation for the carrying out of intrusive surveillance may be made by an individual holding an office, rank or position with that authority only where his office, rank or position is one prescribed by the order.

(5) The Secretary of State may by order impose restrictions—

   (a) on the authorisations for the carrying out of intrusive surveillance that may be granted on the application of an individual holding an office, rank or position with any public authority designated for the purposes of this section; and

   (b) on the circumstances in which, or the purposes for which, such authorisations may be granted on such an application.

(6) The Secretary of State shall not make a designation under subsection (3) unless a draft of the order containing the designation has been laid before Parliament and approved by a resolution of each House.

---

[117] Commencement: 25/9/2000 by SI 2000 No 2543.

[118] But note that by s 81(1) the three military police forces are treated as being police forces rather than part of the armed forces, which implies that the procedures of ss 33–40 are appropriate for them rather than the Secretary of State authorisations procedure in ss 41 and 42.

(7) References in this section to a member of Her Majesty's forces do not include references to any member of Her Majesty's forces who is a member of a police force by virtue of his service with the Royal Navy Regulating Branch, the Royal Military Police or the Royal Air Force Police.

Intelligence services authorisations

42.[119]—(1) The grant by the Secretary of State or, the Scottish Ministers (by virtue of provision under section 63 of the Scotland Act 1998) on the application of a member of one of the intelligence services of any authorisation under this Part must be made by the issue of a warrant.

(2) A single warrant issued by the Secretary of State or, the Scottish Ministers (by virtue of provision under section 63 of the Scotland Act 1998) may combine both—

(a) an authorisation under this Part; and

(b) an intelligence services warrant;

but the provisions of this Act or the Intelligence Services Act 1994 that are applicable in the case of the authorisation under this Part or the intelligence services warrant shall apply separately in relation to the part of the combined warrant to which they are applicable.

(3) Intrusive Surveillance in relation to any premises or vehicle in the British Islands shall be capable of being authorised by a warrant issued under this Part on the application of a member of the Secret Intelligence Service or GCHQ only if the authorisation contained in the warrant is one satisfying the requirements of section 32(2)(a) otherwise than in connection with any functions of that intelligence service in support of the prevention or detection of serious crime.

(4) Subject to subsection (5), the functions of the Security Service shall include acting on behalf of the Secret Intelligence Service or GCHQ in relation to—

(a) the application for and grant of any authorisation under this Part in connection with any matter within the functions of the Secret Intelligence Service or GCHQ; and

(b) the carrying out, in connection with any such matter, of any conduct authorised by such an authorisation.

(5) Nothing in subsection (4) shall authorise the doing of anything by one intelligence service on behalf of another unless—

(a) it is something which either the other service or a member of the other service has power to do; and

(b) it is done otherwise than in connection with functions of the other service in support of the prevention or detection of serious crime.

---

[119] Commencement: 25/9/2000 by SI 2000 No 2543. Amended by the Scotland Act 1998 (Transfer of Functions to the Scottish Ministers etc.) (No 2) Order 2000 (S I 2000 No 3253), Art 4(1), Sch 3, para 7.

(6) In this section "intelligence services warrant" means a warrant under section 5 of the Intelligence Services Act 1994.

Grant, renewal and duration of authorizations

General rules about grant, renewal and duration

43.[120]—(1)[121] An authorisation under this Part—

    (a) may be granted or renewed orally in any urgent case in which the entitlement to act of the person granting or renewing it is not confined to urgent cases; and

    (b) in any other case, must be in writing.

(2) A single authorisation may combine two or more different authorisations under this Part; but the provisions of this Act that are applicable in the case of each of the authorisations shall apply separately in relation to the part of the combined authorisation to which they are applicable.

(3)[122] Subject to subsections (4) and (8), an authorisation under this Part shall cease to have effect at the end of the following period—

    (a) in the case of an authorisation which—

        (i) has not been renewed and was granted either orally or by a person whose entitlement to act is confined to urgent cases, or

        (ii) was last renewed either orally or by such a person,

the period of seventy-two hours beginning with the time when the grant of the authorisation or, as the case may be, its latest renewal takes effect;

    (b) in a case not falling within paragraph (a) in which the authorisation is for the conduct or the use of a covert human intelligence source, the period of twelve months beginning with the day on which the grant of the authorisation or, as the case may be, its latest renewal takes effect; and

---

[120] Commencement: 25/9/2000 by SI 2000 No 2543.

[121] By the RIPA (British Broadcasting Corporation) Order 2001 (SI 2001 No 1057), Art 4, in its application to the detection of television receivers only, s 43 has effect as if in subs (1), for para (a) and (b) there were substituted 'must be in writing'.

[122] By the RIPA (British Broadcasting Corporation) Order 2001 (SI 2001 No 1057), Art 4, in its application to the detection of television receivers only, s 43 has effect as if for subs (3) there were substituted—

  (3) Subject to subsection (4), an authorisation under this Part shall cease to have effect—

    (a) in the case of an authorisation which has not been renewed and in which is specified a period of less than eight weeks beginning with the day on which the grant of the authorisation takes effect, at the end of that period;

    (b) in the case of an authorisation which has not been renewed and to which paragraph (a) does not apply, at the end of the period of eight weeks beginning with the day on which the grant of the authorisation takes effect;

    (c) in the case of an authorisation which has been renewed, and in which is specified a period of less than eight weeks beginning with the day on which the grant of the authorisation takes effect, at the end of a period of the same length beginning with the day on which the latest renewal takes effect;

    (d) in the case of an authorisation which has been renewed, and to which paragraph (c) does not apply, at the end of the period of eight weeks beginning with the day on which the latest renewal takes effect

(c) in any case not falling within paragraph (a) or (b), the period of three months beginning with the day on which the grant of the authorisation or, as the case may be, its latest renewal takes effect.

(4) Subject to subsection (6), an authorisation under this Part may be renewed, at any time before the time at which it ceases to have effect, by any person who would be entitled to grant a new authorisation in the same terms.

(5)[123] Sections 28 to 41 shall have effect in relation to the renewal of an authorisation under this Part as if references to the grant of an authorisation included references to its renewal.

(6) A person shall not renew an authorisation for the conduct or the use of a covert human intelligence source, unless he—

(a) is satisfied that a review has been carried out of the matters mentioned in subsection (7); and

(b) has, for the purpose of deciding whether he should renew the authorisation, considered the results of that review.

(7) The matters mentioned in subsection (6) are—

(a) the use made of the source in the period since the grant or, as the case may be, latest renewal of the authorisation; and

(b) the tasks given to the source during that period and the information obtained from the conduct or the use of the source.

(8) The Secretary of State may by order provide in relation to authorisations of such descriptions as may be specified in the order that subsection (3) is to have effect as if the period at the end of which an authorisation of a description so specified is to cease to have effect were such period shorter than that provided for by that subsection as may be fixed by or determined in accordance with that order.

(9)[124] References in this section to the time at which, or the day on which, the grant or renewal of an authorisation takes effect are references—

(a) in the case of the grant of an authorisation to which paragraph (c) does not apply, to the time at which or, as the case may be, day on which the authorisation is granted;

---

[123] By the RIPA (British Broadcasting Corporation) Order 2001 (SI 2001 No 1057), Art 4, in its application to the detection of television receivers only, s 43 has effect as if for subs (5) there were substituted—

(5) Section 27A shall have effect in relation to the renewal of an authorisation under this Part as if references to the grant of an authorisation included references to its renewal.

[124] By the RIPA (British Broadcasting Corporation) Order 2001 (SI 2001 No 1057), Art 4, in its application to the detection of television receivers only, s 43 has effect as if in subs (9) for paragraphs (a) to (c) there were substituted—

(a) in the case of the grant of an authorisation, to the time at which or, as the case may be, day on which the authorisation is granted;

(b) in the case of the renewal of an authorisation, to the time at which or, as the case may be, day on which the authorisation would have ceased to have effect but for the renewal.

(b) in the case of the renewal of an authorisation to which paragraph (c) does not apply, to the time at which or, as the case may be, day on which the authorisation would have ceased to have effect but for the renewal; and

(c) in the case of any grant or renewal that takes effect under subsection (2) of section 36 at a time or on a day later than that given by paragraph (a) or (b), to the time at which or, as the case may be, day on which the grant or renewal takes effect in accordance with that subsection.

(10) In relation to any authorisation granted by a member of any of the intelligence services, and in relation to any authorisation contained in a warrant issued by the Secretary of State on the application of a member of any of the intelligence services, this section has effect subject to the provisions of section 44.

Special rules for intelligence services authorisations

44.[125]—(1) Subject to subsection (2), a warrant containing an authorisation for the carrying out of intrusive surveillance—

(a) shall not be issued on the application of a member of any of the intelligence services, and

(b) if so issued shall not be renewed,

except under the hand of the Secretary of State or, in the case of a warrant issued by the Scottish Ministers (by virtue of provision made under section 63 of the Scotland Act 1998), a member of the Scottish Executive.

(2) In an urgent case in which—

(a) an application for a warrant containing an authorisation for the carrying out of intrusive surveillance has been made by a member of any of the intelligence services, and

(b) the Secretary of State has himself or the Scottish Ministers (by virtue of provision made under section 63 of the Scotland Act 1998) have themselves expressly authorised the issue of the warrant in that case,

the warrant may be issued (but not renewed) under the hand of a senior official or, as the case may be, a member of the staff of the Scottish Administration who is a member of the Senior Civil Service and is designated by the Scottish Ministers as a person under whose hand a warrant may be issued in such a case (in this section referred to as "a designated official")

(3) Subject to subsection (6), a warrant containing an authorisation for the carrying out of intrusive surveillance which—

(a) was issued, on the application of a member of any of the intelligence services, under the hand of a senior official or, as the case may be, a designated official, and

---

[125] Commencement: 25/9/2000 by SI 2000 No 2543. Amended by the Scotland Act 1998 (Transfer of Functions to the Scottish Ministers etc.) (No 2) Order 2000 (SI 2000 No 3253), Art 4(1), Sch 3, para 8.

(b) has not been renewed under the hand of the Secretary of State or, in the case of a warrant issued by the Scottish Ministers (by virtue of provision made under section 63 of the Scotland Act 1998), a member of the Scottish Executive,

shall cease to have effect at the end of the second working day following the day of the issue of the warrant, instead of at the time provided for by section 43(3).

(4) Subject to subsections (3) and (6), where any warrant for the carrying out of intrusive surveillance which is issued or was last renewed on the application of a member of any of the intelligence services, the warrant (unless renewed or, as the case may be, renewed again) shall cease to have effect at the following time, instead of at the time provided for by section 43(3), namely—

(a) in the case of a warrant that has not been renewed, at the end of the period of six months beginning with the day on which it was issued; and

(b) in any other case, at the end of the period of six months beginning with the day on which it would have ceased to have effect if not renewed again.

(5) Subject to subsection (6), where—

(a) an authorisation for the carrying out of directed surveillance is granted by a member of any of the intelligence services, and

(b) the authorisation is renewed by an instrument endorsed under the hand of the person renewing the authorisation with a statement that the renewal is believed to be necessary on grounds falling within section 32(3)(a) or (c),

the authorisation (unless renewed again) shall cease to have effect at the end of the period of six months beginning with the day on which it would have ceased to have effect but for the renewal, instead of at the time provided for by section 43(3).

(6) The Secretary of State may by order provide in relation to authorisations of such descriptions as may be specified in the order that subsection (3), (4) or (5) is to have effect as if the period at the end of which an authorisation of a description so specified is to cease to have effect were such period shorter than that provided for by that subsection as may be fixed by or determined in accordance with that order.

(7) Notwithstanding anything in section 43(2), in a case in which there is a combined warrant containing both—

(a) an authorisation for the carrying out of intrusive surveillance, and

(b) an authorisation for the carrying out of directed surveillance,

the reference in subsection (4) of this section to a warrant for the carrying out of intrusive surveillance is a reference to the warrant so far as it confers both authorisations.

Cancellation of authorisations

45.[126]—(1)[127]The person who granted or, as the case may be, last renewed an authorisation under this Part shall cancel it if—

    (a) he is satisfied that the authorisation is one in relation to which the requirements of section 28(2)(a) and (b), 29(2)(a) and (b) or, as the case may be, 32(2)(a) and (b) are no longer satisfied; or

    (b) in the case of an authorisation under section 29, he is satisfied that arrangements for the source's case that satisfy the requirements mentioned in subsection (2)(c) of that section no longer exist.

(1A),(1B)[128]

(2) Where an authorisation under this Part was granted or, as the case may be, last renewed—

    (a) by a person entitled to act for any other person, or

    (b) by the deputy of any other person,

that other person shall cancel the authorisation if he is satisfied as to either of the matters mentioned in subsection (1).

(3) Where an authorisation under this Part was granted or, as the case may be, last renewed by a person whose deputy had power to grant it, that deputy shall cancel the authorisation if he is satisfied as to either of the matters mentioned in subsection (1).

(4) The Secretary of State may by regulations provide for the person by whom any duty imposed by this section is to be performed in a case in which it would otherwise fall on a person who is no longer available to perform it.

(5) Regulations under subsection (4) may provide for the person on whom the duty is to fall to be a person appointed in accordance with the regulations.

(6) The references in this section to a person's deputy are references to the following—

    (a) in relation to—

        (i) a chief constable of a police force maintained under section 2 of the Police Act 1996,

        (ii) the Commissioner of Police for the City of London, or

        (iii) a chief constable of a police force maintained under or by virtue of section 1 of the Police (Scotland) Act 1967, to his designated deputy;

    (b) in relation to the Commissioner of Police of the Metropolis, to an Assistant Commissioner of Police of the Metropolis; *and*

    (c) in relation to the Chief Constable of the Royal Ulster Constabulary, to the Deputy Chief Constable of the Royal Ulster Constabulary;

---

[126] Commencement: 25/9/2000 by SI 2000 No 2543.

[127] Note that by the RIPA (British Broadcasting Corporation) Order 2001 (SI 2001 No 1057), Art 5, in its application to the detection of television receivers only, s 45 is amended.

[128] See note to subs (1).

(ca)[129] in relation to the Chairman of the Independent Police Complaints Commission, to his designated deputy;

[(d) in relation to the Director General of the National Criminal Intelligence Service, to his designated deputy; and

(e) in relation to the Director General of the National Crime Squad, to any person designated by him for the purposes of section 32(6)(l) or to his designated deputy.][130]

(7) In this section "designated deputy" has the same meaning as in section 34.

Scotland

Restrictions on authorisations extending to Scotland

46.[131]—(1) No person shall grant or renew an authorisation under this Part for the carrying out of any conduct if it appears to him—

(a) that the authorisation is not one for which this Part is the relevant statutory provision for all parts of the United Kingdom; and

(b) that all the conduct authorised by the grant or, as the case may be, renewal of the authorisation is likely to take place in Scotland.

(2) In relation to any authorisation, this Part is the relevant statutory provision for all parts of the United Kingdom in so far as it—

(a) is granted or renewed on the grounds that it is necessary in the interests of national security or in the interests of the economic well-being of the United Kingdom;

(b) is granted or renewed by or on the application of a person holding any office, rank or position with any of the public authorities specified in subsection (3);

(c) authorises conduct of a person holding an office, rank or position with any of the public authorities so specified;

(d) authorises conduct of an individual acting as a Covert Human Intelligence Source for the benefit of any of the public authorities so specified; or

(e) authorises conduct that is surveillance by virtue of section 48(4).

(3) The public authorities mentioned in subsection (2) are—

(a) each of the intelligence services;

(b) Her Majesty's forces;

(c) the Ministry of Defence;

(d) the Ministry of Defence Police;

---

[129] Inserted by the Independent Police Complaints Commission (Investigatory Powers) Order 2004 (SI 2004 No 815), Art 3(9).

[130] Words in square brackets in (d) and (e) will be omitted and word in italics at end of (b) inserted when Sch 4, para 143 of the SOCAP Act 2005 comes into force.

[131] Commencement: 25/9/2000 by SI 2000 No 2543.

(dza)[132] the Civil Nuclear Constabulary;

(da)[133] the OFT;

(db) *the Serious Organised Crime Agency*[134];

(e) the Commissioners of Customs and Excise; and

(f) the British Transport Police.

(4) For the purposes of so much of this Part as has effect in relation to any other public authority by virtue of—

(a) the fact that it is a public authority for the time being specified in Schedule 1, or

(b) an order under subsection (1)(d) of section 41 designating that authority for the purposes of that section,

the authorities specified in subsection (3) of this section shall be treated as including that authority to the extent that the Secretary of State by order directs that the authority is a relevant public authority or, as the case may be, is a designated authority for all parts of the United Kingdom.

Supplemental provision for Part II

Power to extend or modify authorisation provisions

47.[135]—(1) The Secretary of State may by order do one or both of the following—

(a) apply this Part, with such modifications as he thinks fit, to any such surveillance that is neither directed nor intrusive as may be described in the order;

(b) provide for any description of Directed Surveillance to be treated for the purposes of this Part as intrusive surveillance.

(2) No order shall be made under this section unless a draft of it has been laid before Parliament and approved by a resolution of each House.

Interpretation of Part II

48.[136]—(1)[137] In this Part—

"covert human intelligence source" shall be construed in accordance with section 26(8);

"directed" and "intrusive", in relation to surveillance, shall be construed in accordance with section 26(2) to (6);

"OFT" means the Office of Fair Trading;

---

132 Inserted by the Energy Act 2004, s 69, Sch 14, para 8(1).

133 Inserted by the Enterprise Act, s 199(10).

134 Words in italics inserted when Sch 4, para 144 of the SOCAP Act 2005 comes into force.

135 Commencement: 25/9/2000 by SI 2000 No 2543.

136 Commencement: 25/9/2000 by SI 2000 No 2543.

137 Amended by the Enterprise Act, s 199(11).

"private vehicle" means (subject to subsection (7)(a)) any vehicle which is used primarily for the private purposes of the person who owns it or of a person otherwise having the right to use it;

"residential premises" means (subject to subsection (7)(b)) so much of any premises as is for the time being occupied or used by any person, however temporarily, for residential purposes or otherwise as living accommodation (including hotel or prison accommodation that is so occupied or used);

"senior authorising officer" means a person who by virtue of subsection (6) of section 32 is a senior authorising officer for the purposes of that section;

"surveillance" shall be construed in accordance with subsections (2) to (4);

"surveillance device" means any apparatus designed or adapted for use in surveillance.

(2) Subject to subsection (3), in this Part "surveillance" includes—

(a) monitoring, observing or listening to persons, their movements, their conversations or their other activities or communications;

(b) recording anything monitored, observed or listened to in the course of surveillance; and

(c) surveillance by or with the assistance of a surveillance device.

(3) References in this Part to surveillance do not include references to—

(a) any conduct of a covert human intelligence source for obtaining or recording (whether or not using a surveillance device) any information which is disclosed in the presence of the source;

(b) the use of a covert human intelligence source for so obtaining or recording information; or

(c) any such entry on or interference with property or with wireless telegraphy as would be unlawful unless authorised under—

(i) section 5 of the Intelligence Services Act 1994 (warrants for the intelligence services); or

(ii) Part III of the Police Act 1997 (powers of the police and of Customs officers).

(4) References in this Part to surveillance include references to the interception of a communication in the course of its transmission by means of a postal service or telecommunication system if, and only if—

(a) the communication is one sent by or intended for a person who has consented to the interception of communications sent by or to him; and

(b) there is no interception warrant authorising the interception.

(5) References in this Part to an individual holding an office or position with a public authority include references to any member, official or employee of that authority.

(6) For the purposes of this Part the activities of a covert human intelligence source which are to be taken as activities for the benefit of a particular public

authority include any conduct of his as such a source which is in response to inducements or requests made by or on behalf of that authority.

(7) In subsection (1)—

    (a) the reference to a person having the right to use a vehicle does not, in relation to a motor vehicle, include a reference to a person whose right to use the vehicle derives only from his having paid, or undertaken to pay, for the use of the vehicle and its driver for a particular journey; and

    (b) the reference to premises occupied or used by any person for residential purposes or otherwise as living accommodation does not include a reference to so much of any premises as constitutes any common area to which he has or is allowed access in connection with his use or occupation of any accommodation.

(8) In this section—

"premises" includes any vehicle or moveable structure and any other place whatever, whether or not occupied as land;

"vehicle" includes any vessel, aircraft or hovercraft.

6

DATA PROTECTED BY ENCRYPTION: RIPA, PART III, ss 49–56

A. Discussion

Note: Part III of RIPA was not in force at the date of writing.

Part III creates legal powers to serve notices requiring disclosure of encrypted **6.01** information in an intelligible form or the means (the key) to de-encrypt it, and criminal sanctions for non-compliance. The importance of Part III in the context of RIPA, the Police Act 1997, the Intelligence Service Act 1994 and the Security Service Act 1989 is that the purpose of surveillance or interception could be frustrated if information was not capable of being rendered intelligible in reasonable time once it came into the hands of the authorities.

There is as yet no formal Code of Practice in relation to Part III but a preliminary **6.02** draft Code entitled 'Investigation of Electronic Data protected by Encryption' was circulated by the Home Office during the passage of the RIPA Bill in 1999/2000. The position stated by the Office of the Surveillance Commissioner in 2005 is that:

> A separate Code of Practice on encryption (Part III of RIPA) is being drafted for consultation and then to be brought before Parliament. It is not possible yet to give a timetable for this. Part III of RIPA is not yet in force.

A copy of the preliminary draft is in circulation on the internet from unofficial sources but is not reproduced here because it pre-dates the Act and contains references which do not tally with RIPA as enacted.

Notices requiring disclosure

The effect of s 49 is that certain persons (those having what is described as 'the **6.03** appropriate permission': see para **6.05** below) may, if certain criteria are met, serve upon any person whom they believe has a key to 'protected information' (and can therefore de-encrypt or access it), a disclosure notice requiring disclosure of the information in intelligible form or (sometimes) disclosure of the key(s) to access it. That is the effect of s 49, and its provisions will now be discussed in more detail.

Part III terms defined

6.04 'key'—s 56(1) defines 'key' as:

> . . . any key, code, password, algorithm[1] or other data the use of which (with or without other keys)—
> (a) allows access to the electronic data, or
> (b) facilitates the putting of the data into an intelligible form . . .

'protected information' is then defined in the same section as:

> . . . any electronic data which, without the key to the data—
> (a) cannot, or cannot readily, be accessed, or
> (b) cannot, or cannot readily, be put into an intelligible form . . .

'Person with the appropriate permission'

6.05 This composite expression refers to any 'person'[2] who has 'the appropriate permission' under the provisions of Sch 2. Reference may be had to the text of Sch 2 for the detailed list of who, in what circumstances, will be said to have the appropriate permission to serve a s 49 notice, but the following is a brief summary.

Judicial permission (Sch 2, para 1)

6.06 Schedule 2, para 1 confirms that public authorities may seek permission to serve a s 49 notice from a circuit judge or a district judge (magistrates courts) in England and Wales, a sheriff in Scotland or a county court judge in Northern Ireland. If judicial permission has been granted then further permission is not required in order to serve a s 49 notice.

6.07 Essentially, for public authorities other than the police, Customs and Excise, HM Forces and the security and intelligence agencies (MI5, SIS, GCHQ), permission to serve a s 49 notice must be obtained from one of the above judicial authorities by virtue of paras 4(3) and (4) of Sch 2. For the police, etc the judicial permission avenue under para 1 is available but other avenues for obtaining permission may be available, discussed below. Note that police constables cannot

---

[1] Computational process which will find a solution to the problem or class of problems it is designed to solve.

[2] Section 81(1): any organisation or any association or combination of persons.

have permission under para 1 unless they are of superintendent rank or above, or permission to give a s 49 notice has been given by a person of that rank or above (Sch 2, para 6(2)).[3]

Where data was obtained under warrant or authorisation (Sch 2, para 2)

Where protected information which:[4]   **6.08**

(a) has come into the possession of any person by means of the exercise of a statutory power to seize, detain, inspect, search or otherwise to interfere with documents or other property, or is likely to do so;

(b) has come into the possession of any person by means of the exercise of any statutory power to intercept communications, or is likely to do so;

(c) has come into the possession of any person by means of the exercise of any power conferred by an authorisation under section 22(3) or under Part II, or as a result of the giving of a notice under section 22(4), or is likely to do so . . .[5]

and was obtained under a warrant authorised by the Secretary of State (such as under an interception warrant under Part I of RIPA) then permission to serve a s 49 Notice can be obtained from the Secretary of State in the case of the police, customs, SOCA and persons holding office under the Crown (see Sch 2, para 2).

Similarly where (a)–(c) above apply, where a judicial warrant was given to any   **6.09** body for the obtaining of the data, such as under PACE, then permission to serve a s 49 Notice can be obtained from a judicial office holder of a level which would have been entitled to issue the judicial warrant.[6]

Where (again, in cases within (a)–(c) above) authorisation was obtained under   **6.10** Part III of the Police Act 1997 (by police, customs and SOCA) then permission to serve a s 49 notice may be obtained from a person of a seniority entitled to be an authorising officer under s 93 of that Act (see s 93 of the 1997 Act and the extensive discussion in Chapter 1.

---

[3] This requirement does not apply to SOCA. Instead the requirement is that permission must have been given by the Director General or by a member of staff of SOCA designated by him (Sch 2, para 6(3A)). For customs, an officer does not have permission under para 1 unless the commissioners have also given permission or an officer of a rank above a designated level has given permission to serve a s 49 notice (Sch 2, para 6(4)). In relation to HM Forces, a person of at least the rank of lieutenant colonel must have given permission before an authorisation under para 1 can be effective (unless the person obtaining the judicial permission is in any event of that level of seniority)—Sch 2, para 6(5).

[4] The list which follows is the text of s 49((1)(a)–(c).

[5] Ie the provisions of Part I, Chapter 2 in relation to accessing communications data and those under Part II in relation to covert surveillance and CHIS.

[6] Schedule 2, para 2(8) indicates that this includes (a) any judge of the Crown Court or of the High Court of Justiciary; (b) any sheriff; (c) any justice of the peace; (d) any resident magistrate in Northern Ireland; or (e) any person holding any such judicial office as entitles him to exercise the jurisdiction of a judge of the Crown Court or of a justice of the peace.

Secretary of State's permission (security and intelligence services) (Sch 2, para 3)

6.11   Under Sch 2, para 3 permission to serve a s 49 Notice may be obtained by the security and intelligence services from the Secretary of State where protected material falling within the classes (a)–(c) listed above has been, or is likely to be, obtained by them (or by them and another public authority) under statutory powers without a warrant (ie outside Sch 2, paras 1 and 2).

Police, SOCA, customs and HM Forces permission where data obtained under statute but without warrant (Sch 2, para 4)

6.12   For these bodies, where protected material which *either:*

(a) falls within (a)–(c) above; *or*

(b) is material which came into the possession of any person as a result of being disclosed under a statutory duty,

has been or is likely to be obtained under statutory powers by the above bodies without a warrant, then the body in question has permission to serve a s 49 Notice.

Note that police constables cannot have permission under the above provision unless they are of superintendent rank or above (or permission for them to give a s 49 notice has been given by a person of that rank or above) (Sch 2, para 6(2)).[7]

Data obtained without exercise of statutory powers (Sch 2, para 5) (intelligence services)

6.13   In the case of protected information which has come into the hands of the intelligence services without the exercise of statutory powers (or is likely to come into their hands), the appropriate permission may be obtained from the Secretary of State.

Permission where information obtained under of the Terrorism Act 2000 or the Prevention of Terrorism (Temporary Provisions) Act 1989, s 13B

6.14   In the case of information obtained by the police under s 44 of the Terrorism Act 2000 or ss 13A or 13B of the Prevention of Terrorism (Temporary Provisions) Act 1989 then permission to serve a s 49 notice may be given by persons of or above the ranks set out in those Acts (generally senior officers). See RIPA, Sch 2, para 6(3).

The criteria determining when a person with the appropriate permission may serve a s 49 disclosure notice

6.15   There are several requirements which must be satisfied before a s 49 Notice may be served by a person having the appropriate permission.

---

[7] Similarly, in the case of SOCA see Sch 2, para 6(3A) and in the case of customs and HM Forces, see Sch 2, para 6(4) and (5).

First, the protected information must fall into one of the following categories namely that it:

(a) has come into the possession of any person by means of the exercise of a statutory power to seize, detain, inspect, search or otherwise to interfere with documents or other property[8], or is likely to do so;

(b) has come into the possession of any person by means of the exercise of any statutory power to intercept communications, or is likely to do so;

(c) has come into the possession of any person by means of the exercise of any power conferred by an authorisation under section 22(3) or under Part II, or as a result of the giving of a notice under section 22(4), or is likely to do so[9];

(d) has come into the possession of any person as a result of having been provided or disclosed in pursuance of any statutory duty (whether or not one arising as a result of a request for information), or is likely to do so; or

(e) has, by any other lawful means not involving the exercise of statutory powers, come into the possession of[10] any of the intelligence services, the police, SOCA, [or] the customs and excise, or is likely so to come into the possession of any of those services, the police, SOCA, [or][11] or the customs and excise.

Second, that person must:

- believe on reasonable grounds that a key to the information is in the possession of the person to be served; *and*
- that the imposition of a disclosure requirement is necessary:

— in the interests of national security; or
— for the purpose of preventing or detecting crime;[12] or
— in the interests of the economic well-being of the United Kingdom; or
— for the purpose of securing the effective exercise; or
— proper performance by any public authority of any statutory power or statutory duty; *and*

- that the imposition of a disclosure requirement is proportionate to what is sought to be achieved by its imposition; *and*
- that it is not reasonably practicable for the person with the appropriate permission to obtain possession of the protected information in an intelligible form without the giving of a notice.

(See s 49(2).)

---

[8] Eg under PACE 1984 or an authorisation under the Police Act 1997, Part III.

[9] Ie the provisions of Part I, Chapter 2 in relation to accessing communications data and under Part II in relation to covert surveillance and CHIS.

[10] Eg where disclosed voluntarily to the police.

[11] Words in square brackets will be omitted and references to SOCA inserted when Sch 4, para 145 of the SOCAP Act 2005 comes into force.

[12] The reference to 'crime' is wider than the reference to 'serious crime' in the test applied, for example, under s 32(3).

Who should be served?

6.16 The obvious answer would be 'the person who holds the key', but there will arise circumstances where more than one person is in that position. Section 49(5)–(7) provides that where an employee is in possession, and also a body corporate (company, firm, etc) is in possession, then the notice must be given to a senior officer of the corporate body, or in the case of a firm, to a partner or more senior employee unless it is not reasonably practicable to do so, or unless serving the notice on the senior person would 'in the special circumstances of the case' defeat the purposes for which the key is requested, perhaps where the senior officer is under suspicion.

What may the notice require and how may it be complied with?

6.17 The notice may require the disclosure of the protected information in intelligible form, in other words the information decoded by the person having the key.[13] Section 50(1) is to the effect that a person served with a s 49 notice will have complied with it if he *either* discloses any key in his possession *or* uses the key to obtain access to the information in intelligible form (which he then supplies). The notice has the legal effect that the person served with it is entitled to make use of any key in his possession to access it.

If a person does not have the information (but has a key) or if access cannot be obtained to it without some additional key which the person served does not have, or if the notice itself requires disclosure of the key, then the person served will have complied if he discloses a copy of any key to that information in his possession (s 50(3)).

When can the Notice *require* disclosure of the key as opposed to disclosure of the information accessed by it?

6.18 By s 51 the Notice may require disclosure of the key (without offering the person served any option to serve a copy of the decoded information) if the person who granted permission for service of the notice (or any person who could have given appropriate permission) directs that the disclosure requirement can be complied with only by service of the key. Such a direction[14] may only be given if the person giving it believes:

(a) that there are special circumstances of the case[15] which mean that the purposes for which it was believed necessary to impose the requirement in

---

[13] This does raise the problem of demonstrating compliance where the information after decoding is, in fact, unintelligible.

[14] Section 51(2) imposes requirements as to the seniority of a person making a 'key only' direction, in the cases of the police, customs, SOCA and HM Forces. In such cases either the Intelligence Services Commissioner (in the case of HM Forces) or the Chief Surveillance Commissioner (all other cases), must be notified not more than seven days after the date of the authorisation.

[15] There is no definition of 'special circumstances'.

question would be defeated, in whole or in part, if the direction were not given; and

(b) that the giving of the direction is proportionate to what is sought to be achieved by prohibiting any compliance with the requirement in question otherwise than by the disclosure of the key itself.

Section 51(5) indicates that when considering proportionality, the extent and **6.19** nature of any protected information, in addition to the protected information in respect of which the disclosure requirement is imposed, to which the key is also a key must be considered (analogous to collateral intrusion as applied to keys), as must any adverse effect that the giving of the direction might have on a business carried on by the person on whom the disclosure requirement is imposed.

If a person has more than one key or set of keys to the data in his possession then disclosure of one key or combination of keys which enables the making of the information intelligible will suffice without him having to disclose all of them: s 50(5), (6). On the other hand if more than one key is needed to enable access, the person served must disclose all keys which he has to the protected information (s 50(7)).

Section 55 imposes specific duties upon: **6.20**

- the Secretary of State,
- every Minister of the Crown in charge of a government department,
- every Chief Officer of Police,
- the Commissioners of Customs,
- the Director General of SOCA,
- every person whose officers or employees include persons whose duties involve the giving of disclosure notices

to ensure, among other matters, that there are arrangements to ensure that disclosed keys are not misused (they must be used only in relation to the protected information in respect of which they were directed to be disclosed, or information in respect of which they could have been directed to be disclosed), are used reasonably, that there are secure arrangements for their storage and destruction and that the minimum necessary number of copies are made. People who suffer loss (whether those who comply with a Notice or those whose keys were disclosed) due to breaches of those duties have a cause of action under s 55(4).

Signature keys not required to be disclosed

In the case of keys which are 'signature keys' (keys intended for the sole purpose of **6.21** generating electronic signatures, and not used for anything else), s 49(9) operates so that no disclosure Notice may be given. On the general subject of electronic signatures see EC Directive 1999/93/EC and on a Community framework for electronic signatures, see the Electronic Signatures Regulations (SI 2002 No 0318) and the Electronic Communications Act 2000. Section 49(9) may be open to criticism that disclosure of a key to access data may lead to disclosure of a person's signature key, and there appears to be no protection offered against such indirect access to signature keys.

What form must the Notice take?

6.22 Forms of Notice may be expected to appear when a formal Code of Practice is produced, but the basic requirements are listed in s 49(4), including requirements that the Notice must be in writing, must give details of the person giving the notice, and must impose time limits.

What if the person served no longer has the key?

6.23 By s 50(8), a person served with a Notice but who no longer has the key must disclose information which he has which would facilitate the obtaining or discovery of the key or the putting of the information into intelligible form.

Compensation

6.24 In a manner similar to the compensation arrangements imposed by s 24 of the Act in relation to access to communications data under Part I, the Secretary of State is required to ensure that such arrangements are in force to contribute to the costs incurred by persons complying with disclosure notices (see s 52).

What is the consequence of failure to co-operate?

6.25 Failure to comply with a Notice is an offence[16] if done knowingly: s 53(1). Furthermore a weak evidential presumption in s 53(2) is made to the effect that if it is shown that a person who failed to comply had a key to the data in his possession at any time before the Notice was served, then it is presumed that he had the key at the time of service. That applies unless the defendant adduces enough evidence to raise an issue with respect to his possession of the key and the prosecution then fail to rebut that issue beyond reasonable doubt.

Section 53(4) provides a defence of showing that it was not reasonably practicable to make the disclosure within the time required but that the defendant made the disclosure as soon thereafter as it was reasonably practicable to do so.

Secrecy requirements and tipping-off

6.26 By s 54(2), a requirement may be included on the face of a s 49 notice that the person served must keep *secret* the giving of the notice, its contents or anything done

---

[16] Punishable by up to two years' imprisonment or a fine or both when tried on indictment or imprisonment for up to six months or a fine not exceeding the statutory maximum (or both) when tried summarily (s 53(5)).

in pursuance of it. Such a notice may be included only where the protected information has come into the possession of the police, customs, SOCA or any of the intelligence services (or is likely to come into their hands), by means which it is *reasonable to keep secret* in order to maintain the effectiveness of any investigation or operation, or to maintain the effectiveness of investigatory techniques generally, or in the interests of the safety or well-being of any person.[17] Disclosing to anything covered by a secrecy requirement is an offence punishable by up to five years in prison or a fine or both, when tried on indictment, or imprisonment for up to six months or a fine, or both, when tried summarily (s 54(4)).

There are various specific defences to the charge of tipping-off, such as defences in **6.27** relation to disclosure to legal advisers or commissioners or to others authorised in the notice, and a defence in relation to disclosure caused entirely (and effectively unavoidably) by software designed to detect tampering with keys. It is also a defence to show that the defendant did not know and had no reasonable grounds for suspecting that the notice contained a secrecy requirement covering the information which was disclosed (see s 54(5)–(10)).

The text of RIPA Part III as amended follows.

B. Text of Part III

REGULATION OF INVESTIGATORY POWERS ACT 2000 (AS AMENDED)

Part III[18]
Investigation of Electronic Data Protected by Encryption etc.

Power to require disclosure

Notices requiring disclosure

49.[19]—(1) This section applies where any protected information—
  (a) has come into the possession of any person by means of the exercise of a statutory power to seize, detain, inspect, search or otherwise to interfere with documents or other property, or is likely to do so;
  (b) has come into the possession of any person by means of the exercise of any statutory power to intercept communications, or is likely to do so;

---

[17] Section 54(3).
[18] At the time of writing the whole of Part III of RIPA had not been brought into force (ss 49–56). [19] Section not in force.

(c) has come into the possession of any person by means of the exercise of any power conferred by an authorisation under section 22(3) or under Part II, or as a result of the giving of a notice under section 22(4), or is likely to do so;

(d) has come into the possession of any person as a result of having been provided or disclosed in pursuance of any statutory duty (whether or not one arising as a result of a request for information), or is likely to do so; or

(e) has, by any other lawful means not involving the exercise of statutory powers, come into the possession of any of the intelligence services, the police, *SOCA*, [or] the customs and excise, or is likely so to come into the possession of any of those services, the police, *SOCA*, [or][20] or the customs and excise.

(2) If any person with the appropriate permission under Schedule 2 believes, on reasonable grounds—

(a) that a key to the protected information is in the possession of any person,

(b) that the imposition of a disclosure requirement in respect of the protected information is-

(i) necessary on grounds falling within subsection (3), or

(ii) necessary for the purpose of securing the effective exercise or proper performance by any public authority of any statutory power or statutory duty,

(c) that the imposition of such a requirement is proportionate to what is sought to be achieved by its imposition, and

(d) that it is not reasonably practicable for the person with the appropriate permission to obtain possession of the protected information in an intelligible form without the giving of a notice under this section,

the person with that permission may, by notice to the person whom he believes to have possession of the key, impose a disclosure requirement in respect of the protected information.

(3) A disclosure requirement in respect of any protected information is necessary on grounds falling within this subsection if it is necessary—

(a) in the interests of national security;

(b) for the purpose of preventing or detecting crime; or

(c) in the interests of the economic well-being of the United Kingdom.

(4) A notice under this section imposing a disclosure requirement in respect of any protected information-

(a) must be given in writing or (if not in writing) must be given in a manner that produces a record of its having been given;

---

[20] Words in square brackets will be omitted and references to SOCA inserted when Sch 4, para 145 of the SOCAP Act 2005 comes into force.

   (b) must describe the protected information to which the notice relates;

   (c) must specify the matters falling within subsection (2)(b)(i) or (ii) by reference to which the notice is given;

   (d) must specify the office, rank or position held by the person giving it;

   (e) must specify the office, rank or position of the person who for the purposes of Schedule 2 granted permission for the giving of the notice or (if the person giving the notice was entitled to give it without another person's permission) must set out the circumstances in which that entitlement arose;

   (f) must specify the time by which the notice is to be complied with; and

   (g) must set out the disclosure that is required by the notice and the form and manner in which it is to be made;

and the time specified for the purposes of paragraph (f) must allow a period for compliance which is reasonable in all the circumstances.

(5) Where it appears to a person with the appropriate permission—

   (a) that more than one person is in possession of the key to any protected information,

   (b) that any of those persons is in possession of that key in his capacity as an officer or employee of any body corporate, and

   (c) that another of those persons is the body corporate itself or another officer or employee of the body corporate,

a notice under this section shall not be given, by reference to his possession of the key, to any officer or employee of the body corporate unless he is a senior officer of the body corporate or it appears to the person giving the notice that there is no senior officer of the body corporate and (in the case of an employee) no more senior employee of the body corporate to whom it is reasonably practicable to give the notice.

(6) Where it appears to a person with the appropriate permission—

   (a) that more than one person is in possession of the key to any protected information,

   (b) that any of those persons is in possession of that key in his capacity as an employee of a firm, and

   (c) that another of those persons is the firm itself or a partner of the firm,

a notice under this section shall not be given, by reference to his possession of the key, to any employee of the firm unless it appears to the person giving the notice that there is neither a partner of the firm nor a more senior employee of the firm to whom it is reasonably practicable to give the notice.

(7) Subsections (5) and (6) shall not apply to the extent that there are special circumstances of the case that mean that the purposes for which the notice is given would be defeated, in whole or in part, if the notice were given to

the person to whom it would otherwise be required to be given by those subsections.

(8) A notice under this section shall not require the making of any disclosure to any person other than—

(a) the person giving the notice; or

(b) such other person as may be specified in or otherwise identified by, or in accordance with, the provisions of the notice.

(9) A notice under this section shall not require the disclosure of any key which—

(a) is intended to be used for the purpose only of generating electronic signatures; and

(b) has not in fact been used for any other purpose.

(10) In this section "senior officer", in relation to a body corporate, means a director, manager, secretary or other similar officer of the body corporate; and for this purpose "director", in relation to a body corporate whose affairs are managed by its members, means a member of the body corporate.

(11) Schedule 2 (definition of the appropriate permission) shall have effect.

Effect of notice imposing disclosure requirement

50.[21]—(1) Subject to the following provisions of this section, the effect of a section 49 notice imposing a disclosure requirement in respect of any protected information on a person who is in possession at a relevant time of both the protected information and a means of obtaining access to the information and of disclosing it in an intelligible form is that he—

(a) shall be entitled to use any key in his possession to obtain access to the information or to put it into an intelligible form; and

(b) shall be required, in accordance with the notice imposing the requirement, to make a disclosure of the information in an intelligible form.

(2) A person subject to a requirement under subsection (1)(b) to make a disclosure of any information in an intelligible form shall be taken to have complied with that requirement if—

(a) he makes, instead, a disclosure of any key to the protected information that is in his possession; and

(b) that disclosure is made, in accordance with the notice imposing the requirement, to the person to whom, and by the time by which, he was required to provide the information in that form.

---

[21] Not in force.

(3) Where, in a case in which a disclosure requirement in respect of any protected information is imposed on any person by a section 49 notice—

(a) that person is not in possession of the information,

(b) that person is incapable, without the use of a key that is not in his possession, of obtaining access to the information and of disclosing it in an intelligible form, or

(c) the notice states, in pursuance of a direction under section 51, that it can be complied with only by the disclosure of a key to the information,

the effect of imposing that disclosure requirement on that person is that he shall be required, in accordance with the notice imposing the requirement, to make a disclosure of any key to the protected information that is in his possession at a relevant time.

(4) Subsections (5) to (7) apply where a person ("the person given notice")—

(a) is entitled or obliged to disclose a key to protected information for the purpose of complying with any disclosure requirement imposed by a section 49 notice; and

(b) is in possession of more than one key to that information.

(5) It shall not be necessary, for the purpose of complying with the requirement, for the person given notice to make a disclosure of any keys in addition to those the disclosure of which is, alone, sufficient to enable the person to whom they are disclosed to obtain access to the information and to put it into an intelligible form.

(6) Where—

(a) subsection (5) allows the person given notice to comply with a requirement without disclosing all of the keys in his possession, and

(b) there are different keys, or combinations of keys, in the possession of that person the disclosure of which would, under that subsection, constitute compliance,

the person given notice may select which of the keys, or combination of keys, to disclose for the purpose of complying with that requirement in accordance with that subsection.

(7) Subject to subsections (5) and (6), the person given notice shall not be taken to have complied with the disclosure requirement by the disclosure of a key unless he has disclosed every key to the protected information that is in his possession at a relevant time.

(8) Where, in a case in which a disclosure requirement in respect of any protected information is imposed on any person by a section 49 notice-

(a) that person has been in possession of the key to that information but is no longer in possession of it,

(b) if he had continued to have the key in his possession, he would have been required by virtue of the giving of the notice to disclose it, and

207

(c) he is in possession, at a relevant time, of information to which subsection (9) applies,

the effect of imposing that disclosure requirement on that person is that he shall be required, in accordance with the notice imposing the requirement, to disclose all such information to which subsection (9) applies as is in his possession and as he may be required, in accordance with that notice, to disclose by the person to whom he would have been required to disclose the key.

(9) This subsection applies to any information that would facilitate the obtaining or discovery of the key or the putting of the protected information into an intelligible form.

(10) In this section "relevant time", in relation to a disclosure requirement imposed by a section 49 notice, means the time of the giving of the notice or any subsequent time before the time by which the requirement falls to be complied with.

Cases in which key required

51.[22]—(1) A section 49 notice imposing a disclosure requirement in respect of any protected information shall not contain a statement for the purposes of section 50(3)(c) unless—

(a) the person who for the purposes of Schedule 2 granted the permission for the giving of the notice in relation to that information, or

(b) any person whose permission for the giving of a such a notice in relation to that information would constitute the appropriate permission under that Schedule,

has given a direction that the requirement can be complied with only by the disclosure of the key itself.

(2) A direction for the purposes of subsection (1) by the police, *SOCA,*[23] the customs and excise or a member of Her Majesty's forces shall not be given—

(a) in the case of a direction by the police or by a member of Her Majesty's forces who is a member of a police force, except by or with the permission of a chief officer of police;

(aa) in the case of a direction by SOCA, except by or with the permission of the Director General of the Serious Organised Crime Agency;

(b) in the case of a direction by the customs and excise, except by or with the permission of the Commissioners of Customs and Excise; or

(c) in the case of a direction by a member of Her Majesty's forces who is not a member of a police force, except by or with the permission of a person of or above the rank of brigadier or its equivalent.

---

[22] Not in force.
[23] Reference to SOCA, subs (aa), and the words in italics in subs (3)and (6)inserted with effect from the date when Sch 4, para 146 of the SOCAP Act 2005 comes into force.

(3) A permission given for the purposes of subsection (2) by a chief officer of police, *the Director General of the Serious Organised Crime Agency*, the Commissioners of Customs and Excise or a person of or above any such rank as is mentioned in paragraph (c) of that subsection must be given expressly in relation to the direction in question.

(4) A person shall not give a direction for the purposes of subsection (1) unless he believes—

    (a) that there are special circumstances of the case which mean that the purposes for which it was believed necessary to impose the requirement in question would be defeated, in whole or in part, if the direction were not given; and

    (b) that the giving of the direction is proportionate to what is sought to be achieved by prohibiting any compliance with the requirement in question otherwise than by the disclosure of the key itself.

(5) The matters to be taken into account in considering whether the requirement of subsection (4)(b) is satisfied in the case of any direction shall include—

    (a) the extent and nature of any protected information, in addition to the protected information in respect of which the disclosure requirement is imposed, to which the key is also a key; and

    (b) any adverse effect that the giving of the direction might have on a business carried on by the person on whom the disclosure requirement is imposed.

(6) Where a direction for the purposes of subsection (1) is given by a chief officer of police, *by the Director General of the Serious Organised Crime Agency*, by the Commissioners of Customs and Excise or by a member of Her Majesty's forces, the person giving the direction shall give a notification that he has done so—

    (a) in a case where the direction is given—

        (i) by a member of Her Majesty's forces who is not a member of a police force, and

        (ii) otherwise than in connection with activities of members of Her Majesty's forces in Northern Ireland,

    to the Intelligences Services Commissioner; and

    (b) in any other case, to the Chief Surveillance Commissioner.

(7) A notification under subsection (6)—

    (a) must be given not more than seven days after the day of the giving of the direction to which it relates; and

    (b) may be given either in writing or by being transmitted to the Commissioner in question by electronic means.

Contributions to costs

Arrangements for payments for disclosure

52.[24]—(1)It shall be the duty of the Secretary of State to ensure that such arrangements are in force as he thinks appropriate for requiring or authorising, in such cases as he thinks fit, the making to persons to whom section 49 notices are given of appropriate contributions towards the costs incurred by them in complying with such notices.

(2) For the purpose of complying with his duty under this section, the Secretary of State may make arrangements for payments to be made out of money provided by Parliament.

Offences

Failure to comply with a notice

53. [25]—(1) A person to whom a section 49 notice has been given is guilty of an offence if he knowingly fails, in accordance with the notice, to make the disclosure required by virtue of the giving of the notice.

(2) In proceedings against any person for an offence under this section, if it is shown that that person was in possession of a key to any protected information at any time before the time of the giving of the section 49 notice, that person shall be taken for the purposes of those proceedings to have continued to be in possession of that key at all subsequent times, unless it is shown that the key was not in his possession after the giving of the notice and before the time by which he was required to disclose it.

(3) For the purposes of this section a person shall be taken to have shown that he was not in possession of a key to protected information at a particular time if—

   (a) sufficient evidence of that fact is adduced to raise an issue with respect to it; and

   (b) the contrary is not proved beyond a reasonable doubt.

(4) In proceedings against any person for an offence under this section it shall be a defence for that person to show—

   (a) that it was not reasonably practicable for him to make the disclosure required by virtue of the giving of the section 49 notice before the time by which he was required, in accordance with that notice, to make it; but

   (b) that he did make that disclosure as soon after that time as it was reasonably practicable for him to do so.

---

[24] Not in force.   [25] Not in force.

(5) A person guilty of an offence under this section shall be liable—

    (a) on conviction on indictment, to imprisonment for a term not exceeding two years or to a fine, or to both;

    (b) on summary conviction, to imprisonment for a term not exceeding six months or to a fine not exceeding the statutory maximum, or to both.

Tipping-off

54.[26]—(1) This section applies where a section 49 notice contains a provision requiring—

    (a) the person to whom the notice is given, and

    (b) every other person who becomes aware of it or of its contents,

to keep secret the giving of the notice, its contents and the things done in pursuance of it.

(2) A requirement to keep anything secret shall not be included in a section 49 notice except where—

    (a) it is included with the consent of the person who for the purposes of Schedule 2 granted the permission for the giving of the notice; or

    (b) the person who gives the notice is himself a person whose permission for the giving of such a notice in relation to the information in question would have constituted appropriate permission under that Schedule.

(3) A section 49 notice shall not contain a requirement to keep anything secret except where the protected information to which it relates—

    (a) has come into the possession of the police, *SOCA*,[27] the customs and excise or any of the intelligence services, or

    (b) is likely to come into the possession of the police, *SOCA*, the customs and excise or any of the intelligence services,

by means which it is reasonable, in order to maintain the effectiveness of any investigation or operation or of investigatory techniques generally, or in the interests of the safety or well-being of any person, to keep secret from a particular person.

(4) A person who makes a disclosure to any other person of anything that he is required by a section 49 notice to keep secret shall be guilty of an offence and liable—

    (a) on conviction on indictment, to imprisonment for a term not exceeding five years or to a fine, or to both;

    (b) on summary conviction, to imprisonment for a term not exceeding six months or to a fine not exceeding the statutory maximum, or to both.

---

[26] Not in force.

[27] References to SOCA, inserted with effect from the date when Sch 4, para 147 of the SOCAP Act 2005 comes into force.

(5) In proceedings against any person for an offence under this section in respect of any disclosure, it shall be a defence for that person to show that—

    (a) the disclosure was effected entirely by the operation of software designed to indicate when a key to protected information has ceased to be secure; and

    (b) that person could not reasonably have been expected to take steps, after being given the notice or (as the case may be) becoming aware of it or of its contents, to prevent the disclosure.

(6) In proceedings against any person for an offence under this section in respect of any disclosure, it shall be a defence for that person to show that—

    (a) the disclosure was made by or to a professional legal adviser in connection with the giving, by the adviser to any client of his, of advice about the effect of provisions of this Part; and

    (b) the person to whom or, as the case may be, by whom it was made was the client or a representative of the client.

(7) In proceedings against any person for an offence under this section in respect of any disclosure, it shall be a defence for that person to show that the disclosure was made by a legal adviser—

    (a) in contemplation of, or in connection with, any legal proceedings; and

    (b) for the purposes of those proceedings.

(8) Neither subsection (6) nor subsection (7) applies in the case of a disclosure made with a view to furthering any criminal purpose.

(9) In proceedings against any person for an offence under this section in respect of any disclosure, it shall be a defence for that person to show that the disclosure was confined to a disclosure made to a relevant Commissioner or authorised—

    (a) by such a Commissioner;

    (b) by the terms of the notice;

    (c) by or on behalf of the person who gave the notice; or

    (d) by or on behalf of a person who-

        (i) is in lawful possession of the protected information to which the notice relates; and

        (ii) came into possession of that information as mentioned in section 49(1).

(10) In proceedings for an offence under this section against a person other than the person to whom the notice was given, it shall be a defence for the person against whom the proceedings are brought to show that he neither knew nor had reasonable grounds for suspecting that the notice contained a requirement to keep secret what was disclosed.

(11) In this section "relevant Commissioner" means the Interception of Communications Commissioner, the Intelligence Services Commissioner or any Surveillance Commissioner or Assistant Surveillance Commissioner.

Safeguards

General duties of specified authorities

55.[28]—(1) This section applies to—

    (a) the Secretary of State and every other Minister of the Crown in charge of a government department;

    (b) every chief officer of police;

    (ba) the Director General of the Serious Organised Crime Agency;[29]

    (c) the Commissioners of Customs and Excise; and

    (d) every person whose officers or employees include persons with duties that involve the giving of section 49 notices.

(2) It shall be the duty of each of the persons to whom this section applies to ensure that such arrangements are in force, in relation to persons under his control who by virtue of this Part obtain possession of keys to protected information, as he considers necessary for securing—

    (a) that a key disclosed in pursuance of a section 49 notice is used for obtaining access to, or putting into an intelligible form, only protected information in relation to which power to give such a notice was exercised or could have been exercised if the key had not already been disclosed;

    (b) that the uses to which a key so disclosed is put are reasonable having regard both to the uses to which the person using the key is entitled to put any protected information to which it relates and to the other circumstances of the case;

    (c) that, having regard to those matters, the use and any retention of the key are proportionate to what is sought to be achieved by its use or retention;

    (d) that the requirements of subsection (3) are satisfied in relation to any key disclosed in pursuance of a section 49 notice;

    (e) that, for the purpose of ensuring that those requirements are satisfied, any key so disclosed is stored, for so long as it is retained, in a secure manner;

    (f) that all records of a key so disclosed (if not destroyed earlier) are destroyed as soon as the key is no longer needed for the purpose of enabling protected information to be put into an intelligible form.

(3) The requirements of this subsection are satisfied in relation to any key disclosed in pursuance of a section 49 notice if—

    (a) the number of persons to whom the key is disclosed or otherwise made available, and

    (b) the number of copies made of the key,

---

[28] Not in force.
[29] Subs (1)(ba)and (3A)in italics inserted with effect from the date when Sch 4, para 148 of the SOCAP Act 2005 comes into force.

are each limited to the minimum that is necessary for the purpose of enabling protected information to be put into an intelligible form.

(3A) *Paragraph 11 of Schedule 1 to the Serious Organised Crime and Police Act 2005 does not apply in relation to the duties of the Director General of the Serious Organised Crime Agency under this section.*[30]

(4) Subject to subsection (5), where any relevant person incurs any loss or damage in consequence of—

(a) any breach by a person to whom this section applies of the duty imposed on him by subsection (2), or

(b) any contravention by any person whatever of arrangements made in pursuance of that subsection in relation to persons under the control of a person to whom this section applies,

the breach or contravention shall be actionable against the person to whom this section applies at the suit or instance of the relevant person.

(5) A person is a relevant person for the purposes of subsection (4) if he is—

(a) a person who has made a disclosure in pursuance of a section 49 notice; or

(b) a person whose protected information or key has been disclosed in pursuance of such a notice;

and loss or damage shall be taken into account for the purposes of that subsection to the extent only that it relates to the disclosure of particular protected information or a particular key which, in the case of a person falling with paragraph (b), must be his information or key.

(6) For the purposes of subsection (5)—

(a) information belongs to a person if he has any right that would be infringed by an unauthorised disclosure of the information; and

(b) a key belongs to a person if it is a key to information that belongs to him or he has any right that would be infringed by an unauthorised disclosure of the key.

(7) In any proceedings brought by virtue of subsection (4), it shall be the duty of the court to have regard to any opinion with respect to the matters to which the proceedings relate that is or has been given by a relevant Commissioner.

(8) In this section "relevant Commissioner" means the Interception of Communications Commissioner, the Intelligence Services Commissioner, the Investigatory Powers Commissioner for Northern Ireland or any Surveillance Commissioner or Assistant Surveillance Commissioner.

---

[30] Paragraph 11 of the Schedule referred to (and which is disapplied for the purposes of this section) is to the effect that anything authorised to be done by the Director General may be done by any authorised member of SOCA's staff.

Interpretation of Part III

Interpretation of Part III

56.[31]—(1) In this Part—

"chief officer of police" means any of the following—

(a) the chief constable of a police force maintained under or by virtue of section 2 of the Police Act 1996 or section 1 of the Police (Scotland) Act 1967;

(b) the Commissioner of Police of the Metropolis;

(c) the Commissioner of Police for the City of London;

(d) the Chief Constable of the Royal Ulster Constabulary;

(e) the Chief Constable of the Ministry of Defence Police;

(f) the Provost Marshal of the Royal Navy Regulating Branch;

(g) the Provost Marshal of the Royal Military Police;

(h) the Provost Marshal of the Royal Air Force Police;

(i) the Chief Constable of the British Transport Police;

[(j) the Director General of the National Criminal Intelligence Service;

(k) the Director General of the National Crime Squad;][32]

"the customs and excise" means the Commissioners of Customs and Excise or any customs officer;

"electronic signature" means anything in electronic form which—

(a) is incorporated into, or otherwise logically associated with, any electronic communication or other electronic data;

(b) is generated by the signatory or other source of the communication or data; and

(c) is used for the purpose of facilitating, by means of a link between the signatory or other source and the communication or data, the establishment of the authenticity of the communication or data, the establishment of its integrity, or both;

"key", in relation to any electronic data, means any key, code, password, algorithm or other data the use of which (with or without other keys)—

(a) allows access to the electronic data, or

(b) facilitates the putting of the data into an intelligible form;

"the police" means—

(a) any constable *(except a constable who is a member of the staff of the Serious Organised Crime Agency)*;[33]

---

[31] Not in force.
[32] Words in square brackets will be omitted when para 149 of Sch 4 to the SOCAP Act 2005 comes into force.
[33] Words in italics here and under the definition of SOCA will be added when para 149 of Sch 4 to the SOCAP Act 2005 comes into force.

(b) the Commissioner of Police of the Metropolis or any Assistant Commissioner of Police of the Metropolis; or

(c) the Commissioner of Police for the City of London;

"protected information" means any electronic data which, without the key to the data—

(a) cannot, or cannot readily, be accessed, or

(b) cannot, or cannot readily, be put into an intelligible form;

"section 49 notice" means a notice under section 49;

"SOCA" means the Serious Organised Crime Agency or any member of the staff of the Serious Organised Crime Agency;

"warrant" includes any authorisation, notice or other instrument (however described) conferring a power of the same description as may, in other cases, be conferred by a warrant.

(2) References in this Part to a person's having information (including a key to protected information) in his possession include references—

(a) to its being in the possession of a person who is under his control so far as that information is concerned;

(b) to his having an immediate right of access to it, or an immediate right to have it transmitted or otherwise supplied to him; and

(c) to its being, or being contained in, anything which he or a person under his control is entitled, in exercise of any statutory power and without otherwise taking possession of it, to detain, inspect or search.

(3) References in this Part to something's being intelligible or being put into an intelligible form include references to its being in the condition in which it was before an encryption or similar process was applied to it or, as the case may be, to its being restored to that condition.

(4) In this section—

(a) references to the authenticity of any communication or data are references to any one or more of the following—

(i) whether the communication or data comes from a particular person or other source;

(ii) whether it is accurately timed and dated;

(iii) whether it is intended to have legal effect;

and

(b) references to the integrity of any communication or data are references to whether there has been any tampering with or other modification of the communication or data.

7

THE COMMISSIONERS: RIPA, PART IV, SS 57–64

A. Discussion

The Interception of Communications Commissioner: specific duties under ss 57 and 58

The Interception of Communications Commissioner[1] is charged with keeping **7.01** under review—and reporting upon—the exercise and performance:

- by the Secretary of State of his powers and duties under Chapter I of Part I, ie the interception of communications and related warrantry provisions of the Act;
- by the Scottish ministers (by virtue of s 63 of the Scotland Act 1998) of their powers under ss 5, 9 and 10;[2]
- by the persons on whom they are conferred or imposed, of the powers and duties under the access to communications data provisions of Chapter II of Part I of RIPA;
- *the exercise and performance by the Secretary of State in relation to intercepted communications or communications data of the 'de-encryption' provisions of Part III of RIPA (not in force at time of writing)*;
- the adequacy of the arrangements by virtue of which the 'general safeguards' and 'extra safeguards' of ss 15 and 16 are sought to be discharged by Secretary of State,[3] (see the note entitled *'general safeguards'* in section 3.25), and
- *the adequacy of the arrangements by virtue of which the duties of the Secretary of State are sought to be discharged in relation to disclosed keys to access encrypted data, under s 55 in Part III of RIPA (not in force at time of writing)*.

---

[1] Appointed by the Prime Minister and having held high judicial office (within the Appellate Jurisdiction Act 1876).

[2] Section 5 concerns interception with warrant, s 9: cancellation of a warrant, s 10: modification of a warrant. The reference to s 63 of the Scotland Act 1998 is to a provision which enables the powers of the Secretary of State to be transferred to the Scottish ministers.

[3] Or if appropriate, the Scottish ministers (see s 63 of the Scotland Act 1998 and note above).

See s 58 for details of the categories of person who owe a duty to co-operate with and disclose information to the Interception of Communications Commissioner.

The Intelligence Services Commissioner: specific duties under ss 59 and 60

7.02   The Intelligence Services Commissioner[4] reviews and reports upon the following (to the extent not covered by the responsibilities of the Interception of Communications Commissioner):

- the Secretary of State's exercise[5] of his powers and duties under ss 5–7 ss 5 and 6(3) and (4) of the Intelligence Services Act 1994 (warrants for interference with wireless telegraphy, entry and interference with property);
- the Secretary of State's[6] exercise of powers and duties under Parts II and III of the Act (ie covert surveillance and CHIS, and electronic data protected by encryption, respectively)[7] in relation to the intelligence services, and in relation to activities of the officials of the Ministry of Defence and of members of HM forces, in places other than Northern Ireland;
- the exercise and performance by members of the intelligence services of those powers and duties (ie Parts II and III);
- the exercise and performance by officials of the Ministry of Defence and by members of HM forces, of those powers and duties (Parts II and III) in places other than Northern Ireland;
- *the adequacy of the arrangements for discharging the duty under s 55[8] (in relation to disclosed keys to access encrypted data, under Part III of RIPA), in relation to the members of the intelligence services;*
- *the adequacy of the arrangements for discharging the duty under s.55[9] (in relation to disclosed keys to access encrypted data, under Part III of RIPA), in relation to officials of the Ministry of Defence and members of Her Majesty's forces, in places other than Northern Ireland.*

See s 60 for details of the categories of person who owe a duty to co-operate with and disclose information to the Intelligence Services Commissioner.

The Investigatory Powers Commissioner for Northern Ireland: specific duties under s 61

7.03   The Investigatory Powers Commissioner for Northern Ireland reviews and reports on the exercise, of any powers or duties under Part II which are conferred by an order under s 30 made by the Office of the First Minister and deputy First

---

[4] A person appointed by the Prime Minister and having held high judicial office (within the meaning of the Appellate Jurisdiction Act 1876).

[5] Or of the Scottish ministers (s 63 of the Scotland Act 1998).   [6] Or the Scottish ministers.

[7] Part III not in force.   [8] Not in force.   [9] Not in force.

Minister in Northern Ireland (ie persons decreed by order as being entitled to grant authorisations for directed surveillance and CHIS in Northern Ireland).

See s 61(4) for the categories of person who owe a duty to co-operate with and disclose information to the Investigatory Powers Commissioner for Northern Ireland.

The Chief Surveillance Commissioner: s 62 of RIPA and s 91 of the Police Act 1997

The Chief Surveillance Commissioner's post was created by the Police Act 1997, **7.04** s 91 in relation to authorisations for police access to and interference with property and telegraphy. Section 62 of RIPA adds additional functions in the form of duties to review and report upon the following to the extent that they do not fall within the remit of the Interception of Communications Commissioner, Intelligence Services Commissioner or Investigatory Powers Commissioner for Northern Ireland—note that the items relating to Part III are not in force at the time of writing:

• the exercise and performance, of powers and duties under Part II (covert surveillance and CHIS) (s 62(1)(a));
• *the exercise and performance, by any person other than a judicial authority,*[10] *or with the permission of such an authority, of the powers and duties under Part III*[11] *(s 62(1)(b)); and*
• *the adequacy of the arrangements in Part III for discharging the duties under s 55 (ie duties in relation to keys for de-encrypting encrypted data (s 62(1)(c)).*

The Ordinary Surveillance Commissioners: s 91 of the Police Act 1997

The Police Act 1997, s 91 permits the appointment of ordinary Surveillance **7.05** Commissioners, who must be or have been holders of High Judicial Office. Their roles in relation to authorisations under that Act were discussed in Chapter 6 of this work. By s 62(3)(a) of RIPA any ordinary Surveillance Commissioner may be required by the Chief Surveillance Commissioner to provide him with assistance in carrying out his functions under s 62(1) discussed above.

The Assistant Surveillance Commissioners: s 63

Section 63 permits the Prime Minister to appoint Assistant Surveillance **7.06** Commissioners (not to be confused with ordinary Surveillance Commissioners) who have held at least the position of circuit judge (s 63(2)), and who may be required by the Chief Surveillance Commissioner to assist him in carrying out his functions under s 62(1) or in carrying out equivalent functions under any

---

[10] Ie any judge of the High Court, Crown Court or any circuit judge; judge of the High Court of Justiciary or any sheriff; justice of the peace; county court judge or resident magistrate in Northern Ireland; any person holding any judicial office which entitles him to exercise the jurisdiction of a judge of the Crown Court justice of the peace: s 62(3).   [11] Not in force.

Scottish Act which is equivalent to RIPA, Part II (see the Regulation of Investigatory Powers (Scotland) Act 2000 which is outside the scope of this work).

B. Text of Part IV

REGULATION OF INVESTIGATORY POWERS ACT 2000 (AS AMENDED)

PART IV
SCRUTINY ETC. OF INVESTIGATORY POWERS AND OF THE
FUNCTIONS OF THE INTELLIGENCE SERVICES

Commissioners

Interception of Communications Commissioner

57.[12]—(1) The Prime Minister shall appoint a Commissioner to be known as the Interception of Communications Commissioner.

(2)[13] Subject to subsection (4), the Interception of Communications Commissioner shall keep under review—

(a) the exercise and performance by the Secretary of State of the powers and duties conferred or imposed on him by or under sections 1 to 11;

(aa) the exercise and performance by the Scottish Ministers (by virtue of provision made under section 63 of the Scotland Act 1998) of the powers and duties conferred or imposed on them by or under sections 5, 9 and 10;

(b) the exercise and performance, by the persons on whom they are conferred or imposed, of the powers and duties conferred or imposed by or under Chapter II of Part I;

(c) the exercise and performance by the Secretary of State in relation to information obtained under Part I of the powers and duties conferred or imposed on him by or under Part III; and

(d) the adequacy of the arrangements by virtue of which—

(i) the duty which is imposed on the Secretary of State, or the Scottish Ministers (by virtue of provision under section 63 of the Scotland Act 1998), by section 15, and

---

[12] Commencement: all of this section in force except s 57(2)(b), (c) and (d)(ii) from 2/10/00 by SI 2000 No 2543. Section 57(2)(b) commenced 5/1/04 by SI 2003 No 3140. Section 57(2)(c) and 57(2)(d)(ii) not in force.

[13] Subsection (2)(aa) inserted by, and subs (2)(d)(i) amended by the Scotland Act 1998 (Transfer of Functions to the Scottish Ministers etc.) (No 2) Order 2000 (SI 2000 No 3253), Sch 3.

      (ii) so far as applicable to information obtained under Part I, the duties imposed by section 55,

are sought to be discharged.

(3) The Interception of Communications Commissioner shall give the Tribunal all such assistance (including his opinion as to any issue falling to be determined by the Tribunal) as the Tribunal may require—

    (a) in connection with the investigation of any matter by the Tribunal; or

    (b) otherwise for the purposes of the Tribunal's consideration or determination of any matter.

(4) It shall not be the function of the Interception of Communications Commissioner to keep under review the exercise of any power of the Secretary of State to make, amend or revoke any subordinate legislation.

(5) A person shall not be appointed under this section as the Interception of Communications Commissioner unless he holds or has held a high judicial office (within the meaning of the Appellate Jurisdiction Act 1876).

(6) The Interception of Communications Commissioner shall hold office in accordance with the terms of his appointment; and there shall be paid to him out of money provided by Parliament such allowances as the Treasury may determine.

(7) The Secretary of State, after consultation with the Interception of Communications Commissioner, shall—

    (a) make such technical facilities available to the Commissioner, and

    (b) subject to the approval of the Treasury as to numbers, provide the Commissioner with such staff,

as are sufficient to secure that the Commissioner is able properly to carry out his functions.

(8) On the coming into force of this section the Commissioner holding office as the Commissioner under section 8 of the Interception of Communications Act 1985 shall take and hold office as the Interception of Communications Commissioner as if appointed under this Act-

    (a) for the unexpired period of his term of office under that Act; and

    (b) otherwise, on the terms of his appointment under that Act.

Co-operation with and reports by s 57 Commissioner

58.[14]—(1) It shall be the duty of—

    (a) every person holding office under the Crown,

    [(b) every member of the National Criminal Intelligence Service,

    (c) every member of the National Crime Squad,]

---

[14] Commencement: all of this section except s 58(1)(g) (h) (i) (and (j) insofar as it relates to (h) and (i)) in force from 2/10/00 by SI 2000 No 2543. Subsection (1)(g), (h) and (i) in force 1/5/04 by SI 2003 No 3140. Remainder not in force.

(b) *every member of the staff of the Serious Organised Crime Agency,*[15]

(d) every person employed by or for the purposes of a police force,

(e) every person required for the purposes of section 11 to provide assistance with giving effect to an interception warrant,

(f) every person on whom an obligation to take any steps has been imposed under section 12,

(g) every person by or to whom an authorisation under section 22(3) has been granted,

(h) every person to whom a notice under section 22(4) has been given,

(i) every person to whom a notice under section 49 has been given in relation to any information obtained under Part I, and

(j) every person who is or has been employed for the purposes of any business of a person falling within paragraph (e), (f), (h) or (i), to disclose or provide to the Interception of Communications Commissioner all such documents and information as he may require for the purpose of enabling him to carry out his functions under section 57.

(2) If it at any time appears to the Interception of Communications Commissioner—

(a) that there has been a contravention of the provisions of this Act in relation to any matter with which that Commissioner is concerned, and

(b) that the contravention has not been the subject of a report made to the Prime Minister by the Tribunal,

he shall make a report to the Prime Minister with respect to that contravention.

(3) If it at any time appears to the Interception of Communications Commissioner that any arrangements by reference to which the duties imposed by sections 15 and 55 have sought to be discharged have proved inadequate in relation to any matter with which the Commissioner is concerned, he shall make a report to the Prime Minister with respect to those arrangements.

(4) As soon as practicable after the end of each calendar year, the Interception of Communications Commissioner shall make a report to the Prime Minister with respect to the carrying out of that Commissioner's functions.

(5) The Interception of Communications Commissioner may also, at any time, make any such other report to the Prime Minister on any matter relating to the carrying out of the Commissioner's functions as the Commissioner thinks fit.

(5A)[16] The Interception of Communications Commissioner may also, at any time, make any such other report to the First Minister on any matter relating to

---

[15] Subsections (b) and (c) in square brackets will be replaced by new subs (b) in italics, from the date of coming into force of Sch 4, para 150 of the SOCAP Act 2005.

[16] Section 58(5A), (6A) inserted and s 58(7) amended by the Scotland Act 1998 (Transfer of Functions to the Scottish Ministers etc.) (No 2) Order 2000 (SI 2000 No 3253), Sch 3.

the carrying out of the Commissioner's functions so far as they relate to the exercise by the Scottish Ministers (by virtue of provision made under section 63 of the Scotland Act 1998) of their powers under sections 5, 9(1)(b) and (3), 10(1)(a) and (2) and 15(1) of this Act, as the Commissioner thinks fit.

(6) The Prime Minister shall lay before each House of Parliament a copy of every annual report made by the Interception of Communications Commissioner under subsection (4), together with a statement as to whether any matter has been excluded from that copy in pursuance of subsection (7).

(6A) The Prime Minister shall send a copy of every annual report made by the Interception of Communications Commissioner under subsection (4) which he lays in terms of subsection (6), together with a copy of the statement referred to in subsection (6), to the First Minister who shall forthwith lay that copy report and statement before the Scottish Parliament.

(7) If it appears to the Prime Minister, after consultation with the Interception of Communications Commissioner and, if it appears relevant to do so, with the First Minister, that the publication of any matter in an annual report would be contrary to the public interest or prejudicial to—

(a) national security,

(b) the prevention or detection of serious crime,

(c) the economic well-being of the United Kingdom, or

(d) the continued discharge of the functions of any public authority whose activities include activities that are subject to review by that Commissioner,

the Prime Minister may exclude that matter from the copy of the report as laid before each House of Parliament.

Intelligence Services Commissioner

59.[17]—(1) The Prime Minister shall appoint a Commissioner to be known as the Intelligence Services Commissioner.

(2)[18] Subject to subsection (4), the Intelligence Services Commissioner shall keep under review, so far as they are not required to be kept under review by the Interception of Communications Commissioner—

(a) the exercise by the Secretary of State of his powers under sections 5 to 7 of, or the Scottish Ministers (by virtue of provision made under section

---

[17] Commencement: 2/10/00 by SI 2000 No 2543 but only as regards s 59(1), (2)(a) and (3)–(10). Remainder of subs (2) also in force from the same date insofar as it applies to Part II of the Act only. Remainder not in force.

[18] Amended by the Scotland Act 1998 (Transfer of Functions to the Scottish Ministers etc.) (No 2) Order 2000 (SI 2000 No 3253), Sch 3, para 11.

63 of the Scotland Act 1998) of their powers under sections 5 and 6(3) and (4) of, the Intelligence Services Act 1994 (warrants for interference with wireless telegraphy, entry and interference with property etc.);

(b) the exercise and performance by the Secretary of State or the Scottish Ministers (by virtue of provision made under section 63 of the Scotland Act 1998), in connection with or in relation to—

   (i) the activities of the intelligence services, and

   (ii) the activities in places other than Northern Ireland of the officials of the Ministry of Defence and of members of Her Majesty's forces,[19]

of the powers and duties conferred or imposed on him by Parts II and III of this Act or on them by Part II of this Act;

(c) the exercise and performance by members of the intelligence services of the powers and duties conferred or imposed on them by or under Parts II and III of this Act;

(d) the exercise and performance in places other than Northern Ireland, by officials of the Ministry of Defence and by members of Her Majesty's forces, of the powers and duties conferred or imposed on such officials or members of Her Majesty's forces by or under Parts II and III; and

(e) the adequacy of the arrangements by virtue of which the duty imposed by section 55 is sought to be discharged—

   (i) in relation to the members of the intelligence services; and

   (ii) in connection with any of their activities in places other than Northern Ireland, in relation to officials of the Ministry of Defence and members of Her Majesty's forces.

(3) The Intelligence Services Commissioner shall give the Tribunal all such assistance (including his opinion as to any issue falling to be determined by the Tribunal) as the Tribunal may require—

(a) in connection with the investigation of any matter by the Tribunal; or

(b) otherwise for the purposes of the Tribunal's consideration or determination of any matter.

(4) It shall not be the function of the Intelligence Services Commissioner to keep under review the exercise of any power of the Secretary of State to make, amend or revoke any subordinate legislation.

(5) A person shall not be appointed under this section as the Intelligence Services Commissioner unless he holds or has held a high judicial office (within the meaning of the Appellate Jurisdiction Act 1876).

(6) The Intelligence Services Commissioner shall hold office in accordance with the terms of his appointment; and there shall be paid to him out of money provided by Parliament such allowances as the Treasury may determine.

---

[19] But note that by s 81(1) of RIPA, members of the military police forces are treated as members of police forces and so fall outside this provision and those in subs (2)(d) and (e).

(7)   The Secretary of State shall, after consultation with the Intelligence Services Commissioner and subject to the approval of the Treasury as to numbers, provide him with such staff as the Secretary of State considers necessary for the carrying out of the Commissioner's functions.

(8)   Section 4 of the Security Service Act 1989 and section 8 of the Intelligence Services Act 1994 (Commissioners for the purposes of those Acts) shall cease to have effect.

(9)   On the coming into force of this section the Commissioner holding office as the Commissioner under section 8 of the Intelligence Services Act 1994 shall take and hold office as the Intelligence Services Commissioner as if appointed under this Act—

(a) for the unexpired period of his term of office under that Act; and

(b) otherwise, on the terms of his appointment under that Act.

(10)   Subsection (7) of section 41 shall apply for the purposes of this section as it applies for the purposes of that section.

Co-operation with and reports by s 59 Commissioner

60.[20]—(1)[21] It shall be the duty of—

(a) every member of an intelligence service,

(b) every official of the department of the Secretary of State and every member of staff of the Scottish Administration (by virtue of provision under section 63 of the Scotland Act 1998), and

(c) every member of Her Majesty's forces,

to disclose or provide to the Intelligence Services Commissioner all such documents and information as he may require for the purpose of enabling him to carry out his functions under section 59.

(2)   As soon as practicable after the end of each calendar year, the Intelligence Services Commissioner shall make a report to the Prime Minister with respect to the carrying out of that Commissioner's functions.

(3)   The Intelligence Services Commissioner may also, at any time, make any such other report to the Prime Minister on any matter relating to the carrying out of the Commissioner's functions as the Commissioner thinks fit.

(3A)[22] The Intelligence Services Commissioner may also, at any time, make any such other report to the First Minister on any matter relating to the carrying out of the Commissioner's functions so far as they relate to the exercise by the Scottish Ministers (by virtue of provision made under section 63 of the Scotland Act 1998) of their powers under sections 5 and 6(3) and (4)

---

[20] Commencement: 2/10/00 by SI 2000 No 2543.

[21] Amended by the Scotland Act 1998 (Transfer of Functions to the Scottish Ministers etc.) (No 2) Order 2000 (SI 2000 No 3253), Sch 3, para 12.

[22] Inserted by the Scotland Act 1998 (Transfer of Functions to the Scottish Ministers etc.) (No 2) Order 2000 (SI 2000 No 3253), Sch 3, para 12.

of the Intelligence Services Act 1994 or under Parts I and II of this Act, as the Commissioner thinks fit.

(4) The Prime Minister shall lay before each House of Parliament a copy of every annual report made by the Intelligence Services Commissioner under subsection (2), together with a statement as to whether any matter has been excluded from that copy in pursuance of subsection (5).

(4A)[23] The Prime Minister shall send a copy of every annual report made by the Intelligence Services Commissioner under subsection (2) which he lays in terms of subsection (4), together with a copy of the statement referred to in subsection (4), to the First Minister who shall forthwith lay that copy report and statement before the Scottish Parliament.

(5)[24] If it appears to the Prime Minister, after consultation with the Intelligence Services Commissioner and, if it appears relevant to do so, with the First Minister, that the publication of any matter in an annual report would be contrary to the public interest or prejudicial to—

(a) national security,

(b) the prevention or detection of serious crime,

(c) the economic well-being of the United Kingdom, or

(d) the continued discharge of the functions of any public authority whose activities include activities that are subject to review by that Commissioner,

the Prime Minister may exclude that matter from the copy of the report as laid before each House of Parliament.

(6) Subsection (7) of section 41 shall apply for the purposes of this section as it applies for the purposes of that section.

Investigatory Powers Commissioner for Northern Ireland

61.[25]—(1) The Prime Minister, after consultation with the First Minister and deputy First Minister in Northern Ireland, shall appoint a Commissioner to be known as the Investigatory Powers Commissioner for Northern Ireland.

(2) The Investigatory Powers Commissioner for Northern Ireland shall keep under review the exercise and performance in Northern Ireland, by the persons on whom they are conferred or imposed, of any powers or duties under Part II which are conferred or imposed by virtue of an order under section 30 made by the Office of the First Minister and deputy First Minister in Northern Ireland.

---

[23] Inserted by the Scotland Act 1998 (Transfer of Functions to the Scottish Ministers etc.) (No 2) Order 2000 (SI 2000 No 3253), Sch 3, para 12.

[24] Amended by the Scotland Act 1998 (Transfer of Functions to the Scottish Ministers etc.) (No 2) Order 2000 (SI 2000 No 3253), Sch 3, para 12.

[25] Commencement: 25/9/00 by SI 2000 No 2543.

(3) The Investigatory Powers Commissioner for Northern Ireland shall give the Tribunal all such assistance (including his opinion as to any issue falling to be determined by the Tribunal) as the Tribunal may require—

    (a) in connection with the investigation of any matter by the Tribunal; or

    (b) otherwise for the purposes of the Tribunal's consideration or determination of any matter.

(4) It shall be the duty of—

    (a) every person by whom, or on whose application, there has been given or granted any authorisation the function of giving or granting which is subject to review by the Investigatory Powers Commissioner for Northern Ireland,

    (b) every person who has engaged in conduct with the authority of such an authorisation,

    (c) every person who holds or has held any office, rank or position with the same public authority as a person falling within paragraph (a), and

    (d) every person who holds or has held any office, rank or position with any public authority for whose benefit (within the meaning of Part II) activities which are or may be subject to any such review have been or may be carried out,

to disclose or provide to that Commissioner all such documents and information as he may require for the purpose of enabling him to carry out his functions.

(5) As soon as practicable after the end of each calendar year, the Investigatory Powers Commissioner for Northern Ireland shall make a report to the First Minister and deputy First Minister in Northern Ireland with respect to the carrying out of that Commissioner's functions.

(6) The First Minister and deputy First Minister in Northern Ireland shall lay before the Northern Ireland Assembly a copy of every annual report made by the Investigatory Powers Commissioner for Northern Ireland under subsection (5), together with a statement as to whether any matter has been excluded from that copy in pursuance of subsection (7).

(7) If it appears to the First Minister and deputy First Minister in Northern Ireland, after consultation with the Investigatory Powers Commissioner for Northern Ireland, that the publication of any matter in an annual report would be contrary to the public interest or prejudicial to—

    (a) the prevention or detection of serious crime, or

    (b) the continued discharge of the functions of any public authority whose activities include activities that are subject to review by that Commissioner,

they may exclude that matter from the copy of the report as laid before the Northern Ireland Assembly.

(8) A person shall not be appointed under this section as the Investigatory Powers Commissioner for Northern Ireland unless he holds or has held

office in Northern Ireland—

    (a) in any capacity in which he is or was the holder of a high judicial office (within the meaning of the Appellate Jurisdiction Act 1876); or

    (b) as a county court judge.

(9) The Investigatory Powers Commissioner for Northern Ireland shall hold office in accordance with the terms of his appointment; and there shall be paid to him out of the Consolidated Fund of Northern Ireland such allowances as the Department of Finance and Personnel may determine.

(10) The First Minister and deputy First Minister in Northern Ireland shall, after consultation with the Investigatory Powers Commissioner for Northern Ireland, provide him with such staff as they consider necessary for the carrying out of his functions.

Additional functions of Chief Surveillance Commissioner

62.[26]—(1) The Chief Surveillance Commissioner shall (in addition to his functions under the Police Act 1997) keep under review, so far as they are not required to be kept under review by the Interception of Communications Commissioner, the Intelligence Services Commissioner or the Investigatory Powers Commissioner for Northern Ireland—

    (a) the exercise and performance, by the persons on whom they are conferred or imposed, of the powers and duties conferred or imposed by or under Part II;

    (b) the exercise and performance, by any person other than a judicial authority, of the powers and duties conferred or imposed, otherwise than with the permission of such an authority, by or under Part III; and

    (c) the adequacy of the arrangements by virtue of which the duties imposed by section 55 are sought to be discharged in relation to persons whose conduct is subject to review under paragraph (b).

(2) It shall not by virtue of this section be the function of the Chief Surveillance Commissioner to keep under review the exercise of any power of the Secretary of State to make, amend or revoke any subordinate legislation.

(3) In this section "judicial authority" means—

    (a) any judge of the High Court or of the Crown Court or any Circuit Judge;

    (b) any judge of the High Court of Justiciary or any sheriff;

    (c) any justice of the peace;

    (d) any county court judge or resident magistrate in Northern Ireland;

    (e) any person holding any such judicial office as entitles him to exercise the jurisdiction of a judge of the Crown Court or of a justice of the peace.

---

[26] Commencement: 25/9/00 by SI 2000 No 2543 except for s 62(1)(b) and (c) which is not in force.

Assistant Surveillance Commissioners

63.[27]—(1) The Prime Minister may, after consultation with the Chief Surveillance Commissioner as to numbers, appoint as Assistant Surveillance Commissioners such number of persons as the Prime Minister considers necessary (in addition to the ordinary Surveillance Commissioners) for the purpose of providing the Chief Surveillance Commissioner with assistance under this section.

(2) A person shall not be appointed as an Assistant Surveillance Commissioner unless he holds or has held office as—

(a) a judge of the Crown Court or a Circuit judge;

(b) a sheriff in Scotland; or

(c) a county court judge in Northern Ireland.

(3) The Chief Surveillance Commissioner may—

(a) require any ordinary Surveillance Commissioner or any Assistant Surveillance Commissioner to provide him with assistance in carrying out his functions under section 62(1); or

(b) require any Assistant Surveillance Commissioner to provide him with assistance in carrying out his equivalent functions under any Act of the Scottish Parliament in relation to any provisions of such an Act that are equivalent to those of Part II of this Act.

(4) The assistance that may be provided under this section includes—

(a) the conduct on behalf of the Chief Surveillance Commissioner of the review of any matter; and

(b) the making of a report to the Chief Surveillance Commissioner about the matter reviewed.

(5) Subsections (3) to (8) of section 91 of the Police Act 1997 (Commissioners) apply in relation to a person appointed under this section as they apply in relation to a person appointed under that section.[28]

Delegation of Commissioners' functions

64.[29]—(1) Anything authorised or required by or under any enactment or any provision of an Act of the Scottish Parliament to be done by a relevant Commissioner may be done by any member of the staff of that Commissioner who is authorised for the purpose (whether generally or specifically) by that Commissioner.

(2) In this section "relevant Commissioner" means the Interception of Communications Commissioner, the Intelligence Services Commissioner, the Investigatory Powers Commissioner for Northern Ireland or any Surveillance Commissioner or Assistant Surveillance Commissioner.

---

[27] Commencement: 25/9/00 by SI 2000 No 2543.

[28] Section 91(3)–(8) of the 1997 Act relates to the terms of appointment of ordinary surveillance commissioners and is applied to assistant surveillance commissioners by this subsection.

[29] Commencement: 25/9/00 by SI 2000 No 2543.

8

THE INVESTIGATORY POWERS TRIBUNAL: RIPA, PART IV, SS 65–70

A. Discussion

The Investigatory Powers Tribunal (IPT) is a tribunal created by ss 65–70 of RIPA. **8.01**
The related Rules appear in Chapter 11 and are cross-referenced where appropriate
in this chapter. The reader should note that in this work the Rules of the Tribunal are
generally shortened to 'IPTR' followed by the rule number.

The IPTR were created by the Secretary of State by order under s 69 of RIPA: see **8.02**
the footnotes to that section for details of the types of rules which may be made.

**Standard forms available in Chapter 12 which are relevant to the above (original forms are
available from the IPT).**

A Form T1: Human Rights Complaint Form

B Form T2: Complaint Form

C Tribunal information leaflet

The Tribunal has jurisdiction which will be outlined below but it is worth noting **8.03**
that it replaces and merges previous avenues of complaint about surveillance and
intelligence operations as follows (as well as including an expanded jurisdiction in
relation to matters under RIPA itself):

- the Security Service Tribunal established under s 5 and Sch 1 and 2 of the SSA
  1989 (abolished by s 70(2)(a) of RIPA);
- the Intelligence Services Tribunal established under s 9 and Sch 1 and 2 of the
  Intelligence Services Act 1994 (abolished by s 70(2)(b) of RIPA);
- the Interception of Communications Tribunal under the Interception of
  Communications Act 1985;
- the procedure previously in place under s 102 of the Police Act 1997 for complaints
  to the surveillance commissioner (procedure abolished by s 70(2)(c) of RIPA).

Duties to provide information and documents to the IPT (s 68(6) and (7))

8.04 The various bodies and people listed in s 68(7) are under a duty to disclose or provide the Tribunal with all documents and information which Tribunal requires when exercising its jurisdiction or which are required for the exercise of any other powers or duties given to it. Notably included is the Serious Organised Crime Agency (SOCA) established under the SOCAP Act 2005 expected to be brought into force in 2005–6.

Power to require commissioners to assist the IPT (s 68(2))

8.05 The IPT also has the power to require commissioners to assist it in the discharge of its functions (including by requiring a commissioner to provide an opinion on any issue which is to be determined).

The Tribunal's jurisdiction

8.06 Section 65 establishes the jurisdiction of the Tribunal. At the time of writing not all the subsections of s 65 were in force and the jurisdiction of the Tribunal is accordingly not as wide as it would otherwise be. In particular s 65(1), (2)(a), (b), (3)(a), (b), (d), (4), (5)(a), (b), (c), (d), (f), 8(b), (9), and (11) were in force at time of writing, from which the summary of the Tribunal's jurisdiction given below is derived.[1]

The areas of jurisdiction in force

Human Rights Act 1998, s 7 exclusive jurisdiction (s 65(2)(a), (3), (5))

8.07 The IPT is, by s 65(2)(a) of RIPA the only appropriate tribunal for the purposes of s 7(1)(a) of the Human Rights Act 1998 for certain types of conduct.

A person who alleges that a public authority has unlawfully interfered with any of his Convention rights, and who wishes to sue by means of s 7 of the HRA 1998 *must* therefore, if he proceeds at all, do so via the IPT if the circumstances are those listed below, taken from s 65(3) of RIPA. (In what follows note that the definition of 'public authority' for RIPA which appears in s 81(1) is slightly narrower than the definition under s 6 of the HRA 1998 in that it excludes courts and tribunals.)

8.08 In order to have standing to bring s 7 proceedings at all (whether before the IPT or any other forum) such a person must be a 'victim' of the interference in the sense in which that expression is used in Article 34 of the Convention (see s 7(7) of the HRA 1998 which makes this explicit).

---

[1] And conversely therefore the remainder of the section is not in force, ie s 65(2)(c), (d), (3)(c), (d), (5)(e), (6), (7), (8)(a), (c–f), (10).

Human Rights Act 1998, s 7: the right to sue

7.—(1) A person who claims that a public authority has acted (or proposes to act) in a way which is made unlawful by section 6(1) may—

(a) bring proceedings against the authority under this Act in the appropriate court or tribunal, or

(b) rely on the Convention right or rights concerned in any legal proceedings,

but only if he is (or would be) a victim of the unlawful act.

The restriction requiring s 7(1) proceedings to be brought before the IPT applies to any proceedings for actions incompatible with Convention rights which fall within any of the following categories under s 65(3) of RIPA:[2] **8.09**

(1) proceedings against any of the intelligence services; or

(2) proceedings against any other person in respect of any conduct, or proposed conduct, by or on behalf of any of the intelligence services; or

(3) proceedings relating to the taking place in any 'challengeable circumstances' of any conduct:[3]

- by or on behalf of any of the intelligence services; or
- for or in connection with the interception of communications in the course of their transmission by means of a postal service or telecommunication system; or
- conduct to which Chapter II of Part I applies (ie access to communications data); or
- the carrying out of surveillance by a foreign police or customs officer; or
- other conduct to which Part II applies (ie covert surveillance, covert human intelligence sources); or
- entry on or interference with property or any interference with wireless telegraphy.

'Challengeable circumstances' are defined in s 65(7) and (7)(a). In summary, conduct takes place in challengeable circumstances if:

it takes place with the authority, or purported authority, of:

- an interception warrant or a warrant under the Interception of Communications Act 1985; or

---

[2] S.65(3)(c) which was not in force at time of writing adds to this list proceedings brought by virtue of s.55(4), in other words proceedings in respect of losses suffered by any relevant person arising from a breach of the various duties imposed by s.55 concerning the protection of the keys to encrypted data.

[3] The giving of a disclosure notice or any disclosure or use of a key to protected information is also included in this list by s 65(5)(e).

- an authorisation or notice under Chapter II of Part I of RIPA (access to communications data); or
- an authorisation under Part II of RIPA (covert surveillance and CHIS); or
- an authorisation under s 93 of the Police Act 1997; *or*

the circumstances are such that (whether or not there is authority) it would not have been appropriate for the conduct to take place without it, or at least without proper consideration having been given to whether such authority should be sought; *or*

if it takes place, or purports to take place, under s 76(a) of RIPA (ie foreign surveillance operations).

Conduct does not take place in challengeable circumstances if it is authorised by a judicial authority (s 65(11)).

Complaints jurisdiction (s 65(2)(b),(4),(5))

8.10 The Tribunal has jurisdiction to consider and determine any complaints made to it which are complaints for which the Tribunal is the 'appropriate forum'. The Tribunal will be the 'appropriate forum' for a complaint about conduct in any of the following categories:

- conduct by or on behalf of any of the intelligence services; or
- for or in connection with the interception of communications in the course of their transmission by means of a postal service or telecommunication system; or
- conduct to which Chapter II of Part I applies (ie access to communications data); or
- the carrying out of surveillance by a foreign police or customs officer; or
- other conduct to which Part II applies (ie covert surveillance, covert human intelligence sources); or
- entry on or interference with property or any interference with wireless telegraphy

provided the complainant believes:

- that the conduct complained of took place in relation to him, his property, communications sent by or to him, or intended for him, or his use of any postal or telecommunications service or system; *and*

that the conduct complained of took place:

- *either* in 'challengeable circumstances'; *or*
- was done by or on behalf of any of the intelligence services.

Prospective additional jurisdiction not yet in force

8.11 Provision is made in s 65(2)(c) and (d) for two further areas of jurisdiction which had not been brought into force at time of writing, namely (to paraphrase, in an attempt to clarify poorly drafted wording in the Act):[4]

'References' to the IPT

- to consider and determine any reference to the Tribunal by any person complaining that he has suffered detriment as a consequence of any prohibition or restriction[5] upon him relying on any matter in civil proceedings.

Additional types of HRA proceedings

- to determine other proceedings falling within the list of points 1–3 at para **8.09** above allocated to them by the Secretary of State by order.

The composition of the Tribunal

Schedule 3 of RIPA sets out various practical matters in relation to membership **8.12** and eligibility to sit on the Tribunal. All persons appointed to be members of the Tribunal are appointed by Her Majesty by way of Letters Patent (s 65(1)). Schedule 3 provides that the President of the Tribunal must have held high judicial office (Appellate Jurisdiction Act 1876) whereas the Vice President and other members must meet any of the following qualifications:

- holding or having held a high judicial office; or
- having a 10-year general qualification, within the meaning of s 71 of the Courts and Legal Services Act 1990; or
- being an advocate or solicitor in Scotland of at least 10 years' standing; or
- being a member of the Bar of Northern Ireland or solicitor of the Supreme Court of Northern Ireland of at least 10 years' standing.

Subject to good behaviour, members remain in office for five years but may be reappointed (Sch 3, para. 1(3)).

Special designation of one or more Tribunal members with responsibility for the intelligence services

Schedule 3, para 3 provides that the President must designate one or more members **8.13** as being responsible for matters involving the Intelligence Services (meaning the security service, secret intelligence service and GCHQ: see s 81 of RIPA). The President has a duty to allocate the hearing of complaints involving or alleging matters against those services, to the designated members so that at least one designated member is allocated to the complaint.

The duties of the Tribunal: s 67

The Tribunal has a statutory duty to hear and determine any proceedings brought **8.14** before them within its jurisdiction. When exercising its jurisdiction under s 65(2)(a)

---

[4] Section 65(2)(c) states '. . . to consider and determine any reference to them by any person that he has suffered detriment as a consequence of any prohibition or restriction, by virtue of section 17, on his relying in, or for the purposes of, any civil proceedings on any matter . . .'.

[5] By virtue of RIPA, s 17.

(under the Human Rights Act), the central legal principle is that the Tribunal must apply the same principles for making its determination in those proceedings as would be applied by a court on an application for judicial review (s 67(2)).

8.15　When exercising its jurisdiction under s 65(2)(b), ie when investigating a complaint about activities within its jurisdiction, the Tribunal is obliged to investigate whether the persons against whom any allegations are made in the complaint have engaged in any conduct falling within s 65(5)[6] in relation to the complainant, any of his property, any communications sent by or to him, or intended for him, or his use of any postal service, telecommunications service or telecommunications system.

8.16　If they find that such conduct has taken place the Tribunal must then investigate the authority (if any) for that conduct and must determine the complaint by applying the same principles to their findings as would be applied by a court on an application for judicial review (s 67(3)(a)–(c)).

Number of Tribunal members required

8.17　IPTR, rr 4 and 5 govern how many Tribunal members are required in order to carry out the various Tribunal functions. The general rule (IPTR, r 4) is that the IPT may exercise any of its functions, at any location in the UK, if it is composed of at least two members designated for the purposes of the Tribunal by the President. However the general rule is subject to Sch 3, para 3(2) which requires at least one member designated by the President as having particular responsibility for the intelligence services to sit where the conduct of one of those services is involved or an allegation is made against one of those services.

Certain functions may be carried out by a single member of the Tribunal, and those appear in IPTR, r 5. (The single member must be a designated member with responsibility for the intelligence services if the conduct of those services is involved).

Functions exercisable by a single member sitting alone (r 5(a)–(h))

8.18　A single Tribunal member has:

- the power under rr 7(4) or 8(4) to invite the complainant to supply information or make representations;
- the power under s 68(2) to require a commissioner to provide assistance;
- the power under s 68(6) to require the disclosure or provision of documents or information;

---

[6] Ie conduct by or on behalf of any of the intelligence services, conduct for or in connection with the interception of communications in the course of their transmission, access to communications data, the carrying out of surveillance by a foreign police or customs officer, surveillance and CHIS, and any entry on or interference with property or any interference with wireless telegraphy.

- the power under Sch 3, para 5 (2) to authorise an officer to obtain documents or information on the Tribunal's behalf;
- the power under s 7(5)(b) of the HRA to extend the time limit for HRA, s 7 proceedings;[7]
- the power under s 67(5) to extend the time limit for complaints;[8]
- the duty under r 13 to notify the complainant of any of the determinations described in that rule;[9]
- the duty, in considering a complaint, to investigate (under s 67(3)(a) and (b)) (but the single member may not determine the complaint).

Time limit of one year

In the case of the Tribunal's complaints jurisdiction (s 65(2)(b)) and also its juris-   **8.19**
diction to deal with proceedings under s 7 of the HRA 1998, the Tribunal is obliged not to hear the complaint if it is made more than one year after the conduct complained of *unless* it is satisfied that it would be equitable to do so having regard to all the circumstances (RIPA, s 67(5) and HRA 1998, s 7(5)). IPTR r 5(1)(f) permits an extension of time to be granted by one Tribunal member rather than a full Tribunal.

Presumably an example of such circumstances justifying an extension might be where the complainant could not reasonably have been expected to know the date of the conduct complained of with accuracy. IPTR, r 13(3)(b) requires the Tribunal to notify the complainant if the Tribunal decides not to extend the time limit for a complaint.

The Tribunal procedure generally

The IPT may determine its own procedure subject to any rules, such as the IPTR   **8.20**
themselves, made by the Secretary of State under his rule-making powers in s 69. Sections 68(2) and (3) make it clear that the IPT may require a relevant commissioner to provide assistance to the IPT on any relevant matter as it thinks fit, and keep relevant commissioners informed about matters before it in respect of which the commissioner(s) have functions.

However note that the IPT in the case of *Re Kennedy* (summarised in Chapter 22) ruled that notwithstanding r 9(6) of the IPTR which required it to sit in private, it had the power to sit in public and r 9(6) was ultra vires.

---

[7] Ordinarily the period of one year from the date of the matter complained of, unless it is equitable to extend time.

[8] By s 67(5) ordinarily one year from the date of the conduct complained of, unless it is equitable to extend time.

[9] Relating to notifying the complainant of determinations of frivolous or vexatious complaints, complaints which are out of time where an extension has been refused and complaints where the Tribunal decides that the complainant does not have a right to bring the HRA 1988, s 7 proceedings or to make the complaint.

How to commence HRA 1998, s 7 proceedings

8.21 To commence proceedings the complainant must send a standard form T1[10] to the Tribunal, whose address is:

Investigatory Powers Tribunal

PO Box 33220

London

SWIH 9ZQ

8.22 By IPTR, r 7 it is a requirement that the form is signed by the complainant, giving his name, address and date of birth (IPTR, r 7(2)(a)). The same rule requires the complainant to:

- set out each public authority against which the proceedings are brought (r 7(2)(b));
- describe the nature of the claim (including details of the Convention right which it is alleged has been infringed) and the complainant's interest (r 7(2)(c));
- and to specify the remedy sought (r 7(2)(d)).

In support the complainant is required by IPTR, r 7(3) to supply a summary of the information on which the claim is based, in the T1 form or with it.

Making a complaint (s 65(2)(b)) and IPTR, r 8

8.23 A complaint under the s 65(2)(b) jurisdiction is brought by sending to the Tribunal a completed T2 form[11] signed by the complainant and giving name, address and date of birth (r 8(2)(a)), with other details required by IPTR, r 8 namely:

- the person or authority whose conduct, to the best of the complainant's knowledge or belief, is the subject of the complaint (r 8(2)(b));
- a description of the conduct complained of, given to the best of the complainant's knowledge or belief (r 8(2)(c));
- either in or with the form, a summary of the information on which the claim is based (r 8(3)).

Disposal of frivolous or vexatious cases

8.24 Section 67(4) disapplies the Tribunal's duty to deal with complaints in the case of frivolous or vexatious matters, and that jurisdiction is embodied in r 13(3)(a) which provides that the Tribunal must notify the complainant of the fact that they determine the complaint to be frivolous or vexatious. Notification is one of the functions which may be carried out by a single Tribunal member under (r 5(1)(g)).

---

[10] A copy of this form appears in Chapter 12. Original forms may be obtained from the Tribunal.
[11] See Chapter 12.

Further particulars and interim orders

For both s 7 proceedings and Complaints the Tribunal may at any time invite the **8.25** complainant to supply further information or representations. See IPTR, rr 7(4) and 8(4).

The Tribunal is entitled to make whatever interim orders it thinks fit pending determination of proceedings, subject to any relevant rules (s 67(6)). The general rule is that the Tribunal must invite representations from affected parties before making orders (see IPTR, r 12).

IPTR, r 12(3) includes interim orders when referring to the requirement to give **8.26** the authority (or person) complained against an opportunity to make representations on the proposed order.

The nature of the proceedings and evidence

IPTR, rr 9 and 10 are the key rules governing the form and nature of the proceedings **8.27** and the right to representation. By IPTR, r 9 the Tribunal is not obliged to (but may) hold oral hearings. The complainant may be permitted to make representations, give evidence or call witnesses if an oral hearing is held (r 9(3)). The Tribunal is also given, by IPTR, r 9(4), the power to hold separate oral hearings at which the following classes of person may be required to attend, and at which they may make representations, give evidence or call witnesses:

- the person whose conduct is the subject of the complaint;
- the public authority against which the s 7 proceedings are brought;
- any other person specified in s 68(7) of the Act (ie the persons who are under a duty to disclose and provide information to the Tribunal).

In the event that an oral hearing is to take place the Tribunal may set a date by which it **8.28** must be informed of any witnesses to be called: r 9(5) debars the calling of any other witnesses without leave. The Tribunal's proceedings are on the face of matters required by r 9(6) to be conducted in private but the IPT in the case of *Re Kennedy* (summarised in Chapter 22) ruled that notwithstanding r 9(6) it had the power to sit in public.

Various classes of person have (by IPTR, r 10) rights of audience at any oral hearing if representing a person entitled to make representations or call evidence: **8.29**

- a member of the Bar of England and Wales or of Northern Ireland,
- a solicitor of the Supreme Court in England and Wales or in Northern Ireland,
- a member of the Faculty of Advocates,
- a solicitor within the meaning of the Solicitors (Scotland) Act 1980, or
- any other person with the leave of the Tribunal.

IPTR, r 11 deals with the form of evidence before the IPT and is very broad. The **8.30** IPT may receive evidence in any form, and may receive evidence that would not be admissible in a court of law. Evidence may be required to be given on oath but the IPT cannot compel a complainant to give evidence at an oral hearing (under r 9(3)).

Types of order which may be made by the IPT

8.31 Section 67(7) provides the IPT with the power to:

- award compensation to the complainant;
- quash or cancel warrants or authorizations;
- require destruction of records of information obtained in exercise of powers under a warrant or authorisation.

The Tribunal may also order destruction of records of information held by any public authority concerning any person. (Public authorities are any bodies other than courts or tribunals which fall within the scope of s 6 of the HRA 1998—see RIPA, s 81(1)).

Notifying decisions of the IPT

8.32 The IPT must (subject to any relevant rules which provide for more information to be given to the complainant) notify the complainant of the fact that it has made a determination either in his favour or not in his favour.

IPTR, r 13 supplements this minimal provision by providing that the Tribunal must also provide information to the complainant as follows.

- Where the IPT makes a determination in favour of the complainant, the Tribunal shall provide him with a summary of that determination including any findings of fact (r 13(2)).
- Where the IPT decides that the bringing of HRA, s 7 proceedings or the making of a complaint is frivolous or vexatious, or that they have been brought out of time and that the time limit should not be extended, or that the complainant does not have the right to bring the s 7 proceedings or make the complaint,[12] the Tribunal (or single member) must notify the complainant of that fact.

The reader is referred to para **8.34** below for limitations on the extent to which information may be disclosed (which also applies for the purposes of r 13).

8.33 If the Tribunal's determination is in the complainant's favour and relates to an act or omission by the Secretary of State, or to any conduct authorised by a warrant or authorisation by the Secretary of State, then the IPT must report their findings to the Prime Minister—see s 68(4) and (5).

---

[12] Eg if the person bringing the claim under the HRA 1998, s 7 would not amount to a 'victim' for the purposes of the Convention.

Rules limiting the extent to which the IPT[13] discloses information

IPTR, r 6(1) provides that the Tribunal must operate in such a way as not to **8.34** disclose information either in a manner or to an extent which would be contrary to the public interest or to national security, or to the prevention and detection of serious crime, economic well-being of the UK or to the discharge of the functions of the various intelligence services.

That basic rule is the starting point, but is elaborated upon by the remainder of IPTR, r 6 so that some types of information may not necessarily be disclosed to the complainant or anyone else even if disclosure would not infringe the basic principles of r 6(1). Thus, by r 6(2) and (3) the IPT may not generally disclose to anyone:

- the fact that the Tribunal has held, or proposes to hold, an oral hearing under r 9(4), unless the person required to attend the hearing consents;
- any information or document disclosed in the course of that hearing, or the identity of any witness, unless the witness or the person who disclosed or provided the information or document consents;
- any information or document disclosed to the Tribunal by any person under the duty set out in s 68(6) of the Act, (including where provided voluntarily) unless the person who disclosed or provided the information, etc consents (see also **8.04** above);
- any information or opinion provided to the Tribunal by a commissioner, unless the commissioner in question consents *and*, to the extent that the information or opinion includes information from another person, that other person also consents;
- the fact that any of the above has been disclosed (unless the person concerned consents as above).

A modification to the above applies if the complaint is upheld. In those circum- **8.35** stances it will be recalled that the Tribunal must provide the complainant with a summary of that determination including any findings of fact (r 13(2)).

There is potential tension between the restrictions of r 6(1) and (2) on disclosure **8.36** of information, on the one hand, and the obligation to give a summary and findings of fact where the complaint is successful, under r 13(2).

The IPTR reach a balance that in such circumstances, as a result of r 6(4): **8.37**

- the general restriction in r 6(1) applies come what may (ie the summary and findings may not disclose information contrary to the national interest, etc) but subject to that;
- the types of information set out in r 6(2) may be disclosed as part of the r 13(2) summary and findings (even without consent of the person concerned)

---

[13] The IPT also cannot order any person to disclose information which it itself would not be permitted to disclose: r 6(5).

provided the person whose consent would be required has been given an opportunity to make representations (see r 13(5)).

Additional protection for information provided by the complainant

8.38   IPTR, r 6(6) and (7) affords some additional protection to the privacy of the
complainant against the (mis-)use of information supplied by him as part of the
complaint. The IPT may not (unless the complainant consents) disclose to *any
person holding office under the Crown other than a commissioner* any information
provided either by the complainant or on his behalf, apart from the most basic of
information which is required to be stated on the face of the Tribunal forms,
namely the name, address and date of birth of the complainant, and the details of
the public authorities in question (the information required to be included on the
T1 or T2 forms by r 7(2)(a) and (b) and r 8(2)(a) and (b)).

Appeals against Tribunal decisions

8.39   At the time of writing there was no avenue of appeal or means to question a decision of the IPT in any court, but s 67(8) and (10) provides that the Secretary of
State may provide for avenues of appeal, including the establishment of an appeal
body. The effective result is that a person has no avenue of appeal at present against
IPT decisions even in HRA s 7 proceedings, though it is probable that such a person could apply to the ECHR since the Convention requires contracting States
not to interfere with the right of a person to apply to that court. The full text of the
Tribunal Rules appears in Chapter 11. The standard forms for use in making a
complaint to the Tribunal appear in Chapter 12.

The text of RIPA, Part IV, ss 65–70 as amended follows.

B. Text of Part IV

REGULATION OF INVESTIGATORY POWERS
ACT 2000 (AS AMENDED)

The Tribunal

The Tribunal[14]

65.[15]—(1) There shall, for the purpose of exercising the jurisdiction conferred on
them by this section, be a tribunal consisting of such number of members as Her
Majesty may by Letters Patent appoint—

---

[14] Unless otherwise noted, the parts of s 65 not in force at time of writing are italicised and mostly
relate to matters falling within Part III of the Act which is not in force.
[15] Commencement: s 65(1), (2)(a) and (b), (3)(a), (b) and (d), (4), (5)(a), (b), (d) and (f), (9) and
(11) only from 2/10/00, by SI 2000 No 2543. Section 65(5)(c) and (8)(b) only from 5/1/04 by SI

(2) The jurisdiction of the Tribunal shall be—

    (a) to be the only appropriate tribunal for the purposes of section 7 of the Human Rights Act 1998 in relation to any proceedings under subsection (1)(a) of that section (proceedings for actions incompatible with Convention rights) which fall within subsection (3) of this section;[16]

    (b)[17] to consider and determine any complaints made to them which, in accordance with subsection (4), are complaints for which the Tribunal is the appropriate forum;

    [(c) to consider and determine any reference to them by any person that he has suffered detriment as a consequence of any prohibition or restriction, by virtue of section 17, on his relying in, or for the purposes of, any civil proceedings on any matter; and

    (d) to hear and determine any other such proceedings falling within subsection (3) as may be allocated to them in accordance with provision made by the Secretary of State by order.][18]

(3) Proceedings fall within this subsection if—

    (a) they are proceedings against any of the intelligence services;

    (b) they are proceedings against any other person in respect of any conduct, or proposed conduct, by or on behalf of any of those services;

    [(c) they are proceedings brought by virtue of section 55(4); or][19]

    (d) they are proceedings relating to the taking place in any challengeable circumstances of any conduct falling within subsection (5).

(4) The Tribunal is the appropriate forum for any complaint if it is a complaint by a person who is aggrieved by any conduct falling within subsection (5) which he believes—

    (a) to have taken place in relation to him, to any of his property, to any communications sent by or to him, or intended for him, or to his use of any postal service, telecommunications service or telecommunication system; and

    (b) to have taken place in challengeable circumstances or to have been carried out by or on behalf of any of the intelligence services.

(5) Subject to subsection (6), conduct falls within this subsection if (whenever it occurred) it is—

    (a) conduct by or on behalf of any of the intelligence services;

2003 No 3140. The remainder of the section is not in force (s 65(2)(c), (d), (3)(c), (d), (5)(e), (6), (7), (8)(a), (c–f), (10)).

[16] Note that since no avenue of appeal has been created as yet, at least under domestic law, there is no appeal against HRA, s 7 determinations made by the IPT where it is the only appropriate tribunal, which contrasts with the position generally under the HRA where s 7 proceedings are brought in the courts.

[17] SI 2000 No 2543, Art 6 makes provision for the manner in which complaints of various sorts should be dealt with under this section if they were made before 2/10/00.   [18] Not in force.

[19] Not in force.

   (b)   conduct for or in connection with the interception of communications in the course of their transmission by means of a postal service or
telecommunication system;

   (c)   conduct to which Chapter II of Part I applies;

  (ca)[20] the carrying out of surveillance by a foreign police or customs officer
(within the meaning of section 76A);

   (d)[21] other conduct to which Part II applies;

  *[(e)   the giving of a notice under section 49 or any disclosure or use of a key to
protected information;][22]*

   (f)   any entry on or interference with property or any interference with
wireless telegraphy.

*[(6) For the purposes only of subsection (3), nothing mentioned in paragraph (d) or
(f) of subsection (5) shall be treated as falling within that subsection unless
it is conduct by or on behalf of a person holding any office, rank or position
with—*

   (a)   any of the intelligence services;

   (b)   any of Her Majesty's forces;

   (c)   any police force;

  (ca)[23] the Independent Police Complaints Commission;

  [(d)   the National Criminal Intelligence Service;

   (e)   the National Crime Squad; or]

   (d)   the Serious Organised Crime Agency;[24] or

   (f)   the Commissioners of Customs and Excise;

*and section 48(5) applies for the purposes of this subsection as it applies for the purposes
of Part II.][25]*

(7) For the purposes of this section conduct takes place in challengeable circumstances if—

   (a) it takes place with the authority, or purported authority, of anything
falling within subsection (8); or

   (b) the circumstances are such that (whether or not there is such authority) it
would not have been appropriate for the conduct to take place without it,
or at least without proper consideration having been given to whether
such authority should be sought;

---

[20] Inserted by the Crime (International Co-operation) Act 2003, s 91, Sch 5, para 79 with effect
from 26/4/04 (commenced by SI 2004 No 786).
   [21] Amended by the Crime (International Co-operation) Act 2003, s 91, Sch 5, para 79 with
effect from 26/4/04 (commenced by SI 2004 No 786).   [22] Not in force.
   [23] Inserted by the Independent Police Complaints Commission (Investigatory Powers) Order
2004 (SI 2004 No 815, Art 3(10)) from 1/4/04.
   [24] Subsections (d) and (e) in square brackets are replaced by new subsections (d) with
effect from the date of commencement of Sch 4, para 151 of the SOCAP Act 2005.
   [25] Not in force.

but conduct does not take place in challengeable circumstances to the extent that it is authorised by, or takes place with the permission of, a judicial authority.

(7A)[26] For the purposes of this section conduct also takes place in challengeable circumstances if it takes place, or purports to take place, under section 76A.

(8) The following fall within this subsection—

(a) an interception warrant or a warrant under the Interception of Communications Act 1985;

(b) an authorisation or notice under Chapter II of Part I of this Act;

(c) an authorisation under Part II of this Act or under any enactment contained in or made under an Act of the Scottish Parliament which makes provision equivalent to that made by that Part;

[(d) *a permission for the purposes of Schedule 2 to this Act*];

[(e) *a notice under section 49 of this Act; or*]

(f) an authorisation under section 93 of the Police Act 1997.

(9) Schedule 3 (which makes further provision in relation to the Tribunal) shall have effect.

[(10) *In this section*—

(a) *references to a key and to protected information shall be construed in accordance with section 56;*

(b) *references to the disclosure or use of a key to protected information taking place in relation to a person are references to such a disclosure or use taking place in a case in which that person has had possession of the key or of the protected information; and*

(c) *references to the disclosure of a key to protected information include references to the making of any disclosure in an intelligible form (within the meaning of section 56) of protected information by a person who is or has been in possession of the key to that information;*

and the reference in paragraph (b) to a person's having possession of a key or of protected information shall be construed in accordance with section 56.][27]

(11) In this section "judicial authority" means—

(a) any judge of the High Court or of the Crown Court or any Circuit Judge;

(b) any judge of the High Court of Justiciary or any sheriff;

(c) any justice of the peace;

(d) any county court judge or resident magistrate in Northern Ireland;

(e) any person holding any such judicial office as entitles him to exercise the jurisdiction of a judge of the Crown Court or of a justice of the peace.

---

[26] Inserted by the Crime (International Co-operation) Act 2003, s 91, Sch 5, para 79 with effect from 26/4/04 (commenced by SI 2004 No 786).   [27] Not in force.

Orders allocating proceedings to the Tribunal

66.[28]—(1) An order under section 65(2)(d) allocating proceedings to the Tribunal—

    (a) may provide for the Tribunal to exercise jurisdiction in relation to that matter to the exclusion of the jurisdiction of any court or tribunal; but

    (b) if it does so provide, must contain provision conferring a power on the Tribunal, in the circumstances provided for in the order, to remit the proceedings to the court or tribunal which would have had jurisdiction apart from the order.

(2) In making any provision by an order under section 65(2)(d) the Secretary of State shall have regard, in particular, to—

    (a) the need to secure that proceedings allocated to the Tribunal are properly heard and considered; and

    (b) the need to secure that information is not disclosed to an extent, or in a manner, that is contrary to the public interest or prejudicial to national security, the prevention or detection of serious crime, the economic well-being of the United Kingdom or the continued discharge of the functions of any of the intelligence services.

(3) The Secretary of State shall not make an order under section 65(2)(d) unless a draft of the order has been laid before Parliament and approved by a resolution of each House.

Exercise of the Tribunal's jurisdiction

67.[29]—(1) Subject to subsections (4) and (5), it shall be the duty of the Tribunal-

    (a) to hear and determine any proceedings brought before them by virtue of section 65(2)(a) or (d); and

    (b) to consider and determine any complaint or reference made to them by virtue of section 65(2)(b) or (c).

(2) Where the Tribunal hear any proceedings by virtue of section 65(2)(a), they shall apply the same principles for making their determination in those proceedings as would be applied by a court on an application for judicial review.

(3) Where the Tribunal consider a complaint made to them by virtue of section 65(2)(b), it shall be the duty of the Tribunal—

    (a) to investigate whether the persons against whom any allegations are made in the complaint have engaged in relation to—

        (i) the complainant,

        (ii) any of his property,

        (iii) any communications sent by or to him, or intended for him, or

---

[28] Not in force.
[29] Commencement: 2/10/00 save for subs (9) which is not in force. Subsection (1) is in force from that date only to the extent that it relates to s 65(2)(a) and (b) (SI 2000 No 2543).

      (iv) his use of any postal service, telecommunications service or telecommunication system,

in any conduct falling within section 65(5);

    (b) to investigate the authority (if any) for any conduct falling within section 65(5) which they find has been so engaged in; and

    (c) in relation to the Tribunal's findings from their investigations, to determine the complaint by applying the same principles as would be applied by a court on an application for judicial review.

(4) The Tribunal shall not be under any duty to hear, consider or determine any proceedings, complaint or reference if it appears to them that the bringing of the proceedings or the making of the complaint or reference is frivolous or vexatious.

(5) Except where the Tribunal, having regard to all the circumstances, are satisfied that it is equitable to do so, they shall not consider or determine any complaint made by virtue of section 65(2)(b) if it is made more than one year after the taking place of the conduct to which it relates.

(6) Subject to any provision made by rules under section 69, where any proceedings have been brought before the Tribunal or any reference made to the Tribunal, they shall have power to make such interim orders,[30] pending their final determination, as they think fit.

(7) Subject to any provision made by rules under section 69, the Tribunal on determining any proceedings, complaint or reference shall have power to make any such award of compensation or other order as they think fit; and, without prejudice to the power to make rules under section 69(2)(h), the other orders that may be made by the Tribunal include-

    (a) an order quashing or cancelling any warrant or authorisation; and

    (b) an order requiring the destruction of any records of information which—

      (i) has been obtained in exercise of any power conferred by a warrant or authorisation; or

      (ii) is held by any public authority[31] in relation to any person.

(8) Except to such extent as the Secretary of State may by order otherwise provide, determinations, awards, orders and other decisions of the Tribunal (including decisions as to whether they have jurisdiction) shall not be subject to appeal or be liable to be questioned in any court.[32]

(9) It shall be the duty of the Secretary of State to secure that there is at all times an order under subsection (8) in force allowing for an appeal to a court against any exercise by the Tribunal of their jurisdiction under section 65(2)(c) or (d).

---

[30] See IPTR, r 12(3).

[31] By s 81(1) a public authority is any public authority within the meaning of s 6 of the HRA 1998, other than a court or tribunal.

[32] At the time of writing no avenue of appeal had been put in place.

(10) The provision that may be contained in an order under subsection (8) may include—

(a) provision for the establishment and membership of a tribunal or body to hear appeals;

(b) the appointment of persons to that tribunal or body and provision about the remuneration and allowances to be payable to such persons and the expenses of the tribunal;

(c) the conferring of jurisdiction to hear appeals on any existing court or tribunal; and

(d) any such provision in relation to an appeal under the order as corresponds to provision that may be made by rules under section 69 in relation to proceedings before the Tribunal, or to complaints or references made to the Tribunal.

(11) The Secretary of State shall not make an order under subsection (8) unless a draft of the order has been laid before Parliament and approved by a resolution of each House.

(12) The Secretary of State shall consult the Scottish Ministers before making any order under subsection (8); and any such order shall be laid before the Scottish Parliament.

Tribunal procedure

68.[33]—(1) Subject to any rules made under section 69, the Tribunal shall be entitled to determine their own procedure in relation to any proceedings, complaint or reference brought before or made to them.

(2) The Tribunal shall have power—

(a) in connection with the investigation of any matter, or

(b) otherwise for the purposes of the Tribunal's consideration or determination of any matter,

to require a relevant Commissioner appearing to the Tribunal to have functions in relation to the matter in question to provide the Tribunal with all such assistance (including that Commissioner's opinion as to any issue falling to be determined by the Tribunal) as the Tribunal think fit.

(3) Where the Tribunal hear or consider any proceedings, complaint or reference relating to any matter, they shall secure that every relevant Commissioner appearing to them to have functions in relation to that matter—

(a) is aware that the matter is the subject of proceedings, a complaint or a reference brought before or made to the Tribunal; and

(b) is kept informed of any determination, award, order or other decision made by the Tribunal with respect to that matter.

---

[33] Commencement: 2/10/00 (SI 2000 No 2543) all except (7)(g), (h), (m) and (n) insofar as it relates to (m). Section 68(7)(g) and (h) in force 5/1/04 by SI 2003 No 3140. Subsection (7)(m) not in force.

(4) Where the Tribunal determine any proceedings, complaint or reference brought before or made to them, they shall give notice to the complainant which (subject to any rules made by virtue of section 69(2)(i)) shall be confined, as the case may be, to either—

(a) a statement that they have made a determination in his favour; or

(b) a statement that no determination has been made in his favour.

(5) Where—

(a) the Tribunal make a determination in favour of any person by whom any proceedings have been brought before the Tribunal or by whom any complaint or reference has been made to the Tribunal, and

(b) the determination relates to any act or omission by or on behalf of the Secretary of State or to conduct for which any warrant, authorisation or permission was issued, granted or given by the Secretary of State, they shall make a report of their findings to the Prime Minister.

(6) It shall be the duty of the persons specified in subsection (7) to disclose or provide to the Tribunal all such documents and information as the Tribunal may require for the purpose of enabling them—

(a) to exercise the jurisdiction conferred on them by or under section 65; or

(b) otherwise to exercise or perform any power or duty conferred or imposed on them by or under this Act.

(7) Those persons are—

(a) every person holding office under the Crown;

[(b) every member of the National Criminal Intelligence Service];

(b) every member of the staff of the Serious Organised Crime Agency;[34]

(c) every member of the National Crime Squad;

(d) every person employed by or for the purposes of a police force;

(da)[35] every member and every employee of the Independent Police Complaints Commission;

(e) every person required for the purposes of section 11 to provide assistance with giving effect to an interception warrant;

(f) every person on whom an obligation to take any steps has been imposed under section 12;

(g) every person by or to whom an authorisation under section 22(3) has been granted;

(h) every person to whom a notice under section 22(4) has been given;

(i) every person by whom, or on whose application, there has been granted or given any authorisation under Part II of this Act or under Part III of the Police Act 1997;

---

[34] The text in square brackets will be replaced by the text in italics when Sch 4, para 152 of the SOCAP Act 2005 comes into force.

[35] Inserted by the Independent Police Complaints Commission (Investigatory Powers) Order 2004 (SI 2004 No 815, Art 3(11)).

(j) every person who holds or has held any office, rank or position with the same public authority as a person falling within paragraph (i);

(k) every person who has engaged in any conduct with the authority of an authorisation under section 22 or Part II of this Act or under Part III of the Police Act 1997;

(l) every person who holds or has held any office, rank or position with a public authority for whose benefit any such authorisation has been or may be given;

(m) every person to whom a notice under section 49 has been given;[36] *and*

(n) every person who is or has been employed for the purposes of any business of a person falling within paragraph (e), (f), (h) or (m).

(8) In this section "relevant Commissioner" means the Interception of Communications Commissioner, the Intelligence Services Commissioner, the Investigatory Powers Commissioner for Northern Ireland or any Surveillance Commissioner or Assistant Surveillance Commissioner.

Tribunal rules

69.[37]—(1) The Secretary of State may make rules[38] regulating—

(a) the exercise by the Tribunal of the jurisdiction conferred on them by or under section 65; and

(b) any matters preliminary or incidental to, or arising out of, the hearing or consideration of any proceedings, complaint or reference brought before or made to the Tribunal.

(2) Without prejudice to the generality of subsection (1), rules under this section may—

(a) enable the jurisdiction of the Tribunal to be exercised at any place in the United Kingdom by any two or more members of the Tribunal designated for the purpose by the President of the Tribunal;

(b) enable different members of the Tribunal to carry out functions in relation to different complaints at the same time;

(c) prescribe the form and manner in which proceedings are to be brought before the Tribunal or a complaint or reference is to be made to the Tribunal;

(d) require persons bringing proceedings or making complaints or references to take such preliminary steps, and to make such disclosures, as may be specified in the rules for the purpose of facilitating a determination of whether—

(i) the bringing of the proceedings, or

(ii) the making of the complaint or reference,

is frivolous or vexatious;

---

[36] (m) not in force.   [37] Commencement: 2/10/00 (SI 2000 No 2543).
[38] The current rules were made by SI 2000 No 2665 (the Investigatory Powers Tribunal Rules 2000).

(e) make provision about the determination of any question as to whether a person by whom—
   (i) any proceedings have been brought before the Tribunal, or
   (ii) any complaint or reference has been made to the Tribunal, is a person with a right to bring those proceedings or make that complaint or reference;

(f) prescribe the forms of hearing or consideration to be adopted by the Tribunal in relation to particular proceedings, complaints or references (including a form that requires any proceedings brought before the Tribunal to be disposed of as if they were a complaint or reference made to the Tribunal);

(g) prescribe the practice and procedure to be followed on, or in connection with, the hearing or consideration of any proceedings, complaint or reference (including, where applicable, the mode and burden of proof and the admissibility of evidence);

(h) prescribe orders that may be made by the Tribunal under section 67(6) or (7);

(i) require information about any determination, award, order or other decision made by the Tribunal in relation to any proceedings, complaint or reference to be provided (in addition to any statement under section 68(4)) to the person who brought the proceedings or made the complaint or reference, or to the person representing his interests.

(3) Rules under this section in relation to the hearing or consideration of any matter by the Tribunal may provide—
   (a) for a person who has brought any proceedings before or made any complaint or reference to the Tribunal to have the right to be legally represented;
   (b) for the manner in which the interests of a person who has brought any proceedings before or made any complaint or reference to the Tribunal are otherwise to be represented;
   (c) for the appointment in accordance with the rules, by such person as may be determined in accordance with the rules, of a person to represent those interests in the case of any proceedings, complaint or reference.

(4) The power to make rules under this section includes power to make rules—
   (a) enabling or requiring the Tribunal to hear or consider any proceedings, complaint or reference without the person who brought the proceedings or made the complaint or reference having been given full particulars of the reasons for any conduct which is the subject of the proceedings, complaint or reference;
   (b) enabling or requiring the Tribunal to take any steps in exercise of their jurisdiction in the absence of any person (including the person bringing the proceedings or making the complaint or reference and any legal representative of his);

    (c) enabling or requiring the Tribunal to give a summary of any evidence taken in his absence to the person by whom the proceedings were brought or, as the case may be, to the person who made the complaint or reference;

    (d) enabling or requiring the Tribunal to exercise their jurisdiction, and to exercise and perform the powers and duties conferred or imposed on them (including, in particular, in relation to the giving of reasons), in such manner provided for in the rules as prevents or limits the disclosure of particular matters.

(5) Rules under this section may also include provision—

    (a) enabling powers or duties of the Tribunal that relate to matters preliminary or incidental to the hearing or consideration of any proceedings, complaint or reference to be exercised or performed by a single member of the Tribunal; and

    (b) conferring on the Tribunal such ancillary powers as the Secretary of State thinks necessary for the purposes of, or in connection with, the exercise of the Tribunal's jurisdiction, or the exercise or performance of any power or duty conferred or imposed on them.

(6) In making rules under this section the Secretary of State shall have regard, in particular, to—

    (a) the need to secure that matters which are the subject of proceedings, complaints or references brought before or made to the Tribunal are properly heard and considered; and

    (b) the need to secure that information is not disclosed to an extent, or in a manner, that is contrary to the public interest or prejudicial to national security, the prevention or detection of serious crime, the economic well-being of the United Kingdom or the continued discharge of the functions of any of the intelligence services.

(7) Rules under this section may make provision by the application, with or without modification, of the provision from time to time contained in specified rules of court.

(8) Subject to subsection (9), no rules shall be made under this section unless a draft of them has first been laid before Parliament and approved by a resolution of each House.

(9) Subsection (8) does not apply in the case of the rules made on the first occasion on which the Secretary of State exercises his power to make rules under this section.

(10) The rules made on that occasion shall cease to have effect at the end of the period of forty days beginning with the day on which they were made unless, before the end of that period, they have been approved by a resolution of each House of Parliament.

(11) For the purposes of subsection (10)

  (a) the rules' ceasing to have effect shall be without prejudice to anything previously done or to the making of new rules; and

  (b) in reckoning the period of forty days no account shall be taken of any period during which Parliament is dissolved or prorogued or during which both Houses are adjourned for more than four days.

(12) The Secretary of State shall consult the Scottish Ministers before making any rules under this section; and any rules so made shall be laid before the Scottish Parliament.

Abolition of jurisdiction in relation to complaints

70.[39]—(1) The provisions set out in subsection (2) (which provide for the investigation etc. of certain complaints) shall not apply in relation to any complaint made after the coming into force of this section.

(2) Those provisions are—

  (a) section 5 of, and Schedules 1 and 2 to, the Security Service Act 1989 (investigation of complaints about the Security Service made to the Tribunal established under that Act);

  (b) section 9 of, and Schedules 1 and 2 to, the Intelligence Services Act 1994 (investigation of complaints about the Secret Intelligence Service or GCHQ made to the Tribunal established under that Act); and

  (c) section 102 of, and Schedule 7 to, the Police Act 1997 (investigation of complaints made to the Surveillance Commissioners).

---

[39] Commencement: 2/10/00 (SI 2000 No 2543). This section effectively abolishes the various tribunals under the SSA 1989, Intelligence Services Act 1994 and the complaint process previously in place under s 102 of the Police Act 1997 (complaints to the surveillance commissioner).

9

SECTIONS GOVERNING THE CODES OF PRACTICE: RIPA, PART IV, SS 71–72

Codes reproduced in this work

The following Codes of Practice appear elsewhere in this work and the reader is **9.01** referred to the relevant chapters listed below as well as to the substantive chapters relating to the relevant subject areas.

- The Surveillance Code of Practice 2002 (SI 2002 No 1933)—Chapter 15;
- The Covert Human Intelligence Sources Code of Practice 2002 (SI 2002 No 1932)—Chapter 16;
- Voluntary Retention of Communications Data Code of Practice under Part II: Anti-Terrorism, Crime and Security Act 2001 (SI 2003 No 3175)—Chapter 17;
- Interception of Communications Code of Practice 2002 (SI 2002 No 1693)—Chapter 18;
- Acquisition and Disclosure of Communications Revised Code of Practice (Pre-Consultation draft Code of Practice 2005)—Chapter 19.

For a discussion of the effect of the sections here in the context of their respective subject areas, see the chapters relating to the relevant subject areas.

The text of RIPA, Part IV, ss 71–72 as amended follows.

REGULATION OF INVESTIGATORY POWERS ACT 2000 (AS AMENDED)

Codes of practice

Issue and revision of codes of practice

71.[1]—(1) The Secretary of State shall issue one or more codes of practice relating to the exercise and performance of the powers and duties mentioned in subsection (2).

---

[1] Commencement: 25/9/00 (by SI 2000 No 2543) to the extent that the section relates to Part II of the Act, s 5 of the Intelligence Services Act 1994 or Part III of the Police Act 1997.

(2) Those powers and duties are those (excluding any power to make subordinate legislation) that are conferred or imposed otherwise than on the Surveillance Commissioners by or under—

(a) Parts I to III of this Act;

(b) section 5 of the Intelligence Services Act 1994 (warrants for interference with property or wireless telegraphy for the purposes of the intelligence services); and

(c) Part III of the Police Act 1997 (authorisation by the police or customs and excise of interference with property or wireless telegraphy).

(3) Before issuing a code of practice under subsection (1), the Secretary of State shall—

(a) prepare and publish a draft of that code; and

(b) consider any representations made to him about the draft;

and the Secretary of State may incorporate in the code finally issued any modifications made by him to the draft after its publication.

(4) The Secretary of State shall lay before both Houses of Parliament every draft code of practice prepared and published by him under this section.

(5) A code of practice issued by the Secretary of State under this section shall not be brought into force except in accordance with an order made by the Secretary of State.

(6) An order under subsection (5) may contain such transitional provisions and savings as appear to the Secretary of State to be necessary or expedient in connection with the bringing into force of the code brought into force by that order.

(7) The Secretary of State may from time to time—

(a) revise the whole or any part of a code issued under this section; and

(b) issue the revised code.

(8) Subsections (3) to (6) shall apply (with appropriate modifications) in relation to the issue of any revised code under this section as they apply in relation to the first issue of such a code.

(9) The Secretary of State shall not make an order containing provision for any of the purposes of this section unless a draft of the order has been laid before Parliament and approved by a resolution of each House.

Effect of codes of practice

72.² —(1) A person exercising or performing any power or duty in relation to which provision may be made by a code of practice under section 71 shall, in

---

Commencement on 2/10/00 (SI 2000 No 2543) to the extent that the section relates to Part I, Chapter I. Commencement 13/8/01 to the extent that the section relates to Part I, Chapter II.

² Commencement: 25/9/00 (by SI 2000 No 2543) as regards to the extent that the section relates to Part II of the Act, s 5 of the Intelligence Services Act 1994 or Part III of the Police Act 1997. Commencement on 2/10/00 (SI 2000 No. 2543) to the extent that the section relates to Part I, Chapter I. Commencement 13/8/01 to the extent that the section relates to Part I, Chapter II.

doing so, have regard to the provisions (so far as they are applicable) of every code of practice for the time being in force under that section.

(2) A failure on the part of any person to comply with any provision of a code of practice for the time being in force under section 71 shall not of itself render him liable to any criminal or civil proceedings.

(3) A code of practice in force at any time under section 71 shall be admissible in evidence in any criminal or civil proceedings.

(4) If any provision of a code of practice issued or revised under section 71 appears to—

(a) the court or tribunal conducting any civil or criminal proceedings,

(b) the Tribunal,

(c) a relevant Commissioner carrying out any of his functions under this Act,

(d) a Surveillance Commissioner carrying out his functions under this Act or the Police Act 1997, or

(e) any Assistant Surveillance Commissioner carrying out any functions of his under section 63 of this Act,

to be relevant to any question arising in the proceedings, or in connection with the exercise of that jurisdiction or the carrying out of those functions, in relation to a time when it was in force, that provision of the code shall be taken into account in determining that question.

(5) In this section "relevant Commissioner" means the Interception of Communications Commissioner, the Intelligence Services Commissioner or the Investigatory Powers Commissioner for Northern Ireland.

10

RIPA, PART V AND SCHEDULES

The effects of the sections listed here are dealt with as appropriate in the **10.01** discussions of the subject areas to which they relate.

REGULATION OF INVESTIGATORY POWERS ACT 2000 (AS AMENDED)

Part V
Miscellaneous and Supplemental

Miscellaneous

Conduct in relation to wireless telegraphy

73.[1]—(1) Section 5 of the Wireless Telegraphy Act 1949 (misleading messages and interception and disclosure of wireless telegraphy messages) shall become subsection (1) of that section.

---

[1] Commencement: 2/10/00 (SI 2000 No 2543). This excessively complex amendment to s 5 of the Wireless Telegraphy Act 1949 extensively modifies that section so as to bring its provisions into line with the RIPA scheme and general human rights law. The 1949 Act made it an offence to intercept wireless telegraphy messages (inter alia) without the authority of the Postmaster-General or in the course of Crown duties. This section amends s 5 of the 1949 Act to refer to a 'designated person' who is entitled to grant authorisation to intercept wireless telegraphy. Designated persons are, by the new s 5(12) the Secretary of State, commissioners of Customs and Excise, or any persons designated by order of the Secretary of State: see the Wireless Telegraphy (Interception and Disclosure of Messages) (Designation) Regulations 2000 (SI 2000 No 2409). Section 3(2) minimises the extent of 'overlap' between RIPA and the 1949 Act by providing that the designated person may not authorise interception under the 1949 Act where the conduct to be authorised would fall within the authorisation process of RIPA *unless* necessary for any of the specific purposes set out in s 5(4) or (5) of the amended 1949 Act, and is satisfied that the conduct is proportionate to what it seeks to achieve (s 5(3) of the amended 1949 Act).

(2) In paragraph (b) of that subsection—
   (a) for the words from "under the authority of" to "servant of the Crown," there shall be substituted "under the authority of a designated person"; and
   (b) in sub-paragraph (i), for the words from "which neither" to the end of the sub-paragraph there shall be substituted "of which neither the person using the apparatus nor a person on whose behalf he is acting is an intended recipient,".

(3) In that section, after that subsection there shall be inserted—
   "(2) The conduct in relation to which a designated person may give a separate authority for the purposes of this section shall not, except where he believes the conduct to be necessary on grounds falling within subsection (5) of this section, include—
      (a) any conduct which, if engaged in without lawful authority, constitutes an offence under section 1(1) or (2) of the Regulation of Investigatory Powers Act 2000;
      (b) any conduct which, if engaged in without lawful authority, is actionable under section 1(3) of that Act;
      (c) any conduct which is capable of being authorised by an authorisation or notice granted by any person under Chapter II of Part I of that Act (communications data);
      (d) any conduct which is capable of being authorised by an authorisation granted by any person under Part II of that Act (surveillance etc.).

   (3) A designated person shall not exercise his power to give a separate authority for the purposes of this section except where he believes—
      (a) that the giving of his authority is necessary on grounds falling within subsection (4) or (5) of this section; and
      (b) that the conduct authorised by him is proportionate to what is sought to be achieved by that conduct.

   (4) A separate authority for the purposes of this section is necessary on grounds falling within this subsection if it is necessary—
      (a) in the interests of national security;
      (b) for the purpose of preventing or detecting crime (within the meaning of the Regulation of Investigatory Powers Act 2000) or of preventing disorder;
      (c) in the interests of the economic well-being of the United Kingdom;
      (d) in the interests of public safety;
      (e) for the purpose of protecting public health;
      (f) for the purpose of assessing or collecting any tax, duty, levy or other imposition, contribution or charge payable to a government department; or

(g) for any purpose (not falling within paragraphs (a) to (f)) which is specified for the purposes of this subsection by regulations made by the Secretary of State.

(5) A separate authority for the purposes of this section is necessary on grounds falling within this subsection if it is not necessary on grounds falling within subsection (4)(a) or (c) to (g) but is necessary for purposes connected with—

(a) issue of licences under this Act;

(b) the prevention or detection of anything which constitutes interference with wireless telegraphy; or

(c) the enforcement of any enactment contained in this Act or of any enactment not so contained that relates to such interference.

(6) The matters to be taken into account in considering whether the requirements of subsection (3) of this section are satisfied in the case of the giving of any separate authority for the purposes of this section shall include whether what it is thought necessary to achieve by the authorised conduct could reasonably be achieved by other means.

(7) A separate authority for the purposes of this section must be in writing and under the hand of—

(a) the Secretary of State;

(b) one of the Commissioners of Customs and Excise; or

(c) a person not falling within paragraph (a) or (b) who is designated for the purposes of this subsection by regulations made by the Secretary of State.

(8) A separate authority for the purposes of this section may be general or specific and may be given—

(a) to such person or persons, or description of persons,

(b) for such period, and

(c) subject to such restrictions and limitations,

as the designated person thinks fit.

(9) No regulations shall be made under subsection (4)(g) unless a draft of them has first been laid before Parliament and approved by a resolution of each House.

(10) For the purposes of this section the question whether conduct is capable of being authorised under Chapter II of Part I of the Regulation of Investigatory Powers Act 2000 or under Part II of that Act shall be determined without reference—

(a) to whether the person whose conduct it is is a person on whom any power or duty is or may be conferred or imposed by or under Chapter II of Part I or Part II of that Act; or

(b) to whether there are grounds for believing that the requirements for the grant of an authorisation or the giving of a notice under Chapter II of Part I or Part II of that Act are satisfied.

(11) References in this section to a separate authority for the purposes of this section are references to any authority for the purposes of this section given otherwise than by way of the issue or renewal of a warrant, authorisation or notice under Part I or II of the Regulation of Investigatory Powers Act 2000.

(12) In this section "designated person" means—

(a) the Secretary of State;

(b) the Commissioners of Customs and Excise; or

(c) any other person designated for the purposes of this section by regulations made by the Secretary of State."

(4) In section 16(2) of that Act (regulations and orders), after "the said powers" there shall be inserted ", other than one containing regulations a draft of which has been approved for the purposes of section 5(9),".

Warrants under the Intelligence Services Act 1994

74.[2]—(1) In subsection (2) of section 5 of the Intelligence Services Act 1994 (the circumstances in which the Secretary of State may issue a warrant authorising interference with property or wireless telegraphy)—

(a) in paragraph (a), for "on the ground that it is likely to be of substantial value in" there shall be substituted "for the purpose of"; and

(b) for paragraph (b) there shall be substituted—

"(b) is satisfied that the taking of the action is proportionate to what the action seeks to achieve;".

(2) After that subsection, there shall be inserted—

"(2A) The matters to be taken into account in considering whether the requirements of subsection (2)(a) and (b) are satisfied in the case of any warrant shall include whether what it is thought necessary to achieve by the conduct authorised by the warrant could reasonably be achieved by other means."

(3) In each of sections 6(1)(b) and 7(5)(b) of that Act (warrants issued under the hand of a senior official of the Secretary of State's department), the words "of his department" shall be omitted.

(4) In section 11 of that Act (interpretation), for paragraph (1)(d) there shall be substituted—

"(d) "senior official" has the same meaning as in the Regulation of Investigatory Powers Act 2000;".

---

[2] Commencement: 25/9/00 (by SI 2000 No 2543).

75.[3]—(1) Section 93 of the Police Act 1997 (authorisations to interfere with property etc.) shall be amended as follows.

(2) In subsection (1) (the action that the authorising officer may authorise), for "or" at the end of paragraph (a) there shall be substituted—

"(ab) the taking of such action falling within subsection (1A), in respect of property outside the relevant area, as he may specify, or".

(3) After that subsection there shall be inserted—

"(1A) The action falling within this subsection is action for maintaining or retrieving any equipment, apparatus or device the placing or use of which in the relevant area has been authorised under this Part or Part II of the Regulation of Investigatory Powers Act 2000 or under any enactment contained in or made under an Act of the Scottish Parliament which makes provision equivalent to that made by Part II of that Act of 2000.

(1B) Subsection (1) applies where the authorising officer is a customs officer with the omission of—

(a) the words "in the relevant area", in each place where they occur; and

(b) paragraph (ab)."

(4) In subsection (2) (the grounds on which action may be authorised)—

(a) in paragraph (a), for the words from "on the ground" to "detection of" there shall be substituted "for the purpose of preventing or detecting"; and

(b) for paragraph (b) there shall be substituted—

"(b) that the taking of the action is proportionate to what the action seeks to achieve."

(5) After subsection (2) there shall be inserted—

"(2A) Subsection (2) applies where the authorising officer is the Chief Constable or the Deputy Chief Constable of the Royal Ulster Constabulary as if the reference in subsection (2)(a) to preventing or detecting serious crime included a reference to the interests of national security.

(2B) The matters to be taken into account in considering whether the requirements of subsection (2) are satisfied in the case of any authorisation shall include whether what it is thought necessary to achieve by the authorised action could reasonably be achieved by other means."

---

[3] Commencement: 25/9/00 (by SI 2000 No 2543).

(6) In subsection (5) (the meaning of authorising officer)—

    (a) after paragraph (e) there shall be inserted—

        "(ea) the Chief Constable of the Ministry of Defence Police;

        (eb) the Provost Marshal of the Royal Navy Regulating Branch;

        (ec) the Provost Marshal of the Royal Military Police;

        (ed) the Provost Marshal of the Royal Air Force Police;

        (ee) the Chief Constable of the British Transport Police;";

    [(b) in paragraph (g), after "National Crime Squad" there shall be inserted ", or any person holding the rank of assistant chief constable in that Squad who is designated for the purposes of this paragraph by that Director General"; and]⁴

    (c) in paragraph (h), for the word "the", in the first place where it occurs, there shall be substituted "any".

(7) In subsection (6) (the meaning of relevant area), after paragraph (c) there shall be inserted—

    "(ca) in relation to a person within paragraph (ea), means any place where, under section 2 of the Ministry of Defence Police Act 1987, the members of the Ministry of Defence Police have the powers and privileges of a constable;

    (cb) in relation to a person within paragraph (ee), means the United Kingdom;".

(8) After that subsection there shall be inserted—

    "(6A) For the purposes of any authorisation by a person within paragraph (eb), (ec) or (ed) of subsection (5) property is in the relevant area or action in respect of wireless telegraphy is taken in the relevant area if, as the case may be—

        (a) the property is owned, occupied, in the possession of or being used by a person subject to service discipline; or

        (b) the action is taken in relation to the use of wireless telegraphy by such a person.

    (6B) For the purposes of this section a person is subject to service discipline—

        (a) in relation to the Royal Navy Regulating Branch, if he is subject to the Naval Discipline Act 1957 or is a civilian to whom Parts I and II of that Act for the time being apply by virtue of section 118 of that Act;

        (b) in relation to the Royal Military Police, if he is subject to military law or is a civilian to whom Part II of the Army Act 1955 for the time being applies by virtue of section 209 of that Act; and

---

⁴ The text in square brackets will be omitted when Sch 4, para 153 of the SOCAP Act 2005 is in force.

(c) in relation to the Royal Air Force Police, if he is subject to air-force law or is a civilian to whom Part II of the Air Force Act 1955 for the time being applies by virtue of section 209 of that Act."

Surveillance etc. operations beginning in Scotland

76.[5]—(1) Subject to subsection (2), where—

(a) an authorisation under the relevant Scottish legislation has the effect of authorising the carrying out in Scotland of the conduct described in the authorisation,

(b) the conduct so described is or includes conduct to which Part II of this Act applies, and

(c) circumstances arise by virtue of which some or all of the conduct so described can for the time being be carried out only outwith Scotland,

section 27 of this Act shall have effect for the purpose of making lawful the carrying out outwith Scotland of the conduct so described as if the authorisation, so far as is it relates to conduct to which that Part applies, were an authorisation duly granted under that Part.

(2) Where any such circumstances as are mentioned in paragraph (c) of subsection (1) so arise as to give effect outwith Scotland to any authorisation granted under the relevant Scottish legislation, that authorisation shall not authorise any conduct outwith Scotland at any time after the end of the period of three weeks beginning with the time when the circumstances arose.

(3) Subsection (2) is without prejudice to the operation of subsection (1) in relation to any authorisation on the second or any subsequent occasion on which any such circumstances as are mentioned in subsection (1)(c) arise while the authorisation remains in force.

(4) In this section "the relevant Scottish legislation" means an enactment contained in or made under an Act of the Scottish Parliament which makes provision, corresponding to that made by Part II, for the authorisation of conduct to which that Part applies.

76A[6] Foreign surveillance operations

(1) This section applies where—

(a) a foreign police or customs officer is carrying out relevant surveillance outside the United Kingdom which is lawful under the law of the country or territory in which it is being carried out;

---

[5] Commencement: 25/9/00 (by SI 2000 No 2543).

[6] No order has been made bringing this section into force but the section was inserted by s 83 of the Crime (International Co-operation) Act 2003, on 26/4/04 by the Crime (International Co-operation) Act 2003 (Commencement No 1) Order 2004 (SI 2004 No 786) Art 3(2).

(b) circumstances arise by virtue of which the surveillance can for the time being be carried out only in the United Kingdom; and

(c) it is not reasonably practicable in those circumstances for a United Kingdom officer to carry out the surveillance in the United Kingdom in accordance with an authorisation under Part 2 or the Regulation of Investigatory Powers (Scotland) Act 2000.

(2) "Relevant surveillance" means surveillance which—

(a) is carried out in relation to a person who is suspected of having committed a relevant crime; and

(b) is, for the purposes of Part 2, directed surveillance or intrusive surveillance.

(3) "Relevant crime" means crime which—

(a) falls within Article 40(7) of the Schengen Convention; or

(b) is crime for the purposes of any other international agreement to which the United Kingdom is a party and which is specified for the purposes of this section in an order made by the Secretary of State with the consent of the Scottish Ministers.

(4) Relevant surveillance carried out by the foreign police or customs officer in the United Kingdom during the permitted period is to be lawful for all purposes if—

(a) the condition mentioned in subsection (6) is satisfied;

(b) the officer carries out the surveillance only in places to which members of the public have or are permitted to have access, whether on payment or otherwise; and

(c) conditions specified in any order made by the Secretary of State with the consent of the Scottish Ministers are satisfied in relation to its carrying out;

but no surveillance is lawful by virtue of this subsection if the officer subsequently seeks to stop and question the person in the United Kingdom in relation to the relevant crime.

(5) The officer is not to be subject to any civil liability in respect of any conduct of his which is incidental to any surveillance that is lawful by virtue of subsection (4).

(6) The condition in this subsection is satisfied if, immediately after the officer enters the United Kingdom—

(a) he notifies a person designated by the Director General of the [National Criminal Intelligence Service] *Serious Organised Crime Agency*[7] of that fact; and

(b) (if the officer has not done so before) he requests an application to be made for an authorisation under Part 2, or the Regulation of

---

[7] The reference to NCIA will be replaced by the italicised reference to SOCA with effect from the date when Sch 4, para 154 of the SOCAP Act 2005 is in force.

Investigatory Powers (Scotland) Act 2000, for the carrying out of the surveillance.

(7) "The permitted period" means the period of five hours beginning with the time when the officer enters the United Kingdom.

(8)[8] But a person designated by an order made by the Secretary of State may notify the officer that the surveillance is to cease being lawful by virtue of subsection (4) when he gives the notification.

(9) The Secretary of State is not to make an order under subsection (4) unless a draft of the order has been laid before Parliament and approved by a resolution of each House.

(10) In this section references to a foreign police or customs officer are to a police or customs officer who, in relation to a country or territory other than the United Kingdom, is an officer for the purposes of—

(a) Article 40 of the Schengen Convention; or

(b) any other international agreement to which the United Kingdom is a party and which is specified for the purposes of this section in an order made by the Secretary of State with the consent of the Scottish Ministers.

(11) In this section—

"the Schengen Convention" means the Convention implementing the Schengen Agreement of 14th June 1985;

"United Kingdom officer" means—

(a) a member of a police force;

(b) a member of the [National Criminal Intelligence Service] *staff of the Serious Organised Crime Agency*;[9]

(c) a member of [the National Crime Squad or][10] of the Scottish Crime Squad (within the meaning of the Regulation of Investigatory Powers (Scotland) Act 2000);

(d) a customs officer.

Supplemental

Ministerial expenditure etc.

77.[11] There shall be paid out of money provided by Parliament—

(a) any expenditure incurred by the Secretary of State for or in connection with the carrying out of his functions under this Act; and

(b) any increase attributable to this Act in the sums which are payable out of money so provided under any other Act.

---

[8] The Director General of NCIS was designated from 7 May 2004 for the purposes of s 76A(8) by the RIPA (Foreign Surveillance Operations) Order 2004 (SI 2004 No 1128).

[9] The reference to NCIS will be replaced by the italicised reference to SOCA with effect from the date when Sch 4, para 154 of the SOCAP Act 2005 is in force.

[10] The reference to the NCS will be omitted when Sch 4, para 154 of the SOCAP Act 2005 is in force.

[11] Commencement: 25/9/00 (by SI 2000 No 2543).

Orders, regulations and rules

78.[12]—(1) This section applies to any power of the Secretary of State to make any order, regulations or rules under any provision of this Act.

(2) The powers to which this section applies shall be exercisable by statutory instrument.

(3) A statutory instrument which contains any order made in exercise of a power to which this section applies (other than the power to appoint a day under section 83(2)) but which contains neither—

(a)[13] an order a draft of which has been approved for the purposes of section 12(10), 13(3), 22(9), 25(5), 28(5), 29(6), 30(7), 35(5), 41(6), 47(2), 66(3), 67(11), 71(9) or 76A(9) nor

(b) the order to which section 35(7) applies, shall be subject to annulment in pursuance of a resolution of either House of Parliament.

(4) A statutory instrument containing any regulations made in exercise of a power to which this section applies shall be subject to annulment in pursuance of a resolution of either House of Parliament.

(5) Any order, regulations or rules made in exercise of a power to which this section applies may—

(a) make different provisions for different cases;

(b) contain such incidental, supplemental, consequential and transitional provision as the Secretary of State thinks fit.

Criminal liability of directors etc.

79.[14]—(1) Where an offence under any provision of this Act other than a provision of Part III is committed by a body corporate and is proved to have been committed with the consent or connivance of, or to be attributable to any neglect on the part of—

(a) a director, manager, secretary or other similar officer of the body corporate, or

(b) any person who was purporting to act in any such capacity, he (as well as the body corporate) shall be guilty of that offence and liable to be proceeded against and punished accordingly.

(2) Where an offence under any provision of this Act other than a provision of Part III—

(a) is committed by a Scottish firm, and

(b) is proved to have been committed with the consent or connivance of, or to be attributable to any neglect on the part of, a partner of the firm,

---

[12] Commencement: 25/9/00 (by SI 2000 No 2543).
[13] Amended by the Crime (International Co-operation) Act 2003, sch 5, para 80.
[14] Commencement: 2/10/00 (SI 2000 No 2543).

he (as well as the firm) shall be guilty of that offence and liable to be proceeded against and punished accordingly.

(3) In this section "director", in relation to a body corporate whose affairs are managed by its members, means a member of the body corporate.

General saving for lawful conduct

80.[15] Nothing in any of the provisions of this Act by virtue of which conduct of any description is or may be authorised by any warrant, authorisation or notice, or by virtue of which information may be obtained in any manner, shall be construed—

(a) as making it unlawful to engage in any conduct of that description which is not otherwise unlawful under this Act and would not be unlawful apart from this Act;

(b) as otherwise requiring—

   (i) the issue, grant or giving of such a warrant, authorisation or notice, or

   (ii) the taking of any step for or towards obtaining the authority of such a warrant, authorisation or notice,

before any such conduct of that description is engaged in; or

(c) as prejudicing any power to obtain information by any means not involving conduct that may be authorised under this Act.

General interpretation

81.[16]—(1)[17] In this Act—

"apparatus" includes any equipment, machinery or device and any wire or cable;

"Assistant Commissioner of Police of the Metropolis" includes the Deputy Commissioner of Police of the Metropolis;

"Assistant Surveillance Commissioner" means any person holding office under section 63;

"civil proceedings" means any proceedings in or before any court or tribunal that are not criminal proceedings;

"communication" includes—

(a) (except in the definition of "postal service" in section 2(1)) anything transmitted by means of a postal service;

(b) anything comprising speech, music, sounds, visual images or data of any description; and

---

[15] Commencement: 25/9/00 (by SI 2000 No 2543).
[16] Commencement: 25/9/00 (by SI 2000 No 2543).
[17] Amended by the Justice (Northern Ireland) Act 2002, Sch 4, para 40.

(c) signals serving either for the impartation of anything between persons, between a person and a thing or between things or for the actuation or control of any apparatus;

"criminal", in relation to any proceedings or prosecution, shall be construed in accordance with subsection (4);

"customs officer" means an officer commissioned by the Commissioners of Customs and Excise under section 6(3) of the Customs and Excise Management Act 1979;

"document" includes a map, plan, design, drawing, picture or other image;

"enactment" includes—

(a) an enactment passed after the passing of this Act; and

(b) an enactment contained in Northern Ireland legislation;

"GCHQ" has the same meaning as in the Intelligence Services Act 1994;

"Her Majesty's forces" has the same meaning as in the Army Act 1955;

"intelligence service" means the Security Service, the Secret Intelligence Service or GCHQ;

"interception" and cognate expressions shall be construed (so far as it is applicable) in accordance with section 2;

"Interception warrant" means a warrant under section 5;

"justice of the peace" does not include a justice of the peace in Northern Ireland;

"legal proceedings" means civil or criminal proceedings in or before any court or tribunal;

"modification" includes alterations, additions and omissions, and cognate expressions shall be construed accordingly;

"ordinary Surveillance Commissioner" means a Surveillance Commissioner other than the Chief Surveillance Commissioner;

"person" includes any organisation and any association or combination of persons;

"police force" means any of the following—

(a) any police force maintained under section 2 of the Police Act 1996 (police forces in England and Wales outside London);

(b) the Metropolitan police force;

(c) the City of London police force;

(d) any police force maintained under or by virtue of section 1 of the Police (Scotland) Act 1967

(e) the Royal Ulster Constabulary;

(f) the Ministry of Defence Police;

(g) the Royal Navy Regulating Branch;

(h) the Royal Military Police;

(i) the Royal Air Force Police;

(j) the British Transport Police;

"postal service" and "public postal service" have the meanings given by section 2(1);

"private telecommunication system", "public telecommunications service" and "public telecommunication system" have the meanings given by section 2(1);

"public authority" means any public authority within the meaning of section 6 of the Human Rights Act 1998 (acts of public authorities) other than a court or tribunal;

"senior official" means, subject to subsection (7), a member of the Senior Civil Service or a member of the Senior Management Structure of Her Majesty's Diplomatic Service;

"statutory", in relation to any power or duty, means conferred or imposed by or under any enactment or subordinate legislation;

"subordinate legislation" means any subordinate legislation (within the meaning of the Interpretation Act 1978) or any statutory rules (within the meaning of the Statutory Rules (Northern Ireland) Order 1979);

"Surveillance Commissioner" means a Commissioner holding office under section 91 of the Police Act 1997 and "Chief Surveillance Commissioner" shall be construed accordingly;

"telecommunication system" and "telecommunications service" have the meanings given by section 2(1);

"the Tribunal" means the tribunal established under section 65;

"wireless telegraphy" has the same meaning as in the Wireless Telegraphy Act 1949 and, in relation to wireless telegraphy, "interfere" has the same meaning as in that Act;

"working day" means any day other than a Saturday, a Sunday, Christmas Day, Good Friday or a day which is a bank holiday under the Banking and Financial Dealings Act 1971 in any part of the United Kingdom.

(2) In this Act—

    (a)   references to crime are references to conduct which constitutes one or more criminal offences or is, or corresponds to, any conduct which, if it all took place in any one part of the United Kingdom would constitute one or more criminal offences; and

    (b)   references to serious crime are references to crime that satisfies the test in subsection (3)(a) or (b).

(3) Those tests are—

    (a)[18]   that the offence or one of the offences that is or would be constituted by the conduct is an offence for which a person who has attained the age of twenty-one (eighteen in relation to England and Wales) and has no previous convictions could reasonably be expected to be sentenced to imprisonment for a term of three years or more;

---

[18] Amended by the Criminal Justice and Court Services Act 2000, Sch 7, Part II, para 211.

(b) that the conduct involves the use of violence, results in substantial financial gain or is conduct by a large number of persons in pursuit of a common purpose.

(4) In this Act "criminal proceedings" includes—

(a) proceedings in the United Kingdom or elsewhere before—

(i) a court-martial constituted under the Army Act 1955, the Air Force Act 1955 or the Naval Discipline Act 1957;

(ii)[19] *repealed*

(b) proceedings before the Courts-Martial Appeal Court; and

(c) proceedings before a Standing Civilian Court;

and references in this Act to criminal prosecutions shall be construed accordingly.

(5) For the purposes of this Act detecting crime shall be taken to include—

(a) establishing by whom, for what purpose, by what means and generally in what circumstances any crime was committed; and

(b) the apprehension of the person by whom any crime was committed;

and any reference in this Act to preventing or detecting serious crime shall be construed accordingly, except that, in Chapter I of Part I, it shall not include a reference to gathering evidence for use in any legal proceedings.

(6) In this Act—

(a) references to a person holding office under the Crown include references to any servant of the Crown and to any member of Her Majesty's forces; and

(b) references to a member of a police force, in relation to the Royal Navy Regulating Branch, the Royal Military Police or the Royal Air Force Police, do not include references to any member of that Branch or Force who is not for the time being attached to or serving either with the Branch or Force of which he is a member or with another of those police forces.

(7) If it appears to the Secretary of State that it is necessary to do so in consequence of any changes to the structure or grading of the home civil service or diplomatic service, he may by order make such amendments of the definition of "senior official" in subsection (1) as appear to him appropriate to preserve, so far as practicable, the effect of that definition.

Amendments, repeals and savings etc.

82.[20]—(1) The enactments specified in Schedule 4 (amendments consequential on the provisions of this Act) shall have effect with the amendments set out in that Schedule.

---

[19] Repealed by the Armed Forces Act 2001, Sch 7, Part 1 with effect from 28/2/02 (SI 2002 No 345).

[20] Commencement: s 82(1) and (2) commenced on 25/9/00 by SI 2000 No 2543, Art 2, but only for the purpose of giving effect to Sch 4, paras 4, 6 and 8 and, in Sch 5, the entries relating to ss 6 and 7 of the Intelligence Services Act 1994, the Police Act 1997 and the Crime and

(2) The enactments mentioned in Schedule 5 are hereby repealed to the extent specified in the third column of that Schedule.

(3)[21] For the avoidance of doubt it is hereby declared that nothing in this Act . . . affects any power conferred on a postal operator (within the meaning of the Postal Services Act 2000) by or under any enactment to open, detain or delay any postal packet or to deliver any such packet to a person other than the person to whom it is addressed.

(4) Where any warrant under the Interception of Communications Act 1985 is in force under that Act at the time when the repeal by this Act of section 2 of that Act comes into force, the conduct authorised by that warrant shall be deemed for the period which—

(a) begins with that time, and

(b) ends with the time when that warrant would (without being renewed) have ceased to have effect under that Act,

as if it were conduct authorised by an interception warrant issued in accordance with the requirements of Chapter I of Part I of this Act.

(5) In relation to any such warrant, any certificate issued for the purposes of section 3(2) of the Interception of Communications Act 1985 shall have effect in relation to that period as if it were a certificate issued for the purposes of section 8(4) of this Act.

(6) Sections 15 and 16 of this Act shall have effect as if references to interception warrants and to section 8(4) certificates included references, respectively, to warrants under section 2 of the Interception of Communications Act 1985 and to certificates under section 3(2) of that Act; and references in sections 15 and 16 of this Act to intercepted or certified material shall be construed accordingly.

Short title, commencement and extent

83.[22]—(1) This Act may be cited as the Regulation of Investigatory Powers Act 2000.

(2) The provisions of this Act, other than this section, shall come into force on such day as the Secretary of State may by order appoint; and different days may be appointed under this subsection for different purposes.

(3) This Act extends to Northern Ireland.

Disorder Act 1998. Remainder of section commenced 2/10/00 by SI 2000 No 2543, Art 3 (but subject to some transitional arrangements—see SI 2000 No 2543, Arts 5 and 6). In relation to the Post Office see also transitional arrangements in SI 2001 No 1149, Art 4(8).

[21] Amended by the Postal Services Act 2000 (Consequential Modifications No 1) Order 2001 (SI 2001 No 1149), Sch 1, para 135 and Sch 2.

[22] Commencement: date of passage of RIPA, 28/7/2000.

SCHEDULE 1[23]

RELEVANT PUBLIC AUTHORITIES

PART I
RELEVANT AUTHORITIES FOR THE PURPOSES OF SS. 28 AND 29

Police forces etc.

1.   Any police force.
1A[24]   The Civil Nuclear Constabulary.
[2.   The National Criminal Intelligence Service.
3.   The National Crime Squad.]
2   *The Serious Organised Crime Agency.*[25]
4.   The Serious Fraud Office.
4A.[26] The Independent Police Complaints Commission.
4A.[27] The force comprising the special constables appointed under section 79 of the Harbours, Docks and Piers Clauses Act 1847 on the nomination of the Dover Harbour Board.
4B.   The force comprising the constables appointed under article 3 of the Mersey Docks and Harbour (Police) Order 1975 on the nomination of the Mersey Docks and Harbour Company.

The intelligence services

5.   Any of the intelligence services.

The armed forces

6.   Any of Her Majesty's forces.

The revenue departments

7.   The Commissioners of Customs and Excise.
8.   The Commissioners of Inland Revenue.

Government departments

9.   The Ministry of Agriculture, Fisheries and Food.
10.   The Ministry of Defence.

---

[23] Commencement: 25/9/00 by SI 2000 No 2543.
[24] Substituted by the Energy Act 2004, s 69, Sch 14, para 8(2).
[25] The reference to SOCA will replace the references to NCIS and NCS with effect from the date when Sch 4, para 155 of the SOCAP Act 2005 is in force.
[26] Inserted by the Independent Police Complaints Commission (Investigatory Powers) Order 2004 (SI 2004 No 815), Art. 3(12).
[27] This further para 4A appears to have been inserted along with para 4B by the RIPA (Directed Surveillance and Covert Human Intelligence Sources) (Amendment) Order 2005, SI 2005 No 1084.

The Department for Environment, Food and Rural Affairs[28]

11.[29]   *Repealed*

12.   The Department of Health.

13.   The Home Office.

The Office of the Deputy Prime Minister[30]

13A.[31] The Northern Ireland Office.

14.[32]   *Repealed*

15.   The Department of Trade and Industry.

The Department for Transport

The Department for Work and Pensions[33]

The National Assembly for Wales

16.   The National Assembly for Wales.

Local authorities

17.[34]   Any county council or district council in England, a London borough council, the Common Council of the City of London in its capacity as a local authority, the Council of the Isles of Scilly, and any county council or county borough council in Wales.

17A.   Any fire authority within the meaning of the Fire Services Act 1947 (read with paragraph 2 of Schedule 11 to the Local Government Act 1985.

Other bodies

17B. The Charity Commission.

18.   The Environment Agency.

19.   The Financial Services Authority.

20.   The Food Standards Agency.

20A. The Gaming Board for Great Britain.

20B. The Office of Fair Trading.

---

[28] Inserted by the Ministry of Agriculture, Fisheries and Food (Dissolution) Order 2002 (SI 2002 No 794), Sch 1, para 39 'at the appropriate place'.

[29] Repealed by the Transfer of Functions (Transport, Local Government and the Regions) Order 2002 (SI 2002 No 2626), Sch 2, para 24(a).

[30] Note that this entry and the entry for the Department of Transport were added by the Transfer of Functions (Transport, Local Government and the Regions) Order 2002 (SI 2002 No 2626), Sch 2, para 24(b) 'at the appropriate place' (added in alphabetic order here).

[31] Inserted by the RIPA (Directed Surveillance and Covert Human Intelligence Sources) Order 2003 (SI 2003 No 3171), Art 2.

[32] Repealed by the Secretaries of State for Education and Skills and for Work and Pensions Order 2002 (SI 2002 No 1397), Art 12, Sch, para 16.

[33] Inserted by the Secretaries of State for Education and Skills and for Work and Pensions Order 2002 (SI 2002 No 1397), Art 12, Sch, para 16(b).

[34] No 17 substituted by, and 17A, 17B and 20A–20D inserted by the RIPA (Directed Surveillance and Covert Human Intelligence Sources) Order 2003 (SI 2003 No 3171), Art 2.

20C.   The Office of the Police Ombudsman for Northern Ireland.

20D.   The Postal Services Commission.

21.[35] *Repealed*

22.[36] *Repealed*

23.[37] A universal service provider (within the meaning of the Postal Services Act 2000) acting in connection with the provision of a universal postal service (within the meaning of that Act).

23A.[38] The Office of Communications.

Northern Ireland authorities[39]

23A.   The Department of Agriculture and Rural Development.

23B.   The Department of Enterprise, Trade and Investment.

23C.   The Department of the Environment. 23D. Any district council (within the meaning of section 44 of the Interpretation Act (Northern Ireland) 1954).

PART II

RELEVANT AUTHORITIES FOR THE PURPOSES ONLY OF S. 28

The Health and Safety Executive

24.   The Health and Safety Executive.

NHS bodies in England and Wales

25.   *omitted*[40]

26.   A Special Health Authority established under section 11 of the National Health Service Act 1977.

27.   A National Heath Service trust established under section 5 of the National Health Service and Community Care Act 1990.

27A.[41] Local Health Boards in Wales established under section 6 of the National Health Service Reform and Health Care Professions Act 2002.

---

[35] Repealed by the Intervention Board for Agricultural Produce (Abolition) Regulations 2001 (SI 2001 No 3686), Art 6(17).

[36] Repealed by the Financial Services and Markets Act 2000 (Consequential Amendments) Order 2002 (SI 2002 No 1555), Art 26.

[37] Amended by the Postal Services Act 2000 (Consequential Modifications No 1) Order 2001 (SI 2001 No 1149), Sch 1, para 135.

[38] Inserted by the Communications Act 2003, Sch 17, para 161(3) (the duplicated number 23A appears to be an error in the SI).

[39] Entries 23A–23D below inserted by the RIPA 2000 (Amendment) Order (Northern Ireland) 2002 (SR 2002 No 183), Art 3.

[40] By the RIPA (Directed Surveillance and Covert Human Intelligence Sources) (Amendment) Order 2005, (SI 2005 No 1084), reg 2.

[41] Entries 27A–27D inserted by the RIPA (Directed Surveillance and Covert Human Intelligence Sources) Order 2003 (SI 2003 No 3171), Art 3.

Her Majesty's Chief Inspector of Schools in England

27B.   Her Majesty's Chief Inspector of Schools in England.

The Information Commissioner

27C.   The Information Commissioner.

The Royal Parks Constabulary

27D.   The Royal Parks Constabulary.]⁴²

The Royal Pharmaceutical Society of Great Britain

28.   The Royal Pharmaceutical Society of Great Britain.

Northern Ireland authorities⁴³

29.   The Department of Health, Social Services and Public Safety.
30.   The Department for Regional Development.
31.   The Department for Social Development.
32.   The Department of Culture, Arts and Leisure.
33.   The Foyle, Carlingford and Irish Lights Commission.
34.   The Fisheries Conservancy Board for Northern Ireland.
35.   A Health and Social Services trust established under Article 10 of the Health and Personal Social Services (Northern Ireland) Order 1991.
36.   A Health and Social Services Board established under Article 16 of the Health and Personal Social Services (Northern Ireland) Order 1972.
37.   The Health and Safety Executive for Northern Ireland.
38.   The Northern Ireland Central Services Agency for the Health and Social Services.
39.   The Fire Authority for Northern Ireland.
40.   The Northern Ireland Housing Executive.

SCHEDULE 2⁴⁴

PERSONS HAVING THE APPROPRIATE PERMISSION

Requirement that appropriate permission is granted by a judge

1.—(1) Subject to the following provisions of this Schedule, a person has the appropriate permission in relation to any protected information if, and only

---

⁴² The text in square brackets will be omitted when Sch 13, Part 2, para 10 of the SOCAP Act 2005 is in force.

⁴³ Entries 29–40 below inserted by the RIPA 2000 (Amendment) Order (Northern Ireland) 2002 (SR 2002 No 183), Art 4.   ⁴⁴ Schedule 2 not in force.

if, written permission for the giving of section 49 notices in relation to that information has been granted—

(a)[45] in England and Wales, by a Circuit Judge or a District Judge (Magistrates' Courts);

(b) in Scotland, by a sheriff; or

(c) in Northern Ireland, by a county court judge.

(2) Nothing in paragraphs 2 to 5 of this Schedule providing for the manner in which a person may be granted the appropriate permission in relation to any protected information without a grant under this paragraph shall be construed as requiring any further permission to be obtained in a case in which permission has been granted under this paragraph.

Data obtained under warrant etc.

2.—(1) This paragraph applies in the case of protected information falling within section 49(1)(a), (b) or (c) where the statutory power in question is one exercised, or to be exercised, in accordance with—

(a) a warrant issued by the Secretary of State or a person holding judicial office; or

(b) an authorisation under Part III of the Police Act 1997 (authorisation of otherwise unlawful action in respect of property).

(2) Subject to sub-paragraphs (3) to (5) and paragraph 6(1), a person has the appropriate permission in relation to that protected information (without any grant of permission under paragraph 1) if—

(a) the warrant or, as the case may be, the authorisation contained the relevant authority's permission for the giving of section 49 notices in relation to protected information to be obtained under the warrant or authorisation; or

(b) since the issue of the warrant or authorisation, written permission has been granted by the relevant authority for the giving of such notices in relation to protected information obtained under the warrant or authorisation.

(3) Only persons holding office under the Crown, the police, *SOCA*[46] and customs and excise shall be capable of having the appropriate permission in relation to protected information obtained, or to be obtained, under a warrant issued by the Secretary of State.

(4) Only a person who—

(a) was entitled to exercise the power conferred by the warrant, or

(b) is of the description of persons on whom the power conferred by the warrant was, or could have been, conferred,

---

[45] Amended by the Courts Act 2003, s 65, Sch 4, para 12.

[46] The references to SOCA in this section will be inserted with effect from the date when Sch 4, para 156 of the SOCAP Act 2005 is in force.

shall be capable of having the appropriate permission in relation to protected information obtained, or to be obtained, under a warrant issued by a person holding judicial office.

(5) Only the police, *SOCA* and the customs and excise shall be capable of having the appropriate permission in relation to protected information obtained, or to be obtained, under an authorisation under Part III of the Police Act 1997.

(6) In this paragraph "the relevant authority"—

(a) in relation to a warrant issued by the Secretary of State, means the Secretary of State;

(b) in relation to a warrant issued by a person holding judicial office, means any person holding any judicial office that would have entitled him to issue the warrant; and

(c) in relation to protected information obtained under an authorisation under Part III of the Police Act 1997, means (subject to sub-paragraph (7)) an authorising officer within the meaning of section 93 of that Act.

(7) Section 94 of the Police Act 1997 (power of other persons to grant authorisations in urgent cases) shall apply in relation to—

(a) an application for permission for the giving of section 49 notices in relation to protected information obtained, or to be obtained, under an authorisation under Part III of that Act, and

(b) the powers of any authorising officer (within the meaning of section 93 of that Act) to grant such a permission,

as it applies in relation to an application for an authorisation under section 93 of that Act and the powers of such an officer under that section.

(8) References in this paragraph to a person holding judicial office are references to—

(a) any judge of the Crown Court or of the High Court of Justiciary;

(b) any sheriff;

(c) any justice of the peace;

(d) any resident magistrate in Northern Ireland; or

(e) any person holding any such judicial office as entitles him to exercise the jurisdiction of a judge of the Crown Court or of a justice of the peace.

(9) Protected information that comes into a person's possession by means of the exercise of any statutory power which—

(a) is exercisable without a warrant, but

(b) is so exercisable in the course of, or in connection with, the exercise of another statutory power for which a warrant is required,

shall not be taken, by reason only of the warrant required for the exercise of the power mentioned in paragraph (b), to be information in the case of which this paragraph applies.

Data obtained by the intelligence services under statute but without a warrant

3.—(1) This paragraph applies in the case of protected information falling within section 49(1)(a), (b) or (c) which—

    (a) has come into the possession of any of the intelligence services or is likely to do so; and

    (b) is not information in the case of which paragraph 2 applies.

(2) Subject to paragraph 6(1), a person has the appropriate permission in relation to that protected information (without any grant of permission under paragraph 1) if written permission for the giving of section 49 notices in relation to that information has been granted by the Secretary of State.

(3) Sub-paragraph (2) applies where the protected information is in the possession, or (as the case may be) is likely to come into the possession, of both—

    (a) one or more of the intelligence services, and

    (b) a public authority which is not one of the intelligence services,

as if a grant of permission under paragraph 1 were unnecessary only where the application to the Secretary of State for permission under that sub-paragraph is made by or on behalf of a member of one of the intelligence services.

Data obtained under statute by other persons but without a warrant

4.—(1) This paragraph applies—

    (a) in the case of protected information falling within section 49(1)(a), (b) or (c) which is not information in the case of which paragraph 2 or 3 applies; and

    (b) in the case of protected information falling within section 49(1)(d) which is not information also falling within section 49(1)(a), (b) or (c) in the case of which paragraph 3 applies.

(2) Subject to paragraph 6, where—

    (a) the statutory power was exercised, or is likely to be exercised, by the police, *SOCA*,[47] the customs and excise or a member of Her Majesty's forces, or

    (b) the information was provided or disclosed, or is likely to be provided or disclosed, to the police, *SOCA*, the customs and excise or a member of Her Majesty's forces, or

    (c) the information is in the possession of, or is likely to come into the possession of, the police, *SOCA*, the customs and excise or a member of Her Majesty's forces,

---

[47] The references to SOCA in this section will be inserted with effect from the date when Sch 4, para 156 of the SOCAP Act 2005 is in force.

the police, the customs and excise or, as the case may be, members of Her Majesty's forces have the appropriate permission in relation to the protected information, without any grant of permission under paragraph 1.

(3) In any other case a person shall not have the appropriate permission by virtue of a grant of permission under paragraph 1 unless he is a person falling within sub-paragraph (4).

(4) A person falls within this sub-paragraph if, as the case may be—

(a) he is the person who exercised the statutory power or is of the description of persons who would have been entitled to exercise it;

(b) he is the person to whom the protected information was provided or disclosed, or is of a description of person the provision or disclosure of the information to whom would have discharged the statutory duty; or

(c) he is a person who is likely to be a person falling within paragraph (a) or (b) when the power is exercised or the protected information provided or disclosed.

Data obtained without the exercise of statutory powers

5.—(1) This paragraph applies in the case of protected information falling within section 49(1)(e).

(2) Subject to paragraph 6, a person has the appropriate permission in relation to that protected information (without any grant of permission under paragraph 1) if—

(a) the information is in the possession of any of the intelligence services, or is likely to come into the possession of any of those services; and

(b) written permission for the giving of section 49 notices in relation to that information has been granted by the Secretary of State.

(3) Sub-paragraph (2) applies where the protected information is in the possession, or (as the case may be) is likely to come into the possession, of both—

(a) one or more of the intelligence services, and

(b) the police, *SOCA*[48] or the customs and excise,

as if a grant of permission under paragraph 1 were unnecessary only where the application to the Secretary of State for permission under that sub-paragraph is made by or on behalf of a member of one of the intelligence services.

---

[48] The reference to SOCA will be inserted with effect from the date when Sch 4, para 156 of the SOCAP Act 2005 is in force.

General requirements relating to the appropriate permission

6.—(1) A person does not have the appropriate permission in relation to any protected information unless he is either—

> (a) a person who has the protected information in his possession or is
> likely to obtain possession of it; or
>
> (b) a person who is authorised (apart from this Act) to act on behalf of such
> a person.

(2) Subject to sub-paragraph (3), a constable does not by virtue of paragraph
1, 4 or 5 have the appropriate permission in relation to any protected information unless—

> (a) he is of or above the rank of superintendent; or
>
> (b) permission to give a section 49 notice in relation to that information
> has been granted by a person holding the rank of superintendent, or
> any higher rank.

(3) In the case of protected information that has come into the police's possession by means of the exercise of powers conferred by—

> (a) section 44 of the Terrorism Act 2000 (power to stop and search), or
>
> (b) section 13A or 13B of the Prevention of Terrorism (Temporary
> Provisions) Act 1989 (which had effect for similar purposes before the
> coming into force of section 44 of the Terrorism Act 2000),

the permission required by sub-paragraph (2) shall not be granted by any person
below the rank mentioned in section 44(4) of that Act of 2000 or, as the case may
be, section 13A(1) of that Act of 1989.

[(3A) A member of the staff of the Serious Organised Crime

Agency does not by virtue of paragraph 1, 4 or 5 have the appropriate permission
in relation to any protected information unless permission to give a section 49
notice in relation to that information has been granted—

> (a) by the Director General; or
>
> (b) by a member of the staff of the Agency of or above such level as
> the Director General may designate for the purposes of this sub-
> paragraph.] [49]

(4) A person commissioned by the Commissioners of Customs and Excise
does not by virtue of paragraph 1, 4 or 5 have the appropriate permission
in relation to any protected information unless permission to give a section
49 notice in relation to that information has been granted—

> (a) by those Commissioners themselves; or
>
> (b) by an officer of their department of or above such level as they may
> designate for the purposes of this sub-paragraph.

---

[49] The text in square brackets in sub paras (3A) and at (6) will be inserted when Sch 4, para. 156
of the SOCAP Act 2005 is in force.

(5) A member of Her Majesty's forces does not by virtue of paragraph 1, 4 or 5 have the appropriate permission in relation to any protected information unless—

   (a) he is of or above the rank of lieutenant colonel or its equivalent; or

   (b) permission to give a section 49 notice in relation to that information has been granted by a person holding the rank of lieutenant colonel or its equivalent, or by a person holding a rank higher than lieutenant colonel or its equivalent.

[(6) In sub-paragraph (2) "constable" does not include a constable who is a member of the staff of the Serious Organised Crime Agency.]

Duration of permission

7.—(1) A permission granted by any person under any provision of this Schedule shall not entitle any person to give a section 49 notice at any time after the permission has ceased to have effect.

 (2) Such a permission, once granted, shall continue to have effect (notwithstanding the cancellation, expiry or other discharge of any warrant or authorisation in which it is contained or to which it relates) until such time (if any) as it—

   (a) expires in accordance with any limitation on its duration that was contained in its terms; or

   (b) is withdrawn by the person who granted it or by a person holding any office or other position that would have entitled him to grant it.

Formalities for permissions granted by the Secretary of State

8. A permission for the purposes of any provision of this Schedule shall not be granted by the Secretary of State except—

   (a) under his hand; or

   (b) in an urgent case in which the Secretary of State has expressly authorised the grant of the permission, under the hand of a senior official.

SCHEDULE 3[50]

THE TRIBUNAL

Membership of the Tribunal

1.—(1) A person shall not be appointed as a member of the Tribunal unless he is—

   (a) a person who holds or has held a high judicial office (within the meaning of the Appellate Jurisdiction Act 1876);

---

[50] Commencement 2/10/00 by SI 2000 No 2543.

    (b) a person who has a ten year general qualification, within the meaning of section 71 of the Courts and Legal Services Act 1990;

    (c) an advocate or solicitor in Scotland of at least ten years' standing; or

    (d) a member of the Bar of Northern Ireland or solicitor of the Supreme Court of Northern Ireland of at least ten years' standing.

(2) Subject to the following provisions of this paragraph, the members of the Tribunal shall hold office during good behaviour.

(3) A member of the Tribunal shall vacate office at the end of the period of five years beginning with the day of his appointment, but shall be eligible for reappointment.

(4) A member of the Tribunal may be relieved of office by Her Majesty at his own request.

(5) A member of the Tribunal may be removed from office by Her Majesty on an Address presented to Her by both Houses of Parliament.

(6) If the Scottish Parliament passes a resolution calling for the removal of a member of the Tribunal, it shall be the duty of the Secretary of State to secure that a motion for the presentation of an Address to Her Majesty for the removal of that member, and the resolution of the Scottish Parliament, are considered by each House of Parliament.

President and Vice-President

2.—(1) Her Majesty may by Letters Patent appoint as President or Vice-President of the Tribunal a person who is, or by virtue of those Letters will be, a member of the Tribunal.

(2) A person shall not be appointed President of the Tribunal unless he holds or has held a high judicial office (within the meaning of the Appellate Jurisdiction Act 1876).

(3) If at any time—

    (a) the President of the Tribunal is temporarily unable to carry out any functions conferred on him by this Schedule or any rules under section 69, or

    (b) the office of President of the Tribunal is for the time being vacant,

the Vice-President shall carry out those functions.

(4) A person shall cease to be President or Vice-President of the Tribunal if he ceases to be a member of the Tribunal.

Members of the Tribunal with special responsibilities

3.—(1) The President of the Tribunal shall designate one or more members of the Tribunal as the member or members having responsibilities in relation to matters involving the intelligence services.

(2) It shall be the duty of the President of the Tribunal, in exercising any power conferred on him by rules under section 69 to allocate the members of the

Tribunal who are to consider or hear any complaint, proceedings, reference or preliminary or incidental matter, to exercise that power in a case in which the complaint, proceedings or reference relates to, or to a matter involving—

(a) an allegation against any of the intelligence services or any member of any of those services, or

(b) conduct by or on behalf of any of those services or any member of any of those services,

in such manner as secures that the allocated members consist of, or include, one or more of the members for the time being designated under sub-paragraph (1).

Salaries and expenses

4.—(1) The Secretary of State shall pay to the members of the Tribunal out of money provided by Parliament such remuneration and allowances as he may with the approval of the Treasury determine.

(2) Such expenses of the Tribunal as the Secretary of State may with the approval of the Treasury determine shall be defrayed by him out of money provided by Parliament.

Officers

5.—(1) The Secretary of State may, after consultation with the Tribunal and with the approval of the Treasury as to numbers, provide the Tribunal with such officers as he thinks necessary for the proper discharge of their functions.

(2) The Tribunal may authorise any officer provided under this paragraph to obtain any documents or information on the Tribunal's behalf.

Parliamentary disqualification

6. In Part II of Schedule 1 to the House of Commons Disqualification Act 1975 and in Part II of Schedule 1 to the Northern Ireland Assembly Disqualification Act 1975 (bodies whose members are disqualified) there shall be inserted (at the appropriate places) the following entry—

"The Tribunal established under section 65 of the Regulation of Investigatory Powers Act 2000".

SCHEDULE 4

CONSEQUENTIAL AMENDMENTS

The Post Office Act 1953 (c. 36)

1.[51] *Repealed*

---

[51] Nos 1 and 2 repealed by the Postal Services Act 2000 (Consequential Modifications No 1) Order 2001 (SI 2001 No 1149), Sch 2.

The Post Office Act 1969 (c. 48)

2. *Repealed*

The Telecommunications Act 1984 (c. 12)

3.[52] *Repealed*

The Security Service Act 1989 (c. 5)

4.[53]—(1) In section 1 of the Security Service Act 1989 (functions of the Security Service), after subsection (4) there shall be inserted—

"(5) Section 81(5) of the Regulation of Investigatory Powers Act 2000 (meaning of "prevention" and "detection"), so far as it relates to serious crime, shall apply for the purposes of this Act as it applies for the purposes of the provisions of that Act not contained in Chapter I of Part I."

(2) In section 2(2)(a) of that Act (duty of Director General to secure that information not disclosed except for authorised purposes), for "preventing or detecting" there shall be substituted "the prevention or detection of".

The Official Secrets Act 1989 (c. 6)

5.[54] In section 4(3)(a) of the Official Secrets Act 1989 (offence of disclosing interception information), after "1985" there shall be inserted "or under the authority of an interception warrant under section 5 of the Regulation of Investigatory Powers Act 2000".

The Intelligence Services Act 1994 (c. 13)

6.[55] In section 11 of the Intelligence Services Act 1994 (interpretation), after subsection (1) there shall be inserted—

"(1A) Section 81(5) of the Regulation of Investigatory Powers Act 2000 (meaning of "prevention" and "detection"), so far as it relates to serious crime, shall apply for the purposes of this Act as it applies for the purposes of Chapter I of Part I of that Act."

The Criminal Procedure and Investigations Act 1996 (c. 25)

7.[56]—(1) In each of sections 3(7), 7(6), 8(6) and 9(9) of the Criminal Procedure and Investigations Act 1996 (exceptions for interceptions from obligations to

---

[52] Repealed by the Communications Act 2003, Sch 19.
[53] Commencement: 25/9/00 by SI 2000 No 2543.
[54] Commencement: 2/10/00 by SI 2000 No 2543
[55] Commencement: 25/9/00 by SI 2000 No 2543.
[56] Commencement: 2/10/00 by SI 2000 No 2543

make disclosures to the defence), for paragraphs (a) and (b) there shall be substituted "it is material the disclosure of which is prohibited by section 17 of the Regulation of Investigatory Powers Act 2000."

(2) In section 23(6) of that Act (code of practice not to apply to material intercepted under the Interception of Communications Act 1985), after "1985" there shall be inserted "or under the authority of an interception warrant under section 5 of the Regulation of Investigatory Powers Act 2000".

The Police Act 1997 (c. 50)

8.[57]—(1) In section 91(9) of the Police Act 1997 (staff for Surveillance Commissioners)—
   (a) after "Chief Commissioner" there shall be inserted "and subject to the approval of the Treasury as to numbers"; and
   (b) after "Commissioners" there shall be inserted "and any Assistant Surveillance Commissioners holding office under section 63 of the Regulation of Investigatory Powers Act 2000".
(2) In section 93(3) of that Act (persons who may make an application to an authorising officer within section 93(5))—
   (a) in paragraph (a), for "(e)" there shall be substituted "(ea) or (ee)"; and
   (b) after that paragraph there shall be inserted—
      "(aa) if the authorising officer is within subsection (5)(eb) to (ed), by a member, as the case may be, of the Royal Navy Regulating Branch, the Royal Military Police or the Royal Air Force Police;".
(3) In section 94(1) of that Act (circumstances in which authorisations may be given in absence of authorising officer), in paragraph (b), for ", (f), (g) or (h)" there shall be substituted "or (f)", and after that paragraph there shall be inserted
   "or (c) if the authorising officer is within paragraph (g) of section 93(5), it is also not reasonably practicable for the application to be considered either—
      (i) by any other person designated for the purposes of that paragraph; or
      (ii) by the designated deputy of the Director General of the National Crime Squad."
(4) In section 94(2) of that Act (persons who may act in absence of the authorising officer)—
   (a) after paragraph (d), there shall be inserted—
      "(da) where the authorising officer is within paragraph
      (ea) of that subsection, by a person holding the rank of deputy or assistant chief constable in the Ministry of Defence Police;

---

[57] Commencement: 25/9/00 by SI 2000 No 2543.

(db) where the authorising officer is within paragraph (eb) of that subsection, by a person holding the position of assistant Provost Marshal in the Royal Navy Regulating Branch;

(dc) where the authorising officer is within paragraph (ec) or (ed) of that subsection, by a person holding the position of deputy Provost Marshal in the Royal Military Police or, as the case may be, in the Royal Air Force Police;

(dd) where the authorising officer is within paragraph (ee) of that subsection, by a person holding the rank of deputy or assistant chief constable in the British Transport Police;";

(b) in paragraph (e), the words "or (g)" and "or, as the case may be, of the National Crime Squad" shall be omitted; and

[(c) after that paragraph, there shall be inserted—

"(ea) where the authorising officer is within paragraph (g) of that subsection, by a person designated for the purposes of this paragraph by the Director General of the National Crime Squad as a person entitled to act in an urgent case;".]⁵⁸

[(5) In section 94(3) of that Act (rank of police members of the National Crime Intelligence Squad and National Crime Squad entitled to act), after "(2)(e)" there shall be inserted "or (2)(ea)".]

(6) In section 95 of that Act (authorisations: form and duration etc.)—

(a) in each of subsections (4) and (5), for the words from "the action" onwards there shall be substituted "the authorisation is one in relation to which the requirements of paragraphs (a) and (b) of section 93(2) are no longer satisfied."; and

(b) in subsection (6), for "or (e)" there shall be substituted ", (e) or (g)".

(7) In section 97 of that Act (authorisations requiring approval), in subsection (6), the words from "(and paragraph 7" onwards shall be omitted, and after that subsection there shall be inserted—

"(6A) The reference in subsection (6) to the authorising officer who gave the authorisation or in whose absence it was given shall be construed, in the case of an authorisation given by or in the absence of a person within paragraph (b), (e) or (g) of section 93(5), as a reference to the Commissioner of Police, Chief Constable or, as the case may be, Director General mentioned in the paragraph concerned."

(8) In section 103(7) of that Act (quashing authorisations), for the words from "and paragraph 7" onwards there shall be substituted "and subsection (6A) of section 97 shall apply for the purposes of this subsection as it applies for the purposes of subsection (6) of that section."

---

⁵⁸ The text in square brackets at sub paras (4)(c) and (5) is repealed with effect from the date when Sch 17, Part 2 of the SOCAP Act 2005 is in force.

(9) In section 105 of that Act (appeals by authorising officers: supplementary), in subsection (1)(a), the word "and" shall be inserted at the end of sub-paragraph (i), and sub-paragraph (iii) and the word "and" immediately preceding it shall be omitted.

(10) In section 107 of that Act—

(a) in subsection (2) (report of Chief Surveillance Commissioner on the discharge of his functions under Part III of that Act)—

(i) for "the discharge of functions under this Part" there shall be substituted "the matters with which he is concerned"; and

(ii) for "any matter relating to those functions" there shall be substituted "anything relating to any of those matters";

(b) in subsection (4) (matters that may be excluded from a report), for "the prevention or detection of serious crime or otherwise" there shall be substituted "any of the purposes for which authorisations may be given or granted under this Part of this Act or Part II of the Regulation of Investigatory Powers Act 2000 or under any enactment contained in or made under an Act of the Scottish Parliament which makes provision equivalent to that made by Part II of that Act of 2000 or"; and

(c) after subsection (5) (duty to co-operate with the Chief Surveillance Commissioner) there shall be inserted the subsections set out in sub-paragraph (11).

(11) The subsections inserted after subsection (5) of section 107 of that Act are as follows—

"(5A) It shall be the duty of—

(a) every person by whom, or on whose application, there has been given or granted any authorisation the function of giving or granting which is subject to review by the Chief Commissioner,

(b) every person who has engaged in conduct with the authority of such an authorisation,

(c) every person who holds or has held any office, rank or position with the same public authority as a person falling within paragraph (a),

(d) every person who holds or has held any office, rank or position with any public authority for whose benefit (within the meaning of Part II of the Regulation of Investigatory Powers Act 2000) activities which are or may be subject to any such review have been or may be carried out, and

(e) every person to whom a notice under section 49 of the Regulation of Investigatory Powers Act 2000 (notices imposing a disclosure requirement in respect of information protected by a key) has been given in relation to any information obtained by conduct to which such an authorisation relates, to disclose or provide to the Chief Commissioner all such documents and information as he may require for the purpose of enabling him to carry out his functions.

(5B) It shall be the duty of every Commissioner to give the tribunal established under section 65 of the Regulation of Investigatory Powers Act 2000 all such assistance (including his opinion as to any issue falling to be determined by that tribunal) as that tribunal may require—

(a) in connection with the investigation of any matter by that tribunal; or

(b) otherwise for the purposes of that tribunal's consideration or determination of any matter.

(5C) In this section "public authority" means any public authority within the meaning of section 6 of the Human Rights Act 1998 (acts of public authorities) other than a court or tribunal."

(12) In section 108(1) of that Act after "In this Part-" there shall be inserted— " "Assistant Commissioner of Police of the Metropolis" includes the Deputy Commissioner of Police of the Metropolis;".

(13) In Part VII of that Act, before section 134 there shall be inserted— "Meaning of "prevention" and "detection".

133A. Section 81(5) of the Regulation of Investigatory Powers Act 2000 (meaning of "prevention" and "detection") shall apply for the purposes of this Act as it applies for the purposes of the provisions of that Act not contained in Chapter I of Part I."

The Northern Ireland Act 1998 (c. 47)

9.[59] In paragraph 17(b) of Schedule 2 to the Northern Ireland Act 1998 (excepted matters), for "the Interception of Communications Act 1985" there shall be substituted "Chapter I of Part I of the Regulation of Investigatory Powers Act 2000".

The Electronic Communications Act 2000 (c. 7)

10.[60] In section 4(2) of the Electronic Communications Act 2000 (exception to rules restricting disclosure of information obtained under Part I of that Act), for the word "or" at the end of paragraph (e) there shall be substituted—

"(ea) for the purposes of any proceedings before the tribunal established under section 65 of the Regulation of Investigatory Powers Act 2000; or".

---

[59] Commencement: 2/10/00 by SI 2000 No 2543.
[60] Commencement: 2/10/00 by SI 2000 No 2543.

The Financial Services and Markets Act 2000 (c. 8)

11.[61] In section 394(7) of the Financial Services and Markets Act 2000 (exclusion of material from material of the Authority to which a person must be allowed access), for paragraphs (a) and (b) there shall be substituted—

"(a) is material the disclosure of which for the purposes of or in connection with any legal proceedings is prohibited by section 17 of the Regulation of Investigatory Powers Act 2000; or"

The Terrorism Act 2000 (c. 11)

12.[62]—(1) In section 9(2)(d) of the Terrorism Act 2000 (proceedings under the Human Rights Act 1998), for "8" there shall be substituted "7".

(2) In each of paragraphs 6(3) and 7(5) of Schedule 3 to that Act (references to an organisation and representative in paragraphs 5 and 8 of that Schedule), for "paragraphs 5 and 8" there shall be substituted "paragraph 5".

SCHEDULE 5[63]

REPEALS

Chapter	Short title	Extent of repeal
1975 c. 24.	*The House of Commons Disqualification Act 1975.*	In Part II of Schedule 1, the words "The Tribunal established under the Interception of Communications Act 1985", "The Tribunal established under the Security Service Act 1989", and "The Tribunal established under section 9 of the Intelligence Services Act 1994".
1975 c. 25.	*The Northern Ireland Assembly Disqualification Act 1975.*	In Part II of Schedule 1, the words "The Tribunal established under the Interception of Communications Act 1985", "The Tribunal established under the Security Service Act 1989", and "The Tribunal established under section 9 of the Intelligence Services Act 1994".

---

[61] Commencement: 2/10/00 by SI 2000 No 2543.
[62] Commencement: 2/10/00 by SI 2000 No 2543.
[63] Commencement: 25/9/00 by SI 2000 No 2543 as regards the entries relating to ss 6 and 7 of Intelligence Services Act 1994, the Police Act 1997 and the Crime and Disorder Act 1998. Commencement of the remainder 2/10/00 by the same SI.

291

1985 c. 56.	*The Interception of Communications Act 1985.*
	Sections 1 to 10.
	Section 11(3) to (5).
	Schedule 1.

1989 c. 5.	*The Security Service Act 1989.*
	Sections 4 and 5.
	Schedules 1 and 2.

| 1989 c. 6. | *The Official Secrets Act 1989.* |
| | In Schedule 1, paragraph 3. |

| 1990 c. 41. | *The Courts and Legal Services Act 1990.* |
| | In Schedule 10, paragraphs 62 and 74. |

1994 c. 13.	*The Intelligence Services Act 1994.*
	In section 6(1)(b), the words "of his department".
	In section 7(5)(b), the words "of his department".
	Sections 8 and 9.
	In section 11(1), paragraph (b).
	Schedules 1 and 2.

1997 c. 50.	*The Police Act 1997.*
	In section 93(6), paragraph (f) and the word "and" immediately preceding it.
	In section 94(1), the word "or" at the end of paragraph (a).
	In section 94(2)(e), the words "or (g)" and "or, as the case may be, of the National Crime Squad".
	In section 94(4)—
	(a) the words "in his absence", in each place where they occur; and
	(b) paragraph (d) and the word "and" immediately preceding it.
	In section 97(6), the words from "(and paragraph 7" onwards.
	Sections 101 and 102.
	In section 104—
	(a) in subsection (1), paragraph (g);
	(b) in each of subsections (4), (5) and (6), paragraph (b) and the word "or" immediately preceding it;

(c) in subsection (8), paragraph (b)
and the word "and" immediately
preceding it.
In section 105(1)(a), sub-paragraph (iii) and
the word "and" immediately preceding it.
Section 106.
Section 107(6).
Schedule 7.

1997 c. 68.	*The Special Immigration Appeals Commission Act 1997.*	
	Section 5(7).	
1998 c. 37.	*The Crime and Disorder Act 1998.*	
	Section 113(1) and (3).	
2000 c. 11.	*The Terrorism Act 2000.*	
	In Schedule 3, paragraph 8.	

PART III

THE RULES AND FORMS OF THE INVESTIGATORY POWERS TRIBUNAL

11

THE RULES OF THE INVESTIGATORY POWERS TRIBUNAL[1]

A. Introduction

The Secretary of State is given the power to make rules under s 69 of RIPA. Sections 69(9) and 69(10) provide that the rules made on the first occasion on which the power was exercised did not need to be approved by Parliament, but had to be approved *after* being made in accordance with subs (10). SI 2000 No 2665 was the first exercise of that rule-making power and so the exemption from initial approval applied (the rules were approved by Parliament on the day after they were made).

The explanatory note to the statutory instrument described the Rules as follows: **11.02**

These Rules are for the Tribunal established under Part IV of the Regulation of Investigatory Powers Act 2000. The Tribunal has an extensive jurisdiction, set out in section 65(2) of the Act; these Rules only govern the jurisdiction described in paragraphs (a) and (b) of that subsection. The remainder of the subsection will be brought into force later, and there will be further rules for that purpose.

The Rules therefore cover:

(a) cases brought under section 7(1)(a) of the Human Rights Act 1998 for which the Tribunal is the appropriate tribunal: this category of case is explained in subsections (3) and (5) to (8) of section 65 of the 2000 Act;

(b) complaints for which the Tribunal is the appropriate forum: this function is explained in subsections (4), (5), (7) and (8) of section 65.

Section 68 of the 2000 Act provides that, subject to anything in these Rules, the Tribunal are entitled to determine their own procedure.

Note: Chapter 8 of this work described the Tribunal in detail and that chapter also cross-refers and explains the Rules set out below.

The text of the Rules follows. Annotations are the author's own.

---

[1] The text of the Rules appears formally in SI 2000 No 2665 (the Investigatory Powers Tribunal Rules 2000) which came into force on 2 October 2000.

B. The Rules

Citation and commencement

1. These Rules may be cited as the Investigatory Powers Tribunal Rules 2000, and shall come into force on 2nd October 2000.

Interpretation

2. In these Rules:

"the Act" means the Regulation of Investigatory Powers Act 2000;

"Commissioner" means the Interception of Communications Commissioner, the Intelligence Services Commissioner, the Investigatory Powers Commissioner for Northern Ireland or any Surveillance Commissioner or Assistant Surveillance Commissioner;[2]

"complainant" means a person who brings section 7 proceedings or, as the case may be, makes a complaint;

"complaint" means a complaint for which the Tribunal is the appropriate forum by virtue of section 65(2)(b) and section 65(4) of the Act;

"Convention right" has the same meaning as in the Human Rights Act 1998;[3]

"section 7 proceedings" means proceedings under section 7(1)(a) of the Human Rights Act 1998 in relation to which the Tribunal is the only appropriate tribunal by virtue of section 65(2)(a) of the Act;[4]

"the Tribunal" means the tribunal established under section 65(1) of the Act.

Application of Rules

3. These Rules apply to section 7 proceedings, and to complaints.

Exercise of Tribunal's jurisdiction

4.—(1) The jurisdiction of the Tribunal may be exercised at any place in the United Kingdom, by any two or more members of the Tribunal designated for the

---

[2] Chapter 7 of this work described the commissioners, areas of responsibility and statutory basis.

[3] Extracts from the Human Rights Act 1998 as amended appear in Chapter 23.

[4] A person who alleges that a public authority (definition of public authority for RIPA in s 81(1)—narrower than under s 6 of the HRA 1998 in that it excludes courts and tribunals) has unlawfully interfered with his Convention rights, and who wishes to sue under the HRA 1998 s 7

purpose by the President;[5] and different members of the Tribunal may carry out functions in relation to different complaints at the same time.

(2) This rule is subject to paragraph 3 of Schedule 3 to the Act (members of the Tribunal with special responsibilities).[6]

Functions exercisable by single member

5.—(1) Subject to paragraph (2), the following powers and duties may be exercised or performed by a single member of the Tribunal:

(a) the power under rule 7(4) or rule 8(4) to invite the complainant to supply information or make representations;

(b) the power under section 68(2) of the Act to require a Commissioner to provide assistance;

(c) the power under section 68(6) of the Act to require the disclosure or provision of documents or information;

(d) the power under paragraph 5(2) of Schedule 3 to the Act to authorise an officer to obtain documents or information on the Tribunal's behalf;

(e) the power under section 7(5)(b) of the Human Rights Act 1998 to extend the time limit for section 7 proceedings;[7]

(f) the power under section 67(5) of the Act to extend the time limit for complaints;[8]

(g) the duty under rule 13 to notify the complainant of any of the determinations described in that rule;[9]

(h) the duty, in considering a complaint, to investigate the matters described in paragraphs (a) and (b) of section 67(3) of the Act.

(2) In relation to a case falling within paragraph 3(2) of Schedule 3 to the Act, a single member discharging any of these functions must be a member designated under paragraph 3(1) of that Schedule.[10]

---

must proceed to the IPT if the conduct falls within specified categories—see s 65(3) of RIPA and the discussion in Chapter 8.

[5] The President must be a person who holds or has held high judicial office within the meaning of the Appellate Jurisdiction Act 1876 (see Sch 3 of RIPA).

[6] The Schedule referred to in particular requires at least one member to be designated by the President as having particular responsibility for the intelligence services. See Chapter 7.

[7] Ordinarily the period of one year from the date of the matter complained of, unless it is equitable to extend time (see s 7(5) of the HRA 1998).

[8] By s 67(5) ordinarily one year from the date of the conduct complained of, unless it is equitable to extend time.

[9] Relating to notifying the complainant of determinations of frivolous or vexatious complaints, complaints which are out of time where an extension has been refused and complaints where the Tribunal decides that the complainant does not have a right to bring the HRA 1988, s 7 proceedings or to make the complaint.

[10] Ie in respect of intelligence services matters the single member must be a designated member with responsibility for those services. See the discussion in Chapter 7.

Disclosure of information

6.—(1) The Tribunal shall carry out their functions in such a way as to secure that information is not disclosed to an extent, or in a manner, that is contrary to the public interest or prejudicial to national security, the prevention or detection of serious crime, the economic well-being of the United Kingdom or the continued discharge of the functions of any of the intelligence services.

(2) Without prejudice to this general duty, but subject to paragraphs (3) and (4), the Tribunal may not disclose to the complainant or to any other person:

(a) the fact that the Tribunal have held, or propose to hold, an oral hearing under rule 9(4);

(b) any information or document disclosed or provided to the Tribunal in the course of that hearing, or the identity of any witness at that hearing;

(c) any information or document otherwise disclosed or provided to the Tribunal by any person pursuant to section 68(6) of the Act (or provided voluntarily by a person specified in section 68(7));

(d) any information or opinion provided to the Tribunal by a Commissioner pursuant to section 68(2) of the Act;

(e) the fact that any information, document, identity or opinion has been disclosed or provided in the circumstances mentioned in sub-paragraphs (b) to (d).

(3) The Tribunal may disclose anything described in paragraph (2) with the consent of:

(a) in the case of sub-paragraph (a), the person required to attend the hearing;

(b) in the case of sub-paragraphs (b) and (c), the witness in question or the person who disclosed or provided the information or document;

(c) in the case of sub-paragraph (d), the Commissioner in question and, to the extent that the information or opinion includes information provided to the Commissioner by another person, that other person;

(d) in the case of sub-paragraph (e), the person whose consent is required under this rule for disclosure of the information, document or opinion in question.

(4) The Tribunal may also disclose anything described in paragraph (2) as part of the information provided to the complainant under rule 13(2), subject to the restrictions contained in rule 13(4) and (5).

(5) The Tribunal may not order any person to disclose any information or document which the Tribunal themselves would be prohibited from disclosing by virtue of this rule, had the information or document been disclosed or provided to them by that person.

(6) The Tribunal may not, without the consent of the complainant, disclose to any person holding office under the Crown (except a Commissioner) or to any other person anything to which paragraph (7) applies.

(7) This paragraph applies to any information or document disclosed or provided to the Tribunal by or on behalf of the complainant, except for the statements described in rule 7(2)(a) and (b) or, as the case may be, rule 8(2)(a) and (b).

PART II

PROCEEDINGS AND COMPLAINTS

Bringing section 7 proceedings

7.—(1) Section 7 proceedings are brought by a complainant sending to the Tribunal a form[11] and other information in accordance with this rule.

(2) The form must be signed by the complainant and must:[12]

    (a) state the name, address and date of birth of the complainant;

    (b) state each public authority against which the proceedings are brought;

    (c) describe the nature of the claim (including details of the Convention right which it is alleged has been infringed) and of the complainant's interest; and

    (d) specify the remedy which the complainant seeks.

(3) The complainant must also supply, either in or with the form, a summary of the information on which the claim is based.

(4) At any time, the Tribunal may invite the complainant to supply further information or to make written representations on any matter.

Making a complaint

8.—(1) A complaint is brought by a complainant sending to the Tribunal a form[13] in accordance with this rule.

(2) The form must be signed by the complainant and must:[14]

    (a) state the name, address and date of birth of the complainant;

    (b) state the person or authority whose conduct, to the best of the complainant's knowledge or belief, is the subject of the complaint; and

    (c) describe, to the best of the complainant's knowledge or belief, that conduct.

(3) The complainant must also supply, either in or with the form, a summary of the information on which the claim is based.

(4) At any time, the Tribunal may invite the complainant to supply further information or to make written representations on any matter.

---

[11] Form T1 set out in Chapter 12 of this work.

[12] Note that by r 6(6) and (7), the IPT may not disclose to persons holding office under the Crown other than commissioners, any information given by the complainant save for items (a) and (b)).

[13] Form T2 set out in Chapter 12 of this work.

[14] Note that by r 6(6) and (7), the IPT may not disclose to persons holding office under the Crown other than commissioners, any information given by the complainant save for items (a) and (b)).

Forms of hearing and consideration

9.—(1) The Tribunal's power to determine their own procedure in relation to section 7 proceedings and complaints shall be subject to this rule.

(2) The Tribunal shall be under no duty to hold oral hearings, but they may do so in accordance with this rule (and not otherwise).

(3) The Tribunal may hold, at any stage of their consideration, oral hearings at which the complainant may make representations, give evidence and call witnesses.

(4) The Tribunal may hold separate oral hearings which:

(a) the person whose conduct is the subject of the complaint,

(b) the public authority against which the section 7 proceedings are brought, or

(c) any other person specified in section 68(7) of the Act,

may be required to attend and at which that person or authority may make representations, give evidence and call witnesses.

(5) Within a period notified by the Tribunal for the purpose of this rule, the complainant, person or authority in question must inform the Tribunal of any witnesses he or it intends to call; and no other witnesses may be called without the leave of the Tribunal.

(6) The Tribunal's proceedings, including any oral hearings, shall be conducted in private.[15]

Representation

10.—(1) A person entitled to make representations at an oral hearing may appear in person or may be represented by any person he may appoint for that purpose, subject to paragraph (2).

(2) The leave of the Tribunal is required except where the representative is:

(a) a member of the Bar of England and Wales or of Northern Ireland,

(b) a solicitor of the Supreme Court in England and Wales or in Northern Ireland,

(c) a member of the Faculty of Advocates, or

(d) a solicitor within the meaning of the Solicitors (Scotland) Act 1980.

Evidence

11.—(1) The Tribunal may receive evidence in any form, and may receive evidence that would not be admissible in a court of law.

(2) The Tribunal may require a witness to give evidence on oath.

(3) No person shall be compelled to give evidence at an oral hearing under rule 9(3).

---

[15] This rule was found to be ultra vires in the the IPT decision of *Re Kennedy*, summarised in Chapter 22. The Tribunal determined that it had the power to sit in public.

Remedies

12.—(1) Before exercising their power under section 67(7) of the Act, the Tribunal shall invite representations in accordance with this rule.

(2) Where they propose to make an award of compensation, the Tribunal shall give the complainant and the person who would be required to pay the compensation an opportunity to make representations as to the amount of the award.

(3) Where they propose to make any other order (including an interim order) affecting the public authority against whom the section 7 proceedings are brought, or the person whose conduct is the subject of the complaint, the Tribunal shall give that authority or person an opportunity to make representations on the proposed order.

Notification to the complainant

13.—(1) In addition to any statement under section 68(4) of the Act, the Tribunal shall provide information to the complainant in accordance with this rule.

(2) Where they make a determination in favour of the complainant, the Tribunal shall provide him with a summary of that determination including any findings of fact.

(3) Where they make a determination:

(a) that the bringing of the section 7 proceedings or the making of the complaint is frivolous or vexatious;[16]

(b) that the section 7 proceedings have been brought, or the complaint made, out of time and that the time limit should not be extended;[17] or

(c) that the complainant does not have the right to bring the section 7 proceedings or make the complaint;

the Tribunal shall notify the complainant of that fact.

(4) The duty to provide information under this rule is in all cases subject to the general duty imposed on the Tribunal by rule 6(1).

(5) No information may be provided under this rule whose disclosure would be restricted under rule 6(2) unless the person whose consent would be needed for disclosure under that rule has been given the opportunity to make representations to the Tribunal.

---

[16] Section 67(4) of RIPA absolves the Tribunal of any duty to hear frivolous or vexatious matters.
[17] Section 67(5) imposes a one-year time limit, extendable if it is equitable to do so, to complaints to the Tribunal under its s 65(2)(b) jurisdiction.

12

TRIBUNAL FORMS

A. Form T1: Human Rights Complaint Form

The Investigatory Powers Tribunal

Human Rights Claim Form
Form T1

Use this form if your claim is that your human rights in terms of the Human Rights Act 1998 have been infringed:

(a) by one or more of the Intelligence Services or any person acting on their behalf in any circumstances, or

(b) by any of: Her Majesty's Armed Forces, any police force, the National Criminal Intelligence Service, the National Crime Squad, or the Commissioners of Customs and Excise in circumstances which involved (or which currently involve):

(i) interception of your communications by post or your telecommunications.

(ii) surveillance which has resulted, or is likely to result, inprivate information about you being obtained.

(iii) surveillance concerning you which has been, or is being, carried out in relation to anything taking place on any residential premises or in any private vehicle.

(iv) covert human intelligence which has been, or is being, used in relation to you, e.g. the use of a personal relation ship for the purpose of getting information about you without you knowing about it.

(v) any entry on or interference with property or interference with wireless telegraphy.

If your claim relates to the infringement of your human rights by any other organisation or in other circumstances you should take the matter up with the organisation concerned.

When you have completed the form please sign and date it together with any separate sheets which you wish to submit along with it.

Your Details

Your surname _____

Your surname at birth (if different) _____

Your surname at the date(s) when the events complained of occurred (if different)

Your forenames _____

Any other names by which you were commonly known when the events complained of occurred

Title (Mr, Mrs, Miss etc.) _____

Date of Birth _____

Your present address including your postcode _____

If this form is being submitted by your solicitor or advisor please complete this section.

Surname of solicitor or advisor

Initials _____ Title _____

Name of firm (if applicable) _____

Address including postcode _____

Please answer the following questions to the best of your knowledge and belief. If there is insufficient space on this form please use an additional sheet of paper if you need to, making it clear to which questions the additional information relates.

1   WHICH ORGANISATION OR ORGANISATIONS DO YOU BELIEVE HAS INFRINGED YOUR HUMAN RIGHTS?

2   WHICH OF YOUR HUMAN RIGHTS DO YOU BELIEVE HAS BEEN INFRINGED?

3   AT WHICH PLACE OR PLACES WERE YOUR HUMAN RIGHTS INFRINGED?

4   WHEN DID THE INFRINGEMENT HAPPEN AT EACH PLACE?

5 WHAT HAPPENED? (Please give details of what happened and, if it is not obvious, why you believe that what happened amounted to an infringement of your human rights.)

6 IS THERE EVIDENCE OTHER THAN YOUR OWN IN SUPPORT OF YOUR CLAIM? If so, who could provide that evidence? What is that evidence likely to be?

7 IF THE EVENTS WHICH YOU ARE COMPLAINING ABOUT HAPPENED MORE THAN ONE YEAR AGO IS THERE AN EXPLANATION FOR THE DELAY IN SUBMITTING THIS CLAIM? (See note1 below)

8 IF THE TRIBUNAL UPHOLDS YOUR CLAIM WHAT REMEDIES DO YOU SEEK? (See note2 below)

Do you wish correspondence from the Tribunal to be sent to you or to your solicitor or advisor instead of to you? Please tick one box only

Please send correspondence to me ☐

Please send correspondence to my solicitor/advisor instead of me ☐

Confidentiality

Your claim will be handled in confidence. To carry out its functions, the Tribunal has power to call on any official documents or information it may need. The Tribunal cannot disclose details of your claim in questions 2 to 8 of this form without your permission. If it does not have your permission it may not be possible for the Tribunal to investigate your complaint properly.

Please tick here if you are prepared to give that permission ☐

Declaration

I have answered all the questions on the application form to the best of my knowledge and belief.

Signature _____

Date _____

Notes

1. Normally the Tribunal will only consider claims made within one year of the event(s) to which they relate. The Tribunal can consider older claims if it is equitable to do so. If your claim relates to events more than a year ago you should give an explanation for the delay in submitting your claim if you can.

2. The Tribunal has power in appropriate cases to award compensation, to quash or cancel any warrant or authorisation, to order destruction of records and to make such other order as they think fit.

3. If you wish to consult the legislation relating to your claim you can do so via the website of Her Majesty's Stationery Office www.hmso.gov.uk

    Some of the legislation which you may wish to consult is as follows:

    • Human Rights Act 1998
    • Regulation of Investigatory Powers Act 2000
    • Regulation of Investigatory Powers (Scotland) Act 2000
    • Investigatory Powers Tribunal Rules (Statutory Instrument 2000 No. 2665)

B. Form T2: Complaint Form

The Investigatory Powers Tribunal

Complaint Form
Form T2

Complete this form if your complaint is against any of the Intelligence Services or one or more of the Public Authorities listed at the end of this form and it is not a human rights claim. (If you wish to make a human rights claim please complete Form T1.)

When you have completed the form please sign and date it together with any separate sheets which you wish to submit along with it.

Your Details

Your surname _____

Your surname at birth (if different) _____

Your surname at the date(s) when the events complained of occurred (if different) _____

Your forenames _____

Any other names by which you were commonly known when the events complained of occurred _____

Title (Mr, Mrs, Miss etc.) _____

Date of Birth _____

Your present address including your postcode _____
_____

If this form is being submitted by your solicitor or advisor please complete this section.

Surname of solicitor or advisor _____

Initials _____ Title _____

Name of firm (if applicable) _____

Address including postcode _____
_____

Please answer the following questions to the best of your knowledge and belief. If there is insufficient space on this form please use an additional sheet of paper if you need to, making it clear to which questions the additional information relates.

1 TO WHICH ORGANISATION(S) DOES THE COMPLAINT RELATE AND WHY? (Please refer to the list at the end of this form.) This includes persons acting on behalf of an organisation.

2 AT WHICH PLACE OR PLACES DID THE CONDUCT OF WHICH YOU COMPLAIN HAPPEN? (Please give the full addresses of any properties, telephone numbers and details of any vehicles to which the complaint relates.)

3 WHEN DID THE CONDUCT HAPPEN AT EACH PLACE?

4 WHAT IS YOUR COMPLAINT? (Please give details of the conduct you are complaining about and say why you think your complaint falls with in the category or categories which you have ticked.)

5 WHAT IS THE NATURE OF THE CONDUCT COMPLAINED OF? (The Tribunal can only consider your complaint if it comes under one or more of the following headings. Please tick the box or boxes which apply to your complaint.)

☐ Conduct which you believe to have been carried out in relation to you by or on behalf of any of the Intelligence Services. That conduct may relate to you, your property or your communications. You can complain of that conduct whether or not it involves the use of an investigatory power under the Regulation of Investigatory Powers Act 2000.

☐ Your communications by post or your telecommunications have been intercepted e.g. telephone tapping or interference with your mail.

☐ There has been entry onto or interference with your property or with your wireless telegraphy.

☐ Surveillance by a public authority has taken place which has resulted, or is likely to result, in private information about you being obtained.

☐ Surveillance concerning you has been carried out, or is being carried out, by a public authority in relation to any thing taking place on any residential premises or in any private vehicle.

☐ Covert human intelligence has been used in relation to you, e.g. a public authority has used, or is using, a personal or other relationship for the purpose of getting information about you.

6 IS THERE EVIDENCE OTHER THAN YOUR OWN IN SUPPORT OF YOUR COMPLAINT? If so, who could provide that evidence? What is that evidence likely to be?

7 IF THE EVENTS WHICH YOU ARE COMPLAINING ABOUT HAPPENED MORE THAN ONE YEAR AGO IS THERE AN EXPLANATION FOR THE DELAY IN SUBMITTING YOUR COMPLAINT? (See note2 below)

Do you wish correspondence from the Tribunal to be sent to you or to your solicitor or advisor instead of to you? Please tick *one* box only

Please send correspondence to me ☐

Please send correspondence to my solicitor/advisor instead of me ☐

Confidentiality

Your claim will be handled in confidence. To carry out its functions, the Tribunal has power to call on any official documents or information it may need. The Tribunal cannot disclose details of your claim in questions 1 to 4 and 6 and 7 of this form without your permission. If it does not have your permission it may not be possible for the Tribunal to investigate your complaint properly.

Please tick here if you are prepared to give that permission ☐

Declaration

I have answered all the questions on the application form to the best of my knowledge and belief.

Signature _____

Date _____

Notes

1. If your complaint is not under one of the categories above and is not a human rights claim (for which you must complete a Human Rights Complaint Form) it cannot be considered by the Tribunal and you should make your complaint direct to the Public Authority in question.

2. Normally the Tribunal will only consider complaints made within one year of the event(s) to which it relates. The Tribunal can consider older complaints if it is equitable to do so. If your complaint relates to events more than a year ago you should give an explanation for the delay in submitting your complaint if you can.

3. If you wish to consult the legislation relating to your complaint you can do so via the website of Her Majesty's Stationery Office www.hmso.gov.uk

Some of the legislation which you may wish to consult is as follows:

- Regulation of Investigatory Powers Act 2000
- Regulation of Investigatory Powers (Scotland) Act 2000
- Investigatory Powers Tribunal Rules (Statutory Instrument 2000 No. 2665)

LIST OF ORGANISATIONS ABOUT WHOSE CONDUCT A COMPLAINT MAY BE MADE

1. The Intelligence Services
The Security Service (MI5)
The Secret Intelligence Service (MI6)
Government Communications Headquarters (GCHQ)

2. Public Authorities
Any police force; The National Criminal Intelligence Service; The National Crime Squad; The Scottish Crime Squad; The Scottish Drug Enforcement Agency; The Royal Ulster Constabulary; The Serious Fraud Office; Any of Her Majesty's Armed Forces; The Commissioners of Customs and Excise; The Commissioners of Inland Revenue; The Ministry of Agriculture, Fisheries and Food; The Ministry of Defence; The Department of the Environment, Transport and the Regions; The Department of Health; The Home Office; The Department of Social Security; The Department of Trade and Industry; The Scottish Administration; The National Assembly for Wales; Any local authority (with in the meaning of section 1 of the Local Government Act 1999 or constituted under section 2 of the Local Government etc (Scotland)Act 1994); The Environment Agency; The Scottish Environment Protection Agency; The Financial Services Authority; The Food Standards Agency; The Intervention Board for Agricultural Produce; The Personal Investment Authority; The Post Office; The Health and Safety Executive; A Health Authority established under section 8 of the National Health Service Act 1977; A Special Health Authority established under section 11 of the National Health Service Act 1977; A National Health Service trust established under section 5 of the National Health Service and Community Care Act 1990; The Common Services Agency for the Health Service; A Health Board; A Special Health Board; A National Health Service Trust established under section 12 A of the National Health Service (Scotland) Act 1976; The Royal Pharmaceutical Society of Great Britain; The BBC (TV license detection activities only); The Prison Service; and such other authorities as are granted powers by an order under the Regulation of Investigatory Powers Act or the Regulation of Investigatory Powers (Scotland) Act.

Other public authorities may be added by order making powers under the Acts. Please contact the Secretary to the Tribunal for the latest list.

Alternatively you may wish to consult:
The Regulation of Investigatory Powers (Prescription of Offices, Ranks and Positions) Order 2000 (Statutory Instrument 2000 No. 2417)
The Regulation of Investigatory Powers (Prescription of Offices, Ranks and Positions) (Scotland) Order 2000 (Scottish Statutory Instrument 2000 No. 343)
The Regulation of Investigatory Powers (Prescription of Offices, Ranks and Positions) (Scotland) Amendment Order 2001 (Scottish Statutory Instrument 2001 No. 87)

All are available at www.hmso.gov.uk

C. Tribunal Information Leaflet

Information Leaflet

Regulation of Investigatory Powers Act 2000

Regulation of Investigatory Powers (Scotland) Act 2000

How to apply to the Tribunal

You apply to the Tribunal by completing either Form T1 or Form T2 (or both). Copies of these forms are attached. These forms set out the information which the Tribunal requires in order to commence an investigation.

Please write in black or dark ink so that your complaint can be copied to members of the Tribunal. Please remember to sign and date the form and any separate sheets submitted with it.

You should send the completed form to:

The Investigatory Powers Tribunal, PO Box 33220, London, SW1H 9ZQ

Investigation by the Tribunal

The Tribunal will acknowledge receipt of your claim or complaint. The Tribunal will then, for complaints, investigate whether any authority you have complained about has carried out activities in relation to you, your property or your communications and, if it has, whether its conduct has been properly authorised. It will then consider whether your complaint or claim is justified. The Tribunal can only reveal to other parties your name, address, telephone numbers, date of birth and the identity of the body against whom you are making the claim or complaint. It requires your consent to reveal any other details about you or your claim or complaint. The Tribunal will only reveal such details with your consent to the extent necessary to enable your claim or complaint to be properly investigated. You do not need to give your consent to that but, if you do not, it may prevent a full investigation of our claim or complaint from taking place.

The Outcome

The Tribunal will advise you as soon as possible whether it has found in your favour or not. Where the Tribunal finds in your favour, it will, where permissible, provide you with a summary of its determination and any findings of fact. If it up holds your claim or complaint the Tribunal may, after considering representations by you or on your behalf, also order such remedial action as it considers appropriate.

These Acts establish an independent tribunal to consider all complaints and Human Rights Act claims which fall within its jurisdiction. The Investigatory Powers Tribunal replaces the Interception of Communications Tribunal, the Security Service Tribunal, the Intelligence Services Tribunal and the complaints function of the Commissioner appointed under the Police Act 1997.

What complaints/claims can the Tribunal consider?

Human Rights claims

The Tribunal can consider claims that human rights have been in fringed as a result of actions carried out by or on behalf of any of the Intelligence Services and, *in the circumstances set out below*, by certain Public Authorities. So far as human rights claims are concerned the Tribunal is the body to complain to if you believe that your human rights have been infringed by any of the Intelligence Services or by any of the following Public Authorities: any of Her Majesty's Armed Forces, any police force, the National Criminal Intelligence Service, the National Crime Squad (including the National Hi-Tech Crime Unit) or the Commissioners of Customs and Excise. The Intelligence Services are: the Security Service (commonly known as MI5), the Secret Intelligence Service (SIS- commonly known as MI6) and Government Communications Head quarters (GCHQ). If you consider that your human rights have been in fringed in terms of the Human Rights Act 1998 by any of the Intelligence Services or by one of the Public Authorities listed above please complete Form T1.

Complaints (ie not Human Rights claims)

The Tribunal can also consider complaints about any conduct which you believe to have been carried out in relation to you by or on behalf of any of the Intelligence Services and, *in the circumstances set out below*, of a larger number of Public Authorities than those listed above. The Intelligence Services are as set out above. The Public Authorities in relation to which such complaints may be made are listed at the end of Form T2. For such complaints please complete Form T2.

Whether the claim is a Human Rights claim (Form T1) or another type of complaint (Form T2) the conduct alleged must involve or have involved one or more of the following::

- The interception of communications by post or tele-communications.

- Surveillance which has resulted, or is likely to result, in private information being obtained.

- Surveillance which has been or is being carried out in relation to anything taking place on any residential premises or in any private vehicle.

- Covert human intelligence which has been or is being used in relation to a person, e.g. the use of a personal relationship for the purpose of getting information without that person knowing about it.

- Any entry on or interference with property or interference with wireless telegraphy.

Part IV

RIPA FORMS AND NOTICES

13

PUBLIC AUTHORITY COMMUNICATIONS DATA FORMS[1]

---

[1] Forms for use by additional public authorities listed in the RIPA (Communications Data) Order 2003 (SI No 3172) as amended by SI 2005 No 1083.

A. Application for Communications Data

APPLICATION FOR COMMUNICATIONS DATA
(UNDER PART I, CHAPTER II OF THE REGULATION
OF INVESTIGATORY POWERS ACT 2000)

1. Is this the first application to access communications data in respect of this investigation? If NO, please enter previous SPOC number in the space provided	
Yes ☐	No ☐
	Please provide SPOC number:

SPOC Ref No. (To be completed by SPOC)		Application Ref No. (To be completed by SPOC)	

- This application form is to be used for accessing communications data in respect of either:

    - Subscriber / Account Information
    - Outgoing Call Data (Itemised Billing)

A separate application form must be submitted for each of the services listed above. (i.e. subscriber/account information cannot be applied for on the same application form as outgoing call data).

- The request is subject to the provisions of the Regulation of Investigatory Powers Act 2000. Unlawful disclosure to any person not entitled to receive it may result in prosecution.

- All sections on this form should be completed. Incomplete forms will be returned to the applicant. The SPOC is inspected by the Office of Interception Commissioners who will ensure compliance with RIPA..

- **Once completed by the applicant this form should be forwarded to the SPOC.**

- **The SPOC will assess the application and may reject it and issue a SPOC rejection form, or complete a SPOC report and forward the application for consideration to the Designated Person.**

Applicant Name		Rank / Grade	
Department		Telephone Number	

2. THIS DATA IS NECESSARY FOR ONE OR MORE OF THE FOLLOWING PURPOSES AS SPECIFIED IN THE REGULATION OF INVESTIGATORY POWERS ACT 2000
☐ For the prevention and detection of crime or preventing disorder S22 (2)(b) ☐ In the interests of public safety S22 (2)(d) ☐ For the purpose of protecting public health S22 (2)(e) – not applicable to LEA's ☐ For the purpose, in an emergency, of preventing death or injury or damage to a persons physical or mental health or of mitigating any injury or damage to a persons physical or mental health S22 (2)(g)

Page 1

316

---

3. NATURE OF ENQUIRY / INTELLIGENCE CASE
- **Detail the enquiry or investigation**
- **Where relevant outline the intelligence case indicating how accessing the communications data requested will further the enquiry**
- **Where relevant give the exact date/time/place of the incident under investigation**
- **Include relevant subjects details (date of birth, address and subjects role(s) in the enquiry/investigation)**

---

4.   DETAILS OF SERVICE / DATA REQUIRED

SUBSCRIBER / ACCOUNT INFORMATION [S21 (4)(c)]
(Insert relevant information below e.g. telephone number, e-mail address)
(Please give a date/time period to search on IF you are NOT requesting most current subscriber)

1		2	
3		4	
5		6	

USE MADE OF A COMMUNICATION SERVICE e.g. OUTGOING CALL DATA / ITEMISED BILLING [S21(4)(b)]
(Subscriber/Account details must have been obtained prior to this request)

	Number / Other	Subscriber Details	Date/Time Period From:	Date/Time Period To:
1				

---

5. OUTLINE THE SOURCE OF THE NUMBER/S OR OTHER DATA IN THIS APPLICATION (i.e. how they were identified)

6. NECESSITY
State why it is necessary to the enquiry to obtain this data for the purpose listed at question 2 and what is sought to be achieved from so obtaining it. Explain why you have requested the specific date/time period.

7. PROPORTIONALITY
Ensure the objectives have been defined and how obtaining the data will achieve the objectives. Explain why the objectives cannot reasonably be achieved by less intrusive means.

8. COLLATERAL INTRUSION
Collateral Intrusion is intrusion into the privacy of innocent third parties. It is important to detail any plan to minimise collateral intrusion.

APPLICANT
I, as the applicant, undertake to inform the SPOC of any change in circumstances that no longer supports the lawful acquisition of this data.

Applicant's Details		Date	

Now forward this form to your SPOC.

A SPOC Officer will assess and quality control this application and if it meets the legal threshold for obtaining communications data the SPOC will forward it to the appropriate Designated Person.

If rejected, by the Designated Person or the SPOC, the SPOC will retain this application and inform the applicant in writing of the reason(s) for its rejection.

B. Application for Communications Data—SPoC Rejection Form

INSERT NAME OF AUTHORITY

**APPLICATION FOR
COMMUNICATIONS DATA -
SPOC REJECTION FORM**

SPOC Ref No.		Application Ref No.	

Applicant Name		Rank / Grade	
Department		*Other Ref (if relevant)*	

Your Application for communications data has been REJECTED FOR THE FOLLOWING REASONS:

<u>Insufficient Information in relation to:</u>

☐ **Nature of Enquiry / Investigation (Application Form Question 3)**

☐ **Source of Telephone Number / Other Data (Application Form Question 5)**

☐ **Necessity (Application Form Question 6)**

☐ **Proportionality (Application Form Question 7)**

☐ **Collateral Intrusion (Application Form Question 8)**

☐ **Subscriber / Account Details must be obtained before requesting Outgoing Call Data or Specialist Services**

☐ **The time / date period requested has not been adequately justified**

☐ **The request does not meet the criteria for this type of service. (Specify Reasons)**

☐ **The request has been refused by the Designated Person**

☐ **Other (Specify)**

The original copy of this application is held by the SPOC.

SPOC Name		Date	
Signature			

C. Designated Person's Consideration Form in respect of an Application for Communications Data

INSERT NAME OF AUTHORITY

**DESIGNATED PERSON'S CONSIDERATION FORM
IN RESPECT OF AN APPLICATION FOR COMMUNICATIONS DATA
UNDER THE REGULATION OF INVESTIGATORY POWERS ACT 2000**

SPOC Ref No.		**Application Ref No.**	

I as the Designated Person confirm that I have viewed the above Application Form Ref No and my specific considerations with regard to necessity, proportionality and collateral intrusion are as follows:

1. Whether the matter under investigation justifies the requesting of communications data for one of the purposes listed under the Regulation of Investigatory Powers Act 2000

I confirm that the application is in accordance with the Regulation of Investigatory Powers Act 2000 and that the matter under investigation justifies the requesting of communications data:

☐   For the prevention and detection of crime or preventing disorder S22 (2)(b)
☐   In the interests of public safety S22 (2)(d)
☐   For the purpose of protecting public health S22 (2)(e)
☐   For the purpose, in an emergency, of preventing death or injury or damage to a persons physical or mental health or of mitigating any injury or damage to a persons physical or mental health S22 (2)(g)

2. Outline why the data is necessary for the investigation to progress

3. Where obtaining the communication data is likely to result in collateral intrusion, outline why the circumstances of the case justify that access.

4. Outline why the request is proportionate to the objective(s).

DISCLOSURE OF DATA

I authorise that all data obtained from the Communications Service Provider should be provided to the applicant. If the Communications Service Provider supplies information in excess of that which has been authorised there will be no use, action or dissemination of that material without additional application & authority.   ☐

Page 1

320

RESTRICTED

RIPA permits two ways of accessing communications data.

Firstly, section 22(4) provides that an authority can give a notice to a CSP requiring them to collect or retrieve the data and produce it to the authority. The notice is given by the Designated Person, but served by the SPOC.

Secondly, section 22(3) provides that a Designated Person may grant an authorisation allowing a member of the authority to collect or retrieve the data themselves. An authorisation is granted by the Designated Person, but administered by the SPOC.
The Designated Person will only grant an authorisation when they believe that one or more of the following apply:

If a notice is given then the CSP will be incapable of complying with it and an authorisation will be granted allowing members of the Designated Person's public authority to retrieve the data;
If a notice is given then the enquiry is likely to be prejudiced and an authorisation will be granted allowing members of the Designated Person's public authority to retrieve the data;
There is an existing arrangement in place between the Designated Person's public authority and the CSP for the exchange of data and the SPOC will retrieve the data using an automated system within the Designated Person's public authority.

I as the Designated Person confirm that I have considered the Application Form and have either granted or rejected the authorisations / notices as listed below.
I hereby grant the following authorisations (list the URN of each authorisation and the conduct required to retrieve the data)
I hereby give the following notices (list URN of each notice and the conduct required to retrieve the data)
I hereby refuse the following authorisations (list URN's). Specify reasons for refusal
I hereby refuse the following notices (list URN's). Specify reasons for refusal

DESIGNATED PERSON DETAILS			
Name		**Rank / Grade**	
Signature		**Time/Date**	

Page 2

321

D. Notice under s 22(4) of the Regulation of Investigatory Powers Act 2000 requiring Communications Data to be obtained and disclosed

---

INSERT <u>YOUR</u> PUBLIC AUTHORITY NAME HERE

NOTICE UNDER SECTION 22(4) OF THE REGULATION OF INVESTIGATORY POWERS

ACT 2000 REQUIRING COMMUNICATIONS DATA TO BE OBTAINED AND DISCLOSED

To:	[Insert name of postal or telecommunications service provider and address]

You are required to obtain and disclose the communications data described in this notice to : [Single

Point of Contact name and address] by : -

☐   fax to [number]

☐   e-mail to [address]

☐   post to [address]

☐   hand to [name and position]

SPoC Ref No. (to be completed by SPoC)		Application Ref No. (to be completed by SPoC)		URN of Notice (to be completed by SPoC)	

In accordance with Section 22(4) of the Regulation of Investigatory Powers Act 2000, by this notice I hereby require you:

☐ if not already in possession of the data to which this notice relates, to <u>obtain</u> it;

☐ to <u>disclose</u> all communications data to which this notice relates whether in your possession [or subsequently obtained by you]*

[square bracketed text is only for those cases where data is required to be captured for the duration of the notice - this text should be omitted when the disclosure of historical data only is required]

Description of communications data to which this notice relates:

Enter details of the communications data required (distinguish here between data (a) to be <u>obtained</u> if not already in the possession of the operator [omitting if not relevant] and data (b) to be <u>disclosed</u>. Each should be described separately)

[(a) communications data to be obtained in the future]

[(b) communications data to be disclosed]

A SINGLE FORM CAN ONLY BE USED TO REQUEST EITHER (a) OR (b) NOT A COMBINATION OF BOTH.

This data is necessary for [one or more of] the following purpose[s] specified in the Regulation of Investigatory Powers Act 2000 *[delete those purposes not permitted to your public authority]*

It is necessary for this communications data to be obtained:

☐   For the prevention and detection of crime or preventing disorder S22 (2)(b)

☐   In the interests of public safety S22 (2)(d)

☐   For the purpose of protecting public health S22 (2)(e) (Not applicable to LEA's)

☐   For the purpose, in an emergency, of preventing death or injury or damage to a persons physical or mental health or of mitigating any injury or damage to a persons physical or mental health S22 (2)(g)

Period of Validity

This notice is valid from *[issue date]* to *[end date]*. *[This must be no more than one month from the date of this notice, or earlier if cancelled under section 23(8)]*. This notice may be renewed at any time by the giving of a further notice.

Authorisation			
Designated Person Name		**Division**	
Position in Public Authority		**Department**	
Contact Telephone Number		**Address**	
Date			

This notice may be authenticated by contacting the following:			
SPOC Officer Name		**SPOC Officer Number**	
Position in Public Authority		**Department**	
Contact Telephone Number		**Address**	

Page 4

E. Applicant's Cancellation Request Form under s 22(4) and (8) of RIPA

INSERT NAME OF AUTHORITY

CANCELLATION UNDER SECTION 22(4)(8) OF THE REGULATION OF INVESTIGATORY POWERS ACT 2000

This form must be sent to the Single Point of Contact (SPoC) on completion. Where the activity needs to be ceased immediately, the SPoC must be advised to cease the activity prior to completion of the form to minimise intrusion into the privacy of the subject(s) and innocent third parties. The SPoC on your behal f will verbally inform the CSP to cease the activity and a formal request will follow.

SPoC Ref No.		Application Ref No.		URN of Notice or Authorisation	

TO BE COMPLETED BY THE APPLICANT	
I consider that the obtaining of communications data in respect of the above application is no longer deemed to be necessary and should be cancelled forthwith.	
Applicant Name and Rank / Grade	
Name of SPoC Officer who you informed to cease the activity	
Time and date SPoC informed to cease the activity	

This form must now be forwarded to the SPoC

TO BE COMPLETED BY THE SPoC	
Date/time CSP verbally advised to cease the activity	
Name and Rank of Designated Person that Granted the Notice / Authorisation to be Cancelled	

TO BE COMPLETED BY DESIGNATED PERSO N	
I hereby authorise that the following Notice/s or Authorisation/s should be cancelled forthwith	
Where the original Designated Person (above) is no longer available to cancel the Authorisation or Notice, explain why and specify the name and rank of De signated Person now cancelling the Notice or Authorisation **N.B** *This must be someone who has taken over the DP's roles and responsibilities. Where this person is acting in a temporary capacity they will be performing at the same level as the DP (or higher) and will have been specifically appointed to perform this role for a period of time. Where no such person has been previously appointed to perform the DP's role they must be specifically appointed for this purpose.*	

Designated Person – Name and Rank / Grade	Date and Time

Page 1

F. SPoC's Cancellation Notice under s 22 (4) and (8) of RIPA

INSERT NAME OF AUTHORITY

CANCELLATION OF NOTICE ISSUED UNDER SECTION 22 (4) (8) OF THE
REGULATION OF INVESTIGATORY POWERS ACT 2000

SPoC Ref No.		Application Ref No.		URN of Notice	

TO BE COMPLETED BY THE SPoC	
To CSP (full name & address)	

You are required to cancel the collection of communications data in respect of the above URN.

Date/Time verbally advised to cease activity and by whom	
Telephone Number / or other Communications Data to which this cancellation relates:	

Details of Service / Data to be cancelled

Designated Person Name and Rank / Grade	
Date of requirement to cancel	

This cancellation may be verified by contacting the following:	
SPoC Name		SPoC Telephone Number	

14

FORMS FOR USE BY PUBLIC AUTHORITIES UNDER RIPA, PART II[1]

---

[1] Forms for use by public authorities listed in Sch 1 of RIPA as amended.

A. Application For Authorisation to Carry Out Directed Surveillance

Operation Reference Number* (*Filing Ref)	

PART II OF THE REGULATION OF INVESTIGATORY POWERS ACT (RIPA) 2000

APPLICATION FOR AUTHORISATION TO CARRY OUT DIRECTED SURVEILLANCE

Public Authority *(including full address)*	

Name of Applicant		Unit/Branch /Division	
Full Address			
Contact Details			
Investigation/Oper-ation Name (if applicable)			

Details of application:

1. Give rank or position of authorising officer in accordance with the Regulation of Investigatory Powers (Prescription of Offices, Ranks and Positions) Order 2000; No. 2417.[1]

---

[1] For local authorities: The exact position of the authorising officer should be given. For example, Head of Trading Standards rather than officer responsible for the management of an investigation.

| Operation Reference Number* ^(*Filing Ref) | |

2. Describe the conduct to be authorised and the purpose of the investigation or operation.

3. Identify which grounds the directed surveillance is <u>necessary</u> under Section 28(3) of RIPA. *delete as inapplicable*

- In the interests of national security;

- For the purpose of preventing or detecting crime or of preventing disorder;

- In the interests of the economic well-being of the United Kingdom;

- In the interests of public safety;

- for the purpose of protecting public health;

- for the purpose of assessing or collecting any tax, duty, levy or other imposition, contribution or charge payable to a government department;

4. Explain why directed surveillance is necessary in this particular case.

5. Explain why the directed surveillance is proportionate to what it seeks to achieve.

6. The nature of the surveillance to be authorised, including any premises or vehicles involved.

Operation Reference Number* ^(*Filing Ref)	

7. Investigation or operation to be carried out. The identities, where known, of those to be subject of the directed surveillance.

- Name:
- Address:
- DOB:

- Other information as appropriate:

8. Explanation of the information which it is desired to obtain as a result of the directed surveillance.

9. Details of any potential collateral intrusion and why the intrusion is unavoidable.

INCLUDE A PLAN TO MINIMISE COLLATERAL INTRUSION

10. Confidential information.

INDICATE THE LIKELIHOOD OF ACQUIRING ANY CONFIDENTIAL INFORMATION:

Operation Reference Number* (*Filing Ref)	

11. Anticipated Start.	Date:	Time:

12. Applicant's Details.

Name (print)   Tel No:

Grade/Rank   Date

Signature

13. Authorising officer's comments explaining why in his view the directed surveillance is necessary and proportionate. **This box must be completed**

14. Authorising Officer's Statement.

I, [insert name], hereby authorise the directed surveillance investigation/operation as detailed above. This written authorisation will cease to have effect at the end of a period of 3 months unless renewed (see separate form for renewals).

This authorisation will be reviewed frequently to assess the need for the authorisation to continue.

Name (Print)		Grade / Rank	
Signature		Date	

Date of first review:	
Date of subsequent reviews of this authorisation:	

Operation Reference Number* (*Filing Ref)	

15. Confidential Information Authorisation.

Name (Print)   -   Grade / Rank   - - - - - - - - - - -

Signature   -   Date   - - - - - - - - -

From   Time: Date:

16. Urgent Authorisation: Details of why application is urgent.

Name (Print)   -   Grade/ Rank   - - - - - - - - -

Signature   Date/Time

17. Authorising officers statement. <u>This box must be completed.</u>

18. Please give the reasons why the person entitled to act in urgent cases considered that it was not reasonably practicable for the authorisation to be considered by a person otherwise entitled at act.

Name (Print)   -   Grade/ Rank   - - - - - - - - -

Signature   Date/Time

B. Review of a Directed Surveillance Authorisation

Operation Reference Number* (*Filing Ref)	

PART II OF THE REGULATION OF INVESTIGATORY POWERS ACT (RIPA) 2000

REVIEW OF A DIRECTED SURVEILLANCE AUTHORISATION

Public Authority *(including full address)*	

Applicant		Unit/Branch /Division	
Full Address			
Contact Details			
Operation Name		Operation Number* *Filing Ref	
Date of authorisation or last renewal		Expiry date of authorisation or last renewal	
		Review Number	

Details of review:

1. Review number and dates of any previous reviews.	
Review Number	**Date**

2. Summary of the investigation/operation to date, including what private information has been obtained and the value of the information so far obtained.

Operation Reference Number* (*Filing Ref)	

3. Detail the reasons why it is necessary to continue with the directed surveillance.

4. Explain how the proposed activity is still proportionate to what it seeks to achieve.

5. Detail any incidents of collateral intrusion and the likelihood of any further incidents of collateral intrusions occuring.

6. Give details of any confidential information acquired or accessed and the likelihood of acquiring confidential information.

7. Applicant's Details

Name (Print)		Tel No	
Grade/Rank		Date	
Signature			

8. Review Officer's Comments, including whether or not the directed surveillance should continue.

Operation Reference Number* ^(*Filing Ref)	

9. Authorising Officer's Statement.

I, [insert name], hereby agree that the directed surveillance investigation/operation as detailed above [should/should not] continue [until its next review/renewal][it should be cancelled immediately].

Name (Print) - - - - - - - - - **Grade / Rank**

Signature **Date**

10. Date of next review.	

C. Application for Renewal of a Directed Surveillance Authorisation

Operation Reference Number* (*Filing Ref)	

PART II OF THE REGULATION OF INVESTIGATORY POWERS ACT (RIPA) 2000

APPLICATION FOR RENEWAL OF A DIRECTED SURVEILLANCE AUTHORISATION
(Please attach the original authorisation)

Public Authority *(including full address)*	

Name of Applicant		Unit/Branch /Division	
Full Address			
Contact Details			
Investigation/Operation Name (if applicable)			
Renewal Number			

Details of renewal:

1. Renewal numbers and dates of any previous renewals.	
Renewal Number	Date

Operation Reference Number* (*Filing Ref)	

---

2. Detail any significant changes to the information as listed in the original authorisation as it applies at the time of the renewal.

---

3. Detail the reasons why it is necessary to continue with the directed surveillance.

---

4. Detail why the directed surveillance is still proportionate to what it seeks to achieve.

---

5. Indicate the content and value to the investigation or operation of the information so far obtained by the directed surveillance.

---

6. Give details of the results of the regular reviews of the investigation or operation.

---

7. Applicant's Details

Name (Print)		Tel No	
Grade/Rank		Date	
Signature			

Operation Reference Number* [*Filing Ref]	

8. Authorising Officer's Comments. <u>This box must be completed.</u>

9. Authorising Officer's Statement.

I, [insert name], hereby authorise the renewal of the directed surveillance operation as detailed above. The renewal of this authorisation will last for 3 months unless renewed in writing.

This authorisation will be reviewed frequently to assess the need for the authorisation to continue.

Name (Print)	Grade / Rank

Signature	Date
Renewal From:	Time:	Date:

Date of first review.	
Date of subsequent reviews of this authorisation.	

Page 3

340

D. Cancellation of a Directed Surveillance Authorisation

Operation Reference Number* (*Filing Ref)	

PART II OF THE REGULATION OF INVESTIGATORY POWERS ACT (RIPA) 2000

CANCELLATION OF A DIRECTED SURVEILLANCE AUTHORISATION

Public Authority *(including full address)*	

Name of Applicant		Unit/Branch /Division	
Full Address			
Contact Details			
Investigation/Oper-ation Name (if applicable)			

Details of cancellation:

1. Explain the reason(s) for the cancellation of the authorisation:

Operation Reference Number* (*Filing Ref)	

---

2. Explain the value of surveillance in the operation:

3. Authorising officer's statement.

I, [insert name], hereby authorise the cancellation of the directed surveillance investigation/operation as detailed above.

Name (Print) --- **Grade** ----------------------------

Signature --- **Date** ----------------------------

4. Time and Date of when the authorising officer instructed the surveillance to cease.

Date:		Time:	

5. Authorisation cancelled.	Date:	Time:

Page 2

342

E. Application for Authorisation of the use or conduct of a Covert Human Intelligence Source (CHIS)

Operation Reference Number* (*Filing Ref)	

PART II OF THE REGULATION OF INVESTIGATORY POWERS ACT (RIPA) 2000

APPLICATION FOR AUTHORISATION OF THE USE OR CONDUCT OF A COVERT HUMAN INTELLIGENCE SOURCE (CHIS)

Public Authority *(including full address)*	

Name of Applicant		Unit/Branch /Division	
Full Address			
Contact Details			
Investigation/Oper-ation Name (if applicable)			

Details of application:

1. Give rank or position of authorising officer in accordance with the Regulation of Investigatory Powers (Prescription of Offices, Ranks and Positions) Order 2000/2417.[1]

[1] For local authorities: The exact position of the authorising officer should be given. For example, Head of Trading Standards rather than officer responsible for the management of an investigation.

Operation Reference Number* (*Filing Ref)	

---

2. Identify which grounds the action is <u>necessary</u> under section 29(3) of RIPA: *delete as inapplicable*

- In the interests of national security;

- For the purpose of preventing or detecting crime or of preventing disorder;

- In the interests of the economic well-being of the United Kingdom;

- In the interests of public safety;

- For the purpose of protecting public health;

- For the purpose of assessing or collecting any tax, duty, levy or other imposition, contribution or charge payable to a government department;

---

3. Explain why the use or conduct of a covert human intelligence source (CHIS) is necessary in this particular case.

---

4. Explain why the authorised conduct or use of a source is proportionate to what it seeks to achieve.

---

5. Details of the purpose for which the source will be tasked or deployed.

Operation Reference Number* (*Filing Ref)	

6. Where a specific investigation or operation is involved, details of that investigation or operation.

7. Nature of what the source will be tasked to do.

8. Details of the risk assessment on the security and welfare of using the source

9. Collateral Intrusion.

INDICATE ANY POTENTIAL FOR COLLATERAL INTRUSION ON OTHER PERSONS THAN THOSE TARGETED: INCLUDE A PLAN TO MINIMISE COLLATERAL INTRUSION

10. Confidential Information.

INDICATE THE LIKELIHOOD OF ACQUIRING ANY CONFIDENTIAL INFORMATION.

Page 3

345

	Operation Reference Number* (*Filing Ref)	

11. Anticipated Start	Date:	Time:

12. Applicant's Details

Name (print)   Tel No:

Grade/Rank   Date

Signature

13. Authorising Officer's Comments. This box must be completed.

14. Authorising Officer's Statement.

I, [insert name], hereby authorise the conduct or use of a covert human intelligence source as detailed above. This written authorisation will cease to have effect at the end of a period of 12 months unless renewed (see separate form for renewals).

This authorisation will be reviewed frequently to assess the need for the authorisation to continue.

Name (Print)		Grade / Rank	
Signature		Date	

15. Date of first review:	
16. Date of subsequent reviews of this authorisation:	

17. Confidential Information Authorisation.

Name (Print)   Grade / Rank   ----------------

Signature   -------------------------------   Date   ------------

From	Time:	Date:	

Operation Reference Number* (*Filing Ref)	

18. Urgent Authorisation: Details of why application is urgent.

Name (Print) .... Grade/ Rank ....

Signature Date/Time

19. Authorising officers statement. (This must include why the authorising officer or the person entitled to act in their absence considered the case urgent).

20. Please give the reasons why the person entitled to act in urgent cases considered that it was not reasonably practicable for the authorisation to be considered by a person otherwise entitled at act.

Name (Print) .... Grade/ Rank ....

Signature Date/Time

Page 5

347

F. Review of a Covert Human Intelligence Source (CHIS) Authorisation

Operation Reference Number* (*Filing Ref)	

PART II OF THE REGULATION OF INVESTIGATORY POWERS ACT (RIPA) 2000

REVIEW OF A COVERT HUMAN INTELLIGENCE SOURCE (CHIS) AUTHORISATION

Public Authority *(including full address)*	

Applicant		Unit/Branch /Division	
Full Address			
Contact Details			
Operation Name		Operation Number* *Filing Ref	
Date of authorisation or last renewal		Expiry date of authorisation or last renewal	
		Review Number	

Details of review:

1. Review number and dates of any previous reviews.	
Review Number	Date

Page 1

Operation Reference Number* [(*Filing Ref)]	

2. Summary of the investigation/operation to date, including what information has been obtained and the value of the information so far obtained.

3. Detail the reasons why it is necessary to continue with using a Covert Human Intelligence Source.

4. Explain how the proposed activity is still proportionate to what it seeks to achieve.

5. Detail any incidents of collateral intrusion and the likelihood of any further incidents of collateral intrusions occuring.

6. Give details of any confidential information acquired or accessed and the likelihood of acquiring confidential information.

Operation Reference Number* (*Filing Ref)	

7. Give details of the review of the risk assessment on the security and welfare of using the source.

8. Applicant's Details

Name (Print)		Tel No	
Grade/Rank		Date	
Signature			

9. Review Officer's Comments, including whether or not the use or conduct of the source should continue?

10. Authorising Officer's Statement.

I, [insert name], hereby agree that the use or conduct of the source as detailed above [should/should not] continue [until its next review/renewal][it should be cancelled immediately].

Name (Print)	----------	Grade / Rank	
Signature		Date	
Date of next review:			

G. Application for Renewal of a Covert Human Intelligence Source (CHIS) Authorisation

Operation Reference Number* (*Filing Ref)	

PART II OF THE REGULATION OF INVESTIGATORY

POWERS ACT (RIPA) 2000

APPLICATION FOR RENEWAL OF A COVERT HUMAN INTELLIGENCE SOURCE (CHIS) AUTHORISATION
(please attach the original authorisation)

Public Authority *(including full address)*	

Name of Applicant		Unit/Branch /Division	
Full Address			
Contact Details			
Investigation/Oper-ation Name (if applicable)			
Renewal Number			

Details of renewal:

1. Renewal numbers and dates of any previous renewals.	
Renewal Number	Date

Operation Reference Number* (*Filing Ref)	

2. Detail any significant changes to the information in the previous authorisation

3. Detail any significant changes to the information as listed in the original authorisation as it applies at the time of the renewal.

4. Detail why it is necessary to continue with the authorisation, including details of any tasking given to the source.

5. Detail why the use or conduct of the source is still proportionate to what it seeks to achieve.

6. Detail the use made of the source in the period since the grant of authorisation or, as the case may be, latest renewal of the authorisation.

7. List the tasks given to the source during that period and the information obtained from the conduct or use of the source.

Operation Reference Number* (*Filing Ref)	

8. Detail the results of regular reviews of the use of the source.

9. Give details of the review of the risk assessment on the security and welfare of using the source.

10. Applicant's Details

Name (Print)		Tel No	
Grade/Rank		Date	
Signature			

11. Authorising Officer's Comments. <u>This box must be completed.</u>

12. Authorising Officer's Statement.

I, [insert name], hereby authorise the renewal of the conduct/use of the source as detailed above. The renewal of this authorisation will last for 12 months unless further renewed in writing.

This authorisation will be reviewed frequently to assess the need for the authorisation to continue.

Name (Print)	- - - - - - - - - - - - - - - - - - -	Grade / Rank
Signature		Date
Renewal From:	Time:	Date:

Date of first review:	
Date of subsequent reviews of this authorisation:	

H. Cancellation of an Authorisation for the Use or Conduct of a Covert Human Intelligence Source

Operation Reference Number* (*Filing Ref)	

PART II OF THE REGULATION OF INVESTIGATORY POWERS ACT (RIPA) 2000

CANCELLATION OF AN AUTHORISATION FOR THE USE OR CONDUCT OF A COVERT HUMAN INTELLIGENCE SOURCE

Public Authority *(including full address)*	

Name of Applicant		Unit/Branch /Division	
Full Address			
Contact Details			
Investigation/Operation Name (if applicable)			

Details of cancellation:

1. Explain the reason(s) for the cancellation of the authorisation:

Operation Reference Number* ^(*Filing Ref)	

2. Explain the value of the source in the operation:

3. Authorising officer's statement.
I, [insert name], hereby authorise the cancellation of the use or conduct of the source as detailed above.

Name (Print) -- **Grade** ----------------------------

Signature -- **Date** ----------------------------

4. Time and Date of when the authorising officer instructed the use of the source to cease.			
Date:		Time:	

5. Authorisation cancelled	Date:	Time:

PART V

CODES OF PRACTICE

15

THE COVERT SURVEILLANCE CODE OF PRACTICE 2002* (UNDER SI 2002 NO 1933)

COVERT SURVEILLANCE

Code of Practice

*Pursuant to Section 71 of the
Regulation of Investigatory Powers Act 2000*

Commencement

This code applies to every authorisation of covert surveillance or of entry on or interference with property or with wireless telegraphy carried out under section 5 of the Intelligence Services Act 1994, Part III of the Police Act 1997 or Part II of the Regulation of Investigatory Powers Act 2000 by public authorities which begins on or after the day on which this code comes into effect.

* The text of this Code of Practice is taken from the version published by the Home Office and made under the Regulation of Investigatory Powers (Covert Surveillance: Code of Practice) Order 2002 (SI 2002 No 1933) which came into force on 1 August 2002.

1 BACKGROUND

1.1 In this code the: **15.01**

- "**1989 Act**" means the Security Service Act 1989;
- "**1994 Act**" means the Intelligence Services Act 1994;
- "**1997 Act**" means the Police Act 1997;
- "**2000 Act**" means the Regulation of Investigatory Powers Act 2000;
- "**RIP(S)A**" means the Regulation of Investigatory Powers (Scotland) Act 2000.

1.2 This code of practice provides guidance on the use of covert surveillance by public authorities under Part II of the 2000 Act and on entry on, or interference with, property (or with wireless telegraphy) under section 5 of the 1994 Act or Part III of the 1997 Act. This code replaces the code of practice issued in 1999 pursuant to section 101(3) of the 1997 Act.

1.3 General observation forms part of the duties of many law enforcement officers and other public authorities and is not usually regulated by the 2000 Act. For example, police officers will be on patrol to prevent and detect crime, maintain public safety and prevent disorder or trading standards or HM Customs and Excise officers might covertly observe and then visit a shop as part of their enforcement function to verify the supply or level of supply of goods or services that may be liable to a restriction or tax. Such observation may involve the use of equipment to merely reinforce normal sensory perception, such as binoculars, or the use of cameras, where this does not involve systematic surveillance of an individual.

1.4 Although, the provisions of the 2000 Act or of this code of practice do not normally cover the use of overt CCTV surveillance systems, since members of the public are aware that such systems are in use, there may be occasions when public authorities use overt CCTV systems for the purposes of a specific investigation or operation. In such cases, authorisation for intrusive or directed surveillance may be necessary.

1.5 The 2000 Act provides that all codes of practice relating to the 2000 Act are admissible as evidence in criminal and civil proceedings. If any provision of the code appears relevant to any court or tribunal considering any such proceedings, or to the Investigatory Powers Tribunal established under the 2000 Act, or to one of the Commissioners responsible for overseeing the powers conferred by the 2000 Act, it must be taken into account.

General extent of powers

1.6 Authorisations under the 2000 Act can be given for surveillance both inside **15.02**
and outside the United Kingdom. Authorisations for actions outside the United Kingdom can only validate them for the purposes of proceedings in the United

Kingdom. An authorisation under Part II of the 2000 Act does not take into account the requirements of the country outside the United Kingdom in which the investigation or operation is taking place.

Where the conduct authorised is likely to take place in Scotland, authorisations **1.7** should be granted under RIP(S)A, unless the authorisation is being obtained by those public authorities listed in section 46(3) of the 2000 Act and the Regulation of Investigatory Powers (Authorisations Extending to Scotland) Order 2000; SI No. 2418). Additionally any authorisation granted or renewed for the purposes of national security or the economic well-being of the United Kingdom must be made under the 2000 Act. This code of practice is extended to Scotland in relation to authorisations made under Part II of the 2000 Act which apply to Scotland. A separate code of practice applies in relation to authorisations made under RIP(S)A.

Use of material in evidence

15.03 Material obtained through covert surveillance may be used as evidence in crim- **1.8** inal proceedings. The proper authorisation of surveillance should ensure the admissibility of such evidence under the common law, section 78 of the Police and Criminal Evidence Act 1984 and the Human Rights Act 1998. Furthermore, the product of the surveillance described in this code is subject to the ordinary rules for retention and disclosure of material under the Criminal Procedure and Investigations Act 1996, where those rules apply to the law enforcement body in question.

Directed surveillance, intrusive surveillance and entry on or interference with property or with wireless telegraphy

15.04 Directed surveillance is defined in section 26(2) of the 2000 Act as surveillance **1.9** which is covert, but not intrusive, and undertaken:

a) for the purposes of a specific investigation or specific operation;
b) in such a manner as is likely to result in the obtaining of private information about a person (whether or not one specifically identified for the purposes of the investigation or operation); and
c) otherwise than by way of an immediate response to events or circumstances the nature of which is such that it would not be reasonably practicable for an authorisation under Part II of the 2000 Act to be sought for the carrying out of the surveillance.

Directed surveillance investigations or operations can only be carried out by those **1.10** public authorities who are listed in or added to Part I and Part II of schedule 1 of the 2000 Act.

1.11 Intrusive surveillance is defined in section 26(3) of the 2000 Act as covert surveillance that:

    a) is carried out in relation to anything taking place on any residential premises or in any private vehicle; and

    b) involves the presence of an individual on the premises or in the vehicle or is carried out by means of a surveillance device.

1.12 Applications to carry out intrusive surveillance can only be made by the senior authorising officer of those public authorities listed in or added to section 32(6) of the 2000 Act or by a member or official of those public authorities listed in or added to section 41(1).

1.13 Applications to enter on or interfere with property or with wireless telegraphy can only be made by the authorising officers of those public authorities listed in or added to section 93(5) of the 1997 Act. Under section 5 of the 1994 Act only members of the intelligence services are able to make applications to enter on or interfere with property or with wireless telegraphy.

2 GENERAL RULES ON AUTHORISATIONS

2.1 An authorisation under Part II of the 2000 Act will provide lawful authority for a public authority to carry out surveillance. Responsibility for authorising surveillance investigations or operations will vary, depending on whether the authorisation is for intrusive surveillance or directed surveillance, and which public authority is involved. For the purposes of Chapter 2 and 3 of this code the authorising officer, senior authorising officer or the person who makes an application to the Secretary of State will be referred to as an 'authorising officer'.   **15.05**

2.2 Part II of the 2000 Act does not impose a requirement on public authorities to seek or obtain an authorisation where, under the 2000 Act, one is available (see section 80 of the 2000 Act). Nevertheless, where there is an interference by a public authority with the right to respect for private and family life guaranteed under Article 8 of the European Convention on Human Rights, and where there is no other source of lawful authority, the consequence of not obtaining an authorisation under the 2000 Act may be that the action is unlawful by virtue of section 6 of the Human Rights Act 1998.

2.3 Public authorities are therefore strongly recommended to seek an authorisation where the surveillance is likely to interfere with a person's Article 8 rights to privacy by obtaining private information about that person, whether or not that person is the subject of the investigation or operation. Obtaining an authorisation will ensure that the action is carried out in accordance with law and subject to stringent safeguards against abuse.

Necessity and proportionality

15.06 Obtaining an authorisation under the 2000 Act, the 1997 Act and 1994 Act will **2.4** only ensure that there is a justifiable interference with an individual's Article 8 rights if it is necessary and proportionate for these activities to take place. The 2000 Act first requires that the person granting an authorisation believe that the authorisation is necessary in the circumstances of the particular case for one or more of the statutory grounds in section 28(3) of the 2000 Act for directed surveillance and in section 32(3) of the 2000 Act for intrusive surveillance.

Then, if the activities are necessary, the person granting the authorisation must **2.5** believe that they are proportionate to what is sought to be achieved by carrying them out. This involves balancing the intrusiveness of the activity on the target and others who might be affected by it against the need for the activity in operational terms. The activity will not be proportionate if it is excessive in the circumstances of the case or if the information which is sought could reasonably be obtained by other less intrusive means. All such activity should be carefully managed to meet the objective in question and must not be arbitrary or unfair.

Collateral intrusion

15.07 Before authorising surveillance the authorising officer should also take into **2.6** account the risk of intrusion into the privacy of persons other than those who are directly the subjects of the investigation or operation (collateral intrusion). Measures should be taken, wherever practicable, to avoid or minimise unnecessary intrusion into the lives of those not directly connected with the investigation or operation.

An application for an authorisation should include an assessment of the risk of **2.7** any collateral intrusion. The authorising officer should take this into account, when considering the proportionality of the surveillance.

Those carrying out the surveillance should inform the authorising officer if the **2.8** investigation or operation unexpectedly interferes with the privacy of individuals who are not covered by the authorisation. When the original authorisation may not be sufficient, consideration should be given to whether the authorisation needs to be amended and reauthorised or a new authorisation is required.

Any person granting or applying for an authorisation or warrant will also need to **2.9** be aware of particular sensitivities in the local community where the surveillance is taking place and of similar activities being undertaken by other public authorities which could impact on the deployment of surveillance. In this regard, it is recommended that where the authorising officers in the National Criminal Intelligence Service (NCIS), the National Crime Squad (NCS) and HM Customs and Excise (HMCE) consider that conflicts might arise they should consult a senior officer within the police force area in which the investigation or operation takes place.

2.10   The matters in paragraphs 2.1–2.9 above must also be taken into account when applying for authorisations or warrants for entry on or interference with property or with wireless telegraphy. In particular they must be necessary in the circumstances of the particular case for one of the statutory grounds listed in section 93(2A) of the 1997 Act and section 5(2)(c) of the 1994 Act, proportionate and when exercised, steps should be taken to minimise collateral intrusion.

Combined authorisations

2.11   A single authorisation may combine: **15.08**

- two or more different authorisations under Part II of the 2000 Act;
- an authorisation under Part II of the 2000 Act and an authorisation under Part III of the 1997 Act;
- a warrant for intrusive surveillance under Part II of the 2000 Act and a warrant under section 5 of the 1994 Act.

2.12   For example, a single authorisation may combine authorisations for directed and for intrusive surveillance. The provisions applicable in the case of each of the authorisations must be considered separately. Thus, a police superintendent can authorise the directed surveillance but the intrusive surveillance needs the separate authorisation of a chief constable, and in certain cases the approval of a Surveillance Commissioner will also be necessary. Where an authorisation for directed surveillance or the use or conduct of a covert human intelligence source is combined with a Secretary of State authorisation for intrusive surveillance, the combined authorisation must be issued by the Secretary of State. However, this does not preclude public authorities from obtaining separate authorisations.

2.13   In cases where one agency is acting on behalf of another, it is usually for the tasking agency to obtain or provide the authorisation. For example, where surveillance is carried out by the Armed Forces on behalf of the police, authorisations would be sought by the police and granted by the appropriate authorising officer. In cases where the Security Service is acting in support of the police or other law enforcement agencies in the field of serious crime, the Security Service would normally seek authorisations.

Central Record of all authorisations

15.09 A centrally retrievable record of all authorisations should be held by each public **2.14** authority and regularly updated whenever an authorisation is granted, renewed or cancelled. The record should be made available to the relevant Commissioner or an Inspector from the Office of Surveillance Commissioners, upon request. These records should be retained for a period of at least three years from the ending of the authorisation and should contain the following information:

- the type of authorisation;
- the date the authorisation was given;
- name and rank/grade of the authorising officer;
- the unique reference number (URN) of the investigation or operation;
- the title of the investigation or operation, including a brief description and names of subjects, if known;
- whether the urgency provisions were used, and if so why.
- if the authorisation is renewed, when it was renewed and who authorised the renewal, including the name and rank/grade of the authorising officer;
- whether the investigation or operation is likely to result in obtaining confidential information as defined in this code of practice;
- the date the authorisation was cancelled.

In all cases, the relevant authority should maintain the following documentation **2.15** which need not form part of the centrally retrievable record:

- a copy of the application and a copy of the authorisation together with any supplementary documentation and notification of the approval given by the authorising officer;
- a record of the period over which the surveillance has taken place;
- the frequency of reviews prescribed by the authorising officer;
- a record of the result of each review of the authorisation;
- a copy of any renewal of an authorisation, together with the supporting documentation submitted when the renewal was requested;
- the date and time when any instruction was given by the authorising officer.

Retention and destruction of the product

15.10 Where the product of surveillance could be relevant to pending or future criminal **2.16** or civil proceedings, it should be retained in accordance with established disclosure requirements for a suitable further period, commensurate to any subsequent review.

In the cases of the law enforcement agencies (not including the Royal Navy **2.17** Regulating Branch, the Royal Military Police and the Royal Air Force Police), particular attention is drawn to the requirements of the code of practice issued under the Criminal Procedures and Investigations Act 1996. This requires that material which is obtained in the course of a criminal investigation and which may be relevant to the investigation must be recorded and retained.

2.18 There is nothing in the 2000 Act which prevents material obtained from properly authorised surveillance from being used in other investigations. Each public authority must ensure that arrangements are in place for the handling, storage and destruction of material obtained through the use of covert surveillance. Authorising officers must ensure compliance with the appropriate data protection requirements and any relevant codes of practice produced by individual authorities relating to the handling and storage of material.

The Intelligence Services, MOD and HM Forces

2.19 The heads of these agencies are responsible for ensuring that arrangements exist   **15.11** for securing that no information is stored by the authorities, except as necessary for the proper discharge of their functions. They are also responsible for arrangements to control onward disclosure. For the intelligence services, this is a statutory duty under the 1989 Act and the 1994 Act.

3 SPECIAL RULES ON AUTHORISATIONS

3.1 The 2000 Act does not provide any special protection for 'confidential information'.   **15.12** Nevertheless, particular care should be taken in cases where the subject of the investigation or operation might reasonably expect a high degree of privacy, or where confidential information is involved. Confidential information consists of matters subject to legal privilege, confidential personal information or confidential journalistic material. So, for example, extra care should be given where, through the use of surveillance, it would be possible to acquire knowledge of discussions between a minister of religion and an individual relating to the latter's spiritual welfare, or where matters of medical or journalistic confidentiality or legal privilege may be involved.

3.2 In cases where through the use of surveillance it is likely that knowledge of confidential information will be acquired, the use of surveillance is subject to a higher level of authorisation. Annex A lists the authorising officer for each public authority permitted to authorise such surveillance.

Communications subject to legal privilege

3.3 Section 98 of the 1997 Act describes those matters that are subject to legal privilege in England and Wales. In Scotland, the relevant description is contained in   **15.13**

section 33 of the Criminal Law (Consolidation) (Scotland) Act 1995. With regard to Northern Ireland, Article 12 of the Police and Criminal Evidence (Northern Ireland) Order 1989 should be referred to.

Legal privilege does not apply to communications made with the intention of **3.4** furthering a criminal purpose (whether the lawyer is acting unwittingly or culpably). Legally privileged communications will lose their protection if there are grounds to believe, for example, that the professional legal adviser is intending to hold or use them for a criminal purpose. But privilege is not lost if a professional legal adviser is properly advising a person who is suspected of having committed a criminal offence. The concept of legal privilege applies to the provision of professional legal advice by any individual, agency or organisation qualified to do so.

The 2000 Act does not provide any special protection for legally privileged infor- **3.5** mation. Nevertheless, such information is particularly sensitive and surveillance which acquires such material may engage Article 6 of the ECHR (right to a fair trial) as well as Article 8. Legally privileged information obtained by surveillance is extremely unlikely ever to be admissible as evidence in criminal proceedings. Moreover, the mere fact that such surveillance has taken place may lead to any related criminal proceedings being stayed as an abuse of process. Accordingly, action which may lead to such information being acquired is subject to additional safeguards under this code.

In general, an application for surveillance which is likely to result in the acquisi- **3.6** tion of legally privileged information should only be made in exceptional and compelling circumstances. Full regard should be had to the particular proportionality issues such surveillance raises. The application should include, in addition to the reasons why it is considered necessary for the surveillance to take place, an assessment of how likely it is that information subject to legal privilege will be acquired. In addition, the application should clearly state whether the purpose (or one of the purposes) of the surveillance is to obtain legally privileged information.

This assessment will be taken into account by the authorising officer in deciding **3.7** whether the proposed surveillance is necessary and proportionate under section 28 of the 2000 Act for directed surveillance and under section 32 for intrusive surveillance. The authorising officer may require regular reporting so as to be able to decide whether the authorisation should continue. In those cases where legally privileged information has been acquired and retained, the matter should be reported to the relevant Commissioner or Inspector during his next inspection and the material be made available to him if requested.

A substantial proportion of the communications between a lawyer and his **3.8** client(s) may be subject to legal privilege. Therefore, any case where a lawyer is the subject of an investigation or operation should be notified to the relevant Commissioner during his next inspection and any material which has been retained should be made available to him if requested.

3.9 Where there is any doubt as to the handling and dissemination of information which may be subject to legal privilege, advice should be sought from a legal adviser within the relevant public authority before any further dissemination of the material takes place. Similar advice should also be sought where there is doubt over whether information is not subject to legal privilege due to the "in further-ance of a criminal purpose" exception. The retention of legally privileged infor-mation, or its dissemination to an outside body, should be accompanied by a clear warning that it is subject to legal privilege. It should be safeguarded by taking rea-sonable steps to ensure there is no possibility of it becoming available, or its con-tents becoming known, to any person whose possession of it might prejudice any criminal or civil proceedings related to the information. Any dissemination of legally privileged material to an outside body should be notified to the relevant Commissioner or Inspector during his next inspection.

Communications involving confidential personal information and confidential journalistic material

3.10 Similar consideration must also be given to authorisations that involve confiden-tial personal information and confidential journalistic material. In those cases where confidential personal information and confidential journalistic material has been acquired and retained, the matter should be reported to the relevant Commissioner or Inspector during his next inspection and the material be made available to him if requested. Confidential personal information is information held in confidence relating to the physical or mental health or spiritual coun-selling concerning an individual (whether living or dead) who can be identified from it. Such information, which can include both oral and written communica-tions, is held in confidence if it is held subject to an express or implied undertak-ing to hold it in confidence or it is subject to a restriction on disclosure or an obligation of confidentiality contained in existing legislation. Examples might include consultations between a health professional and a patient, or information from a patient's medical records. **15.14**

3.11 Spiritual counselling means conversations between an individual and a Minister of Religion acting in his official capacity, where the individual being counselled is seeking or the Minister is imparting forgiveness, absolution or the resolution of conscience with the authority of the Divine Being(s) of their faith.

3.12 Confidential journalistic material includes material acquired or created for the purposes of journalism and held subject to an undertaking to hold it in confi-dence, as well as communications resulting in information being acquired for the purposes of journalism and held subject to such an undertaking.

4 AUTHORISATION PROCEDURES
FOR DIRECTED SURVEILLANCE

15.15 Directed surveillance is desfined in section 26(2) of the 2000 Act as surveillance **4.1**
which is covert, but not intrusive, and undertaken:

a) for the purposes of a specific investigation or specific operation;

b) in such a manner as is likely to result in the obtaining of private information
about a person (whether or not one specifically identified for the purposes of
the investigation or operation); and

c) otherwise than by way of an immediate response to events or circumstances
the nature of which is such that it would not be reasonably practicable for an
authorisation under Part II of the 2000 Act to be sought for the carrying out
of the surveillance.

Covert surveillance is defined in section 26(9)(a) of the 2000 Act as any surveil- **4.2**
lance which is carried out in a manner calculated to ensure that the persons subject to the surveillance are unaware that it is or may be taking place.

Private information is defined in section 26(10) of the 2000 Act as including any **4.3**
information relating to a person's private or family life. The concept of private
information should be broadly interpreted to include an individual's private or
personal relationship with others. Family life should be treated as extending
beyond the formal relationships created by marriage.

Directed surveillance does not include covert surveillance carried out by way of **4.4**
an immediate response to events or circumstances which, by their very nature,
could not have been foreseen. For example, a police officer would not require an
authorisation to conceal himself and observe a suspicious person that he came
across in the course of a patrol.

By virtue of section 48(4) of the 2000 Act, surveillance includes the interception **4.5**
of postal and telephone communications where the sender or recipient consents
to the reading of or listening to or recording of the communication (as the case
may be). For further details see paragraphs 4.30–4.32 of this code.

Surveillance in residential premises or in private vehicles is defined as intrusive **4.6**
surveillance in section 26(3) of the 2000 Act and is dealt with in chapter 5 of this
code. However, where surveillance is carried out by a device designed or adapted
principally for the purpose of providing information about the location of a vehicle, the activity is directed surveillance and should be authorised accordingly.

Directed surveillance does not include entry on or interference with property **4.7**
or with wireless telegraphy. These activities are subject to a separate regime of
authorisation or warranty, as set out in chapter 6 of this code.

4.8 Directed surveillance includes covert surveillance within office premises, (as defined in paragraph 6.31 of this code). Authorising officers are reminded that confidential information should be afforded an enhanced level of protection. Chapter 3 of this code provides that in cases where the likely consequence of surveillance is to acquire confidential information, the authorisation should be given at a higher level.

Authorisation procedures

4.9 Under section 28(3) of the 2000 Act an authorisation for directed surveillance **15.16** may be granted by an authorising officer where he believes that the authorisation is necessary in the circumstances of the particular case:

- in the interests of national security;[1,2]
- for the purpose of preventing and detecting[3] crime or of preventing disorder;
- in the interests of the economic well-being of the UK;
- in the interests of public safety;
- for the purpose of protecting public health;[4]
- for the purpose of assessing or collecting any tax, duty, levy or other imposition, contribution or charge payable to a government department; or
- for any other purpose prescribed by an order made by the Secretary of State.[5]

4.10 The authorising officer must also believe that the surveillance is proportionate to what it seeks to achieve.

4.11 The public authorities entitled to authorise directed surveillance are listed in Schedule 1 to the 2000 Act. Responsibility for authorising the carrying out of directed surveillance rests with the authorising officer and requires the personal

---

[1] One of the functions of the Security Service is the protection of national security and in particular the protection against threats from terrorism. These functions extend throughout the United Kingdom, save that, in Northern Ireland, where the lead responsibility for investigating the threat from terrorism related to the affairs of Northern Ireland lies with the Police Service of Northern Ireland. An authorising officer in another public authority should not issue an authorisation under Part II of the 2000 Act or under Part III of the 1997 Act where the operation or investigation falls within the responsibilities of the Security Service, as set out above, except where it is a directed surveillance investigation or operation that is to be carried out by a Special Branch or where the Security Service has agreed that another public authority can carry out a directed surveillance operation or investigation which would fall within the responsibilities of the Security Service.

[2] HM Forces may also undertake operations in connection with a military threat to national security and other operations in connection with national security in support of the Security Service, the Police Service of Northern Ireland or other Civil Powers.

[3] Detecting crime is defined in section 81(5) of the 2000 Act and is applied to the 1997 Act by section 134 of that Act (as amended).

[4] This could include investigations into infectious diseases, contaminated products or the illicit sale of pharmaceuticals.

[5] This could only be for a purpose which satisfies the criteria set out in Article 8(2) of the ECHR.

authority of the authorising officer. The Regulation of Investigatory Powers (Prescriptions of Offices, Ranks and Positions) Order 2000; SI No: 2417 designates the authorising officer for each different public authority and the officers entitled to act only in urgent cases. Where an authorisation for directed surveillance is combined with a Secretary of State authorisation for intrusive surveillance, the combined authorisation must be issued by the Secretary of State.

The authorising officer must give authorisations in writing, except that in urgent **4.12** cases, they may be given orally by the authorising officer or the officer entitled to act in urgent cases. In such cases, a statement that the authorising officer has expressly authorised the action should be recorded in writing by the applicant as soon as is reasonably practicable.

A case is not normally to be regarded as urgent unless the time that would elapse **4.13** before the authorising officer was available to grant the authorisation would, in the judgement of the person giving the authorisation, be likely to endanger life or jeopardise the investigation or operation for which the authorisation was being given. An authorisation is not to be regarded as urgent where the need for an authorisation has been neglected or the urgency is of the authorising officer's own making.

Authorising officers should not be responsible for authorising investigations or **4.14** operations in which they are directly involved, although it is recognised that this may sometimes be unavoidable, especially in the case of small organisations, or where it is necessary to act urgently. Where an authorising officer authorises such an investigation or operation the central record of authorisations (see paragraphs 2.14–2.15) should highlight this and the attention of a Commissioner or Inspector should be invited to it during his next inspection.

Authorising officers within the Police, NCIS and NCS may only grant authorisa- **4.15** tions on application by a member of their own force, Service or Squad. Authorising officers in HMCE may only grant an authorisation on application by a customs officer.[6]

Information to be provided in applications for authorisation

15.17 A written application for authorisation for directed surveillance should describe **4.16** any conduct to be authorised and the purpose of the investigation or operation. The application should also include:

- the reasons why the authorisation is necessary in the particular case and on the grounds (e.g. for the purpose of preventing or detecting crime) listed in Section 28(3) of the 2000 Act;

---

[6] As defined in section 81(1) of the 2000 Act.

- the reasons why the surveillance is considered proportionate to what it seeks to achieve;
- the nature of the surveillance;
- the identities, where known, of those to be the subject of the surveillance;
- an explanation of the information which it is desired to obtain as a result of the surveillance;
- the details of any potential collateral intrusion and why the intrusion is justified;
- the details of any confidential information that is likely to be obtained as a consequence of the surveillance.
- the level of authority required (or recommended where that is different) for the surveillance; and
- a subsequent record of whether authority was given or refused, by whom and the time and date.

4.17 Additionally, in urgent cases, the authorization should record (as the case may be):

- the reasons why the authorising officer or the officer entitled to act in urgent cases considered the case so urgent that an oral instead of a written authorisation was given; and/or
- the reasons why it was not reasonably practicable for the application to be considered by the authorising officer.

4.18 Where the authorisation is oral, the detail referred to above should be recorded in writing by the applicant as soon as reasonably practicable.

Duration of authorisations

4.19 A written authorisation granted by an authorising officer will cease to have effect (unless renewed) at the end of a period of three months beginning with the day on which it took effect.   **15.18**

4.20 Urgent oral authorisations or written authorisations granted by a person who is entitled to act only in urgent cases will, unless renewed, cease to have effect after seventy-two hours, beginning with the time when the authorisation was granted or renewed.

Reviews

4.21 Regular reviews of authorisations should be undertaken to assess the need for the surveillance to continue. The results of a review should be recorded on the central record of authorisations (see paragraphs 2.14–2.15). Particular attention is drawn   **15.19**

to the need to review authorisations frequently where the surveillance provides access to confidential information or involves collateral intrusion.

In each case the authorising officer within each public authority should determine **4.22** how often a review should take place. This should be as frequently as is considered necessary and practicable.

Renewals

If at any time before an authorisation would cease to have effect, the authori- **4.23** sing officer considers it necessary for the authorisation to continue for the purpose for which it was given, he may renew it in writing for a further period of three months unless it is a case to which paragraph 4.25 applies. Renewals may also be granted orally in urgent cases and last for a period of seventy-two hours.

A renewal takes effect at the time at which, or day on which the authorisation **4.24** would have ceased to have effect but for the renewal. An application for renewal should not be made until shortly before the authorisation period is drawing to an end. Any person who would be entitled to grant a new authorisation can renew an authorisation. Authorisations may be renewed more than once, provided they continue to meet the criteria for authorisation.

If at any time before an authorisation for directed surveillance, granted on the **4.25** grounds of it being in the interests of national security or in the interests of the economic well-being of the UK, would cease to have effect, an authorising officer who is a member of the intelligence services considers it necessary for it to continue, he may renew it for a further period of six months, beginning with the day on which it would have ceased to have effect but for the renewal.

All applications for the renewal of an authorisation for directed surveillance **4.26** should record:

- whether this is the first renewal or every occasion on which the authorisation has been renewed previously;
- any significant changes to the information in paragraph 4.16;
- the reasons why it is necessary to continue with the directed surveillance;
- the content and value to the investigation or operation of the information so far obtained by the surveillance;
- the results of regular reviews of the investigation or operation.

Authorisations may be renewed more than once, if necessary, and the renewal **4.27** should be kept/recorded as part of the central record of authorisations (see paragraphs 2.14–2.15).

Cancellations

4.28   The authorising officer who granted or last renewed the authorisation must   **15.20**
cancel it if he is satisfied that the directed surveillance no longer meets the
criteria upon which it was authorised. Where the authorising officer is no longer
available, this duty will fall on the person who has taken over the role of authorising officer or the person who is acting as authorising officer (see the Regulation
of Investigatory Powers (Cancellation of Authorisations) Order 2000; SI
No: 2794).

Ceasing of surveillance activity

4.29   As soon as the decision is taken that directed surveillance should be discontinued,   **15.21**
the instruction must be given to those involved to stop all surveillance of the sub-
ject(s). The date and time when such an instruction was given should be recorded
in the central record of authorisations (see paragraphs 2.14–2.15) and the notification of cancellation where relevant.

Additional Rules

Recording of telephone conversations

4.30   Subject to paragraph 4.31 below, the interception of communications sent by   **15.22**
post or by means of public telecommunications systems or private telecommunications systems attached to the public network may be authorised only by the
Secretary of State, in accordance with the terms of Part I of the 2000 Act. Nothing
in this code should be taken as granting dispensation from the requirements of
that Part of the 2000 Act.

4.31   Part I of the 2000 Act provides certain exceptions to the rule that interception of
telephone conversations must be warranted under that Part. This includes, where
one party to the communication consents to the interception, it may be authorised in accordance with section 48(4) of the 2000 Act provided that there is no
interception warrant authorising the interception. In such cases, the interception
is treated as directed surveillance.

4.32   The use of a surveillance device should not be ruled out simply because it may
incidentally pick up one or both ends of a telephone conversation, and any such
product can be treated as having been lawfully obtained. However, its use would
not be appropriate where the sole purpose is to overhear speech which, at the time
of monitoring, is being transmitted by a telecommunications system. In such
cases an application should be made for an interception of communication warrant under section 5 of the 2000 Act.

5 AUTHORISATION PROCEDURES FOR INTRUSIVE SURVEILLANCE

15.23 Intrusive surveillance is defined in section 26(3) of the 2000 Act as covert surveillance that: **5.1**

a) is carried out in relation to anything taking place on any residential premises or in any private vehicle; and
b) involves the presence of an individual on the premises or in the vehicle or is carried out by means of a surveillance device.

Covert surveillance is defined in section 26(9)(a) of the 2000 Act as any surveillance which is carried out in a manner calculated to ensure that the persons subject to the surveillance are unaware that it is or may be taking place. **5.2**

Where surveillance is carried out in relation to anything taking place on any residential premises or in any private vehicle by means of a device, without that device being present on the premises, or in the vehicle, it is not intrusive unless the device consistently provides information of the same quality and detail as might be expected to be obtained from a device actually present on the premises or in the vehicle. Thus, an observation post outside premises, which provides a limited view and no sound of what is happening inside the premises would not be considered as intrusive surveillance. **5.3**

Residential premises are defined in section 48(1) of the 2000 Act. The definition includes hotel rooms, bedrooms in barracks, and police and prison cells but not any common area to which a person is allowed access in connection with his occupation of such accommodation e.g. a hotel lounge. **5.4**

A private vehicle is defined in section 48(1) of the 2000 Act as any vehicle which is used primarily for the private purposes of the person who owns it or of a person otherwise having the right to use it. A person does not have a right to use a motor vehicle if his right to use it derives only from his having paid, or undertaken to pay, for the use of the vehicle and its driver for a particular journey. **5.5**

In many cases, a surveillance investigation or operation may involve both intrusive surveillance and entry on or interference with property or with wireless telegraphy. In such cases, both activities need authorisation. This can be done as a combined authorisation (see paragraph 2.11). **5.6**

An authorisation for intrusive surveillance may be issued by the Secretary of State (for the intelligence services, the Ministry of Defence, HM Forces and any other public authority designated under section 41(1)) or by a senior authorising officer (for police, NCIS, NCS and HMCE). **5.7**

5.8 All authorisations require the personal authority of the Secretary of State or the senior authorising officer. Any members or officials of the intelligence services, the Ministry of Defence and HM Forces can apply to the Secretary of State for an intrusive surveillance warrant. Under section 32(2) of the 2000 Act neither the Secretary of State or the senior authorising officer may authorise intrusive surveillance unless he believes—

    a)   that the authorisation is necessary in the circumstances of the particular case on the grounds that it is:
- in the interests of national security;[7]
- for the purpose of preventing or detecting serious crime; or
- in the interests of the economic well-being of the UK;

    and

    b)   the authorising officer must also believe that the surveillance is proportionate to what it seeks to achieve.

5.9 A factor which must be taken into account in deciding whether an authorisation is necessary and proportionate is whether the information which it is thought necessary to obtain by means of the intrusive surveillance could reasonably be obtained by other less intrusive means.

Authorisations procedures for police, National Criminal Intelligence Service, the National Crime Squad and HM Customs and Excise

5.10 The senior authorising officer should generally give authorisations in writing. **15.24** However, in urgent cases, they may be given orally. In an urgent oral case, a statement that the senior authorising officer has expressly authorised the conduct should be recorded in writing by the applicant as soon as is reasonably practicable.

5.11 If the senior authorising officer is absent then, as provided for in section 12(4) of the Police Act 1996, section 5(4) of the Police (Scotland) Act 1967, section 25 of the City of London Police Act 1839, or sections 8 or 54 of the 1997 Act, an authorisation can be given in writing or, in urgent cases, orally by the designated deputy.

5.12 In an urgent case, where it is not reasonably practicable having regard to the urgency of the case for the designated deputy to consider the application, a written authorisation may be granted by a person entitled to act under section 34(4) of the 2000 Act.

---

    [7] A senior authorising officer of a law enforcement agency should not issue an authorisation for intrusive surveillance or entry on or interference with property or with wireless telegraphy where the operation is within the responsibilities of one of the intelligence services and properly falls to be authorised by warrant issued by the Secretary of State under Part II of the 2000 Act or the 1994 Act. Also see footnotes 1 and 2.

A case is not normally to be regarded as urgent unless the time that would elapse **5.13** before the authorising officer was available to grant the authorisation would, in the judgement of the person giving the authorisation, be likely to endanger life or jeopardise the investigation or operation for which the authorisation was being given. An authorisation is not to be regarded as urgent where the need for an authorisation has been neglected or the urgency is of the authorising officer's own making.

The consideration of an authorisation by the senior authorising officer is only to **5.14** be regarded as not reasonably practicable (within the meaning of section 34(2) of the 2000 Act) if he is on annual leave, is absent from his office and his home, or is for some reason not able within a reasonable time to obtain access to a secure telephone or fax machine. Pressure of work is not normally to be regarded as rendering it impracticable for a senior authorising officer to consider an application. Where a designated deputy gives an authorisation this should be made clear and the reason for the absence of the senior authorising officer given.

A police, NCIS or NCS authorisation cannot be granted unless the application is **5.15** made by a member of the same force, service or squad. For HMCE an authorisation cannot be granted unless the application is made by a customs officer. Where the surveillance is carried out in relation to any residential premises, the authorisation cannot be granted unless the residential premises are in the area of operation of the force, service, squad or organisation.

Information to be provided in applications for authorisation

15.25 Applications should be in writing and describe the conduct to be authorised and **5.16** the purpose of the investigation or operation. The application should specify:

- the reasons why the authorisation is necessary in the particular case and on the grounds (e.g. for the purpose of preventing or detecting serious crime) listed in section 32(3) of the 2000 Act;
- the reasons why the surveillance is considered proportionate to what it seeks to achieve;
- the nature of the surveillance;
- the residential premises or private vehicle in relation to which the surveillance will take place;
- the identities, where known, of those to be the subject of the surveillance;
- an explanation of the information which it is desired to obtain as a result of the surveillance;
- details of any potential collateral intrusion and why the intrusion is justified;
- details of any confidential information that is likely to be obtained as a consequence of the surveillance.
- A subsequent record should be made of whether authority was given or refused, by whom and the time and date.

5.17 Additionally, in urgent cases, the authorisation should record (as the case may be):

- the reasons why the authorising officer or designated deputy considered the case so urgent that an oral instead of a written authorisation was given; and/or
- the reasons why it was not reasonably practicable for the application to be considered by the senior authorising officer or the designated deputy.

5.18 Where the application is oral, the detail referred to above should be recorded in writing as soon as reasonably practicable.

Approval of Surveillance Commissioners

5.19 Except in urgent cases a police, NCIS, NCS or HMCE authorisation granted **15.26** for intrusive surveillance will not take effect until it has been approved by a Surveillance Commissioner and written notice of the Commissioner's decision has been given to the person who granted the authorisation. This means that the approval will not take effect until the notice has been received in the office of the person who granted the authorisation within the relevant force, service, squad or HMCE.

5.20 When the authorisation is urgent it will take effect from the time it is granted provided notice is given to the Surveillance Commissioner in accordance with section 35(3)(b) (see section 36(3) of the 2000 Act).

5.21 There may be cases that become urgent after approval has been sought but before a response has been received from a Surveillance Commissioner. In such a case, the authorising officer should notify the Surveillance Commissioner that the case is now urgent (pointing out that it has become urgent since the notification). In these cases, the authorisation will take effect immediately.

Notifications to Surveillance Commissioners

5.22 Where a person grants, renews or cancels an authorisation, he must, as soon as is **15.27** reasonably practicable, give notice in writing to a Surveillance Commissioner, in accordance with whatever arrangements have been made by the Chief Surveillance Commissioner.

5.23 In urgent cases, the notification must specify the grounds on which the case is believed to be one of urgency. The urgency provisions should not be used routinely. If the Surveillance Commissioner is satisfied that there were no grounds for believing the case to be one of urgency, he has the power to quash the authorisation

5.24 The information to be included in the notification to the Surveillance Commissioner is set out in the Regulation of Investigatory Powers (Notification of Authorisations etc.) Order 2000; SI No: 2563.

Authorisation procedures for secretary of state authorisations

Authorisations

15.28 An intrusive surveillance authorisation for any of the intelligence services, the **5.25**
Ministry of Defence, HM Forces or any other public authority designated for this
purpose requires a Secretary of State authorisation/warrant, unless they are acting
on behalf of another public authority that has obtained an authorisation. In this
context, Secretary of State can mean any Secretary of State, although an authorisation or warrant should be obtained from the Secretary of State of the relevant
department.

Intelligence services authorisations must be made by issue of a warrant. Such war- **5.26**
rants will generally be given in writing by the Secretary of State. In urgent cases, a
warrant may be signed (but not renewed) by a senior official, provided the
Secretary of State has expressly authorised this.

Applications to the Secretary of State for authorisations should specify those mat- **5.27**
ters listed in paragraph 5.16.

All intrusive surveillance authorisations

15.29 Paragraphs 5.29 to 5.42 deal with the duration, renewal and cancellation of authori- **5.28**
sations. Unless otherwise specified, the guidance below applies to all authorisations.

Duration of authorisations

All authorisations except Secretary of State Intelligence Services authorisations

15.30 A written authorisation granted by a Secretary of State, a senior authorising offi- **5.29**
cer or a designated deputy will cease to have effect (unless renewed) at the end of
a period of three months, beginning with the day on which it took effect.

Oral authorisations given in urgent cases by a Secretary of State, a senior authori- **5.30**
sing officers or their designated deputies, and written authorisations given by
those only entitled to act in urgent cases (see paragraph 5.11), will cease to have
effect (unless renewed) at the end of the period of seventy-two hours beginning
with the time when they took effect.

Secretary of State intelligence services authorisations

15.31 A warrant issued by the Secretary of State will cease to have effect at the end of a **5.31**
period of six months beginning with the day on which it was issued.

Warrants expressly authorised by a Secretary of State, and signed on his behalf by **5.32**
a senior civil servant, will cease to have effect at the end of the second working day
following the day of issue of the warrant, unless renewed by the Secretary of State.

Renewals

All authorisations except Secretary of State Intelligence Services authorisations

5.33   If at any time before an authorisation expires the senior authorising officer or, in   **15.32**
his absence, the designated deputy considers the authorisation should continue to
have effect for the purpose for which it was issued, he may renew it in writing for
a further period of three months.

5.34   As with the initial authorisation, the senior authorising officer must (unless it is a
case to which the urgency procedure applies) seek the approval of a Surveillance
Commissioner. This means that the renewal will not take effect until the notice of
it has been received in the office of the person who granted the authorisation within
the relevant force, service, squad or HMCE (but not before the day on which the
authorisation would have otherwise ceased to have effect). In urgent cases, a
renewal can take effect immediately (provided this is not before the day on which
the authorisation would have otherwise ceased to have effect). See section 35 and
36 of the 2000 Act and the Regulation of Investigatory Powers (Notification of
Authorisations etc.) Order 2000; SI No 2563.

5.35   Subject to paragraph 5.36, if at any time before the day on which a Secretary of
State authorisation expires, the Secretary of State considers it necessary for the
warrant to be renewed for the purpose for which it was issued, he may renew it in
writing for a further period of three months, beginning with the day on which it
would have ceased to have effect, but for the renewal.

Secretary of State intelligence services authorisations

5.36   If at any time before an intelligence service warrant expires, the Secretary of State   **15.33**
considers it necessary for the warrant to be renewed for the purpose for which it
was issued, he may renew it in writing for a further period of six months, beginning with the day on which it would have ceased to have effect, but for the
renewal.

5.37   All applications for a renewal of an authorisation or warrant should record:

• whether this is the first renewal or every occasion on which the warrant/
authorisation has been renewed previously;
• any significant changes to the information listed in paragraph 5.16;
• the reasons why it is necessary to continue with the intrusive surveillance;
• the content and value to the investigation or operation of the product so far
obtained by the surveillance;
• the results of regular reviews of the investigation or operation.

5.38   Authorisations may be renewed more than once, if necessary, and the renewal
should be kept/recorded as part of the central record of authorisations (see
paragraphs 2.14–2.15).

Reviews

15.34 Regular reviews of authorisations should be undertaken to assess the need for the   **5.39**
surveillance to continue. The results of a review should be recorded on the central
record of authorisations (see paragraphs 2.14–2.15). Particular attention is drawn
to the need to review authorisations frequently where the intrusive surveillance
provides access to confidential information or involves collateral intrusion.

The senior authorising officer or, for those subject to Secretary of State authorisa-   **5.40**
tion, the member or official who made the application within each public authority should determine how often a review should take place. This should be as
frequently as is considered necessary and practicable.

Cancellations

15.35 The senior authorising officer who granted or last renewed the authorisation must   **5.41**
cancel it, or the person who made the application to the Secretary of State must
apply for its cancellation, if he is satisfied that the surveillance no longer meets the
criteria upon which it was authorised. Where the senior authorising officer or person who made the application to the Secretary of State is no longer available, this
duty will fall on the person who has taken over the role of senior authorising officer
or taken over from the person who made the application to the Secretary of State or
the person who is acting as the senior authorising officer (see the Regulation of
Investigatory Powers (Cancellation of Authorisations) Order 2000; SI No 2794).

The Surveillance Commissioners must be notified where police, NCIS, NCS or   **5.42**
HMCE authorisations are cancelled (see the Regulation of Investigatory Powers
(Notification of Authorisations etc.) Order 2000; SI No 2563).

Ceasing of surveillance activity

15.36 As soon as the decision is taken that the intrusive surveillance should be discon-   **5.43**
tinued, instructions must be given to those involved to stop all surveillance of the
subject(s). The date and time when such an instruction was given should be
recorded in the central record of authorisations (see paragraphs 2.14–2.15) and
the notification of cancellation where relevant.

*Police, National Criminal Intelligence Service, the National Crime Squad and HM
Customs and Excise authorisations*

15.37 In cases where an authorisation is quashed or cancelled by a Surveillance   **5.44**
Commissioner, the senior authorising officer must immediately instruct those
carrying out the surveillance to stop monitoring, observing, listening or recording
the activities of the subject of the authorisation. The date and time when such an
instruction was given should be recorded on the central record of authorisations
(see paragraphs 2.14–2.15).

6 AUTHORISATION PROCEDURES FOR ENTRY ON OR INTERFERENCE WITH PROPERTY OR WITH WIRELESS TELEGRAPHY

6.1 The 1994 Act and 1997 Act provide lawful authority for entry on or interference **15.38** with property or with wireless telegraphy by the intelligence services and the police, NCIS, NCS and HMCE.

6.2 In many cases a covert surveillance operation may involve both intrusive surveillance and entry on or interference with property or with wireless telegraphy. This can be done as a combined authorisation, although the criteria for authorisation of each activity must be considered separately (see paragraph 2.11).

Authorisations for entry on or interference with property or with wireless telegraphy by the police, National Criminal Intelligence Service, the National Crime Squad and HM Customs and Excise

6.3 Responsibility for such authorisations rests with the authorising officer as defined in section 93(5) of the 1997 Act, that is the chief constable or equivalent. Authorisations require the personal authority of the authorising officer (or his designated deputy) except in urgent situations, where it is not reasonably practicable for the application to be considered by such person. The person entitled to act in such cases is set out in section 94 of the 1997 Act.

6.4 Authorisations under the 1997 Act may not be necessary where the public authority is acting with the consent of a person able to give permission in respect of relevant property, although consideration should still be given to the need to obtain an authorisation under Part II of the 2000 Act.

6.5 Authorisations for the police, NCIS and NCS may only be given by an authorising officer on application by a member of his own force, Service or Squad for entry on or interference with property or with wireless telegraphy within the authorising officer's own area of operation. For HMCE an authorisation may only be given by an authorising officer on application by a customs officer. An authorising officer may authorise the taking of action outside the relevant area solely for the purpose of maintaining or retrieving any device, apparatus or equipment.

Any person giving an authorisation for entry on or interference with property or **6.6** with wireless telegraphy under section 93(2) of the 1997 Act must believe that:

- it is necessary for the action specified to be taken for the purpose of preventing or detecting serious crime (or in the case of the Police Service of Northern Ireland, in the interests of national security);[8] and
- that the taking of the action is proportionate to what the action seeks to achieve.

The authorising officer must take into account whether what it is thought necessary **6.7** to achieve by the authorised conduct could reasonably be achieved by other means.

Any person granting or applying for an authorisation or warrant to enter on or **6.8** interfere with property or with wireless telegraphy will also need to be aware of particular sensitivities in the local community where the entry or interference is taking place and of similar activities being undertaken by other public authorities which could impact on the deployment. In this regard, it is recommended that the authorising officers in NCIS, NCS and HMCE should consult a senior officer within the police force in which the investigation or operation takes place where the authorising officer considers that conflicts might arise. The Chief Constable of the Police Service of Northern Ireland should be informed of any surveillance operation undertaken by another law enforcement agency which involve its officers in maintaining or retrieving equipment in Northern Ireland.

Authorisation procedures for entry on or interference with property or with wireless telegraphy by the police, National Criminal Intelligence Service, the National Crime Squad and HM Customs and Excise

Authorisations will generally be given in writing by the authorising officer. **6.9** However, in urgent cases, they may be given orally by the authorising officer. In such cases, a statement that the authorising officer has expressly authorised the action should be recorded in writing by the applicant as soon as is reasonably practicable. This should be done by the person with whom the authorising officer spoke.

If the authorising officer is absent then, as provided for in section 12(4) of the **6.10** Police Act 1996, section 5(4) of the Police (Scotland) Act 1967, section 25 of the City of London Police Act 1839, or sections 8 or 54 of the 1997 Act, an authorisation can be given in writing or, in urgent cases, orally by the designated deputy.

Where, however, in an urgent case, it is not reasonably practicable for the desig- **6.11** nated deputy to consider an application, then written authorisation may be given by the following:

- in the case of the police, by an assistant chief constable (other than a designated deputy);

---

[8] See footnotes 1 and 2.

- in the case of the Metropolitan Police and City of London Police, by a commander;
- in the case of NCIS and NCS, by a person designated by the relevant Director General;[9]
- in the case of HMCE, by a person designated by the Commissioners of Customs and Excise.[10]

6.12 Applications to the authorising officer for authorisation must be made in writing by a police or customs officer or a member of NCIS or NCS (within the terms of section 93(3) of the 1997 Act) and should specify:

- the identity or identities of those to be targeted (where known);
- the property which the entry or interference with will affect;
- the identity of individuals and/or categories of people, where known, who are likely to be affected by collateral intrusion;
- details of the offence planned or committed;
- details of the intrusive surveillance involved;
- how the authorisation criteria (as set out in paragraphs 6.6 and 6.7) have been met;
- any action which may be necessary to retrieve any equipment used in the surveillance;
- in case of a renewal, the results obtained so far, or a full explanation of the failure to obtain any results; and
- whether an authorisation was given or refused, by whom and the time and date.

6.13 Additionally, in urgent cases, the authorisation should record (as the case may be):

- the reasons why the authorising officer or designated deputy considered the case so urgent that an oral instead of a written authorisation was given; and
- the reasons why (if relevant) the person granting the authorisation did not consider it reasonably practicable for the application to be considered by the senior authorising officer or the designated deputy.

6.14 Where the application is oral, the information referred to above should be recorded in writing by the applicant as soon as reasonably practicable.

Notifications to Surveillance Commissioners

6.15 Where a person gives, renews or cancels an authorisation, he must, as soon as is rea-　**15.39** sonably practicable, give notice of it in writing to a Surveillance Commissioner, in accordance with arrangements made by the Chief Surveillance Commissioner. In

---

[9] For police members of NCIS or NCS, this will be an officer who holds the rank of assistant chief constable in that service or squad. Additionally, in the case of NCIS, this may be an assistant chief investigation officer of HMCE.

[10] This will be an officer of the rank of assistant chief investigation officer.

urgent cases which would otherwise have required the approval of a Surveillance Commissioner, the notification must specify the grounds on which the case is believed to be one of urgency.

There may be cases which become urgent after approval has been sought but **6.16** before a response has been received from a Surveillance Commissioner. In such a case, the authorising officer should notify the Surveillance Commissioner that the case is urgent (pointing out that it has become urgent since the previous notification). In these cases, the authorisation will take effect immediately.

Notifications to Surveillance Commissioners in relation to the authorisation, **6.17** renewal and cancellation of authorisations in respect of entry on or interference with property should be in accordance with the requirements of the Police Act 1997 (Notifications of Authorisations etc) Order 1998; SI No 3241.

Duration of authorisations

15.40 Written authorisations given by authorising officers will cease to have effect at the end **6.18** of a period of three months beginning with the day on which they took effect. In cases requiring prior approval by a Surveillance Commissioner this means from the time the Surveillance Commissioner has approved the authorisation and the person who gave the authorisation has been notified. This means that the approval will not take effect until the notice has been received in the office of the person who granted the authorisation within the relevant force, service, squad or HMCE. In cases not requiring prior approval, this means from the time the authorisation was given.

Oral authorisations given in urgent cases by: **6.19**

- authorising officers;
- or designated deputies

and Written authorisations given by:

- assistant chief constables (other than a designated deputy);
- commanders in the Metropolitan Police and City of London Police;
- the person designated to act by the Director General of NCIS or of NCS;
- the person designated for the purpose by the Commissioners of Customs and Excise;

will cease at the end of the period of seventy-two hours beginning with the time when they took effect.

Renewals

15.41 If at any time before the day on which an authorisation expires the authorising **6.20** officer or, in his absence, the designated deputy considers the authorisation should continue to have effect for the purpose for which it was issued, he may renew it in writing for a period of three months beginning with the day on which the authorisation would otherwise have ceased to have effect. Authorisations may be renewed more than once, if necessary, and the renewal should be recorded on the authorisation record (see paragraph 6.27).

6.21 Commissioners must be notified of renewals of authorisations. The information to be included in the notification is set out in the Police Act 1997 (Notifications of Authorisations etc) Order 1998; SI No 3241.

6.22 If, at the time of renewal, the criteria in paragraph 6.30 exist, then the approval of a Surveillance Commissioner must be sought before the renewal can take effect. The fact that the initial authorisation required the approval of a Commissioner before taking effect does not mean that its renewal will automatically require such approval. It will only do so if, at the time of the renewal, it falls into one of the categories requiring approval (and is not urgent).

Reviews

6.23 Authorising officers should regularly review authorisations to assess the need for the entry on or interference with property or with wireless telegraphy to continue. This should be recorded on the authorisation record (see paragraph 6.27). The authorising officer should determine how often a review should take place when giving an authorisation. This should be as frequently as is considered necessary and practicable and at no greater interval than one month. Particular attention is drawn to the need to review authorisations and renewals regularly and frequently where the entry on or interference with property or with wireless telegraphy provides access to confidential information or involves collateral intrusion. **15.42**

Cancellations

6.24 The senior authorising officer who granted or last renewed the authorisation must cancel it, or the person who made the application to the Secretary of State must apply for its cancellation, if he is satisfied that the authorisation no longer meets the criteria upon which it was authorised. Where the senior authorising officer or person who made the application to the Secretary of State is no longer available, this duty will fall on the person who has taken over the role of senior authorising officer or taken over from the person who made the application to the Secretary of State or the person who is acting as the senior authorising officer (see the Regulation of Investigatory Powers (Cancellation of Authorisations) Order 2000; SI No 2794). **15.43**

6.25 The Surveillance Commissioners must be notified of cancellations of authorisations. The information to be included in the notification is set out in the Police Act 1997 (Notifications of Authorisations etc.) Order 1998; SI No 3421.

The Surveillance Commissioners have the power to cancel an authorisation if they are satisfied that, at any time after an authorisation was given or renewed, there were no reasonable grounds for believing the matters set out in paragraphs 6.6 and 6.7 above. In such circumstances, a Surveillance Commissioner may order the destruction of records, in whole or in part, other than any that are required for pending criminal or civil proceedings. **6.26**

Authorisation record

15.44 An authorisation record should be created which records: **6.27**

- the time and date when an authorisation is given;
- whether an authorisation is in written or oral form;
- the time and date when it was notified to a Surveillance Commissioner;
- and the time and date when the Surveillance Commissioner notified his approval (where appropriate).

The authorisation record should also record:

- every occasion when entry on or interference with property or with wireless telegraphy has occurred;
- the result of periodic reviews of the authorisation;
- the date of every renewal; and
- it should record the time and date when any instruction was given by the authorising officer to cease the interference with property or with wireless telegraphy.

Ceasing of entry on or interference with property or with wireless telegraphy

15.45 Once an authorisation or renewal expires or is cancelled or quashed, the authorising officer must immediately instruct those carrying out the surveillance to cease all the actions authorised for the entry on or interference with property or with wireless telegraphy. The time and date when such an instruction was given should be recorded on the authorisation record (see paragraph 6.27). **6.28**

Retrieval of equipment

15.46 Where a Surveillance Commissioner quashes or cancels an authorisation or renewal, he will, if there are reasonable grounds for doing so, order that the authorisation remain effective for a specified period, to enable officers to retrieve anything left on the property by virtue of the authorisation. He can only do so if the authorisation or renewal makes provision for this. A decision by the Surveillance Commissioner not to give such an order can be the subject of an appeal to the Chief Surveillance Commissioner. **6.29**

Special Rules

Cases requiring prior approval of a Surveillance Commissioner

6.30 In certain cases, an authorisation for entry on or interference with property will   **15.47**
not take effect until a Surveillance Commissioner has approved it and the notice
has been received in the office of the person who granted the authorisation within
the relevant force, service, squad or HMCE (unless the urgency procedures are
used). These are cases where the person giving the authorisation believes that any
of the property specified in the authorisation:

- is used wholly or mainly as a dwelling or as a bedroom in a hotel; or
- constitutes office premises; or
- the action authorised is likely to result in any person acquiring knowledge of:
- matters subject to legal privilege;
- confidential personal information; or
- confidential journalistic material.

6.31 Office premises are defined as any building or part of a building whose sole or principal use is as an office or for office purposes (which means purposes of administration, clerical work, handling money and telephone or telegraph operation).

**Authorisations for entry on or interference with property or with wireless
telegraphy by the intelligence services**

6.32 Before granting a warrant, the Secretary of State must: **15.48**

- think it necessary for the action to be taken for the purpose of assisting the relevant agency in carrying out its functions;
- be satisfied that the taking of the action is proportionate to what the action
  seeks to achieve;
- take into account in deciding whether an authorisation is necessary and proportionate is whether the information which it is thought necessary to obtain
  by the conduct authorised by the warrant could reasonably be obtained by
  other means; and
- be satisfied that there are satisfactory arrangements in force under the 1994 Act
  or the 1989 Act in respect of disclosure of any material obtained by means of the
  warrant, and that material obtained will be subject to those arrangements.

6.33 An application for a warrant must be made by a member of the intelligence ser-
vices for the taking of action in relation to that agency. In addition, the Security
Service may make an application for a warrant to act on behalf of the Secret
Intelligence Service (SIS) and the Governments Communication Headquarters
(GCHQ). SIS and GCHQ may not be granted a warrant for action in support of
the prevention or detection of serious crime which relates to property in the
British Islands.

A warrant shall, unless renewed, cease to have effect if the warrant was under the **6.34** hand of the Secretary of State, at the end of the period of six months beginning with the day on which it was issued. In any other case, at the end of the period ending with the second working day following that day.

If at any time before the day on which a warrant would cease to have effect the **6.35** Secretary of State considers it necessary for the warrant to continue to have effect for the purpose for which it was issued, he may by an instrument under his hand renew it for a period of six months beginning with that day. The Secretary of State shall cancel a warrant if he is satisfied that the action authorised by it is no longer necessary.

The intelligence services should provide the same information as the police, as **6.36** and where appropriate, when making applications, requests for renewal and requests for cancellation of property warrants.

Retrieval of equipment

15.49 Because of the time it can take to remove equipment from a person's property it **6.37** may also be necessary to renew a property warrant in order to complete the retrieval. Applications to the Secretary of State for renewal should state why it is being or has been closed down, why it has not been possible to remove the equipment and any timescales for removal, where known.

7 OVERSIGHT BY COMMISSIONERS

15.50 The 1997 and 2000 Acts require the Chief Surveillance Commissioner to keep **7.1** under review (with the assistance of the Surveillance Commissioners and Assistant Surveillance Commissioners) the performance of functions under Part III of the 1997 Act and Part II of the 2000 Act by the police (including the Royal Navy Regulating Branch, the Royal Military Police and the Royal Air Force Police and the Ministry of Defence Police and the British Transport Police), NCIS, the NCS, HMCE and of the 2000 Act the other public authorities listed in Schedule 1 and in Northern Ireland officials of the Ministry of Defence and HM Forces.

The Intelligence Services Commissioner's remit is to provide independent over- **7.2** sight of the use of the powers contained within Part II of the 2000 Act and the 1994 Act by the Security Service, Secret Intelligence Service, GCHQ and the Ministry of Defence and HM Forces (excluding the Royal Navy Regulating Branch, the Royal Military Police and the Royal Air Force Police, and in Northern Ireland officials of the Ministry of Defence and HM Forces);

7.3 This code does not cover the exercise of any of the Commissioners' functions. It is the duty of any person who uses these powers to comply with any request made by a Commissioner to disclose or provide any information he requires for the purpose of enabling him to carry out his functions.

7.4 References in this code to the performance of review functions by the Chief Surveillance Commissioner and other Commissioners apply also to Inspectors and other members of staff to whom such functions have been delegated.

8 COMPLAINTS

8.1 The 2000 Act establishes an independent Tribunal. This Tribunal will be made up **15.51** of senior members of the judiciary and the legal profession and is independent of the Government. The Tribunal has full powers to investigate and decide any case within its jurisdiction.

This code does not cover the exercise of the Tribunal's functions. Details of the relevant complaints procedure can be obtained from the following address:

Investigatory Powers Tribunal
PO Box 33220
London
SW1H 9ZQ

☎   020 7273 4514

Annex A

Authorisation levels when knowledge of confidential information is likely to be acquired

Relevant Public Authorities	Authorisation level
Police Forces—Any police force maintained under section 2 of the Police Act 1996 (police forces in England and Wales outside London).	Chief Constable
Police Forces—Any police force maintained under or by virtue of section 1 of the Police (Scotland) Act 1967.	Chief Constable
The Metropolitan Police Force	Assistant Commissioner
The City of London Police Force	Commissioner
The Police Service of Northern Ireland	Deputy Chief Constable
The Royal Navy Regulating Branch	Provost Marshal
The Royal Military Police	Provost Marshal
The Royal Air Force Police	Provost Marshal
National Criminal Intelligence Service (NCIS)	Director General
National Crime Squad (NCS)	Director General or Deputy Director General
Serious Fraud Office	Director or Assistant Director
The Intelligence Services:	
Government Communications Headquarters	A Director of GCHQ
Security Service	Deputy Director General
Secret Intelligence Service	A Director of the Secret Intelligence Service
HM Forces:	
Royal Navy	Rear Admiral
Army	Major General
Royal Air Force	Air-Vice Marshall
HM Customs and Excise	Director Investigation or Regional Heads of Investigation
Inland Revenue	Deputy Chairman of Inland Revenue
Department for Environment, Food and Rural Affairs:	
DEFRA Investigation Branch	Immediate Senior Officer of Head of DEFRA Prosecution Division
Horticultural Marketing Inspectorate	Immediate Senior Officer of Head of DEFRA Prosecution Division
Plant Health and Seed Inspectorate	Immediate Senior Officer of Head of DEFRA Prosecution Division
Egg Marketing Inspectorate	Immediate Senior Officer of Head of DEFRA Prosecution Division
Sea Fisheries Inspectorate (SFI)	Immediate Senior Officer of Head of DEFRA Prosecution Division
Centre for Environment, Fisheries & Aquaculture Science (CEFAS)	Immediate Senior Officer of Head of DEFRA Prosecution Division

Ministry of Defence—	Director General or equivalent
Department for Transport, Local Government and Regions:	
Vehicle Inspectorate	No
Transport Security (Transec)	Director of Transport Security
Department of Health:	
Medical Devices Agency	Chief Executive
Relevant Public Authorities	**Authorisation level**
Medicine Control Agency	Chief Executive
Welfare Foods Policy Unit	Deputy Chief Medical Officer
Directorate of Counter Fraud Services (DFCS)	Director of Counter Fraud Services
Home Office:	
HM Prison Service	Deputy Director General of the Prison Service
Immigration Service	Chief Inspector of the Immigration Service
Department of Work and Pensions:	
Benefits Agency	Chief Executive of the Benefits Agency
Department of Trade and Industry:	
Radiocommunications Agency	No
British Trade International	No
Coal Health Claims Unit	Director of Coal Health Claims unit
Companies Investigation Branch	The Inspector of Companies
Legal Services Directorate D	The Director of Legal Service D
National Assembly for Wales	Head of NHS Directorate in the National Assembly for Wales Head of NHS Finance Division in the National Assembly for Wales Head of Common Agricultural Policy Management Division in the National Assembly for Wales
Local Authorities	The Head of Paid Service or (in his absence) a Chief Officer
Environment Agency	Chief Executive of the Environment Agency
Financial Services Authority	Chairman of the Financial Services Authority
Food Standards Agency	Head of Group, Deputy Chief Executive and Chief Executive of the Foods Standards Agency
The Intervention Board for Agricultural Produce	Chief Executive of the Intervention Board for Agricultural Produce
Personal Investment Authority	Chairman of the Personal Investment Authority
Post Office	Director of Security
Health & Safety Executive	Director of Field Operations, Director of Hazardous Installations Directorate, Her Majesty's Chief Inspector of Nuclear Installations.

NHS bodies in England and Wales:

A health authority established under section 8 of the National Health Service Act 1977	Chief Executive
A Special Health Authority established under section 11 of the National Health Service 1977	Chief Executive
A National Health Service Trust established under section 5 of the National Health Service and Community Care Act 1990	Chief Executive
Royal Pharmaceutical Society of Great Britain	Director of Professional Standards

16

THE COVERT HUMAN INTELLIGENCE SOURCES CODE OF PRACTICE* 2002 (UNDER SI 2002 NO 1932)

COVERT HUMAN INTELLIGENCE SOURCES

Code of Practice

Pursuant to Section 71 of the
Regulation of Investigatory Powers Act 2000

Commencement

This code applies to every authorisation of the use or conduct by public authorities of covert human intelligence sources carried out under Part II of the Regulation of Investigatory Powers Act 2000 which begins on or after the day on which this code comes into effect.

---

* The text of this Code of Practice is taken from the version published by the Home Office and made under the Regulation of Investigatory Powers (Covert Human Intelligence Sources: Code of Practice) Order 2002 (SI 2002 No 1932) which came into force on 1 August 2002.

1 GENERAL

1.1 In this code the: **16.01**

- "**1989 Act**" means the Security Service Act 1989;
- "**1994 Act**" means the Intelligence Services Act 1994;
- "**1997 Act**" means the Police Act 1997;
- "**2000 Act**" means the Regulation of Investigatory Powers Act 2000;
- "**RIP(S)A**" means the Regulation of Investigatory Powers (Scotland) Act 2000;

1.2 This code of practice provides guidance on the authorisation of the use or conduct of covert human intelligence sources ("a source") by public authorities under Part II of the 2000 Act.

1.3 The provisions of the 2000 Act are not intended to apply in circumstances where members of the public volunteer information to the police or other authorities, as part of their normal civic duties, or to contact numbers set up to receive information (such as Crimestoppers, Customs Confidential, the Anti Terrorist Hotline, or the Security Service Public Telephone Number). Members of the public acting in this way would not generally be regarded as sources.

1.4 Neither Part II of the 2000 Act or this code of practice is intended to affect the practices and procedures surrounding criminal participation of sources.

1.5 The 2000 Act provides that all codes of practice relating to the 2000 Act are admissible as evidence in criminal and civil proceedings. If any provision of the code appears relevant to any court or tribunal considering any such proceedings, or to the Investigatory Powers Tribunal established under the 2000 Act, or to one of the Commissioners responsible for overseeing the powers conferred by the 2000 Act, it must be taken into account.

General extent of powers

1.6 Authorisations can be given for the use or conduct of a source both inside and out-   **16.02**
side the United Kingdom. Authorisations for actions outside the United Kingdom can only validate them for the purposes of proceedings in the United Kingdom. An authorisation under Part II of the 2000 Act does not take into account the requirements of the country outside the United Kingdom in which the investigation or operation is taking place.

1.7 Members of foreign law enforcement or other agencies or sources of those agencies may be authorised under the 2000 Act in the UK in support of domestic and international investigations.

Where the conduct authorised is likely to take place in Scotland, authorisations **1.8** should be granted under RIP(S)A, unless the authorisation is being obtained by those public authorities listed in section 46(3) of the 2000 Act and the Regulation of Investigatory Powers (Authorisations Extending to Scotland) Order 2000). Additionally, any authorisation granted or renewed for the purposes of national security or the economic well-being of the UK must be made under the 2000 Act. This code of practice is extended to Scotland in relation to authorisations made under Part II of the 2000 Act which apply to Scotland. A separate code of practice applies in relation to authorisations made under RIP(S)A.

Use of material in evidence

16.03 Material obtained from a source may be used as evidence in criminal proceedings. **1.9** The proper authorisation of a source should ensure the suitability of such evidence under the common law, section 78 of the Police and Criminal Evidence Act 1984 and the Human Rights Act 1998. Furthermore, the product obtained by a source described in this code is subject to the ordinary rules for retention and disclosure of material under the Criminal Procedure and Investigations Act 1996, where those rules apply to the law enforcement body in question. There are also well-established legal procedures that will protect the identity of a source from disclosure in such circumstances.

2 GENERAL RULES ON AUTHORISATIONS

16.04 An authorisation under Part II of the 2000 Act will provide lawful authority for **2.1** the use of a source. Responsibility for giving the authorisation will depend on which public authority is responsible for the source.

Part II of the 2000 Act does not impose a requirement on public authorities to seek **2.2** or obtain an authorisation where, under the 2000 Act, one is available (see section 80 of the 2000 Act). Nevertheless, where there is an interference by a public authority with the right to respect for private and family life guaranteed under Article 8 of the European Convention on Human Rights, and where there is no other lawful authority, the consequences of not obtaining an authorisation under the 2000 Act may be that the action is unlawful by virtue of section 6 of the Human Rights Act 1998.

Public authorities are therefore strongly recommended to seek an authorisation **2.3** where the use or conduct of a source is likely to interfere with a person's Article 8 rights to privacy by obtaining information from or about a person, whether or not that person is the subject of the investigation or operation. Obtaining an authorisation will ensure that the action is carried out in accordance with law and subject to stringent safeguards against abuse.

Necessity and proportionality

2.4 Obtaining an authorisation under the 2000 Act will only ensure that the author- **16.05**
ised use or conduct of a source is a justifiable interference with an individual's
Article 8 rights if it is necessary and proportionate for the source to be used. The
2000 Act first requires that the person granting an authorisation believe that the
authorisation is necessary in the circumstances of the particular case for one or
more of the statutory grounds in section 29(3) of the 2000 Act.

2.5 Then, if the use of the source is necessary, the person granting the authorisation
must believe that the use of a source is proportionate to what is sought to be
achieved by the conduct and use of that source. This involves balancing the intrusiveness of the use of the source on the target and others who might be affected by
it against the need for the source to be used in operational terms. The use of a
source will not be proportionate if it is excessive in the circumstances of the case
or if the information which is sought could reasonably be obtained by other less
intrusive means. The use of a source should be carefully managed to meet the
objective in question and sources must not be used in an arbitrary or unfair way.

Collateral intrusion

2.6 Before authorising the use or conduct of a source, the authorising officer should **16.06**
also take into account the risk of intrusion into the privacy of persons other than
those who are directly the subjects of the operation or investigation (collateral
intrusion). Measures should be taken, wherever practicable, to avoid unnecessary
intrusion into the lives of those not directly connected with the operation.

2.7 An application for an authorisation should include an assessment of the risk of
any collateral intrusion. The authorising officer should take this into account,
when considering the proportionality of the use and conduct of a source.

2.8 Those tasking a source should inform the authorising officer if the investigation
or operation unexpectedly interferes with the privacy of individuals who are not
covered by the authorisation. When the original authorisation may not be sufficient, consideration should be given to whether the authorisation needs to be
amended and reauthorised or a new authorisation is required.

2.9 Any person granting or applying for an authorisation will also need to be aware
of any particular sensitivities in the local community where the source is being
used and of similar activities being undertaken by other public authorities

which could impact on the deployment of the source. Consideration should also be given to any adverse impact on community confidence or safety that may result from the use or conduct of a source or of information obtained from that source. In this regard, it is recommended that where the authorising officers in the National Criminal Intelligence Service (NCIS), the National Crime Squad (NCS) and HM Customs and Excise (HMCE) consider that conflicts might arise they should consult a senior officer within the police force area in which the source is deployed. Additionally, the authorising officer should make an assessment of any risk to a source in carrying out the conduct in the proposed authorisation.

In a very limited range of circumstances an authorisation under Part II may, by **2.10** virtue of sections 26(7) and 27 of the 2000 Act, render lawful conduct which would otherwise be criminal, if it is incidental to any conduct falling within section 26(8) of the 2000 Act which the source is authorised to undertake. This would depend on the circumstances of each individual case, and consideration should always be given to seeking advice from the legal adviser within the relevant public authority when such activity is contemplated. A source that acts beyond the limits recognised by the law will be at risk from prosecution. The need to protect the source cannot alter this principle.

Combined authorisations

16.07 A single authorisation may combine two or more different authorisations under **2.11** Part II of the 2000 Act. For example, a single authorisation may combine authorisations for intrusive surveillance and for the conduct of a source. In such cases the provisions applicable to each of the authorisations must be considered separately. Thus, a police superintendent can authorise the conduct of a source but an authorisation for intrusive surveillance by the police needs the separate authority of a chief constable, and in certain cases the approval of a Surveillance Commissioner will also be necessary. Where an authorisation for the use or conduct of a covert human intelligence source is combined with a Secretary of State authorisation for intrusive surveillance, the combined authorisation must be issued by the Secretary of State. However, this does not preclude public authorities from obtaining separate authorisations.

Directed surveillance against a potential source

16.08 It may be necessary to deploy directed surveillance against a potential source as **2.12** part of the process of assessing their suitability for recruitment, or in planning how best to make the approach to them. An authorisation under this code authorising an officer to establish a covert relationship with a potential source could be combined with a directed surveillance authorisation so that both the officer and potential source could be followed. Directed surveillance is defined in section 26(2) of the 2000 Act. See the code of practice on Covert Surveillance.

Central Record of all authorisations

2.13 A centrally retrievable record of all authorisations should be held by each public **16.09** authority and regularly updated whenever an authorisation is granted, renewed or cancelled. The record should be made available to the relevant Commissioner or an Inspector from the Office of Surveillance Commissioners, upon request. These records should be retained for a period of at least three years from the ending of the authorisation.

2.14 Proper records must be kept of the authorisation and use of a source. Section 29(5) of the 2000 Act provides that an authorising officer must not grant an authorisation for the use or conduct of a source unless he believes that there are arrangements in place for ensuring that there is at all times a person with the responsibility for maintaining a record of the use made of the source. The Regulation of Investigatory Powers (Source Records) Regulations 2000; SI No 2725 details the particulars that must be included in the records relating to each source.

2.15 In addition, records or copies of the following, as appropriate, should be kept by the relevant authority:

- a copy of the authorisation together with any supplementary documentation and notification of the approval given by the authorising officer;
- a copy of any renewal of an authorisation, together with the supporting documentation submitted when the renewal was requested;
- the reason why the person renewing an authorisation considered it necessary to do so;
- any authorisation which was granted or renewed orally (in an urgent case) and the reason why the case was considered urgent;
- any risk assessment made in relation to the source;
- the circumstances in which tasks were given to the source;
- the value of the source to the investigating authority;
- a record of the results of any reviews of the authorisation;
- the reasons, if any, for not renewing an authorisation;
- the reasons for cancelling an authorisation.
- the date and time when any instruction was given by the authorising officer to cease using a source.

2.16 The records kept by public authorities should be maintained in such a way as to preserve the confidentiality of the source and the information provided by that source. There should, at all times, be a designated person within the relevant public authority who will have responsibility for maintaining a record of the use made of the source.

Retention and destruction of the product

16.10 Where the product obtained from a source could be relevant to pending or future **2.17** criminal or civil proceedings, it should be retained in accordance with established disclosure requirements for a suitable further period, commensurate to any subsequent review.

In the cases of the law enforcement agencies (not including the Royal Navy **2.18** Regulating Branch, the Royal Military Police and the Royal Air Force Police), particular attention is drawn to the requirements of the code of practice issued under the Criminal Procedure and Investigations Act 1996. This requires that material which is obtained in the course of a criminal investigation and which may be relevant to the investigation must be recorded and retained.

There is nothing in the 2000 Act which prevents material obtained from properly **2.19** authorised use of a source being used in other investigations. Each public authority must ensure that arrangements are in place for the handling, storage and destruction of material obtained through the use of a source. Authorising officers must ensure compliance with the appropriate data protection requirements and any relevant codes of practice produced by individual authorities in the handling and storage of material.

The Intelligence services, MOD and HM Forces

16.11 The heads of these agencies are responsible for ensuring that arrangements exist to **2.20** ensure that no information is stored by the authorities, except as necessary for the proper discharge of their functions. They are also responsible for arrangements to control onward disclosure. For the intelligence services, this is a statutory duty under the 1989 Act and the 1994 Act.

3 SPECIAL RULES ON AUTHORISATIONS

Confidential information

16.12 The 2000 Act does not provide any special protection for 'confidential informa- **3.1** tion'. Nevertheless, particular care should be taken in cases where the subject of the investigation or operation might reasonably expect a high degree of privacy, or where confidential information is involved. Confidential information consists of matters subject to legal privilege, confidential personal information or confidential journalistic material.

3.2 In cases where through the use or conduct of a source it is likely that knowledge of confidential information will be acquired, the deployment of the source is subject to a higher level of authorisation. Annex A lists the authorising officer for each public authority permitted to authorise such use or conduct of a source.

Communications subject to legal privilege

3.3 Section 98 of the 1997 Act describes those matters that are subject to legal privilege in England and Wales. In Scotland, the relevant description is contained in section 33 of the Criminal Law (Consolidation) (Scotland) Act 1995. With regard to Northern Ireland, Article 12 of the Police and Criminal Evidence (Northern Ireland) Order 1989 should be referred to. **16.13**

3.4 Legal privilege does not apply to communications made with the intention of furthering a criminal purpose (whether the lawyer is acting unwittingly or culpably). Legally privileged communications will lose their protection if there are grounds to believe, for example, that the professional legal adviser is intending to hold or use them for a criminal purpose. But privilege is not lost if a professional legal adviser is properly advising a person who is suspected of having committed a criminal offence. The concept of legal privilege applies to the provision of professional legal advice by any individual, agency or organisation qualified to do so.

3.5 The 2000 Act does not provide any special protection for legally privileged information. Nevertheless, such information is particularly sensitive and any source which acquires such material may engage Article 6 of the ECHR (right to a fair trial) as well as Article 8. Legally privileged information obtained by a source is extremely unlikely ever to be admissible as evidence in criminal proceedings. Moreover, the mere fact that use has been made of a source to obtain such information may lead to any related criminal proceedings being stayed as an abuse of process. Accordingly, action which may lead to such information being obtained is subject to additional safeguards under this code.

3.6 In general, an application for the use or conduct of a source which is likely to result in the acquisition of legally privileged information should only be made in exceptional and compelling circumstance. Full regard should be had to the particular proportionality issues such a use or conduct of a source raises. The application should include, in addition to the reasons why it is considered necessary for the use or conduct of a source to be used, an assessment of how likely it is that information subject to legal privilege will be acquired. The application should clearly state whether the purpose (or one of the purposes) of the use or conduct of the source is to obtain legally privileged information.

3.7 This assessment will be taken into account by the authorising officer in deciding whether the proposed use or conduct of a source is necessary and proportionate for a purpose under section 29 of the 2000 Act. The authorising officer may require regular reporting so as to be able to decide whether the authorisation should continue. In those cases where legally privileged information has been acquired and retained, the matter should be reported to the relevant Commissioner or Inspector during his next inspection and the material should be made available to him if requested.

A substantial proportion of the communications between a lawyer and his **3.8** client(s) may be subject to legal privilege. Therefore, any case where a lawyer is the subject of an investigation or operation should be notified to the relevant Commissioner or Inspector during his next inspection and any material which has been retained should be made available to him if requested.

Where there is any doubt as to the handling and dissemination of information **3.9** which may be subject to legal privilege, advice should be sought from a legal adviser within the relevant public authority before any further dissemination of the material takes place. Similar advice should also be sought where there is doubt over whether information is not subject to legal privilege due to the "in furtherance of a criminal purpose" exception. The retention of legally privileged information, or its dissemination to an outside body, should be accompanied by a clear warning that it is subject to legal privilege. It should be safeguarded by taking reasonable steps to ensure there is no possibility of it becoming available, or its contents becoming known to any person whose possession of it might prejudice any criminal or civil proceedings related to the information. Any dissemination of legally privileged material to an outside body should be notified to the relevant Commissioner or Inspector during his next inspection.

Communications involving confidential personal information and confidential journalistic material

16.14 Similar consideration must also be given to authorisations that involve confidential **3.10** personal information and confidential journalistic material. In those cases where confidential personal information and confidential journalistic material has been acquired and retained, the matter should be reported to the relevant Commissioner or Inspector during his next inspection and the material be made available to him if requested. Confidential personal information is information held in confidence relating to the physical or mental health or spiritual counselling concerning an individual (whether living or dead) who can be identified from it. Such information, which can include both oral and written communications is held in confidence if it is held subject to an express or implied undertaking to hold it in confidence or it is subject to a restriction on disclosure or an obligation of confidentiality contained in existing legislation. Examples might include consultations between a health professional and a patient, or information from a patient's medical records.

Spiritual counselling means conversations between an individual and a Minister **3.11** of Religion acting in his official capacity, where the individual being counselled is seeking or the Minister is imparting forgiveness, absolution or the resolution of conscience with the authority of the Divine Being(s) of their faith.

3.12 Confidential journalistic material includes material acquired or created for the purposes of journalism and held subject to an undertaking to hold it in confidence, as well as communications resulting in information being acquired for the purposes of journalism and held subject to such an undertaking.

Vulnerable individuals

3.13 A 'vulnerable individual' is a person who is or may be in need of community care **16.15** services by reason of mental or other disability, age or illness and who is or may be unable to take care of himself, or unable to protect himself against significant harm or exploitation. Any individual of this description should only be authorised to act as a source in the most exceptional circumstances. In these cases, the attached table in Annex A lists the authorising officer for each public authority permitted to authorise the use of a vulnerable individual as a source.

Juvenile sources

3.14 Special safeguards also apply to the use or conduct of juvenile sources; that is **16.16** sources under the age of 18 years. **On no occasion should the use or conduct of a source under 16 years of age be authorised to give information against his parents or any person who has parental responsibility for him.** In other cases, authorisations should not be granted unless the special provisions contained within The Regulation of Investigatory Powers (Juveniles) Order 2000; SI No 2793 are satisfied. Authorisations for juvenile sources should be granted by those listed in the attached table at Annex A. The duration of such an authorisation is **one month** instead of twelve months.

4 AUTHORISATION PROCEDURES FOR COVERT HUMAN INTELLIGENCE SOURCES

4.1 Under section 26(8) of the 2000 Act a person is a source if: **16.17**

a) he establishes or maintains a personal or other relationship with a person for the covert purpose of facilitating the doing of anything falling within paragraph (b) or (c);

b) he covertly uses such a relationship to obtain information or to provide access to any information to another person; or

c) he covertly discloses information obtained by the use of such a relationship or as a consequence of the existence of such a relationship.

A source may include those referred to as agents, informants and officers working undercover. **4.2**

By virtue of section 26(9)(b) of the 2000 Act a purpose is covert, in relation to the establishment or maintenance of a personal or other relationship, if and only if, the relationship is conducted in a manner that is calculated to ensure that one of the parties to the relationship is unaware of the purpose. **4.3**

By virtue of section 26(9)(c) of the 2000 Act a relationship is used covertly, and information obtained as mentioned in paragraph 4.1(c) above is disclosed covertly, if and only if it is used or, as the case may be, disclosed in a manner that is calculated to ensure that one of the parties to the relationship is unaware of the use or disclosure in question. **4.4**

The use of a source involves inducing, asking or assisting a person to engage in the conduct of a source or to obtain information by means of the conduct of such a source. **4.5**

The conduct of a source is any conduct falling within section 29(4) of the 2000 Act, or which is incidental to anything falling within section 29(4) of the 2000 Act. **4.6**

Authorisation procedures

16.18 Under section 29(3) of the 2000 Act an authorisation for the use or conduct of a source may be granted by the authorising officer where he believes that the authorisation is necessary: **4.7**

- in the interests of national security;[1,2]
- for the purpose of preventing and detecting[3] crime or of preventing disorder;

---

[1] One of the functions of the Security Service is the protection of national security and in particular the protection against threats from terrorism. These functions extend throughout the United Kingdom, save that, in Northern Ireland, where the lead responsibility for investigating the threat from terrorism related to the affairs of Northern Ireland lies with the Police Service of Northern Ireland. An authorising officer in another public authority should not issue an authorisation under Part II of the 2000 Act where the operation or investigation falls within the responsibilities of the Security Service, as set out above, except where it is to be carried out by a Special Branch or where the Security Service has agreed that another public authority can authorise the use or conduct of a source which would normally fall within the responsibilities of the Security Service.

[2] HM Forces may also undertake operations in connection with a military threat to national security and other operations in connection with national security in support of the Security Service, the Police Service of Northern Ireland or other Civil Powers.

[3] Detecting crime is defined in section 81(5) of the 2000 Act.

- in the interests of the economic well-being of the UK;
- in the interests of public safety;
- for the purpose of protecting public health;[4]
- for the purpose of assessing or collecting any tax, duty, levy or other imposition, contribution or charge payable to a government department; or
- for any other purpose prescribed in an order made by the Secretary of State.[5]

4.8 The authorising officer must also believe that the authorised use or conduct of a source is proportionate to what is sought to be achieved by that use or conduct.

4.9 The public authorities entitled to authorise the use or conduct of a source are those listed in Schedule 1 to the 2000 Act. Responsibility for authorising the use or conduct of a source rests with the authorising officer and all authorisations require the personal authority of the authorising officer. An authorising officer is the person designated under section 29 of the 2000 Act to grant an authorisation for the use or conduct of a source. The Regulation of Investigatory Powers (Prescriptions of Offices, Ranks and Positions) Order 2000; SI No: 2417 designates the authorising officer for each different public authority and the officers entitled to act only in urgent cases. In certain circumstances the Secretary of State will be the authorising officer (see section 30(2) of the 2000 Act).

4.10 The authorising officer must give authorisations in writing, except that in urgent cases, they may be given orally by the authorising officer or the officer entitled to act in urgent cases. In such cases, a statement that the authorising officer has expressly authorised the action should be recorded in writing by the applicant as soon as is reasonably practicable.

4.11 A case is not normally to be regarded as urgent unless the time that would elapse before the authorising officer was available to grant the authorisation would, in the judgement of the person giving the authorisation, be likely to endanger life or jeopardise the operation or investigation for which the authorisation was being given. An authorisation is not to be regarded as urgent where the need for an authorisation has been neglected or the urgency is of the authorising officer's own making.

4.12 Authorising officers should not be responsible for authorising their own activities, e.g. those in which they, themselves, are to act as the source or in tasking the source. However, it is recognised that this is not always possible, especially in the cases of small organisations. Where an authorising officer authorises his own activity the authorisation record (see paragraphs 2.13–2.15) should highlight this and the attention of a Commissioner or Inspector should be invited to it during his next inspection.

---

[4] This could include investigations into infectious diseases, contaminated products or the illicit sale of pharmaceuticals.

[5] This could only be for a purpose which satisfies the criteria set out in Article 8(2) of the ECHR.

The authorising officers within the police, NCIS and NCS may only grant autho- **4.13**
risations on application by a member of their own force, Service or Squad.
Authorising officers in HMCE may only grant authorisations on application by a
customs officer.[6]

Information to be provided in applications for authorisation

16.19 An application for authorisation for the use or conduct of a source should be in **4.14**
writing and record:

- the reasons why the authorisation is necessary in the particular case and on the
  grounds (e.g. for the purpose of preventing or detecting crime) listed in section
  29(3) of the 2000 Act;
- the reasons why the authorisation is considered proportionate to what it seeks
  to achieve;
- the purpose for which the source will be tasked or deployed (e.g. In relation to
  an organised serious crime, espionage, a series of racially motivated crimes etc);
- where a specific investigation or operation is involved, nature of that investigation or operation;
- the nature of what the source will be tasked to do;
- the level of authority required (or recommended, where that is different).
- the details of any potential collateral intrusion and why the intrusion is justified;
- the details of any confidential information that is likely to be obtained as a consequence of the authorisation; and
- a subsequent record of whether authority was given or refused, by whom and
  the time and date.

Additionally, in urgent cases, the authorisation should record (as the case may be): **4.15**

- the reasons why the authorising officer or the officer entitled to act in urgent
  cases considered the case so urgent that an oral instead of a written authorisation was given; and/or
- the reasons why it was not reasonably practicable for the application to be considered by the authorising officer.

Where the authorisation is oral, the detail referred to above should be recorded in **4.16**
writing by the applicant as soon as reasonably practicable.

Duration of authorisations

16.20 A written authorisation will, unless renewed, cease to have effect at the end of a **4.17**
period of **twelve months** beginning with the day on which it took effect.

---

[6] As defined in section 81(1) of the 2000 Act.

4.18 Urgent oral authorisations or authorisations granted or renewed by a person who is entitled to act only in urgent cases will, unless renewed, cease to have effect after **seventy-two hours**, beginning with the time when the authorisation was granted or renewed.

Reviews

4.19 Regular reviews of authorisations should be undertaken to assess the need for the use of a source to continue. The review should include the use made of the source during the period authorised, the tasks given to the source and the information obtained from the source. The results of a review should be recorded on the authorisation record (see paragraphs 2.13–2.15). Particular attention is drawn to the need to review authorisations frequently where the use of a source provides access to confidential information or involves collateral intrusion.   **16.21**

4.20 In each case the authorising officer within each public authority should determine how often a review should take place. This should be as frequently as is considered necessary and practicable.

Renewals

4.21 Before an authorising officer renews an authorisation, he must be satisfied that a review has been carried out of the use of a source as outlined in paragraph 4.19.   **16.22**

4.22 If at any time before an authorisation would cease to have effect, the authorising officer considers it necessary for the authorisation to continue for the purpose for which it was given, he may renew it in writing for a further period of **twelve months**. Renewals may also be granted orally in urgent cases and last for a period of **seventy-two hours**.

4.23 A renewal takes effect at the time at which, or day on which the authorisation would have ceased to have effect but for the renewal. An application for renewal should not be made until shortly before the authorisation period is drawing to an end. Any person who would be entitled to grant a new authorisation can renew an authorisation. Authorisations may be renewed more than once, if necessary, provided they continue to meet the criteria for authorisation. The renewal should be kept/recorded as part of the authorisation record (see paragraphs 2.13–2.15).

4.24 All applications for the renewal of an authorisation should record:

- whether this is the first renewal or every occasion on which the authorisation has been renewed previously;
- any significant changes to the information in paragraph 4.14;
- the reasons why it is necessary to continue to use the source;

- the use made of the source in the period since the grant or, as the case may be, latest renewal of the authorisation;
- the tasks given to the source during that period and the information obtained from the conduct or use of the source;
- the results of regular reviews of the use of the source;

Cancellations

16.23 The authorising officer who granted or renewed the authorisation must cancel it if **4.25** he is satisfied that the use or conduct of the source no longer satisfies the criteria for authorisation or that satisfactory arrangements for the source's case no longer exist. Where the authorising officer is no longer available, this duty will fall on the person who has taken over the role of authorising officer or the person who is acting as authorising officer (see the Regulation of Investigatory Powers (Cancellation of Authorisations) Order 2000; SI No: 2794). Where necessary, the safety and welfare of the source should continue to be taken into account after the authorisation has been cancelled.

Management of Sources

Tasking

16.24 Tasking is the assignment given to the source by the persons defined at sections **4.26** 29(5)(a) and (b) of the 2000 Act, asking him to obtain information, to provide access to information or to otherwise act, incidentally, for the benefit of the relevant public authority. Authorisation for the use or conduct of a source is required prior to any tasking where such tasking requires the source to establish or maintain a personal or other relationship for a covert purpose.

The person referred to in section 29(5)(a) of the 2000 Act will have day to day **4.27** responsibility for:

— dealing with the source on behalf of the authority concerned;
— directing the day to day activities of the source;
— recording the information supplied by the source; and
— monitoring the source's security and welfare;

The person referred to in section 29(5)(b) of the 2000 Act will be responsible for **4.28** the general oversight of the use of the source.

In some instances, the tasking given to a person will not require the source to estab- **4.29** lish a personal or other relationship for a covert purpose. For example a source may be tasked with finding out purely factual information about the layout of commercial premises. Alternatively, a trading standards officer may be involved in the test purchase of items which have been labelled misleadingly or are unfit for consumption. In such cases, it is for the relevant public authority to determine where, and in what circumstances, such activity may require authorisation.

4.30 It is not the intention that authorisations be drawn so narrowly that a separate authorisation is required each time the source is tasked. Rather, an authorisation might cover, in broad terms, the nature of the source's task. If this changes, then a new authorisation may need to be sought.

4.31 It is difficult to predict exactly what might occur each time a meeting with a source takes place, or the source meets the subject of an investigation. There may be occasions when unforeseen action or undertakings occur. When this happens, the occurrence must be recorded as soon as practicable after the event and, if the existing authorisation is insufficient it should either be updated and reauthorised (for minor amendments only) or it should cancelled and a new authorisation should be obtained before any further such action is carried out.

4.32 Similarly where it is intended to task a source in a new way or significantly greater way than previously identified, the persons defined at section 29(5)(a) or (b) of the 2000 Act must refer the proposed tasking to the authorising officer, who should consider whether a separate authorisation is required. This should be done in advance of any tasking and the details of such referrals must be recorded.

Management responsibility

4.33 Public authorities should ensure that arrangements are in place for the proper oversight and management of sources, including appointing individual officers as defined in section 29(5)(a) and (b) of the 2000 Act for each source. **16.25**

4.34 The person responsible for the day-to-day contact between the public authority and the source will usually be of a rank or position below that of the authorising officer.

4.35 In cases where the authorisation is for the use or conduct of a source whose activities benefit more than a single public authority, responsibilities for the management and oversight of that source may be taken up by one authority or can be split between the authorities.

Security and welfare

4.36 Any public authority deploying a source should take into account the safety and welfare of that source, when carrying out actions in relation to an authorisation or tasking, and to foreseeable consequences to others of that tasking. Before authorising the use or conduct of a source, the authorising officer should ensure that a **16.26**

risk assessment is carried out to determine the risk to the source of any tasking and the likely consequences should the role of the source become known. The ongoing security and welfare of the source, after the cancellation of the authorisation, should also be considered at the outset.

The person defined at section 29(5)(a) of the 2000 Act is responsible for bringing **4.37** to the attention of the person defined at section 29(5)(b) of the 2000 Act any concerns about the personal circumstances of the source, insofar as they might affect:

- the validity of the risk assessment
- the conduct of the source, and
- the safety and welfare of the source.

Where deemed appropriate, concerns about such matters must be considered by **4.38** the authorising officer, and a decision taken on whether or not to allow the authorisation to continue.

Additional Rules

Recording of telephone conversations

16.27 Subject to paragraph 4.40 below, the interception of communications sent by **4.39** post or by means of public telecommunications systems or private telecommunications systems attached to the public network may be authorised only by the Secretary of State, in accordance with the terms of Part I of the 2000 Act. Nothing in this code should be taken as granting dispensation from the requirements of that Part of the 2000 Act.

Part I of the 2000 Act provides certain exceptions to the rule that interception of **4.40** telephone conversations must be warranted under that Part. This includes, where one party to the communication consents to the interception, it may be authorised in accordance with section 48(4) of the 2000 Act provided that there is no interception warrant authorising the interception. In such cases, the interception is treated as directed surveillance (see chapter 4 of the Covert Surveillance code of practice).

Use of covert human intelligence source with technical equipment

16.28 A source, whether or not wearing or carrying a surveillance device and invited into **4.41** residential premises or a private vehicle, does not require additional authorisation to record any activity taking place inside those premises or vehicle which take place in his presence. This also applies to the recording of telephone conversations other than by interception which takes place in the source's presence. Authorisation for the use or conduct of that source may be obtained in the usual way.

4.42 However, if a surveillance device is to be used, other than in the presence of the source, an intrusive surveillance authorisation and if applicable an authorisation for interference with property should be obtained.

5 OVERSIGHT BY COMMISSIONERS

5.1 The 2000 Act requires the Chief Surveillance Commissioner to keep under review **16.29** (with the assistance of the Surveillance Commissioners and Assistant Surveillance Commissioners) the performance of functions under Part III of the 1997 Act and Part II of the 2000 Act by the police (including the Royal Navy Regulating Branch, the Royal Military Police and the Royal Air Force Police and the Ministry of Defence Police and the British Transport Police), NCIS, NCS, HMCE and of the 2000 Act the other public authorities listed in Schedule 1 and in Northern Ireland officials of the Ministry of Defence and HM Forces

5.2 The Intelligence Services Commissioner's remit is to provide independent oversight of the use of the powers contained within Part II of the 2000 Act by the Security Service, Secret Intelligence Service (SIS), the Governments Communication Headquarters (GCHQ) and the Ministry of Defence and HM Forces (excluding the Royal Navy Regulating Branch, the Royal Military Police and the Royal Air Force Police, and in Northern Ireland officials of the Ministry of Defence HM Forces).

5.3 This code does not cover the exercise of any of the Commissioners' functions. It is the duty of any person who uses these powers to comply with any request made by a Commissioner to disclose or provide any information he requires for the purpose of enabling him to carry out his functions.

5.4 References in this code to the performance of review functions by the Chief Surveillance Commissioner and other Commissioners apply also to Inspectors and other members of staff to whom such functions have been delegated.

6 COMPLAINTS

6.1 The 2000 Act establishes an independent Tribunal. This Tribunal will be made up **16.30** of senior members of the judiciary and the legal profession and is independent of the Government. The Tribunal has full powers to investigate and decide any case within its jurisdiction.

This code does not cover the exercise of the Tribunal's functions. Details of the rel- **6.2**
evant complaints procedure can be obtained from the following address:

Investigatory Powers Tribunal
PO Box 33220
London
SW1H 9ZQ
☎ 020 7273 4514

Annex A

Authorisation levels when knowledge of confidential information is likely to be acquired or when a vulnerable individual or juvenile is to be used as a source

Government Department / Public Authority	Authorisation level for when knowledge of Confidential Information is likely to be acquired	Authorisation level for when a vulnerable individual or a Juvenile is to be used as a source
Police Forces—Any police force maintained under section 2 of the Police Act 1996 (police forces in England and Wales outside London).	Chief Constable	Assistant Chief Constable
Police Forces—Any police force maintained under or by virtue of section 1 of the Police (Scotland) Act 1967.	Chief Constable	Assistant Chief Constable
The Metropolitan Police Force	Assistant Commissioner	Commander
The City of London Police Force	Commissioner	Commander
The Police Service of Northern Ireland	Deputy Chief Constable	Assistant Chief Constable
The Royal Navy Regulating Branch	Provost Marshal	Provost Marshal
Royal Military Police	Provost Marshal	Provost Marshal
Royal Air Force Police	Provost Marshal	Provost Marshal
National Criminal Intelligence Service (NCIS)	Director General	Assistant Chief Constable or Assistant Chief Investigation Officer
National Crime Squad (NCS)	Director General or Deputy Director General	Assistant Chief Constable
Serious Fraud Office	Director or Assistant Director	Director or Assistant Director
The Intelligence Services:		
Government Communications Headquarters	A Director of GCHQ	A Director of GCHQ
Security Service	Deputy Director General	Deputy Director General
Secret Intelligence Service	A Director of the Secret Intelligence Service	A member of the Secret Intelligence Service not below the equivalent rank to that of a Grade 5 in the Home Civil Service)

Government Department / Public Authority	Authorisation level for when knowledge of Confidential Information is likely to be acquired	Authorisation level for when a vulnerable individual or a Juvenile is to be used as a source
HM Forces: Royal Navy	Rear Admiral	Rear Admiral
Army	Major General	Major General
Royal Air Force	Air-Vice Marshall	Air-Vice Marshall
HM Customs and Excise	Director Investigation or Regional Heads of Investigation	Band 11 (Intelligence)
Inland Revenue	Deputy Chairman of Inland Revenue	Head of Special Compliance Office
Department for the Environment, Food and Rural Affairs:		
DEFRA Investigation Branch	Immediate Senior Officer of Head of DEFRA Prosecution Division	Head of DEFRA Prosecution Division
Horticultural Marketing Inspectorate	Immediate Senior Officer of Head of DEFRA Prosecution Division	No
Plant Health and Seed Inspectorate	Immediate Senior Officer of Head of DEFRA Prosecution Division	No
Egg Marketing Inspectorate	Immediate Senior Officer of Head of DEFRA Prosecution Division	No
Sea Fisheries Inspectorate (SFI)	Immediate Senior Officer of Head of DEFRA Prosecution Division	No
Centre for Environment, Fisheries & Aquaculture Science (CEFAS)	Immediate Senior Officer of Head of DEFRA Prosecution Division	Head of DEFRA Prosecution Division
Ministry of Defence	Director General or equivalent	Director General or equivalent
Department for Transport, Local Government and the Regions: Vehicle Inspectorate	No	No
Transport Security (Transec)	Director of Transport Security	Deputy Director of Transport Security

Government Department / Public Authority	Authorisation level for when knowledge of Confidential Information is likely to be acquired	Authorisation level for when a vulnerable individual or a Juvenile is to be used as a source
Department of Health: Medical Devices Agency	Chief Executive	No
Medicine Control Agency	Chief Executive	Head of Division for Inspection and Enforcement
Medicine Control Agency	Chief Executive	
Welfare Foods Policy Unit	Deputy Chief Medical Officer	No
Directorate of Counter Fraud Services (DFCS)	Director of Counter Fraud Services	Director of Counter Fraud Services
Home Office: HM Prison Service	Deputy Director General	Area Managers
Immigration Service	Chief Inspector	Director
Department of Work and Pensions:		
Benefits Agency	Chief Executive	Head of Fraud Investigation
Department of Trade and Industry: Radiocommunications Agency	No	No
British Trade International	No	No
Coal Health Claims Unit	Director of Coal Health Claims unit	No
Companies Investigation Branch	The Inspector of Companies	The Inspector of Companies
Legal Services Directorate D	The Director of Legal Service D	The Director of Legal Service D
National Assembly for Wales	Health—Director, NHS Wales	Health—Director, NHS Wales
	Agriculture—Head, National Assembly for Wales Agriculture Department	Agriculture—Head, National Assembly for Wales Agriculture Department
Local Authorities	The Head of Paid Service or (in his absence) a Chief Officer	The Head of Paid Service or (in his absence) a Chief Officer
Environment Agency	Chief Executive	Executive Managers

Government Department / Public Authority	Authorisation level for when knowledge of Confidential Information is likely to be acquired	Authorisation level for when a vulnerable individual or a Juvenile is to be used as a source
Financial Services Authority	Chairman	Chairman
Food Standards Agency	Head of Group, Deputy Chief Executive and Chief Executive	Head of Group, Deputy Chief Executive and Chief Executive
The Intervention Board for Agricultural Produce	Chief Executive	Legal Director
Personal Investment Authority	Chairman	Chairman
Post Office	Director of Security	Head of Corporate Security/Head of Security for the Royal Mail/Head of Security for Counter Business

17

VOLUNTARY RETENTION OF COMMUNICATIONS DATA CODE OF PRACTICE[1,2] UNDER PART II: ANTI-TERRORISM, CRIME AND SECURITY ACT 2001 (UNDER SI 2003 NO 3175)

Foreword

17.01 The Anti-Terrorism, Crime & Security Act was passed in December 2001 (the Act). Part 11 of the Act aims to allow for the retention of communications data to ensure that the UK security, intelligence and law enforcement agencies have sufficient information available to them to assist them in protecting the UK's national security and to investigate terrorism.

Communications data are retained by the communications service providers to enable them to carry out their business effectively. Such information could be divided into three broad categories these being subscriber information (identifies user); traffic data (identifies whom was called etc); and use made of service (identifies what services are used). The Act recognises that communications data are an essential tool for the security, intelligence and law enforcement agencies in carrying out their work to safeguard United Kingdom national security. These agencies, which are authorised to acquire communications data under statutory provisions, would be greatly assisted if they could rely on the communications data being available when they required it.

---

[1] This Code of Practice came into force on 5 December 2003 by virtue of the Retention of Communications Data (Code of Practice) Order 2003 (SI 2003 No 3175) the relevant regulation of which read '2. The draft code of practice entitled "Voluntary Retention of Communications Data under Part 11: Anti-terrorism, Crime and Security Act 2001-Voluntary Code of Practice", . . . shall come into force on the day after the day on which this Order is made.'

[2] The text here is a re-typeset version of the text promulgated by the Home Office and HMSO but omits Appendix B and the annex (produced by a non-Government third party) which was attached to the official version. Readers are directed to the Home Office Website for the full text.

Part 11 of the Act provides only for the retention of data that communication service providers already retain for business purposes. Its object is not to enlarge the fields of data which a communication service provider may (or must) retain, but to encourage communication service providers to retain that data for longer than they would otherwise need to do so for their own commercial purposes. The Act identifies that the purpose of the retention period is the safeguarding of national security or for the prevention or detection of crime or the prosecution of offences which relate directly or indirectly to national security.

This Code of Practice relates specifically to the need for communications service providers to retain data for extended periods of time in order to assist the security, intelligence and law enforcement agencies in carrying out their work of safeguarding national security or in the prevention or detection of crime or the prosecution of offences which relate directly or indirectly to national security.

This Code of Practice does not address issues relating to disclosure of data, it simply addresses the issues of what types of data can be retained and for how long it will be retained beyond a particular company's existing business practice. The Code explains why communications service providers have the ability to retain data beyond their normal business purposes for the reasons outlined in the Act.

Communications data may be obtained by security, intelligence and law enforcement agencies under the Regulation of Investigatory Powers Act 2000 and other statutory powers.

This Code does not deal with these provisions.

The Data Protection Act 1998 requires that personal data are processed lawfully. In retaining communications data for longer than needed for their own business purposes and for the purposes identified in the Act communication service providers will process personal data. The Information Commissioner's Office (ICO) has accepted that such processing will not, on human rights grounds, contravene this requirement of the Act.

However, individual communication service providers must satisfy themselves that the processing is "necessary" for one of a range of functions. In doing so they are entitled to rely heavily on the Secretary of State's assurance that the retention of communications data for the periods as specified in this Code is necessary for the government's function of safeguarding national security, and on the fact that the Code has been approved by Parliament.

The ICO has though expressed concern about such retained data being acquired for purposes that do not relate to national security. Acquisition of communications data is not addressed in the Act and therefore is not within the proper ambit of this Code.

CONTENTS

Purpose of the Code

17.02 1. In section 102 of the Act,[3] Parliament has given the Secretary of State the power to issue a Code of Practice relating to the retention of communications data by communication service providers. This Code of Practice is intended to outline how communication service providers can assist in the fight against terrorism by meeting agreed time periods for retention of communications data that may be extended beyond those periods for which their individual company currently retains data for business purposes.

2. After consultation with the security, intelligence and law enforcement agencies, the Secretary of State has determined that retention of communications data by communication service providers in line with the Appendix to this Code of Practice is necessary for the purposes set out in section 102(3) of the Act, namely; (a) the purposes of safeguarding national security (b) the purposes of prevention or detection of crime or the prosecution of offenders which may relate directly or indirectly to national security.

3. The Code of Practice is intended to ensure that communication service providers may retain data for the two purposes identified at 2 a & b, after the need for retention for business purposes has elapsed and there is otherwise an obligation to erase or anonymise retained data. It does not provide guidance on the manner in which data retained for these purposes should be processed; nor does the Secretary of State consider it necessary to impose new standards on the conditions in which the data are stored, e.g. technical media, security, ease of access, indexing or other.

4. The Code does not relate to the powers of public authorities to obtain communications data retained in accordance with the Appendix to the Code. Acquisition of communications data is provided for by Chapter II of Part I of the Regulation of Investigatory Powers Act 2000, as well as other relevant statutory powers. See paragraphs 25 to 28.

---

[3] Editorial note: The Act referred to is the Anti-Terrorism, Crime and Security Act 2001.

Human rights and data protection considerations

5. This Code has been drawn up in accordance with existing legislation, including the Human Rights Act 1998, and the Data Protection Act 1998, and the Telecommunications (Data Protection and Privacy) Regulations 1999, together with their parent directives.

6. Data retained under the Code are subject to the data protection principles found in the Data Protection Act 1998. Under the first data protection principle personal data may only be processed if at least one of the conditions in Schedule 2 to the 1998 Act is met. The processing of data retained under this Code falls within paragraph 5 of Schedule 2 of the Data Protection Act 1998 in that it is necessary for the communication service provider to retain data to enable the Secretary of State to fulfil his function for the protection of national security. Some communications data may in certain circumstances constitute sensitive personal data.

Processing of such data is permitted by virtue of Schedule 3, paragraph 7 of the 1998 Act.

7. Data retained under the Code will, at least for a certain period, be data that are needed by the communication service provider for business purposes. Its processing will therefore initially be undertaken for a dual purpose: (a) business purposes, (b) national security purposes, where "national security purposes" includes both the purposes set out in section 102(3) of the Act. Since both purposes of retention will apply to all data simultaneously during the 'business purpose time period, there is no need for separate storage systems for "business data" and "national security data" under this dual-purpose scheme.

However, once an individual company has exceeded the business purpose time period then data will be retained specifically for the purposes described in Section 102(3) of the Act. The system deployed by individual companies will need to identify that the data has exceeded the business purpose time period. Individual communication service providers will need to ensure that they do not access those data for their own purposes. At the end of the retention period necessary for 'business purposes' the only data that a communication service provider should retain are that data identified in the 'Technical Specification' attached as Appendix A to this Code.

8. The fifth data protection principle provides that personal data processed for any purpose or purposes shall not be kept for any longer than is necessary for that purpose or those purposes. The periods for which it appears necessary to the Secretary of State for communication service providers to retain communications data for national security purposes are those set out in Appendix A. The periods for which it is necessary for communication service providers to retain communications data for business purposes is a matter for each communication service provider, and they might be longer or shorter than the retention

periods the Secretary of State has set out are necessary for national security. Compliance with the fifth data protection principle under the dual-purpose scheme requires that after the expiry of the shorter of these two periods, communications data may only be retained further for the period required by the remaining purpose. When the retention periods for both purposes have expired, the data must be either anonymised or erased.

9. As indicated the Secretary of State considers the retention of data in accordance with Appendix A to be necessary for the purpose of national security and accordingly retention for those periods should comply with the fifth data protection principle. However, because the purpose of retention is to safeguard national security were it to be suggested that retention in accordance with this Code did not comply with the fifth principle, the national security exemption in s 28 of the Data Protection Act 1998 could be relied on to exempt such data from the fifth principle so enabling it to be retained in accordance with the Code. If necessary the Secretary of State would issue a certificate under s 28.2 confirming the same.

10. The data subject access provisions set out in the Data Protection Act 1998 continue to apply to communications data retained under this Code, that is to say that data subjects may request access to their personal data whether it is held for national security purposes or for the communication service provider's business purposes. In addition, subscribers should be notified where their personal data will be retained for the purpose of the Act, as well as for the communication service providers business purposes, and that it may be disclosed to relevant public authorities, as set out in paragraph 27 of this Code. Every effort should be made to ensure that this is brought to the attention of the subscriber for example this could be added to billing information or sent by way of text message or e-mail.

NB. Communication service providers will need to ensure that their entry in the register of data controllers maintained by the Information Commissioner describes the processing of personal data involved in retention of communications data for the national security purposes. The Information Commissioner's advice is that they should notify that they are processing for the following purpose:

> *"NATIONAL SECURITY:– Retention of communications data for the purpose of safeguarding national security or for the purposes of prevention or detection of crime or the prosecution of offenders which may relate directly or indirectly to national security".*

This is not one of the standard purpose descriptions that the Information Commissioner provides so communication service providers will need to complete it in full, together with details of the associated data subjects, classes and recipients, when they apply to add a new purpose to their existing notification.

11. The retention specification set out in Appendix A to this Code has been drafted taking into account a number of factors, including the right to respect for private life under Article 8 of the European Convention of Human Rights. The Secretary of State considers the retention periods set out in Appendix A to be both necessary and proportionate in light of the individual's right to respect for private life and the national security purposes for which the retention of data is required.

Jurisdiction and types of operators covered by the Code of Practice

12. The Code of Practice applies to all communication service providers who, provide a public telecommunications service in the United Kingdom as defined in section 2 of the Regulation of Investigatory Powers Act 2000, and who retain communications data in line with the provisions of the Act. The Secretary of State considers it necessary for the national security purposes outlined in the Act, for communications data held by communication service providers, which relates to subscribers resident in the UK or subscribing to or using a UK-based service, to be retained in accordance with the provisions of the Code, whether the data are generated or processed in the UK or abroad. However, if data relating to a service provided in the UK are stored in a foreign jurisdiction it may be subject to conflicting legal requirements prohibiting the retention of data in accordance with this Code. In such cases, it is accepted that it may not be possible to adhere to the terms of this Code in respect of that communications data. **17.04**

13. The data categories and retention periods in the Appendix to this Code have been determined with regard to considerations of necessity and proportionality. The data categories and retention periods relate to communications data generated and retained by communication service providers who provide a service to the general public in the United Kingdom. This Code is not intended to apply to individuals or organisations who do not provide such a public service (e.g. private networks).

14. In some cases, two or more legal entities may be involved in the provision of a public telecommunications service, e.g. backbone/virtual service provider model. In such cases, the provisions of this Code apply to data retained by each legal entity for their own business purposes.

Types of data and retention periods

15. Communications data can be divided into three broad categories, corresponding to the definitions in section 21(4) of the Regulation of Investigatory Powers Act 2000, which can be summarised as follows: **17.05**
    a) **traffic data**—including telephone numbers called, email addresses, and location data etc;
    b) **use made of service**—including services subscribed to, etc;
    c) **other information relating to the subscriber**—including installation address, etc.

"*communications data*" as defined by RIPA means any of the following:
>   (i) any traffic data comprised in or attached to a communication (whether by the sender or otherwise) for the purposes of any postal service or telecommunication system by means of which it is being or may be transmitted;
>   (ii) any information which includes none of the contents of a communication [apart from any information falling within paragraph (i)] and is about the use made by any person:
>>   (1) of any telecommunications service; or
>>   (2) in connection with the provision to or use by any person of any telecommunications service, of any part of a telecommunication system.
> (iii) any information not falling within paragraph (i) or (ii) that is held or obtained, in relation to persons to whom he provides the service, by a person providing a telecommunications service.

"*traffic data*", as defined by the Regulation of Investigatory Powers Act 2000 in relation to any communication, means:
>   (i) any data identifying, or purporting to identify, any person, apparatus or location to or from which the communication is or may be transmitted;
>   (ii) any data identifying or selecting, or purporting to identify or select, apparatus through which, or by means of which, the communication is or may be transmitted;
> (iii) any data comprising signals for the actuation of apparatus used for the purposes of a telecommunication system for effecting (in whole or in part) the transmission of any communication; and
>   (iv) any data identifying the data or other data as data comprised in or attached to a particular communication, but that expression includes data identifying a computer file or computer program access to which is obtained, or which is run, by means of the communication to the extent only that the file or program is identified by reference to the apparatus in which it is stored.

References, in relation to traffic data comprising signals for the actuation of apparatus, to a telecommunication system by means of which a communication is being or may be transmitted include references to any telecommunication system in which that apparatus is comprised; and references to traffic data being attached to a communication include references to the data and the communication being logically associated with each other.

16. The maximum retention period for data held under the provisions of this Code is 12 months, without prejudice to any longer retention period which may be justified by the business practices of the communication service provider.
17. For data categories 15(a) and 15 (b) above the period of retention begins at the point when the call ends, for subscriber-related data category 15 (c) the period of retention begins when the data are changed or subscriber leaves the service.

18. The retention periods given in Appendix A recognise that types of communications data, as personal data, vary with respect both to their usefulness to the agencies, and to their sensitivity. It is recognised that the usefulness of different types of communications data for the purpose of safeguarding national security will vary and this is reflected in the different retention periods.

19. The data categories listed in Appendix A will not all be relevant to every communication service provider. Whether or not a data type will be relevant to a communication service provider and therefore retained will depend on the services which it provides, for example, an internet service provider will not retain IMEI data. Communication service providers will not be expected to retain additional categories of data to those which they routinely retain for business purposes. In other words if a data type is not already captured for the business purposes of an individual company then there will be no expectation that this data type is retained for the purposes of the Act.

Agreements

20. The Secretary of State may enter into agreements with individual communication service providers who receive requests for communications data stored under these provisions. The purpose of these agreements is to communicate the retention practices of those communication service provider to public authorities listed in Chapter II of Part I of the Regulation of Investigatory Powers Act 2000. **17.06**

They will play the role of Service Level Agreements (SLAs) and will include any arrangements for payments to cover retention costs. These SLAs will be based on an open document outlining the agreement between the Secretary of State and the company concerned.

Each of these will differ with respect to the appendices which will outline the services that a particular provider is able to deliver. Those parts of these agreements that do not contain commercially sensitive material will be publicly available. The appendices will remain commercially sensitive.

21. The agreements will be drafted within the framework provided by this Code. An agreement may not set a retention period for any type of data which is greater than the period set out in Appendix A to this Code.

22. Any agreement will be made between the Secretary of State and the communication service provider and must be entered into voluntarily by both sides. It may be terminated by either side subject to a period of notice set out in the agreement.

Costs arrangements

23. Where the period of retention of data for national security purposes is not substantially larger than the period of retention for business purposes, the retention costs will continue to be borne by the communication service provider. **17.07**

24. Where data retention periods are significantly longer for national security purposes than for business purposes, the Secretary of State will contribute a reasonable proportion of the marginal cost as appropriate. Marginal costs may include, for example, the design and production of additional storage and searching facilities. This may be in the form of capital investment into retention and retrieval equipment or may include running costs.

Acquisition of data retained under the terms of this Code of Practice

17.08   25. It is outside of the scope of this Code of Practice to address the issue of acquisition of data after it has been retained. It can only address the issue of retention of data for the purposes of the Act. The Act establishes the framework for communication service providers to retain data for the purposes of safeguarding national security and for the prevention or detection of crime and prosecution of offenders which may relate directly or indirectly to national security.

26. The Code sets out a retention specification which is designed to meet the two aims set out above, both relating to national security. That is to say that any particular piece of data is retained because it belongs to a certain data type, and it is necessary to retain all data of that type for the purpose of safeguarding national security or for the purpose of the prevention or detection of crime or the prosecution of offenders which may relate directly or indirectly to national security.

27. The retention of such data is necessary so that it is available to be acquired by relevant public authorities under Chapter II of Part I of the Regulation of Investigatory Powers Act 2000, or otherwise, to assist them in safeguarding national security. However, whilst restrictions exist elsewhere, this Code cannot itself place restrictions on the ability of these bodies or other persons to acquire data retained under the Code for other purposes through the exercise of any statutory power. In particular, this Code cannot place any restrictions on the ability of the public authorities listed in Chapter II of Part I of the Regulation of Investigatory Powers Act 2000 to acquire data retained under this Code for any of the purposes set out in section 22 of that Act which do not relate to national security.

28. In addition data access requests can also be received from data subjects under the Data Protection Act 1998 and from civil litigants.

Oversight mechanism

17.09   29. The retention of communications data is a form of personal data processing. As such, it is subject to the Data Protection Act 1998. Oversight of the 1998 Act is by the Information Commissioner.

Transitional arrangements

30. All data collected after the communication service provider adopts the Code **17.10** should be processed in accordance with both the national security purposes and the business purposes from the point that it is generated. Data already held by the communication service providers at the time of adopting the Code will be processed only in accordance with the purpose for which it was originally collected.

31. Subscribers should be notified of the new purpose for which data is being retained. This may be done by sending out a general notification to all customers. The national security purpose must be made clear to any new subscribers at the time they subscribe.

32. During the period of time that a communications service provider is building the technical capacity to extend retention of specified data beyond their normal business time periods, the company's standard retention practice takes precedence. Once the individual communication service provider has the technical capacity to retain data for the extended time periods set out in this voluntary Code of Practice, then the communication service provider shall inform existing and new customers that the purpose for retention and the periods of retention have been varied to meet with the needs of the Act. Only after this information has been passed on to existing customers and new customers can the communication service provider then retain the data for the extended time periods for the purposes of national security. There may be a period after the communication service provider has adopted the Code when he cannot retain data for the full period set out in Appendix A owing to the need to introduce technical adaptations. The agreement with the communication service provider will set out how long it will take to reach full compliance.

Criteria for assessing the effectiveness of the Code of Practice

33. The Code will be reviewed three months from the date when it first receives **17.11** parliamentary approval, in accordance with the following criteria:
    (i) has it improved investigative work?
    (ii) how many request for data have been made?
    (iii) is the voluntary system working?
    (iv) what percentage of the market is covered by communication service providers who have adopted the Code of Practice?
    (v) are sectors of the industry which have not adopted the Code enjoying an unfair commercial advantage?

The SLAs introduced under this Code will require communication service providers to keep records of all enquiries made for data retained under the Act from the date an individual service provider enters into a voluntary agreement with the Secretary of State, in order to enable a comprehensive survey to be undertaken.

APPENDIX A

Data retention: expansion of data categories

SUBSCRIBER INFORMATION   **12 months**
(From end of subscription/last change)

Subscriber details relating to the person
e.g. Name, date of birth, installation and billing address, payment methods, account/credit card details

Contact information (information held about the subscriber but not verified by the CSP)
e.g. Telephone number, email address

Identity of services subscribed to (information determined by the communication service provider)
Customer reference/account number, list of services subscribed to

Telephony:	telephone number(s), IMEI, IMSI(s)
Email:	email address(es), IP at registration
Instant messaging:	Internet Message Handle, IP at registration
ISP—dial-in:	Log-in, CLI at registration (if kept)
ISP—always-on:	Unique identifiers, MAC address (if kept), ADSL end points, IP tunnel address

TELEPHONY DATA   **12 months**
All numbers (or other identifiers e.g. name@bt) associated with call (e.g. physical/presentational/network assigned CLI, DNI, IMSI, IMEI, exchange/divert numbers)
Date and time of start of call
Duration of call/date and time of end of call
Type of call (if available)
Location data at start and/or end of call, in form of lat/long reference.
Cell site data from time cell ceases to be used.
IMSI/MSISDN/IMEI mappings.
For GPRS & 3G, date and time of connection, IMSI, IP address assigned.
Mobile data exchanged with foreign operators; IMSI & MSISDN, sets of GSM triples, sets of 3G quintuples, global titles of equipment communicating with or about the subscriber.

SMS, EMS and MMS DATA   **6 months**
Calling number, IMEI
Called number, IMEI
Date and time of sending
Delivery receipt—if available
Location data when messages sent and received, in form of lat/long reference.

EMAIL DATA   **6 months**
Log-on (authentication user name, date and time of log-in/log-off, IP address logged-in from)
Sent email (authentication user name, from/to/cc email addresses, date and time sent)
Received email (authentication user name, from/to email addresses, date and time received)

ISP DATA   **6 months**

Log-on (authentication user name, date and time of log-in/log-off, IP address assigned)
Dial-up: CLI and number dialled
Always-on: ADSL end point/MAC address (If available)

WEB ACTIVITY LOGS   **4 days**

Proxy server logs (date/time, IP address used, URL's visited, services)
The data types here will be restricted **solely to Communications Data and exclude content of communication**. This will mean that storage under this code can only take place to the level of www.homeoffice.gov.uk/ . . . .

OTHER SERVICES

Retention relative to service provided
Instant Message Type Services (log-on/off time) If available.

COLLATERAL DATA

Retention relative to data to which it is related
Data needed to interpret other communications data for example—the mapping between cell mast identifiers and their location—translation of dialling (as supported by IN networks)

Notes:
All times should include an indication of which time zone is being used (Universal Co-ordinated Time is preferred).
An indication should also be given of the accuracy of the timing.
To assist in the interpretation of Internet terminology the Home Office have, with the permission of the Internet Crime Forum, reproduced at Appendix D the document written by the Data Retention Project Group of the Internet Crime Forum.[4]
The Home Office recognises the effort that has gone into producing this document and would thank all those responsible for its production.

---

[4] Not reproduced in this work.

18

INTERCEPTION OF COMMUNICATIONS CODE OF PRACTICE 2002 (UNDER SI 2002 NO 1693)[1]

Pursuant to Section 71 of the Regulation of Investigatory Powers Act 2000

---

[1] The text of this Code of Practice is taken from the version published by the Home Office and made under the Regulation of Investigatory Powers (Interception of Communications: Code of Practice) Order 2002 (SI 2002 No 1693) which came into force on 1 July 2002.

1 GENERAL

1.1 This code of practice relates to the powers and duties conferred or imposed under   **18.01**
Chapter I of Part I of the Regulation of Investigatory Powers Act 2000 ("the Act").
It provides guidance on the procedures that must be followed before interception of
communications can take place under those provisions. It is primarily intended for
use by those public authorities listed in section 6(2) of the Act. It will also prove useful to postal and telecommunication operators and other interested bodies to
acquaint themselves with the procedures to be followed by those public authorities.

1.2 The Act provides that all codes of practice relating to the Act are admissible as evidence in criminal and civil proceedings. If any provision of this code appears relevant before any court or tribunal considering any such proceedings, or to the
Tribunal established under the Act, or to one of the Commissioners responsible
for overseeing the powers conferred by the Act, it must be taken into account.

2 GENERAL RULES ON INTERCEPTION
WITH A WARRANT

2.1 There are a limited number of persons by whom, or on behalf of whom, applic-   **18.02**
ations for interception warrants may be made. These persons are:

- The Director-General of the Security Service.
- The Chief of the Secret Intelligence Service.
- The Director of GCHQ.
- The Director-General of the National Criminal Intelligence Service (NCIS
  handle interception on behalf of police forces in England and Wales).
- The Commissioner of the Police of the Metropolis (the Metropolitan Police
  Special Branch handle interception on behalf of Special Branches in England
  and Wales).
- The Chief Constable of the Police Service of Northern Ireland.
- The Chief Constable of any police force maintained under or by virtue of sec-
  tion 1 of the Police (Scotland) Act 1967
- The Commissioners of Customs and Excise.
- The Chief of Defence Intelligence.

A person who, for the purposes of any international mutual assistance agreement,
is the competent authority of a country or territory outside the United Kingdom.

Any application made on behalf of one of the above must be made by a person holding office under the Crown.

All interception warrants are issued by the Secretary of State. Even where the **2.2** urgency procedure is followed, the Secretary of State personally authorises the warrant, although it is signed by a senior official.

Before issuing an interception warrant, the Secretary of State must believe that what **2.3** the action seeks to achieve is necessary for one of the following section 5(3) purposes:

- in the interests of national security;
- for the purpose of preventing or detecting serious crime; or
- for the purpose of safeguarding the economic well-being of the UK

and that the conduct authorised by the warrant is proportionate to what is sought to be achieved by that conduct.

Necessity and proportionality

18.03 Obtaining a warrant under the Act will only ensure that the interception autho- **2.4** rised is a justifiable interference with an individual's rights under Article 8 of the European Convention of Human Rights (the right to privacy) if it is necessary and proportionate for the interception to take place. The Act recognises this by first requiring that the Secretary of State believes that the authorisation is necessary on one or more of the statutory grounds set out in section 5(3) of the Act. This requires him to believe that it is necessary to undertake the interception which is to be authorised for a particular purpose falling within the relevant statutory ground.

Then, if the interception is necessary, the Secretary of State must also believe that **2.5** it is proportionate to what is sought to be achieved by carrying it out. This involves balancing the intrusiveness of the interference, against the need for it in operational terms. Interception of communications will not be proportionate if it is excessive in the circumstances of the case or if the information which is sought could reasonably be obtained by other means. Further, all interception should be carefully managed to meet the objective in question and must not be arbitrary or unfair.

Implementation of warrants

18.04 After a warrant has been issued it will be forwarded to the person to whom it is **2.6** addressed, in practice the intercepting agency which submitted the application. The Act (section 11) then permits the intercepting agency to carry out the interception, or to require the assistance of other persons in giving effect to the warrant. Warrants cannot be served on those outside the jurisdiction of the UK.

Provision of reasonable assistance

2.7 Any postal or telecommunications operator (referred to as communications service   **18.05** providers) in the United Kingdom may be required to provide assistance in giving effect to an interception. The Act places a requirement on postal and telecommunications operators to take all such steps for giving effect to the warrant as are notified to them (section 11(4) of the Act). But the steps which may be required are limited to those which it is reasonably practicable to take (section 11(5)). What is reasonably practicable should be agreed after consultation between the postal or telecommunications operator and the Government. If no agreement can be reached it will be for the Secretary of State to decide whether to press forward with civil proceedings. Criminal proceedings may also be instituted by or with the consent of the Director of Public Prosecutions.

2.8 Where the intercepting agency requires the assistance of a communications service provider in order to implement a warrant, they should provide the following to the communications service provider:

- A copy of the warrant instrument signed and dated by the Secretary of State (or in an urgent case, by a senior official);
- The relevant schedule for that service provider setting out the numbers, addresses or other factors identifying the communications to be intercepted;
- A covering document from the intercepting agency requiring the assistance of the communications service provider and specifying any other details regarding the means of interception and delivery as may be necessary. Contact details with respect to the intercepting agency will either be provided in this covering document or will be available in the handbook provided to all postal and telecommunications operators who maintain an intercept capability.

Provision of intercept capability

2.9 Whilst all persons who provide a postal or telecommunications service are obliged   **18.06** to provide assistance in giving effect to an interception, persons who provide a public postal or telecommunications service, or plan to do so, may also be required to provide a reasonable intercept capability. The obligations the Secretary of State considers reasonable to impose on such persons to ensure they have such a capability will be set out in an order made by the Secretary of State and approved by Parliament. The Secretary of State may then serve a notice upon a communications service provider setting out the steps they must take to ensure they can meet these obligations. A notice will not be served without consultation over the content of the notice between the Government and the service provider having previously taken place. When served with such a notice, a communications service provider, if he feels it unreasonable, will be able to refer that notice to the Technical Advisory Board (TAB) on the reasonableness of the technical requirements and capabilities that are being sought. Details of how to submit a notice to the TAB will be provided either before or at the time the notice is served.

2.10 Any communications service provider obliged to maintain a reasonable intercept capability will be provided with a handbook which will contain the basic information they require to respond to requests for reasonable assistance for the interception of communications.

Duration of interception warrants

18.07 **2.11** All interception warrants are valid for an initial period of three months. Upon renewal, warrants issued on serious crime grounds are valid for a further period of three months. Warrants renewed on national security/economic well-being grounds are valid for a further period of six months. Urgent authorisations are valid for five working days following the date of issue unless renewed by the Secretary of State.

2.12 Where modifications take place, the warrant expiry date remains unchanged. However, where the modification takes place under the urgency provisions, the modification instrument expires after five working days following the date of issue unless renewed following the routine procedure.

2.13 Where a change in circumstance prior to the set expiry date leads the intercepting agency to consider it no longer necessary or practicable for the warrant to be in force, it should be cancelled with immediate effect.

Stored communications

18.08 **2.14** Section 2(7) of the Act defines a communication in the course of its transmission as also encompassing any time when the communication is being stored on the communication system in such a way as to enable the intended recipient to have access to it. This means that a warrant can be used to obtain both communications that are in the process of transmission and those that are being stored on the transmission system.

2.15 Stored communications may also be accessed by means other than a warrant. If a communication has been stored on a communication system it may be obtained with lawful authority by means of an existing statutory power such as a production order (under the Police and Criminal Evidence Act 1984) or a search warrant.

3 SPECIAL RULES ON INTERCEPTION WITH A WARRANT

Collateral intrusion

3.1 Consideration should be given to any infringement of the privacy of individuals **18.09** who are not the subject of the intended interception, especially where communications relating to religious, medical, journalistic or legally privileged material may be involved. An application for an interception warrant should draw attention to any circumstances which give rise to an unusual degree of collateral infringement of privacy, and this will be taken into account by the Secretary of State when considering a warrant application. Should an interception operation reach the point where individuals other than the subject of the authorisation are identified as directly relevant to the operation, consideration should be given to applying for seperate warrants covering those individuals.

3.2 Particular consideration should also be given in cases where the subject of the interception might reasonably assume a high degree of privacy, or where confidential information is involved. Confidential information consists of matters subject to legal privilege, confidential personal information or confidential journalistic material (see paragraphs 3.9–3.11). For example, extra consideration should be given where interception might involve communications between a minister of religion and an individual relating to the latter's spiritual welfare, or where matters of medical or journalistic confidentiality or legal privilege may be involved.

Communications subject to legal privilege

3.3 Section 98 of the Police Act 1997 describes those matters that are subject to legal priv- **18.10** ilege in England and Wales. In relation to Scotland, those matters subject to legal privilege contained in section 33 of the Criminal Law (Consolidation) (Scotland) Act 1995 should be adopted. With regard to Northern Ireland, Article 12 of the Police and Criminal Evidence (Northern Ireland) Order 1989 should be referred to.

3.4 Legal privilege does not apply to communications made with the intention of furthering a criminal purpose (whether the lawyer is acting unwittingly or culpably). Legally privileged communications will lose their protection if there are grounds to believe, for example, that the professional legal advisor is intending to hold or use the information for a criminal purpose. But privilege is not lost if a professional legal advisor is properly advising a person who is suspected of having committed a criminal offence. The concept of legal privilege applies to the provision of professional legal advice by any individual, agency or organisation qualified to do so.

The Act does not provide any special protection for legally privileged commun- **3.5** ications. Nevertheless, intercepting such communications is particularly sensitive and is therefore subject to additional safeguards under this Code. The guidance set out below may in part depend on whether matters subject to legal privilege have been obtained intentionally or incidentally to some other material which has been sought.

In general, any application for a warrant which is likely to result in the interception of **3.6** legally privileged communications should include, in addition to the reasons why it is considered necessary for the interception to take place, an assessment of how likely it is that communications which are subject to legal privilege will be intercepted.

In addition, it should state whether the purpose (or one of the purposes) of the interception is to obtain privileged communications. This assessment will be taken into account by the Secretary of State in deciding whether an interception is necessary under section 5(3) of the Act and whether it is proportionate. In such circumstances, the Secretary of State will be able to impose additional conditions such as regular reporting arrangements so as to be able to exercise his discretion on whether a warrant should continue to be authorised. In those cases where communications which include legally privileged communications have been intercepted and retained, the matter should be reported to the Interception of Communications Commissioner during his inspections and the material be made available to him if requested.

Where a lawyer is the subject of an interception, it is possible that a substantial **3.7** proportion of the communications which will be intercepted will be between the lawyer and his client(s) and will be subject to legal privilege. Any case where a lawyer is the subject of an investigation should be notified to the Interception of Communications Commissioner during his inspections and any material which has been retained should be made available to him if requested.

In addition to safeguards governing the handling and retention of intercept material **3.8** as provided for in section 15 of the Act, caseworkers who examine intercepted communications should be alert to any intercept material which may be subject to legal privilege. Where there is doubt as to whether the communications are subject to legal privilege, advice should be sought from a legal adviser within the intercepting agency.

Similar advice should also be sought where there is doubt over whether communications are not subject to legal privilege due to the "in furtherance of a criminal purpose" exception.

Communications involving confidential personal information and confidential journalistic material

18.11 Similar consideration to that given to legally privileged communications must **3.9** also be given to the interception of communications that involve confidential personal information and confidential journalistic material. Confidential personal information is information held in confidence concerning an individual (whether living or dead) who can be identified from it, and the material in question relates to his physical or mental health or to spiritual counselling. Such information can include both oral and written communications. Such information as described above is held in confidence if it is held subject to an express or implied undertaking to hold it in confidence or it is subject to a restriction on disclosure or an obligation of confidentiality contained in existing legislation. For example, confidential personal information might include consultations between a health professional and a patient, or information from a patient's medical records.

3.10 Spiritual counselling is defined as conversations between an individual and a Minister of Religion acting in his official capacity, and where the individual being counselled is seeking or the Minister is imparting forgiveness, absolution or the resolution of conscience with the authority of the Divine Being(s) of their faith.

3.11 Confidential journalistic material includes material acquired or created for the purposes of journalism and held subject to an undertaking to hold it in confidence, as well as communications resulting in information being acquired for the purposes of journalism and held subject to such an undertaking.

4 INTERCEPTION WARRANTS (SECTION 8(1))

4.1 This section applies to the interception of communications by means of a warrant complying with section 8(1) of the Act. This type of warrant may be issued in respect of the interception of communications carried on any postal service or telecommunications system as defined in section 2(1) of the Act (including a private telecommunications system). **18.12**

Responsibility for the issuing of interception warrants rests with the Secretary of State.

Application for a Section 8(1) warrant

4.2 An application for a warrant is made to the Secretary of State. **18.13**

Interception warrants, when issued, are addressed to the person who submitted the application. This person may then serve a copy upon any person who may be able to provide assistance in giving effect to that warrant. Each application, a copy of which must be retained by the applicant, should contain the following information:

- Background to the operation in question.
- Person or premises to which the application relates (and how the person or premises feature in the operation).
- Description of the communications to be intercepted, details of the communications service provider(s) and an assessment of the feasibility of the interception operation where this is relevant.
- Description of the conduct to be authorised as considered necessary in order to carry out the interception, where appropriate.
- An explanation of why the interception is considered to be necessary under the provisions of section 5(3).
- A consideration of why the conduct to be authorised by the warrant is proportionate to what is sought to be achieved by that conduct.
- A consideration of any unusual degree of collateral intrusion and why that intrusion is justified in the circumstances. In particular, where the communications in question might affect religious, medical or journalistic confidentiality or legal privilege, this must be specified in the application.
- Where an application is urgent, supporting justification should be provided.
- An assurance that all material intercepted will be handled in accordance with the safeguards required by section 15 of the Act.

Authorisation of a Section 8(1) warrant

18.14 Before issuing a warrant under section 8(1), the Secretary of State must believe the warrant is necessary   **4.3**

- in the interests of national security;
- for the purpose of preventing or detecting serious crime; or
- for the purpose of safeguarding the economic well-being of the United Kingdom.

In exercising his power to issue an interception warrant for the purpose of safe-   **4.4** guarding the economic well-being of the United Kingdom (as provided for by section 5(3)(c) of the Act), the Secretary of State will consider whether the economic well-being of the United Kingdom which is to be safeguarded is, on the facts of each case, directly related to state security. The term "state security", which is used in Directive 97/66/EC (concerning the processing of personal data and the protection of privacy in the telecommunications sector), should be interpreted in the same way as the term "national security" which is used elsewhere in the Act and this Code. The Secretary of State will not issue a warrant on section 5(3)(c) grounds if this direct link between the economic well-being of the United Kingdom and state security is not established. Any application for a warrant on section 5(3)(c) grounds should therefore explain how, in the applicant's view, the economic well-being of the United Kingdom which is to be safeguarded is directly related to state security on the facts of the case.

4.5 The Secretary of State must also consider that the conduct authorised by the warrant is proportionate to what it seeks to achieve (section 5(2)(b)). In considering necessity and proportionality, the Secretary of State must take into account whether the information sought could reasonably be obtained by other means (section 5(4)).

Urgent Authorisation of a Section 8(1) warrant

4.6 The Act makes provision (section 7(1)(b)) for cases in which an interception warrant   **18.15** is required urgently, yet the Secretary of State is not available to sign the warrant. In these cases the Secretary of State will still personally authorise the interception but the warrant is signed by a senior official, following discussion of the case between officials and the Secretary of State. The Act restricts issue of warrants in this way to urgent cases where the Secretary of State has himself expressly authorised the issue of the warrant (section 7(2)(a)), and requires the warrant to contain a statement to that effect (section 7(4)(a)). A warrant issued under the urgency procedure lasts for five working days following the day of issue unless renewed by the Secretary of State, in which case it expires after 3 months in the case of serious crime or 6 months in the case of national security or economic well-being in the same way as other non-urgent section 8(1) warrants. An urgent case is one in which interception authorisation is required within a twenty four hour period.

Format of a Section 8(1) warrant

4.7 Each warrant comprises two sections, a warrant instrument signed by the Secretary   **18.16** of State listing the subject of the interception or set of premises, a copy of which each communications service provider will receive, and a schedule or set of schedules listing the communications to be intercepted. Only the schedule relevant to the communications that can be intercepted by the specified communications service provider will be provided to that service provider.

4.8 The warrant instrument should include:

- The name or description of the interception subject or of a set of premises in relation to which the interception is to take place
- A warrant reference number
- The persons who may subsequently modify the scheduled part of the warrant in an urgent case (if authorised in accordance with section 10(8) of the Act)

4.9 The scheduled part of the warrant will comprise one or more schedules. Each schedule should contain:

- The name of the communication service provider, or the other person who is to take action

- A warrant reference number
- A means of identifying the communications to be intercepted

Modification of Section 8(1) warrant

18.17 Interception warrants may be modified under the provisions of section 10 of the **4.10**
Act. The unscheduled part of a warrant may only be modified by the Secretary of
State or, in an urgent case, by a senior official with the express authorisation of the
Secretary of State. In these cases, a statement of that fact must be endorsed on the
modifying instrument, and the modification ceases to have effect after five work-
ing days following the day of issue unless it is renewed by the Secretary of State.
The modification will then expire upon the expiry date of the warrant.

Scheduled parts of a warrant may be modified by the Secretary of State, or by a **4.11**
senior official acting upon his behalf. A modification to the scheduled part of the
warrant may include the addition of a new schedule relating to a communication
service provider on whom a copy of the warrant has not been previously served.
Modifications made in this way expire at the same time as the warrant expires. There
also exists a duty to modify a warrant by deleting a communication identifier if it is
no longer relevant. When a modification is sought to delete a number or other communication identifier, the relevant communications service provider must be
advised and interception suspended before the modification instrument is signed.

In an urgent case, and where the warrant specifically authorises it, scheduled parts **4.12**
of a warrant may be modified by the person to whom the warrant is addressed (the
person who submitted the application) or a subordinate (where the subordinate is
identified in the warrant). Modifications of this kind are valid for five working days
following the day of issue unless the modification instrument is endorsed by a
senior official acting on behalf of the Secretary of State. Where the modification is
endorsed in this way, the modification expires upon the expiry date of the warrant.

Renewal of a Section 8(1) warrant

18.18 The Secretary of State may renew a warrant at any point before its expiry date. **4.13**
Applications for renewals must be made to the Secretary of State and should contain an update of the matters outlined in paragraph 4.2 above. In particular, the
applicant should give an assessment of the value of interception to the operation
to date and explain why he considers that interception continues to be necessary
for one or more of the purposes in section 5(3).

Where the Secretary of State is satisfied that the interception continues to meet **4.14**
the requirements of the Act he may renew the warrant.

Where the warrant is issued on serious crime grounds, the renewed warrant is valid for a further three months. Where it is issued on national security/economic well-being grounds, the renewed warrant is valid for six months. These dates run from the date of signature on the renewal instrument.

4.15 A copy of the warrant renewal instrument will be forwarded by the intercepting agency to all relevant communications service providers on whom a copy of the original warrant instrument and a schedule have been served, providing they are still actively assisting. A warrant renewal instrument will include the reference number of the warrant and description of the person or premises described in the warrant.

Warrant cancellation

4.16 The Secretary of State is under a duty to cancel an interception warrant if, at any time before its expiry date, he is satisfied that the warrant is no longer necessary on grounds falling within section 5(3) of the Act. Intercepting agencies will therefore need to keep their warrants under continuous review. In practice, cancellation instruments will be signed by a senior official on his behalf. **18.19**

4.17 The cancellation instrument should be addressed to the person to whom the warrant was issued (the intercepting agency) and should include the reference number of the warrant and the description of the person or premises specified in the warrant. A copy of the cancellation instrument should be sent to those communications service providers who have held a copy of the warrant instrument and accompanying schedule during the preceding twelve months.

Records

4.18 The intercepting agency should keep the following to be made available for scrutiny by the Commissioner as he may require: **18.20**

- all applications made for warrants complying with section 8(1) and applications made for the renewal of such warrants.
- all warrants, and renewals and copies of schedule modifications (if any).
- where any application is refused, the grounds for refusal as given by the Secretary of State.
- the dates on which interception is started and stopped.

4.19 Records shall also be kept of the arrangements by which the requirements of section 15(2) (minimisation of copying and destruction of intercepted material) and section 15(3) (destruction of intercepted material) are to be met. For further details see section on "Safeguards".

4.20 The term "intercepted material" is used throughout to embrace copies, extracts or summaries made from the intercepted material as well as the intercept material itself.

5 INTERCEPTION WARRANTS (SECTION 8(4))

18.21 This section applies to the interception of external communications by means of a **5.1** warrant complying with section 8(4) of the Act. External communications are defined by the Act to be those which are sent or received outside the British Islands. They include those which are both sent and received outside the British Islands, whether or not they pass through the British Islands in course of their transit. They do not include communications both sent and received in the British Islands, even if they pass outside the British Islands en route. Responsibility for the issuing of such interception warrants rests with the Secretary of State.

Application for a Section 8(4) warrant

18.22 An application for a warrant is made to the Secretary of State. Interception warrants, **5.2** when issued, are addressed to the person who submitted the application. This person may then serve a copy upon any person who may be able to provide assistance in giving effect to that warrant. Each application, a copy of which must be retained by the applicant, should contain the following information:

- Background to the operation in question.
- Description of the communications to be intercepted, details of the communications service provider(s) and an assessment of the feasibility of the operation where this is relevant.
- Description of the conduct to be authorised, which must be restricted to the interception of external communications, or to conduct necessary in order to intercept those external communications, where appropriate.
- The certificate that will regulate examination of intercepted material.
- An explanation of why the interception is considered to be necessary for one or more of the section 5(3) purposes.
- A consideration of why the conduct to be authorised by the warrant is proportionate to what is sought to be achieved by that conduct.
- A consideration of any unusual degree of collateral intrusion, and why that intrusion is justified in the circumstances. In particular, where the communications in question might affect religious, medical or journalistic confidentiality or legal privilege, this must be specified in the application.
- Where an application is urgent, supporting justification should be provided.
- An assurance that intercepted material will be read, looked at or listened to only so far as it is certified, and it meets the conditions of sections 16(2)–16(6) of the Act.
- An assurance that all material intercepted will be handled in accordance with the safeguards required by sections 15 and 16 of the Act.

Authorisation of a Section 8(4) warrant

5.3 Before issuing a warrant under section 8(4), the Secretary of State must believe **18.23** that the warrant is necessary:

- in the interests of national security;
- for the purpose of preventing or detecting serious crime; or
- for the purpose of safeguarding the economic well-being of the United Kingdom;

5.4 In exercising his power to issue an interception warrant for the purpose of safeguarding the economic well-being of the United Kingdom (as provided for by section 5(3)(c) of the Act), the Secretary of State will consider whether the economic well-being of the United Kingdom which is to be safeguarded is, on the facts of each case, directly related to state security. The term "state security", which is used in Directive 97/66/EC (concerning the processing of personal data and the protection of privacy in the telecommunications sector), should be interpreted in the same way as the term "national security" which is used elsewhere in the Act and this Code. The Secretary of State will not issue a warrant on section 5(3)(c) grounds if this direct link between the economic well-being of the United Kingdom and state security is not established. Any application for a warrant on section 5(3)(c) grounds should therefore explain how, in the applicant's view, the economic well-being of the United Kingdom which is to be safeguarded is directly related to state security on the facts of the case.

5.5 The Secretary of State must also consider that the conduct authorised by the warrant is proportionate to what it seeks to achieve (section 5(2)(b)). In considering necessity and proportionality, the Secretary of State must take into account whether the information sought could reasonably be obtained by other means (section 5(4)).

5.6 When the Secretary of State issues a warrant of this kind, it must be accompanied by a certificate in which the Secretary of State certifies that he considers examination of the intercepted material to be necessary for one or more of the section 5(3) purposes. The Secretary of State has a duty to ensure that arrangements are in force for securing that only that material which has been certified as necessary for examination for a section 5(3) purpose, and which meets the conditions set out in section 16(2) to section 16(6) is, in fact, read, looked at or listened to. The Interception of Communications Commissioner is under a duty to review the adequacy of those arrangements.

Urgent authorisation of a Section 8(4) warrant

5.7 The Act makes provision (section 7(1)(b)) for cases in which an interception warrant **18.24** is required urgently, yet the Secretary of State is not available to sign the warrant. In these cases the Secretary of State will still personally authorise the interception but the warrant is signed by a senior official, following discussion of the case between officials and the Secretary of State. The Act restricts issue of warrants in this way to urgent cases where the Secretary of State has himself expressly authorised the issue of the warrant (section 7(2)(a)), and requires the warrant to contain a statement to that effect (section 7(4)(a)).

A warrant issued under the urgency procedure lasts for five working days following **5.8** the day of issue unless renewed by the Secretary of State, in which case it expires after 3 months in the case of serious crime or 6 months in the case of national security or economic well-being in the same way as other section 8(4) warrants.

Format of a Section 8(4) warrant

18.25 Each warrant is addressed to the person who submitted the application. This person **5.9** may then serve a copy upon such providers of communications services as he believes will be able to assist in implementing the interception. Communications service providers will not receive a copy of the certificate.

The warrant should include the following:

- a description of the communications to be intercepted;
- the warrant reference number;
- the persons who may subsequently modify the scheduled part of the warrant in an urgent case (if authorised in accordance with section 10(8) of the Act)

Modification of a section 8(4) warrant

18.26 Interception warrants may be modified under the provisions of section 10 of the **5.10** Act. The warrant may only be modified by the Secretary of State or, in an urgent case, by a senior official with the express authorisation of the Secretary of State. In these cases a statement of that fact must be endorsed on the modifying instrument, and the modification ceases to have effect after five working days following the day of issue unless it is endorsed by the Secretary of State.

The certificate must be modified by the Secretary of State, save in an urgent case **5.11** where a certificate may be modified under the hand of a senior official provided that the official holds a position in respect of which he is expressly authorised by provisions contained in the certificate to modify the certificate on the Secretary of State's behalf, or the Secretary of State has himself expressly authorised the modification and a statement of that fact is endorsed on the modifying instrument. Again the modification shall cease to have effect after five working days following the day of issue unless it is endorsed by the Secretary of State.

Renewal of a Section 8(4) warrant

18.27 The Secretary of State may renew a warrant at any point before its expiry date. **5.12** Applications for renewals are made to the Secretary of State and contain an update of the matters outlined in paragraph 5.2 above. In particular, the applicant must give an assessment of the value of interception to the operation to date and explain why he considers that interception continues to be necessary for one or more of purposes in section 5(3).

5.13   Where the Secretary of State is satisfied that the interception continues to meet the requirements of the Act he may renew the warrant. Where the warrant is issued on serious crime grounds, the renewed warrant is valid for a further three months. Where it is issued on national security/ economic well-being grounds the renewed warrant is valid for six months. These dates run from the date of signature on the renewal instrument.

5.14   In those circumstances where the assistance of communications service providers has been sought, a copy of the warrant renewal instrument will be forwarded by the intercepting agency to all those on whom a copy of the original warrant instrument has been served, providing they are still actively assisting. A warrant renewal instrument will include the reference number of the warrant and description of the communications to be intercepted.

Warrant cancellation

5.15   The Secretary of State shall cancel an interception warrant if, at any time before its **18.28** expiry date, he is satisfied that the warrant is no longer necessary on grounds falling within Section 5(3) of the Act. In practice, cancellation instruments will be signed by a senior official on his behalf.

5.16   The cancellation instrument will be addressed to the person to whom the warrant was issued (the intercepting agency). A copy of the cancellation instrument should be sent to those communications service providers, if any, who have given effect to the warrant during the preceding twelve months.

Records

5.17   The oversight regime allows the Interception of Communications Commissioner **18.29** to inspect the warrant application upon which the Secretary of State based his decision, and the applicant may be required to justify the content. Each intercepting agency should keep, so to be made available for scrutiny by the Interception of Communications Commissioner, the following:

- all applications made for warrants complying with section 8(4), and applications made for the renewal of such warrants.
- all warrants and certificates, and copies of renewal and modification instruments (if any).
- where any application is refused, the grounds for refusal as given by the Secretary of State.
- the dates on which interception is started and stopped.

Records shall also be kept of the arrangements in force for securing that only material which has been certified for examination for a purpose under section 5(3) and which meets the conditions set out in section 16(2)–16(6) of the Act in accordance with section 15 of the Act. Records shall be kept of the arrangements by which the requirements of section 15(2) (minimisation of copying and distribution of intercepted material) and section 15(3) (destruction of intercepted material) are to be met. For further details see the section on "Safeguards".

6 SAFEGUARDS

18.30 All material (including related communications data) intercepted under the **6.1** authority of a warrant complying with section 8(1) or section 8(4) of the Act must be handled in accordance with safeguards which the Secretary of State has approved in conformity with the duty imposed upon him by the Act. These safeguards are made available to the Interception of Communications Commissioner, and they must meet the requirements of section 15 of the Act which are set out below. In addition, the safeguards in section 16 of the Act apply to warrants complying with section 8(4). Any breach of these safeguards must be reported to the Interception of Communications Commissioner.

Section 15 of the Act requires that disclosure, copying and retention of intercept **6.2** material be limited to the minimum necessary for the authorised purposes. The authorised purposes defined in section 15(4) of the Act include:

- if the material continues to be, or is likely to become, necessary for any of the purposes set out in section 5(3)—namely, in the interests of national security, for the purpose of preventing or detecting serious crime, for the purpose of safeguarding the economic well-being of the United Kingdom.
- if the material is necessary for facilitating the carrying out of the functions of the Secretary of State under Chapter I of Part I of the Act.
- if the material is necessary for facilitating the carrying out of any functions of the Interception of Communications Commissioner or the Tribunal.
- if the material is necessary to ensure that a person conducting a criminal prosecution has the information he needs to determine what is required of him by his duty to secure the fairness of the prosecution.
- if the material is necessary for the performance of any duty imposed by the Public Record Acts.

Section 16 provides for additional safeguards in relation to material gathered **6.3** under section 8(4) warrants, requiring that the safeguards:

- ensure that intercepted material is read, looked at or listened to by any person only to the extent that the material is certified.
- regulate the use of selection factors that refer to individuals known to be for the time being in the British Islands.

The Secretary of State must ensure that the safeguards are in force before any interception under warrants complying with section 8(4) can begin. The Interception of Communications Commissioner is under a duty to review the adequacy of the safeguards.

Dissemination of intercepted material

6.4 The number of persons to whom any of the material is disclosed, and the extent of disclosure, must be limited to the minimum that is necessary for the authorised purposes set out in section 15(4) of the Act. This obligation applies equally to disclosure to additional persons within an agency, and to disclosure outside the agency. It is enforced by prohibiting disclosure to persons who do not hold the required security clearance, and also by the need-to-know principle: intercepted material must not be disclosed to any person unless that person's duties, which must relate to one of the authorised purposes, are such that he needs to know about the material to carry out those duties. In the same way only so much of the material may be disclosed as the recipient needs; for example if a summary of the material will suffice, no more than that should be disclosed. **18.31**

6.5 The obligations apply not just to the original interceptor, but also to anyone to whom the material is subsequently disclosed. In some cases this will be achieved by requiring the latter to obtain the originator's permission before disclosing the material further. In others, explicit safeguards are applied to secondary recipients.

Copying

6.6 Intercepted material may only be copied to the extent necessary for the of the identities of the persons to or by whom the intercepted material was sent. The restrictions are implemented by requiring special treatment of such copies, extracts and summaries that are made by recording their making, distribution and destruction. **18.32**

Storage

6.7 Intercepted material, and all copies, extracts and summaries of it, must be handled and stored securely, so as to minimise the risk of loss or theft. It must be held so as to be inaccessible to persons without the required level of security clearance. This requirement to store intercept product securely applies to all those who are responsible for the handling of this material, including communications service providers. The details of what such a requirement will mean in practice for communications service providers will be set out in the discussions they will be having with the Government before a Section 12 Notice is served (see paragraph 2.9). **18.33**

Destruction

18.34 Intercepted material, and all copies, extracts and summaries which can be identified **6.8**
as the product of an interception, must be securely destroyed as soon as it is no
longer needed for any of the authorised purposes. If such material is retained, it
should be reviewed at appropriate intervals to confirm that the justification for its
retention is still valid under section 15(3) of the Act.

Personnel security

18.35 Each intercepting agency maintains a distribution list of persons who may have **6.9**
access to intercepted material or need to see any reporting in relation to it. All such
persons must be appropriately vetted. Any person no longer needing access to perform his duties should be removed from any such list. Where it is necessary for an
officer of one agency to disclose material to another, it is the former's responsibility
to ensure that the recipient has the necessary clearance.

7 DISCLOSURE TO ENSURE FAIRNESS IN CRIMINAL PROCEEDINGS

18.36 Section 15(3) of the Act states the general rule that intercepted material must be **7.1**
destroyed as soon as its retention is no longer necessary for a purpose authorised
under the Act. Section 15(4) specifies the authorised purposes for which retention
is necessary.

This part of the Code applies to the handling of intercepted material in the context **7.2**
of criminal proceedings where the material has been retained for one of the purposes authorised in section 15(4) of the Act. For those who would ordinarily have
had responsibility under the Criminal Procedure and Investigations Act 1996 to
provide disclosure in criminal proceedings, this includes those rare situations
where destruction of intercepted material has not taken place in accordance with
section 15(3) and where that material is still in existence after the commencement
of a criminal prosecution, retention having been considered necessary to ensure
that a person conducting a criminal prosecution has the information he needs to
discharge his duty of ensuring its fairness (section 15(4)(d)).

Exclusion of matters from legal proceedings

18.37 The general rule is that neither the possibility of interception nor intercepted mate- **7.3**
rial itself plays any part in legal proceedings. This rule is set out in section 17 of the
Act, which excludes evidence, questioning, assertion or disclosure in legal proceedings likely to reveal the existence (or the absence) of a warrant issued under this Act

(or the Interception of Communications Act 1985). This rule means that the intercepted material cannot be used either by the prosecution or the defence. This preserves "equality of arms" which is a requirement under Article 6 of the European Convention on Human Rights.

7.4 Section 18 contains a number of tightly-drawn exceptions to this rule. This part of the Code deals only with the exception in subsections (7) to (11).

Disclosure to a prosecutor

7.5 Section 18(7)(a) provides that intercepted material obtained by means of a warrant **18.38** and which continues to be available, may, for a strictly limited purpose, be disclosed to a person conducting a criminal prosecution.

7.6 This may only be done for the purpose of enabling the prosecutor to determine what is required of him by his duty to secure the fairness of the prosecution. The prosecutor may not use intercepted material to which he is given access under section 18(7)(a) to mount a cross-examination, or to do anything other than ensure the fairness of the proceedings.

7.7 The exception does not mean that intercepted material should be retained against a remote possibility that it might be relevant to future proceedings. The normal expectation is, still, for the intercepted material to be destroyed in accordance with the general safeguards provided by section 15. The exceptions only come into play if such material has, in fact, been retained for an authorised purpose. Because the authorised purpose given in section 5(3)(b) ("for the purpose of preventing or detecting serious crime") does not extend to gathering evidence for the purpose of a prosecution, material intercepted for this purpose may not have survived to the prosecution stage, as it will have been destroyed in accordance with the section 15(3) safeguards. There is, in these circumstances, no need to consider disclosure to a prosecutor if, in fact, no intercepted material remains in existence.

7.8 Be that as it may, section 18(7)(a) recognises the duty on prosecutors, acknowledged by common law, to review all available material to make sure that the prosecution is not proceeding unfairly. 'Available material' will only ever include intercepted material at this stage if the conscious decision has been made to retain it for an authorised purpose.

7.9 If intercepted material does continue to be available at the prosecution stage, once this information has come to the attention of the holder of this material the prosecutor should be informed that a warrant has been issued under section 5 and that material of possible relevance to the case has been intercepted.

Having had access to the material, the prosecutor may conclude that the material **7.10** affects the fairness of the proceedings. In these circumstances, he will decide how the prosecution, if it proceeds, should be presented.

Disclosure to a judge

18.39 Section 18(7)(b) recognises that there may be cases where the prosecutor, having **7.11** seen intercepted material under subsection (7)(a), will need to consult the trial Judge. Accordingly, it provides for the Judge to be given access to intercepted material, where there are exceptional circumstances making that disclosure essential in the interests of justice.

This access will be achieved by the prosecutor inviting the judge to make an order **7.12** for disclosure to him alone, under this subsection. This is an exceptional procedure; normally, the prosecutor's functions under subsection (7)(a) will not fall to be reviewed by the judge. To comply with section 17(1), any consideration given to, or exercise of, this power must be carried out without notice to the defence. The purpose of this power is to ensure that the trial is conducted fairly.

The judge may, having considered the intercepted material disclosed to him, **7.13** direct the prosecution to make an admission of fact. The admission will be abstracted from the interception; but, in accordance with the requirements of section 17(1), it must not reveal the fact of interception. This is likely to be a very unusual step. The Act only allows it where the judge considers it essential in the interests of justice.

Nothing in these provisions allows intercepted material, or the fact of interception, to be disclosed to the defence.

8 OVERSIGHT

18.40 The Act provides for an Interception of Communications Commissioner whose **8.1** remit is to provide independent oversight of the use of the powers contained within the warranted interception regime under Chapter I of Part I of the Act.

This Code does not cover the exercise of the Commissioner's functions. However, **8.2** it will be the duty of any person who uses the above powers to comply with any request made by the Commissioner to provide any information as he requires for the purpose of enabling him to discharge his functions.

9 COMPLAINTS

9.1 The Act establishes an independent Tribunal. This Tribunal will be made up of senior members of the judiciary and the legal profession and is independent of the Government. The Tribunal has full powers to investigate and decide any case within its jurisdiction. **18.41**

9.2 This code does not cover the exercise of the Tribunal's functions. Details of the relevant complaints procedure can be obtained from the following address:

The Investigatory Powers Tribunal
PO Box 33220
London
SW1H 9ZQ
0207 273 4514

10 INTERCEPTION WITHOUT A WARRANT

10.1 Section 1(5) of the Act permits interception without a warrant in the following circumstances: **18.42**

- where it is authorised by or under sections 3 or 4 of the Act (see below);
- where it is in exercise, in relation to any stored communication, of some other statutory power exercised for the purpose of obtaining information or of taking possession of any document or other property, for example, the obtaining of a production order under Schedule 1 to the Police and Criminal Evidence Act 1984 for stored data to be produced.

Interception in accordance with a warrant under section 5 of the Act is dealt with under parts 2, 3, 4 and 5 of this Code.

10.2 For lawful interception which takes place without a warrant, pursuant to sections 3 or 4 of the Act or pursuant to some other statutory power, there is no prohibition in the Act on the evidential use of any material that is obtained as a result. The matter may still, however, be regulated by the exclusionary rules of evidence to be found in the common law, section 78 of the Police and Criminal Evidence Act 1984, and/or pursuant to the Human Rights Act 1998.

Interception with the consent of both parties

10.3 Section 3(1) of the Act authorises the interception of a communication if both the person sending the communication and the intended recipient(s) have consented **18.43**

to its interception, or where the person conducting the interception has reasonable grounds for believing that all parties have consented to the interception.

Interception with the consent of one party

18.44 Section 3(2) of the Act authorises the interception of a communication if either **10.4**
the sender or intended recipient of the communication has consented to its interception, and directed surveillance by means of that interception has been authorised under Part II of the Act. Further details can be found in chapter 4 of the Covert Surveillance Code of Practice and in chapter 2 of the Covert Human Intelligence Sources Code of Practice.

Interception for the purposes of a communication service provider

18.45 Section 3(3) of the Act permits a communication service provider or a person acting **10.5**
upon their behalf to carry out interception for purposes connected with the operation of that service or for purposes connected with the enforcement of any enactment relating to the use of the communication service.

Lawful business practice

18.46 Section 4(2) of the Act enables the Secretary of State to make regulations setting out **10.6**
those circumstances where it is lawful to intercept communications for the purpose of carrying on a business. These regulations apply equally to public authorities.

These Lawful Business Practice Regulations can be found on the following Department of Trade and Industry website: www.dti.gov.uk/cii/regulation.html

19

ACQUISITION AND DISCLOSURE OF COMMUNICATIONS REVISED CODE OF PRACTICE (HOME OFFICE PRE-CONSULTATIVE DOCUMENT, 2005)*

[2005 PRE-CONSULTATION EDITION]

ACQUISITION AND DISCLOSURE OF COMMUNICATIONS DATA REVISED DRAFT CODE OF PRACTICE

Pursuant to Section 71 of the Regulation of Investigatory Powers Act 2000

* Editorial note: this draft Code is taken from the copy promulgated by the Home Office in 2005 as a pre-consultative document. Note that it is therefore not in force at time of writing. Footnotes throughout the remainder of this chapter are the official footnotes forming part of that document. The Home Office published it in March 2005.

Pre-consultation Revised Draft

1 INTRODUCTION

1.1 This code of practice relates to the powers and duties conferred or imposed under **19.01** Chapter II of Part I of the Regulation of Investigatory Powers Act 2000 ('the Act'). It provides guidance on the procedures to be followed when acquisition of communications data takes place under those provisions.

1.2 This code applies to relevant public authorities within the meaning of the Act: those listed in section 25 or specified in an order made by the Secretary of State.[1]

1.3 The code should be readily available to members of a relevant public authority involved in the acquisition of communications data under the Act and to communications service operators involved in the disclosure of data to public authorities under the Act. Throughout this code an operator who provides a postal or telecommunications service is described as a communications service provider (CSP).

1.4 The Act provides that the code is admissible in evidence in criminal and civil proceedings. If any provision of the code appears relevant to a question before any court or tribunal hearing any such proceedings, or to the Tribunal established under the Act,[2] or to one of the Commissioners responsible for overseeing the powers conferred by the Act, it must be taken into account.

1.5 The exercise of powers and duties under Chapter II of Part I of the Act is kept under review by the Interception of Communications Commissioner ('the Commissioner') appointed under section 57 of the Act.

1.6 This code does not relate to the interception of communications nor to the acquisition or disclosure of the contents of communications. The Interception of Communications Code of Practice pursuant to Section 71 of the Regulation of Investigatory Powers Act 2000 provides guidance on procedures to be followed in relation to the interception of communications.[3]

Any information, including communications data, that is product of an interception **1.7** warrant and any communications data acquired or obtained directly as a consequence of the execution of an interception warrant is intercept material. Any such communications data, and any other communications data derived directly from it, must be treated in accordance with the restrictions on the use of the material associated with the warrant.

This code extends to the United Kingdom. **1.8**

---

[1] For example, the Regulation of Investigatory Powers (Communications Data) Order 2003, SI No. 3172
[2] The Investigatory Powers Tribunal
[3] ISBN 0-11-341281-9

2 GENERAL EXTENT OF POWERS

Scope of powers, necessity and proportionality

19.02 The acquisition of communications data under the Act will be a justifiable interfer- **2.1** ence with an individual's human rights under Article 8 of the European Convention on Human Rights only if it is both necessary and proportionate that the conduct being authorised or required take place.

The Act stipulates that conduct to be authorised or required must be necessary for **2.2** one or more of the purposes set out in section 22(2) of the Act:[4]

- in the interests of national security;
- for the purpose of preventing or detecting crime[5] or of preventing disorder;
- in the interests of the economic well-being of the United Kingdom (see paragraph 2.11);
- in the interests of public safety;
- for the purpose of protecting public health;
- for the purpose of assessing or collecting any tax, duty, levy or other imposition, contribution or charge payable to a government department;
- for the purpose, in an emergency, of preventing death or injury or any damage to a person's physical or mental health, or of mitigating any injury or damage to a person's physical or mental health.

The purposes for which some public authorities may seek to acquire communica- **2.3** tions data are restricted by order.[6] The designated person (see paragraph 3.7) may only consider necessity on grounds open to his or her public authority and only in relation to matters that are the statutory or administrative function of their respective public authority.

⁴ The Act permits the Secretary of State to add further purposes to this list by means of an Order subject to the affirmative resolution procedure in Parliament.

⁵ Detecting crime includes establishing by whom, for what purpose, by what means and generally in what circumstances any crime was committed, the gathering of evidence for use in any legal proceedings and the apprehension of the person (or persons) by whom any crime was committed, see section 81(5) of the Act.

⁶ See paragraph 6, SI 2003/3172

2.4 There is a further restriction upon the acquisition of communications data:

- in the interests of public safety;
- for the purpose of protecting public health;
- for the purpose of assessing or collecting any tax, duty, levy or other imposition, contribution or charge payable to a government department.

Only communications data within the meaning of section 21(4)(c) of the Act' may be acquired for these purposes and only by those public authorities permitted by order to acquire communications data for one or more of those purposes.

2.5 The designated person must believe that the conduct required by any authorisation or notice is necessary. He or she must also believe that conduct to be proportionate to what is sought to be achieved by obtaining the specified communication data— that the conduct is no more than is required in the circumstances. This involves balancing the extent of the intrusiveness of the interference with an individual's right of respect for their private life against a specific benefit to the investigation or operation being undertaken by a relevant public authority in the public interest.

2.6 Consideration should also be given to any actual or potential infringement of the privacy of individuals who are not the subject of the investigation or operation. An application for the acquisition of communications data should draw attention to any circumstances which give rise to a meaningful degree of collateral intrusion.

2.7 Taking all these considerations into account in a particular case, an interference with the right to respect of individual privacy may still not be justified because the adverse impact on the privacy of an individual or group of individuals is too severe.

2.8 Any conduct that is excessive in the circumstances of both the interference and the aim of the investigation or operation, or is in any way arbitrary will not be proportionate.

⁷ See paragraph 7, SI 2003/3172

2.9 Exercise of the powers in the Act to acquire communications data is restricted to designated persons in relevant public authorities. A designated person is someone holding a prescribed office, rank or position within a relevant public authority that has been designated for the purpose of acquiring communications data by order.⁸

The relevant public authorities for Chapter II of Part I of the Act are set out in section **2.10** 25(1). They are:

- a police force (as defined in section 81(1) of the Act);[9]
- the National Criminal Intelligence Service;
- the National Crime Squad;
- HM Customs and Excise;
- the Inland Revenue;
- the Security Service;
- the Secret Intelligence Service;
- the Government Communications Headquarters.

These and additional relevant public authorities are listed in schedules to the Regulation of Investigatory Powers (Communications Data) Order 2003.[10]

Where acquisition of communications data is necessary in the interests of the **2.11** economic well-being of the United Kingdom, a designated person must take into account whether the economic well-being of the United Kingdom is, on the facts of the specific case, directly related to State security. The term "State security", which is used in Directive 97/66/EC (concerning the processing of personal data and the protection of privacy in the telecommunications sector), should be interpreted in the same way as the term "national security" which is used elsewhere in the Act and this code.

[8] See paragraphs 2 and 4, SI 2003/3172. By virtue of paragraph 5 of the order all more senior personnel to the designated office, rank or position are also allowed to grant authorisations or give notices.
[9] Each police force is a separate relevant public authority which has implications for the separation of roles in the acquisition of data under the Act. See paragraph 3.1
[10] SI 2003/3172

Communications data

19.03 The code covers any conduct relating to the exercise of powers and duties under Part I **2.12** Chapter II of the Act to acquire or disclose communications data. Communications data is defined in section 21(4) of the Act.

The term 'communications data' embraces the 'who', 'when' and 'where' of a com- **2.13** munication but not the content, not what was said or written. It includes the manner in which, and by what method, a person or machine communicates with another person or machine. It excludes what they say or what data they pass on within that communication (with the exception of data required to investigate crimes such as 'dial through' fraud, where data is passed on to activate communications equipment in order to fraudulently obtain communications services).

Communications data is generated, held or obtained in the provision, delivery **2.14** and maintenance of communications services, those being postal services[11] or telecommunications services.[12]

2.15 Communications service providers do not include those persons who provide a communications service which is ancillary to the provision of a service which is not a communications service or is necessarily incidental to the provision of a service which is not a communications service.[13]

2.16 For example, the provision of communications services is ancillary to the services provided by a hotel or restaurant to its guests, by a public library to members of the public, or by an airport authority to travellers. Similarly retailers or financial services which provide their services online, or provide access to their services online, will not ordinarily be communications service providers.

Traffic data

2.17 The Act defines certain communications data as 'traffic data' in sections 21(4)(a) and 21(6) of the Act. This is data that is comprised in or attached to a communication for the purpose of transmitting the communication and 'in relation to any communication' which: **19.04**

- identifies, or appears to identify, any person, equipment[14] or location to or from which a communication is or may be transmitted;
- identifies or selects, or appears to identify or select, transmission equipment;
- comprises signals that activate equipment used, wholly or partially, for the transmission of any communication (such as data generated in the use of carrier pre-select or redirect communication services or data generated in the commission of, what is known as, 'dial through' fraud);
- identifies data as data comprised in or attached to a communication. This includes data which is found at the beginning of each packet in a packet switched network that indicates which communications data attaches to which communication.

[11] Any service which consists in the collection, sorting, conveyance, distribution and delivery of postal items and is offered or provided as a service the main purpose of which, or one of the main purposes of which, is to transmit postal items from place to place. (See section 2(1) of the Act.)

[12] Any service which consists in the provision of access to, and for making use of, any telecommunication system (whether or not one provided by the person providing the service) the purpose of which is to transmit communications using electrical or electro-magnetic energy. (See section 2(1) of the Act.)

[13] See section 12(4) of the Act.

[14] In this code equipment is used, and has the same meaning as 'apparatus', which is defined in section 81(1) of the Act to mean 'any equipment, machinery, device, wire or cable'.

2.18 Traffic data includes data identifying a computer file or a computer programme to which access has been obtained, or which has been run, by means of the communication—but only to the extent that the file or programme is identified by reference to the apparatus in which the file or programme is stored. In relation to internet communications, this means traffic data stops at the apparatus within which files or programmes are stored, so that traffic data may identify a server but not a website or page.

Examples of traffic data, within the definition in section 21(6), include: **2.19**

- information tracing the origin or destination of a communication that is in transmission;
- information identifying the location of equipment when a communication is or has been made or received (such as the location of a mobile phone);
- information identifying the sender and recipient (including copy recipients) of a communication from data comprised in or attached to the communication;
- routing information identifying equipment through which a communication is or has been transmitted (for example, dynamic IP address allocation, web postings and e-mail headers—to the extent that content of a communication, such as the subject line of an e-mail, is not disclosed);
- web browsing information to the extent that only the host machine, server or domain is disclosed;
- anything, such as addresses or markings, written on the outside of a postal item (such as a letter, packet or parcel) that is in transmission;
- online tracking of communications (including postal items and parcels).

Post cards are an exception. Any message written on a post card which is in transmission is content and falls within the scope of the provisions for interception of communications. All other information contained on the post card, for example the address of the recipient and the post-mark, is communications data within section 21(4) of the Act. **2.20**

Service use information

19.05 Data relating to the use made by any person of a postal or telecommunications service, or any part of it, is widely known as 'service use information' and falls within section 21(4)(b) of the Act. **2.21**

Examples of data within the definition at section 21(4)(b) include: **2.22**

- itemised telephone call records (numbers called);
- itemised records of connections to internet services;
- itemised timing and duration of service usage (calls and/or connections);
- information about amounts of data downloaded and/or uploaded;
- information about the connection, disconnection and reconnection of services;
- information about the provision and use of forwarding/redirection services (by postal and telecommunications service providers);
- information about the provision of conference calling, call messaging, call waiting and call barring telecommunications services;
- information about selection of preferential numbers or discount calls;
- records of postal items, such as records of registered, recorded or special delivery postal items, records of parcel consignment, delivery and collection.

Subscriber information

2.23 The third type of communication data, widely known as 'subscriber information', is set out in section 21(4)(c) of the Act. This relates to information held or obtained by a CSP about persons[15] to whom the CSP provides or has provided a communications service. Those persons will include people who are subscribers to a communications service without necessarily using that service and persons who use a communications service without necessarily subscribing to it.

19.06

2.24 Examples of data within the definition at section 21(4) (c) include:

- 'subscriber checks' (also known as 'reverse look ups') such as "who is the subscriber of phone number 012 345 6789?", "who is the account holder of e-mail account xyz@xyz.anyisp.co.uk?" or "who is entitled to post to web space www.xyz.anyisp.co.uk?";
- subscribers or account holders' account information, including payment method(s) and any services to which the subscriber or account holder is allocated or has subscribed;
- addresses for installation and billing;
- information provided by a subscriber or account holder to a CSP, such as demographic information or sign-up data (to the extent that information, such as a password, giving access to the content of any stored communications is not disclosed).

[15] 'Person' includes any organisation and any association or combination of persons, as defined in section 81(1) of the Act

3 GENERAL RULES ON THE GRANTING OF AUTHORISATIONS AND GIVING OF NOTICES

3.1 Acquisition of communications data under the Act involves three roles with a relevant public authority:

19.07

- the applicant
- the designated person
- the single point of contact

3.2 The Act provides two alternative means for acquiring communications data, by way of:

- an authorisation under section 22(3), or
- a notice under section 22(4).

The applicant

19.08 The applicant is a person involved in conducting an investigation or operation **3.3** who makes an application in writing or electronically for the acquisition of communications data. The applicant completes an application form, setting out for consideration by the designated person, the necessity and proportionality of a specific requirement for acquiring communications data.

Applications may be made orally in exceptional circumstances,[16] but a record of that **3.4** application must be made in writing or electronically as soon as possible.

Applications, which must be retained[17] by the public authority, must:

- include the name (or designation)[18] and the office, rank or position held by the **3.5** person making the application;
- include a unique reference number;
- include the operation name (if applicable) to which the application relates;
- specify the purpose for which the data is required, by reference to a statutory purpose under 22(2) of the Act;
- describe the communications data required, specifying, where relevant, any historic or future date(s) and, where appropriate, time period(s);
- explain why the acquisition of that data is considered necessary and proportionate to what is sought to be achieved by acquiring it;
- consider and, where appropriate, describe any meaningful collateral intrusion—the extent to which the privacy of any individual not under investigation may be infringed and why that intrusion is justified in the circumstances, and
- identify and explain the time scale within which the data is required.

---

[16] See paragraph 3.42–3.45
[17] See paragraphs 5.1 to 5.5
[18] The use of a designation rather than a name will be appropriate only for designated persons in one of the security and intelligence agencies.

The application should record subsequently whether it was approved or not by a **3.6** designated person, by whom and when that decision was made. If approved, the application form should, to the extent necessary, be crossreferenced to any authorisation granted[19] or notice given.

The Designated Person

19.09 The Designated Person is a person holding a prescribed office[20] in the same public **3.7** authority as the applicant, who considers the application and records his considerations at the time (or as soon as is reasonably practicable) in writing or electronically. If the Designated Person believes it appropriate, both necessary and proportionate in the specific circumstances, an authorisation is granted or a notice is given.

3.8 Designated Persons must ensure that they grant authorisations or give notices only for purposes and only in respect of types of communications data that a designated person of their office, rank or position in the relevant public authority may grant or give.

3.9 The Designated Person shall assess the necessity for any conduct to acquire or obtain communications data taking account of any advice provided by the single point of contact (SPoC).[21]

3.10 Designated Persons should not be responsible for granting authorisations or giving notices in relation to investigations or operations in which they are directly involved, although it is recognised that this may sometimes be unavoidable, especially in the case of small organisations or where it is necessary to act urgently or for security reasons.

3.11 Individuals who undertake the role of a Designated Person must have current working knowledge of human rights principles, specifically those of necessity and proportionality, and how they apply to the acquisition of communications data under Chapter II of Part I of the Act and this code.

[19] Cross-referencing will be unnecessary in circumstances where the grant of an authorisation is recorded in the same document as the relevant application.

[20] The offices, ranks or positions of designated persons are prescribed by order. See paragraphs 4 and 5, SI 2003/3172

[21] See paragraph 3.12

The single point of contact

3.12 The single point of contact (SPoC) is either an accredited individual or a group of accredited individuals trained to facilitate lawful acquisition of communications data and effective co-operation between a public authority and CSPs. To become accredited an individual must complete a course of training appropriate for the role of a SPoC. Details of all accredited individuals are available to CSPs for authentication purposes. **19.10**

3.13 An accredited SPoC promotes efficiency and good practice in ensuring only practical and lawful requirements for communications data are undertaken. This encourages the public authority to regulate itself. The SPoC provides objective judgement and advice to both the applicant and the designated person. In this way the SPoC provides a "guardian and gatekeeper" function ensuring that public authorities act in an informed and lawful manner.

3.14 The SPoC should be in a position to:

- assess whether the acquisition of specific communications data from a CSP is reasonably practical or whether the specific data required is inextricably linked to other data;[22]

- advise applicants and designated persons on the interpretation of the Act, particularly whether an authorisation or notice is appropriate;
- provide assurance to designated persons that authorisations and notices are lawful under the Act and free from errors;
- provide assurance to CSPs that authorisations and notices are authentic and lawful;
- assess any cost and resource implications to both the public authority and the CSP of data requirements.

Public authorities unable to call upon the services of an accredited SPoC should not undertake the acquisition of communications data.   **3.15**

The SPoC may be an individual who is also a designated person.   **3.16**

Authorisations

19.11 An authorisation provides for persons within a public authority to engage in specific conduct, relating to a postal service or telecommunications system, to obtain communications data.   **3.17**

[22] In the event that the required data is inextricably linked to, or inseparable from, other data the designated person must take that into account in their consideration of necessity, proportionality and collateral intrusion.

Any designated person in a public authority may only authorise persons working in the same public authority to engage in specific conduct. This will normally be the public authority's SPoC.   **3.18**

The decision of a designated person whether to grant an authorisation shall be based upon information presented to them in an application.   **3.19**

An authorisation may be appropriate where: **3.20**

- a CSP is not capable of obtaining or disclosing the communications data;[23]
- a designated person believes the investigation or operation may be prejudiced if the CSP is required to obtain or disclose the data;
- there is an agreement in place between a public authority and a CSP relating to appropriate mechanisms for disclosure of communications data, or
- a designated person considers there is a requirement to conduct a telephone subscriber check but a CSP has yet to be conclusively determined as the holder of the communications data.

An authorisation is not served upon a CSP, although there may be circumstances where a CSP may require or may be given an assurance that conduct being undertaken is lawful. That assurance may be given by disclosing details of the authorisation or the authorisation itself.[24]   **3.21**

3.22 An authorisation must:

- be granted in writing or, if not, in a manner that produces a record of it having been granted;[25]
- describe the conduct which is authorised and describe the communications data to be acquired by that conduct specifying, where relevant, any historic or future date(s) and, where appropriate, time period(s);
- specify the purpose for which the conduct is authorised, by reference to a statutory purpose under 22(2) of the Act;
- specify the office, rank or position held by the designated person granting the authorisation. The designated person should also record their name (or designation) on any authorisation they grant;
- record the date and, when appropriate to do so, the time[26] when the authorisation was granted by the designated person.

[23] Where possible, this assessment will be based upon information provided by the CSP.
[24] See also paragraph 3.38
[25] See also paragraph 5.1
[26] Recording of the time an authorisation is granted (or a notice is given) will be appropriate in urgent and time critical circumstances.

Notices

3.23 Giving of a notice is appropriate where a CSP is able to retrieve or obtain specific **19.12** data, and to disclose that data, unless the grant of an authorisation is more appropriate. A notice may require a CSP to obtain any communications data, if that data is not already in its possession.

3.24 The decision of a designated person whether to give a notice shall be based upon information presented to them in an application.

3.25 The notice, the original of which must be retained by the public authority, should contain enough information to allow the CSP to comply with the requirements of the notice.

3.26 A notice must:

- be given in writing or, if not, in a manner that produces a record, within the public authority, of its having been granted;
- include a unique reference number that also identifies the public authority;[27]
- specify the purpose for which the notice has been given, by reference to a statutory purpose under 22(2) of the Act;
- describe the communications data to be obtained or disclosed under the notice specifying, where relevant, any historic or future date(s)and, where appropriate, time period(s);
- include an explanation that compliance with the notice is a requirement of the Act;
- specify the office, rank or position held by the designated person giving the notice. The designated person should also record their name (or designation) on any notice they give;

- specify the manner in which the data should be disclosed. The notice should contain sufficient information to enable a CSP to confirm the notice is authentic and lawful;
- record the date and, when appropriate to do so, the time when the notice was given by the designated person, and
- where appropriate, the notice should provide an indication of any urgency or time within which the CSP is requested to comply with the requirements of the notice.

---

[27] This can be a code or an abbreviation. For police services it will be appropriate to use the Police National Computer (PNC) force coding. See also paragraph 5.1.

3.27 A notice must not place a CSP under a duty to do anything which is not reasonably practicable for the CSP to do.

3.28 In giving notice a designated person may only require a CSP to disclose the communications data to the designated person or to a specified person working within the same public authority. This will normally be the public authority's SPoC.

Duration of authorisations and notices

19.13 **3.29** Relevant to all authorisations and notices is the date upon which authorisation is granted or notice given. From that date, when the authorisation or notice becomes valid, it has a validity of a maximum of one month.[28] This means the conduct authorised should have been commenced or the notice served within that month.

3.30 All authorisations and notices must relate to the acquisition or disclosure of data for a specific date or period.[29] Any period should be clearly indicated in the authorisation or notice. The start date and end date should be given, and where a precise start and end time are relevant these must be specified. Where no date is specified it should be taken to be the date on which the authorisation was granted or the notice given.

3.31 Where an authorisation or a notice relates to the acquisition or obtaining of specific data that will or may be generated in the future, the future period is restricted to no more than one month by section 23(4) of the Act.

Renewal of authorisations and notices

19.14 **3.32** Any valid authorisation or a notice may be renewed for a period of up to one month by the grant of a further authorisation or the giving of a further notice. A renewed authorisation or notice takes effect upon the expiry of the authorisation or notice it is renewing.

3.33 Renewal may be appropriate where there is a continuing requirement to acquire or obtain data that will or may be generated in the future. The reasoning for seeking renewal should be set out by an applicant in an addendum to the application upon which the authorisation or notice being renewed was granted or given.

> [28] Throughout this Code, a month means a calendar month or a period of time extending from a date in one calendar month to the corresponding date in the following month. (When there is no corresponding date the period shall end on the day that would have been the corresponding date had a new month not begun.)
>
> [29] For example, details of traffic data or service use on a specific date or for a specific period or the details of a subscriber on a specific date or for a specific period.

3.34 Where a designated person is granting a further authorisation or giving a further notice to renew an earlier authorisation or notice,[30] the designated person should:

- consider the reasons why it is necessary and proportionate to continue with the acquisition of the data being generated;
- record the date and, when appropriate to do so, the time when the authorisation or notice is renewed.

3.35 Designated persons should give particular consideration to any periods of days or shorter periods of time for which they may approve for the acquisition or disclosure of historic or future data. They should specify the shortest period in which the objective for which the data is sought can be achieved. To do otherwise will impact on the proportionality of the authorisation or notice and impose unnecessary burden upon a CSP.

Cancellation of notices and withdrawal of authorisations

3.36 A designated person who has given notice to a CSP under section 22(4) of the Act **19.15** shall cancel the notice if, at any time after giving the notice,[31] it is no longer necessary for the CSP to comply with the notice or the conduct required by the notice is no longer proportionate to what was sought to be achieved. Equally where a designated person considers an authorisation[32] should cease to have effect, because the conduct authorised becomes unnecessary or no longer proportionate to what was sought to be achieved, the authorisation shall be withdrawn.

3.37 Notification to a CSP of the cancellation of a notice can be undertaken by the designated person directly or, on that person's behalf, by the public authority's SPoC. Where human rights considerations are such that a notice should be cancelled with immediate effect a SPoC may notify the CSP to suspend compliance with the notice pending notification that the designated person has cancelled the notice.

3.38 When it is appropriate to do so a CSP should be advised of the withdrawal of an authorisation.[33]

3.39 Where the designated person who gave the notice is no longer available, this duty should fall on a person who has temporarily or permanently taken over the role of the designated person.

30 This can include an authorisation or notice that has been renewed previously.
31 This can include a renewed notice.
32 This can include a renewed authorisation.
33 See also paragraph 3.21

Cancellation of a notice must: **3.40**

- be undertaken in writing or, if not, in a manner that produces a record of it having been cancelled;
- identify, by reference to its unique reference number, the notice being cancelled;
- record the date and, when appropriate to do so, the time when the notice was cancelled, and
- specify the office, rank or position held by the designated person cancelling the notice. The designated person should also record their name (or designation) on any cancellation they make.

Withdrawal of an authorisation should: **3.41**

- be undertaken in writing or, if not, in a manner that produces a record of it having been withdrawn;
- identify, by reference to its unique reference number, the authorization being withdrawn;
- record the date and, when appropriate to do so, the time when the authorisation was cancelled;
- record the name and the office, rank or position held by the designated person withdrawing the authorisation.

Urgent oral giving of notice or grant of authorisation

19.16 In exceptional urgent circumstances, application for the giving of a notice or the **3.42** grant of an authorisation may be made by an applicant, approved by a designated person and either notice given to a CSP or an authorisation granted orally. The circumstances in which an oral notice or authorisation may be appropriate include those where this is an immediate threat to life such that a person's life might be endangered if the application procedure were undertaken in writing from the outset.

Particular care must be given to the use of the urgent oral process. When notice is **3.43** given orally, the SPoC or (in the case of an emergency call) the emergency service controller must provide a unique reference number for the notice (or emergency call) and provide the name of the designated person (or authorising officer in the case of an emergency call). Where telephone numbers (or other identifiers) are being relayed, the relevant number must be read twice and repeated back by the CSP to confirm the correct details have been taken.

When, in a matter of urgency, a designated person decides that the oral giving of **3.44** a notice or grant of an authorisation is appropriate, that notice should be given or the authorised conduct undertaken as soon as practicable after the making of that decision.

3.45 After the period of urgency, the normal written process must be completed:

- the applicant must complete a retrospective application[34] which includes an explanation of why the urgent process was undertaken;
- the designated person must make a record of the oral grant of an authorisation or the oral giving of a notice, including the time at which the oral decision was made;
- and, in the case of an oral notice, written notice[35] must be given to the CSP retrospectively within one working day[36] of the oral notice being given. Failure to do so will constitute an error reportable to the Commissioner.

[34] See paragraph 3.5
[35] See paragraphs 3.25–3.28
[36] Working day means any day other than a Saturday, a Sunday, Christmas Day, Good Friday or a day which is a bank holiday under the Banking and Financial Dealings Act 1971 in any part of the United Kingdom.

4 SPECIAL RULES ON THE GRANTING OF AUTHORISATIONS AND GIVING OF NOTICES IN SPECIFIC MATTERS OF PUBLIC INTEREST

Sudden deaths, serious injuries and vulnerable persons

4.1 There are circumstances when the police undertake enquiries in relation to specific matters of public interest where the disclosure of communications data may be necessary and proportionate. For example: **19.17**

- locating and notifying next of kin following a sudden or unexpected death;
- locating and notifying the next of kin of a seriously injured person;
- locating and notifying the next of kin or responsible adult of a child or other vulnerable person where there is a concern for the child's or the vulnerable person's welfare.

4.2 Often a telephone, telephone number or other communications details may be the only information available to identify a person or to identify their next of kin or a person responsible for their welfare.

4.3 Under the Act communications data may be obtained and disclosed in serious and urgent welfare cases where it is necessary within the meaning of section 22(2)(g) and the conduct authorised or required is proportionate to what is sought to be achieved by obtaining the data.

Public Emergency Call Service (999/112 calls)

19.18 Certain CSPs have obligations under the Communications Act 2003[37] in respect   **4.4**
of emergency calls made to 999 and 112 emergency numbers. They must ensure
that any service user can access the emergency authorities by using the emergency
numbers and, to the extent technically feasible, make caller location information
available to the emergency authorities for all 999/112 calls.

Caller location information, which provides the geographic position of the equip-   **4.5**
ment being used by the person making the emergency call, facilitates a fast
response in emergency situations where the caller is unable to give their position
(either because the caller does not know, is panicking or is incapacitated).

[37] General Conditions of Entitlement

Handling of an emergency call involves five phases: **4.6**

- connection of the caller to the Emergency Operator using the 999/112 number;
- selection by the Emergency Operator of the required Emergency Authority
  Control Room (Police, Fire, Ambulance or Coastguard)('the emergency service');
- connection of the caller to the Emergency Authority Control Room;
- listening by the Emergency Operator to ensure the caller is connected to the
  correct emergency service and to provide further assistance to the caller or the
  emergency service when required.[38]

Best practice dictates that the emergency operator will disclose location information   **4.7**
to the emergency service during the initial call hand-over. In many cases this will
be done automatically by the call handling system.

In automated cases, data relating to the emergency call is automatically displayed   **4.8**
at the relevant emergency service, the instant a call is routed from the Emergency
Operator. This data is available to the emergency service throughout the duration
of the emergency call, but disappears once the call has ended unless retained by the
emergency service.

The Privacy and Electronic Communications (EC Directive) Regulations   **4.9**
2003 (SI 2003 No. 2426)[39] allows telephone users the choice whether or not
their telephone number is displayed or can be accessed by the recipient of a call
they make. However when an emergency call using 999 or 112 is made, the
option to withhold the number making the call is not available. Instead the
calling line identity and location data (fixed or mobile) are automatically disclosed to the emergency services in order to facilitate a rapid response to the
emergency call.

[38] This can also include silent emergency calls where the call is connected but the caller, for
whatever reason, is unable to speak to the emergency operator or the emergency service.

[39] http://www.legislation.hmso.gov.uk/si/si2003/20032426.htm

Dropped 999/112 calls

4.10 There are situations where the Emergency Operator may become aware of the **19.19** premature termination of an emergency call. There are a number of reasons for these 'dropped' emergency calls, which cannot be reconnected. For example:

- there is a fault on the line
- the emergency service requests to be reconnected where the caller was incapacitated or unable to maintain the call (and reconnection is tried and fails)
- the Emergency Operator diagnoses a problem with the call or the strength of a mobile phone signal

4.11 If an emergency call is disconnected prematurely for any reason, technical or otherwise, and the Emergency Operator is aware or is made aware of this, then the Emergency Operator can elect to represent the data disclosed when the call was put to the emergency service initially. This voluntary disclosure would fall outside the scope of the Act. This can also include silent emergency calls where the call is connected but the caller, for whatever reason, is unable to speak to the emergency operator or the emergency service.

4.12 The Emergency Operator can anticipate the needs of the emergency service and represent the information disclosed automatically to the emergency service without prompting.

4.13 The Emergency Operator can choose to represent the data, whether prompted or unprompted, only for the period of time that the data is held specifically as emergency call data. This period is not normally longer than one hour from the termination of the emergency call.

4.14 There are circumstances where the Emergency Operator cannot automatically present the emergency service with communications data about the maker of an emergency call. For example, because the emergency service does not have equipment to receive the data automatically or the data is held by a third party service provider and not readily available to the Emergency Operator. In those circumstances, and in order to provide an effective emergency service, the Emergency Operator may disclose the data it has orally.

4.15 The emergency service can call upon the Emergency Operator or relevant service provider to disclose that data within the emergency period (within one hour of the termination of the emergency call) outside the scope of the Act. The emergency service controller must provide a unique reference number for the emergency call and provide the name of the authorizing officer). Where telephone numbers (or other identifiers) are being relayed, the relevant number must be read twice and repeated back by the CSP to confirm the correct details have been taken.

4.16 Should an emergency service require communications data relating to the making of any emergency call after the expiry of the emergency period of one hour from the termination of the call, that data must be acquired or obtained under the provisions of the Act.

Where communications data about a third party (other than the maker of an **4.17** emergency call) is required to deal effectively with an emergency call, the emergency service may make an oral application for the data. In the case of an oral notice, written notice under the provisions of the Act must be given to the CSP retrospectively, within 24 hours of the oral notice being given. Particular care must be taken with the use of the oral giving of notice (see paragraph 3.41).

5 KEEPING OF RECORDS

19.20 Applications, authorisations and copies of notices must be retained by the rele- **5.1** vant public authority in written or electronic form, and physically attached or cross-referenced where they are associated to each other.[40] The public authority should also keep a record of the date and, when appropriate to do so, the time when each notice or authorisation is given or granted, renewed or cancelled.

These records must be available for annual inspection by the Interception of **5.2** Communications Commissioner and retained to allow the Investigatory Powers Tribunal, established under Part IV of the Act, to carry out its functions.[41]

This code does not affect any other statutory obligations placed on public author- **5.3** ities to keep records under any other enactment. For example, where applicable in England and Wales, the relevant test given in the Criminal Procedure and Investigations Act 1996 as amended. This requires that material which is obtained in the course of an investigation and which may be relevant to the investigation must be recorded and retain.

Each relevant public authority must also keep a record of the following items: **5.4**

- number of applications submitted to a designated person for a decision to (i) give a notice or (ii) grant an authorisation;
- number of notices requiring disclosure of communications data within the meaning of each subsection of section 21(4) of the Act or any combinations of data;
- number of authorisations for conduct to acquire communications data within the meaning of each subsection of section 21(4) of the Act or any combinations of data;
- number of times an urgent notice is given orally, or an urgent authorisation granted orally, requiring disclosure of communications data within the meaning of each subsection of section 21(4) of the Act or any combinations of data.

5.5 This record must be sent in written or electronic form to the Interception of Communications Commissioner annually. Where appropriate, guidance on format or timing may be sought from the Commissioner.

[40] Including records of the withdrawal of authorisations and the cancellation of notices.
[41] The Tribunal will consider complaints made up to one year after the conduct to which the complaint relates and, where it is satisfied it is equitable to do so, may consider complaints made more than one year after the conduct to which the complaint relates. See section 67(5) of the Act.

Errors

5.6 Proper application of the Act and thorough procedures for operating its provisions, including the careful preparation and checking of applications, notices and authorisations, should reduce the scope for making errors whether by public authorities or by CSPs.   **19.21**

5.7 Where any error occurs, in the grant of an authorisation, the giving of a notice or as a consequence of any authorised conduct or any conduct undertaken to comply with a notice, a record should be kept and a report made to the Commissioner. Recording and reporting of errors will draw attention to those aspects of the process of acquisition and disclosure of communications data that require further improvement to eliminate errors and the risk of undue interference with any individual's rights.

5.8 An error can only occur after a designated person has granted an authorisation or given a notice that has been served on a CSP in writing or orally and the acquisition or disclosure of data has been initiated.

5.9 Any failure by a public authority to correctly apply the process of acquiring or obtaining communications data set out in this code will increase the likelihood of an error occurring. This section of the code cannot provide an exhaustive list of possible causes of errors. They can, for example, fall into one of the following categories:

- an authorisation or notice made for a purpose, or for a type of data, which the relevant public authority cannot call upon, or seek, under the Act;
- human error, such as incorrect transposition of information from an application to an authorisation or notice or the acquisition or disclosure of communications data other than that specified on an authorisation or notice;
- an authorisation granted requiring a public authority to engage in impractical conduct or a notice given which is impractical for a CSP to comply with;
- disclosure or acquisition of data in excess of that required, where a SPoC may have failed to identify that the required data is inextricably linked to or inseparable from other data and/or the CSP failed to identify that compliance with the notice entailed the disclosure of data outside of the scope of the notice;
- failure to review information already held, for example seeking the acquisition or disclosure of data already acquired or obtained for the same investigation or

operation, or data for which the requirement to acquire or obtain it is known to be no longer valid.

Communications identifiers can be readily transferred, or 'ported', between CSPs. When a correctly completed authorisation or notice results in a CSP indicating to a public authority that, for example, a telephone number has been 'ported' to another CSP does not constitute an error—unless the fact of the porting was already known to the public authority. **5.10**

When an error has been made the public authority which made the error, or established that the error had been made, must report the error to the Commissioner in written or electronic form as soon as is practical. All errors should be reported individually. The report sent to the Commissioner must include details of the error, explain how the error occurred, indicate whether any unintended collateral intrusion has taken place and provide an indication of what steps have been, or will be, taken to ensure that a similar error does not reoccur. **5.11**

Within every relevant public authority a senior responsible officer, at or above the seniority of a designated person, should oversee the reporting of errors to the Commissioner and the identification of both the cause(s) of errors and the implementation of processes to minimise repetition of reported errors. **5.12**

Where a CSP discloses communications data in error it must report each error to the Commissioner. It is appropriate for a person holding a suitably senior position within a CSP to do so. Errors by service providers could include responding to a notice by disclosing incorrect or excessive data or by disclosing the required data or excessive data to the wrong public authority. **5.13**

Where authorised conduct by a public authority results in the acquisition of excess data, or a CSP discloses data in excess of that required by a notice, all the data acquired or disclosed should be retained by the public authority and the error reported. **5.14**

After the error has been reported the designated person must review all the data and consider whether it is necessary and proportionate to make use of that material in the course of the investigation or operation. **5.15**

There is always a duty upon any investigator, in England and Wales, to comply with the requirements of the Criminal Procedure and Investigations Act 1996 (as amended) and its Codes and where excessive data comes into their possession they have a duty to record and retain that material. **5.16**

Where material is disclosed by a CSP in error which has no connection or relevance to any investigation or operation undertaken by the public authority receiving it, that material and any copy of it should be destroyed as soon as the report to the Commissioner has been made. **5.17**

6 DATA PROTECTION SAFEGUARDS

6.1 Communications data acquired or obtained under the provisions of the Act, and all copies, extracts and summaries of it, must be handled and stored securely. In addition, the requirements of the Data Protection Act 1998 ('the DPA')[42] and its data protection principles should be adhered to. **19.22**

Disclosure of communications data and subject access rights

6.2 This section of the Code provides guidance on the relationship between disclosure of communications data under the Act and the provisions for subject access requests under the DPA, and the balance between CSPs obligations to comply with a notice to disclose data and individuals' right of access under section 7 of the DPA to personal data held about them. **19.23**

6.3 There is no provision in the Act preventing CSPs from informing individuals about whom they have been required by notice to disclose communications data in response to a Subject Access Request made under section 7 of the DPA. However a CSP may exercise certain exemptions to the right of subject access under Part IV of the DPA.

6.4 Section 28 provides that data are always exempt from section 7 where such an exemption is required for the purposes of safeguarding national security.

6.5 Section 29 provides that personal data processed for the purposes of the prevention and detection of crime; the apprehension or prosecution of offenders, or the assessment or collection of any tax or duty or other imposition of a similar nature are exempt from section 7 to the extent to which the application of the provisions for rights of data subjects would be likely to prejudice any of those matters.

6.5 The exercise of the exemption to subject access rights possible under section 29 does not automatically apply to notices given under the Act. In the event that a CSP receives a subject access request where the fact of a disclosure under the Act might itself be disclosed the CSP concerned must carefully consider whether in the particular case disclosure of the fact of the notice would be likely to prejudice the prevention or detection of crime.

6.6 Where a CSP is uncertain whether disclosure of the fact of a notice would be likely to prejudice an investigation or operation, it should approach the SPoC of the public authority which gave the notice—and do so in good time to respond to the subject access request. The SPoC can determine within the public authority whether disclosure of the fact of the notice would be likely to be prejudicial to the matters in section 29.

[42] Further guidance is available from http://www.lcd.gov.uk/foi/datprot.htm or from http://www.informationcommissioner.gov.uk

Where a CSP withholds a piece of information in reliance on the exemption in **6.7** section 29 of the DPA, it is not obliged to inform an individual that any information has been withheld. It can simply leave out that piece of information and make no reference to it when responding to the individual who has made the subject access request.

CSPs should keep a record of the steps they have taken in determining whether **6.8** disclosure of the fact of a notice would prejudice apprehension or detection of offenders. This might be useful in the event of the data controller having to respond to enquiries made subsequently by the Information Commissioner or by the courts.

Acquisition of communication data on behalf of overseas authorities

19.24 Whilst the majority of public authorities which obtain communications data **6.9** under the Act have no need to disclose that data to any authority outside the United Kingdom, there can be occasions when it is necessary, appropriate and lawful to do so in matters of international co-operation.

There are two methods by which communications data, whether obtained under **6.10** the Act or not, can be acquired and disclosed to overseas public authorities:

- Judicial co-operation;
- Non-judicial co-operation.

Neither method compels United Kingdom public authorities to disclose data to overseas authorities. Data can only be disclosed when a United Kingdom public authority is satisfied that it is in the public interest to do so and all the conditions imposed by domestic legislation have been fulfilled.

Judicial co-operation

19.25 If the United Kingdom receives a formal request from an overseas court or other **6.11** prosecuting authority that appears to have a function of making requests for legal assistance, the Secretary of State (in Scotland the Lord Advocate) will consider the request under the Crime (International Co-operation) Act 2003. In order to assist he must be satisfied that the request is made in connection with criminal proceedings or a criminal investigation being carried on outside the United Kingdom.

If such a request is accepted, that request will be passed to a nominated court in the **6.12** United Kingdom. That court may make an order requiring a CSP to disclose the relevant information to the court for onward transmission to the overseas authority.

Non-judicial co-operation

6.13 Public authorities in the United Kingdom can receive direct requests for assistance **19.26** from their counterparts in other countries. These can include requests for the acquisition and disclosure of communications data. On receipt of such a request the United Kingdom public authority may consider seeking the acquisition or disclosure of the requested data under the provisions of Chapter II of Part I of the Act.

6.14 The United Kingdom public authority must be satisfied that the request complies with United Kingdom obligations under human rights legislation. The necessity and proportionality of each case must be considered before the authority processes the authorisation or notice.

Disclosure of communications data to overseas authorities

6.15 Where a United Kingdom public authority is considering the acquisition of communications data on behalf of an overseas authority and transferring the data to that authority it must consider whether the data will be adequately protected outside the United Kingdom and what safeguards may be needed to ensure that.[43] Such safeguards might include attaching conditions to the processing, storage and destruction of the data. **19.27**

6.16 If the proposed transfer of data is to an authority within the European Union that authority will be bound by the European Data Protection Directive (95/46/EC) and its national data protection legislation. Any data disclosed will be protected there without need for additional safeguards.

6.17 If the proposed transfer is to an authority outside of the European Union and the European Economic Area (Norway, Liechtenstein and Iceland) then it must not be disclosed unless the overseas authority can ensure an adequate level of data protection. The European Commission has determined that certain countries, including Canada and Switzerland, have laws providing an adequate level of protection where data can be transferred without need for further safeguards.

6.18 In all other circumstances the United Kingdom public authority must decide in each case, before transferring any data overseas, whether the data will be adequately protected there. If necessary the Information Commissioner can give guidance.

[43] The eighth data protection principle is: 'Personal data shall not be transferred to a country or territory outside the European Economic Area unless that country or territory ensures an adequate level of protection for the rights and freedoms of data subjects in relation to the processing of personal data.' (Paragraph 8, Schedule 1, DPA 1998)

6.19 The DPA recognises that it will not always be possible to ensure adequate data protection in third countries and there are exemptions to the principle, for example if the transfer of data is necessary for reasons of 'substantial public interest'.[44] There may be circumstances when it is necessary, for example in the interests of national security, for communications data to be disclosed to a third party country, even though that country does not have adequate safeguards in place to protect the data. That is a decision that can only be taken by the public authority holding the data on a case by case basis.

[44] Paragraph 4, Schedule 4, DPA 1998

7 OVERSIGHT

19.28 The Act provides for an Interception of Communications Commissioner ('the **7.1** Commissioner') whose remit is to provide independent oversight of the exercise and performance of the powers and duties contained under Chapter II of Part I of the Act.

This code does not cover the exercise of the Commissioner's functions. It is the **7.2** duty of any person who uses the powers conferred by Chapter II of Part I of the Act, or on whom duties are conferred, to comply with any request made by the Commissioner to provide any information he requires for the purposes of enabling him to discharge his functions.

Should the Commissioner establish that an individual has been adversely affected **7.3** by any wilful or reckless failure by any person exercising or complying with the powers and duties under the Act in relation to the acquisition or disclosure of communications data, he shall inform the affected individual of the existence of the Tribunal and its role. The Commissioner should disclose sufficient information to the affected individual to enable him or her to effectively engage the Tribunal.

8 COMPLAINTS

19.29 The Act established an independent Tribunal. The Tribunal is made up of senior **8.1** members of the judiciary and the legal profession and is independent of the Government. The Tribunal has full powers to investigate and decide any case within its jurisdiction.

This code does not cover the exercise of the Tribunal's functions. Details of the rel- **8.2** evant complaints procedure can be obtained from the following address:

The Investigatory Powers Tribunal,

PO Box 33220
London
SW 1H 9ZQ
020 7273 4514

Part VI

CASE LAW SUMMARIES[1]

[1] Cases here are restricted to those decided after RIPA came into force and which refer to the Act. For a more general list of cases on surveillance see the OSC website.

20

RIPA, PART I CASE LAW

A. Interception of Communications

R v Hardy and Hardy [2002] EWCA Crim 3012

Recorded telephone conversation to which officer is a party—whether 'interception'—RIPA s 1(1), s 2(6)—'while being transmitted'

The defendants were charged with conspiracy to supply cannabis, and the **20.01** Crown's evidence included taped conversations (face to face and telephone) between the defendants and police officers posing as lorry drivers. The defence sought disclosure of the RIPA surveillance authorities so that the lawfulness of the obtaining of the evidence could be challenged. The Crown disclosed edited versions of the authorities, and the defence argued that the authorities disclosed did not permit telephone interception, so that accordingly the police activities breached RIPA, s 1. Stay of proceedings was refused. The defendants pleaded guilty but appealed on the basis that the evidence had been obtained by unlawful telephone intercepts.

Held, on appeal to the Court of Appeal (Rose LJ, Hughes J, Royce J) that there was **20.02** no abuse of process. The surveillance, including tape-recording, had been authorised under RIPA and was lawful. It was surveillance, not interception. Since a police officer had been a party to the conversations on the telephone, there was no interception within the meaning of s 1 of RIPA. The recording did not occur while the contents of the communications were being transmitted, and tape-recording the conversations did not render it unlawful (the court observed that tape-recording was a safeguard against mistaken recollections). There was good reason for the definition of 'interception' to require interception in the course of transmission, since a person who knowingly spoke to another knew that the conversation could be related later to someone else whereas the overhearing of a conversation by a third party using interception unknown to either party was different. To hold otherwise would make it an offence for any householder to record his private telephone; this was not the intention of Parliament.[1] (Appeals dismissed.)

AG's Ref No 5 of 2002 sub nom W [2004] UKHL 40

RIPA, ss 1(5)(c), 2, 3, 4, 17, 18—extent to which a criminal court may investigate lawfulness of interception and questions whether interception was over a public or private telecommunications system—PACE 1984, s 78

20.03   Under s 36(1) of the Criminal Justice Act 1972 the A-G sought the opinion of the Court of Appeal on the correct construction of RIPA, s 17(1). The relevant question was whether, and if so to what extent, a criminal court could investigate whether intercept material relied on by the Crown had been obtained by intercepting a private as opposed to a public telecommunications system. The Court of Appeal (Clarke LJ, Morison J and Dame Heather Steel) referred the questions to the House of Lords.

20.04   The underlying facts were that in the course of an investigation as to whether police officers had been supplying sensitive information to journalists, the police arranged for calls to be intercepted. The Crown's case at trial was that the interceptions had taken place within a private telecommunications system. The defence case was that the interception had taken place on a public system. The defence had submitted that RIPA, s 17[2] prevented any investigation into the circumstances of the interception and, in particular, into whether the interception had taken place on the public side of the telecommunications system. The judge ruled that s 17 prevented the defence from asserting that the interception had taken place on the public side of the system, but did not prevent the prosecution from adducing evidence that it had taken place on the private side. The judge then acceded to a request from the defence that the judge should exclude the prosecution evidence under s 78 of PACE 1984 since it would not be fair to admit prosecution evidence that it had taken place on the private side but shut out the defence evidence that it had taken place on the public side of such a system. The Crown offered no evidence and the defendants were acquitted at the judge's direction.

20.05   **Held**, (Lord Bingham of Cornhill, Lord Nicholls of Birkenhead, Lord Steyn, Lord Hope of Craighead, Lord Walker of Gestingthorpe), that there was nothing in RIPA which suggested an intention to depart from the principle that the issue

---

[1] Had there been interception properly so-called, it may well have been treated as surveillance under Part II if the police officer as a party to the call consented to the interception (s 3(2) of RIPA).

[2] Section 17 imposes a prohibition (subject to exceptions in s 18) that no evidence shall be adduced, question asked, etc for purposes of or in connection with any legal proceedings, which (broadly) discloses that information has its origins in intercepted communications or which discloses the content of intercepted communications.

of warrants and matters pertaining to them should not be the subject of enquiry in the course of a criminal trial, but there was nothing which threw doubt on the decisions in *R v Ahmed*[3] and *R v Effik*[4] in which the court had examined whether an interception had been made within a public or a private system following enactment of the Interception of Communications 1985 Act. Since RIPA had been passed, there had been further Court of Appeal decisions in which the same enquiry had been conducted: *R v Allan;*[5] *R v Goodman.*[6]

Per Lord Nicholls of Birkenhead at 27–28:   **20.06**

> . . . if the prosecution seeks to give evidence of the contents of an intercept as properly admissible on the basis that the interception was of a communication in the course of transmission by means of a private telecommunication system carried out with the consent of the person in charge of that system, can the defence advance a case that the place where the intercept occurred was part of a public telecommunication system even though this might involve the suggestion that an offence had been committed under section 1(1) by a person mentioned in section 17(3)? . . .
>
> . . . I am in no doubt that the answer to this question is 'yes'. Investigating this issue, essential to the conduct of a fair trial, would not imperil the secrecy of the warrant system. . . . Section 17 must therefore be interpreted as inapplicable as much in the type of case now under consideration as it is in the cases specifically mentioned in section18(4).

R v E [2004] EWCA Crim, 1243, (2004) 2 Cr App R 29 (also known as R v X)

Listening device in vehicle—entry to property—Police Act 1997, ss 91(5), 7(1)—whether unlawful interception to record one side of a telephone conversation—intrusive surveillance—RIPA, ss 1(1), 2(1), 2(2), 2(8), 5, 17(1)—PACE 1984, s 78—Directive 97/66—Telecommunications and Data Protection Directive—Art 8

The appellant was charged with conspiracy to supply controlled drugs. At a   **20.07**
preparatory hearing the judge ruled admissible evidence of recordings made by a device placed in the accused's car by the police. The facts were that the police obtained permission under the Police Act 1997 and RIPA to place a listening device in the car which provided recordings of words spoken by in the car including words spoken by the accused in the car using a mobile telephone. The device recorded the accused's end of any such telephone conversations. It did not pick up any speech from the other end of the call.

The defence argued that the recorded telephone conversation was unlawful interception and that s 17 of RIPA rendered evidence of the product of the device inadmissible. Furthermore it was argued that a lack of candour in the police

---

[3] Court of Appeal, 29 March 1994.   [4] [1995] 1 AC 309, 314.
[5] [2001] EWCA Crim 1027, 6 April 2001, unrep.
[6] [2002] EWCA Crim 903, 4 March 2002, unrep.

application for authorisation for intrusive surveillance (failing to mention that most of the recordings would involve one side of a telephone conversation) meant that the entire product of the recordings should be excluded under s 78 of PACE.

20.08   **Held**, on appeal to the Court of Appeal (Rose LJ, Hughes J, Gloster J) that placing the device involved entry into a private vehicle, and that was lawful under s 92 of the Police Act 1997 if it was properly authorised (ss 91(5) and 97(1) of the Police Act 1997). Intrusive surveillance using the device had been authorised under RIPA.

20.09   The court was satisfied that if what happened had been interception, then evidence of the content of any telephone calls would be rendered inadmissible by RIPA, s 17(1)(a). If it had been interception, it would be unnecessary to get as far as the discretionary power to exclude evidence pursuant to s 78 of PACE. But the critical words were 'in the course of its transmission' in RIPA, s 2(2) as part of the definition of interception. In the court's judgment the natural meaning of the expression denoted some inference or abstraction of the signal, whether it was passing along wires or by wireless telegraphy, during the process of transmission. The recording of a person's voice, independently of the fact that at the time he was using a telephone, did not become interception simply because what he said went not only into the recorder, but, by separate process, was transmitted by a telecommunications system. Interception was concerned with what happened in the course of transmission by 'a telecommunications system', and s 2(1) defined a telecommunications system such that the system began with the conversion of sound waves from the maker of the call into electrical or electromagnetic energy.

20.10   What had been recorded in the instant case was what happened independently of the operation of the telecommunications system. What was being recorded was the words of the accused taken from the sound waves in the car. In the circumstances the recordings had not amounted to interception of communications. *R v Effik*,[7] *DPP v Morgans*,[8] *R v Smart & Beard*,[9] *R v Alan, Bunting and Boodo*,[10] *Attorney-General's Reference No 5 of 2002*,[11] *R v Hammond, McIntosh & Gray*[12] and in *R v Hardy & Hardy*,[13] *R v MacDonald*,[14] *R v Ahmed*,[15] referred to. Directive 97/66 of the European Parliament and of the Council of the European Community of 15th December 1997 (the Telecommunications and Data Protection Directive) also considered. (Appeal dismissed.)

---

[7] [1995] 1 AC 309.   [8] [2000] 2 Cr App R 113.   [9] [2002] EWCA Crim 772.
[10] [2001] EWCA 1005.   [11] [2004] 1 Cr App R(S) No 2.
[12] [2002] EWCA Crim 1243.   [13] [2003] 1 Cr App R(S) No 30, 494.
[14] Woolwich Crown Court, 23 April 2002.
[15] Court of Appeal, 29 March 1994.

R v Ipswich Crown Court ex parte NTL Group Ltd [2002] EWHC 1585
(Divisional Court)

Unlawful interception—PACE, Sch 1—special procedure material—whether copying
to an email address is 'interception'—whether PACE, Sch 1, para 11 provides implicit
authority to intercept—RIPA, s 1(1), (2), (5)(c)

In the course of investigation into suspected conspiracy to defraud, the police **20.11**
applied for an order under PACE, s 9 and Sch 1 whereby NTL (an email service
provider) would be obliged to produce or provide access to various emails passing
through customer email accounts. By virtue of para 11 of the schedule, NTL, as
soon as it was served with notice of the application, was obliged not to destroy alter
or dispose of the material without leave of the judge or written permission of a
constable, until the disposal of the application or until it had disclosed the material
or provided access to it.

The emails were subject to an automatic system whereby they were deleted **20.12**
after being read, and it was not practicable for NTL to change its system. The
only way in which the emails could be preserved was by copying them to a third
email address. NTL sought an order permitting them to allow the destruction
of the emails, on the basis that the only way in which it could comply would be
by what amounted to the offence of unlawful interception within under RIPA,
s 1. They argued that the diversion or copying of email would be interception
as a result of RIPA, s 1(7) and (8) which referred to any time when the system
was used for storing messages in a manner that enabled the intended recipient
to collect it, and to diversion or recording of messages so as to be available
subsequently.

Held, (Lord Woolf of Barnes LCJ, Curtis J) that while the court had considerable **20.13**
doubts as to whether it was intended that s 1 of RIPA should have the effect of
making what happened an offence, the language of s 2 was clear, and an offence of
unlawful interception would have been committed by NTL if they were not entitled
to rely upon some lawful authority for doing what they were required to do to
comply with Sch 1, para 11 of PACE.

Under s 1(5) of RIPA, it was not the police, but NTL, who required lawful **20.14**
authority for the action which they were taking. If NTL were not in a position
to take that action without committing an offence then the power under PACE
would be almost worthless. The court found it impossible to accept that it
was the intention of Parliament in legislating in the terms that it did in RIPA,
s 1 for all practical purposes to defeat the powers of the police under PACE in
this area.

20.15 It was implicit in the terms of para 11 that the body subject to an application (NTL) had the necessary power (arising implicitly from the language of PACE, Sch 1, para 11 read together with PACE, s 9), to take the action which they apparently had to take to conserve the communications within the system until the court decided whether or not to make an order. That provided the lawful authority for the purposes of RIPA, s 1(5) and no offence would be committed.

21

RIPA, PART II CASE LAW

A. Intrusive Surveillance

R v GS and Others [2005] EWCA Crim 887

Intrusive surveillance—recorded conversations—status of surveillance commissioners' approval forms—RIPA, ss 27, 32, 36—Police Act 1997, s 91(10)—whether underlying material may be ordered to be disclosed in order for lawfulness to be examined

The defendants were charged with conspiracy to supply drugs. The Crown sought **21.01** to adduce evidence of covertly recorded telephone using devices at the homes of three defendants, obtained using the intrusive surveillance authorisation procedures under RIPA, Part II. The Crown sought to rely on the surveillance commissioners' approvals for the surveillance as proof of the lawfulness of the process by which the evidence was obtained. The defence sought an order that the prosecution do produce the material which had been placed before the commissioners when seeking the approval and argued that without the material they would be unable properly to formulate argument for evidential exclusion of the recordings. The defence argued at a preliminary hearing that the proceedings should be stayed for abuse of process or covert recording evidence be excluded in the absence of disclosure of the material. In the alternative they sought a decision that the judge himself would consider the material as undisclosed material.

The judge below held that RIPA (ss 32 and 36) was provided with a rigorous high **21.02** level machinery for securing that intrusive surveillance was permissible in the interests of national security and for serious crime, where the evidence could not be obtained by other means and where the surveillance was proportionate. Section 91(10) of the Police Act 1997 rendered commissioners' approvals conclusive as to lawfulness. The effect was to substitute the commissioners' approval in place of the court's responsibility to determine whether the evidence was lawfully obtained. The judge held that there was no abuse of process or prejudice.

.03 **Held**, on appeal to the Court of Appeal (Auld LJ, Beatson J, Wakerley J) that the 1997 and 2000 Acts provided independent verification at a very high judicial level and that there was a high level Tribunal[1] to inquire into complaints. The Tribunal's jurisdiction covered both the legality of the authorisation and whether the surveillance had been carried out in accordance with that authorisation. Section 91(10) of the 1997 Act was designed to prevent re-litigation of the protective regime of authorisation and approval of it.

21.04 The protection of s 91(10) of the 1997 Act and s 27 of RIPA went beyond protecting chief officers and surveillance commissioners from civil proceedings. Section 27 was important in that it provided that the conduct covered by the authorisation was lawful 'for all purposes', so that s 91(10) of the 1997 Act, providing that commissioners should not be subject to appeal or liable to be questioned in any court, applied equally to criminal trials. (*R v SL*,[2] *R v Hardy and Hardy*[3] referred to). The judge below had been correct to rely upon the approval forms to satisfy himself that the surveillance had been lawfully authorised. He was not required to accede to the defence request for disclosure or judicial examination of the underlying material. The provisions of RIPA, Part II affected the lawfulness of the evidence obtained but not its admissibility, which remained a matter for the court. (Appeals dismissed.)

R v Allsopp and Others [2005] EWCA Crim 703

Intrusive surveillance—RIPA, ss 26 and 32—modified telephone used as listening device in vehicle—whether amounting to an 'intercept' within the meaning of RIPA, ss 1, 2 and 81—application for disclosure of material supporting intrusive surveillance authorisation—meaning of 'communication'—Surveillance Code of Practice, para 4.32

21.05 The defendants were charged with conspiracy to supply drugs. Use was made of transcripts of conversations taking place within a vehicle which had been recorded by the police using a device inside the vehicle. The device was in the nature of a mobile telephone which could be remotely activated to transmit sound from the vehicle to police who could record the sound. Copies of surveillance authorisations under ss 26 and 32 of RIPA were disclosed.[4] The defence sought an order excluding the evidence unless the underlying material on which the authorisation was based was disclosed, and on the ground that there had been an unlawful telephone intercept under s 1 of RIPA. The trial judge held that there was no unfairness caused by non-disclosure of the material, and that the conversation between the

---

[1] Ie the IPT.   [2] [2001] EWCA Crim 1829.   [3] [2002] EWCA Crim 3012.

[4] The judgment refers to these as having been signed by an interception of communications commissioner. It is unclear whether this is a slip and whether the reference is intended to be to a surveillance commissioner.

defendants had been a face to face communication transmitted orally and not by way of the telephone network, such that the police were recording not carrying out a telephone intercept.

Held, on appeal to the Court of Appeal (Gage LJ, Nelson J, Sir Douglas Brown) that **21.06** the authorisations were properly countersigned by commissioners and on their face were valid. The correct procedure had been followed and the defendants' Article 8 and 6 rights had been protected by the RIPA procedures and the public interest immunity procedures in relation to the non-disclosed supporting material. On the question of whether the recordings were obtained by unlawful telephone intercept rather than intrusive surveillance, it was accepted that if the information had been obtained by unlawful telephone intercept then RIPA, s 17 had the effect that it would be prohibited from use in evidence. However the conversation between the men was a face to face one and had not passed between them through any telecommunications system. *R v E*[5] applied. (Appeals dismissed.)

B. Directed Surveillance

R v Sutherland and Others Nottingham Crown Court Case T20027203 *(29/1/2002)*[6]

Abuse of process—directed surveillance—recording privileged conversations deliberately—recording outside scope of authorisation

Defendants in a murder trial applied to stay the indictment on the basis of abuse of **21.07** process relying on, inter alia, complaints that police officers leading the investigation deliberately placed a microphone in the exercise yard at police stations, so that any privileged conversations taking placed between a solicitor and the suspects held there would be recorded. The officer in charge of the investigation had (inter alia) made applications for authority under RIPA, Part II for directed surveillance at the police stations, but did not refer to recording in the yard areas.

Held, (Newman J), staying the indictment, the covert surveillance led to the record- **21.08** ing of conversations between suspects and their solicitors whilst in the exercise yards. The suspects were there to be interviewed by the police, and it was obvious the solicitors were there to advise them in connection with their arrests. The conversations were occasions which attracted privilege. Privileged conversations had been listened to, recorded and subsequently listened to by second-hand listeners.

Circumstances could arise in which the police came into possession of privileged **21.09** material by mistake. However the applications in the instant case were not made

---

[5] [2004] EWCA Crim 1243. [6] See *R v Grant* [2005] EWCA Crim 108.

on the basis of mistake. In the court's judgment even if it was not intended from the outset, in this case there could be no answer the proposition that the listening to privileged material deliberately and intentionally continued after it was known that there was a risk that the microphones would pick up privileged conversations. The RIPA, Part II applications as made did not seek authority to place a surveillance device in the exercise yards, nor was authority granted for such. The authority granted was in terms, referring to 'communal passage area of the cell complex at the respective police stations in respect of conversations from one cell to another via the communal passage area'.

21.10 No steps had been taken to ensure that the surveillance did not give rise to the interception of privileged material, no action taken when privileged material was obtained other than to continue recording, and no procedures existed for review or re-assessment to be made of the risks in relation to privileged material being obtained. The microphones had been placed with the intention of capturing any conversation which might take place between the detained persons and the solicitors. Flagrant breaches of the law had occurred. The procedure for regulation under RIPA was deliberately manipulated by an intentional material non-disclosure, and no authority would have been granted for the exercise yards in the light of the state of affairs prevailing at each of the police stations. There was a fundamental principle at play, namely that a person could not be deprived of his right to private consultation with his solicitor in connection with threatened criminal proceedings. (Indictment stayed.)

C. Covert Human Intelligence Sources

R v Brett [2005] EWCA Crim 983

Covert human intelligence Source—investigation while defendant on trial for similar offences—whether 'necessary'—RIPA, s 29(2), (3)—Code of Practice, paras 2.4, 2.5—abuse of process

21.11 The defendant operated a shop which sold electrical goods. In an undercover operation a police officer with a concealed camera attended her home at her invitation and posed as a person seeking to sell stolen goods (which were not in fact stolen) which she purchased. She was charged with attempting to handle stolen goods. The defence sought to stay the prosecution for abuse since the defendant had been on bail at the time in respect of offences of handling stolen goods which the police knew were stolen, and accordingly the use of CHIS to gather evidence for a further prosecution was 'unnecessary' and oppressive. The court below refused to stay the proceedings and the defendant pleaded guilty but appealed.

21.12 **Held,** on appeal to the Court of Appeal, (Laws LJ, Owen J, Judge Moss QC) that the expression 'necessary' in RIPA, s 29(2) meant necessary for one of the stated statutory purposes (including the prevention or detection of crime). Authorisation under s 29 was only lawfully given if the authorising officer genuinely believed that the action was necessary for one of the statutory purposes (CHIS Code of Practice, paras 2.4 and 2.5 referred to). The test of necessity in RIPA and the Codes was not the test to be applied for abuse of process, which was that in *R v Looseley*,[7] namely whether the conduct was so seriously improper as to bring the administration of justice into disrepute.

21.13 The court accepted that if the provisions of s 29 had been shown to have been flouted or ignored then that might give rise to the implication that their conduct was seriously improper. However in this case the officers reasonably regarded the operation as necessary. It was not possible to come to a conclusion that the police were guilty of seriously improper conduct. (Appeal dismissed.)

R v Hans-Constantin Paulssen [2003] EWCA Crim 3109

Covert human intelligence sources—failure to review or renew authorisation but continuing to use CHIS—whether abuse to rely on evidence so obtained—whether operation had been 'in accordance with the law'—Art 8(2)—whether affront to public conscience to allow guilty plea to stand

21.14 The accused was charged with two counts of soliciting to murder. The prosecution evidence included evidence from a CHIS to the effect that the accused solicited him to murder a woman. An application under RIPA, Part II for 'authority to deploy an under cover officer and to use technical equipment to obtain further evidence of soliciting to murder' was granted by a police commander on 16 March 2001. Authority was given until 14 June 2001 but no reviews took place and no renewal was sought despite the operation continuing until 4 July 2001. The defence sought (among other arguments unrelated to RIPA) to argue that the use of the CHIS had not been 'in accordance with the law'.

21.15 The judge declined to stay the proceedings for abuse and held inter alia that apart from minor infractions to the provisions of RIPA, the undercover operation had been 'in accordance with the law', necessary in the interests of a democratic society and proportionate to the aims of the operation. The defendant pleaded guilty but sought permission to appeal against conviction.

21.16 **Held**, on application for permission to appeal to the Court of Appeal (Waller LJ, Hughes J, Roderick Evans J), on the issues relating to RIPA, that under the authorisation for use of CHIS, if the undercover operation was to continue after its expiry then a further authority would have been needed. The applicant officer had been

---

[7] *R v Looseley: Attorney-General's reference (No 3 of 2000)* [2001] UKHL 53 reported at [2002] 1 Cr App R 29, [2001] 4 All ER 897.

told that he must give to the commander who authorised the operation a report on it by 17 April 2001. No report had been provided and although the undercover operation went on until 4 July 2001, no further authorisation had been sought for operations after 14 June 2001.

21.17 The judge had found that the authorisation complied with the terms of RIPA and he was satisfied for the purposes of Article 8(2) that the authorisation had been a response to a pressing social need and proportionate. So far as supervision was concerned there were legitimate criticisms and he had appreciated that strictly speaking the whole operation was not 'in accordance with law' for the purposes of Article 8(2). In the court's judgment the whole operation had been duly authorised and the judge was entitled to find that any infractions of the provisions of RIPA had been minor. The judge's conclusion that there was 'no affront to the public conscience' had been justified. His reasons were unassailable. (Application dismissed.)

22

RIPA, PART IV CASE LAW

A. The Tribunal

Ewing v Security Service, QBD (Unrep 30/7/2003)

Investigatory Powers Tribunal—whether 'court' for the purposes of s 42 of the Supreme Court Act 1981—Rule 11(1) of the Tribunal Rules—RIPA, s 67(4)

The claimant was the subject of a civil proceedings order under s 42 of the **22.01** Supreme Court Act 1981. The effect was that he needed leave, from the High Court, to institute any civil proceedings 'in a court'. He desired to apply to the Investigatory Powers Tribunal under RIPA, s 65(2)(a) and (3)(a) alleging breaches of his rights by the security service when dealing with his application under ss 7(1) and 82 of the Data Protection Act 1998.

He argued (on the question whether the Investigatory Powers Tribunal was 'a **22.02** court'), inter alia that r 11(1) of the Tribunal Rules[1] was a statutory recognition that the Tribunal was not a formal court of law. The nature of the Tribunal was that the proceedings might not always be in public, the claimant might sometimes not be permitted to be present, and the Tribunal could hear witnesses without the claimant having an opportunity to question witnesses or make representations. Even if oral hearings were heard, they would normally be in private. There was no proper reasoned decision at the end of the hearing, unless the claimant succeeded when there was a summary.

Held (Brown J) that as regarded the question whether the Investigatory Powers **22.03** Tribunal was a court within s 42 the starting point for both sides had been *AG v the BBC*[2] where Lord Diplock, stated at 338:

> I do not think that the Divisional Court's jurisdiction extends to all courts created by the state for I think that a distinction has to be drawn between courts which

---

[1] Ie 'The tribunal may receive evidence in any form and may receive evidence that would not be admissible in a court of law.'   [2] [1981] Appeal Cases 303.

discharge judicial functions and those which discharge administrative ones, between courts of law which form part of the judicial system of the country on the one hand and courts which are constituted to resolve problems which arise in the administration of the government of this country.

22.04 A body which had a judicial function was a court, whereas if it had an administrative function, albeit carried out judicially, it would not be a court. *Peach Gray and Company v Summers* [1995] ICR 549, referred to.

22.05 The Tribunal's jurisdiction provided the exclusive venue for a human rights complaint against the intelligence services. The Tribunal was a court exercising its judicial function and not any administrative function. The court was satisfied that there were reasonable grounds for the claimant to make his application to the Tribunal and if in the end the claim was devoid of merit, the Tribunal had procedures to deal with that situation (RIPA, s 67(4) referred to).

Re Kennedy and other cases, Investigatory Powers Tribunal Ruling[3] *23/1/03*

Investigatory Powers Tribunal—procedure—open court—status of the Tribunal Rules

22.06 Liberty and others pursued complaints to the IPT concerning interception activities by the intelligence services (inter alia alleging 'blanket' monitoring of telecommunications and monitoring of privileged material). In a separate case Mr Kennedy, a businessman, alleged police were interfering with his telephone communications.

22.07 The Tribunal Rules as to the private nature of the hearings were challenged in legal argument. The Tribunal ruled that notwithstanding IPTR, r 9(6) it could hear some parts of cases in public, allow the complainant and his lawyers to be present and could give reasons for decisions. The Tribunal stated in open court:

> The challenge to r.9(6) and to most of the other rules governing the basic procedures of the Tribunal have made this the most significant case ever to come before the Tribunal. The Tribunal are left in no doubt that their rulings on the legal issues formulated by the parties have potentially important consequences for dealing with and determining these and future proceedings and complaints.

---

[3] It is anticipated that an official full text of the judgment will be made available shortly via the IPT website. The summary here is based upon informal reports.

Part VII

OTHER STATUTES

23

THE HUMAN RIGHTS ACT 1998[1]
(s 6 AND ECHR, ARTS 6 AND 8)

Public authorities

Acts of public authorities.

6.—(1) It is unlawful for a public authority to act in a way which is incompatible **23.01**
with a Convention right.

(2) Subsection (1) does not apply to an act if—

    (a) as the result of one or more provisions of primary legislation, the authority
could not have acted differently; or

    (b) in the case of one or more provisions of, or made under, primary legislation
which cannot be read or given effect in a way which is compatible with the
Convention rights, the authority was acting so as to give effect to or enforce
those provisions.

(3) In this section "public authority"[2] includes—

    (a) a court or tribunal, and

    (b) any person certain of whose functions are functions of a public nature,
but does not include either House of Parliament or a person exercising functions in connection with proceedings in Parliament.

(4) In subsection (3) "Parliament" does not include the House of Lords in its
judicial capacity.

(5) In relation to a particular act, a person is not a public authority by virtue only
of subsection (3)(b) if the nature of the act is private.

(6) "An act" includes a failure to act but does not include a failure to—

    (a) introduce in, or lay before, Parliament a proposal for legislation; or

    (b) make any primary legislation or remedial order.

---

[1] Enacted 9 November 1998. Original commencement date for parts here was 2 October 2000
(SI 2000 No 1851).

[2] Cf the sections of RIPA which use the expression 'public authority' and provide the definition
in s 81(1) of RIPA, which is that a public authority is any public authority within the meaning of s 6
of the HRA 1998 *other than a court or tribunal.*

SCHEDULES

SCHEDULE 1
THE ARTICLES

PART I

THE CONVENTION
RIGHTS AND FREEDOMS

[. . .]

Article 6
Right to a Fair Trial

23.02 1. In the determination of his civil rights and obligations or of any criminal charge against him, everyone is entitled to a fair and public hearing within a reasonable time by an independent and impartial tribunal established by law. Judgment shall be pronounced publicly but the press and public may be excluded from all or part of the trial in the interest of morals, public order or national security in a democratic society, where the interests of juveniles or the protection of the private life of the parties so require, or to the extent strictly necessary in the opinion of the court in special circumstances where publicity would prejudice the interests of justice.

2. Everyone charged with a criminal offence shall be presumed innocent until proved guilty according to law.

3. Everyone charged with a criminal offence has the following minimum rights:
    (a) to be informed promptly, in a language which he understands and in detail, of the nature and cause of the accusation against him;
    (b) to have adequate time and facilities for the preparation of his defence;
    (c) to defend himself in person or through legal assistance of his own choosing or, if he has not sufficient means to pay for legal assistance, to be given it free when the interests of justice so require;
    (d) to examine or have examined witnesses against him and to obtain the attendance and examination of witnesses on his behalf under the same conditions as witnesses against him;
    (e) to have the free assistance of an interpreter if he cannot understand or speak the language used in court.

[. . .]

Article 8
Right to Respect for Private and Family Life

23.03 1. Everyone has the right to respect for his private and family life, his home and his correspondence.

2. There shall be no interference by a public authority with the exercise of this right except such as is in accordance with the law and is necessary in a democratic society in the interests of national security, public safety or the economic well-being of the country, for the prevention of disorder or crime, for the protection of health or morals, or for the protection of the rights and freedoms of others.

24

ANTI-TERRORISM, CRIME AND SECURITY ACT 2001 (PART 11)[1]

PART II
RETENTION OF COMMUNICATIONS DATA

102 Codes and agreements about the retention of communications data

(1) The Secretary of State shall issue, and may from time to time revise, a code of **24.01** practice relating to the retention by communications providers of communications data obtained by or held by them.[2]

(2) The Secretary of State may enter into such agreements as he considers appropriate with any communications provider about the practice to be followed by that provider in relation to the retention of communications data obtained by or held by that provider.

(3) A code of practice or agreement under this section may contain any such provision as appears to the Secretary of State to be necessary—

(a) for the purpose of safeguarding national security; or

---

[1] The sections reproduced here came into force upon enactment on 14 December 2001.
[2] A Code of Practice (reproduced in Chapter 17) was published entitled 'Voluntary Retention of Communications Data under Part 11: Anti-terrorism, Crime and Security Act 2001—Voluntary Code of Practice' and was brought into force by the Retention of Communications Data (Code of Practice) Order 2003 (SI 2003 No 3175) with effect from 5 December 2001.

(b) for the purposes of prevention or detection of crime or the prosecution of offenders which may relate directly or indirectly to national security.

(4) A failure by any person to comply with a code of practice or agreement under this section which is for the time being in force shall not of itself render him liable to any criminal or civil proceedings.

(5) A code of practice or agreement under this section which is for the time being in force shall be admissible in evidence in any legal proceedings in which the question arises whether or not the retention of any communications data is justified on the grounds that a failure to retain the data would be likely to prejudice national security, the prevention or detection of crime or the prosecution of offenders.[3]

103 Procedure for codes of practice

24.02 (1) Before issuing the code of practice under section 102 the Secretary of State shall—

(a) prepare and publish a draft of the code; and

(b) consider any representations made to him about the draft;

and the Secretary of State may incorporate in the code finally issued any modifications made by him to the draft after its publication.

(2) Before publishing a draft of the code the Secretary of State shall consult with—

(a) the Information Commissioner; and

(b) the communications providers to whom the code will apply.

(3) The Secretary of State may discharge his duty under subsection (2) to consult with any communications providers by consulting with a person who appears to him to represent those providers.

(4) The Secretary of State shall lay before Parliament the draft code of practice under section 102 that is prepared and published by him under this section.

(5) The code of practice issued by the Secretary of State under section 102 shall not be brought into force except in accordance with an order made by the Secretary of State by statutory instrument.

(6) An order under subsection (5) may contain such transitional provisions and savings as appear to the Secretary of State to be necessary or expedient in connection with the coming into force of the code to which the order relates.

(7) The Secretary of State shall not make an order under this section unless a draft of the order has been laid before Parliament and approved by resolution of each House.

---

[3] See the note to subs (1) above.

(8) The Secretary of State may from time to time—
    (a) revise the whole or any part of the code issued under section 102; and
    (b) issue the revised code.

(9) The preceding provisions of this section shall apply (with appropriate modifications) in relation to the issue of any revised code under section 102 as they apply in relation to the first issuing of the code.

(10) Subsection (9) shall not, in the case of a draft of a revised code, require the Secretary of State to consult under subsection (2) with any communications providers who would not be affected by the proposed revisions.

104 Directions about retention of communications data

(1) If, after reviewing the operation of any requirements contained in the code of **24.03** practice and any agreements under section 102, it appears to the Secretary of State that it is necessary to do so, he may by order made by statutory instrument authorise the giving of directions under this section for purposes prescribed in section 102(3).

(2) Where any order under this section is in force, the Secretary of State may give such directions as he considers appropriate about the retention of communications data—
    (a) to communications providers generally;
    (b) to communications providers of a description specified in the direction; or
    (c) to any particular communications providers or provider.

(3) An order under this section must specify the maximum period for which a communications provider may be required to retain communications data by any direction given under this section while the order is in force.

(4) Before giving a direction under this section the Secretary of State shall consult—
    (a) with the communications provider or providers to whom it will apply; or
    (b) except in the case of a direction confined to a particular provider, with the persons appearing to the Secretary of State to represent the providers to whom it will apply.

(5) A direction under this section must be given or published in such manner as the Secretary of State considers appropriate for bringing it to the attention of the communications providers or provider to whom it applies.

(6) It shall be the duty of a communications provider to comply with any direction under this section that applies to him.

(7) The duty imposed by subsection (6) shall be enforceable by civil proceedings by the Secretary of State for an injunction, or for specific performance of a statutory duty under section 45 of the Court of Session Act 1988 (c. 36), or for any other appropriate relief.

(8) The Secretary of State shall not make an order under this section unless a draft of it has been laid before Parliament and approved by a resolution of each House.

105 Lapsing of powers in section 104

24.04 (1) Section 104 shall cease to have effect at the end of the initial period unless an order authorising the giving of directions is made under that section before the end of that period.

(2) Subject to subsection (3), the initial period is the period of two years beginning with the day on which this Act is passed.

(3) The Secretary of State may by order made by statutory instrument extend, or (on one or more occasions) further extend the initial period.[4]

(4) An order under subsection (3)—

    (a) must be made before the time when the initial period would end but for the making of the order; and

    (b) shall have the effect of extending, or further extending, that period for the period of two years beginning with that time.

(5) The Secretary of State shall not make an order under subsection (3) unless a draft of it has been laid before Parliament and approved by a resolution of each House.

106 Arrangements for payments

24.05 (1) It shall be the duty of the Secretary of State to ensure that such arrangements are in force as he thinks appropriate for authorising or requiring, in such cases as he thinks fit, the making to communications providers of appropriate contributions towards the costs incurred by them—

    (a) in complying with the provisions of any code of practice, agreement or direction under this Part, or

    (b) as a consequence of the retention of any communications data in accordance with any such provisions.

(2) For the purpose of complying with his duty under this section, the Secretary of State may make arrangements for the payments to be made out of money provided by Parliament.

107 Interpretation of Part 11

24.06 (1) In this Part—

"communications data" has the same meaning as in Chapter 2 of Part 1 of the Regulation of Investigatory Powers Act 2000 (c. 23);

"communications provider" means a person who provides a postal service or a telecommunications service;

---

[4] Orders under this subs: the Retention of Communications Data (Extension of Initial Period) Order 2003 (SI 2003 No 3173) in force 5 December 2003, which extended the initial period for a further period of two years from the date it would otherwise expire (which would otherwise have been two years after enactment on 14 December 2001).

"legal proceedings", "postal service" and "telecommunications service" each has the same meaning as in that Act;

and any reference in this Part to the prevention or detection of crime shall be construed as if contained in Chapter 2 of Part 1 of that Act.

(2) References in this Part, in relation to any code of practice, agreement or direction, to the retention by a communications provider of any communications data include references to the retention of any data obtained by that provider before the time when the code was issued, the agreement made or the direction given, and to data already held by that provider at that time.

. . . .

Part VIII

STATUTORY INSTRUMENTS[1]

---

[1] Note that commencement instruments and revoked Orders are not reproduced here (see footnotes
to each RIPA section for commencement dates and commencement SIs).

25

STATUTORY INSTRUMENTS (1998)

A. SI 1998 No 3241 The Police Act 1997 (Notification of Authorisations etc.) Order 1998[1]

Made 22nd December 1998

Coming into force in accordance with article 1(1)

Whereas—

(1) A notice under section 96 of the Police Act 1997 ("the 1997 Act") (notification of authorisations etc.) shall specify such matters as the Secretary of State may by order prescribe;

(2) And whereas a draft of this Order has been approved by each House of Parliament;

Now, therefore, the Secretary of State, in exercise of the powers conferred on him by section 96(2) of the 1997 Act, hereby orders as follows:

Citation, commencement etc.

25.01 1.—(1) This Order may be cited as the Police Act 1997 (Notification of Authorisations etc.) Order 1998 and shall come into force on the date on which Part III of the Police Act 1997 comes fully into force.

(2) In this Order, references to authorisations are references to authorisations under section 93 of the 1997 Act (authorisations to interfere with property etc.) and references to a notice are references to a notice required to be given to a Commissioner under section 96(1) of that Act (notifications of authorisations etc.).

---

[1] Made on 22 December 1998, coming into force in accordance with Art 1(1), ie at the date of coming into force of the remainder of Part III of the Police Act 1997 (22/2/99).

Notice of authorisation

2. Where a person gives an authorisation, the notice thereof to a Commissioner **25.02**
shall specify the following matters—
   (a) whether section 97 of the 1997 Act (requiring the approval of a
       Commissioner in certain cases before an authorisation can take effect)
       applies;
   (b) where that section does not apply by virtue of subsection (3) of that section,
       the grounds on which the case is believed to be one of urgency;
   (c) the grounds on which the authorising officer believes the matters specified
       in section 93(2) of the 1997 Act;
   (d) the identity, where known, of persons to be the subject of the action
       authorised;
   (e) where the action authorised involves an interference with property, the
       property to which the authorisation applies;
   (f) the nature of the case and the reason why action of the kind and extent
       authorised is considered to be necessary;
   (g) whether the authorising officer considers that the action to be authorised
       is likely to lead to intrusion on the privacy of persons other than any per-
       son who is to be the subject of that action; and
   (h) whether it will be necessary to retrieve any equipment used in the action
       to be authorised.

Notice of renewal of authorisation

3. Where a person renews an authorisation, the notice thereof to a Commissioner **25.03**
shall specify the following matters—
   (a) whether the authorisation is being renewed for the first time, or, where it
       has been previously renewed, each occasion on which it has been
       renewed;
   (b) the matters required by article 2 above, as they apply at the time of notice
       of renewal;
   (c) every respect in which the information provided in the previous notifica-
       tion has changed;
   (d) the reason why it is considered to be necessary to renew the authorisation;
   (e) the content, and value to the investigation, of the information obtained to
       date through the action authorised;
   (f) the results of any reviews by the authorising officer; and
   (g) the period for which the authorisation is considered likely to continue to
       be necessary.

Notice of cancellation of authorisation

25.04 4. Where a person cancels an authorisation, the notice thereof to a Commissioner shall specify the following matters—

(a) the date and time when he gave the instructions to cease the action authorised;

(b) the reasons for cancelling the authorisation;

(c) the outcome of the investigation to which the authorisation related, and details of any criminal proceedings instituted or intended to be instituted; and

(d) what arrangements have been made for the storage of material obtained as a result of the action authorised, for its review and its destruction when its retention is no longer required, and for the immediate destruction of any material unrelated to the purposes for which the action was authorised.

26

STATUTORY INSTRUMENTS (2000)

A. SI 2000 No 2409 The Wireless Telegraphy (Interception and Disclosure of Messages) (Designation) Regulations 2000

Made	*6th September 2000*
Laid before Parliament	*7th September 2000*
Coming into force	*2nd October 2000*

26.01 The Secretary of State, in exercise of the powers conferred on him by section 5(7)(c) and (12)(c) of the Wireless Telegraphy Act 1949 (hereinafter referred to as "the Act") and of all other powers enabling him in that behalf, hereby makes the following Regulations—

1. These Regulations may be cited as the Wireless Telegraphy (Interception and Disclosure of Messages) (Designation) Regulations 2000 and shall come into force on 2nd October 2000.

2. The persons for the time being who hold the respective positions of Chief Executive of the Radiocommunications Agency of the Department of Trade and Industry and Director of the Customer Services Executive of that Agency (and, when they are both absent from the principal establishment of that Agency, any other person for the time being holding the position of a Director of an Executive of that Agency) are hereby designated for the purposes of section 5(7)(c) and (12)(c) of the Act.

Patricia Hewitt,

Minister of State for Small Business and E-Commerce, Department of Trade and Industry

6th September 2000

B. SI 2000 No 2417 The Regulation of Investigatory Powers (Prescription of Offices, Ranks and Positions) Order 2000 [*Revoked*]

[This SI has been revoked and is omitted, see SI 2003 No 3171 The Regulation of **26.02**
Investigatory Powers (Directed Surveillance and Covert Human Intelligence Sources)
Order 2003, Chapter 29]

C. SI 2000 No 2418 The Regulation of Investigatory Powers (Authorisations Extending to Scotland) Order 2000

Made	*7th September 2000*
Laid before Parliament	*8th September 2000*
Coming into force	*2nd October 2000*

The Secretary of State, in exercise of the power conferred on him by section 46(4) **26.03**
of the Regulation of Investigatory Powers Act 2000, hereby makes the following
Order:

Citation and commencement

1. This Order may be cited as the Regulation of Investigatory Powers **26.04**
   (Authorisations Extending to Scotland) Order 2000 and shall come into force
   on 2nd October 2000.

Relevant public authorities for all parts of the United Kingdom

2.—(1) Subject to paragraph (2), the public authorities listed in column 1 of the **26.05**
   Schedule to this Order (being public authorities for the time being specified
   in Schedule 1 to the Regulation of Investigatory Powers Act 2000) are relevant public authorities for all parts of the United Kingdom.
   (2) Where there is an entry in column 2 against a particular authority, that
   authority is a relevant public authority for all parts of the United Kingdom
   only to the extent specified in that column.

Charles Clarke
Minister of State

Home Office
7th September 2000

SCHEDULE

Article 2

(1)	(2)
The National Criminal Intelligence Service	
The Commissioners of Inland Revenue	
The Department of the Environment, Transport and the Regions	
The Department of Health	
The Home Office	The Immigration Service
The Department of Social Security	
The Department of Trade and Industry	
The Environment Agency	
The Financial Services Authority	
The Personal Investment Authority	
The Post Office	
The Health and Safety Executive	
The Royal Pharmaceutical Society of Great Britain	

D. SI 2000 No 2563 The Regulation of Investigatory Powers (Notification of Authorisations etc.) Order 2000

Approved by both Houses of Parliament

Made	*20th September 2000*
Laid before Parliament	*22nd September 2000*
Coming into force	*25th September 2000*

26.06 Whereas the Secretary of State may make an order under section 35(2)(c) of the Regulation of Investigatory Powers Act 2000;

And whereas subsections (6) and (7) of section 35 provide that the order made on the first occasion on which the power is exercised does not need to be approved by

Parliament before being made, but must be approved after being made in accordance with subsection (7);

And whereas this is the first occasion on which the Secretary of State exercises the power;

Now, therefore, the Secretary of State, in exercise of the power conferred on him by section 35(2)(c) of the Regulation of Investigatory Powers Act 2000, hereby makes the following Order:

Citation and commencement

1. This Order may be cited as the Regulation of Investigatory Powers (Notification **26.07** of Authorisations etc.) Order 2000 and shall come into force on 25th September 2000.

Interpretation

2. In this Order— **26.08**
   "the 2000 Act" means the Regulation of Investigatory Powers Act 2000;
   "authorisation" means a police or customs authorisation for the carrying out of intrusive surveillance;
   "Commissioner" means an ordinary Surveillance Commissioner; and
   "notice to a Commissioner" means the notice required to be given under section 35(1) of the 2000 Act.

Notice of authorisation

3. Where a person grants an authorisation, the notice to a Commissioner shall, **26.09** in addition to the statement required by section 35(3) of the 2000 Act specify the following matters:
   (a) the grounds on which he believes the matters specified in section 32(2)(a) and (b) of the 2000 Act;
   (b) the nature of the authorised conduct including the residential premises or private vehicle in relation to which the conduct is authorised and the identity, where known, of persons to be the subject of the authorised conduct; and
   (c) whether the conduct to be authorised is likely to lead to intrusion on the privacy of persons other than any person who is to be the subject of that conduct.

Notice of renewal of authorisation

4. Where a person renews an authorisation, the notice to a Commissioner shall, **26.10** in addition to the statement required by section 35(3) of the 2000 Act, specify the following matters:
   (a) whether the authorisation is being renewed for the first time, or, where it has been previously renewed, each occasion on which it has been renewed;

(b) the matters required by article 3, as they apply at the time of notice of renew

(c) every respect in which the information provided in the previous notice ha changed;

(d) the reason why it is considered to be necessary to renew the authorisation;

(e) the content, and value to the investigation, of the information obtained to date by the conduct authorised;

(f) the results of any reviews of the authorisation and

(g) the period for which the authorisation is considered likely to continue to be necessary.

Notice of cancellation of authorisation

26.11 5. Where a person cancels an authorisation, the notice to a Commissioner shall specify the following matters:

(a) the date and time when he gave the instructions to cease the conduct authorised;

(b) the reasons for cancelling the authorisation;

(c) the outcome of the investigation to which the authorisation related, and details of any criminal proceedings instituted or intended to be instituted; and

(d) what arrangements have been made for the storage of material obtained as a result of the conduct authorised, for its review and its destruction when its retention is no longer required, and for the immediate destruction of any material unrelated to the purposes for which the conduct was authorised.

Charles Clarke
Minister of State

Home Office
20th September 2000

E. SI 2000 No 2665 Investigatory Powers Tribunal Rules

26.12 *[The Rules appear in Chapter 11 and are discussed in Chapter 8]*

F. SI 2000 No 2699 The Telecommunications (Lawful Business Practice) (Interception of Communications) Regulations 2000

Made	*2nd October 2000*
Laid before Parliament	*3rd October 2000*
Coming into force	*24th October 2000*

The Secretary of State, in exercise of the powers conferred on him by sections 4(2) **26.13**
and 78(5) of the Regulation of Investigatory Powers Act 2000 ("the Act"), hereby
makes the following Regulations:—

Citation and commencement

1. These Regulations may be cited as the Telecommunications (Lawful Business **26.14**
   Practice) (Interception of Communications) Regulations 2000 and shall come
   into force on 24th October 2000.

Interpretation

2. In these Regulations— **26.15**
   (a) references to a business include references to activities of a government
   department, of any public authority or of any person or office holder on
   whom functions are conferred by or under any enactment;
   (b) a reference to a communication as relevant to a business is a reference to—
      (i) a communication—
         (aa) by means of which a transaction is entered into in the course of
         that business, or
         (bb) which otherwise relates to that business, or
      (ii) a communication which otherwise takes place in the course of the
      carrying on of that business;
   (c) "regulatory or self-regulatory practices or procedures" means practices or
   procedures—
      (i) compliance with which is required or recommended by, under or by
      virtue of—
         (aa) any provision of the law of a member state or other state within
         the European Economic Area, or
         (bb) any standard or code of practice published by or on behalf of a
         body established in a member state or other state within the
         European Economic Area which includes amongst its objec-
         tives the publication of standards or codes of practice for the
         conduct of business, or
      (ii) which are otherwise applied for the purpose of ensuring compliance
      with anything so required or recommended;
   (d) "system controller" means, in relation to a particular telecommunication
   system, a person with a right to control its operation or use.

Lawful interception of a communication

3.—(1) For the purpose of section 1(5)(a) of the Act, conduct is authorised, sub- **26.16**
   ject to paragraphs (2) and (3) below, if it consists of interception of a communication, in the course of its transmission by means of a telecommunication

system, which is effected by or with the express or implied consent of the system controller for the purpose of—

(a) monitoring or keeping a record of communications—
  (i) in order to—
    (aa) establish the existence of facts, or
    (bb) ascertain compliance with regulatory or self-regulatory practices or procedures which are—
      applicable to the system controller in the carrying on of his business or
      applicable to another person in the carrying on of his business where that person is supervised by the system controller in respect of those practices or procedures, or
    (cc) ascertain or demonstrate the standards which are achieved or ought to be achieved by persons using the system in the course of their duties, or
  (ii) in the interests of national security, or
  (iii) for the purpose of preventing or detecting crime, or
  (iv) for the purpose of investigating or detecting the unauthorised use of that or any other telecommunication system, or
  (v) where that is undertaken—
    (aa) in order to secure, or
    (bb) as an inherent part of,
    the effective operation of the system (including any monitoring or keeping of a record which would be authorised by section 3(3) of the Act if the conditions in paragraphs (a) and (b) thereof were satisfied); or
(b) monitoring communications for the purpose of determining whether they are communications relevant to the system controller's business which fall within regulation 2(b)(i) above; or
(c) monitoring communications made to a confidential voice-telephony counselling or support service which is free of charge (other than the cost, if any, of making a telephone call) and operated in such a way that users may remain anonymous if they so choose.

(2) Conduct is authorised by paragraph (1) of this regulation only if—
(a) the interception in question is effected solely for the purpose of monitoring or (where appropriate) keeping a record of communications relevant to the system controller's business;
(b) the telecommunication system in question is provided for use wholly or partly in connection with that business;
(c) the system controller has made all reasonable efforts to inform every person who may use the telecommunication system in question that communications transmitted by means thereof may be intercepted; and

(d) in a case falling within—

  (i) paragraph (1)(a)(ii) above, the person by or on whose behalf the interception is effected is a person specified in section 6(2)(a) to (i) of the Act;

  (ii) paragraph (1)(b) above, the communication is one which is intended to be received (whether or not it has been actually received) by a person using the telecommunication system in question.

(3) Conduct falling within paragraph (1)(a)(i) above is authorised only to the extent that Article 5 of Directive 97/66/EC of the European Parliament and of the Council of 15 December 1997 concerning the processing of personal data and the protection of privacy in the telecommunications sector so permits.

Patricia Hewitt,
Minister for Small Business and E-Commerce, Department of Trade and Industry

2nd October 2000

G. SI 2000 No 2725 The Regulation of Investigatory Powers (Source Records) Regulations 2000

Approved by both Houses of Parliament
Made   20th September 2000
Laid before Parliament 22nd September 2000
Coming into force   25th September 2000

Whereas the Secretary of State may make an order under section 35(2)(c) of the **26.17** Regulation of Investigatory Powers Act 2000;

And whereas subsections (6) and (7) of section 35 provide that the order made on the first occasion on which the power is exercised does not need to be approved by Parliament before being made, but must be approved after being made in accordance with subsection (7);

And whereas this is the first occasion on which the Secretary of State exercises the power;

Now, therefore, the Secretary of State, in exercise of the power conferred on him by section 35(2)(c) of the Regulation of Investigatory Powers Act 2000, hereby makes the following Order:

Citation and commencement

1. This Order may be cited as the Regulation of Investigatory Powers **26.18** (Notification of Authorisations etc.) Order 2000 and shall come into force on 25th September 2000.

Interpretation

26.19 2. In this Order—

"the 2000 Act" means the Regulation of Investigatory Powers Act 2000;

"authorisation" means a police or customs authorisation for the carrying out of intrusive surveillance;

"Commissioner" means an ordinary Surveillance Commissioner; and

"notice to a Commissioner" means the notice required to be given under section 35(1) of the 2000 Act.

Notice of authorisation

26.20 3. Where a person grants an authorisation, the notice to a Commissioner shall, in addition to the statement required by section 35(3) of the 2000 Act, specify the following matters:

(a) the grounds on which he believes the matters specified in section 32(2)(a) and (b) of the 2000 Act;

(b) the nature of the authorised conduct including the residential premises or private vehicle in relation to which the conduct is authorised and the identity, where known, of persons to be the subject of the authorised conduct; and

(c) whether the conduct to be authorised is likely to lead to intrusion on the privacy of persons other than any person who is to be the subject of that conduct.

Notice of renewal of authorisation

26.21 4. Where a person renews an authorisation, the notice to a Commissioner shall, in addition to the statement required by section 35(3) of the 2000 Act, specify the following matters:

(a) whether the authorisation is being renewed for the first time, or, where it has been previously renewed, each occasion on which it has been renewed;

(b) the matters required by article 3, as they apply at the time of notice of renewal;

(c) every respect in which the information provided in the previous notice has changed;

(d) the reason why it is considered to be necessary to renew the authorisation;

(e) the content, and value to the investigation, of the information obtained to date by the conduct authorised;

(f) the results of any reviews of the authorisation and

(g) the period for which the authorisation is considered likely to continue to be necessary.

Notice of cancellation of authorisation

5. Where a person cancels an authorisation, the notice to a Commissioner shall **26.22**
specify the following matters:
  (a) the date and time when he gave the instructions to cease the conduct
  authorised;
  (b) the reasons for cancelling the authorisation;
  (c) the outcome of the investigation to which the authorisation related, and
  details of any criminal proceedings instituted or intended to be instituted; and
  (d) what arrangements have been made for the storage of material obtained as
  a result of the conduct authorised, for its review and its destruction when
  its retention is no longer required, and for the immediate destruction of any
  material unrelated to the purposes for which the conduct was authorised.

Charles Clarke
Minister of State

Home Office
20th September 2000

H. SI 2000 No 2793 The Regulation of Investigatory Powers (Juveniles) Order 2000

Made   *10th October 2000*
Laid before Parliament   *16th October 2000*
Coming into force   *6th November 2000*

The Secretary of State, in exercise of the powers conferred on him by sections **26.23**
29(2)(c), 29(7)(a) and (b) and 43(8) of the Regulation of Investigatory Powers Act
2000, hereby makes the following Order:

Citation and commencement

1. This Order may be cited as the Regulation of Investigatory Powers (Juveniles) **26.24**
Order 2000 and shall come into force on 6th November 2000.

Interpretation

2. In this Order—   **26.25**
  "the 2000 Act" means the Regulation of Investigatory Powers Act 2000;
  "guardian", in relation to a source, has the same meaning as is given to
  "guardian of a child" by section 105 of the Children Act 1989;

"relative" has the same meaning as it is given by section 105 of the Children Act 1989;

"relevant investigating authority" has the meaning given by section 29(8) of the 2000 Act, and where the activities of a source are to be for the benefit of more than one public authority, each of these authorities is a relevant investigating authority;

"source" means covert human intelligence source.

Sources under 16: prohibition

26.26   3. No authorisation may be granted for the conduct or use of a source if:

(a) the source is under the age of sixteen; and

(b) the relationship to which the conduct or use would relate is between the source and his parent or any person who has parental responsibility for him.

Sources under 16: arrangements for meetings

26.27   4.—(1) Where a source is under the age of sixteen, the arrangements referred to in section 29(2)(c) of the 2000 Act must be such that there is at all times a person holding an office, rank or position with a relevant investigating authority who has responsibility for ensuring that an appropriate adult is present at meetings to which this article applies.

(2) This article applies to all meetings between the source and a person representing any relevant investigating authority that take place while the source remains under the age of sixteen.

(3) In paragraph (1), "appropriate adult" means:

(a) the parent or guardian of the source;

(b) any other person who has for the time being assumed responsibility for his welfare; or

(c) where no person falling within paragraph (a) or (b) is available, any responsible person aged eighteen or over who is neither a member of nor employed by any relevant investigating authority.

Sources under 18: risk assessments etc.

26.28   5. An authorisation for the conduct or use of a source may not be granted or renewed in any case where the source is under the age of eighteen at the time of the grant or renewal, unless:

(a) a person holding an office, rank or position with a relevant investigating authority has made and, in the case of a renewal, updated a risk assessment sufficient to demonstrate that:

(i) the nature and magnitude of any risk of physical injury to the source arising in the course of, or as a result of, carrying out the conduct described in the authorisation have been identified and evaluated; and

(ii) the nature and magnitude of any risk of psychological distress to the source arising in the course of, or as a result of, carrying out the conduct described in the authorisation have been identified and evaluated;

(b) the person granting or renewing the authorisation has considered the risk assessment and has satisfied himself that any risks identified in it are justified and, if they are, that they have been properly explained to and understood by the source; and

(c) the person granting or renewing the authorisation knows whether the relationship to which the conduct or use would relate is between the source and a relative, guardian or person who has for the time being assumed responsibility for the source's welfare, and, if it is, has given particular consideration to whether the authorisation is justified in the light of that fact.

Sources under 18: duration of authorisations

6. In relation to an authorisation for the conduct or the use of a source who is **26.29** under the age of eighteen at the time the authorisation is granted or renewed, section 43(3) of the 2000 Act shall have effect as if the period specified in paragraph (b) of that subsection were one month instead of twelve months.

Charles Clarke
Minister of State

Home Office
10th October 2000

I. SI 2000 No 2794 The Regulation of Investigatory Powers (Cancellation of Authorisations) Regulations 2000

Made   *10th October 2000*
Laid before Parliament   *16th October 2000*
Coming into force   *6th November 2000*

The Secretary of State, in exercise of the powers conferred on him by section 45(4) **26.30** and (5) of the Regulation of Investigatory Powers Act 2000, hereby makes the following Regulations:

Citation and commencement

1. These Regulations may be cited as the Regulation of Investigatory Powers **26.31** (Cancellation of Authorisations) Regulations 2000, and shall come into force on 6th November 2000.

Performance of duty to cancel

26.32 2.—(1) Where any duty imposed by section 45 of the Regulation of Investigatory Powers Act 2000(a) would otherwise fall on a person who is no longer available to perform it, that duty is to be performed by—

    (a) the person, if any, appointed for the purpose of these Regulations in accordance with paragraph (2);

    (b) where no such person has been appointed, the person, if any, who holds the same office, rank or position in the same public authority as was held by the person who is no longer available and who has taken over that person's responsibilities or most of them.

(2) The person making an appointment for the purpose of these Regulations, and the person appointed, must each be a person holding the same office, rank or position (or a more senior one) in the same public authority as was held by the person who is no longer available.

Charles Clarke
Minister of State

Home Office
10th October 2000

27

STATUTORY INSTRUMENTS (2001)

A. SI 2001 No 1057 The Regulation of Investigatory Powers (British Broadcasting Corporation) Order 2001

Made   *15th March 2001*
Coming into force   *16th March 2001*

27.01   The Secretary of State, in exercise of the powers conferred on him by section 47(1) of the Regulation of Investigatory Powers Act 2000, hereby makes the following Order, of which a draft has, in accordance with section 47(2) of that Act, been laid before and approved by resolution of each House of Parliament:

Citation, commencement and interpretation

27.02   1.—(1) This Order may be cited as the Regulation of Investigatory Powers (British Broadcasting Corporation) Order 2001.

(2) This Order shall come into force on the day after the day on which it is made.

(3) In this Order "the 2000 Act" means the Regulation of Investigatory Powers Act 2000.

Application of Part II of the 2000 Act to the detection of television receivers

27.03   2.—(1) Part II of the 2000 Act (surveillance and covert human intelligence sources) shall apply to surveillance which—

(a) is carried out by means of apparatus designed or adapted for the purpose of detecting the installation or use in any residential or other premises of a television receiver (within the meaning of section 1 of the Wireless Telegraphy Act 1949), and

(b) is carried out from outside those premises exclusively for that purpose,

and such surveillance is referred to in this Order as "the detection of television receivers".

(2) In its application to the detection of television receivers, Part II of the 2000 Act shall have effect as if—

    (a) the following provisions were omitted, namely, sections 28 to 42, in section 43, subsections (2), (6) to (8) and (10) and in subsection (4) the words "Subject to subsection (6)", section 44, section 45(2) to (7) and section 46, and

    (b) the modifications set out in articles 3 to 5 were made.

New section 27A

3. In its application to the detection of television receivers, Part II of the 2000 Act **27.04** shall have effect as if the following section were inserted after section 27—

" Authorisation of detection of television receivers

27A.—(1) Subject to the following provisions of this Part, the persons designated for the purposes of this section shall each have power to grant authorisations for the detection of television receivers, that is to say, surveillance which—

    (a) is carried out by means of apparatus designed or adapted for the purpose of detecting the installation or use in any residential or other premises of a television receiver (within the meaning of section 1 of the Wireless Telegraphy Act 1949), and

    (b) is carried out from outside those premises exclusively for that purpose.

(2) The persons designated for the purposes of this section are—

    (a) any person holding the position of head of sales or head of marketing within the Television Licence Management Unit of the British Broadcasting Corporation, and

    (b) any person holding a position within that Unit which is more senior than the positions mentioned in paragraph (a).

(3) A person shall not grant an authorisation for the detection of television receivers unless he believes—

    (a) that the authorisation is necessary—

        (i) for the purpose of preventing or detecting crime constituting an offence under section 1 or 1A of the Wireless Telegraphy Act 1949; or

        (ii) for the purpose of assessing or collecting sums payable to the British Broadcasting Corporation under regulations made under section 2 of the Wireless Telegraphy Act 1949; and

    (b) that the authorised surveillance is proportionate to what is sought to be achieved by carrying it out.

(4) The conduct that is authorised by an authorisation for the detection of television receivers is any conduct that—

    (a) consists in the carrying out of the detection of television receivers, and

    (b) is carried out by the persons described in the authorisation in the circumstances described in the authorisation."

Modifications of section 43

27.05 4. In its application to the detection of television receivers, section 43 of the 2000 Act (general rules about grant, renewal and duration) shall have effect as if—
  (a) in subsection (1), for paragraphs (a) and (b) there were substituted "must be in writing";
  (b) for subsection (3) there were substituted—
" (3) Subject to subsection (4), an authorisation under this Part shall cease to have effect—
    (a) in the case of an authorisation which has not been renewed and in which is specified a period of less than eight weeks beginning with the day on which the grant of the authorisation takes effect, at the end of that period;
    (b) in the case of an authorisation which has not been renewed and to which paragraph (a) does not apply, at the end of the period of eight weeks beginning with the day on which the grant of the authorisation takes effect;
    (c) in the case of an authorisation which has been renewed, and in which is specified a period of less than eight weeks beginning with the day on which the grant of the authorisation takes effect, at the end of a period of the same length beginning with the day on which the latest renewal takes effect;
    (d) in the case of an authorisation which has been renewed, and to which paragraph (c) does not apply, at the end of the period of eight weeks beginning with the day on which the latest renewal takes effect.";
  (c) for subsection (5) there were substituted—
" (5) Section 27A shall have effect in relation to the renewal of an authorisation under this Part as if references to the grant of an authorisation included references to its renewal."; and
  (d) in subsection (9) for paragraphs (a) to (c) there were substituted—
"(a) in the case of the grant of an authorisation, to the time at which or, as the case may be, day on which the authorisation is granted;
  (b) in the case of the renewal of an authorisation, to the time at which or, as the case may be, day on which the authorisation would have ceased to have effect but for the renewal."

Modification of section 45(1)

27.06 5. In its application to the detection of television receivers, section 45 of the 2000 Act (cancellation of authorisations) shall have effect as if—
  (a) in subsection (1) for the words from "if" to the end there were substituted "if he is satisfied that the authorisation is one in relation to which the requirements of section 27A(3)(a) and (b) are no longer satisfied"; and
  (b) after subsection (1) there were inserted—

"(1A) Where any duty imposed by subsection (1) would otherwise fall on a person who is no longer available to perform it, that duty is to be performed by—

   (a) the person, if any, appointed for the purpose of this subsection in accordance with subsection (1B);

   (b) where no such person has been appointed, the person (if any) holding a position within the British Broadcasting Corporation who has taken over the responsibilities of the person who is no longer available, or most of them.

(1B) The person making an appointment for the purpose of subsection (1A), and the person appointed, must each be—

   (a) a person designated for the purposes of section 27A, or

   (b) a person holding a more senior position within the British Broadcasting Corporation than was held by the person who is no longer available."

Charles Clarke
Minister of State

Home Office
15th March 2001

B. SI 2001 No 1126 Designation of Public Authorities for the Purposes of Intrusive Surveillance Order 2001

Made   *21st March 2001*

Coming into force   *22nd March 2001*

The Secretary of State, in exercise of the powers conferred on him by section 41(3) and (4) of the Regulation of Investigatory Powers Act 2000, hereby makes the following Order of which a draft has, in accordance with section 41(6) of that Act, been laid before and approved by resolution of each House of Parliament: **27.07**

Citation and commencement

1. This Order may be cited as the Regulation of Investigatory Powers (Designation of Public Authorities for the Purposes of Intrusive Surveillance) Order 2001 and shall come into force on the day after the day on which it is made. **27.08**

Designated public authority

2. The Home Office is hereby designated for the purposes of section 41 of the Regulation of Investigatory Powers Act 2000, as a public authority whose activities may require the carrying out of intrusive surveillance. **27.09**

Prescribed offices, ranks and positions

27.10 3.—(1) In relation to the Home Office, an application for an authorisation for the carrying out of intrusive surveillance may be made by an individual holding an office, rank or position with the Home Office only where his office, rank or position is prescribed by paragraph (2).

(2) The offices, ranks and positions prescribed by this paragraph are all offices, ranks and positions in Her Majesty's Prison Service.

Minister of State
Charles Clarke

Home Office
21st March 2001

C. SI 2001 No 3734 The Regulation of Investigatory Powers (Technical Advisory Board) Order 2001

Made   *21st November 2001*

Coming into force   *22nd November 2001*

27.11 Whereas a draft of this Order has been laid before Parliament and approved by a resolution of each House:

Now, therefore, the Secretary of State, in exercise of the powers conferred on him by section 13(1) and (2) of the Regulation of Investigatory Powers Act 2000, hereby makes the following Order:

Citation, commencement and interpretation

27.12 1.—(1) This Order may be cited as the Regulation of Investigatory Powers (Technical Advisory Board) Order 2001 and shall come into force on the day after the day on which it is made.

(2) In this Order, "the 2000 Act" means the Regulation of Investigatory Powers Act 2000.

Membership of the Board

27.13 2.—(1) The Technical Advisory Board established by section 13(1) of the 2000 Act shall consist of 13 persons.

(2) Of that number one person, who does not fall within paragraph (3), shall be appointed chairman.

(3) Of the remaining number—

    (a) six shall be persons holding an office, rank or position with either—

        (i) a person on whom obligations may be imposed under section 12 of the 2000 Act, or

        (ii) a body representing the interests of such persons, and

    (b) six shall be persons holding an office, rank or position with either—

        (i) a person by or on whose behalf applications for interception warrants may be made, or

        (ii) a body representing the interests of such persons.

Bob Ainsworth
Parliamentary Under-Secretary of State

Home Office
21st November 2001

28

STATUTORY INSTRUMENTS (2002)

A. SI 2002 No 1298 The Regulation of Investigatory Powers (Prescription of Offices, Ranks and Positions) (Amendment) Order 2002

28.01 *[This SI has been revoked by operation of SI 2003 No. 3171 The Regulation of Investigatory Powers (Directed Surveillance and Covert Human Intelligence Sources) Order 2003 which revoked SI 2000 No. 2417 to which this SI was an amending order. See Chapter 29.]*

B. SI 2002 No 1693 The Regulation of Investigatory Powers (Interception of Communications: Code of Practice) Order 2002

Made 28th   June 2002

Coming into force   1st July 2002

28.02 Whereas—

(1) in pursuance of section 71 of the Regulation of Investigatory Powers Act 2000 (hereinafter referred to as "the 2000 Act") the Secretary of State is under a duty to prepare codes of practice containing provisions relating to the exercise and performance of the powers and duties mentioned in subsection (2) of that section;

(2) in pursuance of section 71(3) of the 2000 Act the Secretary of State published the code prepared by him under section 71 of the 2000 Act relating to the interception of communications under Chapter I of Part I of the 2000 Act in the form of a draft and has considered representations made to him about the draft and modified the draft accordingly;

(3) in pursuance of section 71(4) of the 2000 Act the Secretary of State has laid that code before both Houses of Parliament;

(4) a draft of this Order has been laid before Parliament and approved by a resolution of each House:

Now, therefore, the Secretary of State, in exercise of the powers conferred on him by section 71(5) of the 2000 Act, hereby makes the following Order:

Citation and commencement

1. The Order may be cited as the Regulation of Investigatory Powers (Interception of Communications: Code of Practice) Order 2002 and shall come into force on 1st July 2002.   **28.03**

Interception of Communications Code of Practice   **28.04**

2. The draft code of practice entitled "Interception of Communications", laid before each House of Parliament on 8th May 2002, relating to the interception of communications under Chapter I of Part I of the 2000 Act, shall come into force on 1st July 2002.

Bob Ainsworth
Parliamentary Under-Secretary of State

Home Office
28th June 2002

C. SI 2002 No 1931 The Regulation of Investigatory Powers (Maintenance of Interception Capability) Order 2002

Made   *22nd July 2002*

Coming into force   *1st August 2002*

Whereas the Secretary of State has consulted the persons listed in section 12(9) and (11) of the Regulation of Investigatory Powers Act 2000 about this Order;   **28.05**

And whereas a draft of this Order has been laid before Parliament and approved by a resolution of each House;

Now, therefore, the Secretary of State, in exercise of the powers conferred on him by section 12(1), (2) and (5) and section 78(5) of that Act, hereby makes the following Order:

Citation, commencement and interpretation

1.—(1) This Order may be cited as the Regulation of Investigatory Powers (Maintenance of Interception Capability) Order 2002 and shall come into force on 1st August 2002.   **28.06**

(2) In this Order "service provider" means a person providing a public postal service or a public telecommunications service, or proposing to do so.

Interception capability

28.07 2.—(1) The Schedule to this Order sets out those obligations which appear to the Secretary of State reasonable to impose on service providers for the purpose of securing that it is and remains practicable for requirements to provide assistance in relation to interception warrants to be imposed and complied with.

(2) Subject to paragraph (3) the obligations in—

(a) Part I of the Schedule only apply to service providers who provide, or propose to provide, a public postal service; and

(b) Part II of the Schedule only apply to service providers who provide, or propose to provide, a public telecommunications service.

(3) The obligations in Part II of the Schedule shall not apply to service providers who—

(a) do not intend to provide a public telecommunications service to more than 10,000 persons in any one or more parts of the United Kingdom and do not do so; or

(b) only provide, or propose to provide, a public telecommunications service in relation to the provision of banking, insurance, investment or other financial services.

28.08 **Interception capability notices**

3.—(1) The Secretary of State may give a service provider a notice requiring him to take all such steps falling within paragraph (2) as may be specified or described in the notice.

(2) Those steps are ones appearing to the Secretary of State to be necessary for securing that the service provider has the practical capability of meeting the obligations set out in the Schedule to this Order.

28.09 **Referral of notices to the Technical Advisory Board**

4. The period within which any person to whom a notice has been given under article 3 may refer the notice to the Technical Advisory Board is specified as being before the end of 28 days from the date of the notice.

Bob Ainsworth
Parliamentary Under-Secretary of State

Home Office
22nd July 2002

SCHEDULE

Article 2

OBLIGATIONS ON SERVICE PROVIDERS

PART I

INTERCEPTION CAPABILITY FOR PUBLIC POSTAL SERVICES

1. To ensure the interception and temporary retention of postal items destined **28.10** for addresses in the United Kingdom for provision to the person on whose application the interception warrant was issued.
2. To provide for the interception and retention of postal items sent by identified persons where the carrier keeps records of who sent which item in the course of their normal business.
3. To maintain a system of opening, copying and resealing of any postal item carried for less than £1.
4. To comply with the obligations set out in paragraphs 1 to 3 above in such a manner that the chance of the interception subject or other unauthorised persons becoming aware of any interception is minimised.

PART II

INTERCEPTION CAPABILITY FOR PUBLIC TELECOMMUNICATION SERVICES

5. To provide a mechanism for implementing interceptions within one working **28.11** day of the service provider being informed that the interception has been appropriately authorised.
6. To ensure the interception, in their entirety, of all communications and related communications data authorised by the interception warrant and to ensure their simultaneous (i.e. in near real time) transmission to a hand-over point within the service provider's network as agreed with the person on whose application the interception warrant was issued.
7. To ensure that the intercepted communication and the related communications data will be transmitted so that they can be unambiguously correlated.
8. To ensure that the hand-over interface complies with any requirements communicated by the Secretary of State to the service provider, which, where practicable and appropriate, will be in line with agreed industry standards (such as those of the European Telecommunications Standards Institute).

9. To ensure filtering to provide only the traffic data associated with the warranted telecommunications identifier, where reasonable.

10. To ensure that the person on whose application the interception warrant was issued is able to remove any electronic protection applied by the service provider to the intercepted communication and the related communications data.

11. To enable the simultaneous interception of the communications of up to 1 in 10,000 of the persons to whom the service provider provides the public telecommunications service, provided that those persons number more than 10,000.

12. To ensure that the reliability of the interception capability is at least equal to the reliability of the public telecommunications service carrying the communication which is being intercepted.

13. To ensure that the intercept capability may be audited so that it is possible to confirm that the intercepted communications and related communications data are from, or intended for the interception subject, or originate from or are intended for transmission to, the premises named in the interception warrant.

14. To comply with the obligations set out in paragraphs 5 to 13 above in such a manner that the chance of the interception subject or other unauthorised persons becoming aware of any interception is minimised.

D. SI 2002 No 1932 The Regulation of Investigatory Powers (Covert Human Intelligence Sources: Code of Practice) Order

Made   *22nd July 2002*

Coming into force   *1st August 2002*

28.12 Whereas—

(1) in pursuance of section 71 of the Regulation of Investigatory Powers Act 2000 ("the 2000 Act") the Secretary of State is under a duty to prepare codes of practice containing provisions relating to the exercise and performance of the powers and duties mentioned in subsection (2) of that section;

(2) in pursuance of section 71(3) of the 2000 Act the Secretary of State published the code prepared by him under section 71 of the 2000 Act relating to the conduct and use of covert human intelligence sources under Part II of the 2000 Act in the form of a draft and has considered representations made to him about the draft and modified the draft accordingly;

(3) in pursuance of section 71(4) of the 2000 Act the Secretary of State has laid that code before both Houses of Parliament;

(4) a draft of this Order has been laid before Parliament and approved by a resolution of each House;

Now, therefore, the Secretary of State, in exercise of the powers conferred on him by section 71(5) of the 2000 Act, hereby makes the following Order:

Citation and commencement

1. The Order may be cited as the Regulation of Investigatory Powers (Covert **28.13** Human Intelligence Sources: Code of Practice) Order 2002 and shall come into force on 1st August 2002.

Covert Human Intelligence Sources Code of Practice

2. The draft code of practice entitled "Covert Human Intelligence Sources", laid **28.14** before each House of Parliament on 10th June 2002, relating to the conduct and use of covert human intelligence sources under Part II of the 2000 Act, shall come into force on 1st August 2002.

Bob Ainsworth
Parliamentary Under-Secretary of State

Home Office
22nd July 2002

E. SI 2002 No 1933 The Regulation of Investigatory Powers (Covert Surveillance: Code of Practice) Order 2002

Made   *22nd July 2002*

Coming into force   *1st August 2002*

Whereas—   **28.15**

(1) in pursuance of section 71 of the Regulation of Investigatory Powers Act 2000 ("the 2000 Act") the Secretary of State is under a duty to prepare codes of practice containing provisions relating to the exercise and performance of the powers and duties mentioned in subsection (2) of that section;

(2) in pursuance of section 71(3) of the 2000 Act the Secretary of State published the code prepared by him under section 71 of the 2000 Act relating to covert surveillance under Part II of the 2000 Act in the form of a draft and has considered representations made to him about the draft and modified the draft accordingly;

(3) in pursuance of section 71(4) of the 2000 Act the Secretary of State has laid that code before both Houses of Parliament;

(4) a draft of this Order has been laid before Parliament and approved by a resolution of each House;

Now, therefore, the Secretary of State, in exercise of the powers conferred on him by section 71(5) of the 2000 Act, hereby makes the following Order:

Citation and commencement

28.16 **1.** The Order may be cited as the Regulation of Investigatory Powers (Covert Surveillance: Code of Practice) Order 2002 and shall come into force on 1st August 2002.

Covert Surveillance Code of Practice

28.17 **2.** The draft code of practice entitled "Covert Surveillance", laid before each House of Parliament on 10th June 2002, relating to covert surveillance under Part II of the 2000 Act, shall come into force on 1st August 2002.

Bob Ainsworth
Parliamentary Under-Secretary of State

Home Office
22nd July 2002

29

STATUTORY INSTRUMENTS (2003)

A. SI 2003 No 3171 The Regulation of Investigatory Powers (Directed Surveillance and Covert Human Intelligence Sources) Order 2003[1]

Made   5th December 2003

Coming into force   5th January 2004

29.01   Whereas a draft of this Order has been approved by a resolution of each House of Parliament;

Now, therefore, the Secretary of State, in exercise of the powers conferred on him by sections 30(1), (3), (5) and (6) and 78(5) of the Regulation of Investigatory Powers Act 2000, hereby makes the following Order:

Citation, commencement and interpretation

29.02   **1.**—(1) This Order may be cited as the Regulation of Investigatory Powers (Directed Surveillance and Covert Human Intelligence Sources) Order 2003 and shall come into force one month after the day on which it is made.

(2) In this Order "the 2000 Act" means the Regulation of Investigatory Powers Act 2000.

Amendments to Schedule 1 to the 2000 Act

29.03   **2.**—(1) Part I of Schedule 1 to the 2000 Act shall be amended as follows.

(2) After paragraph 1 add the words—

"**1A.** The United Kingdom Atomic Energy Authority Constabulary.".

---

[1] Note that this SI is amended by SI 2005 No 1084 The Regulation of Investigatory Powers (Directed Surveillance and Covert Human Intelligence Sources) (Amendment) Order 2005. The amendments have not been inserted into this copy of this SI (which is reproduced as originally made) and the reader is advised to consult the amending SI in Chapter 31 of this work.

(3) After paragraph 13 add the words—

"**13A.** The Northern Ireland Office.".

(4) For paragraph 17 substitute—

"**17.** Any county council or district council in England, a London borough council, the Common Council of the City of London in its capacity as a local authority, the Council of the Isles of Scilly, and any county council or county borough council in Wales.".

(5) After paragraph 17 add the words—

"**17A.** Any fire authority within the meaning of the Fire Services Act 1947 (read with paragraph 2 of Schedule 11 to the Local Government Act 1985).".

(6) After the heading "*Other bodies*" add the words—

"**17B.** The Charity Commission.".

(7) After paragraph 20 add the words—

"**20A.** The Gaming Board for Great Britain.

20B. The Office of Fair Trading.

20C. The Office of the Police Ombudsman for Northern Ireland.

20D. The Postal Services Commission.".

3.—(1) Part II of Schedule 1 to the 2000 Act shall be amended as follows.

(2) After paragraph 27 add the words—

"**27A.** Local Health Boards in Wales established under section 6 of the National Health Service Reform and Health Care Professions Act 2002.

Her Majesty's Chief Inspector of Schools in England

27B. Her Majesty's Chief Inspector of Schools in England.

The Information Commissioner

27C. The Information Commissioner.

The Royal Parks Constabulary

27D. The Royal Parks Constabulary.".

Prescribed offices, ranks and positions

4.—(1) The offices, ranks and positions listed in column 2 of Part I of the **29.04** Schedule to this Order (being offices, ranks or positions with the relevant public authorities listed in column 1 of Part I of that Schedule which are relevant public authorities for the purposes of sections 28 and 29 of the 2000 Act) are hereby prescribed for the purpose of section 30(1) of the 2000 Act, subject to the restrictions in articles 7, 8 and 9.

(2) The offices, ranks and positions listed in column 2 of Part II of the Schedule to this Order (being offices, ranks or positions with the relevant public authorities listed in column 1 of Part II of that Schedule which are relevant

public authorities for the purposes only of section 28 of the 2000 Act) are hereby prescribed for the purpose of section 30(1) of the 2000 Act, subject to the restrictions in articles 7, 8 and 9.

More senior offices, ranks and positions

29.05 5.—(1) Where an office, rank or position with a relevant public authority is prescribed by virtue of article 4, all more senior offices, ranks or positions with that authority are also prescribed for the purpose of section 30(1) of the 2000 Act, subject to article 10.

(2) Where an office, rank or position with a relevant public authority is described in column 2 of the Schedule to this Order by reference to an agency, unit, branch, division or other part of that authority, the reference in paragraph (1) to all more senior offices, ranks or positions with that authority is a reference to all more senior offices, ranks or positions with that agency, unit, branch, division or part.

Additional offices, ranks and positions prescribed for urgent cases

29.06 6.—(1) The additional offices, ranks and positions listed in column 3 of the Schedule to this Order (being offices, ranks or positions with the relevant public authorities listed in column 1) are hereby prescribed for the purposes of section 30(1) of the 2000 Act, subject to the restrictions in articles 7, 8 and 9 in the circumstances described in paragraph (2).

(2) An individual holding an office, rank or position which is listed in column 3 of the Schedule to this Order may only grant an authorisation where it is not reasonably practicable, having regard to the urgency of the case, for the application to be considered by an individual with the same authority holding an office, rank or position listed in column 2 of the Schedule to this Order.

(3) Where an office, rank or position with a relevant public authority is described in column 3 of the Schedule to this Order by reference to an agency, unit, branch, division or other part of that authority, the reference in paragraph (2) to an individual with the same authority is a reference to an individual with that agency, unit, branch, division or part.

Restrictions on the granting of authorisations

29.07 7. The restriction in this article is that an individual holding an office, rank or position which is listed in column 2 or 3 of the Schedule to this Order may not grant an authorisation unless he believes it is necessary on the grounds set out in one or more of the paragraphs of sections 28(3) and 29(3) of the 2000 Act listed in the corresponding entry in column 4 of that Schedule.

8. The restriction in this article is that where any entry in column 2 or 3 of Part I of the Schedule to this Order is headed by a reference to an authorisation under section 28 or section 29 of the 2000 Act, an individual holding an office, rank or position which is listed in that entry may only grant an authorisation under the section of the 2000 Act with which that entry is headed.

9. The restriction in this article is that an individual holding an office, rank or position with the Food Standards Agency or the Rural Payments Agency may not grant an authorisation for conduct in Northern Ireland.

10. The restrictions on the granting of authorisations under section 28 and 29 of the 2000 Act that apply to an individual holding an office, rank or position with a relevant public authority listed in column 2 of the Schedule to this Order shall also apply to individuals holding all more senior offices, ranks or positions with that authority that are prescribed by article 5.

Revocation

11. The Regulation of Investigatory Powers (Prescription of Offices, Ranks and Positions) Order 2000 is hereby revoked. **29.08**

Caroline Flint
Parliamentary Under-Secretary of State

Home Office
5th December 2003

Schedule

Article 4

Part I (Prescriptions for public authorities in Part I of Schedule 1 to the 2000 Act **29.09** that are relevant public authorities for the purposes of sections 28 and 29 of the 2000 Act)

(1) Relevant public authorities in Part I of Schedule 1 to the 2000 Act	(2) Prescribed offices etc.	(3) Urgent cases	(4) Grounds set out in the paragraphs of sections 28(3) and 29(3) of the 2000 Act for which an authorisation can be given
A police force maintained under section 2 of the Police Act 1996 (police forces in	Superintendent	Inspector	(a)(b)(c)(d)(e)

England and Wales outside London)			
A police force maintained under or by virtue of section 1 of the Police (Scotland) Act 1967	Superintendent	Inspector	(a)(b)(c)(d)(e)
The metropolitan police force	Superintendent	Inspector	(a)(b)(c)(d)(e)
The City of London police force	Superintendent	Inspector	(a)(b)(c)(d)(e)
The Police Service of Northern Ireland	Superintendent	Inspector	(a)(b)(c)(d)(e)
The Ministry of Defence Police	Superintendent	Inspector	(a)(b)(c)
The Royal Navy Regulating Branch	Provost Marshal		(a)(b)(c)
The Royal Military Police	Lieutenant Colonel	Major	(a)(b)(c)
The Royal Air Force Police	Wing Commander	Squadron Leader	(a)(b)(c)
The British Transport Police	Superintendent	Inspector	(a)(b)(c)(d)(e)
The United Kingdom Atomic Energy Authority Constabulary	Superintendent	Inspector	(a)(b)
The National Criminal Intelligence Service	Superintendent, Level 2 or any individual on secondment to the National Criminal Intelligence Service who holds any office, rank or position in any other relevant public authority listed in column 2 of Part I of the Schedule to this Order	Inspector, Level 4 or any individual on secondment to the National Criminal Intelligence Service who holds any office, rank or position in any other relevant public authority listed in column 3 of Part I of the Schedule to this Order	(a)(b)(c)(d)(e)

The National Crime Squad	Superintendent	Inspector	(a)(b)(c)(d)(e)
The Serious Fraud Office	Assistant Director		(b)
Government Communications Headquarters	GC8		(a)(b)(c)
The Security Service	General Duties 3 or any other Officer at Level 3		(a)(b)(c)
The Secret Intelligence Service	Grade 6 or equivalent		(a)(b)(c)
The Royal Navy	Commander	Lieutenant Commander	(a)(b)(c)(d)(e)
The Army	Lieutenant Colonel	Major	(a)(b)(c)(d)(e)
The Royal Air Force	Wing Commander	Squadron Leader	(a)(b)(c)(d)(e)
The Commissioners of Customs and Excise	Band 9	Band 7 or 8	(a)(b)(c)(d)(e)(f)
The Commissioners of Inland Revenue	Band C1	Band C2	(b)(c)(f)
Ministry of Defence	Band C1	Band C2	(b)
Department for Environment, Food and Rural Affairs	Senior Investigation Officer in DEFRA Investigation Branch		(b)
	Senior Counter Fraud Officer in the Counter Fraud and Compliance Unit of the Rural Payments Agency		(b)
	Senior Investigation Officer in Centre for Environment, Fisheries and Aquaculture Science		(b)
	Section 28 Authorisation Regional Horticultural Marketing		(b)

	Inspector in Horticultural Marketing Inspectorate		
	Section 28 authorisation Senior Plant Health and Seed Inspector in Plant Health and Seed Inspectorate		(b)
	Section 28 authorisation Chief Egg Marketing Inspector in Egg Marketing Inspectorate		(b)
	Section 28 authorisation District Inspector in Sea Fisheries Inspectorate		(b)
The Department of Health	Integrated Payband 3 (Standard 2) in Medicines and Healthcare Products Regulatory Agency		(b)(d)(e)
The Home Office	**Section 28 authorisation** Area Manager in HM Prison Service		(a)(b)(d)
	Section 29 authorisation Prison Source System Manager in HM Prison Service	**Section 29 authorisation** A Governor, Duty Governor or Deputy Controller in HM Prison Service	(a)(b)(d)
	Immigration Inspector in the Immigration Service	Chief Immigration Officer in the Immigration Service	(b)(c)
	Section 28 authorisation The Head of the Unit responsible for Security and Anti Corruption within the Immigration and Nationality Directorate	**Section 28 authorisation** Senior Executive Officer within the Unit responsible for Security and Anti Corruption within the	(b)

		Immigration and Nationality Directorate	
The Northern Ireland Office	Deputy Principal or Governor 3 in the Northern Ireland Prison Service	Staff Officer or Governor 4 in the Northern Ireland Prison Service	(b)(d)
The Department of Trade and Industry	Deputy Inspector of Companies in Companies Investigation Branch		(b)
	Chief Investigation Officer in the Investigation Officers Section of Legal Services Directorate D or a member of the Senior Civil Service in Legal Services Directorate D		(b)
	Section 28 authorisation Radio Specialist 5 or Range 9 Officer in Radiocommunications Agency	**Section 28 authorisation** Radio Specialist 4 or Range 8 Officer in Radiocommunica-tions Agency	(b)
	Section 29 authorisation Member of Senior Civil Service in Radiocommunications Agency		(b)
	Section 28 authorisation Member of Senior Civil Service in British Trade International		(b)
	Section 28 authorisation Range 10 Officer in Coal Health Claims Unit	**Section 28 authorisation** Range 9 Officer in Coal Health Claims Unit	(b)
The Department for Transport	Head of Maritime Section		(b)(d)
	Assistant Director Transport Security		(b)(d)

	Head of Operational Support		(b)(d)
	Head of Land Transport Security		(b)(d)
	Head of Aviation Security Compliance		(b)(d)
	Head of Aviation Security Domestic Policy		(b)(d)
	Head of Aviation Security International Policy		(b)(d)
	Senior Transport Security Inspector		(b)(d)
	Section 28 authorisation Area Manager or National Intelligence Co-ordinator in the Vehicle and Operator Services Agency	**Section 28 authorisation** Senior Vehicle Examiner or Senior Traffic Examiner or Intelligence Officer in the Vehicle and Operator Services Agency	(b)(d)
	Section 29 authorisation Enforcement Manager in the Vehicle and Operator Services Agency	**Section 29 authorisation** Area Manager in the Vehicle and Operator Services Agency	(b)(d)(b)(d)
	Principal Enforcement Officer in the Maritime and Coastguard Agency	Enforcement Officer in the Maritime and Coastguard Agency	(b)(d)
The Department for Work and Pensions	Senior Executive Officer or equivalent grades in Jobcentre Plus	Higher Executive Officer or equivalent grades in Jobcentre Plus	(b)
	Senior Executive Officer or equivalent grades in DWP Internal Assurance Services		(b)
	Senior Executive Officer or equivalent grades in Child Support Agency	Higher Executive Officer or equivalent grades in Child Support Agency	(b)

National Assembly for Wales	Head of NHS Directorate	Member of NHS Directorate at a level equivalent to Grade 7	(b)(d)(e)
	Head of NHS Finance Division	Member of NHS Finance Division at a level equivalent to Grade 7	(b)(d)(e)
	Head of Common Agricultural Policy Management Division	Member of Common Agricultural Policy Management Division at a level equivalent to Grade 7	(b)(e)
	Regional Director in the Care Standards Inspectorate for Wales	Senior Inspector in the Care Standards Inspectorate for Wales	(b)(d)(e)
Any county council or district council in England, a London Borough Council, the Common Council of the City of London in its capacity as a local authority, the Council of the Isles of Scilly, and any county council or county borough council in Wales	Assistant Chief Officer, Assistant Head of Service, Service Manager or equivalent		(b)
Any fire authority within the meaning of the Fire Services Act 1947 (read with paragraph 2 of Schedule 11 to the Local Government Act 1985)	Divisional Officer 2	Divisional Officer 3	(b)(d)
The Charity Commission	Senior Investigations Manager	Investigations Manager	(b)
The Environment Agency	**Section 28 authorization** Area Management Team Member	**Section 28 authorisation** Area Team Leader	(b)(d)(e)

	Section 29 **authorisation** Area Manager	Section 29 **authorisation** Area Management Team Member	(b)(d)(e)
The Financial Services Authority	Head of Department in Enforcement Division	Manager in Enforcement Division	(b)
The Food Standards Agency	**Section 28** **authorisation** Head of Division or equivalent grade		(b)(d)(e)
	Section 29 **authorisation** Deputy Director of Legal Services or any Director		(b)(d)(e)
The Gaming Board for Great Britain	Chief Inspector	Deputy Chief Inspector	(b)
The Office of Fair Trading	Director of Cartel Investigations	Principal Investigation Officer in the Cartel Investigation Branch	(b)(c)
The Office of the Police Ombudsman for Northern Ireland	Senior Investigating Officer	Deputy Senior Investigating Officer	(b)
The Postal Services Commission	**Section 28** **authorisation** Legal Adviser	**Section 28** **authorisation** Deputy Director	(b)
	Section 29 **authorisation** Chief Legal Adviser		(b)
A Universal Service Provider within the meaning of the Postal Services Act 2000	Senior Investigation Manager in Royal Mail Group plc		(b)

Part II (Prescriptions for public authorities in Part II of Schedule 1 to the 2000 Act that are relevant public authorities for the purposes only of section 28 of the 2000 Act)

(1) Relevant public authorities in Part II of Schedule 1 to the 2000 Act	(2) Prescribed etc.	(3) Urgent cases	(4) Grounds set out in the paragraphs of section 28(3) of the 2000 Act for which an authorisation can be given
The Health and Safety Executive	Band 2 Inspector		(b)(d)(e)
A Special Health Authority established under section 11 of the National Health Service Act 1977	Chief Executive		(b)(e)
	Senior Manager (Senior Manager Pay Range 14) in the Counter Fraud and Security Management Service		(b)
A National Health Service trust established under section 5 of the National Health Service and Community Care Act 1990	Chief Executive		(b)(e)
Local Health Boards in Wales established under section 6 of the National Health Service Reform and Health Care Professions Act 2002	Chief Officer or Finance Officer		(b)(e)
Her Majesty's Chief Inspector of Schools in England	Band A in the Complaints, Investigation and Enforcement Team in the Office of Her Majesty's Chief Inspector of Schools in England (OFSTED)	Band B1 in the Complaints, Investigation and Enforcement Team in the Office of Her Majesty's Chief Inspector of Schools in England (OFSTED)	(b)

The Information Commissioner	Head of Investigations	Senior Investigating Officer	(b)
The Royal Parks Constabulary	Chief Officer	Inspector	(b)
The Royal Pharmaceutical Society of Great Britain	Director of Fitness to Practice and Legal Affairs or Director of Practice and Quality Improvement		(b)(d)(e)

B. SI 2003 No 3172 The Regulation of Investigatory Powers (Communications Data) Order 2003[2]

Made   *5th December 2003*

Coming into force   *5th January 2004*

29.10 Whereas a draft of this Order has been approved by resolution of each House of Parliament;

Now, therefore, the Secretary of State, in exercise of the powers conferred on him by paragraph (g) of the definition of "relevant public authority" in section 25(1) of the Regulation of Investigatory Powers Act 2000 and by sections 25(2) and (3) and 78(5) of that Act, hereby makes the following Order:

Citation, commencement and interpretation

29.11 **1.**—(1) This Order may be cited as the Regulation of Investigatory Powers (Communications Data) Order 2003 and shall come into force one month after the day on which it is made.

(2) In this Order—

"the 2000 Act" means the Regulation of Investigatory Powers Act 2000;

"authorisation" means an authorisation under section 22(3) of the 2000 Act; and

"notice" means a notice under section 22(4) of the 2000 Act.

Prescribed offices, ranks and positions

29.12 **2.** The offices, ranks and positions listed in columns 2 and 3 of Schedule 1 (being offices, ranks and positions with the relevant public authorities in column 1 of

---

[2] Note that this SI is amended by the Regulation of Investigatory Powers (Communications Data) (Amendment) Order 2005 (SI 2005 No 1083). The amendments have not been inserted into this copy of this SI (which is reproduced as originally made) and the reader is advised to consult the amending SI in Chapter 31 of this work.

that Schedule) are hereby prescribed for the purposes of section 25(2) of the 2000 Act, subject to the restrictions in articles 6, 7 and 10.

Additional public authorities

3. The public authorities set out in column 1 of Parts I, III and IV of Schedule 2 **29.13** are hereby specified as relevant public authorities for the purposes of section 25(1) of the 2000 Act.

Prescribed offices, ranks and positions in the additional public authorities

4. The offices, ranks and positions listed in columns 2 and 3 of Parts I, II, III and **29.14** IV of Schedule 2 (being offices, ranks and positions with the relevant public authorities in column 1 of that Schedule) are hereby prescribed for the purposes of section 25(2) of the 2000 Act, subject to the restrictions in articles 6, 7, 8 and 9.

More senior offices, ranks and positions

5.—(1) Where an office, rank or position with a relevant public authority listed **29.15** in column 2 of Schedule 1 or column 2 of Schedule 2 is prescribed by virtue of article 2 or 4, all more senior offices, ranks or positions with that authority are also prescribed for the purposes of section 25(2) of the 2000 Act, subject to article 11.

(2) Where an office, rank or position with a relevant public authority is described in column 2 of Schedule 1 or column 2 of Schedule 2 by reference to an agency, unit, branch, division or other part of that authority, the reference in paragraph (1) to all more senior offices, ranks or positions with that authority is a reference to all more senior offices, ranks or positions with that agency, unit, branch, division or part.

Restrictions on the granting of authorisations or the giving of notices

6. The restriction in this article is that an individual holding an office, rank or **29.16** position which is listed in column 2 or 3 of Schedule 1 or column 2 or 3 of Schedule 2 may not grant an authorisation or give a notice unless he believes it is necessary on the grounds set out in one or more of the paragraphs of section 22(2) of the 2000 Act listed in the corresponding entry in column 4 of those Schedules.

7.—(1) The restriction in this paragraph is that an individual holding an office, rank or position which is listed in column 2 of Schedule 1 or column 2 of Schedule 2 may only grant an authorisation or give a notice that he believes is necessary on grounds other than those set out in paragraphs (a), (b), (c) and (g) of section 22(2) of the 2000 Act where that authorisation or notice satisfies the condition in paragraph (3).

(2) The restriction in this paragraph is that an individual holding an office, rank or position which is listed in column 3 of Schedule 1 or column 3 of Schedule 2 may only grant an authorisation or give a notice which satisfies the condition set out in paragraph (3).

(3) The condition referred to in paragraphs (1) and (2) is that the only communications data authorised to be obtained by the authorisation, or required to be obtained or disclosed by the notice, is communications data falling within section 21(4)(c) of the 2000 Act.

8.—(1) The restriction in this article is that an individual holding an office, rank or position which is listed in column 2 of Part II or Part III of Schedule 2 may only grant an authorisation or give a notice which satisfies the condition set out in paragraph (2).

(2) The condition referred to in paragraph (1) is that the only communications data authorised to be obtained by the authorisation, or required to be obtained or disclosed by the notice, is communications data falling within section 21(4)(b) or (c) of the 2000 Act.

9.—(1) The restriction in this article is that an individual holding an office, rank or position which is listed in column 2 of Part IV of Schedule 2 may only grant an authorisation or give a notice which satisfies the condition set out in paragraph (2).

(2) The condition referred to in paragraph (1) is that the only communications data authorised to be obtained by the authorisation, or required to be obtained or disclosed by the notice, is communications data relating to a postal service.

10.—(1) The restriction in this article is that an individual holding an office, rank or position with the Commissioners of Inland Revenue (being a relevant public authority listed in Schedule 1) may only grant an authorisation or give a notice which satisfies the condition set out in paragraph (2).

(2) The condition referred to in paragraph (1) is that the only communications data falling with section 21(4)(a) of the 2000 Act authorised to be obtained by the authorisation, or required to be obtained or disclosed by the notice is communications data relating to a postal service.

11. The restrictions on the granting of authorisations and the giving of notices that apply to an individual holding an office, rank or position with a relevant public authority listed in column 2 of Schedule 1 or column 2 of Schedule 2 shall also apply to all individuals holding all more senior offices, ranks or positions with that authority that are prescribed by article 5.

Caroline Flint
Parliamentary Under-Secretary of State

Home Office
5th December 2003

Schedule 1

Article 2

Individuals in Public Authorities Within Section 25(1) of the 2000 Act

(1) Relevant public authorities	(2) Prescribed offices etc (All authorisations/notices)	(3) Additional prescribed offices etc (Authorisations/notices relating solely to communications data falling within section 21(4)(c))	(4) Purposes within section 22(2) for which an authorization may be granted or a notice given
Police Forces			
A police force maintained under section 2 of the Police Act 1996 (police forces in England and Wales outside London)	Superintendent	Inspector	(a)(b)(c)(d)(e)(g)
A police force maintained under or by virtue of section 1 of the Police (Scotland) Act 1967	Superintendent	Inspector	(a)(b)(c)(d)(e)(g)
The Metropolitan police force	Superintendent	Inspector	(a)(b)(c)(d)(e)(g)
The City of London police force	Superintendent	Inspector	(a)(b)(c)(d)(e)(g)
The Police Service of Northern Ireland	Superintendent	Inspector	(a)(b)(c)(d)(e)(g)
The Ministry of Defence Police	Superintendent	Inspector	(a)(b)(c)(g)
The Royal Navy Regulating Branch	Provost Marshal	—	(a)(b)(c)(g)
The Royal Military Police	Lieutenant Colonel	Major	(a)(b)(c)(g)

The Royal Air Force Police	Wing Commander	Squadron Leader	(a)(b)(c)(g)
The British Transport Police	Superintendent	Inspector	(a)(b)(c)(d)(e)(g)
The National Criminal Intelligence Service	Superintendent, Level 2 or any individual on secondment to the National Criminal Intelligence Service who holds any other office, rank or position in any relevant public authority listed in column 2 of Schedule 1	Inspector, Level 4 or any individual on secondment to the National Criminal Intelligence Service who holds any other office, rank or position in any relevant public authority listed in column 3 of Schedule 1	(a)(b)(c)(d)(e)(g)
The National Crime Squad	Superintendent, Band I or any individual on secondment to the National Crime Squad who holds any other office, rank or position in any relevant public authority listed in column 2 of Schedule 1	Inspector, Band F or any individual on secondment to the National Crime Squad who holds any other office, rank or position in any relevant public authority listed in column 3 of Schedule 1	(a)(b)(c)(d)(e)(g)
The Commissioners of Customs and Excise	Band 9	Band 7 or 8	(b)(f)
The Commissioners of Inland Revenue	Band C1	Band C2	(b)(f)
The Intelligence Services			
Government Communications Headquarters	GC8	—	(a)(b)(c)
The Security Service	General Duties 3 or any other Officer at Level 3	General Duties 4	(a)(b)(c)
The Secret Intelligence Service	Grade 6 or equivalent	—	(a)(b)(c)

Schedule 2

Article 3

Individuals in Additional Public Authorities Specified by this Order

Part I

(Individuals in additional public authorities that may acquire all types of communications data within section 21(4) of the 2000 Act)

(1)	(2)	(3)	(4)
Additional public authorities specified for the purposes of section 25(1) of the 2000 Act	*Prescribed offices etc (All authorisations/notices)*	*Additional prescribed offices etc (Authorisations/notices relating solely to communications data falling within section 21(4)(c))*	*Purposes within section 22(2) for which an authorization may be granted or a notice given*
The Financial Services Authority	Head of Department in Enforcement Division	—	(b)
The Scottish Crime Squad within the meaning of the Regulation of Investigatory Powers (Scotland) Act 2000	Superintendent	Inspector	(b)(d)(g)
The United Kingdom Atomic Energy Authority Constabulary	Superintendent	Inspector	(a)(b)
The Department of Trade and industry	Range 9 Officer in Radiocommunications Agency	—	(b)
The Office of the Police Ombudsman for Northern Ireland	Senior Investigating Officer	—	(b)
Emergency Services			
A National Health Service trust established under	Duty Officer responsible for the Control Function	—	(g)

29.18

section 5 of the National Health Service and Community Care Act 1990 whose functions, as specified in its Establishment Order, include the provision of emergency ambulance services			
The Welsh Ambulance Services NHS Trust	Regional Control Manager	—	(g)
The Scottish Ambulance Service Board	Emergency Medical Dispatch Centre Officer in Charge	—	(g)
The Northern Ireland Ambulance Service Health and Social Services Trust	Control Supervisor in Ambulance Control Room	—	(g)
The Department for Transport	Area Operations Manager in the Maritime and Coastguard Agency	—	(g)
Any fire authority within the meaning of the Fire Services Act 1947 (read with paragraph 2 of Schedule 11 to the Local Government Act 1985)	Fire Control Officer	—	(g)
A council constituted under section 2 of the Local Government etc. (Scotland) Act 1994	Fire Control Officer	—	(g)
A joint Board constituted by an administration scheme under section 36 of the	Fire Control Officer	—	(g)

Fire Services Act 1947 or section 147 of the Local Government (Scotland) Act 1973			
The Fire Authority for Northern Ireland	Fire Control Officer	—	(g)

Part II

(Individuals in the public authorities specified in Part I that may only acquire communications data falling within sections 21(4)(b) and (c) of the 2000 Act)

(1)	(2)	(3)	(4)
Additional public authorities specified for the purposes of section 25(1) of the 2000 Act	*Prescribed offices etc (All authorisations/notices) relating to communications data falling within sections 21(4)(b)and(c))*	*Additional prescribed offices etc (Authorisations/notices relating solely to communications data falling within section 21(4)(c))*	*Purposes within section 22(2) for which an authorization may be granted or a notice given*
The Department of Trade and Industry	Deputy Inspector of Companies in Companies Investigation Branch	— —	(b) (b)
	Deputy Chief Investigation Officer in the Investigation Officers Section of Legal Services Directorate D		
Emergency Services			
A National Health Service Trust established under section 5 of the National Health Service and Community Care Act 1990 whose functions, as specified in its	Director of operations or Director of Control and Communications	—	(b)

Establishment Order, include the provision of emergency ambulance services			
The Welsh Ambulance Services NHS Trust	Director of Operations	—	(b)
The Scottish Ambulance Service Board	Director of Operations	—	(b)
The Northern Ireland Ambulance Service Health and Social Services Trust	Director of Operations	—	(b)
The Department for Transport	Principal Enforcement Officer in the Maritime and Coastguard Agency	—	(b)(d)
Any fire authority within the meaning of the Fire Services Act 1947 (read with paragraph 2 of Schedule 11 to the Local Government Act 1985)	Principal Fire Control Officer or Divisional Officer 2	—	(b)(d)
A council constituted under section 2 of the Local Government etc. (Scotland) Act 1994	Assistant Chief Officer, Assistant Head of Service, Service Manager or equivalent Principal Fire Control Officer or Divisional Officer 2	— —	(b) (b)(d)
A joint Board constituted by an administration scheme under section 36 of the Fire Services Act 1947 or section 147 of the Local Government (Scotland) Act 1973	Principal Fire Control Officer or Divisional Officer 2	—	(b)(d)
The Fire Authority for Northern	Principal Fire Control Officer or Divisional	—	(b)(d)

PART III

(INDIVIDUALS IN FURTHER ADDITIONAL PUBLIC AUTHORITIES THAT MAY ONLY ACQUIRE COMMUNICATIONS DATA FALLING WITHIN SECTIONS 21(4) (B) AND (C) OF THE 2000 ACT)

29.19

(1)	*(2)*	*(3)*	*(4)*
Additional public authorities specified for the purposes of section 25(1) of the 2000 Act	*Prescribed offices etc (All authorisations/notices relating to communications data falling within sections 21(4)(b) and (c))*	*Additional prescribed offices etc (Authorisations/notices relating solely to communications data falling within section 21(4)(c))*	*Purposes within section 22(2) for which an authorisation may be granted or a notice given*
Government Departments			
The Department for Environment, Food and Rural Affairs	Senior Investigation Officer in DEFRA Investigation Branch	—	(b)
		—	(b)
	Senior Investigation Officer in the Centre for Environment, Fisheries and Aquaculture Science	—	(b)
	Senior Counter Fraud Officer in the Counter Fraud and Compliance Unit of the Rural Payments Agency		
The Food Standards Agency	Deputy Director of Legal Services or any Director	—	(b)(d)(e)
The Department of Health	Integrated Payband 3 (Standard 2) in the Medicines and Healthcare Products Regulatory Agency	—	(b)(d)(e)
The Home Office	Immigration Inspector in the Immigration Service	—	(b)
The Department of Enterprise, Trade and Investment for Northern Ireland	Deputy Chief Inspector in Trading Standards Service	—	(b)

Local Authorities			
Any county council or district council in England, a London borough council, the Common Council of the City of London in its capacity as a local authority, the Council of the Isles of Scilly, and any county council or county borough council in Wales	Assistant Chief Officer, Assistant Head of Service, Service Manager or equivalent	—	(b)
A district council with in the meaning of the Local Government Act (Northern Ireland) 1972	Assistant Chief Officer	—	(b)
NHS Bodies			
The Counter Fraud and Security Management Service	Senior Manager (Senior Manager Pay Range 14)	—	(b)
The Common Services Agency for the Scottish Health Service	Head of NHS Scotland Counter Fraud Services	—	(b)
The Northern Ireland Health and Social Services Central Services Agency	Head of the Counter Fraud Unit	—	(b)
Other Bodies			
The Charity Commission	Senior Investigations Manager	—	(b)
The Environment Agency	Area Management Team Member	—	(b)(d)(e)
The Gaming Board for Great Britain	Chief Inspector	—	(b)
The Health and Safety Executive	Band 2 Inspector	—	(b)(d)(e)(g)

The Information Commissioner	Head of Investigations	—	(b)
The Office of Fair Trading	Director of Cartel Investigations	—	(b)
The Serious Fraud Office	Assistant Director	—	(b)
The Scottish Environment Protection Agency	Director of Operations, any other Director	—	(b)(d)(e)
A Universal Service Provider within the meaning of the Postal Services Act 2000	Senior Investigation Manager in Royal Mail Group plc	—	(b)

PART IV

(INDIVIDUALS IN ADDITIONAL PUBLIC AUTHORITIES THAT MAY ONLY ACQUIRE COMMUNICATIONS DATA WITHIN SECTION 21(4) OF THE 2000 ACT RELATING TO A POSTAL SERVICE)

(1)	*(2)*	*(3)*	*(4)*	**29.20**
Additional public authorities specified for the purposes of section25(1) of the 2000 Act	*Prescribed offices etc (All authorisations/notices relating to communications data relating to postal services*	*Additional prescribed offices etc (Authorisations/notices relating solely to communications data falling within section 21(4)(c))*	*Purposes within section 22(2) for which an authorization may be granted or a notice given*	
Postal Services Commission	Legal Adviser	—	(b)	

C. SI 2003 No 3173 Retention of Communications Data (Extension of Initial Period) Order 2003

Made   *4th December 2003*

Coming into force   *5th December 2003*

Whereas a draft of this Order has been laid before Parliament and approved by   **29.21**
resolution of each House;

Now, therefore, the Secretary of State, in exercise of the powers conferred on him by section 105(3) of the Anti-terrorism, Crime and Security Act 2001, hereby makes the following Order:

1. This Order may be cited as the Retention of Communications Data (Extension of Initial Period) Order 2003 and shall come into force on the day after the day on which it is made.
2. The initial period specified in section 105(2) of the Anti-terrorism, Crime and Security Act 2001 shall be extended for the period of two years beginning with the time when that period would end but for the making of this Order.

Caroline Flint
Parliamentary Under-Secretary of State

Home Office
4th December 2003

D. SI 2003 No 3174 The Regulation of Investigatory Powers (Intrusive Surveillance) Order 2003

Made   *5th December 2003*

Coming into force   *5th January 2004*

29.22   Whereas a draft of this Order has been laid before Parliament and approved by a resolution of each House;

Now, therefore, the Secretary of State, in exercise of the powers conferred on him by section 41(3) and (4) of the Regulation of Investigatory Powers Act 2000, hereby makes the following Order:

Citation and commencement

29.23   1. This Order may be cited as the Regulation of Investigatory Powers (Intrusive Surveillance) Order 2003 and shall come into force one month after the day on which it is made.

Designated public authority

29.24   2. The Northern Ireland Office is hereby designated for the purposes of section 41 of the Regulation of Investigatory Powers Act 2000 as a public authority whose activities may require the carrying out of intrusive surveillance.

Prescribed offices, ranks and positions

3. An application for an authorisation for the carrying out of intrusive surveil- **29.25**
lance may be made only by an individual holding an office, rank or position in
the Northern Ireland Prison Service.

Caroline Flint
Parliamentary Under-Secretary of State

Home Office
5th December 2003

E. SI 2003 No 3175 The Retention of Communications Data (Code of Practice) Order 2003

Made   *4th December 2003*

Coming into force   *5th December 2003*

Whereas—   **29.26**

(1) in pursuance of section 102(1) of the Anti-terrorism, Crime and Security Act
2001 ("the 2001 Act") the Secretary of State is under a duty to issue a code of
practice containing provisions relating to the retention by communications
providers of communications data obtained by or held by them;

(2) in pursuance of section 103(2) of the 2001 Act the Secretary of State has
consulted with the Information Commissioner and the communications
providers to whom the code will apply;

(3) in pursuance of section 103(1) of the 2001 Act the Secretary of State has
prepared and published the code in the form of a draft and has considered
representations made to him about the draft and modified the draft
accordingly;

(4) in pursuance of section 103(4) of the 2001 Act the Secretary of State has laid
that draft code before both Houses of Parliament; and

(5) a draft of this Order has been laid before Parliament and approved by a resolution of each House:

Now, therefore, the Secretary of State, in exercise of the powers conferred on him
by section 103(5) of the 2001 Act, hereby makes the following Order:

Citation and commencement

1. The Order may be cited as the Retention of Communications Data (Code of **29.27**
Practice) Order 2003 and shall come into force on the day after the day on
which it is made.

Retention of Communications Data Code of Practice

29.28 2. The draft code of practice entitled "Voluntary Retention of Communications Data under Part 11: Anti-Terrorism, Crime and Security Act 2001— Voluntary Code of Practice", laid before each House of Parliament on 11th September 2003, relating to the retention by communications providers of communications data obtained by or held by them, shall come into force on the day after the day on which this Order is made.

Caroline Flint
Parliamentary Under-Secretary of State

Home Office
4th December 2003

30

STATUTORY INSTRUMENTS (2004)

A. SI 2004 No 157 The Regulation of Investigatory Powers (Conditions for the Lawful Interception of Persons outside the United Kingdom) Order 2004

Made   *27th January 2004*

Laid before Parliament   *3rd February 2004*

Coming into force in accordance with regulation 2

30.01 The Secretary of State, in exercise of the powers conferred on him by section 4(1)(d) of the Regulation of Investigatory Powers Act 2000, hereby makes the following Regulations:

Citation

30.02 1. These Regulations may be cited as the Regulation of Investigatory Powers (Conditions for the Lawful Interception of Persons outside the United Kingdom) Regulations 2004.

Commencement

30.03 2.—(1) These Regulations shall come into force—

    (a) if the United Kingdom is one of the first eight Member States of the European Union to ratify the Convention on Mutual Assistance in Criminal Matters established by Council Act of 29th May 2000 (2000/C197/01) ("the Convention"), 90 days after the day on which the eighth Member State ratifies; or

    (b) otherwise, 90 days after the day on which the United Kingdom ratifies the Convention.

  (2) For the purposes of paragraph (1)—

    (a) a Member State ratifies the Convention when it notifies the Secretary-General of the Council of the European Union of the completion of its constitutional procedures for the adoption of the Convention, in accordance with Article 27(2) of the Convention;

  (b) the reference to a "Member State" is only to a state that was a Member State on 29th May 2000.

Conditions for the lawful interception of persons outside the United Kingdom

3. For the purposes of section 4(1)(d) of the Regulation of Investigatory Powers Act 2000, the following conditions are prescribed—   **30.04**

  (a) the interception is carried out for the purposes of a criminal investigation;

  (b) the criminal investigation is being carried out in a country or territory that is party to an international agreement designated for the purposes of section 1(4) of that Act.

Caroline Flint
Parliamentary Under-Secretary of State

Home Office
27th January 2004

B. SI 2004 No 158 The Regulation of Investigatory Powers (Designation of an International Agreement) Order 2004

Made   *27th January 2004*

Laid before Parliament   *3rd February 2004*

Coming into force   *1st April 2004*

The Secretary of State, in exercise of the powers conferred on him by section 1(4)(c) of the Regulation of Investigatory Powers Act 2000, hereby makes the following Order: **30.05**

Citation and commencement

1. This Order may be cited as the Regulation of Investigatory Powers (Designation of an International Agreement) Order 2004 and shall come into force on 1st April 2004.   **30.06**

Designation of an international agreement

2. The Convention on Mutual Assistance in Criminal Matters between the Member States of the European Union established by Council Act of 29th   **30.07**

May 2000 (2000/C197/01) is hereby designated for the purposes of section 1(4) of the Regulation of Investigatory Powers Act 2000.

Home Office   *Caroline Flint*
27th January 2004   Parliamentary Under-Secretary of State

C. SI 2004 No 815 The Independent Police Complaints Commission (Investigatory Powers) Order 2004

Made   *11th March 2004*

Coming into force   *1st April 2004*

30.08 The Secretary of State, in exercise of the powers conferred on him by section 19(1) and (2) of the Police Reform Act 2002 hereby makes the following Order, a draft of which has been laid before and approved by resolution of each House of Parliament:

Citation, commencement and interpretation

30.09 1.—(1) This Order may be cited as the Independent Police Complaints Commission (Investigatory Powers) Order 2004 and shall come into force on 1st April 2004.

(2) In this Order—
"the 1997 Act" means the Police Act 1997
"the 2000 Act" means the Regulation of Investigatory Powers Act 2000.

Modifications to the 1997 Act

30.10 2.—(1) For the purposes of the carrying out of the functions of the Independent Police Complaints Commission, Part 3 of the 1997 Act shall have effect with the following modifications.

(2) In section 93 (authorisations to interfere with property etc.)—
  (a) after subsection (3)(aa) insert the following paragraph—
    "(ab) if the authorising officer is within subsection (5)(ef), by a member of staff of the Independent Police Complaints Commission who has been designated under paragraph 19(2) of Schedule 3 to the Police Reform Act 2002,";
  (b) after subsection (5)(ee) insert the following paragraph—
    "(ef) the Chairman of the Independent Police Complaints Commission;";
  (c) in subsection (6)(e) after the words "in relation to" insert the words "the Chairman of the Independent Police Complaints Commission or".

(3) In section 94 (authorisations given in absence of authorising officer)—
  (a) in subsection (1)(b) after the words "paragraph (a), (c), (d)" insert ", (ef)";

(b) after subsection (2)(dd) insert the following paragraph—

"(de) where the authorising person is within paragraph (ef) of that subsection, by any other member of the Independent Police Complaints Commission;";

(c) after subsection (4)(c) insert the following paragraph—

"(d) in the case of an authorising officer within paragraph (ef) of section 93(5), means a person appointed as deputy chairman of the Independent Police Complaints Commission under paragraph 3(1) of Schedule 2 to the Police Reform Act 2002.".

(4) In section 95(7) (authorisations: form and duration etc.) after the words "paragraph (a), (c), (d)," insert "(ef),".

(5) In section 105(3) (appeals by authorising officer: supplementary) after the words "paragraph (a), (c), (d)," insert "(ef),".

(6) In section 107(4) (supplementary provisions relating to Commissioners) after paragraph (a) insert the following paragraph—

"(aa) the functions of the Independent Police Complaints Commission,".

Modifications to the 2000 Act

3.—(1) For the purposes of the carrying out of the functions of the Independent Police Complaints Commission, Parts 2 and 4 of the 2000 Act shall have effect with the following modifications. **30.11**

(2) After section 32(6)(j) (authorisation of intrusive surveillance) insert the following paragraph—

"(ja) the Chairman of the Independent Police Complaints Commission;".

(3) In section 33 (rules for grant of authorisations)—

(a) after subsection (1) insert the following subsection—

"(1A) A person who is a designated person for the purposes of section 28 or 29 by reference to his office or position with the Independent Police Complaints Commission shall not grant an authorisation under that section except on an application made by a member of staff of the Commission who has been designated under paragraph 19(2) of Schedule 3 to the Police Reform Act 2002.";

(b) after subsection (3) insert the following subsection—

"(3A) A person who is a senior authorising officer by reference to the Independent Police Complaints Commission shall not grant an authorisation for the carrying out of intrusive surveillance except—

(a) on an application made by a member of staff of the Commission who has been designated under paragraph 19(2) of Schedule 3 to the Police Reform Act 2002; and

(b) in the case of an authorisation for the carrying out of intrusive surveillance in relation to any residential premises, where those premises are in England and Wales.";

(c) in subsection (5)(a) after the words "National Crime Squad," insert "or who is a member of staff of the Independent Police Complaints Commission,".

(4) In section 34 (grant of authorisations in the senior officer's absence)—

(a) in subsection (1)(a) after the words "National Crime Squad," insert "or by a member of staff of the Independent Police Complaints Commission who has been designated under paragraph 19(2) of Schedule 3 to the Police Reform Act 2002";

(b) in subsection (2)(a) after the words "Squad in question" insert "or the Independent Police Complaints Commission";

(c) after subsection (4)(m) insert the following paragraph—

"(n) person is entitled to act for the Chairman of the Independent Police Complaints Commission if he is any other member of the Independent Police Complaints Commission.";

(d) after subsection (6)(c) insert the following paragraph—

"(d) in relation to the Chairman of the Independent Police Complaints Commission, means a person appointed as deputy chairman of the Independent Police Complaints Commission under paragraph 3(1) of Schedule 2 to the Police Reform Act 2002.".

(5) In section 35(10)(a) (notification of authorisations for intrusive surveillance) after "a police force," insert "the Independent Police Complaints Commission,".

(6) In section 36 (approval required for authorisations to take effect)—

(a) after subsection (1)(a) insert the following paragraph—

"(aa) a member of staff of the Independent Police Complaints Commission who has been designated under paragraph 19(2) of Schedule 3 to the Police Reform Act 2002;";

(b) after subsection (6)(b) insert the following paragraph—

"(ba) where the authorisation was granted by the Chairman of the Independent Police Complaints Commission, by the designated deputy of the Chairman of the Independent Police Complaints Commission or by another member of that Commission entitled to act for that Chairman by virtue of section 34(4)(m), that Chairman;".

(7) After section 37(1)(a) (quashing of police and customs authorisations etc.) insert the following paragraph—

"(aa) a member of staff of the Independent Police Complaints Commission who has been designated under paragraph 19(2) of Schedule 3 to the Police Reform Act 2002;".

(8) After section 40(a) (information to be provided to Surveillance Commissioners) insert the following paragraph—

"(aa) every member and every employee of the Independent Police Complaints Commission,".

(9) After section 45(6)(c) (cancellation of authorisation) insert the following paragraph—
"(ca) in relation to the Chairman of the Independent Police Complaints Commission, to his designated deputy;".

(10) After section 65(6)(c) (the Tribunal) insert the following paragraph—
"(ca) the Independent Police Complaints Commission;".

(11) After section 68(7)(d) (Tribunal procedure) insert the following paragraph—
"(da) every member and every employee of the Independent Police Complaints Commission;".

(12) After paragraph 4 of Schedule 1 (authorisation of surveillance and covert human intelligence sources: relevant public authorities for the purposes of sections 28 and 29) insert the following paragraph—
"4A. The Independent Police Complaints Commission.".

Authorisation of surveillance and human intelligence sources: persons entitled to grant authorisations

4.—(1) The offices and positions of member, Regional Director, Director of Investigations and Deputy Director of Investigations of the Independent Police Complaints Commission are hereby prescribed for the purposes of section 30(1) of the 2000 Act (persons entitled to grant authorisations under sections 28 and 29) as if prescribed by an order under that section. **30.12**

(2) An individual holding an office or position mentioned in paragraph (1) may not grant an authorisation unless he believes it is necessary on the grounds set out in section 28(3)(b) or 29(3)(b) of the 2000 Act (authorisation necessary for the purpose of preventing or detecting crime or of preventing disorder).

Urgentcases

5.—(1) The additional position of Senior Investigating Officer of the Independent Police Complaints Commission is hereby prescribed for the purposes of section 30(1) of the 2000 Act, for the cases described in paragraph (2) as if prescribed by an order under that section. **30.13**

(2) An individual prescribed by virtue of paragraph (1) may grant an authorisation only where it is not reasonably practicable having regard to the urgency of the case for the application to be considered by an individual holding an office or position prescribed by article 4(1).

Hazel Blears
Minister of State

Home Office
11th March 2004

D. SI 2004 No 1128 The Regulation of Investigatory Powers (Foreign Surveillance Operations) Order 2004

Made   *13th April 2004*

Laid before Parliament *16th April 2004*

Coming into force *7th May 2004*

30.14 In exercise of the powers conferred upon him by section 76A(8) of the Regulation of Investigatory Powers Act 2000[1], the Secretary of State hereby makes the following Order:

1. This Order may be cited as the Regulation of Investigatory Powers (Foreign Surveillance Operations) Order 2004 and shall come into force on 7th May 2004.
2. The Director General of the National Criminal Intelligence Service[2] is hereby designated for the purposes of section 76A(8) of the Regulation of Investigatory Powers Act 2000.

Caroline Flint
Parliamentary Under-Secretary of State

Home Office
13th April 2004

31

STATUTORY INSTRUMENTS (2005)

A. SI 2005 No 1083 The Regulation of Investigatory Powers (Communications Data) (Amendment) Order 2005

Made   *4th April 2005*
Coming into force in accordance with article 1(2) and (3)

31.01 The Secretary of State, in exercise of the powers conferred upon him by paragraph (g) of the definition of "relevant public authority" in section 25(1) of the Regulation of Investigatory Powers Act 2000 and by sections 25(2), (3) and (4) and 78(5) of that Act, hereby makes the following Order (a draft of which has been approved by resolution of each House of Parliament):

Citation and commencement

31.02 1.—(1) This Order may be cited as the Regulation of Investigatory Powers (Communications Data) (Amendment) Order 2005.

(2) Subject to paragraph (3), this Order shall come into force one month after the day on which it is made.

(3) Article 2(3) of this Order shall come into force on the day on which either—

(a) the other provisions of this Order come into force, or

(b) paragraph 8 of Schedule 14 to the Energy Act 2004 comes into force, whichever is the later.

Amendment of the Regulation of Investigatory Powers (Communications Data) Order 2003

31.03 2.—(1) Part 1 of Schedule 2 (individuals in additional public authorities that may acquire all types of communications data within section 21(4) of the Regulation of Investigatory Powers Act 2000) to the Regulation of Investigatory Powers (Communications Data) Order 2003 is amended as follows.

(2) For the entry for the Scottish Crime Squad, substitute—

The Scottish Drug Enforcement Agency, meaning the organisation known by that name and established under section36(1)(a)(ii) of the Police (Scotland) Act 1967	Superintendent, Grade PO7 or any individual on secondment to the Scottish Drug Enforcement Agency who holds the rank of Superintendent or Grade PO7 with the police force from which that person is seconded	Inspector or any individual on secondment to the Scottish Drug Enforcement Agency who holds the rank of Inspector with the police force from which that person is seconded	(b)(d)(g)

(3) For the entry for the United Kingdom Atomic Energy Authority Constabulary, substitute—

The Civil Nuclear Constabulary	Superintendent	Inspector	(a)(b)

(4) Delete the entry for the Department of Trade and Industry.

(5) After the entry for the Office of the Police Ombudsman for Northern Ireland, add the following entries—

The Independent Police Complaints Commission	Commissioner, Regional Director, Director of Investigations or Deputy Director of Investigations	—	(b)
The Office of Communications	Senior Enforcement Policy Manager	—	(b)
The force comprising the special constables appointed under section 79 of the Harbours, Docks and Piers Clauses Act 1847 on the nomination of the Dover Harbour Board	Superintendent	Inspector	(a)(b)(d)(e)
The force comprising the constables appointed under article 3 of the Mersey Docks and Harbour (Police) Order 1975 on the nomination of the Mersey Docks and Harbour Company	Superintendent	Inspector	(a)(b)(d)(e)

Caroline Flint
Parliamentary Under-Secretary of State

Home Office
4th April 2005

B. SI 2005 No 1084 The Regulation of Investigatory Powers (Directed Surveillance and Covert Human Intelligence Sources) (Amendment) Order 2005

Made   4th April 2005
Coming into force in accordance with article 1(2) and (3)

31.04 The Secretary of State, in exercise of the powers conferred upon him by sections 30(1), (3), (5)(a) and (b), and (6) and 78(5) of the Regulation of Investigatory Powers Act 2000 hereby makes the following Order (a draft of which has been approved by resolution of each House of Parliament):

Citation, commencement and interpretation

31.05 1.—(1) This Order may be cited as the Regulation of Investigatory Powers (Directed Surveillance and Covert Human Intelligence Sources) (Amendment) Order 2005.

(2) Subject to paragraph (3), this Order shall come into force one month after the day on which it is made.

(3) Article 3(3) of this Order shall come into force on the day on which either—

(a) the other provisions of this Order come into force, or

(b) paragraph 8 of Schedule 14 to the Energy Act 2004 comes into force, whichever is the later.

(4) In this Order "the Act" means the Regulation of Investigatory Powers Act 2000.

Amendment of Schedule 1 to the Act

31.06 2.—(1) After paragraph 4 of Part 1 of Schedule 1 to the Act, add the words—

" 4A. The force comprising the special constables appointed under section 79 of the Harbours, Docks and Piers Clauses Act 1847 on the nomination of the Dover Harbour Board.

4B. The force comprising the constables appointed under article 3 of the Mersey Docks and Harbour (Police) Order 1975 on the nomination of the Mersey Docks and Harbour Company."

(2) Paragraph 25 of Part 2 of Schedule 1 to the Act is omitted.

Amendment of the Regulation of Investigatory Powers (Directed Surveillance and Covert Human Intelligence Sources) Order 2003

31.07 3.—(1) Part 1 of the Schedule (prescriptions for public authorities in Part 1 of Schedule 1 to the Act that are relevant authorities for the purposes of sections 28 and 29 of the Act) to the Regulation of Investigatory Powers (Directed

Surveillance and Covert Human Intelligence Sources) Order 2003 is amended as follows.

(2) After the entry for the British Transport Police, insert—

The force comprising the special constables appointed under section 79 of the Harbours, Docks and Piers Clauses Act 1847 on the nomination of the Dover Harbour Board	Superintendent	Inspector	(a)(b)(d)(e)
The force comprising the constables appointed under article 3 of the Mersey Docks and Harbour (Police) Order 1975 on the nomination of the Mersey Docks and Harbour Company	Superintendent	Inspector	(a)(b)(d)(e)

(3) For the entry for the United Kingdom Atomic Energy Authority Constabulary, substitute—

The Civil Nuclear Constabulary	Superintendent	Inspector	(a)(b)

(4) In the entry for the Department of Trade and Industry, omit all references to individuals holding office, rank or position in the Radiocommunications Agency.

(5) In the entry for the Department for Transport, omit the first eight references in columns 2 and 4 (Head of Maritime Section to and including the Senior Transport Security Inspector).

(6) At the end, insert—

The Office of Communication	**Section 28 authorisation** Manager of Spectrum Operations or Head of Enforcement and Interference Policy **Section 29 authorisation** Head of Field operation	**Section 28 authorisation** Area Manager or Senior Enforcement Policy Manager	(b) (b)

Caroline Flint
Parliamentary Under-Secretary of State

Home Office
4th April 2005

PART IX

INTERNATIONAL MATERIALS

32

THE CONVENTION ON MUTUAL ASSISTANCE IN CRIMINAL MATTERS BETWEEN THE MEMBER STATES OF THE EUROPEAN UNION ESTABLISHED BY COUNCIL ACT OF 29TH MAY 2000 (2000/C197/01)[1]

(Annex Titles relating to Interception of Telecommunications, Covert Investigation and Data Sharing)

ANNEX

TITLE I

GENERAL PROVISIONS

[. . .]

Article 3

Proceedings in connection with which mutual assistance is also to be afforded

32.01 1. Mutual assistance shall also be afforded in proceedings brought by the administrative authorities in respect of acts which are punishable under the national law of the requesting or the requested Member State, or both, by virtue of being infringements of the rules of law, and where the decision may give rise to proceedings before a court having jurisdiction in particular in criminal matters.

---

[1] This Convention and Annex has been designated by SI 2004 No 158 The RIPA (Designation of an International Agreement) Order 2004 as an international agreement for the purposes of s 1(4) of RIPA. See Official Journal C 197, 12/07/2000 P 0003–0023.

2. Mutual assistance shall also be afforded in connection with criminal proceedings and proceedings as referred to in paragraph 1 which relate to offences or infringements for which a legal person may be held liable in the requesting Member State.

Article 7

Spontaneous exchange of information

1. Within the limits of their national law, the competent authorities of the **32.02** Member States may exchange information, without a request to that effect, relating to criminal offences and the infringements of rules of law referred to in Article 3(1), the punishment or handling of which falls within the competence of the receiving authority at the time the information is provided.
2. The providing authority may, pursuant to its national law, impose conditions on the use of such information by the receiving authority.
3. The receiving authority shall be bound by those conditions.

TITLE II
REQUEST FOR CERTAIN SPECIFIC FORMS OF MUTUAL ASSISTANCE

[. . .]

Article 14

Covert investigations

1. The requesting and the requested Member State may agree to assist one **32.03** another in the conduct of investigations into crime by officers acting under covert or false identity (covert investigations).
2. The decision on the request is taken in each individual case by the competent authorities of the requested Member State with due regard to its national law and procedures. The duration of the covert investigation, the detailed conditions, and the legal status of the officers concerned during covert investigations shall be agreed between the Member States with due regard to their national law and procedures.
3. Covert investigations shall take place in accordance with the national law and procedures of the Member States on the territory of which the covert investigation takes place. The Member States involved shall co-operate to ensure that the covert investigation is prepared and supervised and to make arrangements for the security of the officers acting under covert or false identity.
4. When giving the notification provided for in Article 27(2), any Member State may declare that it is not bound by this Article. Such a declaration may be withdrawn at any time.

[. . .]

TITLE III
INTERCEPTION OF TELECOMMUNICATIONS

Article 17

Authorities competent to order interception of telecommunications

32.04   For the purpose of the application of the provisions of Articles 18, 19 and 20, "competent authority" shall mean a judicial authority, or, where judicial authorities have no competence in the area covered by those provisions, an equivalent competent authority, specified pursuant to Article 24(1)(e) and acting for the purpose of a criminal investigation.

Article 18

Requests for interception of telecommunications

32.05   1.   For the purpose of a criminal investigation, a competent authority in the requesting Member State may, in accordance with the requirements of its national law, make a request to a competent authority in the requested Member State for:
  (a)   the interception and immediate transmission to the requesting Member State of telecommunications; or
  (b)   the interception, recording and subsequent transmission to the requesting Member State of the recording of telecommunications.
  2.   Requests under paragraph 1 may be made in relation to the use of means of telecommunications by the subject of the interception, if this subject is present in:
  (a)   the requesting Member State and the requesting Member State needs the technical assistance of the requested Member State to intercept his or her communications;
  (b)   the requested Member State and his or her communications can be intercepted in that Member State;
  (c)   a third Member State which has been informed pursuant to Article 20(2)(a) and the requesting Member State needs the technical assistance of the requested Member State to intercept his or her communications.
  3.   By way of derogation from Article 14 of the European Mutual Assistance Convention and Article 37 of the Benelux Treaty, requests under this Article shall include the following:
  (a)   an indication of the authority making the request;
  (b)   confirmation that a lawful interception order or warrant has been issued in connection with a criminal investigation;
  (c)   information for the purpose of identifying the subject of this interception;
  (d)   an indication of the criminal conduct under investigation;
  (e)   the desired duration of the interception; and

(f) if possible, the provision of sufficient technical data, in particular the relevant network connection number, to ensure that the request can be met.

4. In the case of a request pursuant to paragraph 2(b), a request shall also include a summary of the facts. The requested Member State may require any further information to enable it to decide whether the requested measure would be taken by it in a similar national case.

5. The requested Member State shall undertake to comply with requests under paragraph 1(a):
   (a) in the case of a request pursuant to paragraph 2(a) and 2(c), on being provided with the information in paragraph 3. The requested Member State may allow the interception to proceed without further formality;
   (b) in the case of a request pursuant to paragraph 2(b), on being provided with the information in paragraphs 3 and 4 and where the requested measure would be taken by it in a similar national case. The requested Member State may make its consent subject to any conditions which would have to be observed in a similar national case.

6. Where immediate transmission is not possible, the requested Member State shall undertake to comply with requests under paragraph 1(b) on being provided with the information in paragraphs 3 and 4 and where the requested measure would be taken by it in a similar national case. The requested Member State may make its consent subject to any condition which would have to be observed in a similar national case.

7. When giving the notification provided for in Article 27(2), any Member State may declare that it is bound by paragraph 6 only when it is unable to provide immediate transmission. In this case the other Member State may apply the principle of reciprocity.

8. When making a request under paragraph 1(b), the requesting Member State may, where it has a particular reason to do so, also request a transcription of the recording. The requested Member State shall consider such requests in accordance with its national law and procedures.

9. The Member State receiving the information provided under paragraphs 3 and 4 shall keep that information confidential in accordance with its national law.

Article 19

Interceptions of telecommunications on national territory by the use of service providers

1. Member States shall ensure that systems of telecommunications services **32.06** operated via a gateway on their territory, which for the lawful interception of the communications of a subject present in another Member State are not

directly accessible on the territory of the latter, may be made directly accessible for the lawful interception by that Member State through the intermediary of a designated service provider present on its territory.

2. In the case referred to in paragraph 1, the competent authorities of a Member State shall be entitled, for the purposes of a criminal investigation and in accordance with applicable national law and provided that the subject of the interception is present in that Member State, to carry out the interception through the intermediary of a designated service provider present on its territory without involving the Member State on whose territory the gateway is located.

3. Paragraph 2 shall also apply where the interception is carried out upon a request made pursuant to Article 18(2)(b).

4. Nothing in this Article shall prevent a Member State from making a request to the Member State on whose territory the gateway is located for the lawful interception of telecommunications in accordance with Article 18, in particular where there is no intermediary in the requesting Member State.

Article 20

Interception of telecommunications without the technical assistance of another Member State

32.07 1. Without prejudice to the general principle of international law as well as to the provisions of Article 18(2)(c), the obligations under this Article shall apply to interception orders made or authorised by the competent authority of one Member State in the course of criminal investigations which present the characteristics of being an investigation following the commission of a specific criminal offence, including attempts in so far as they are criminalised under national law, in order to identify and arrest, charge, prosecute or deliver judgment on those responsible.

2. Where for the purpose of a criminal investigation, the interception of telecommunications is authorised by the competent authority of one Member State (the "intercepting Member State"), and the telecommunication address of the subject specified in the interception order is being used on the territory of another Member State (the "notified Member State") from which no technical assistance is needed to carry out the interception, the intercepting Member State shall inform the notified Member State of the interception:

(a) prior to the interception in cases where it knows when ordering the interception that the subject is on the territory of the notified Member State;

(b) in other cases, immediately after it becomes aware that the subject of the interception is on the territory of the notified Member State.

3. The information to be notified by the intercepting Member State shall include:
   (a) an indication of the authority ordering the interception;
   (b) confirmation that a lawful interception order has been issued in connection with a criminal investigation;
   (c) information for the purpose of identifying the subject of the interception;
   (d) an indication of the criminal conduct under investigation; and
   (e) the expected duration of the interception.

4. The following shall apply where a Member State is notified pursuant to paragraphs 2 and 3:
   (a) upon receipt of the information provided under paragraph 3 the competent authority of the notified Member State shall, without delay, and at the latest within 96 hours, reply to the intercepting Member State, with a view to:
      (i) allowing the interception to be carried out or to be continued. The notified Member State may make its consent subject to any conditions which would have to be observed in a similar national case;
      (ii) requiring the interception not to be carried out or to be terminated where the interception would not be permissible pursuant to the national law of the notified Member State or for the reasons specified in Article 2 of the European Mutual Assistance Convention. Where the notified Member State imposes such a requirement, it shall give reasons for its decision in writing;
      (iii) in cases referred to in point (ii), requiring that any material already intercepted while the subject was on its territory may not be used, or may only be used under conditions which it shall specify. The notified Member State shall inform the intercepting Member State of the reasons justifying the said conditions;
      (iv) requiring a short extension, of up to a maximum period of eight days, to the original 96 hour deadline, to be agreed with the intercepting Member State, in order to carry out internal procedures under its national law. The notified Member State shall communicate, in writing, to the intercepting Member State, the conditions which, pursuant to its national law, justify the requested extension of the deadline;
   (b) until a decision has been taken by the notified Member State pursuant to points (i) or (ii) of subparagraph (a), the intercepting Member State:
      (i) may continue the interception; and
      (ii) may not use the material already intercepted, except:
      —if otherwise agreed between the Member States concerned; or
      —for taking urgent measures to prevent an immediate and serious threat to public security. The notified Member State shall be informed of any such use and the reasons justifying it;

(c) The notified Member State may request a summary of the facts of the case and any further information necessary to enable it to decide whether interception would be authorised in a similar national case. Such a request does not affect the application of subparagraph (b), unless otherwise agreed between the notified Member State and the intercepting Member State.

(d) the Member States shall take the necessary measures to ensure that a reply can be given within the 96 hour period. To this end they shall designate contact points, on duty 24 hours a day, and include them in their statements under Article 24(1)(e).

5. The notified Member State shall keep the information provided under paragraph 3 confidential in accordance with its national law.

6. Where the intercepting Member State is of the opinion that the information to be provided under paragraph 3 is of a particularly sensitive nature, it may be transmitted to the competent authority through a specific authority where that has been agreed on a bilateral basis between the Member States concerned.

7. When giving its notification under Article 27(2), or at any time thereafter, any Member State may declare that it will not be necessary to provide it with information on interceptions as envisaged in this Article.

Article 21

Responsibility for charges made by telecommunications operators

32.08 Costs which are incurred by telecommunications operators or service providers in executing requests pursuant to Article 18 shall be borne by the requesting Member State.

Article 22

Bilateral arrangements

32.09 Nothing in this Title shall preclude any bilateral or multilateral arrangements between Member States for the purpose of facilitating the exploitation of present and future technical possibilities regarding the lawful interception of telecommunications.

TITLE IV

Article 23

Personal data protection

32.10 1. Personal data communicated under this Convention may be used by the Member State to which they have been transferred:

(a) for the purpose of proceedings to which this Convention applies;

(b) for other judicial and administrative proceedings directly related to proceedings referred to under point (a);

(c) for preventing an immediate and serious threat to public security;

(d) for any other purpose, only with the prior consent of the communicating Member State unless the Member State concerned has obtained the consent of the data subject.

2. This Article shall also apply to personal data not communicated but obtained otherwise under this Convention.

3. In the circumstances of the particular case, the communicating Member State may require the Member State to which the personal data have been transferred to give information on the use made of the data.

4. Where conditions on the use of personal data have been imposed pursuant to Articles 7(2), 18(5)(b), 18(6) or 20(4), these conditions shall prevail. Where no such conditions have been imposed, this Article shall apply.

5. The provisions of Article 13(10) shall take precedence over this Article regarding information obtained under Article 13.

6. This Article does not apply to personal data obtained by a Member State under this Convention and originating from that Member State.

7. Luxembourg may, when signing the Convention, declare that where personal data are communicated by Luxembourg under this Convention to another Member State, the following applies:

Luxembourg may, subject to paragraph 1(c), in the circumstances of a particular case require that unless that Member State concerned has obtained the consent of the data subject, the personal data may only be used for the purposes referred to in paragraph 1(a) and (b) with the prior consent of Luxembourg in respect of proceedings for which Luxembourg could have refused or limited the transmission or use of the personal data in accordance with the provisions of this Convention or the instruments referred to in Article 1.

If, in a particular case, Luxembourg refuses to give its consent to a request from a Member State pursuant to the provisions of paragraph 1, it must give reasons for its decision in writing.

TITLE V

FINAL PROVISIONS

[. . .]

Declaration by the United Kingdom on Article 20

32.11 This Declaration shall form an agreed, integral part of the Convention.

In the United Kingdom, Article 20 will apply in respect of interception warrants issued by the Secretary of State to the police service or HM Customs and Excise where, in accordance with national law on the interception of communications, the stated purpose of the warrant is the detection of serious crime. It will also apply to such warrants issued to the Security Service where, in accordance with national law, it is acting in support of an investigation presenting the characteristics described in Article 20(1).

APPENDIX

Useful Sources of Information

ECHELON—European Parliament report on:[1]
   http://www.europarl.eu.int/oeil/FindByProcnum.do?lang=2&procnum=INI/2001/2098
European Convention on Human Rights http://www.humanrights.coe.int/
Europol http://www.europol.eu.int/
Government Communications Headquarters (GCHQ)
   http://www.gchq.gov.uk/about/index.html
HM Revenue and Customs (formerly Inland Revenue and Customs and Excise)
   http://www.hmrc.gov.uk/
Independent Police Complaints Authority http://www.ipcc.gov.uk
Interpol http://www.interpol.int/
Investigatory Powers Tribunal http://www.ipt-uk.com
MI6/SI http://www.mi6.gov.uk
National Crime Squad and the National Crime Squad Service Authority
   http://www.nationalcrimesquad.police.uk/
National Criminal Intelligence Service (NCIS) and the NCIS Service Authority
   www.ncis.co.uk
National Infrastructure Security Co-ordination Centre website
   http://www.niscc.gov.uk/niscc/index-en.html
Office of Fair Trading www.oft.gov.uk
Office of the Surveillance Commissioners
http://www.surveillancecommissioners.gov.uk/
RIPA Technical Advisory Board
http://www.technicaladvisoryboard.org.uk/
Security Service ('MI5') www.mi5.gov.uk
Secret Intelligence Service (SIS) (sometimes called 'MI6') see 'MI6'
Serious Organised Crime Agency (SOCA) and the Centre for Child Protection on the Internet
   http://www.ncis.co.uk/organisedcrimeagency.asp
   http://www.homeoffice.gov.uk/n_story.asp?item_id=1287
Sirene UK http://www.sirene.gov.uk/
Special Branch www.met.police.uk/so/special_branch.htm

---

[1] The author is grateful to the staff of the European Parliament for assistance in locating the appropriate source link.

INDEX

be

I will get a flat
at the side of the
will building

I will get a flat at
the back of the
will building

343|172|335|224|5 21

469 59 83   74 1314

11271   282
                    48%

I will get a
flat at
the back of the
will building

345|73|224|244|112 1

4662 117 434   38%

891092 10181 281

Aidan

I will get a flat at the
side of the will building

444|823|24|133|3 121

664 11546   1210957

57%   27002
                471

44|182224|334 121

565 41546

1101051   261 37%

444|82924|3|34|121

565 11536 1191061   91%

2791 316